Jews and Medicine

An Epic Saga

Also by Frank Heynick:

Language and Its Disturbances in Dreams: The Pioneering Work of Freud and Kraepelin Updated.

Jews and Medicine

An Epic Saga

Dr. Frank Heynick

KTAV Publishing House, Inc.

Heynick, Frank
Jews and medicine: an epic saga/ by Frank Heynick.
    p. cm.
Includes bibliographical references and index.
 ISBN 0-88125-773-7

Distributed by
Ktav Publishing House, Inc.
900 Jefferson Street
Hoboken, NJ 07030
201-963-9524 FAX 201-963-0102
www.ktav.com
Email orders@ktav.com

Contents

Acknowledgments

When, in 1993, after many years of mental preparation, I embarked on the actual writing of this work, little did I envisage a tome of some six hundred pages. But it became more and more apparent that, even with a lot of trimming, nothing less could do justice to the sweeping, unending epic that is the story of Jews and medicine.

The book was written mostly in a period in my life when I was in New York only three or so months of the year, and living, lecturing and writing in Europe the rest of the time. On any given week in the Old Country, I could be found in five or six different locations with my laptop, books and documents. For the pleasant atmosphere so conducive for the carrying out of this project, I wish to express my general thanks to the folks of the Dutch cities and towns of Rotterdam, Eindhoven, Amsterdam, and Groningen. (In the latter case, my special appreciation goes to the staff of Motel-Restaurant Westerbroek, and to its managers Walter and Suzie van der Valk, where I spent six or more hours virtually every Sunday with my laptop.) Similar general thanks are due the people of the northwest German cities and towns of Bremen, Leer, and Oldenburg, and their environs.

Particular appreciation goes to my mother, Betty S. Heynick, for providing such a good pied-à-terre for my activities in New York during the writing of this book and for her steadfast moral support during the publication process.

While most of the bibliographical material for this work is drawn from among the many thousands of books I've collected in the course of time, this project would have been incomplete indeed without the help of several library sources. My thanks go to the New York Public Library (Research Division), the New York University medical library (particularly librarian Arthur Strange), the library of the Rockefeller University, and the library of the New York Academy of Medicine. Most of all, I'm grateful for the considerable help of Leon Osinski, chief librarian of the Faculty of Philosophy and Social Sciences (as it was then called) of the Eindhoven University of Technology in the Netherlands.

Dr. Sherwin B. Nuland of Yale University so very kindly took the time from his busy book-writing, clinical, and teaching schedule in order to look over most of the previous draft of this book with the keen eye of a surgeon and the vast knowledge of a medical historian. I am indebted to him for his valuable suggestions and comments. Similar thanks go to Renate Fuks-Mansfeld, professor emeritus of Jewish studies at the University of Amsterdam, for vetting most of a previous draft from the Jewish historical side. Of course, any and all faults in the present version are my responsibility alone.

I much appreciate Dr. Jerry Baum, Dr. Baruj Benacerraf, and Dr. Mike Nevins, for having, along with Dr. Nuland, kindly provided such thoughtful pre-publication reviews.

To Bernie Scharfstein, the publisher of KTAV, much gratitude is due for bringing to this project his personal enthusiastism and his wonderfully efficient, hands-on way of getting things done.

My thanks go as well to Bernie Hoenig, esq., family friend and counselor, who contributed such expertise that he became my virtual literary agent.

That this book should first see the light of day after the turn of the new millennium was as unanticipated as the book's length when I began the project. But this, too, is all for the best. There can hardly be a better time than now to look back at this great Jewish medical saga as we take stock of where we are going and what we might hope to achieve in the future.

Introduction
The Wandering Jew as Doctor

"I beheld [at my door] a proper, tall, grave old man . . . his beard and head were white, and he had a white stick in his hand. The day was rainy from morning to night, but he had not one spot of dirt upon his clothes. . . . Thus he said: 'Friend, I pray thee, give an old pilgrim a cup of small beere!' . . . After finishing the beere, 'Friend,' he said, 'thou art not well.' I said, 'No, truly, Sir, I have not been well these many years.' He said, 'What is thy disease?' I said, 'A deep consumption, Sir; our doctors say past cure . . . .' 'Then,' he said, 'I will tell thee what thou shalt do; and by the help and power of Almighty God above, thou shalt be well. Tomorrow, when thou riseth up, go into thy garden, and get there two leaves of red sage, and one of bloodwort, and put them into a cup of thy small beere.'". . . So saying he departed, and was never more heard of; but the patient got well within the given time, and for many a long day there was war hot and fierce among the divines of Stamford, as to whether the stranger was an angel or a devil."
—England, 1658, collected in "The Legend of the Wandering Jew"

The Wandering Jew, the Eternal Jew. . . . In a thousand folktales, legends, and literary renderings through the centuries, this restless wayfarer has assumed dozens of names and appeared in countless locales.

He had his thematic roots in the story of Cain, the archetypal eternal wanderer of biblical tradition. At the time of Jesus, his name was Cartaphilus, a shoemaker along the Via Dolorosa in Jerusalem, whom a Christian curse doomed to roam the earth, never resting or dying until Judgment Day.

Six centuries later, at the dawn of the Moslem era in Arabia, the Wandering Jew made an appearance before the armies of the Prophet, dressed as a dervish named Zerib, speaking Arabic, and seated between two moun-

1

tains. The ancient folklore of the Aegean islands of Lesbos and Syme tells of frequent sightings of Koutetes, the Short One, a ceaselessly moving Israelite, crying out to passing ships and carrying a lantern at night.

In Italy in the late Middle Ages and early Renaissance, the Wandering Jew appeared in various places under several names. He was perhaps first sighted in Forli in 1267, where he was called Johannes Buttadeus. During a raging snowstorm a century and a half later, he appeared wearing the habit of a Franciscan friar but barefoot, at an inn at Scaricalasino, bearing the name Votaddio and effecting an amazing rescue. At sightings in Sicily, where he was known as Arributa-Diu, the Wanderer wasn't barefoot but wore shoes striped yellow, red, and black. Thunder and lightning accompanied him everywhere. Other Italian witnesses reported the Wandering Jew as wearing a dirty broad-brimmed hat and a topcoat of dragon-blood red.

The Jew's roamings from Italy to France turned wheat fields into snowy fir forests. In Provence and elsewhere in France, he was known as Isaac Laquedem, Boutedieu, or Malc, and his exploits were depicted in Medieval passion plays. On the Iberian peninsula the comings and goings of the Wandering Jew were particularly evident in the fifteenth and sixteenth centuries. Among his appellations were Juan Espera en Dios, or in Portugese João Espera em Dios, and he was said to have the power of an all-knowing necromancer.

In the German-speaking lands, the Wandering Jew was best known as Ahasuerus, and his career flourished in folklore and literature for centuries. Frankfurt am Main, Oldenburg, Bamberg, and Würzburg were just some of the places where legends of his visitation took root. Ahasuerus usually wore a turban and a tunic, threadbare from his travels. He carried a long staff. His gray beard was down to his waist and he cast a shadow the length of a half-hour's walk. His visit to Hamburg in 1542 was described by respectable witnesses in some detail. In Elberfeld he was known for frantically engaging in business each Christmas day. His weeping created the Grimselmeer in Switzerland. He made a fatal prediction at a tavern in Lübeck. He drew lots with the witch Langtüttin at the Oetzhaler Glacier in Austria. He bore an indecipherable inscription on his hat when he appeared in Breslau in 1646. He related his firsthand accounts of the history of the past seventeen centuries to visitors at the Leipzig fair. In literary manifestations in more recent centuries, Ahasuerus, now sometimes clad in respectable bourgeois attire, served as a foil for a spectrum of opinions on Germany's burning "Jewish question."

The folklore and legends of the Wandering Jew extended to the periphery of the European continent. In England he was known as John Puttidew or (curiously) Mr. Ferguson. In the Ukraine and Russia he was called Phanyas. But the Wandering Jew's roamings have by no means been restricted to Europe and the Near East. A pamphlet published in Cambridge in 1757 entitled "The History of Israel Jobson, the Wandering Jew" and dealing with astronomy and cosmology was purportedly "translated from the Original Chinese." An early twentieth-century German literary rendering of the legend has Ahasuerus, with doctoral diplomas from thirteenth-century Bologna and eighteenth-century Köningsberg in hand, driven from Europe to assume a professorship in China.

But more important are the Wandering Jew's migrations to the New World. Perhaps the earliest recorded sighting was in Charleston, South Carolina, in 1845, when the Wanderer, said to have come from Poland or Russia, was seen wearing a blue skull cap and a long, faded, and frayed purple cloak, scribbling warning passages from the Old Testament on the sidewalks in chalk. A blast of wind accompanied him wherever he went. Postbellum Mormon sources told of the discovery of the Wandering Jew in a cave in upstate New York. Similar legends grew up in the Finger Lakes region. As recently as 1948 Ahasuerus was spotted—twice—in the men's room of the main New York Public Library.

Through most of his career, this Eternal Wanderer was typically regarded with disdain by Christians for his supposed insult to Jesus on the Via Dolorosa, which resulted in the curse. Some gentiles, however, felt sympathy for his plight. Others sought in his story a parable of redemption applicable to broader humanity. But all who believed the legend felt awe for the Wandering Jew. He carried with him firsthand knowledge of historical events since the time of Jesus and was unsurpassed by any mortal in learning. He had powers of divination and could read indecipherable texts. He spoke like a native the language of every land through which he passed. Dramatic meteorological phenomena and supernatural events attended his comings and goings.

Perhaps only to be expected was that the Wandering Jew's visitation should sometimes be accompanied by seemingly miraculous healings. His appearance in Stamford in mid-seventeenth-century England, as related in the introductory epigraph, was one instance of this. An early eighteenth-century French *Dictionnaire de la Bible* told how the Wandering Jew could cure men merely by touching them. Literary treatments of the legend have similarly had our Eternal Wanderer appear in the guise of a physician. The play *Der gelbe Ring*, written around the turn of the twentieth century, had Ahasuerus incarnated as a young physician in Medieval Germany who treated the local *Bürgermeister* and won the love of his daughter—with tragic consequences. A late nineteenth-century novel, *Der neue Ahasver*, had the title character reincarnated as a neat young doctor who served with distinction in the Franco-Prussian War of 1870 but remained the target of anti-Semitism.

The eternal Wandering Jew was taken as very real through the ages, and we may assume that many of the hundreds of sightings involved flesh-and-blood mortals who were mistaken for the Wanderer or who deliberately impersonated him. But part of the legend's appeal to the imagination of even those folks—gentile and Jew, friend and foe—who gave it no literal credence lay in its powerful symbolism. Ahasuerus's career since the time of Jesus represented the trials and tribulations of all Jewry, roaming from country to country through centuries in the Diaspora, seeing everything and acquiring all knowledge, while remaining undying and indestructible despite all prejudices and hostility.

Similarly, we may assume that whoever it was who supposedly cured by touch or by a miracle formula of bloodwort and red sage was not really Ahasuerus. Yet in view of the truly overwhelming contributions of Jews to medicine throughout the centuries, the image of the Wandering Jew as Doctor is as powerful a symbol as that of the Wandering Jew of legend. In the analytical psychology of the (gentile) Swiss psychiatrist Carl Gustav Jung, the Physician is one of the so-called archetypes in mankind's collective unconscious. As such, he can take many forms but is in essence beyond time and space. With a little imagination, one can see some of the great and not-so-great figures in Jewish medicine as manifestations and incarnations of a particularly Jewish archetype of the Eternal Doctor.

He appears in third-century Babylon as Samuel, an Aramaic-speaking talmudic sage whose knowledge of anatomy and detailed interpretation of Jewish hygienic regulations lead him to believe that he knows the cure for all ailments but three.

In twelfth-century Cairo, he's an Arabic speaking, turbaned rabbi-philosopher named Moses, a great interpreter and codifier of Jewish law, who also masters and elucidates the ancient Greco-Roman medical theories to such an extent that the Christian and Moslem sovereigns battling each other in the War of the Crusades both bid for his services.

He's called Angelo at the Vatican around the turn of the fifteenth century, the personal physician and "beloved son" of Pope Boniface IX—one of a long line of Israelite doctors to serve the Holy See (and as such be exempted from wearing the Jew-badge), despite an array of Church edicts through the centuries forbidding the faithful from being treated by Jews.

He makes an appearance at the Chinese capital, Kaifeng, early in the fifteenth century as physician An Cheng, major of the Brocaded Robe Corps, whom the physician Prince of Zhou honors with incense money for the rebuilding of the synagogue.

In late fifteenth-century Iberia his name is Rodrig, a member of a medical dynasty, clad as grandee, who is held in awe for his arcane medical knowledge by the Spanish and Portuguese monarchs but who proves unable to avert the Expulsion and Inquisition, which puts an end to centuries of Ibero-Jewish glory.

Some accounts have him reappear as Maestro Bernel, a ship's doctor on the Santa Maria, who, wearing a plumed cap on that fateful day in 1492, sets foot on the soil of the New World before Columbus does.

In sixteenth-century Provence his name is Michel and he wears the four-sided hat of an academic doctor and bears the Catholic family name of Our Lady, yet he claims descent from ancient Hebrew star-gazers as well as from recent court physicians and he writes down in his native Provençal a thousand verses of prophesy, which will be translated into all the world's languages and believed by multitudes for centuries to come.

Sporting the cloak and broad-brimmed hat made famous by the seventeenth-century Dutch masters, he appears as Juan, one of many refugee physician-scholars from Iberia who are contributing mightily to Holland's Golden Age; but he also serves as mentor to a young philosopher named Spinoza and so gets caught up in one of the greatest intellectual crises in Jewish history.

Again he's Samuel, this time a Jew-doctor in early nineteenth-century England, flaunting a medical diploma he shamelessly purchased in Aberdeen and becoming fabulously wealthy by selling his flavored brandy as a universal cure-all—which at least does his patients less harm than the toxins prescribed by his more reputable colleagues.

He appears as Ferdinand, a professor in Breslau, who having once worn the black, red and gold patriotic all-German colors of the ill-fated revolution in Berlin in 1848, now devotes his idealism and energy to a scientific revolution as he tries to convince the world of the enormous influence of infinitesimal organisms on the fate of men and nations.

In the smoke of the battle of Gettysburg during the American Civil War, his name is Simon, a 23-year-old German immigrant, wearing Confederate gray and operating on both Southern and Northern wounded for thirty-six hours at a stretch while musing about a future that will bring far gentler therapies.

On a beach in southern Italy in the latter nineteenth century his name is Eli and he's sticking a thorn into a starfish egg, observing the effects through his microscope and exclaiming in his native Russian that he's unlocked the secret of how the body defends itself against armies of subvisible invaders.

In Vienna around the turn of the twentieth century he's an absolutely irreligious yet proud Jew named Sigmund, who abandons his pioneering investigation of the nervous system in order to elucidate the labyrinth of the human conscious and unconscious mind in daringly novel metapsychological terms.

He takes the form of a little bespectacled cigar-addicted professor wearing a high collar in Frankfurt early in the twentieth century, a great pioneer in immunology, who is now looking with the power of his intellect and imagination into patients desperately ill with a disease whose very name is unmentionable but that he dreams of curing by shooting a tamed poison into their bodies.

Once again, he's an American named Simon, but this time he's on Manhattan's Upper East Side, founding and heading a multi-departmental research institute that would do more than any other to make the twentieth century the American Century.

He's a world-renowned pioneer in hematology named Ludwik, a Polish-Jewish convert to Catholicism, ordered to the Warsaw ghetto by the German invaders during World War Two because of his Jewish "blood," and refusing offers of sanctuary from his Catholic coreligionists so as to provide medical help to the doomed Jews, with whom he now identifies more than ever before.

At Oxford in England, he's Ernst, an exuberant refugee chemist from Nazi Germany with a bushy moustache, who's the driving force behind a top-secret project to derive from the squishy green mold of a rotting cantaloupe a juice to annihilate mankind's greatest invisible foes.

At war's end he's back in America, as a Russian immigrant biologist named Selman, who, clad in a white lab coat, wrings from a microorganism in the soil of the New World the cure for the Black Death and the White Plague, which had claimed untold millions of lives since the dawn of time.

And the previous are just some of the many names the Wandering Jewish Doctor takes throughout the centuries in our story. In the chapters that follow we will see him appear also as Antoine, Balthasar, Cesare, David, Ezechiel, Francisco, Gabriel, Hisdai, Isaac, Jacques, Karl, Leslie, Moritz, Nathan, Otto, Philotheus, Robert, Solomon, Tobias, Ulrich, Vitale, Waldemar, Xiansheng, Yuceff, and Zekekias. And one could go through the alphabet of the Wanderer's aliases again and again. But just as important is the fact that for every Jewish doctor named in our story, there were countless others throughout the ages who go unmentioned. Indeed, as the famed essayist on Jewish medicine Harry Friedenwald noted over half a century ago: "The reputation of Jewish physicians was such that at one time it was believed essential to skill in medicine to be of Jewish descent."

One might almost say that for some 1,000 years and counting, medicine has been *the* Jewish profession. The only other occupations to rival it in the Diaspora as particularly Jewish are commerce and, to a lesser extent, finance. This almost unique status of medicine may come as a surprise to many who are familiar with the various Jewish professional accomplishments of the last hundred years or so but who are less knowledgeable about Jewish livelihoods in ages past.

It's fairly common knowledge that since the late nineteenth century Jews have been wildly overrepresented among the world's great scientists, as indexed by such markers as the number of Nobel Prizes received. Yet this explosion of scientific discovery and creativity is a recent development in Jewish history. One would be hard-pressed to write of the Wandering Jew as Scientist if such a history were to extend back more than a century and a half from the present day. There was no Jewish Copernicus, Newton, or Galileo in ages past, or even particularly noteworthy lesser greats. (Only the science of astronomy and its pseudoscientific precursor astrology formed somewhat of an exception to this restriction.)

Similarly with the profession of law, with which Jews today are so strongly identified. True, rabbis throughout the ages were expert in analyzing and dissecting the fine points of talmudic law. But, again, one would have much difficulty in writing a long history of the Wandering Jew as professional Jurist. For the transfer by the Jews of their countless generations of keen legal thinking to the jurisprudence of larger society stems likewise from the post-emancipation era of the last century and a half or so.

Likewise with letters and its journalistic offshoot. Throughout the ages Jews in the Diaspora have been exceptionally literate—always in Hebrew, but often in other languages besides. Yet, with some exceptions—the great flowering of Judeo-Arabic literature in Moslem Spain comes most readily to mind—Jewish writing up to comparatively recent times has been largely concerned with religious matters. Today, Jews are great literati and even the more mundane Jewish authors are prominent on the best-seller lists of fiction. But in ages past there was no Jewish Shakespeare, Goethe, or Hugo—or if there was, his works have remained well hidden from the wider world. Similar comments can be made about Jewish artists, musicians, and theaterical directors before their explosive appearance on the world stage in comparatively recent times.

Not so with medicine. For more than a millennium, in so many lands, under all varieties of circumstances, and even in the most intolerant surroundings, Jewish physicians have been the medical superstars of society at large, and their less renowned brethren were as much as fifty times—5,000 percent—overrepresented in the profession. The Wandering Jew as Doctor has had a long lifespan, indeed.

How did this come about? When searching for answers, one quickly finds that explanations that are apparent in one era or country are often not readily applicable to other times and places.

Let's begin by considering a rather recent literary text, a passage from Philip Roth's classic novel *Portnoy's Complaint,* published in the mid-1960s.

We find the protagonist, the 30-something lawyer Alexander Portnoy, free-associating for his psychoanalyst: "Oh, that's one of the words they [Jewish mothers] just love, almost as much as *doctor*, Doctor. And *residency*. And best of all, *his own office*. . . . 'Do you remember Seymour Schmuck, Alex,' she [my mother] asks me. . . . Well, I met his mother on the street today, and she told me that Seymour is now the biggest brain surgeon in the entire Western Hemisphere. He owns six different split-level ranch-type houses made all of fieldstone in Livingston, and belongs to the boards of eleven synagogues, all brand-new and designed by Marc Kugel, and last year with his wife and two little daughters, . . . he took them all to Europe for an eighty-million-dollar tour of seven thousand countries, some of them you never heard of, that they made up just to honor Seymour. . . ."

Medicine in contemporary America is, of course, an extremely lucrative field. The Jewish community—highly literate and intelligent—has traditionally produced far more than its share of excellent and even phenomenal students. So it seems only natural that when American universities offered them—albeit with restrictions—the opportunity to study medicine and become doctors, young Jews should flock to the medical faculties in as large numbers as were allowed. This would ensure them—even as children and grandchildren of immigrants—entrée into the upper-middle socioeconomic stratum, with split-level ranch houses and all the other trappings.

Yet this alone doesn't quite explain Portnoy's *kvetching* about his mother's disappointment that he did not become a physician rather than a lawyer. After all, lawyers in contemporary America have a range of earnings comparable with that of doctors, and so do successful businessmen, entrepreneurs, and politicians. Perhaps the best of the many my-son-the-doctor jokes involves the Jewish mother flying to Washington to attend her son's inauguration as president of the United States, the first Jew to be elected to the office. She strikes up a conversation with the stranger sitting next to her on the plane, who at a certain point inquires as to why she's flying to Washington. "Well, my son Melvin is a doctor," replies the proud Jewish mother, "and I'm on my way to the Capitol to attend his brother's swearing in as president." The point is that the obsession with "my son the doctor" transcends wealth and even power. Indeed, in her own day the *grandmothers* of Portnoy and of our fictional Jewish president no doubt held the profession of medical doctor in just as high esteem. Yet early in the twentieth century, even in America, medicine was, with some individual exceptions, by no means the lucrative profession it would later become. It promised only a quite modest and at times uncertain prosperity in exchange for long working hours and much interrupted sleep.

Consider also a thoroughly noncapitalist system such as that of the former USSR, where forces other than Adam Smith's "invisible hand" guided the citizens into their various lines of work. By the mid-twentieth century a whopping 35,000 of all 215,000 Soviet physicians were Jewish—this despite the Jews being less than 1 percent of the total population and there having been a return to some form of the restrictive university quota system that had been abolished by the Revolution. Moreover, the Jewish doctors in the USSR were far more wildly overrepresented in the highest echelons of their profession—as became all too evident in the so-called Doctors' Plot of 1953, when an increasingly paranoid Stalin arrested the top Kremlin physicians, who were almost all Jewish. Yet this was under a system where the accumulation of any real monetary wealth could hardly have been a motivation in career choice, since it was virtually impossible.

In fact, there have been times and places when not the pursuit of wealth but some embarrassment about already having it was a contributing factor for Jews entering the medical profession. In Germany in the course of the nineteenth century, rapid industrialization and liberal capitalism, together with gradual legal emancipation and integration into wider society, brought much prosperity to the Jewish community in general and fabulous wealth to individual Jews in particular, as they moved from being traders in secondhand goods and petty money-lenders to captains of industry and grand investment bankers. Yet the social status of the Israelites lagged behind their meteoric economic rise. Professions such as military officer, judge, and high-ranking bureaucrat, held in such respect and even awe by German society, were restricted for members of the Mosaic faith. Careers in medicine were, however, open to Jews. Toward the end of the nineteenth century, Jewish doctors made up a sixth of the entire German medical profession (this from an overall population where Jews numbered less than 1 percent). In the capital, Berlin, they accounted for a third and eventually half of all doctors. In at least some cases, it appears that the motivation for entering medicine was the opposite of economic advancement, namely the prestige that the Jewish *nouveau riche* families felt by having their sons pursue an avocation untainted by commercialism. As a contemporary commentator put it: "We may spurn the millionaire for once having been a ragpicker, even while we drink his martinis. No one spurns the surgeon for being the son of a ragpicker."

A similar, if more general point was made at the end of the nineteenth century by the founder of the Zionist movement, Theodor Herzl, who wrote in his book *Die Judenstaat*: "The great majority of Jewish businessmen give their sons a superior education. Hence the so-called 'Judaizing' of all intellectual professions." Yet we must bear in mind that if all intellectual professions—science, literature, journalism, law, and medicine—were "Judaized" in Herzl's specific time and place, the latter and only the latter had already been "Judaized" for some 1,000 years and on all continents. Evidently, more has been involved in the Jewish participation in medicine than economic drive or intellectual prestige.

Consider a passage from the life story of the journalist Paul Cowan, as related in his book *An Orphan in History*. Growing up in a highly assimilated Jewish family on the WASPy Upper East Side of Manhattan, Paul was sent by his father (once a Cohen, now a Cowan and president of CBS) to prestigious Episcopalian prepschools. Paul's mother was a socialite and social activist, who, although the family didn't convert to Christianity, made a tradition of celebrating Christmas and gathering for an Easter dinner, while never once conducting a Seder. Nothing of the ancient Jewish tradition was consciously transmitted, not even the Bar Mitzvah ritual. Yet although Paul's mother's family had roots in the relative tolerance and freedom of America, already extending back for several generations, centuries of previous persecution had laid down a residue in what might almost be called her racial unconscious. "She seemed to agree when my father urged me to get a Ph.D.," Paul writes, "but in quieter conversation, when we were shopping together or talking late at night, she'd insist that I learn a trade—not a profession, but a trade—since she secretly believed that one day we'd have to leave all our goods and money behind and flee to some strange foreign land, where my survival would be ensured by a skill that didn't depend on language."

Although doctoring is nowadays certainly not considered a "trade," for much of its history it was often associated with physical skills. In ancient Greece, physicians were typically traveling artisans, on a par with cobblers and potters. Surgery was quite literally "hand-work" (*cheir-urgia*). In the

Middle Ages and beyond, although some physicians were university educated and may have been "doctors" in the academic sense, the vast majority of healers received their training by other means, usually as apprentices. The barber-surgeons in particular retained their manual worker status, and many healers among the gentiles weren't even literate. This contrasted sharply with, for example, the legal profession, which always required literacy and almost always a university diploma.

Of the learned professions even at the turn of the twenty-first century, medicine more than any other—its great prestige notwithstanding—has something of a physical rather than a purely intellectual or language-dependent nature. As such, it is a skill that the Wandering Jew most easily carries across borders. This was apparent in the Nazi era when German-Jewish refugee doctors could transfer their expertise to their new homes—human physiology being basically the same all over the world. Refugee lawyers, by contrast, were faced with the prospect of having to learn a whole different legal system, and refugee intellectuals and writers had to acquire the ins and outs of a new language, culture, and means of expression. Many times in the centuries before Hitler, whole Jewish communities had found themselves forced to flee to other countries, and the Wandering Jewish Doctor among them was particularly grateful that his skills were portable and transferable.

Yet once more we must be wary of generalizing. True, medicine in ages past was basically a physical skill for many healers. But the Jewish doctors as a group were the most highly literate and esoteric, and least manual, members of the profession. Telling is also the fact that when whole Jewish communities were exiled by the powers that be, the doctors often *didn't* have to leave. As Winston Churchill succinctly wrote in his *History of the English-Speaking Peoples*, with regard to events in early thirteenth-century England under King Edward I: "The Jews, held up to universal hatred, were pillaged, maltreated, and finally expelled from the realm. Exception was made for certain physicians without whose skill persons of consequence might have lacked due attention." Such privileged exemptions were accorded to many a Jewish doctor by monarchs in various times and places.

Jewish physicians were not the only Israelites at court. There was also the Jewish financier, who likewise had a privileged status, even under sovereigns who otherwise maintained harsh policies toward the Jewish community at large. At first sight, this tempts one to speculate that historical forces similar to those that placed Jews in the role of financiers likewise guided them to become doctors. As is well known, the Church in the Middle Ages forbade good Christians to lend money at interest, a restriction that left the market wide open to Israelites. But there was in fact precious little of a parallel in the case of medicine. The Church never prohibited Christians from practicing medicine (although it condemned monks and canons for doing so, especially if for temporal gain). On the other hand, from the seventh century onward, the Church *did* explicitly and repeatedly restrict and even outright forbid Christians, under pain of excommunication, from seeking the medical services of Jews. Yet in the late Middle Ages, when the most stringent provisions of the ban were in force, the Israelites, who accounted for only about 1 percent of the European population, supplied half of Europe's doctors. And their clientele included not only temporal monarchs but great men of the cloth, as well as various segments of Christian society in general.

What did Jews possess in gentile eyes that drove half of all Christian patients—and particularly the ecclesiastic and temporal princes—to consult Jewish doctors and thereby risk losing their souls in the next world in the hope of gaining a lease on life in the present one?

Again, we find that extrapolation of the modern situation to ages past can be deceptive. For the last 150 years or so, Jews have been known as great innovators in all fields of science and the arts. Einstein's relativity, Bohr's quantum physics, Schönberg's atonal music, Wittgenstein's logical positivism, Mendelsohn's sculptured architecture, and Chagall's poetic paintings are just a sampling of the Jewish contribution to modernism. As the famed socioeconomist Thorstein Veblen wrote early in the twentieth century with reference to this Jewish phenomenon, the first requisite for great science—and great intellectual and cultural achievements in general— is a skeptical frame of mind, freed of hard-and-fast preconceptions and the "dead hand of conventional finality." Such was the condition of many Jews in the wake of their legal emancipation and integration into larger society 100 or so years ago. Set loose from their own traditional moorings, coming to the gentile world as outsiders unfettered by those preconceptions about truth and beauty that Christians by centuries of habit took to be givens, many a modern Jew became, in Veblen's words, which resonate so well with our Wandering Jew theme: "a disturber of the intellectual peace, but only at the cost of becoming an intellectual wayfaring man, a wanderer in an intellectual no-man's land, seeking another place to rest, farther along the road, somewhere over the horizon."

So it was also with the Jewish contribution to modern medicine. Freud's psychoanalysis comes most readily to mind as a revolutionary concept that greatly influenced twentieth-century thought. More mainstream medical contributions made by Jews included their pioneering of the germ theory, immunology, chemotherapy, and antibiotics. Given the reputation of Jews as great innovators, Jewish doctors, even of the more run-of-the-mill variety, have understandably attracted patients who see them as being on the cutting edge of medical science and perhaps even capable—in a last resort—of coming up with an experimental miracle cure.

But such was hardly the case in eras past. Throughout the Middle Ages and even throughout most of the Renaissance and Enlightenment, Jews—with few exceptions—were far from innovators in any field, medical or otherwise. (Telling is the fact that the greatest exception, the seventeenth-century philosopher Baruch Spinoza, was excommunicated by the rabbis.) Indeed, for centuries, first in the Islamic world and then in Christian Europe, Jewish physicians were the great bearers of the classical medical doctrines of Hippocrates and Galen, which were already 1,000 years old or more. Although some of the commentaries and elucidation by Jewish doctors showed a certain independence and novelty, on balance it can easily be argued that Jewish medical scholarship was an inhibiting factor in Europe's transition from the moribund classical medical doctrines to the free inquiry of the Renaissance.

Yet in its time and place, the undisputed mastery of the ancient Greco-Roman medical texts by the tradition-bound, backward-looking rather than innovating Jewish physicians of the Middle Ages was reason enough for their appeal to masses of Christian patients in an era of general illiteracy among the gentiles. Furthermore, the gentile population knew that the multiliterate Israelites had more than just Greek and Latin books among the hidebound works at their disposal; there were also more than a millennium of Hebrew and Aramaic texts, most notably the Talmud, the codification of rabbinical law and opinion in the Diaspora. And the Wandering Jew as Doctor had also spent centuries among the Arabic books of the Moslem infidels from Cordoba to Baghdad. In many Christian eyes, this gave him powers and abilities—real or imagined, for good or evil—far beyond those of his Christian colleagues.

Not least important in this regard was the contrast in the overall attitude toward things corporal in the Jewish and Christian traditions. While the Church didn't prohibit the faithful from practicing medicine, Christian ideology from St. Augustine onward was generally permeated by a certain disdain for the body. Such an attitude was foreign to Jewish thinking. Talmudic writings neither venerated the body (as did the ancient Greeks, with their cult of nude statues) nor despised it, but endeavored to keep it—and not least of all its reproductive apparatus—in good working order so as better to serve higher goals. With such a millennium-long tradition on his side, the Jewish doctor, even in the often bigoted climate of the Middle Ages, had the competitive edge in attracting Christian patients, especially in a potentially life-or-death situation.

And aside from his general attitude toward the body, the Jewish doctor with his talmudic texts was the bearer of centuries of specific observations and discussion on health, hygiene, and anatomy among Jewish sages. Most of this had its origins in religion rather than rational science or natural philosophy. A wealth of knowledge of ritual animal physiology and food purity was obtained indirectly by adhering to the kosher dietary laws, which sooner had its roots in animal sacrifices at the Temple in the biblical era and in Mosaic ethical considerations than in matters of health per se. Even Jewish concerns with contamination were in large measure a carry-over from a biblical—indeed, prebiblical and prehistoric—concept of contagion in the magico-religious sense.

No matter. In the religious and superstitious climate of the Middle Ages, the presumed mystical powers of the Jewish doctor were as great an asset in Christian eyes as was his mastery of the rational texts of Hippocrates and Galen. The Wandering Jew of legend was cursed for insulting Jesus on his way to the crucifixion. The Jewish doctor shared with all his coreligionists the Christian contempt for his continued rejection of the Savior. Yet the Wandering Jew and the Jewish doctor were both held in awe not only for their centuries of accumulated knowledge but also for the supernatural phenomena that accompanied their actions. The Jewish physician was widely presumed to be in league with Satan. He was suspected of being under a religious obligation to secretly poison one out of every ten Christian patients and of withholding last rights from the dying. Yet these were odds and risks the gentile patient—even the cleric—was willing to accept, in the hope that the Jewish doctor, accessing dark powers of which a good Christian couldn't and shouldn't have knowledge, would effect a miracle cure.

In the terms of depth psychology, one could say that the Jungian archetype of the Physician meets the Freudian Oedipal complex of the Father in the gentile unconscious. The Wandering Jew of legend was traditionally depicted as an old fatherly image, his long great beard befitting one who has roamed the earth for centuries. So, too, the Antoines, Balthasars, Cesares, and all the others in our history of the Wandering Jewish Doctor, whatever their physical age in a given time and place, evoked a mental icon of an ancient father. As psychoanalyst Ernst Van den Haag put it in his classic book *The Jewish Mystique:* "Omnipotent, threatening, or reassuring—we depend on his power and are afraid of it. He may turn out to be the bad father who will punish us for our sins—though we hope he is the good father who will save us from them. The Jews . . . bear the burden of being the fathers of our civilization, who imposed their moral values on our reluctant impulses. The Jewish doctor thus becomes a father figure because of both his origin and his profession, provoking negative and fearful feelings, as well as positive and hopeful feelings, just as a father might."

The Jewish doctor has roamed the earth for ages, and the first chapter of the story that follows will, in fact, open at the very dawn of mankind. But much of our history—more than half—will take place from around the mid-nineteenth to the mid-twentieth century. This was truly the Heroic Age of medicine. In a radical break from past doctrines, physicians began for the first time in history to gain the knowledge and power to actually conquer the scourges of mankind. And the Jewish doctors, drawn from a people who were but a minuscule part of the world's population, played a pivotal role in this drama, particularly in the victory of man over microbe. "One of the noblest chapters in the history of mankind" was the description given to the heyday of the microbe hunters by the great (gentile) journalist H. L. Mencken, a man otherwise known for his cynicism. (Mencken was also known for harboring some anti-Semitic feelings, but prudently he never extended these to the medical field. "I go only to a Jewish doctor," he said. "Medicine requires brains, and the Jews got it. Goyim make bum doctors.")

Yet even in our chapters of triumphal medical science, there still remains something of the awe and mystery that have surrounded the Wandering Jewish Doctor through the ages. It is perhaps fitting that today's chemotherapeutic agents, antibiotics, and genetically manipulated drugs should so often be referred to as "*magic* bullets," a name with superstitious Medieval resonances, coined by the greatest of all Jewish doctors when he ushered in the age of molecular-based therapy at the dawn of the twentieth century.

Chapter 1
A Serpent upon a Pole

Every thing that may abide the fire, ye shall make it go through the fire, and it shall be clean: nevertheless it shall be purified with the water of separation: and all that abideth not the fire ye shall make go through the water. And ye shall wash your clothes on the seventh day and ye shall be clean, and afterwards ye shall come into the camp.

(Numbers 31:19–24)

And the Lord said unto Moses, Make thee a fiery serpent, and set it upon a pole: and it shall come to pass, that everyone that is bitten, when he looketh upon it, shall live. And Moses made a serpent of brass, and put it upon a pole, and it came to pass, that if a serpent had bitten any man, when he beheld the serpent of brass, he lived.

(Numbers 21:5–9)

From the northern reaches of the land of Israel, the Great Rift Valley makes its way along the River Jordan, across the Dead Sea basin, down into the Gulf of Aqaba, and over the Red Sea. From there it continues for over 1,000 miles through Ethiopia, Kenya, and Tanzania. This East African stretch of the Rift Valley is generally considered today to have been the evolutionary counterpart of the biblical creation myth and the Garden of Eden—the place where the species *Homo sapiens* arose in the course of a few million years of genetic mutations under the pressure of natural selection. An earthly paradise sub-Saharan Africa certainly was, with regard to the vast variety of life forms its tropical ecology could sustain. Man's quickly evolving intelligence, planning ability, and tool- and weapon-making skills brought about his transition from vegetarian to omnivore and placed him in a dominant position in the food chain. (In the biblical parable: "And the fear of you and the dread of you shall be upon every beast of the earth, and upon every fowl of the air, upon all that moveth upon the earth, and upon all the fishes of the sea; into your hands they are delivered"—Genesis 9:2).

But not all was paradise for *Homo sapiens* in this African homeland. Man's acquiring of an intellect, a mere moment in the biblical account of Adam at the tree of knowledge, went hand in hand with an increase in brain size that in terms of the evolutionary clock was hardly less dramatic in its speed—by some estimates, just a million years. So rapid was this development that adaptations in the woman's pelvis could only imperfectly keep pace with the size of the baby's brain at term. "In sorrow thou shalt bring forth children" (Genesis 3:16) has ever since been part of the human condition. So also is the particularly vulnerable infant, needing far longer nurturing than its simian relatives. And so, too, are the slipped disc, inguinal hernias, hemorrhoids, digestive system blockages, and a host of other ailments that, even several thousand generations later, *Homo sapiens* continues to pay as the price of early man's perhaps too rapid evolution from horizontal four-footer to upright biped.

And although club- and spear-wielding man may have had relatively little to fear from hungry predators, he was less secure from insults from other creatures. The serpent in the biblical parable was deceitful, but in the Rift Valley he was also likely to be poisonous. So, too, were various spiders, scorpions, and plants. The bush also teemed with parasitic insects and worms. But most important for our story was the fact that for every single plant or animal that man could see, there were countless trillions more that he could not. Among the members of this invisible zoo were entities so simple that they were virtually unchanged from the very first forms of life on earth that had emerged some four billion years earlier. For the next million years or so, no member of the species *Homo sapiens* would ever set eyes on any of them, and only a handful of humans would even conceive of their existence. Yet the influence of these infinitesimal creatures on the lives of men and the course of human history would be enormous.

So warm and lush were the rain forests of Africa that a broad spectrum of microorganisms could flourish without needing any animal host. The microbes were not quite so independent on the savanna of the Rift Valley and the tropical grasslands and shrubs. One such strain, however, which would one day be visualized and given the names *Trypanosoma gambiense* and *Trypanosoma rhodesiense,* was particularly hostile to man. Transmitted by the tsetse fly, these germs had long lived in a fairly benign and stable relationship to the herds of antelope they infested. But when they entered the human bloodstream, their effect was usually devastating.

With the number of humans increasing due to their skills in tool- and weapon-making, but their expansion into much of the rest of Africa inhibited by the trypanosomes and other hostile microorganisms, the time was ripe—around 100,000 years ago—for an exodus of some *Homo sapiens* out of Africa. Their gateway to the other continents was along the Rift Valley, across the Sinai Peninsula, and into the land that countless millennia later would be known as Israel. Skeletal remains at Mount Carmal, near Haifa, attest to this Israeli route out of Africa. In taking this path, *Homo sapiens* followed in the already million-year-old footsteps of the nearly human primate *Homo erectus*. (The account in Genesis in fact speaks of a first creation of humans, who were not capable of agriculture ["there was not a man to till the ground" (2:5)], followed by a second creation of humans, who later were ["Therefore the Lord God sent him forth from the Garden of Eden, to till the ground from whence he was taken" (3:23)].) *Homo sapiens* was also traveling the route that some of his distant descendants, called Hebrews, would again trace in their Exodus from Egypt.

In leaving the tropical Eden for more temperate climes, the hunter bands distanced themselves from the extraordinary spectrum of parasitic microorganisms that flourish so well in warm and moist conditions. Of course, diseases such as rabies and tetanus could still be transferred to humans from wild animals and from the soil. But such infections were now scarcer than in mankind's tropical African cradle. Other afflictions such as yaws and herpes, which are spread by transmission of the *Treponema pertenue* spirochete and *Herpesvirus hominis* by direct human-to-human body contact, might have more or less permanently accompanied the wandering hunting communities. But even then, the human migrants had an advantage. Only those strains of microorganism that were fairly benign and chronic (or, at least, capable of remaining long dormant in the body) would have stood much chance of surviving for longer than a human generation or so. A quick-acting, virulent strain would result in the death or abandonment of the victim or else the annihilation of the whole migratory group before they could infect other bands. In either scenario, the virulent strain itself comes to a dead end. A mild, long-lasting strain, by contrast, allows a continual chain of infection between individuals and between groups. At the same time, it often provides the carriers or recovered people with a degree of immunity to the more virulent strains, thus beating them out in the competition for survival.

Yet even so, there were enough afflictions to plague primitive man. New mutant strains of pathogenic microbes could have devastatingly rapid effects. Deviant gene expression in the cells of man's own body triggered malignant cancers. The finely tuned human immune system, whose function is to guard against all such foreign and home-grown enemies, could go awry and turn against the very body it was supposed to defend, resulting in arthritis and other autoimmune disorders. Wandering man's search for new foods in new environments often entailed various degrees of trade-off between nutritional benefits, on the one hand, and toxicity and digestive disorders, on the other. Slight deviations in the amounts of hormones secreted by one of the body's glands could have major effects on the entire system.

The primitive hunter-gatherers who fanned out from the African Rift Valley had a cerebral capacity similar to our own. As such, they had the concomitant mental abilities to learn to engage in formal reasoning using major and minor premises and syllogisms; manipulate random variables in controlled experiments; compute chi-square tests or establish statistical reliability; and balance organic chemistry equations involving double displacement reactions. But such things are, of course, very recent cultural developments in human history and would remain beyond the ken, though not beyond the intelligence, of *Homo sapiens* for tens of thousands of generations to come.

The way in which our Paleolithic ancestors sought to understand the world in general—and illness and cure in particular—is shrouded in the mists of prehistory. Yet there are even today Stone Age hunter-gatherers whose lifestyle has apparently evolved the least since the time of the exodus out of Africa. If we may extrapolate from the studies by the famed anthropologist James Frazer of Stone Age people early in the twentieth century, much of the primeval hunter-gatherers' understanding of cause and effect was dominated by two types of "sympathetic" relations between events: imitation and contagion. In the case of imitation, what happens to one object can supposedly influence a distant object merely by virtue of some physical similarity between the two. With contagion, on the other hand, the presumed influence between the distant objects is based on their once having been in physical contact (contagion and contact being derived from the Latin for "touching"). These prescientific concepts—overgeneralizations of the principle of association—formed the basis of many beliefs and practices that the modern mind calls magical. Added to this was the notion that one's thoughts and wishes, be they benevolent or malevolent, are able to cause or influence events—a vestigial unconscious memory (if one may trust psychoanalytic theory) of the infantile stage of cognitive development when the baby needed only feel hunger and desire food for it to appear.

Magical belief shaded into religious belief with the concept, still common to primitive peoples on all continents, of a world of transcendental spirits. The increasing mental capacities of *Homo sapiens* made him all the more aware of himself as a being with feelings and motivations and consciousness—a soul. Apparently inspired by his nightly experience of dreaming, in which he often encountered the dead in various settings far removed from the bed in which he was sleeping, primitive man further conceived of the soul or spirit as not indissolubly connected with a physical body and as capable of persisting after death. An extension of this was the concept of animism—primitive man's belief that combinations of substance and conscious spirit resided not only in himself and other humans and animals, but also in objects that the modern mind views as inanimate (e.g., trees) and even nonliving (rivers, rain) and nonmotile (rocks). Such spirits and ghosts were often called upon as intermediary agents in the carrying out of magical procedures.

The primitive attribution of animate and anthropomorphic characteristics to the spirits of even inanimate objects may be reflected in the gender markers that are still very present in many languages throughout the world, including those of the Semitic and Indo-European families (though only vestigially in the English branch). The earth, whose fertility brings forth the bounties of nourishment, was typically identified with a great female or mother spirit. Yet, in line with an extremely powerful predisposition toward religious belief among virtually all peoples stretching from the present back to the Stone Age, there also commonly emerged among the hunter-gatherers some dominant god of the masculine gender to be worshiped. This deity may at some time have been identified with the sky but was more commonly given plastic representation closer to home in the form of a carved statue of a sacred totem animal. Endowed with anthropomorphic properties, the totem typically evolved into an authoritative father-like god, derived (if we may again draw from psychoanalytic theory) from the universality of a father-figure in the infant stage of cognitive development and the ambiguous feelings of love and fear felt toward him.

Inhabiting a universe of anthropomorphic spirits and parent-like gods, primitive man understandably sought to placate these entities and turn their force to his advantage. Inherent in this quest was the drawing up of positive rules and rituals (commandments) for worship and offerings and negative rules (prohibitions or taboos) on such things as the killing of the totem animal. Taboos on the consumption of certain foods may have had an instinctual basis or have derived in part from a process of trial and error as migrating bands entered new environments and tested new food sources. Other dietary taboos may have derived merely from cultural tastes that, like genetic drift, just happened to evolve differently in various groups but may then have been incorporated into the religious system and taken on the force of law. Similarly, laws of social interaction evolved partly on the basis of instinctual forces and revulsion that were more or less consciously recognized, partly due to forces that (if, again, we trust psychoanalytic theory) were sublimated and suppressed from collective awareness, and partly on the basis of each given culture's attempt to reconcile these pressures with the need for a suitable modus vivendi among the hunter-gatherers. The social rules as they evolved were likewise incorporated into the broader supernatural system and attained the power of religious commandments, prohibitions, and taboos.

It was largely within this prescientific, magico-religious framework that primitive man, and particularly the *Ur*-physician, the "medicine man," first sought to explain and cure disease. The term—derived from American Indian languages—belies the greater spiritual and political role he played, in accordance with the structure of primitive society and the nature of the transcendental world. The prehistoric medicine man was probably often chief of the band. He (or, in the case of a medicine woman, she) might also have been the bard, entrusted with preserving and recounting the history of his people and the myths surrounding the creation of the world. As priest and sorcerer, he used his transcendental powers to ensure victory in war and a sufficient food supply, as well as to cure the sick. For these purposes the medicine man knew special songs, prayers, rites, and fetishes. Medicine men were seers, who derived much of their knowledge and abilities from a guardian spirit that spoke to them. Or they were shamans, voluntarily possessed by a spirit that worked through them.

When a tribe member fell ill, the medicine man's first task was to determine the etiology by taking a kind of case history. His attention was likely directed toward finding out what taboos might have been broken; what spirits, ghosts, or deities offended; or what totem animal killed or eaten, by either the patient or his family. Confession itself was the first step toward healing, to be followed by purification, prayers of atonement, and sacrifices. Inquiries into the patient's dreams were highly appropriate, for his nocturnal interaction with the world of spirits, ghosts, and even his fellow man was considered part of reality. The medicine man might himself enter a trance state in order to commune with the spirits and obtain from them a diagnosis and prognosis. Or he might search for omens in waking life. If no broken taboo or offended spirit could be discovered, then the medicine man inquired about human enemies who might have fashioned an effigy of the patient in order to mutilate it (imitative magic) or who may have gained control of his nail clippings, hair, or other body products carelessly left around in order to harm them and thereby the patient (contagious magic). Furthermore, any unusual object the patient may have noticed, say, at the entrance to his hut, would be suspect as a fetish invested with malevolent powers.

Whatever the etiology, it was commonly assumed in hunter-gatherer societies that a person was sick because either something vital was removed from the body or something bad was introduced—general concepts quite reasonable even by modern standards. The removal or loss of the soul was typically suspected in the case of chronic or degenerative diseases that cause the patient to wither away or afflictions that cause him to lose consciousness. The soul may, for instance, have been trapped by a malevolent sorcerer who hung a noose above the path of the unsuspecting victim. Or someone may have gained control of his shadow, the spiritual counterpart of his body. Alternatively, in its nocturnal wanderings the soul may have failed to return to the sleeping body, either because it lost its way, met with an accident, or was bewitched and lured away by the laughter of ghosts of virgins. Or the soul may have been expelled from the body by a sudden fright or sneeze. The medicine man, initiated in the appropriate chants, spells, and prayers, was adept at navigating his way in the world of the spirits, had a variety of soul-capturing devices, and knew how to lure or trick a lost soul into re-entering the patient's body either directly or through an intermediary object or creature.

As for more acute or localized diseases, these were sooner attributed to the patient's acquiring something malevolent, be it spiritual or tangible, rather than his losing something vital (his soul). The Paleolithic medicine man's treatment was correspondingly based on expelling the pathogenic agent. Trepanation—the grooving or boring out of a section of the skull— may have had some origin in practical measures: the removal of arrow- heads or the relief of pressure of intracranial bleeding from other trauma. But in the transcendental universe, the procedure was widely used to re- lease the evil spirits assumed to be causing headaches, epilepsy, psychoses, and probably a variety of non-neurological afflictions as well. Similarly, the very widespread Paleolithic therapeutic practice of drawing blood from a sick person by means of venesection or scarification may have owed some of its origin to practical observations—namely, the relief felt by some fe- brile patients when a spontaneous hemorrhage, nosebleed, or menstrua- tion decongested their systems. Bloodletting also accompanied the medi- cine man's sucking out of the body of tangible objects such as arrowheads, splinters, and worms. But no doubt most important within the magico- religious framework of the prehistoric hunter-gatherers was the assump- tion that pathogenic spirits left the body along with the patient's blood. Less pleasant were the prehistoric procedures involving the whipping and fumigating of the patient—to the accompaniment of jarring noises and frightening masks—in order to made the bodily abode so inhospitable to the malevolent spirit that he abandoned it. Patient-friendlier procedures involved enticing the spirit out of the body with food or the use of magical chants and commands to exorcise the demon and call upon more powerful and benevolent spirits and deities to intervene.

It was within the magico-religious conceptual framework that Paleolithic pharmacology had its origins, as bands of *Homo sapiens* migrating to the four corners of the earth continually encountered new flora, fauna, and miner- als. The simple principle of association gave rise to the doctrine of signa- tures, whereby some external characteristic of a plant or mineral suppos- edly made it appropriate for strengthening a certain body part or treating a certain affliction (red flowers or coral for the blood, the weasel plant to ease childbirth, the mandrake root as an aphrodisiac, and so on). In some remedies an incipient homeopathic (like-cures-like) principle was also at work (yellow plants and emeralds to treat jaundice, toads to eliminate boils, spotted white snake skins to cure leprosy, red-speckled blood-stone to staunch bleeding). Other drugs arose from trial and error rather than outward signs. Vomitives and evacuants supposedly purged a patient of malevolent spirits along with the contents of his digestive system. Various stimulants, intoxicants, and hallucinogens found in leaves, seeds, barks, and roots were used in communal religious ceremonies and helped the medicine man in particular to enter the trance state and consult the spirits.

Some of the diverse drugs chosen for their influence in the transcendental scheme of things in fact had pharmacologically useful properties. Certain psychotropic drugs relieved pain, stimulated the appetite, had aphrodisiac effects, and countered indigestion. Evacuants purged the body of worms. Some fumigants eased the distress of asthma or other respiratory afflictions.

Even in the transcendental universe of the Paleolithic hunter-gatherers, magic and religion gave way to empirical and pragmatic concepts, particularly with regard to afflictions that were endemic—that "everybody" seemed to get. The counter-irritation provided by the massaging of aching muscles or the swelling reduction afforded by the application of a poultice of warm cow dung to a sprained ankle were practical measures hardly needing rationalization in terms of the driving or drawing out a spirit. Where malaria, yaws, certain venereal diseases, and tuberculosis were commonplace, sufferers were likely to seek the services of a herbalist woman rather than the medicine man, as were patients with colds, dyspepsia, common rashes, diarrhea, and the like. Visible parasites such as ringworm and hookworm were likewise sooner viewed in a mundane rather than transcendental light. Instead of being ceremoniously anointed, the tribesmen's feet were smeared with common oil to protect against infestation. Broken bones were splinted or put in casts of clay, dislocations were reduced by manipulation, and hemorrhaging was staunched by direct pressure of sand, down, or animal hides on the wound.

In the transcendental world, no less than in the age of modern rational medicine, an ounce of prevention was worth a pound of cure. On all continents, the wearing of tiger teeth, eagle claws, sharp flints, and the like served to fend off evil spirits. Malodorous substances repelled them. Phallic and vaginal symbols afforded protection through, respectively, their masculine potency and their live-giving forces. The glittering of diamonds and other precious jewels neutralized the evil eye. Collective dancing and hostile displays with weapons and frightening masks provided a prophylactic effect against evil spirits that was greater than the sum of individual efforts. For the potentially benign spirits and protective gods, placation in the form of offerings of food and drink were called for.

Just as some curative medical practices based on a magico-religious worldview may have had real physiological benefit, so, too, may certain pre- or unscientific preventative measures have had a positive effect on the health of those who observed them. Lest an enemy gain control over them by means of sympathetic magic, primitive people typically engaged in the quite hygienic practice of covering up their excrement and rubbish. Fear of contagion in the magical sense led to some customs whose practical value would only be fully appreciated in the age of microbiology, such as the avoidance of the clothes and possessions of a sick or dead person. A corpse was buried deeply and securely, lest it turn into a vampire who, lonesome for company, would lure the living to the grave. Or the corpse and its dwelling were burned so that the pathogenic evil spirit would not go on to claim another victim. Lest a river god be offended, primitive animists refrained from urinating in or otherwise fouling the water—and thus they inadvertently ensured a healthy source for drinking.

Unfortunately, not all primitive magico-religious practices—even those that have stood the test of time—necessarily had a positive effect on health. For example, bathing in a common source for the purposes of ritual purification—laudable in principle—could have devastating consequences for the practitioners in spreading infectious and parasitic diseases in certain geographic areas. And when autopsies of sorts were performed, as when the abdomen of the deceased was searched for the witchcraft object supposed to have caused his demise, this was more likely to expose the dissector and others to further disease than to yield meaningful anatomical knowledge—especially when the search concentrated only on finding some tangible malevolent object.

∼

The human epidemiological picture underwent dramatic changes, thanks to the descendants who, a few thousand generations after the original exodus across the Sinai, found themselves back in the Middle Eastern extension of the Rift Valley and were the first on earth to develop agriculture. It was some nine millennia ago, apparently around the fertile banks of the River Jordan, that the advent of farming heralded the end to man's nomadic lifestyle. With this advance came a ten- to twenty-fold population increase within the space of a few centuries and the beginning of civilization, in the quite literal sense of the building of cities (Latin *civitas*). People not directly engaged in food-production, but rather in administration, management, food storage, planning, distribution, taxation, and trade, took up residence in centers whose populations numbered in the hundreds and then in the thousands. Nine millennia ago the thick foundation walls of Jericho, the first city on earth, were laid down. They have survived to the present day.

From a medical point of view, the advent of civilization had profound consequences, as previously unimaginable numbers of sedentary people were concentrated in a given area. The population of the united kingdom of Sumer and Akkad in Mesopotamia probably topped the half million mark by around 3000 B.C.E. Within the cities the concentration was, of course, far higher still, reaching a certain critical mass that permitted infectious diseases to become endemic. From that point on, as long as the urban population remained large enough through new births and immigration, various pathogenic microbes could always find someone new to infect, usually children. So it was that perhaps from the very dawn of civilization, measles, mumps, whooping cough, smallpox, and other typically childhood diseases were transferred directly from town-dweller to town-dweller, often borne by droplets sneezed into the air. This had the long-term advantage of allowing the development of individual immunity, acquired early in life. Furthermore, as we have noted, it was typically the more attenuated strain of a given pathogenic germ that found a niche in the population, beating out its more virulent competitors. The urban situation also allowed the local human gene pool to develop a degree of communal immunity to the local pathogens in the course of generations by the process of natural selection—the survival and reproduction of the members of the community with greatest natural resistance.

But counterbalancing the apparent advantage of this modus vivendi between sedentary humans and local pathogenic microbes, civilization also brought enormous disadvantages, not least for the large towns that engaged in commerce. The thick walls around Jericho and similar cities may have repelled hostile marauders, but they were useless against unfamiliar and devastating microorganisms borne over perhaps hundreds of miles by friendly traders and migrants. The effect of such germs on populations that had not developed individual or communal immunity to them were potentially as bad as any wrought by an invading army.

The concentration of people in an agricultural and urban environment allowed the spread of disease in many more ways than merely by droplets sneezed into the air or direct physical contact. Contamination of food by human fecal matter now gave certain pathogens their chance to establish a niche denied them by the mobile hunter-gatherers. Cities and agricultural areas also provided a haven for a range of parasites that could not be transmitted from person to person but required some animal intermediary or reservoir. Schistosomaisis, a disease of humans caused by the schistosome fluke or flatworm, can complete its life cycle only outside the human body with the help of snails that breed in shallow, still water, especially in warm climes. Such were the conditions in the African forests that the ancestors of the Middle Eastern agriculturists had left behind eons earlier, and such were the conditions their descendants now artificially recreated. The schistosome blood flukes found in Egyptian mummies dating from 1200 B.C.E. had probably already been infesting wading cultivators of the Nile and Mesopotamia for millennia.

Similarly, the anopheline mosquito that transmits malaria, so at home in the swamps of Africa, found a suitable niche in the stagnant bodies of water created by Middle Eastern farmers. So, too, did its cousin the aedine mosquito, the carrier of yellow fever. Later, the accumulation of human waste along river banks and the damming of streams made a highly hospitable environment for the simulium flies transmitting the filarial worms that cause onchocerciasis (river blindness). Fleas, which typically contaminate human homes and animal nests and were therefore of little concern to nomads who regularly abandoned their makeshift dwellings, now became a permanent part of the human scene. So did rats and mice, which could feed on the stored grain.

Disease-carrying snails, insects, and rodents were the unintended and unwanted company of the changes in the landscape brought about by farming. Domestic animals, by contrast, were one of the purposes of farming. There are, unfortunately, dozens of diseases—some common, some rare— that humans came to share with domesticated animals. The pig ranked fairly high on the list of carriers of infective agents. In a natural setting, a microbe strain tends to evolve so that it parasitizes a particular species of host. Thus in the hunter-gatherer era, a disease common to wild boars would be unlikely to infect a human, even when man and beast happened to come into close contact. With the development of farming, as groups of men lived for generations with a given species of animal such as pigs, the microbes, especially the rapidly mutating viruses, could readily evolve a strain capable of infecting and being transmitted across the two species. So it has been in recent times with the swine-flu epidemics, and so it was with the advent of agriculture in the ancient Middle East.

But it was the pig's scavenging habits that presented particular health problems for humans, most notably in regard to parasitic worms. Larvae of the nematode (roundworm) *Trichinella spiralis* are often encysted in the muscles of infected pork. When the meat is insufficiently cooked and then consumed by humans, the larvae are liberated from their cysts by the digestive juices and grow to maturity in the gut, where they reproduce sexually and their larvae is in turn carried by the blood and lymphatics to the muscles. The result is an uncomfortable, though usually passing period of debilitation. When pigs ingest fecal material from infected humans or scraps of meat from other, infected pigs, the cycle begins anew. Similarly, tapeworms (which unlike most pathogens are quite visible, often growing to over a meter or yard in length) often transfer from pig intestines to human intestines and back again.

The development of agriculture was a boon to mankind, in that the increased food supply allowed vastly more people to inhabit the planet. Whereas hunter-gatherers deliberately employed various means to keep their numbers low, with the advent of civilization early marriage and many children were signs of divine favor even before the injunction to be fruitful and multiply appeared in the Bible. But for each individual person, the development of civilization was, nutritionally speaking, sooner a step backward. Quantity came at the expense of quality. The hunter-gatherers had access to a great variety of nuts, fruits, and vegetables, as well as meat, which they consumed fresh, year round. The civilized sedentary diet, by contrast, meant a greater reliance on a limited number of stored, typically starchy, foods as sources of cheap calories. The proportion of meat in the diet declined, as did the variety, freshness, and fiber content. Archaeological evidence points to increased incidence of anemia, rickets, and (perhaps) scurvy—the consequences, we now know, of deficiency in, respectively, iron, vitamin D, and vitamin C. Most likely, the incidence of appendicitis and intestinal cancers increased. The lower fiber diet allowed longer contact of the intestinal walls with microbes associated with decay and carcinogenic substances, and the reduction of fruit and nut intake meant lesser amounts of possibly anticarcinogenic ellagic acid. Hypertension and other cardiovascular disturbances and diabetes are likewise millennia-old legacies of the advent of civilization.

Virtually everything that has been related up to this point in our story belongs to prehistory and has been deduced from skeletal, mummified, and fossil remains of prehistoric humans and from observation of present-day primitive peoples. With the development of writing in the Middle East some three millennia B.C.E. came the dawn of recorded history. Not long afterward (relatively speaking), the first Jews made their appearance on the world stage. Around 2000 B.C.E. the merchant Terah; his son Abraham; Abraham's wife, Sarah; and their nephew Lot journeyed from the port city of Ur on the Persian Gulf northwestward along the Tigris and Euphrates Rivers in present-day Iraq, an area where the city-states of Sumer a few centuries earlier had been conquered and united by the Semitic-speaking Akkadians, thus forming the Kingdom of Babylonia.

Mesopotamia, the Land Between the Rivers, would figure larger in Jewish history than merely as its starting point. In succeeding centuries the Babylonian Empire would exert a strong cultural influence on Israel, as it did on the rest of the Middle East and Western Asia. It was from Babylonian myths that various elements of the Bible borrowed, particularly the story of Creation and the tale of an ark and a great Deluge. In the sixth century B.C.E., the spiritual and genealogical descendants of Abraham and Sarah would spend almost fifty years by the Rivers of Babylon as forced exiles from their Zion homeland. And it was in Mesopotamia in the third, fourth, and fifth centuries C.E. that Jewish scholars, now in for a much longer, worldwide exile following the destruction of the Temple by the Romans, developed the Babylonian Talmud—the body of oral law derived from exposition and adaptations of the Bible's five books of Moses—and eventually committed it to written form.

Tens of thousands of Babylonian clay tablets from around 3000 B.C.E. impressed with cuneiform characters have withstood the ravages of five millennia by laying low underground. It is from them that much of our knowledge of ancient Mesopotamia is derived, including a thousand or so items of medical interest. As with all cuneiform texts, these medical notes are open to varying interpretations. Furthermore, the relevant tablets were in no way comparable to modern textbooks for the education of healers but were merely intended as notes and memory aids. At the time when Abraham and his family journeyed through the Babylonian Empire, its population had for several centuries already been above the critical threshold of about half a million needed for acute human-to-human contagion to be indefinitely sustained. The clay tablets appear to make reference to smallpox and tuberculosis as well as gonorrhea. There are also descriptions of diseases of the eye and intestines and reference to the presence of malaria in the swampy regions.

The Babylonians were no different from every society, before and since, in wanting to combat the medical afflictions that befell them. They made recourse to medicines of vegetable, mineral, and other origins. Their medicinal resins and spices probably included cassia, frankincense, and myrrh. Oils, wines, beer, milk, honey, fats, and wax were common bases, and some of the compounding procedures may have yielded soap. A few of the plant extracts and alcoholic spirits may have had at least a mild bactericidal effect on wounds. The more fragrant ingredients had in any case the advantage of counteracting malodorous smells. Not so the various types of dung the Babylonians used for wound treatment, perhaps under the assumption that since the proteolytic enzymes served to bate hides before tanning, they would similarly reduce the swelling of wounds. Living as they did in the Bronze Age, the Babylonians also made some references on their tablets to knives and lancets for surgical procedures. To the Babylonians also goes the honor of history's first medico-legal texts. Etched in stone rather than clay, the Code of Hammurabi stipulated the generous fees to be paid the physician for a successful procedure but also the penalties and compensations to be exacted from him if he caused the patient's death.

The presence of such practical and rational medical items belies the otherworldly universe that the Babylonians inhabited and the supernatural basis for their healing. There was no dramatic break with the primitive and prehistoric mentality. The use of oils for wound treatment had its origin in religious anointing, and the aromatic spices in drugs had a similar ceremonial origin, regardless of medicinal properties they might possess. Healing was basically an empowerment of the priestly class, since illness was conceived of as punishment for sin or impurity. These transgressions had deprived the patient of divine protection and made him prey to one or more of the hordes of demons and malevolent spirits (some 6,000 of them, by one reckoning) that haunted the Babylonian universe. The precise supernatural treatment would depend on the determination of the specific supernatural etiology of the illness.

As for the Babylonian knowledge of anatomy, it probably extended no further than what could be seen in the entrails of butchered animals. The Babylonians wrongly conceived the heart to be the site of intelligence and the kidneys the source of strength. They also had strangely detailed conceptualizations of the livers of sheep. It was believed that when a person blew into a sheep's nose and the animal was then slaughtered, an examination of the form of the liver could reveal all sorts of information, particularly about the future. As is written in Ezekiel (21:21) ". . . the king of Babylon stood at the parting of the ways, at the head of the two ways, to use divination: he made his arrows bright, he consulted with images, he looked in the liver." Sheep heptoscopy was likewise used for diagnosing human medical ailments. Clay models of sheep livers were constructed in several variations as standards for comparison. Yet if the Mesopotamians ever gained from this any real knowledge about the functions or dysfunctions of the liver in man or beast, this is nowhere reflected in the cuneiform tablets that have been deciphered.

Nor can much scientific knowledge be said to have come from the many other prognostic practices of the Babylonian physicians. For example, they also made diagnoses by examining the number of openings on an expectant mother's nipple (five and six, bad; seven to ten, good). This was not an inherently illogical practice—the modern-day obstetrician, for example, counts the number of tubes in the severed umbilical cord for signs of possible genetic birth defects—but was nonetheless baseless.

Most important among the Babylonian pseudosciences was astrology. The Babylonians were gifted astronomers, capable of predicting the movements of the heavens and heavenly bodies. Their interpreting of events in the skies as omens of occurrences on earth, including diseases, was—although not inherently irrational—likewise completely false. Nevertheless, it established an astrological tradition that was to exert a powerful influence on medicine for more than 2,000 years.

But there was a very real aspect of certain diseases that even the supernatural-minded Babylonians undoubtedly noticed through simple experience. In sparse hunter-gather societies, where all strains of parasitic microorganisms were slow-acting, chronic, and relatively benign, the idea of "catching" a disease from another person may never have occurred to anyone. In densely inhabited Babylonia, by contrast, the concept of contagion—more in the modern medical, rather than in the prescientific magical, sense—began to dawn. Someone came into contact with a sick person, was himself soon acutely stricken, and in turn transmitted the disease to someone else. Tangentially related to this was the Babylonians' awe of Baal-Zebub, the Lord of the Flies (as well as of gnats and other insects), who was blamed for diseases among the Philistines and Phoenicians. A Babylonian court physician would later write: "Beware of flies and shun lice in the interest of good health"—perhaps the dawning of the concept of natural disease transmission through animate vectors.

It was such a mix of supernatural beliefs, a bit of chance practical knowledge, and some concept of contagion that Abraham most likely took with him on his journey from Ur. In Haran, in the southern part of present-day Turkey, the 75-year-old patriarch had his encounter with Jehovah. In their covenant, Abraham and his descendants, given the name Hebrews, were promised the land of Canaan. For four centuries the patriarchs Isaac, Jacob, and Joseph, and their rapidly expanding families wandered through the Promised Land. Then, in the sixteenth century B.C.E. a famine struck the areas to the northeast of Egypt, and many of Abraham's descendants migrated to the fertile Nile Valley, where they were welcomed by the pharaoh, whose viceroy, Joseph, was himself a Hebrew. There they would remain for another 400 years and absorb various aspects of Egyptian culture, including medical concepts.

Although the history of the Middle East during the Egyptian New Kingdom, which began in the sixteenth century B.C.E., tells of military and diplomatic relations and commercial contacts between Egypt and Mesopotamia, the two great river civilizations—800 miles apart—had their distinct traditions, not least of all in medicine.

Our knowledge of Egyptian medicine is derived largely from seven papyri devoted to healing. Five of them date from the fifteenth to the twelfth centuries B.C.E., the time of the Hebrew sojourn in Egypt. One of the other texts perhaps slightly predates this period and the remaining one, the oldest of all, originated in the nineteenth century B.C.E. Instead of cuneiform script, the Egyptians used a complex hieroglyphic system: partly ideographic, when signs stood for the things or concepts they depicted; and partly phonetic, when signs stood for particular consonant sounds. Although far from complete, the Egyptian papyri clearly come closer to our concept of a medical textbook than do the Mesopotamian tablets.

Like everyone else, the Egyptians viewed the etiologiy of disease in a basically supernatural way. Spirits and demons were working their mischief along the Nile, just as they were along the Tigris and Euphrates. But by a certain theological evolution, demonology in Egypt came to be replaced by a belief that *deities* caused disease and that other gods (or sometimes the same god) could cure it. Egypt was originally home to many local deities and these often fused with one another, some of them attaining cosmic importance. Ra, the sun-god, was the chief deity. The female Isis, representing the earth-mother, was worshiped as a goddess of healing. Her brother, Osiris, the personification of the Nile, was dismembered by another brother, Seth, but was revived when Isis lay upon him. Together— sibling mating was as common among the Egyptian deities as it was among Egyptian mortals—Osiris and Isis conceived Horus, the falcon-god. But Seth tore out Horus's eye (of which today's Rx prescription symbol is believed to be a stylized representation), thus giving a boost to his reputation as a major bringer of afflictions to humans. The eye was, however, healed by Thoth, the physician to the gods and source of all wisdom. In the course of centuries, Thoth was replaced by Imhotep, an actual historical figure of many talents, who was known more for his architectural and poetic accomplishments but was nevertheless deified as chief healing god and given a divine father.

As for the mortal physicians of ancient Egypt, they were grouped into a hierarchical pyramid of specialists. As the Father of History, the Greek Herodotus, related in the fifth century B.C.E.: "Medicine with them [the Egyptians] is distributed in the following way: every physician is for one disease and not for several, and the whole country is full of physicians of the eyes; others of the head; others of the belly; and others of obscure diseases." The pharaoh's physician stood at the top of the hierarchy, followed by lesser palace physicians and supervisors and inspectors, and then by the physicians to the quarry, serfs, temple, and military. Prestigious was the position of "Keeper of the King's Rectum." This was in line with the Egyptian obsession with the anus, which in their anatomical conceptions was apparently second only to the heart as a center where blood (and other) vessels met. Decay was assumed to occur in the intestines, and the excremental rot was capable of being transported to other parts of the body and thus cause disease. Hence the Egyptian obsession with enemas. To cite Herodotus again: "For three consecutive days in every month they purge themselves, pursuing after health by means of emetics and drenches; for they think it is from the food they eat that all sickness comes to men."

A most important event in the history of the Jews and Jewish medicine took place in the fourteenth century B.C.E., at a time when the Hebrews were living and working in Egypt and had not yet been reduced to bondage. The pharaoh Amenhotep IV rejected the ancient array of gods and demons and established as the state religion the worship of the god Aton, the Disc of the Sun. Amenhotep changed his name to Ikhnaton; chiseled off the stone monuments all references to Ammon, as the top god was then currently known; and moved the capital from Thebes to a new site downstream, Akhetaton. Some thirty-two centuries later, a Jewish medical doctor named Sigmund Freud would author a psychoanalytic-anthropological study on *Moses and Monotheism* and speculate that Ikhnaton's new religion strictly involved only One God and brought with it a rejection of all magic, sorcery, anthropomorphism, as well as the afterlife. This was probably an exaggeration of what really happened; but most historians agree that a shift toward monotheism was wrought by the worship of the Sun God, a vestigial reference to whom would be found even centuries later in Psalms 104 of the Hebrew Bible, where the Lord "coverest thyself with light as with a garment, . . . layeth the beams of his chamber [and] maketh . . . his ministers a flaming fire." In any case, with the death of Ikhnaton, his son-in-law and successor moved the court back to Thebes and reestablished Ammon as the top god among many others, thus ending for the time being the monotheistic trend.

So the concept of an afterlife, presumably downplayed in Ikhnaton's short-lived new religion, continued to obsess the Egyptians. The very symbol of ancient Egypt, the pyramids, were in fact gargantuan funeral monuments. An assumption among the Egyptians was that although some divine spark departed the body at the moment of death, the soul continued to be housed in the body. The Egyptians removed the liver, lungs, stomach, intestines, and brains of the deceased and kept them in separate stone jars. (These were dissections of sorts, affording information—however erroneously interpreted—of internal human anatomy.) The shell of the body, however, had to be maintained intact. Since around 2000 B.C.E. or earlier, the Egyptians had used drying and salting as a means of preserving fish and meat. But for preserving humans on their journey through the afterlife, the Egyptians embalmers opted for natron, a naturally available mixture of sodium carbonate and bicarbonate, also containing sodium sulfate and sodium chloride impurities. This represented perhaps the first systematic use of antibacterial agents on the human body, albeit on corpses. (The custom of mummification would also provide—at the time of the Crusades, some 2,000 years later—a very lucrative business for an enterprising Alexandrian Jew named Elmagar, who sold mummy remains as a wonder drug to Crusaders and Saracens alike. The fad caught on, to such an extent that Renaissance popes and kings relied on the stuff, and less honest apothecaries were not above using corpses of recently deceased convicts instead of the real thing.) Serendipitously when it came to living bodies, copper oxides, prized for their green color (which represented life to the people of the verdant Nile Valley, hemmed in on both sides by the desert), were used as women's make-up and then in ointments for wound treatment. This copper may have had a beneficial effect in combating the microorganisms today known as streptococci.

Long predating even the oldest papyrus is a bas-relief in Memphis from around the twenty-third century B.C.E. of a young man or adult being circumcised. The knife was almost certainly not of metal but of flint. (Copper first made its way through Mesopotamia to Egypt after the start of the Middle Kingdom, around 2000 B.C.E. And until the New Kingdom, which began a half millennium later, iron was an extremely precious commodity obtained from an occasional meteorite.) Various kinds of circumcision have been practiced since time immemorial by widely disparate peoples, ranging from the Bantu of South Africa to the Aborigines of Australia to the Islanders of the South Pacific to the Indians of South America. This practice seems to owe at least some of its origin to an association with agricultural fertility, as manifested by the ceremonial strewing of the severed foreskins on the earth. In a more general vein, the Creator of All was offered a part of the human organ of creation.

Such ritual symbolic offerings obviously required the actual severing of the foreskin. If the purpose of the operation was purely hygienic (the prevention of infection under the foreskin, known as balanitis), a simple lengthwise dorsal cut rather than removal of the ring, would suffice to loosen the prepuce and permit thorough cleaning. In Egypt, however, although there was actual severing of the foreskin in accordance with religious ritual, hygienic considerations certainly did play a role in circumcision. It was probably first the privilege of the priesthood, later extended to the pharaoh and his family, and then to the nobles. From there, it filtered down to other layers of cleanliness-conscious Egyptian society.

The Egyptian practice of circumcision certainly became an obsession to Moses, who set in motion a trend that would elevate the severing of the male baby's foreskin into one of Judaism's most central rituals. (True, the Book of Genesis presents circumcision as part of Jehovah's covenant with Abraham centuries earlier; but this pedigree is suspected of having been added retrospectively by the compilers of the Bible.) Freud, of course, had his own views of the circumcision ritual as symbolic castration. Yet no less interesting were his speculations—not entirely original with him—that, unlike in the biblical account, Moses was not born a Hebrew and raised as an Egyptian prince but was in fact an Egyptian by birth who was deeply impressed by the discredited cult of the One God, Aton. Unsuccessful in reviving the cult among the Egyptians, he turned to the Hebrews (who had, in the meantime, been enslaved under "a new king . . . who did not know Joseph" [Exodus 1:8]) and promised them freedom in return for their accepting monotheism. Whatever the case, it seems reasonable to assume that during their 400-year sojourn in Egypt, the Hebrews were influenced by Egyptian medical views. There cannot, however, be any doubt that Jewish thinking on religion and disease also represented a momentous break with all that had come before in the Middle East. As the first nation to embrace monotheism, the Jews were the first to inhabit a universe that did not swarm with hordes of demons and evil spirits, or with more benevolent supernatural beings. In medical matters, monotheism signaled a dramatic reduction in the multitude of practices that we would sooner call "superstitious" rather than merely "religious."

Jewish monotheism didn't, however, mean a rejection of the supernatural concept of the causation and cure of disease—at least, not at initially. To a modern microbiologist, the description of the beginning of the ten plagues of Egypt ("the waters which are in the river . . . shall be turned to blood. And the fish that is in the river shall die, and the river shall stink; and the Egyptians shall lothe to drink of the water of the river" [Exodus 7:17–18]) sounds like a tide of red algae (*Dinoflagellida*) causing mass paralytic poisoning of marine life. This in turn apparently led to vermin devastating the Nile region ("lice in man, and in beast . . . a grievous swarm of flies into the house of Pharaoh . . . a boil breaking forth with blains upon man, and upon beast, throughout the land of Egypt" [Exodus 8:17, 24; 9:9]). Be this as it may, the Scriptures leave no doubt that it was Jehovah Himself Who brought about the pestilence in order to compel Pharaoh to release the Hebrews from bondage. On later occasions He would smite the enemies of the Children of Israel with various other afflictions. Some form of hemorrhoids (perhaps in combination with the bubonic plague) was a particular expression of His wrath, as on the occasion of the Philistines' capture of the Ark ("[T]here was a deadly destruction throughout the city; the hand of God was heavy there. And the men that died not were smitten with the emerods: and the cry of the city went up to heaven" [1 Samuel 5:11–12]).

As for His Chosen People, Jehovah promised and cajoled: "If thou wilt diligently hearken to the voice of the Lord thy God, and wilt do that which is right in His sight, and wilt give ear to His commandments, and keep all His statutes, I will put none of these diseases upon thee, which I have brought upon the Egyptians" (Exodus 15:26). When, nevertheless, Moses' sister

Miriam broke a commandment by defaming him, the Lord made her "lep-rous, white as snow" (Numbers 12:10). On Moses' pleading, He commuted this punishment to seven days' banishment. Years later, as the Jews were about to cross the Jordan, Jehovah reminded them: "Take heed in the plague of leprosy, that thou observe diligently, and do according to all that the priests the Levites shall teach you: as I commanded them, so ye shall ob-serve to do. Remember what the Lord thy God did unto Miriam by the way, after that ye were come forth out of Egypt" (Deuteronomy 24:8–9).

Subsequently, Michal's mocking of her husband, David, for leaping and dancing in public on the occasion of the Ark's arrival in Jerusalem resulted in her having "no child until the day of her death" (2 Samuel 7:23). Women accused by their husbands of adultery were made to drink holy water mixed with dust from the temple. If they were guilty, "the Lord doth make a curse and an oath among thy people, when the Lord doth make thy thigh to rot, and thy belly to swell" (Numbers 5:21). The dreaded hemorrhoids awaited those who "tempted and provoked the most high God and kept not his testimonies, [for] he smote his enemies in the hinder parts: he put them to a perpetual reproach" (Psalms 78:66). The threatened punishment for idol-worshipers in the second commandment—"I the Lord thy God am a jeal-ous God, visiting the iniquity of the fathers upon the children unto the third and fourth generation of them that hate me" (Exodus 20:5)—may have reflected a recognition on the part of the compilers of hereditary afflictions or of congenitally transmitted venereal disease; but the agent was Jehovah.

Most dramatic of all was Jehovah's angry reaction during the Exodus when the Children of Israel protested to Moses about His swallowing up the rebellious Korah, Dathan, Abiram, and their followers in a fiery pit the day before. "There is a wrath gone out from the Lord; the plague is begun. . . . Now they that died in the plague were fourteen thousand and seven hundred." The disaster would apparently have been worse had it not been for an offering: "And Aaron took as Moses commanded, and ran into the midst of the congregation; and behold, the plague was begun among the people: and he put on incense, and made an atonement for the people. And he stood between the dead and the living; and the plague was stayed" (Numbers 16:46–49). If the compilers got the figures right, then the plague Jehovah wrought during the Exodus was but a fifth as severe as the one during the reign of David, when "the Lord sent a pestilence upon Israel from the morning even unto the time appointed: and there died the people from Dan even to Beersheba seventy thousand men." (2 Samuel 24:15)

The Bible is not without some seeming reversion to the demonic etiology of disease when the Devil in the form of the Babylonian Lord of the Flies, Baal-Zebub (or Beelzebub), or in the form of Satan puts in an occasional appearance. In the Book of Job we find echoes of the primitive concept of disease as a projectile-like entity forced into the body of the sufferer, in this case by Jehovah: "For the arrows of the Almighty are within me, the poison whereof drinketh my spirit" (6:4). But, more than God himself, it was Satan who tested Job's faith by (among other things) having him smitten "with sore boils from the sole of his foot unto his crown" (Job 3:6–7). Nevertheless, all Satan's tormenting of Job was carried out with God's permission and within set limits. "Behold," God says to Satan, "he is in thine hand; but save his life" (Job 3:6).

In view of the preeminent role that Jews would one day play as doctors to the hundreds of millions of adherents of Judaism's daughter religions, Christianity and Islam, it is ironic that the physician was held in low esteem early in Jewish history. If, according to the Books of Moses, disease came from the Almighty, so cure was likewise to be found in Him. "I am the Lord that healeth thee," says God during the flight from Egypt (Exodus 15:26), and this is reiterated in later centuries. The Bible speaks disparagingly of King Asa, who ruled Judah in the late tenth and early ninth centuries B.C.E.: "And Asa in the thirty and ninth year of his reign was diseased in his feet, until his disease was exceedingly great; yet in his disease he sought not to the Lord, but to the physicians. And Asa slept with his fathers, and died in the one and fortieth year of his reign" (2 Chronicles 16:12–13). Clearly, the primitive concept of the cure of disease—as well as its causation—as emanating from otherworldly sources was as strong among the ancient Hebrews as among other ancient peoples. But it was in keeping with the Jewish tendency toward monotheism and away from idolatry to eschew lower-level magical and superstitious practices. "There shall not be found among you any one that . . . useth divination, or an observer of times, or an enchanter, or a witch. Or a charmer, or a consulter with familiar spirits, or a wizard, or a necromancer. For all that do these are an abomination unto the Lord" was the warning in Deuteronomy (18:10–12). And Leviticus (19:31) reiterated: "Regard not them that have familiar spirits, neither seek after wizards, to be defiled by them."

Yet if there was no great contribution to be made by the biblical Jews to medical science in the therapeutic sphere, they were nevertheless great pioneers in a different area: public health. In 1893 C.E., when the germ theory of communicable disease had become established, a French Christian writer, Anatole Leroy-Beaulieu, would remark on the better resistance of Jews to certain diseases and their low infant mortality, and lament "that the controversies of the Early Church about ritual observances had not resulted in the triumph of the Law and of the Judeo-Christians." He then asked rhetorically whether "the writer of the Pentateuch [the five Books of Moses] had not anticipated Monsieur Pasteur?" As we shall see, Jews did indeed anticipate Louis Pasteur's germ theory—but they did so by three decades, rather than by three millennia. Still, one can appreciate Leroy-Beaulieu's tendency toward hyperbole when one considers the anticontagion regulations mandated in the Law of Moses at a time of when knowledge of pathogenic microorganisms and their vectors lay a hundred generations in the future.

Cleanliness was next to Godliness for the Children of Israel. Contamination or pollution by a corpse was of particular concern: "He that toucheth the dead body of any man shall be unclean seven days. He shall purify himself on the third day. . . . When a man dieth in a tent: all that come into the tent, and all that is in the tent, shall be unclean seven days. And every open vessel, which hath no covering bound upon it, is unclean" (Numbers 19:12–15). Sanitary measures were especially important in military camps during campaigns outside Israel: "Thou shalt have a place also without the camp, whither thou shalt go forth abroad: And thou shalt have a paddle upon thy weapon; and it shall be, when thou wilt ease thyself abroad, thou shalt dig therewith, and shalt turn back and cover that which cometh from thee. . . . For the Lord, thy God, walketh in the midst of thy camp, to deliver thee and to give up thine enemies before thee; therefore shall thy camp be holy: that he see no unclean thing in thee, and turn away from thee" (Deuteronomy 23:12–14).

The possibility of contamination from abroad called for special measures. Returning soldiers, along with their equipment, captives, and booty, were subject to a quarantine and a disinfection, of sorts:

And do ye abide without the camp seven days: whosoever hath killed any person, and whosoever hath touched any slain, purify both yourselves and your captives on the third day and the seventh day. And purify all your raiment, and all that is made of skins, and all work of goats' hair, and all things made of wood. . . . Only the gold, and the silver, the brass, the iron, the tin, and the lead. Every thing that may abide the fire, ye shall make it go through the fire, and it shall be clean: nevertheless it shall be purified with the water of separation: and all that abideth not the fire ye shall make go through the water. And ye shall wash your clothes on the seventh day and ye shall be clean, and afterwards ye shall come into the camp. (Numbers 31:19–24)

Most impressive are the long passages in Leviticus (12–14) dealing with "leprosy" (Hebrew *tzaraath*), a collective term apparently referring to dermatological manifestations of a variety of diseases as well as the one now known to be caused by *Mycobactetrium leprae*. Rules were provided for the priest examining a lesion of a potentially unclean "leper," which are so detailed that they might be turned into a modern algorithmic flowchart, complete with yes-no nodes. Diagnostic factors included the color, texture, extent, and depth of the dermatological manifestations and their changes upon reexamination by the priest at seven-day intervals. In line with the therapeutic nihilism of the ancient Hebrews, Leviticus prescribed isolation for the "unclean" skin patient but no treatment. If disease was divine punishment for sin, then cure might follow from prayers for the "separated" leper offered by friends, just as Moses' intercession with Jehovah on behalf of his wayward and leprous wife, Miriam, resulted in a lighter punishment.

The readmission into society of the healed leper (when healing indeed occurred) was preceded by some curious rituals. No obvious hygienic value can today be discerned in the sprinkling of a bird's blood, cedar, scarlet, and hyssop upon the former leper, or from the complicated sacrifice of two lambs (or just one for the less affluent outcast) as a sin-offering and a trespass-offering. But the ritual cleansing and shaving of the healed leper, along with the washing of his clothes (if these have not already been burned), was significant from the point of view of public health, apart from the spiritual connotations.

Perhaps most strongly associated with day-to-day Jewish regulations in the gentile public mind, even at the turn of the third millennium of the Common Era, is the prohibition against eating pork. This dates back to the

passage in Leviticus (11:7) "And the swine . . . is unclean to you." No further explanation is offered for this or for the many other dietary restrictions. The pig is in fact not only apparently unclean; compared to other
domestic species, it was and is a poor economic investment in the environment and climate of the Near East. Unlike cattle, sheep, and goats, pigs
require shade and damping down with water (a scarce Middle Eastern
commodity). Rather than consume grass and other shrubs unappetizing to
man, pigs eat grains that could be used for breadstuffs and other human
foods. And in return for all this investment, pigs ungratefully refuse to be
milked or to pull plows. From a more narrowly medical point of view, the
prejudice against the consumption of pork is obvious, certainly in retrospect. As we have seen, the scavenging pig is a prime vehicle for the transmission of the roundworm *Trichinella spiralis* and tapeworm to humans.
(Unfortunately, many of the other dietary prohibitions in the Books of Moses
are far less amenable to rationalization.)

Anticontagion measures and dietary fastidiousness notwithstanding, the
biblical story of the Jews, from Abraham to Moses to the Prophets, gives
precious little indication of the role their biological and spiritual descendants would play in centuries to come as physicians to all humanity. Hebrew medicine was in the hands of priests, and, as we have seen, their role
was diagnostic and preventative, not therapeutic, and was still bound up
with ancient concepts of supernatural causation, calling for correspondingly otherworldly rituals such as animal sacrifice. It hardly augured well
for the future of Jews in medicine that the most positive references to
doctors and drugs in the ancient Hebrew scriptures were to be found in
the Apocrypha. For it is only in Ecclesiastes, a book *excluded* from canoni-
zation by the compilers of the Jewish Bible, that we read: "Pray unto the
Lord . . . then give place to the physician, for the Lord hath created him
(and) thou hast need of him. . . . God hath created medicines out of the
earth, and let not a discerning man reject them" (38).

Yet early on, the Hebrew Bible relates an incident that, anomalous as it
was at the time, would in later ages come to be seen as powerfully prophetic in its significance and symbolism for a hundred generations of Jewish doctors. It was during the grueling hardships of the Exodus that "the
people spake against God, and against Moses, Wherefore have ye brought
us up out of Egypt to die in the wilderness? for there is no bread, neither

is there any water, and our soul loatheth this light bread." (Certainly, their bodies were at a disadvantage, for leavening reduces the bread's phytate content and thereby facilitates the absorption of minerals from the wheat.) What came next was fully in keeping with the tradition of the gods—for the monotheistic Jews the One God, Jehovah—visiting disease upon the wayward: "And the Lord sent fiery serpents among the people, and they bit the people; and much people of Israel died." There followed, accordingly, the penitence of the transgressors so that God might remove the afflictions He was causing: "Therefore the people came to Moses, and said, We have sinned for we have spoken against the Lord, and against thee; pray unto the Lord, that he take away the serpents from us. And Moses prayed for the people."

What happened next, however, was far less in keeping with the general spirit of the Books of Moses: "And the Lord said unto Moses, Make thee a fiery serpent, and set it upon a pole: and it shall come to pass, that everyone that is bitten, when he looketh upon it, shall live. And Moses made a serpent of brass, and put it upon a pole, and it came to pass, that if a serpent had bitten any man, when he beheld the serpent of brass, he lived" (Numbers 21:5–9).

It is one of the great contradictions of the Bible that the order to Moses to make a brass serpent should have come from the same God Who earlier in the Exodus on Mount Sinai had placed at the very top of His list of commandments delivered to Moses: "Thou shalt have no other gods before me. Thou shalt not make unto thee any graven image, or any likeness of any thing that is in heaven above, or that is in the earth beneath, or that is in the water under the earth. Thou shalt not bow down thyself to them, nor serve them . . ." (Exodus 20:3–5). To show He meant it, Jehovah soon had Moses and his Levite army slaughter no fewer than 3,000 fellow Hebrews who worshiped the golden calf and He further "plagued the people" for their sin. In erecting a serpent image to be viewed in awe, Moses might have known—certainly, the omniscient Jehovah must have—that this symbol would so easily lend itself to idol worship. In fact, Jews in the eighth century B.C.E. would still be burning incense to it in the Jerusalem Temple, when King Hezekiah finally "did that which was right in the sight of the Lord . . . and brake in pieces the brasen serpent that Moses had made" (2 Kings 18:3–4). Later generations of embarrassed medical historians, drawing upon epidemiology, would seek some rational explanation of the serpent of brass. So, it has been speculated that the fiery serpents that bit the people were the worm *Dracunculus medinensis,* a threadlike parasite that burrows under human skin, particularly the legs, and can grow to a length of half a meter. The worm, which today still infests wide areas of the globe, particularly Africa and India, produces toxins that result in reactions of fever, nausea, and vomiting. The Hebrews on the Exodus devised a method of removing the worms by means of a peg, and this was supposedly given plastic representation by the brass serpent coiled around the pole.

Sigmund Freud, who called himself "completely godless," recoiled from scenes of Hebrew idolatry as much as would even the most pious of his fellow Jews, albeit for different reasons. Freud prided himself in the comparative rationality of Jewish monotheism as opposed to the polytheism and idol-worship of other ancient peoples. As a medical doctor, Freud knew that the healing practices of the Hebrews were particularly affected by the monotheistic antipathy toward idolatry and toward the superstitious practices of neighboring peoples. Freud sought to brush off incidents of magic among the Old Testament Jews as mere relics of an earlier belief in volcanic demon-gods that had not yet been entirely eradicated from the new monotheism. If the superstitious power of incantations, amulets, and charms, so strong among the peoples of the Middle East, was not always irresistible to the Jews, at least such practices were never tolerated to the point of idolatry. But what, then, to make of the scene of Moses himself erecting a brass image of a snake? Freud was perhaps more willing to forgive this lapse, in view of the powerful significance with which the serpent—with its phallic associations—is laden in everyone's personal unconscious, according to psychoanalytic theory. (Freud's onetime pupil, Carl Jung, excavated even deeper in the psyche and saw the snake as evoking memories of our reptilian evolutionary heritage in some collective unconscious.)

But the ancient cultures of the Middle East, in touch as they were with the land, somewhat more consciously perceived the snake as possessing arcane knowledge of healing from the underworld, due to its intimate connection with the caves and crevices of the earth. Furthermore, they consciously associated the snake's shedding of its skin with the earth's power of seasonal renewal and restoration. So it was that prior to the second millennium B.C.E., the Sumerians had a god of healing with origins in the snake cult, and the Phoenicians in turn worshiped a god-snake healer called

Eschmun. So it was that Genesis (3:1) described the snake that tempted Eve as "more subtil than any beast of the field which the Lord God had made." And so it was that the Egyptian pharaoh was typically depicted as holding alternatively a rod or an erect snake, and we read how "Aaron cast down his [Moses'] rod before Pharaoh, and before his servants, and it became a serpent," which swallowed up all other rod-serpents of the Egyptian magicians.

A serpent and a rod. This is the eternal symbol of the medical profession. The sign is known to us as the staff of Asklepios (or, in the Latinized version, Aesculapius). This was the name of a legendary Greek physician in Homer's day, around the ninth or eighth century B.C.E., who was subsequently mythologized and given semi-divine status. Yet we find Asklepios's symbol elevated by Moses in the Exodus of the Hebrews a few hundred years earlier. Call it an omen. But little could the Hebrews have imagined at the time how much their distant descendants would come to be identified with the Asklepios symbol, or why.

Chapter 2
Hellas and Talmud

For all things I know the cure except the following three: eating bitter dates on an empty stomach, girding one's loins with a damp flaxen cord, and eating and not walking at least four cubits after it.

—Mar Samuel

The best of physicians is destined for Hell.

—The Talmud (*Kiddishun* 4:14)

*I*n the latter nineteenth century, the legal emancipation of the Jews in Germany brought about their dramatic rise to prominence in various fields of endeavor, not least of all in medical science. It also brought about a certain backlash at the universities of what was at the time the world's leading academic nation. Anti-Semitic feeling clouded the works of even some otherwise quite distinguished German scholars of archaeology and ancient cultures—most notably with regard to the great pride of Western civilization, the Golden Age of ancient Greece.

Already in the late eighteenth century, philologists had established that the German and Greek languages, as well as Latin, Sanskrit, Persian, Gaelic, Slavic, and several others, had derived from a common ancestor, which they called "Indo-European" or "Aryan." Hebrew, Akkadian, Arabic, and other Near Eastern languages, were, by contrast, of the unrelated Semitic linguistic family. The corollary assumption was that the Germans and ancient Greeks, along with speakers of other Indo-European languages, also derived biologically from a common Aryan racial stock, from which the Semitic Jews, past and present, were excluded. Some of the nineteenth-

century German archaeologists were ready to take their anti-Semitic prejudice in the everyday sense of anti-Jewish and broaden it to encompass the
whole range of ancient Semitic cultures and languages, particularly when
considering the phenomenal achievements in the arts and sciences that
characterized Greek civilization for so much of the first millennium B.C.E.
This theoretical juxtaposition of the Aryan and the Semitic in the ancient
world carried with it the biased assumption that although the Greeks were
a Mediterranean people, their Golden Age owed very little to the peoples
of the Middle East.

The unbiased truth, of course, is that Hellenic art and science inherited
much from the East. The Greek system of writing was derived and adapted
from the script of the Semitic Phoenicians in the eighth and seventh centuries B.C.E. Homeric epics had counterparts in the East, particularly in
the Semitic literary forms from Ugarit in Mesopotamia. The Pythagorean
theorem was known to the Babylonians 1,000 years before Pythagoras, and
Greek astronomy drew much from centuries of Mesopotamian knowledge
of the heavens.

Likewise in the realm of religion, the Semitic East had its influence on
Hellas. Of course, the Greek-speaking tribes that had migrated into the
Greek peninsula—sometimes peacefully, sometimes aggressively—in the
first half of the second millennium B.C.E. had brought with them a pantheon of gods that was shared to a greater or lesser degree by other Indo-
European peoples. This can be seen in the etymology of some divine names.
So, for example, the Greek Zeus corresponds with the Jovis of the Italic
tribes and the Dyaus of the Sanskrit-speaking Aryans who invaded India.
The common root in the original (and long lost) proto-Indo-European
language is assumed to have been something like Dyeus, which relates to
the Indo-European word for "sky." But the fact that the Sky-god assumed
a top position in the religion of the Greeks and Romans but occupied a
lower rung in other Indo-European mythologies indicates an influence of
the earlier, non-Indo-European Mediterranean religions. Also noteworthy
is that the Greek statues of Zeus bearing a thunderbolt are derived from
effigies of weather-gods in the Near East. We also have an ancient inscription referring to Zeus Atabyrios, which relates to Mount Atabyrion (Ta-
bor) in Palestine. Similarly, some Greek rituals connected with Apollo
include celebrations of the day of the new moon and of the seventh day of
the month—typical Semitic customs.

Greek medical thinking was likewise fertilized by contacts with the ancient civilizations of the Middle East. Ceramic remains tell us that Phoenician traders, the bearers of Middle Eastern cultural as well as material goods, were active on the Greek isle of Cos, the home of the Hippocratic school of medicine. Across the straits in Asia Minor (present-day Turkey) the influential medical school of the Greek colony of Cnidus developed from the seventh century B.C.E. onward a medical doctrine based mostly on the classification, diagnosis, and local treatment of disease, which apparently drew in part from Egyptian sources. Hepatoscopy—the Babylonian pseudoscience of divination through analysis of the livers of slaughtered animals—was widely practiced in Greece from around the sixth century B.C.E. In the statue at the temple at Epidaurus, we find a dog standing next to Asklepios, the Greek god of healing, just as centuries earlier the Babylonians had constructed a shrine at Samos with bronze effigies of dogs accompanying their healing goddess Gula.

But when it comes to the great flowering of philosophy and science—including medical science—in the Golden Age of ancient Greece, any discussion of "Aryan" origins and Semitic influences pales into insignificance next to the spontaneous creative achievements of the Greeks themselves. For the Greeks introduced a rationalist approach that was a dramatic departure from all that went before, whether in the East or the West.

Inhabiting a peninsula broken up by barren mountain ranges into a number of valleys, an archipelago fragmented by the waters of the Aegean into a multitude of islands, the ancient Greeks never attained the political unity characteristic of other ancient civilizations. Likewise, they knew no unified priesthood. A mercantile people, with trading colonies that by the sixth century B.C.E. extended from Sicily and southern Italy to the shores of the Black Sea, the Greeks' contact with so many diverse and even contradictory beliefs apparently made them skeptical of religion in general. Hellas did, of course, have a pantheon of gods and also impressive temples such as the Parthenon on the Acropolis in Athens. But the Greeks, particularly the intellectuals, were the first in history not to take their deities very seriously. There were no sacred texts or infallible priests. Zeus, Apollo, Nike, and the rest were playful or mischievous entities hovering around Mount Olympus, rather than creators of the universe, shapers of laws, or bearers of immutable revelations.

Thus the Greeks, like the Jews, brought about a radical revolution in thinking about the world and the heavenly powers that be—*but each in a quite distinct way.* The Jews basically eliminated the array of gods and spirits, just as the Greek intellectuals downplayed their pantheon of dieties. But whereas the Jews had the One God, Jehovah, Who was conceived of in anthropomorphic terms, and Whom they took very seriously indeed every day of their lives, Greek philosophers, notably Aristotle, conceived of a Supreme Being as some intellectual construct quite removed from the affairs of men.

Yet despite this apparent gulf between the Jewish and the Greek revolutions in theology, we have every reason in our present story to dwell a while on Hellenic philosophy, science, and medicine. For centuries, Jewish philosophers, having voraciously absorbed the philosophical and scientific ideas of Hellas, would endeavor to reconcile them with the religion of Moses. And long after Greece itself had passed from its Golden Age into the Dark Ages and its architectural monuments fell into ruin, Jewish physician-philosophers would be instrumental in keeping the flame of ancient learning alive and would be the acknowledged masters of Hellenic medical science.

Unwilling to rely on myth or divine revelation, Greek thinkers took it upon themselves to answer by thought and observation some of the most fundamental questions about existence, not least of all the ultimate substance and fabric of the universe. The philosopher Thales of the Greek town of Miletus in Asia Minor astonished his contemporaries in the sixth century B.C.E. by informing them that the sun and stars, once worshiped as gods, were in fact mere balls of fire. Yet Thales's ultimate substance was something other than fire: "All things are made of water," he declared. This theory, perhaps based on observations of meteorological cycle of evaporation, condensation, and rain, was quite rational, even if incorrect. (At least, it may be said that all elements can in theory be synthesized from hydrogen, the main element of water.)

Thales's fellow Melisian philosopher Anaximenes reasoned differently. The human soul is of air, and this is also the basic substance that keeps the world in being. Next came the Ionian philosopher Heraclitus, a man particularly contemptuous of religious ritual. ("They [worshipers] vainly purify themselves by defiling themselves with blood," he wrote, "just as if one who had stepped into the mud were to wash his feet in mud. Any man who

marked him doing this would deem him mad.") Observing the transformations that matter undergoes in the process of combustion, Heraclitus took
yet another view of the basic stuff of the world. Employing a mercantile
simile sure to appeal to the Greek traders, he declared: "All things are an
exchange for Fire, and Fire for all things, even as wares for gold and gold
for wares."

It was the physician Empedocles of Acragas who, in the fifth century
B.C.E., achieved a compromise by accepting all three substances—water,
air, and fire—as basic, and adding to them a fourth, earth. He further
theorized the existence of two active principles of nature—love and strife—
which respectively united and divided the basic substances, thus account-
ing, in a way, for the various actions taking place in the world. This included the process of biological evolution. For nature, according to
Empedocles, is continually combining organs in various trials, only some
of which combinations successfully meet the challenges of their environments and reproduce their kind.

Similar secular and rational thinking came to dominate the Hellenic
approach to medicine. Asklepios, the Greek god of healing, was only a half-
hearted concession to the otherworldly. Asklepios had been merely a mortal
(albeit very competent) physician in the ninth or eighth century B.C.E. and
was subsequently mythologized. (According to the divine legend, Zeus,
jealous of Asklepios's powers over life and death, smote him with a thunderbolt. But Asklepios's daughters, Panacea and Hygeia, carried on his good
work.) Furthermore, even the religiously inclined viewed the god Asklepios,
unlike the God Jehovah, as solely the curer, never the bringer, of disease.
(Only on occasion might the latter function be taken up by Apollo or some
other god, as when in the Oedipus Rex myth Thebes was devastated by
plague as divine punishment for the king's unwitting incest.) The Greeks
had their temples of healing, where Asklepios might appear in a dream to
a sleeping patient and prescribe a remedy or effect a cure on the spot. But
even if "prayer is indeed good," as a contemporary physician conceded,
"while calling upon the gods a man should himself lend a hand."

The Greek skepticism of the supernatural in medicine—and all the more
of the concept of gods visiting disease—was most notable with regard to
epileptic seizures, an affliction that, more than any other, appeared to have
a supernatural etiology. Indeed, the very name seizure, still used in the age
of nuclear medicine, is a vestige of the once prevailing concept of spirit

possession. The Bible tells of King Saul, who "fell down the entire day and the entire night" (1 Samuel 19:24). And accounts of seeming possession that fit the epileptic pattern are found in the New Testament of the Christians. But the author of the Greek book *On the Sacred Disease* took an entirely different view. "I, at any rate, do not believe that the human body is defiled by a god," he wrote. "It appears to me to be nowise more divine or sacred than any other diseases, but has a natural cause from which it originates like other affections. Men regard its nature and cause as divine from ignorance and wonder, because it is not at all like other diseases." This rationalist author, by contrast, suggested that a phlegmatic discharge blocks the vessels communicating with the brain, thereby causing the epileptic fit. Accordingly, he condemned the use of charms and incantations for this as for any other physical ailments.

On the Sacred Disease is one of seventy or so books and texts that make up the Hippocratic corpus, written in the fifth and fourth centuries B.C.E. Although the whole collection bears the name of Hippocrates, who came to be known as the Father of Medicine, analysis of the texts reveals them to have been written by many different authors, only one of whom was (presumably) Hippocrates himself. To complicate matters further, the extant corpus is assumed to be only part of a much larger library of the medical academy, which might be called the Hippocratic school, on the island of Cos, off the coast of Asia Minor. Precious little is known for certain about Hippocrates himself or his life. He was born on Cos around 460 B.C.E., is said to have traveled widely as a physician and lecturer, effected wondrous cures, received many honors, and lived to be 100 or so. Although idolized and sanctified in his own day, and certainly by more than a hundred generations of doctors to come, what was no less important was how Hippocrates *didn't* come to be viewed: he was recognized as not divine or possessing supernatural powers but as a mere mortal. This was in keeping with the purely rational and naturalistic approach to health and disease that permeates the whole Hippocratic corpus. "Each disease has a natural cause, and nothing happens without a natural cause," declared a Hippocratic physician-author.

Much Greek medical thinking, from Hippocrates onward, was based on the theory of the four fundamental elements. As already mentioned, Empedocles, the philosopher who established the four-element system, was a physician—and a contemporary of Hippocrates. In fact, Empedocles was regarded as so skilled at his craft that a coin was struck in the city of Selinus commemorating his supposed staying of the plague there. From another physician, Alcmaeon of Croton, Empedocles adopted the theory that health derives from a balance of the four elements in the body and that disease is a consequence of their imbalance. The biological corollaries of the four elements were the four body humors: blood, yellow bile, black bile, and phlegm. These were assumed to be produced and secreted by, respectively, the heart, liver, spleen, and brain. In broad lines the Greeks brilliantly anticipated our modern endocrinology, that is, the secretion of hormones by glands, and the importance of their being in the proper quantities. But, almost inevitably in view of the state of the art of their medical technology, the Greek physicians got virtually every detail wrong.

As the theory developed, each humor was linked to one of the four seasons, which were each in turn associated with two of the four primary properties: hot, cold, dry, and wet. Thus, for example, phlegm = winter = wet and cold, which made some observational sense, since mucous discharges were most prevalent during the rains and chills of the Greek winter. "All diseases," wrote a Hippocratic author, "come to be, as regards things inside the body, from bile and phlegm, and as regards external things, from exercise and wounds, from the hot being too hot, the cold too cold, the dry too dry, and the wet too wet. And bile and phlegm . . . exist, in greater or lesser quantities, in the body, and they bring about diseases, both those arising from food and drink and those from excess of hot and cold."

The concept of illness as caused by natural external sources was reflected in the Hippocratic concept of epidemiology. "When a large number of people all catch the same disease at the same time, the cause must be ascribed to something common to all and which they all use" or to which they are all exposed. By this was meant, among other things, the air, waters, winds, even the angle of the sun in any given place or time. "However," the writer continued, "when many different diseases appear at the same time, it is plain that the regimen [diet, exercise] is responsible in individual cases."

Connected with the belief in the natural causation of disease was the healing power of nature or *physis*. An internal process of *pepsis*, or coction (cooking), was nature's way of reestablishing the balance of humors. The Hippocratic *iatròs* (physician) brought about a fundamental advance in medical thinking by emphasizing the role of proper diet in maintaining the body in a healthy equilibrium. In practice, however, these healers once again got the details all wrong, due to their faulty theoretical basis. Thus they did more harm than good for their own contemporary patients and for patients in the Western world for almost two millennia to come. If diseases were due to an excess of some humor, then starving the patient by limiting his food intake to some watered-down barley slop was the theoretical way to prevent the formation of new humors while the body struggled to re-establish an equilibrium. As for the healthy, the Greek physicians were strongly prejudiced against vegetables and fruit. We find this reflected several centuries later in the encyclopedia *Historia naturalis* of Pliny the elder, who declared spring apples to be bad, pears to be indigestible, plums and cherries to harm the stomach, and walnuts (perhaps due to some reverse sympathetic or homeopathic principle based on external resemblance) to be poisonous for the brain. It was the wealthier Greeks' misfortune to be able to afford to follow such medical advice and restrict their food intake mostly to meat (and cereals)—and thus incur a range of vitamin deficiencies.

An excess of blood humor in particular was seen by the Greek physicians as the cause of many ills. As we have noted, this was a primitive notion that long predated the sophisticated four-humor theory. The misconception was apparently reinforced by observations of wound inflammation. The Greek *iatròs* correctly assumed that inflammation around wounds was due to increased blood flow to that area, but he erred in thinking that the blood then rotted there and that this increase was therefore ipso facto harmful. Such reasoning as to local afflictions, already faulty, was extended to systemic diseases and eventually led to the practice of letting the blood of all patients, and even, in later centuries, to the prophylactic bleeding of healthy people.

Hippocrates was the father of rational medicine. But early in the fourth century, a few decades after Hippocrates' death, Greece brought forth a greater thinker, who, although not primarily known as a physician, would for millennia to come exert a comparably powerful influence Western medicine.

Aristotle was the son of the physician to Amyntas, the king of Macedon, and it is said that Aristotle himself was a member of the medical fraternity of the Asklepiads. According to one account, he practiced medicine in his hometown of Stagira before going off to Athens at age 30 to study philosophy under Plato. It was Aristotle who gave the name *elements* to the four basic substances and by his authority ensured that they would remain a foundation of the natural sciences in the West, particularly in matters of chemistry, for some 2,000 years. But it was especially in his role as the founder of the science of biology that Aristotle had the greatest influence on subsequent medical thinking. Aristotle brilliantly concluded that man is an extension of the animal kingdom. Humans, he declared, belong to the group that also encompasses the viviparous quadrupeds (roughly, the mammals). The monkey is intermediate between man and the four-footers, and the human soul in infancy is hardly distinguishable from that of the beasts.

Yet, as in the case of Hippocrates, very many of Aristotle's biological observations and theorizations were off the mark. For Aristotle, the seat of intelligence was the heart rather than the brain, the latter organ having merely the function of cooling the blood. He made no distinction between arteries and veins, and the muscles and their function went unnoticed. Such errors were at least partly due to the fact that there were no human dissections in Greece. But some of Aristotle's misconceptions are less forgivable, as when he pronounced that man had only eight ribs on each side and that women had fewer teeth than men. As Bertrand Russell is said to have remarked, the latter misconception might have been avoided by a simple inspection of the mouth of Mrs. Aristotle. But this was considered work, and, as a matter of pride, the Greek intellectuals far preferred mental reasoning. Another unfortunate aspect of Aristotle's biology was his belief in spontaneous generation: that creatures could come into being due to physical processes occurring in dunghills or the hardening of dew. This quite understandable misconception, which could only have been remedied by controlled experimentation (another form of work), would dog Western science until it was finally overthrown in the nineteenth century and would cause much controversy on theological grounds among Christians and Jews alike.

Aristotle himself was not devoid of religious beliefs, but these were likewise based on rational speculation and as such they differed profoundly from any religion practiced up to that time. A problem for Aristotle and his physics was the movement taking place in the universe. While he conceived matter to have always existed and to be everlasting, he felt that motion must have an origin, a Prime Mover Unmoved. This God—although having powered the inherent drive, purpose, and growth in the natural world—was conceived of by Aristole as devoid of any desires, emotions or intentions. There was no question of his otherwise interfering with the natural processes of the world. Yet he was conscious, or more precisely, self-conscious, in that he contemplated the essences of all things, which was in fact himself. Such a God required no worship from humans. He was in fact an extension of Aristotle's Ideal Man.

From his natural and theological concepts, Aristotle derived his teleological beliefs, particularly that man has a purpose in the world. Such a view accorded more with religious thinking, past and present, than with modern biology. He took as a truism that man's happiness is the supreme good. He saw as his task a clarification of happiness and the road to it. His conclusion was that those functions that are uniquely human are most worthy of being engaged in by humans, and then for their own sake. "The operation of the intellect," he wrote, "aims at no end beyond itself, and finds in itself the pleasure which stimulates it to further operation." On a more mundane level of activity, Aristotle advocated the golden mean: self-control rather than indecisiveness or impulsiveness; ambition rather than sloth or greed; good humor rather than moroseness or buffoonery, and so on down the list. The good "humor" in the last example can be taken literally, for the Greeks saw a parallel between the proper balance of body fluids and ideal equilibrium of mental qualities.

In 334 B.C.E. Aristotle's most famous pupil, Alexander the Great, defeated the Persian armies of Darius III and then led his host east to the gates of India, thus becoming ruler of virtually all the known world. Alexander's vast empire included Israel, Egypt, and the other Middle Eastern lands on the Mediterranean his armies swept through. While in Egypt, Alexander, on the strength of a dream, established a new city, appropriately called Alexandria, on the barren strip of coast west of the Nile delta. Alexander died in 323 B.C.E. following a drinking bout in Babylon, which issued in fever, a seizure, and lavish medical attention of which he was not particularly appreciative. ("I die by the help of too many physicians," were Alexander's final words.)

One of Alexander's generals, Ptolemy I, took over Egypt and declared himself pharaoh, with Alexandria as his residence. Ptolemy established in Alexandria a House of the Muse, called Mousion in Greek and Museum in

Latin. This was the B.C.E. counterpart of the twentieth century's Rockefeller Institute in New York or the Institute for Advanced Studies in Princeton. Scholars in all fields of knowledge were paid to dine together when they were not otherwise engaged in thinking, reading, and writing in a library containing hundreds of thousands of books. Among the great intellectual achievements to derive from the Museum in its heyday was a highly accurate calculation of the diameter of the earth, the mathematical theorems of Euclid, and the physical principles of Archimedes. On the tangible level, the clever scholars produced such inventions as screws, levers, pulleys, pumps, and valves.

Although such devices most often were applied to the production of adult toys, in the field of medicine they found application as orthopedic aids, syringes, and the Alexandrian water clock, used for the first reasonably accurate registration of pulse rates. But it was mostly on a more theoretical level that Alexandrian mechanics had its strongest impact upon the course of medical science. This was the only period in the history of Greek medicine when human dissections were legal. The physician Erasistratos, apparently inspired by the hydraulic inventions of his fellow Alexandrians, gained renown for describing the heart as a pump and the heart valves as one-way flaps. It was perhaps under this influence that the Alexandrians introduced the life-saving technique of ligation (tying off of severed blood vessels).

Nevertheless, a multitude of misconceptions reigned in Erasistratos's view of the cardiovascular system. Opposing the Dogmatists—the adherents of the humoral view of health and sickness—Erasistratos assumed the body to be composed of solid atoms. These were supposedly vitalized by the system of arteries, which he (adopting a Cosean misconception) assumed to carry air. Blood flow was confined to the veins. One of the Alexandrian medical schools, the Pneumatists, went so far as to base their entire theoretical system of health and disease on highly complex speculation about the interaction of air (*pneuma*) with warmth and moisture inside the body.

"Captive Greece took Rome, her captor, captive," wrote the Roman poet Horace in the first century C.E. For although the military might of Rome had by then overrun the Greek peninsula and all the Hellenic dominions in the Eastern Mediterranean, the Romans were no match for Greek arts and sciences, which they were glad to adopt—not least, the science of medicine. Hippocrates achieved a semi-divine status in the Roman Empire, and

Greek physicians were prized above all others. The widely recognized fact that the Hippocratic corpus was written by many authors and was often contradictory permitted subsequent medical writers in the Roman Empire to attribute to the "real" Hippocrates those texts that they personally favored and on which they elaborated, thus presenting themselves as Hippocrates' true heir. Greco-Roman physicians of various schools—the Empiricists, the Dogmatists, the Pneumatists, and others—vied for this title. But in the second century C.E., one doctor, Claudius Galenus (Galen), by force of his often arrogant rhetoric and an enormous literary output amounting to over 10,000 pages, secured for himself the status of the new Hippocrates. For better or worse, Galen's works would have virtual canonical authority for some fifteen centuries to come.

A Hellenic Roman citizen born in Pergamum on the coast of Asia Minor, Galen trained in medicine for four years at the school of the Asklepieion and then journeyed to Alexandria and elsewhere for some eight more years of learning, a remarkable academic background in an age when boys of 17 could call themselves *medici* (physicians) after only six months of study. Although he styled himself an Eclectic physician—one who drew upon the best of each of the often conflicting schools of medicine—Galen was enchanted most of all by the theory of the four elements and their corresponding bodily humors. This concept had played only a marginal role in the Hippocratic corpus, but Galen made it the touchstone of what he considered to be the true Hippocrates.

Galen gleefully proceeded to elaborate on the four-humor theory, by associating earth (black bile) with sour bodily qualities, quartan fever, the afternoon, and, in anticipation of endocrino-psychiatry, stubbornness and insolence (later melancholia). He linked the Greek fire (yellow bile) with bitter bodily qualities, tertian fever, the noontime, and a bold, exuberant (choleric) personality. Air (blood) was associated with sweetness, continuous fever, the morning, and a serene, unruffled (sanguine) temperament, while water (phlegm) became linked with saltiness, quotidian fever, the evening, and an idle, foolish (phlegmatic) personality.

For all his tomes of abstract reasoning—impressive today as a monument to brilliantly eloquent theories largely divorced from reality—Galen also filled thousands of pages with details of very concrete and purposeful experiments. Dissections of humans—even corpses—were taboo in the Roman Empire, and Galen perhaps performed one in his whole lifetime.

But there was no law against animal dissections, even of man's cousin the Barbary ape. And the fastidiousness of the Romans with regard to human dissections was more than compensated for by the carnage of their gladiatorial games. This allowed Galen, in his capacity as surgeon to the gladiators in Pergamum, to conduct experiments "from nature," if such a term may be used in these circumstances.

Perhaps Galen's most important observation was his determining once and for all that intelligence or the soul resides not in the heart but in the brain. "If the ventricle of the heart is wounded, a gladiator dies very soon," he wrote. "If the wound is slight, he may die the following day. While he lives, he is of sane mind; this is testimony that the heart is not the seat of the mind." Galen further showed that lesions on the side of the brain produced disturbances on the other side of the body (due to cross-wiring of the nerve channels in the brain stem). He distinguished between sensory and motor nerves leading, as it were, respectively to and from the brain, and he showed that various forms of paralysis result from the severing of the spinal cords at different levels. Among Galen's other contributions were his demonstrating that the arteries contain blood, not air, and that urine comes from the kidneys.

But Galen was also quite ready to repeat previous misconceptions and to introduce his share of new ones, all of which became virtual dogma for over 1,000 years. Perhaps most notable, in view of his positive contributions to the understanding of the heart, blood, and arteries, was Galen's lack of any concept of circulation—let alone dual circulation—and his insistence that the blood sloshed back and forth. He also had no proper understanding of the purpose served by blood flow. Worse still, Galen was a great advocate of bloodletting, having inherited the assumption from his Greek predecessors that since raised veins and accumulated stagnating blood appeared in some wounds, bleeding should be carried out for any wound as a prophylactic measure. By extension, systemic ailments could be relieved at least in part by the draining off of an excess of the blood humor. Excesses of other humors were, however, likewise of concern to Galen, particularly due to the unfavorable qualitative changes they supposedly underwent. He accordingly prescribed all manner of purges and evacuants.

But mere voiding was a bit too negative and crude for Galen's ever-theorizing mind. A proper balance of body humors should ideally be achieved by administering drugs that were the exact opposite of whatever humors and respective qualities were deemed to be in excess in a given patient. So, whereas the Hippocratic doctors relied on simple drugs, Galen, having added layers of theoretical complexity to the Greek four-humor concept, proceeded to introduce compound drugs into the pharmacopoeia. If in Galen's scheme of things, some form of, for example, tertian fever were diagnosed as due to an excess of yellow bile producing warmth in the third degree, dryness in the first degree, and bitterness in the second degree, thus affecting vital powers and functions in a certain manner, then a concoction of drugs theoretically possessing the exact opposite qualities needed to be prescribed.

At the time Galen wrote his monumental works in the second half of the second century C.E., much had taken place in the story of the Jews. The biblical age had more or less ended some 600 years earlier—around the fifth century B.C.E.—with the visions of the last of the Prophets, who preached that Israel become "a light unto the nations" (Isaiah 49:6). The universalistic message of the Prophets rose above the tribal religious rituals of Judaism, such as animal sacrifices to Jehovah in the Jerusalem Temple. Jews would still have to keep the physical commandments, but the spiritual and moral message of their religion as expressed by the Prophets was extended to embrace all humanity.

The time was indeed right for this universalistic vision among the Jews. For the Hebrews had already begun their dispersion from their biblical homeland, which would take them to the four corners of the earth in the course of 2,000 years. The Babylonian exile under King Nebuchadrezzar in the sixth century B.C.E. left many Jews voluntarily behind in Babylon even after they were permitted to return to Israel in the wake of the Persian conquest. Contemporary records show that there was a Jewish community of mercenaries at Elephantine in the Middle Nile and of merchants at Sardis on the west coast of Asia Minor. Some Jews settled in northern Persia under Artaxerxes III.

Alexander the Great's swift displacement of Persian might in the fourth century B.C.E. and the establishment of Greek hegemony throughout the known world—including the Holy Land itself—stimulated the formation of Jewish communities in the Diaspora (a word, fittingly enough, taken from the Greek). In Alexandria on the mouth of the Nile, the meeting point between the European and the Middle Eastern, a large hellenized Jewish community—numbering in the hundreds of thousands, and including many Greek converts—grew up alongside Ptolemy's House of the Muses. The influence of Hellenic philosophy, literature, and science on Egyptian Jewish thought was powerful. Early in the second century B.C.E., the Alexandrian Jewish philosopher Aristobulus, a follower of Aristotle, published (in Greek) his *Explanation of the Mosaic Scripture,* in which he adopted a nonanthropomorphic view of God and further sought a nonliteral interpretation of the Bible. Both the Greek philosopher and the religious Jew sought wisdom and the proper rules of conduct, Aristobulus declared. The apparent differences in achieving this—rational analysis of nature as opposed to God-given commandments—could be reconciled by delving below the surface of the Hebrew Scriptures.

In Alexandria 300 years later, at a time when the Greek world had long since come under Roman domination but Hellenic thinking and the Greek language still reigned supreme in the civilized world, the Jewish philosopher Philo similarly endeavored to reconcile Judaism with Greek thinking, particularly the Platonic and Stoic philosophies. Philo adapted Plato's concept of man as a spiritual being pent up in a material body—this in contrast to the more Jewish notion of *nefesh*, the unity of body and soul. Philo's intellectual Judaism won many additional converts in the Hellenic world and had a particular impact on that current of Jewish thinking that eventually split off into Christianity, with its disdain for the corporal. The Alexandrian Jewish tradition of viewing the biblical text as allegorical and, as such, reconcilable at a deeper level of analysis with Greek intellectual concepts would be followed by other great Jewish thinkers in later eras and various lands. So enamored were some Jews with Hellenic philosophy that a legend began to grow that had Aristotle accompanying his pupil Alexander the Great to Jerusalem, there to come into possession of the original works of King Solomon, which supposedly served as the basis for Aristotle's metaphysical system. (At least, one may say of this myth that it is no more absurd than the anti-"Semitic" arguments that the Golden Age of Greece owed nothing to the Near East.)

By the time Galen entered the scene in the latter part of the second century C.E., the Jews had been completely and forcibly dispersed from what had been the Roman province of Judea. This was in the aftermath of the unsuccessful Jewish revolts against Roman rule, first in 70 C.E. (which resulted in the destruction of the Temple in Jerusalem), and again, under Bar Kochba, in 135 C.E. Rome's concern now no longer came from a concentrated military force in Judea, but from six or seven million Jews (about a tenth of the Empire's total population!) now living throughout the whole Mediterranean area, whose economic activities were vital but who might cause disturbances and dislocations if their religious sensibilities were offended. Even decades before the Bar Kochba revolt, a synagogue already stood in Ostia, Rome's harbor at the mouth of the Tiber river. Wisely, the Roman authorities accorded Judaism the special status of *religio licita* (legal religion), which absolved the Jews of obligations to make even token offerings to the Roman pagan deities or the divine emperor.

How did the Jews feel about Greco-Roman medicine as embodied by the great Galen? Although a pagan and very much a scientist in the non-supernatural Greek tradition, Galen may have been invested with a semi-religious awe by Jews in the Hellenic-Jewish milieu. This was aided by Galen's presenting himself as a priest-like figure and by the reverence he showed in his writings for the Creator and His works. As Galen wrote in *On the Use-fulness of the Parts of the Body:* "I want you now to pay closer attention to me than if you were being initiated into the mysteries of Eleusis or Samothrace or some other sacred rite. . . . You should consider that the mystery is in no way inferior to those and no less able to show you the wisdom, foresight, and power of the Creator of animals. . . . Accordingly, even if you have not done so before, fix your mind now on holier things. . . ."

Galen himself made a few references to Judaism in his writings. As a Hellenic philosopher-scientist, he took issue with Moses, who arbitrarily "framed laws for the tribe of the Jews, since it is his method to write without offering proofs, saying 'God commanded, God spoke.'" Galen was particularly displeased with the biblical doctrine of *creatio ex nihilo:* "It seems enough [for Moses] to say that God simply willed the arrangement of matter and it was presently arranged in due order, for he believes everything to be possible with God. . . . We say that certain things are impossible and that God does not even attempt such things." Yet Galen was aware of the work, at the turn of his own (second) century, of the Alexandrian Jewish physician Rufus of Samaria, known for his commentaries on Hippocrates and his anatomical observations. Galen also conceded that "one might more easily teach novelties to the followers of Moses [. . .] than to the physicians and philosophers who cling fast to their schools."

Yet in the eyes of the inhabitants of the Roman Empire, there was more to Jewish healers than the intellectual theories they may have picked up from Galen. For the Jews and other Orientals, especially the Egyptians, were often seen as possessing mysterious powers. As we have noted, the overall tendency of the Bible was an advance away from magic and sorcerers and toward the concept of One God controlling the universe. But as we shall see on many occasions in our story, the trends in Jewish thought through the ages are more complex than a unidirectional evolution toward rational monotheism. In the time of the Roman Empire, Jewish thought was probably also influenced by the apocryphal *Book of Enoch,* with its accounts of good and evil angels, unclean spirits, and idolatry. The number of Jewish *magi* in ancient Rome may have been small in an absolute sense, but those Jewish magicians who did ply their trade were evidently conspicuous and in demand, due not least of all to the mystery and awe the Romans felt for the religions of the Near East. In the first century of the Common Era, the satiric poet Juvenal told of Jewish fortunetellers on Rome's Appian Way. In the second century, the time of Galen, Lucius of Samasate condemned "the fool who submits himself to the incantations of a Jew" to cure his gout. Nevertheless, in the same century, the famed Roman physician Celsus told how the posts of *archiatri* (physicians) were among the positions occupied by Jews at the Imperial Palace.

The awe of the magical or superstitious in healing, however, was not just for Jews in pagan eyes but also the other way around. Except among the intelligentsia, Greco-Roman healing practices were far from being dominated by purely rationalistic concepts. And just as Greek philosophy, science, and medicine made inroads among Jewish thinkers, so some of the less rational practices of the Greeks infiltrated to some extent the lives of the Jewish common folk. Thus, for example, there is still to be seen today at the pagan alter in Oropus a stone slab presented by the former slave Moschion, son of Moschion, to Hygeia, the Greek goddess of health, in gratitude for an oracle dream foretelling that he would be freed by his master. Indeed, Rabbi Akiba, famed for his anointing of Bar Kochba as the

Messiah in his ill-fated revolt against the Romans early in the second century, noted with some dismay how healings at pagan temples impressed the Jews and seduced them into idolatry.

As the Jewish priests were the dominant force in the spiritual life of the Israelites before the destruction of the Temple, so the rabbis—the Hebrew word for "teachers"—assumed the mantle of religious leaders in the Diaspora. And whereas the priests had only the Bible—and particularly the first five Books of Moses, the Torah—as their written spiritual texts, the rabbis in exile eventually set about committing to parchment and papyrus the vast amount of oral law hitherto handed down by word of mouth from generation to generation.

Already for centuries before the expulsion from Israel by the Romans, Hebrew sages had engaged in vigorous analyses, discussions, disputations, and linguistic interpretations of various lines and passages in the Torah in order to determine their implications for the Jews in their religious and secular lives. This scholarly activity was intense during the Greek hegemony over the Middle East and Israel, which was also a time of tension among the Jews themselves. There was generally much mutual admiration between Israel and Hellas in their respective spheres. But arriving at some synthesis of the two civilizations was a different matter. The more hellenized Jews, especially among the upper socioeconomic strata, not only adopted the trappings of Greek civilization, but also endeavored to subject the Holy Book to the logic of Aristotle. Other Jews opposed any deviation from the oldtime religion of Moses. The Book of the Maccabees chronicled the various conflicts between the Jews and their Seleucid Greek overlords and between the Jews themselves. In such times of tension the Jewish spiritual authorities were wary lest a book of commentaries on the Torah supplant the Torah itself.

Having been canonized and committed to definitive written form in the fifth century B.C.E., the Torah itself could not be added to. Commentary, however, was not quite the same as addition, but the religious authorities prohibited it from taking written form. Thus there arose in the course of centuries a couple of million words of Oral Law, transmitted only by word of mouth and committed to memory rather than to papyrus. For the increasing number of Jews living outside Israel, the Oral Law expanded to encompass circumstances not known on the Exodus from Egypt or the centuries of life in the Promised Land.

With the weakening and impending dissolution of the Roman Empire, the rabbis now became concerned that the 2.5 million or so words of commentary existing only in the heads of those scholars capable of storing such vast amounts of information might perish in the chaos before they could be transmitted to new generations. Reluctantly, the rabbis allowed the Oral Law to be committed to folios. The result, called the *Mishnah* (Teachings) was then canonized just as the Torah had once been and likewise preserved from any further amendment. And so there began in the third century C.E.—particularly at the Jewish yeshivot (academies) of Babylon—the home of the majority of the world's Jews, which replaced Israel as the focus of Jewish intellectual life—a new cycle of commentaries on both the Torah and the *Mishnah,* eventually to be called the *Gemara* (Supplement). It in turn would be canonized in written form in the sixth century when a fanatical Zoroastrian sect known as the Magii gained power in Babylonia and again threatened the survival of the hitherto orally transmitted and memorized texts. The *Mishnah* and the *Gemara* were together called the Talmud (Learning).

The Talmud contains no medical tractates. Yet it would have a profound influence on a hundred generations of Jewish doctors and would be instrumental in establishing medicine as the Jewish profession par excellence. There were various reasons for this. Hundreds of medical references are to be found in the Talmud. Although scattered unsystematically, they formed a body of medical knowledge to complement that of the Greeks. The Talmud furthermore reinforced among the Jews a healthily balanced attitude toward the body, which contrasted with the cult of naked body worship of the pagan Greeks and the disdain for the corporal on the part of the Christians (more about which, below).

The talmudic rabbis furthermore began the codification of ethical principles, some of which had particular relevance to Jewish doctors. And last but not least, the development of the folios of esoteric Hebrew writings could not but strengthen the image in the gentile mind of the Jewish physicians as being privy to secret sources and powers not accessible to the gentiles. But for all that, we shall see that when the talmudic era ended, it was still by no means evident that the Jews were destined for a 1,000-year reign as the greatest of physicians.

In metaphysical matters, Galen, as was noted, criticized the Jews for simply declaring "God commanded, God spoke," rather than offering proofs. Underlying Galen's Greco-Roman systems of philosophy, natural sciences, and medicine were beautifully rational and secular doctrines—built upon fictitious speculation about four basic elements and four basic body humors and their various interactions. The Jewish system, by contrast, had a religious foundation that was unashamedly supernatural and was built upon presumably divinely revealed truths. (The talmudic sages and rabbis prided themselves in the precision and logic they applied to their analyses of the biblical texts. But the Scriptures themselves were not considered to be the product of human intellect.) Yet when it came to supplying down-to-earth details of anatomy as an aid to fulfilling Jewish religious obligations, the talmudic sages were often just as on or off the mark as was the rationalist Galen.

It was the kosher dietary regulations that provided perhaps the most important contribution of talmudic learning to medicine—albeit indirectly. Jewish law, as it evolved, mandated that animals intended for consumption be slaughtered in the quickest manner possible, while also being rendered optimally free of blood, which the Bible prohibited Jews from eating or drinking. The rabbis, with their knowledge of medicine and anatomy, enjoined the Jewish slaughterers (*shohets*) to kill their animals by a single unblemished cut through the jugular vein and the carotid artery. The rationale was partly humane consideration for the animal, but the strictures also harked back to the earlier biblical concept of animal slaughter as a sacrifice for God in the Jerusalem Temple, as well as a source of food for man. (While such practices are considered rather barbaric by modern standards, we must bear in mind that human sacrifice was widespread in ancient times. God's order to Abraham to sacrifice a ram instead of Isaac was a milestone in the advance of civilization.) Strict regulations were in force to ensure that the Almighty not be offended by an imperfect or unhealthy animal. Thus it was ruled that for an animal to be deemed kosher, it had to be viable at the moment of slaughtering—its demise being due solely to its being killed in the prescribed manner and not to any preexisting affliction.

To meet these demands, the Jewish slaughterers had to be versed in what would today be called veterinary medicine. But the ultimate resolution of potential disputes between possibly lax butchers and possibly overly prudent Jewish housewives rested with the rabbis. It was they who in the course of time described and classified a wide range of animal diseases on the basis of both their outward manifestations and investigation of the corresponding internal conditions—autopsies, as it were. And if some of the regulations seem arbitrary as to what might offend the Almighty and what not, the general finickiness at least had a positive effect in preventing the Jews from consuming a diseased or otherwise harmful animal. So, for example, any perforation of the stomach or intestinal system (which might allow the contamination of the meat by fecal matter) was deemed to render the animal *terefah* (literally "torn," and thus unkosher). But it should be noted that here as elsewhere, the sages and rabbis themselves recognized the lack of obvious rationale for many strictures and they generally eschewed providing any medical or health justifications for their pronouncements on rituals, lest their interpretations of the sacred Jewish obligations be degraded into mundane hygienic considerations. This attitude prevailed despite the fact that talmudic scholars were themselves often quite knowledgeable in the various sciences and were literate in Greek as well as other languages. In later generations, as we shall see, some rabbis were not averse to providing a Greco-Roman medical interpretation to some Jewish laws.

Many other veterinary observations and rulings in the Talmud, although not necessarily of immediate benefit to the health of the consumer, provided medical science with anatomical observations that were among the most advanced in the world. The condition of the lungs of slaughtered animals was of particular concern to the rabbis. The Talmud contains descriptions of the two "skins" (pleura) of the lung, and the opinion is stated that both had to be perforated before a pneumothorax (which is fatal and therefore renders the animal nonkosher) can be said to be present. A variety of tests for pneumothorax included submerging the slaughtered animal in lukewarm water, blowing into its trachea, and watching for bubbles. Yet even if they appeared, the possibility had to be excluded that the inner lung membrane was still intact and that the bubbles were coming not from the lung but from air in the space between the two coats—a nonfatal injury that would not in itself invalidate the animal's kosher status. In a similar vein, descriptions were given of peripneumonia, cheesiness, pus, fistulae, and cysts of the lungs, with commentary as to their seriousness. The Talmud itself cautions against extrapolations from animal to human anatomy and pathology. Yet such extrapolations were inevitable, and more often than not were justified. For example, the human esophagus has two coats and the human kidneys a special layer of fat, just as the Talmud relates with regard to slaughtered animals.

The Talmud also contains human anatomical information not derived from veterinary kosher commentary, though, of course, virtually none of this was based on dissection of corpses. From the *Berakhot* we learn that "The kidneys prompt, the heart discerns, the tongue shapes [words], the mouth articulates, the gullet takes in and lets out all kinds of food, the windpipe produces the voice, the lung absorbs all kinds of liquids, the liver is the seat of anger, the gall lets a drop fall into it and allays it, the spleen produces laughter, the large intestines grind [the food], the maw brings sleep, the nose awakens." There is also much information on human disease in the Talmud, but its place in the modern nosological scheme of things is problematical. Thus "heaviness of heart" (*yukra de'libba* in Aramaic, the Semitic sister-tongue of Hebrew that became the Jewish vernacular) may pertain to asthma but perhaps to mental depression instead. Since the heart is often referred to as the literal seat of emotions (and sometimes of decision-making as well), melancholy caused by "heaviness of heart" would be viewed as a genuine cardiac problem. "Weakness of the heart" (*hulsha de'libba*), on the other hand, seems to refer to hunger pangs or hypoglycemia and could be alleviated by consuming the right flank of a male beast roasted on a willow twig, supplemented, if need be, by excrement of cattle cast in the month of Nissan. As for "pressure of the heart" (*kira de'libba*)— perhaps in fact a stomach ailment—mint, camon, and sesame were prescribed. A terminological confusion also surrounds the illness *yerakon*, mentioned in both the Bible and the Talmud, a name derived from the word *yerok*, meaning "green" (as in plants) but perhaps shading off into yellow. As such, it had been interpreted alternatively as chlorosis (greenish coloration in adolescent girls, due to iron deficiency) and jaundice. One recommended treatment was the urine of an ass, apparently a homeopathic remedy, especially since jaundice is sometimes mentioned as being due to urine retention.

The names of various physicians are specifically mentioned in the Talmud. Yet one stands out above the rest. He is the great authority on civil law known as Mar (that is, "master") Samuel, and also as Samuel the physician, due to his expertise in medicine. Born to a wealthy silk merchant in Babylon about 180 C.E., Samuel was a contemporary of Galen. But unlike Galen, Samuel inhabited the area on the eastern fringe of the Roman Empire. He was educated at the rabbinical academy in Netzivim (Nisibis), the capital city of the Armenian kings, which was also home to a medical school. Samuel subsequently pursued his studies in both religion and medicine in Tzipori (Sepphoris). While still studying medicine, Samuel cured Rabbi Judah of an eye ailment, whereupon the grateful Patriarch wished to bestow the title "rabbi" on the young physician. When, for unclear reasons, this did not come to pass, Samuel told Judah: "Let it not grieve thee, for I have seen written in the book of Adam that I will be called *chacham* [sage]." Indeed, Samuel would serve as rector of the school of higher learning in Nehardea in Babylon and go on the become personal physician to, among other greats, King Shapur I of Persia.

Mar Samuel contributed to the kosher and veterinary store of knowledge of the Talmud, most notably in neurology. He pronounced *terefah* (nonviable, and thus forbidden) those animals with perforation of the *dura mater* of the brain or severance of the spinal cord at the level of the first sacral nerve. (By contrast, he declared severance at the third sacral nerve not to affect viability.) Samuel also discussed the consequences for an animal's kosher status when the aorta (the great artery from the heart) is punctured, and he wrote about leg fractures, the Achilles tendon, and injuries to the pharynx (foodpipe), gullet, and rumen.

As for specifically human anatomy, Mar Samuel tells of a dissection of a condemned prostitute. Such human dissections, if they occurred at all, were quite rare. Interesting is how the *Mishnah*, in enumerating all the bones of the human skeleton, comes up with a total of 248 (excluding the teeth). This is considerably more than the 205 recognized by more modern anatomists, but corresponds quite conveniently to the number of lunar days in the year and also to the number of positive commandments in Jewish law.

Procreation has forever been of great concern to the Jews, so it is understandable that many of Mar Samuel's notes should have been devoted to obstetrics and gynecology. Samuel made some firsthand observations on breast development by examining his maidservant at intervals around puberty. (He quite properly paid her four *zuz* as "shame money," reasoning that although the right to her labor was his, the right to such invasion of her modesty was not.) But far more important to Samuel were the women's primary sexual organs and not least the vaginal discharges.

In the Books of Moses, a menstruating woman was hardly more welcome than a leper—a view that reflected the awe and loathing in which menstrual blood has traditionally been held in primitive societies. "And if a woman have an issue, and her issue in her flesh be blood, she shall be put apart seven days: and whosoever toucheth her shall be unclean until the eve," commanded the Lord to Moses and Aaron in Leviticus (15:19–21). "And every thing that she lieth upon in her separation shall be unclean: every thing also that she sitteth upon shall be unclean. And whoso ever toucheth her bed shall wash his clothes, and bathe himself in water, and be unclean until the even." Under such circumstances, differentiation of a menstrual discharge from other vaginal bleeding was of great importance. Mar Samuel accordingly perfected a cotton-tipped, soft lead device to determine whether vaginal blood after intercourse was from the "fountain" (uterus) or from abrasions in the walls. In the latter case, the discharge was "clean," although perhaps an indication of vaginal disease (or an overendowed husband). Even if pathological, such nonmenstrual bleeding did not evoke the same degree of primitive horror among Jews and did not render the woman untouchable.

When the vaginal discharge was indeed menstrual blood, a ritual bath (*mikveh*) had to follow the end of the period before intercourse could resume. Mar Samuel was particularly obsessive with regard to this. Purification required that all of the woman's body surface be in contact with the water, so Samuel took the precaution of placing a mat on the sand bed of his daughters' *mikveh*, lest some loose grain adhere, block contact with the water on a minute part of her skin, and render the whole ritual invalid. Such finickiness had at least the advantage of ensuring that the *mikveh*, where so many women bathed together, remained free of any visible contaminant. (Men, too, were required to take ritual baths, if they ate a forbidden food, touched a corpse, had an involuntary ejaculation, or were cured of leprosy or gonorrhea. The same stringent rules applied to them as well.)

All this notwithstanding, in some ways vaginal bleeding, of both the unclean and clean variety, was a blessing to the woman. Rabbinical opinion opposed letting women marry who have not menstruated (unclean blood). Furthermore, if on the wedding night the "tokens of the damsel's virginity" (clean blood) were not to be found on the sheets, this was cause for the annulment of the marriage, if not necessarily also the stoning to death of the "whore" prescribed in Deuteronomy (22:15–21). Yet Mar Samuel pointed out that such tokens were not a foolproof sign of the first loss of virginity (the hymen may have survived several previous episodes of intercourse); likewise, the absence of bleeding was not necessarily proof that there had been no *virgo intacta*.

Understandably, in view of the great importance Jewish law attached to the presence or absence of hymen blood, the Talmud gives various reagents for determining whether a red spot on the women's undergarment was blood or just some dye. Among them are hot bean soup, the spittle of someone who has not eaten or spoken since the previous night, fermented urine, and the soapwort plant, which, Samuel tells us, could be extracted by an iron nail from the cracks of pearls. (These reagents supposedly lighten or remove blood stains but not dyes.)

For fertilization to take place, the sperm ejaculated during intercourse must, according to Samuel, "shoot forth like an arrow." He therefore looked askance at stories of pregnancies resulting from a woman bathing in tub water where a man had recently ejaculated. Samuel was also concerned with penile injuries that might render a man impotent and therefore forbidden to marry under Jewish law. But to the relief of monorchid men, he stated that the absence of one testicle did not prevent procreation.

Samuel set the length of a normal pregnancy, from conception to birth, at 271 to 273 days. He considered 212 days to be the minimum for infant vitality. The distinguishing of a miscarried fetus from other vaginal discharges was, of course, important. Samuel declared that a discharged sac was not a miscarried fetus as long as it was so transparent that a single hair placed on the other side of it could still be seen. As for the sex of a fetus in the early stages, Samuel stated that this could be determined only by the presence or absence of hair on its head. Among the possible teratologies (birth abnormalities) of a fetus brought to term, Samuel made mention of an otherwise normal baby with wing-like appendages resembling the night-spirit Lilith. Less deviant was a newborn with extremely long hair. Samuel ruled that the baby could have its hair cut even on a half-holiday (the intermediate days of Passover and Tabernacles), since this is also permitted by talmudic law to those just released from jail, and the newborn has, after all, just come free from a prison of sorts.

As for the cutting of the foreskin, this takes place on the eighth day, even if it falls on the Sabbath. Mar Samuel, however, cautiously recommended that this be postponed until the thirtieth day if the baby has had a fever, even if it lasted only an hour. The genetic, maternally transmitted basis of hemophilia was apparently recognized in the Babylonian Talmud. Concern for life was placed above religious ritual, so that baby boys whose older brothers had died from bleeding were exempted from circumcision. The unquestionable expertise in this ritual that the Jews built up through the ages and codified on paper—for example, on the proper cutting techniques, the blood supply in the area to be operated on, and the means of staunching the bleeding wound—no doubt had some relevance for other surgical and wound treatment procedures.

In the realm of preventative medicine, Samuel strongly advised consistency from day to day in one's eating habits. Change of diet brought dangers to health, particularly dysentery. So the poor man, much to his chagrin, was cautioned to stick to his meager fare, even on festival days when he was offered rich foods, lest the bountiful change cause illness. Various talmudic authors stressed the importance of eating simply, slowly, and in moderation, as well as regularly and with dietary consistency. If after eating one goes directly to bed rather than first going for a walk, the food will putrefy without being digested. "For all things I know the cure except the following three," declared Samuel: "eating bitter dates on an empty stomach, girding one's loins with a damp flaxen cord, and eating and not walking at least four cubits after it." But as bad as eating the wrong way was not eating at all. In contrast to Christian tendencies toward asceticism, Samuel generally condemned the idea of fasting other than on Yom Kippur (the Day of Atonement), since this might weaken one's health. Elsewhere in the Talmud (Yoma, 8:83a) we are told: "If the patient says, I need [food], whilst the physician says: He does not need it, we hearken to the patient." This

Jewish view contrasted sharply with the Greco-Roman practice of starving the illness.

As for elimination, Mar Samuel was of the opinion that the urge to urinate should be heeded with minimal delay—even in public, if need be. Heeding the call to defecate was socially more problematic. But talmudic scholars ruled that the commandment in Leviticus (28:25) that "ye shall not make your souls abominable" applied not just to avoidance of unclean animals but also the avoidance of too laden a colon. The snout of the pig—the unclean animal par excellence—was compared with a wandering toilet, which was declared to be a great source of contagious disease. So the Talmud stated that evacuation in the early morning was good for the body as hardening is to iron, and it mandated that "when your pot is boiling, empty it out." Rabbi Judah ben Illay was proud of the fact that "on the road from my house to the house of study there are 24 lavatories, and at each I can think whether nature is calling and, if so, can relieve myself immediately."

Mar Samuel's views on those diseases now known to be spread by microorganisms were a particularly interesting mix of some ancient folk superstitions and hints of modern microbiology. He spoke of demons (or wind) causing disease and of the evil spirit resting upon a rabid dog. Yet Samuel apparently had some awareness of the chain of transmission of pestilence, as when he was concerned that an epidemic raging in far-off Be Hozae might be brought to his own town by the active caravan route linking the two locations. (He prudently ordered a fast of supplication.) Samuel warned that untidiness (neglect) causes blindness by contamination. (Another talmudic writer warned: "Whoever eats bread without previously washing the hands is as though he had intercourse with a harlot" [*Sotah* 1:4b].) Fearing that water might be contaminated by the poison of a snake, Mar Samuel made a habit of boiling it before drinking. Whether any supposed snake venom was indeed rendered nonvirulent by the fire is questionable, but pathogenic microorganisms were undoubtedly destroyed in the process. (The *Abudah Zarah* and the *Midrash Rabbah* were incredibly more prescient when they stated, respectively, that "water suspected of containing germs should be boiled before drinking" and that "the harm-producing minute organisms are everywhere in abundance, if we would see them we could not exist.")

Whereas grains of truth are to be found in many of Samuel's pronouncements, it is hard to find one in his favorite diagnostic technique. This involved a tiny *betza tormita* or hard-boiled egg passed through the digestive system. "The work required to prepare one is worth a thousand denars," he stated. "For the egg must be placed a thousand times in hot water and a thousand times in cold water until it is small enough to be swallowed whole." (Samuel is said to have tested less labor-intensive substitutes for the *betza tormita,* such as a cabbage-stalk, but this caused such a bad reaction that he was at first thought to have died.) If an illness is present in the person," Samuel stated, "it is attracted to the egg, and when the egg is passed out per rectum, the physician knows which medication is required for the patient and how to treat him."

Indeed, when it came to treatments, there were legions of medicines and cures scattered through the pages of the Talmud, from which the physicians might choose. As Rabbi Judah stated: "The Holy One has created nothing useless in the world. He created the snail as a remedy for a sore, the fly for the sting of a wasp, mosquito for the bite of a serpent, the serpent for . . ." and so on. A look at some of Mar Samuel's cures reveals a motley collection, with some treatments based on sound sense, some on harmless misinformation, and some on outright superstition. Samuel recommended treatment of wounds with oil and warm water, and of peeling skin with water of mangold beets. He had concoctions (collyriums) for healing the eye and preferred water as a base since this would not weaken the eyesight. (The rabbis graciously ruled that if flour was added to the collyrium to make a paste, this, unlike all other sour dough, did not have to be destroyed before Passover.) Samuel prescribed fat meat for bulimia, and he hoped that an infusion of fat and charcoal-broiled meat together with stimulants such as undiluted wine might allow someone stuck by a poisoned Persian lance to live at least long enough to arrange his affairs. He proclaimed the healthiness of asafetida (*chiltith*)—despite its dreadful smell, its nickname "devil's dirt," and the opinion of some rabbis that it was poisonous. Samuel maintained that the best time to drink liquid healing concoctions was between Passover and Pentecost. He advocated the use of dust from the grave of the talmudic sage Rab as antidote for quotidian fever. Any superstitious use of the remains of the corpse itself or its clothes was, however, strictly prohibited.

Mar Samuel was by no means unaffected by the ancient concept of the tangible removal of disease, which was further developed in the Greco-Roman medical theories. So, for example, he saw the value of steam baths in the release of sweat and hot vapor from the body. As for bloodletting, the Jerusalem Talmud (*Bechorath* 3:17) not unreasonably recommended venesection for an animal that is "overtaken by blood," that is, has plethora (and further stated that the blemish thus caused renders it unfit for sacrifice). But Samuel, like Galen and so many others before and since, used bloodletting for many ailments and for the removal of poisons. Samuel extended the practice to include prophylactic bleeding of the healthy person every thirty days.

In retrospect, the most charitable thing that one can say about bloodletting is that it may have lowered the iron level and thus deprived bacteria of a nutrient needed for their replication. And the best that could be said about Mar Samuel with regard to bloodletting was that he took a noteworthy precaution. In marked contrast with Greco-Roman practices that compounded the ordeal of phlebotomy with fasting in order to starve the illness, Samuel provided sufficient nourishment to his patients after the procedure. He was especially partial to the consumption of spleen and red wine, since the former is rich in blood (here the Mosaic prohibition seems to have been suspended) and the latter supposedly helps produce new blood. (By contrast, the patient's eating of fowl after bloodletting was prohibited by Samuel, since "his heart will flutter like a bird.") Should a person get the chills after bloodletting, Samuel prescribed warming by fire even on the dog days of summer—when Sirius rises and sets with the sun.

Furthermore, Samuel limited the days on which bloodletting could be carried out. As we know with the wisdom of hindsight, the more such restrictions, so much the better for the patient. Sunday and Friday were the approved times for venesection, Samuel declared, but not on the first three days of the month. Monday and Thursday were forbidden because both the celestial and human courts were in session and "the accuser (Satan) accuses during time of danger." Tuesday, for its part, was similarly prohibited, since it was associated with Mars, the planet of murderers. As for Wednesday, Samuel prohibited bloodletting if it fell on the fourth, fourteenth, twenty-fourth or on one of the last four days of the month. He furthermore forbade venesection on the eve of any festival, apparently because one was already weakened by all the preparations.

The sun's course through the heavens determined the length of the day, the four seasons, and the year. The planets supposedly held sway over the weekdays. The moon's cycle determined the length of the month. The path of Sirius governed the dog days. And so it went. But most important of all for the Jews were the celestial circumstances determining the Sabbath days, the prayer days, the holy days, and the festivals. No people's calendar was more governed by the present and future position of the heavenly bodies than that of the Jews. And no people had a more intimate knowledge of the skies or keener mathematical skills. From this has arisen an unbroken tradition of great Jewish astronomers from antiquity right through to the era of orbiting telescopes. Mar Samuel was one of these. That a great physician should also be a great astronomer may seem anomalous in our day; but it wasn't so in Samuel's time or for a millennium and a half thereafter.

Much of the early astronomical skill of the Jews derived from contacts with the Babylonians, who in biblical times built towers on their flat plains from which better to observe occurrences in the heavens. It was the Babylonians who, on the basis of the monthly lunar cycle, conceived of the zodiac by dividing into twelve signs the celestial band along which the planets travel and by attaching a special correspondence between the conjunctions of the heavenly bodies within the signs and the present and future affairs of men and nations on earth. In Numbers, a Mesopotamian astrologer prophesied that "There shall come a Star out of Jacob, and a scepter shall rise out of Israel, and shall smite the corners of Moab and destroy all the children of Seth." Amos urges his followers to "Seek him that maketh the seven stars in Orion, and turneth the shadow of death into the morning." The same constellation is referred to in Job (38:31–32) when God asks him: "Canst thou bind the sweet influences of Pleiades, or loose the bands of Orion?; canst thou bring forth Mazzaroth in his season? or canst thou guide Arcturus with his sons?" The Babylonian king Nebuchadrezzar had the young Daniel instructed in the language and learning of the Chaldean soothsayers—so well, in fact, that he became "ten times better than all the magicians and astrologers that were in all his realm" (Daniel 1:20).

But in contrast to the Jews with their monotheism, the Babylonians viewed the stars and planets as gods, even if they later adopted the modified concept that the planets were merely controlled by their respective deities. The Jewish aversion to such star-struck concepts as part and parcel of Babylonian idolatry is reflected in Zephenia's pronouncement: "I will cut off the remnant of Baal from this place . . . and them that worship the host of heaven upon the housetops." In Jeremiah (10:2) the Hebrews are told: "Do not dread the signs of heaven, like the heathens, who fear them." Thus arose alongside a tradition of Jewish astronomy a healthy skepticism toward astrology.

Alexandria, the Egyptian center of Greek learning, was the site of great accomplishments in the field of astronomy. It was there in the third century B.C.E. that the mathematician Eratosthenes made impressively accurate calculations of the Earth's circumference and the distance to the Moon, and even estimated the distance to the Sun within a quite respectable order of magnitude. The most influential of the Alexandrian astronomers was Ptolemy, who lived in the second century C.E. and whose model of a universe of clocklike concentric spheres predicted the motions of the heavenly bodies with an accuracy that is all the more impressive in that his model suffered from immense unnecessary complications—epicycles and eccentrics—due to its being earth-centered rather than helio-centered.

The large hellenized Jewish community of Alexandria, enthralled as they were by Greek science, were only too glad to believe the legend that one of their own ancestors, the stargazing Abraham, had anticipated the sophisticated cosmology of Eratosthenes and Ptolemy. As one story had it, the Patriarch astronomer was first with the theory of stars attached to uniformly moving concentric spheres, which he took as proof of divine intelligence governing the universe. Alternatively, a legend propagated by the great Roman Jewish historian Josephus had Abraham happily pointing to the peculiar *irregularities* in the otherwise perfect celestial order, viewing these as God's signs of the subordination of the working of the cosmos to His will.

The influence not only of the Sun on terrestrial life but also of the Moon upon the tides was as self-evident to the Jews as to the Greeks, indeed as to all people living near the coast. But the four-element theory was a Greek, not a Jewish, construct, and it was the Greek scientists and philosophers who used this to develop a sophisticated system of interrelations between astronomy and biology. The Greeks identified the Sun with the element fire and the Moon with the element water. Aristotle, by holding the movement of the Sun and Moon through the skies responsible for keeping these two elements on earth in a state of activity, credited the two main heavenly bodies for the processes of terrestrial life, growth, and decay, as opposed to static immobility. Ptolemy and his followers took the dubious liberty of extending the celestial movers and shakers to include the fixed stars and the wandering planets. These heavenly objects "cause heats, winds, and storms, to the influence of which earthy things are comfortably subjected." "From these premises," Ptolemy went on to state, "it follows not only that all bodies, which may be already compounded, are subjected to the motions of the stars, but also that the impregnation and growth of the seeds from which all bodies proceed are formed and molded by the quality existing in the ambient at the time of such impregnation and growth." So it was that the stars and planets had a role in what Ptolemy called "medical mathematics," by which process "remedies for the present and preservations against future disorders are to be acquired: for without astronomical knowledge, medical aid would be most frequently unavailing."

So for Mar Samuel, being a great physician went hand in hand with being a famed astronomer. He was, in his own words, "as familiar with the paths of heaven as with the streets of Nehardea." Indeed, along with the titles *Mar* (master) and *Chacham* (sage), he was accorded the appellation *Yarchinai* (astrologer). Although he modestly expressed his ignorance of comet trajectories, he could "make a calendar [of leap years] for the whole Diaspora," and he calculated the intercalation of months for sixty years. We have seen how Samuel combined his astronomical and medical skills—pseudoscientific though they were—to determine the do-not-bleed days of the month. But astrology and horoscopes had no place in Samuel's worldview, at least as far as Jews were concerned, for he argued that Israelites were exempt from planetary influences. This accorded with one of the legends in the Talmud (*Nedarim* 32a), which has Abraham saying, "I have seen in the stars that I will have only one son," to which God retorted: "Leave your astrology; for Israel there are no stars."

In an era of pseudoscience and woeful ignorance of the true bases of human pathology, which would endure until the nineteenth century, skepticism of astrology ranks as a major contribution of the talmudic Jews to medical science, albeit a negative one. The rabbis did, however, set in motion a major positive contribution to medicine. Not, strictly speaking, to medical science, but to medical ethics.

The school of Hippocratic physicians made a point of distinguishing it-self from the many rival medical sects not only by its rational theories but by its rules of ethical conduct. These were embodied in the Hippocratic Oath. The talmudic rabbis, for their part, began systematizing a Jewish code of ethics that would have particular relevance to the Jewish physician. In some details, these resembled the Hippocratic commandments. Notably, the rabbinical rulings that prohibited tale-bearing (*rechilut*) and malicious gossip (*lashon hara*) placed ethical constraints on the Jewish physician simi-lar to those on the Hippocratic physician, who swore that "whatever you shall see or hear of the lives of men which is not fitting to be spoken, you shall keep inviolably secret."

But more fundamental and far-reaching was the principle first given form by the talmudic rabbis that places an infinite value on a person's life. This principle would be strengthened and expanded by various responsa (rab-binical rulings) for the next thousand years or so. For the Jewish physician this mandated that he place the treatment of patients whose lives are in danger (*pikuach nefesh*) or even potentially in danger (*sofek pikuach nefesh*), above the observance of religious obligations such as the honoring of the Sabbath. Only the observance of three prohibitions, namely, those against murder, idolatry, and incest, were deemed by the rabbis to take precedence over the saving of a human life. Patients were similarly enjoined to put the preservation of their own lives above religious ritual; even among the well-bodied the preservation of health in the threat of dangerous illness could take priority over religious observance, as when during a cholera outbreak a rabbi (Yisroel Salanter) commanded his congregation to eat on Yom Kip-pur to strengthen their resistance.

Although the Jewish physician's life-saving imperative was originally binding only with respect to fellow Jews, various responsa would affirm his obligation to come to the aid of dangerously ill or suffering gentiles, even if doing so means the suspension of biblical and rabbinical command-ments. The killing of one person—Jew or gentile—to save the life of an-other, no matter how humble or mean the former or how great and noble the latter, was strictly prohibited. "Your blood is not redder than that of your neighbor," says the *Pesachim*. So the supposedly therapeutic practice indulged in by kings in the ancient world of bathing in the blood of their slain subjects received only condemnation from the Jewish sages.

The only taking of one human life for the sake of another sanctioned by

Jewish medical scriptures was the abortion of a fetus to save the mother, and even this trade-off is not permitted should the baby's head already be born. The Jews came to condemn the practice, accepted as a matter of course by the Greeks at the height of their intellectual development, of infanticide of superfluous or undesired newborn. The Jewish reverence for human life was in fact generally deemed to encompass even severely defective babies—although with some leeway, as when a rabbinical ruling advised against the desecration of the Sabbath for a premature neonate considered to be nonviable. Other rabbinical pronouncements endeavored to distinguish between the passive or active shortening of life by the physician, which was prohibited outright, and his non-interference in, or even his deliberate shortening of, the process of impending death. The latter case was more problematical and remains so even at the dawn of the third millennium.

When Mar Samuel wrote his commentaries, Judaism was no longer the only religion to hold sacred the Jewish Bible and the figures of Abraham, Moses, and the Hebrew Prophets. Christianity, which had originally started out as a Jewish sect whose adherents worshiped and preached their doctrines in synagogues, had by the end of the first century C.E. become a distinct religion of its own. Although most of the early Christians were Jewish, they soon despaired of convincing the mass of their fellow Jews that the Messiah prophesied in the Hebrew Bible had indeed appeared on earth in the form of Jesus of Nazareth. So, the Christians actively sought converts among the gentiles. Early on, the Jewish kosher dietary laws were suspended, as was the rite of circumcision. The latter lapse gave the Christians decided advantages. For although, as we have seen, gentile Greeks and Romans were attracted to Judaism, adult males were understandably reluctant to have their prepuces cut off as the price for full entry into the Jewish community.

As for medicine, the New Testament or Gospel—the Christian supplement to the Jewish Bible—has its full share of healing lore, based largely on the same primitive concept of supernatural causation and cure of disease common to Judaism. The pages of the Gospel are filled with accounts of healing wrought not by drugs but by the miraculous powers of Jesus. Those who were possessed by devils and cruelly shunned by their fellows had their evils spirits exorcised by the Nazarene—a cure that in modern thinking is sooner attributable to the hysterical nature of the afflictions and the great kindness and charisma of Jesus' personality. The Nazarene also cured ailments of a more physical (though perhaps psychosomatic) nature, as when he brought sight back to the blind and caused withered hands to move again. Lepers and sufferers from dropsy were likewise given a new lease on life. The apostle Luke, unlike the other three, was himself a physician and as such he sprinkled his accounts of Jesus' miracle cures with Hippocratic terms such as hydropokis, atrophy, and apoplexy. The Christians proclaimed it their duty "To preach the kingdom of God and to heal the sick." As James (5:14–15) declared: "Is any sick among you? let him call for the elders of the Church; and let them pray over him, anointing him with oil in the name of the Lord. And the prayer of faith shall save the sick, and the Lord shall raise him up. . . ."

If much of the Christian concept of disease causation and cure was consistent with Old Testament views, there was a fundamental element in the biological thinking of the early Church Fathers—most notably Paul—that had little basis in Jewish tradition, namely, the despising of the corporal. Religious Jews, it is true, rejected the Hellenic cult of the body as reflected in nude Greek statues. But, notwithstanding such Platonic philosophizing as that of Philo, Judaism traditionally struck a balance between worshiping the body and despising it. The body—including its sexual functions—was respected and the concept of a mind-body unity was maintained. By contrast, St. Paul boasted: "I keep under my body and bring it into subjection" (1 Corinthians 9:27). He warned his followers that "if ye live after the flesh, ye shall die: but if ye through the spirit do mortify the deeds of the body, ye shall live" (Romans 8:13). With the Second Coming and the End of the World supposedly in sight, and his eyes fixed on the Hereafter, Paul even declared: "I take pleasure in infirmities . . . in distresses for Christ's sake: for when I am weak, then I am strong" (2 Corinthians 12:10).

The first few centuries of the Christian era saw intermittent persecution of the followers of Christ by suspicious Roman emperors. By the end of the fourth century, however, the proverbial shoe—or jackboot—was on the other foot. In 313 C.E. Christianity was granted the status of *religio licita,* which had already been enjoyed by Judaism for well over a century. In 391 C.E., under Emperor Theodosius, Christianity was proclaimed the State Religion, all others being declared *illicita,* to the particular detriment of Judaism—and to classical learning.

Around the fifth century the great library at Alexandria, as well as the city's already much diminished Jewish community, came to an end. The library was burned to the ground by Christian fanatics and a mob spurred on by Bishop Cyril took to a church and lynched the Museum's last scholar—a woman—and soon destroyed the Jewish quarter. It boded further ill for medical science in Christendom when, in 431 C.E., the Council of Ephesos excommunicated as heretical the Patriarch of Constantinople, Nestorios, who with his followers and their knowledge of classical learning, fled eastward to beyond the confines of the former Roman Empire.

By then the empire had already been sundered into an eastern and western half, under the control of two sons of Theodosius, the last ruler of a united empire and the one who had made Christianity the sole religion. The disintegration continued rapidly as the Western Empire became so politically and economically weakened as to succumb to the invasions of the Germanic hordes from northeastern Europe. (One medical theory has it that the lead in the Roman plumbing contributed to the demise of the upper classes in particular, and thus to the imperial collapse.) When in the fifth century Rome was sacked by barbarian Germanic tribes—first by the Visigoths and then by the Vandals—Europe began its rapid descent into the Dark Ages. The violence, pestilence, and general social chaos that accompanied the breakdown provided fertile ground for the strengthening of the Christian faith, with its concepts of brotherly love and pity and a promise of a better life in the Hereafter.

As Christian Europe groped in darkness, there was still precious little hint of the 1,000-year reign to come of Jews as doctors to the gentile world. Even among the Jews themselves, the place of the physician was far from secure. True, the Talmud contained the laudatory reference to the "faithful physician" and enjoined the Jews to "honor thy physician before thou hast need of him" (*Taanit*). But the Talmud also contained the perplexing statement—offered without any further explanation—that "the best of physicians is destined for hell (*Gehenna*)" (*Kiddishun* 4:14). Later generations of Jewish scholars—some of whom were also great doctors—would ponder its meaning. It would be variously interpreted as a caution against overconfidence, quackery, careless administration of harmful drugs without regard to side effects, neglect of poor patients, refusal to consult with colleagues, commercialization, or lack of attention to individual differences among

patients. Perhaps the line was no more than a cryptic play on some Hebrew words, *rophim* ("physicians") sounding like *r'pho'im* ("dwellers of the
netherworld"). Some have seen the remark as a reminder that God and not
man, no matter how skilled, is the Ultimate Healer. In a similar vein, it has
been interpreted as a warning to Jewish physicians who were too enamored of the rational medicine of the Greeks.

While Christianity spread to the northernmost and easternmost reaches
of a Europe stumbling through the Dark Ages, much of the southern realm
of the former Roman Empire would remain predominantly Christian for
only two or three centuries after the fall of Rome. For there would appear
in the Arabian peninsula yet another religion born of Jewish Scriptures and
Jewish memory. As it swept from the Middle East through the former
imperial domains of North Africa and then into Spain, it would rekindle
the flame of ancient learning even as Greece and Rome themselves lay in
shadow. In this radiance a bond between Jews and medicine would be forged,
to remain indissoluble up to the present day.

Chapter 3

The Doctor Who Could Stop the Crescent from Waning

Should [a person's] soul become sick, he must follow the same course of treating it as in the medical treatment for bodies. For when the body gets out of equilibrium, we look to which side it inclines in becoming unbalanced, and then oppose it with its contrary until it returns to equilibrium.

—Maimonides

Semen is the strength of the body and its life, and is the light of the eyes. Whenever too much is ejaculated, the body decays, its strength is spent, and its life destroyed. . . . [Circumcision aims to] weaken the organ of generation as far as possible and thus cause men to be moderate.

—Maimonides

Galen's art heals only the body,
But [Maimonides's] heals the body and soul.
His knowledge has made him the physician of the century.
With his wisdom, he could heal the sickness of ignorance.
Were he to attend the moon,
He would free her of her spots when she was full,
He would heal her of her periodic defects,
And at the time of her weakness save her from waning.

—Said ben Sana Almulk

When around 950 B.C.E. the Queen of Sheba journeyed from the southern tip of the Arabian peninsula "with camels that bare spices, and very much gold, and precious stones" to visit King Solomon in Jerusa-

87

lem (1 Kings 10:2), she traveled along the same incense route that carried from her kingdom and from nearby Hadramawt the myrrh and frankincense so prized by the Jews and other peoples of the Mediterranean. These incense resins were valued not just for their fragrance, but also for their soothing, wound-healing, and anti-decay properties, the latter due (we now know) to their bacteriostatic action. The inland incense route ran parallel to the Red Sea for some 1,200 miles along a verdant stretch dotted by trading towns, one of which was Mecca. Beyond lay, then as now, some half million square miles of sand, sparsely inhabited by hardy nomadic Bedouin tribes.

These Arab desert dwellers shared with the Jews some common Semitic mythological heritage, not least of which was an adoration of Ibrahim (Abraham), whom they, too, regarded as their ancestor—through his second son, Ishmael. But for over fifteen centuries after the Jews had evolved their religion into a rigorous monotheism, Allah, the top deity of the Arabs, or at least of those living in the area around Mecca, had to share power with a multitude of other supernatural entities: the spirits of trees, rocks, and watersprings worshiped by the animist nomadic tribes; the moon-god, symbol of the blessed coolness of the desert night; a black rock that fell from heaven as a meteorite and was enshrined in Mecca; and a host of benevolent gods and malevolent jinns and ghuls.

However, during this millennium and a half of Arab paganism, the influence of Jewish thought extended far beyond some common Semitic remembrance. After the destruction of the Temple in 70 c.e., and especially in the fifth and sixth centuries, the Diaspora Jews brought their commercial skills in handicrafts, goldworking, and even date palm cultivation to the Arabian peninsula, thus helping to transform villages into cities. They also brought their religion, to which tribes of Arabian pagans voluntarily converted. Around the turn of the seventh century c.e., Mohammed, a prosperous Meccan camel driver, apparently came under the influence of groups of men known as *hanifs*, who rejected pagan idolatry and sexual symbols in favor of an ascetic monotheism such as practiced by the Jews. A trip to Syria by caravan further exposed Mohammed to Jewish thinking and the Hebrew Bible. When, around 610 c.e. the Prophet, as Mohammed would forever after be known, began to have his revelations, these were, he declared, transmitted to him from God by the archangel Gabriel, and they abounded with Old Testament names and references: the Creation, the Fall, the Flood; Adam, Noah, Lot, Joseph, Saul, David, Solomon, Elijah, Job; and, of course, Abraham and Moses, who together are mentioned over a hundred times. In his fabled Night Journey in 620 C.E. the dreaming Mohammed flew to the Wailing Wall in Jerusalem, whence he ascended to Seventh Heaven to meet God.

By the time of his death in 632, Mohammed had managed, with the sword and the pen, to unite all the tribes of Arabia under his Islam, meaning submission to the will of God and apparently derived from Abraham's theoretical willingness to submit (*aslama* in Arabic) to Jehovah's command to sacrifice his son Isaac. Where necessary, however, the Prophet had assimilated pagan symbols—the crescent moon, the black meteor—to the monotheistic creed. The hardy tribes of Arab horsemen, imbued by a religious fanaticism, and an appetite for riches in the world outside the desert, and now forbidden to wage their traditional wars against one another, burst out of their homeland and swept through the Middle East and North Africa, wielding swords and the holy Koran, the compilation of the Mohammed's revelations. In spite of the quarrels that soon arose about succession and doctrinal matters, by the year 711 the Prophet's disciples had made Islam the dominant religion of an area stretching from present-day Morocco to Pakistan.

Despite, or because of, Islam's deep roots in Jewish tradition, events during Mohammed's early years of struggle appeared to auger ill for the future of the Jews who fell under the domain of the new faith. The Prophet first sought to win over the people of the Old Testament by commanding his followers to pray to Jerusalem, honor the Saturday Sabbath, and fast on Yom Kippur. But soon despairing of his attempts to convert the Jews, Mohammed substituted Mecca for prayer, Friday for the Sabbath day, and Ramadan for the fasting period. In the decade following the night flight to the City of David in 620, the Jewish Arabian communities of al-Nadhir, Qurayza, and Khaybar were massacred, enslaved, or (if they were lucky) exiled, for not accepting Mohammed's claim to being the ultimate prophet in a line extending from Abraham and Moses. But in his lifetime Mohammed also concluded treaties of protection with Jewish tribes in Southern Arabia in exchange for their payment of a poll tax. This set a comparatively tolerant precedent, which the armies of Islam wisely followed upon more or less reaching their geographic limits after their lightning expansion. Not coincidentally, this also marked the beginning of glorious centuries of Islamic civilization.

In principle, the world of the Moslems, as the followers of Mohammed were known, remained divided into the House of Islam *(dar el-Islam)* and the still-to-be-conquered and converted House of War *(dar el-Harb)*. Yet Jews residing in Mohammedan lands, although inferior to Moslems, could be viewed as occupying a third estate, the House of Truce *(dar al-Sulh)* or House of the Convent *(dar el-Ahd)*. Jews who continued to accept only the Hebrew Bible might at least be granted partial salvation based on their partial revelation. In this regard, Islamic theologians were generally prepared to concede more to the People of the Book than were the Christian theologians across the Mediterranean in a Europe sunk in the Dark Ages.

Although the Prophet had ultimately rejected certain Jewish customs, Islam tended more than did the Christian Church to carry over Jewish practices, including those tangentially related to health and medicine. Mohammedans retained the Old Testament concept of prohibited foods, particularly pork, and in fact Moslems were allowed by their religious authorities to partake of kosher meat when traveling outside the House of Islam. Moslems also inherited the Hebrew concern with hygiene ("Truly Allah . . . loveth those who have a care for cleanliness"). And like the Jews before them, the Islamized Arabs elevated the ancient Semitic practice of circumcision to a sacred rite.

Already prominent in trade and commerce for centuries, the Jews now found a particularly prosperous niche in a world where Moslems were often barred from Christian lands and Christians from Mohammedan waters. Exchanging the furs and timber of Christian Europe for the textiles of Spain and Egypt and the spices and medicinal herbs of the Orient, the Jews also served as diplomatic intermediaries between the House of Islam, the House of Truce, and the House of War. But Jews held in highest esteem the concept of journeys undertaken not for the purposes of trade and diplomacy but for the pursuit of learning. This sentiment, too, found resonance with the Moslems. Just as the commandment "Go and learn" figures prominently in the Talmud, so Mohammed is quoted as saying, "Those who go out in search of knowledge will be in the path of God until they return."

Travel by sea was particularly appealing to Jews, not least because the rabbis deemed sailing on the Sabbath not to be a violation of the biblical commandment. But, whatever the day of the week, there were the dangers of Mediterranean pirates and the consequent obligation of the local Jewish communities to ransom their coreligionists from the slave market. As a leader of the Cairo Jews wrote in request of financial help from other communities: "We turn to you today on behalf of a captive woman who has been brought from Byzantine. . . . Soon afterwards sailors brought two other prisoners, one of them a fine young man possessing knowledge of the Torah. . . . We had hardly settled this, when another ship arrived carrying many prisoners, among them a physician. . . . "

That Jewish physicians should be sailing back and forth in the Mediterranean relates to a key reason they were held in such high regard in the Medieval world. To the great credit of the fierce and rough-hewn Arabian conquerors—whose only cultural achievement in their harsh desert homeland had lain in their gifted tongues and oral traditions—they quickly became enamored of the arts and sciences of the peoples of the former Persian, Greek, Roman, and Byzantium Empires whom they subjugated. A major activity at the great centers of learning of the House of Islam, notably Baghdad and Cairo in the Middle East as well as Cordoba in conquered Spain, was the translation of the disparate philosophical and medical texts of ancient Greece and Rome into the new imperial language of Arabic, sometimes first through the other Semitic languages of Syriac (Aramaic) and Hebrew. The scholars of the Islamic world were greatly aided in this endeavor by the multilingual talents of non-Muslims, and not just the Jews. For Islam also gained enormously from the intolerance of the Christian powers even toward their fellow believers in Christ.

In 431 C.E. the Council of Ephesos had excommunicated the Patriarch of Constantinople, Nestorios, for his supposedly heretical belief that there were two distinct, rather than merged, persons in Christ—the divine and the human—and that Mary should not be called the Mother of God. Nestorios's followers had fled eastward, some as far as India and China, while a significant number of Nestorians found refuge under the tolerant Persian king at his capital Jundi Shapur, not far north of Ur, where the story of Abraham began. Jundi Shapur was home to a university and a hospital and as such was a beacon of light at a time when Europe was sliding into the Dark Ages. It was there that the Nestorians translated the ancient works, not least those of Hippocrates and Galen, into the form of Aramaic that was the language of the university.

When in the wake of the Moslem conquest things settled down in Persia, the Christian minority, too, was viewed as dwelling in *dar el-Ahd,* the House of the Convent, having accepted the partial revelation of the Old Testament, plus those of Jesus, whom the Koran recognized as a minor prophet. Now began the task of translating Hippocrates and Galen—including those of their works that are today forever lost in their original Greek or Latin—into Arabic, which in a matter of decades had risen from a peninsular tongue to become the universal language of an empire stretching over thousands of miles. Jundi Shapur, where Greek, Alexandrian, Persian, Hindu, and even Chinese thought converged, was home to Jewish scholars, whose roots and contacts extended East and West, indeed throughout all the known world.

But the conveying of the ideas of the ancients into the second millennium involved more than literal translation. The Jewish, Islamic, and Nestorian scholars provided extensive commentaries on the texts they were preserving and transmitting. The translation process, in and of itself, provided a basis for further philosophizing and extrapolations, especially since the Indo-European languages such as Greek and Latin have certain grammatical characteristics in common that the Arabic and Hebrew languages, being of the Semitic family, do not share.

The importance of particular languages is evident in the work of the great physician-philosopher Avicenna, whose life spanned six decades around the turn of the second millennium. Although he was to become one of the greatest of Moslem philosophers (as well as one of the greatest physicians of the Middle Ages), it has occasionally been speculated that Avicenna was at least partly of Jewish descent, through his maternal line. The Bokkhara region of Persia from which he hailed had been home to a substantial Jewish community since time immemorial, and late in the tenth century there were converted to Islam thousands of Jews, as well as Nestor Christians and Zoroastrians (the latter being adherents of the ancient Iranian religion, which contained elements of both monotheism and polytheism).

The very name Avicenna is a Latinization not of the Arabic form of his name, Ibn Sina, but of the Hebrew version, Aven Sina. This was a custom followed with several other important names in the medical and philosophical literature and does not necessarily argue for his Jewish origin. It does, however, highlight the importance of the Jews and their ancestral language in Avicenna's milieu. Indeed, as Avicenna recalled:

> Jacob the Jew, a man of penetrating mind, also taught me many things, and I shall repeat to you what he taught me: if you want to be a philosopher of nature, to whichever religion you belong, listen to the instructed man of whatever religion, because the law of the philosopher says: thou shalt not kill, thou shalt not steal, thou shalt not commit adultery, do unto others as you do to yourself, and don't utter blasphemies.

Likewise in the medical sphere, Avicenna drew upon the work of a Jewish scholar, the physician-philosopher Isaac Israeli (also known as Isaac Judaeus), whose life spanned over a hundred years from the mid-ninth to the mid-tenth centuries. Although active in court life, Isaac has come down to us from accounts by his Moslem contemporaries as being indifferent to wealth and personal advancement. Among his surviving works are *On Definitions,* an Aristotelian logical treatise that influenced later Medieval Christian scholasticism, and *On the Elements,* an exposition of Aristotelian physics. In the field of healing, Isaac was particularly active in spreading medical knowledge in North Africa. His contributions included his studies on fever and his authoritative work on pharmacology, which was given the Latin title *De Gradibus Simplicum* by the translator Constantine the African, himself probably of Jewish birth. An important concept of Isaac Israeli was the "duel between nature and disease." This reappears in the writings of Avicenna and, as we shall see, attains greater importance in Moses Maimonides' caution against unnecessary or excessive treatment. Among Isaac's aphorisms (translated from the Hebrew): "Most illnesses are cured without the physician's help through the aid of Nature." "If you can cure the patient by dietary means, do not turn to drugs." "Do not rely on cure-alls, for they mostly rest on ignorance and superstition." "Always make the patient feel he will be cured when you are not convinced of it, for it aids the healing effort of Nature."

With his way to the understanding of the classics partially paved by the likes of Isaac Israeli, Avicenna set out on his life's work in philosophy and medicine. In the former field he endeavored to reconcile the concepts of the Islamic teachings (influenced in large measure by the Hebrew Bible) with the logic of Aristotle and the neo-Platonists. Particularly vexing were the concepts of contingency and necessity and the related matters of freedom and futurity, temporality and timelessness. Avicenna argued that God is a necessarily existent being and that the world is an eternal process of emanation by a world-soul (or intelligence) acting on eternal matter. The thinking human soul was for Avicenna a substance independent of the body and hence capable of surviving alone.

Although almost all of Avicenna's great works were composed in Arabic, his native tongue was Persian, an Indo-European rather than Semitic language, and therefore related, however distantly, to Latin, Greek, and most of the other tongues of Europe, as well as to the Sanskrit of India. Among the contributions of Avicenna's philosophizing was a distinction between essence (what a thing is) and existence (that a thing is), a distinction not evident in Aristotle or Latin scholars. It has been speculated that the nature of the verb "to be" (*wujud*) in the Arabic language in which he wrote, stimulated Avicenna to think along these lines, since, unlike the Indo-European languages of Latin, Greek, and even Avicenna's native Persian, the Arabic verb "to be" signifies existence but not essence. (The concept of specific linguistic forms determining or influencing the thought processes of their respective speakers would be given its strongest formulation early in the twentieth century by the Jewish linguist Edward Sapir and his (gentile) pupil Benjamin Lee Whorf.)

In the Medieval as in the ancient world, philosophy and medicine were interrelated. But Avicenna found the latter field decidedly the easier of the two. When in his early teens he was having a hard time digesting Aristotle's *Physics* and *Metaphysics,* Avicenna turned for relaxation to Galen's medical texts, which, like the philosophy treatises, had been translated and commented upon by Moslem and Jewish scholars. Never one for false modesty, Avicenna would later write of this period in his life: "Medicine isn't one of the difficult sciences and so I excelled in it before long, so much so in fact that famous physicians came to study with me. I treated sick people, and indescribable possibilities were revealed to me which can only be acquired from experience. . . . I turned sixteen."

It would, however, take another two years for Avicenna to master phi-losophy, during which time he assimilated (so he tells us in his autobiog-raphy) all the books in the library of Sultan Nuh ibn-Mansur, to whose court he was summoned as personal physician. Finally, at the age of 21, he could declare himself to have pretty much absorbed everything that was known up to that moment in human history. (When the library at Bukhara went up in flames, Avicenna's enemies accused him of starting the blaze, while his friends consoled themselves with the thought that all the per-ished contents were preserved in his head.) Avicenna now set himself the task of synthesizing and expanding man's knowledge, first and foremost in the field of medicine.

Seeing that neither the Greeks nor the Arabs had produced a textbook to teach the art and science of medicine as an integrated whole, this be-came Avicenna's prime goal. The results were the five books comprising his *Canon of Medicine*. From head to toe, the physiology and pathology of the twenty-one organs and systems (by Avicenna's reckoning) were sur-veyed. Attention was, however, also paid to general conditions such as fever, not necessarily associated with a particular body part. Symptoms, diagnos-tics, and prognostics were discussed, as was the concept of crisis (the criti-cal moment in the course of the disease that is either the turning point if the disease breaks or the point of no return if it doesn't). In the ancient tradition, Avicenna viewed diseases as imbalances of the temperaments, bodily malformations, or dissolutions of the bodily order (for example, obstructions). The etiology could involve problems with diet, air, motion and rest, sleep or the passions of the soul. The *Canon* also discussed various external insults—wounds, bruises, sprains, dislocation, fractures—as well as poisons, whether deliberately administered or from bites and stings.

When it came to treatment, Avicenna recommended a range of regi-mens, as well as emetics, cathartics, enemas, and sedatives. Manual proce-dures included bleeding, blistering, and cauterizing. (The latter, which in-volved the application of searing heat, was the only surgical option in accord with the Islamic prohibition on the shedding of blood). The *Canon*'s phar-macopoeia contained some 760 drugs of animal, vegetable, and mineral origin, in both simple and compound prescriptions, with specifications for their use for any given disease. There were, for example, some eighty medicines for various heart ailments (palpitations, angina, fainting), including silk cocoon, saffron, ruby, pearl, Egyptian clover, wild ginger, silver, gold, musk, ambergris, egg yolk, and meat soup.

Avicenna also had his share to say on the mind-body issue as it relates to mental afflictions. At the court of Majd-al-Dawla he treated the prince for melancholia. The Greek term literally means "black bile," an excess of which was the theoretical cause of the depression, as supposedly evidenced by a dark stool. Yet in his *Situation of the Human Soul,* written at the prince's court, Avicenna emphasized the psychological, by advancing the philosophical-religious argument that the immortal soul has hegemony over the body rather than being dependent on it. Similarly, Avicenna opposed too much mind-body determinism with relation to the heart. The term *sanguine* (from *sanguis,* the Latin word for "blood") denoted that the hopeful temperament was due to a surfeit of the blood humor. But Avicenna observed that a sanguine person need not be physiologically strong-hearted, a view shared by his younger Jewish contemporary Ibn Gabriol.

Avicenna's *Canon* has been called the most influential textbook ever written, medical or otherwise. Translated into Latin in the second half of the twelfth century, it served as a virtual Bible for European and Eastern physicians up to the Renaissance. Between 1470 and 1500 the work went through fourteen editions in Latin. More important from the point of view of the present story, it saw numerous translations into Hebrew, the most influential of which were by Nathan Meati of Rome in the thirteenth century and Zerahiah ben Isaac in the fifteenth. Yet, as in philosophy, the importance of the medical contributions of Avicenna and the Arabs to the history of Western civilization lay not in any great originality. The *Canon* is basically a systematic synthesis of Galen (himself to a good extent a synthesizer of earlier Greek works). As such, it accepted as its foundation the concept of the four elements and four humors. And like Galen, Avicenna has been condemned for producing scriptures so authoritative as to impede fresh inquiry for centuries to come. Yet the state of the art in chemistry in the Medieval period was such that nothing was capable of replacing the ancient concepts as a basis for medical science. Indeed, not until the advent of molecular biochemistry late in the nineteenth century would such a foundation be available. To Avicenna must at least go the credit for upholding the rational basis of medicine at a time when Europe was still struggling to emerge from the Dark Ages. And although Avicenna didn't explicitly advocate experimentation, his *Canon* did encourage careful observation for the gathering of new facts.

At the time when Avicenna was making medical history in the Middle East, not far from the Arabic homeland that gave birth to Mohammed, the Islamic world had long since expanded some 3,000 miles to the West. Back in the eighth century, after their sweep through North Africa, the armies of the Prophet had barely paused for breath before the Straits of Gibraltar. Under the command of Tariq ibn Ziyad, and spearheaded by the native Berbers with a fierceness and fanaticism so common among new converts, the Arabs swiftly conquered most of Christian Iberia. Wherever they marched, they encountered another people of Semitic heritage, who had already been in Iberia for centuries and who had little reason to bemoan the fall of their Christian overlords.

Even before the destruction of the Temple in Jerusalem by Titus's legions in 70 C.E., Jewish merchant colonies had dotted the Iberian coast. After the exile, Jewish life in Hispania flourished under the *Pax Romana* as elsewhere in the Empire, but only until the conversion of Constantine to Christianity early in the fourth century and the ensuing anti-Jewish legislation. With the collapse of the empire came the sacking of Iberia by the barbarian Germanic tribes, one of which, the Vandals, lent their name to southernmost province of Andalusia and to the vocabulary of many languages as a synonym for wreakers of wanton destruction. Jewish life in Spain was to suffer not only from the dislocation of trade and commerce but from two centuries of anti-Jewish edicts following the conversion to Catholicism in 587 C.E. of the strongman of the Germanic invaders, the Visigoth Reccard I, who established himself as Iberian king. In the unruly conditions of the peninsula in the Dark Ages, the Visigoths promoted the concept of a unitary Spain and a monolithic religion. Jews were forbidden to hold public office or to employ Christian workers. In some cases Israelites were declared to be slaves and saw their children forcibly removed, to be raised as Catholics. Such pressure, although apparently applied intermittently rather than systematically, resulted in tens of thousands of at least nominal conversions and the beginning of a phenomenon that would be typically Spanish for centuries to come: the "crypto-Jew." It also gave rise to Jewish migration across the border to southern France, the first of several waves over the next 800 years.

The chaos and disunity of Visigoth Catholic Spain gave way to relative stability under the crescent of Islam at the beginning of the eighth century. The Arab invaders soon formed an upper class controlling the economy and the state bureaucracy. They brought with them an attitude towards the subject Jewish population which was not only more tolerant than that of Christendom, but also generally more lenient than elsewhere in the Islamic world. Whereas the Jews in North Africa and the Middle East might be prohibited from building new houses of worship or even repairing old ones, in Spain these *Ahl ed-dhimma* (protected people) constructed spectacular synagogues with the wealth their merchants amassed through international trade. The multilingual literacy of the Jews, in combination with their foreign contacts and financial talents, made them an especially valuable asset to the new rulers of Spain in domestic and international affairs.

But it was in the literary sphere that the Jewish-Islamic symbiosis of Medieval Spain found its highest expression, and it was largely the Jewish physicians doubling as poets and philosophers who brought this about. Never before in their history had even the People of the Book been so literate. The private collections of books in the homes of the Jewish merchants were exceeded only by the 400,000 volumes in the library of the caliph. The Spanish-Jewish physician Judah ben Saul ibn Tibbon, known as "the father of translators," waxed: "Make thy books thy companions, let thy cases and shelves be thy pleasure-grounds and gardens. Bask in their paradise, gather their fruit, pluck their roses, take their spices and their myrrh." He further commanded: "Examine thy Hebrew books at every new moon, the Arabic volumes once in two months, and the bound codices once every quarter." Citing the verse from the Book of Proverbs (3:27) to "Withhold not good from him to whom it is due," Ibn Tibbon further enjoined: "Never refuse to lend books to anyone who has not the means to purchase books for himself." Here he made no explicit distinction between Jew and gentile. Indeed, the contemporary *Sefer Hasidim,* the Book of the Pious, required Jewish merchants to "sell [books] to a non-Jew, if one knows that he lends his books, rather than to a Jew, even though it be one's brother, who does not. . . ."

Before books could be read or lent, they had to be written. The beauty of the spoken word was the only cultural achievement of the Arabians before they burst out of their desert homeland. In Spain the Arab élite continued to hold poetry in highest regard. So, too, did their Jewish subjects. The Spanish-Jewish poets, even when writing in the Hebrew language, gladly adopted the rhymes and meters of the Arabic literary tradition, a synthesis facilitated by the historical kinship of the two Semitic languages. The Hebrew poets also made use of the stunningly beautiful Arabic calligraphy into the development of which the Moslems, who inherited the Jewish commandment against the making of graven images of anything earthly, poured their artistic talents so as to adorn the words of the Prophet. Most notable of the Jewish poets was the physician-philosopher Judah ha-Levi, who as a philosopher-physician was also given to prose comments on quacks and the placebo effect. ("Every ill man fears death and hopes that he may be cured; and when told that the physician is coming he feels happy and he longs to wait for the utterances of his mouth. For this reason any fool and inexperienced man finds it possible to be a physician.") Of another of the many Jewish physician-poets, Abraham ben Meir ibn Kammial, court physician and vizier to King Ali of Seville, it was said, "His poems gave voice to the dumb and sight to the blind."

Arguably, no city in the whole history of Medieval Islamic Spain matched the cultural splendor of tenth-century Cordoba, seat of the Caliphate. "The majesty and adornment of the world, the wondrous capital . . . radiating in affluence of all earthly blessings," was how a contemporary visiting German nun described this "Bride of Andalusia." This was the age of Hasdai ibn Shaprut, physician, astronomer, and minister of finance to the Caliph Abn al-Rahman III, whom he also served as diplomat to the Christian potentates. Hasdai became known for his translation into Arabic (in collaboration with a Greek monk) of the work of Dioscorides, the first-century Greco-Roman military physician whose campaigns in exotic climes resulted in the granddaddy of all subsequent *Materiae Medicae,* describing some 600 medicinal plants, perhaps 100 of which are today considered to indeed be medically active. Hasdai also established in Cordoba a Jewish school of higher learning. Among his notable coreligionist fellow physicians was Ibn Janah, born in Cordoba a few years before the second millennium, who wrote a classic treatise on Hebrew grammar as well as a handbook of *Simple Remedies*.

The first century of the new millennium saw the waning of the Golden Age of Arabic culture and the dimming of Cordoba's brilliance. Still, the Bride of Andalusia radiated a twilight glow. Hundreds of colorful villas still lined the ten-mile stretch of the Guadalquivir. The markets bustled with dyed silk and linen; gold- and silversmith stalls crowded the alleyways; and the scent of spices and medicinal herbs from India and China mingled with the sound of lutes. Along the river still stood, as indeed it does to this day, the colonnaded great mosque, adorned with ornamentation of porphyry, jasper, marble, and glass mosaics. These bore testimony to the cultural splendor that had surrounded the ancestors, a long line of *dayans* (official rabbis or "judges"), of Maimon, a talmudist disciple of the Jewish scholar Joseph ibn Migash. A writer of stirringly beautiful religious allegories, Maimon believed in the existence of angels and prophetic dreams. But being also a scholar of the Medieval Islamic enlightenment, he was an accomplished astronomer and mathematician. On Passover Eve of 1135, a son was born to Maimon, whom he named Moses and who was destined almost by design to have an enormous impact on Jewish theology—and by accident also to be one of the greatest doctors in the history of medicine.

Not all Moslem sects were tolerant, even in the Golden Age of Islamic culture. Just as Moses reached Bar Mitzvah age, the tranquil life of the family of Maimon was shattered by the fall of Cordoba to the fanatical sect known as the Almohades, who had invaded Spain from North Africa. Their leader, Abdalluh ibn Tumart, and his successors toppled the lenient Almoravid dynasty and ruled Spain for the next half century. The intolerance of the Almohades toward lax and worldly Moslems was exceeded only by their fanatical antipathy toward Jews and Christians. "No church and no synagogue," was their battle cry. At first, the infidels were prohibited from emigrating for fear of, among other things, the potential benefit of the Jews to the rival kings. Their choice was thus between martyrdom and Islam. Some Jews accepted the former alternative, but many thousands merely became crypto-Jews, riding out the storm by outwardly adopting the trappings of Islam. As the Spanish rabbi Avraham ibn Ezra lamented: "Great evil has descended on Spain from heaven. . . . Our hands are weakened and our eyes are filled with tears. . . . How abandoned is Cordoba, like a stormy sea. . . . The Jews have been injured and dealt a terrible blow. I will cry out, I will speak bitterly, I will sigh and groan. I will wail in deepest sadness."

Young Moses, as part of the family of Maimon, began a decade of wandering through Spain, first seeking refuge in the Christian-held port of Almera, 130 miles to the southwest of Cordoba, and then moving through other towns on the peninsula. When, after the death of Ibn Tumart, a third alternative, emigration, was opened up, the family of Maimon eventually opted for it, crossing the Straits of Gibraltar and settling in Fez, Morocco, in 1160.

According to tradition, Jews had lived in Morocco since biblical times, when they came to buy gold and fight the Plishtim. Later, before the Moslem conquest, whole tribes of Berbers were said to have abandoned idol worship for Judaism. In the ninth and tenth centuries, the Jewish communities in Morocco had experienced their equivalent of the Golden Age of their Spanish brethren. But now Fez was the very capital of the fanatical Almohades and as such a seemingly strange choice as a place of refuge for the family of Maimon. True, there had been some recent relaxation on the part of the ruler Abd Almumin. But more important, the Moroccans might have been expected to assume as a matter of course that any newcomers just had to be Moslems. If so, the family of Maimon could hope to avoid having to make much of an outward show of Islamic faith, while they very discreetly continued to practice Judaism.

Through all the disruptions and dislocations, the erudite Maimon saw to it that his son, whose exceptional brilliance was readily apparent, received alongside his religious upbringing a liberal arts education encompassing mathematics, philosophy, natural science, logic, metaphysics, and medicine. By the time he reached his mid-twenties, Moses was already an esteemed rabbinical scholar whose advice was prized by his imperiled coreligionists. In his "Letter of Consolation," Maimonides (i.e., the son of Maimon) urged his fellow Jews not to yield under political and social pressure to the temptation of seeing Islam as God's intended substitute for Judaism. "We must no more doubt God's promise than we doubt His existence," he wrote.

"God does not desire a thing and then despise it; He does not favor it and then reject it." Rather, Maimonides reasoned, the tribulations of the Jews were God's stern but loving chastisement for their wayward tendencies. But Maimonides, who himself may have had to make certain compromises, was understanding of the dilemma facing his coreligionists. A fellow rabbi, citing the talmudic verse in *Yirmiyahu* (2:13) that "My people have committed two evils against me: they have bowed to an image and bowed to a [Jewish] temple," likened the entering of a mosque to idol worship and condemned the subsequent praying at a synagogue as a double sin. But Maimonides urged his fellow rabbi not to judge the pseudo-converts to Islam so harshly, as long as they avoided actively transgressing God's commandments. "We are not asked to render service to heathenism," wrote Maimonides, "but only to recite an empty formula which the Moslems themselves know we utter insincerely in order to circumvent a bigot. . . . If a man asks me: Shall I be slain or utter the formula of Islam? I answer, Utter the formula and live."

It was during his sojourn in Fez that Maimonides began to do for Jewish theology what Avicenna had done for the Islamic, namely, the application of Aristotelian logic. The Rambam, as he also became known (an acronym formed from the Hebrew letters for Rabbi Moses ben Maimon), undertook his first major work, the *Commentary on the Mishnah*. This book had an impact on Jewish communal life that was immediate and enduring. Characteristic of the *Mishnah*, the first of the two books of the Talmud, is its lack of an orderly system. Yet Maimonides saw this as only a superficial defect and was determined to bring about a codification of the rabbinical scriptures by applying his vast knowledge and intense logical powers. ("Logic is to intellect as grammar is to language," he declared.) Essential in this regard was the distinguishing between that which was to be taken literally in the Talmud and that which had esoteric meaning. The sages deliberately hid some things, Maimonides maintained, choosing "not to reveal them openly, so that the mind of the student might be sharpened, and so that these matters might remain a secret from those whose intellect was inadequate to receive truth in its purity." The Rambam drew up general principles from which the laws flow and he demonstrated how the exceptions to the rule were to be accommodated.

One principle advanced by Maimonides in his *Commentary*, to be reinforced by other great Jewish thinkers in later centuries, was the doing of good for its own sake, rather than out of hope of reward or fear of punishment. "The reward of a mitzvah [good deed] is a mitzvah," wrote the Rambam, "and the punishment for a sin is a sin." But like Spinoza centuries later, Maimonides recognized that only a few could intellectually reach such a level of comprehension. Thus he understood the need for preaching reward and punishment to the masses, and agreed with the sages who had written: "A person should always be involved with the Torah even not for the proper intent, for out of this, he will come to the proper intent."

For all the weight of his pronouncements, Maimonides was known for a certain modesty and he took to heart the injunction "Teach thy tongue to say, I do not know." His own writings often enough included the phrase, "I do not see how to explain this matter," and in his *Commentary* he welcomed constructive criticism. The Rambam also begged the reader's pardon for his errors, stating that "While my mind was ever troubled amid the God-decreed expatriations from one end of heaven to the other, I wrote notes on many a halachah [religious-legal point] on journeys by land, or while tossed on the stormy waves at sea."

The storm-swept sea in question was the Mediterranean, which almost claimed the lives of the family of Maimon when they sailed to Palestine in 1165, after five years in Morocco. The departure took place in the dead of night, after a crackdown on pseudo-Moslems who were secret Judiazers led to the execution of the rabbinical scholar Judah ibn Sosan, who was probably Maimonides' teacher. (The Rambam himself was granted only a fragile reprieve from arrest and possible execution due to the intervention of a friend, the Moslem poet-theologian with the improbable name Abul-Arab ibn Moisha.)

In Palestine Maimonides made a pilgrimage to the Wailing Wall in Jerusalem and the graves of the Patriarchs in Hebron, visits he would commemorate every year for the rest of his life. But Palestine was under the control of the Crusaders, and the whole territory contained only 1,000 or so relatively poor and nonintellectual Jewish families. Nearby Egypt, by contrast, was home to some 30,000 Jews, who generally prospered as artisans, merchants, and shipowners. Furthermore, the Moslem rulers of this part of North Africa and the Near East, the Empire of the Ayyuubids, were unaffected by the fanaticism of the Almohades to the west and allowed the Jews a degree of communal autonomy unmatched in any other country.

Maimonides first sojourned in the port city of Alexandria and then moved to the Cairo suburb of Fostat, an administrative and business center that boasted fourteen-story skyscrapers and was home to thousands of government officials. Fostat had recently been put to the torch as a defensive maneuver against the invading Christian Crusaders and was now being rebuilt. Maimonides would live in this Cairo suburb until his death some forty years later. It was there than he completed in 1180 his fourteen-volume *Mishneh Torah,* a complete codification and digest of biblical and rabbinical law. He then went on in the next decade to compose the work for which he became best known, the *Guide for the Perplexed.*

Who were the "perplexed" in need of the Rambam's guidance? They were not so much those Jews who may have been vaguely skeptical of their faith but rather those who, living as they were in an enlightened society whose intellectuals held ancient Greek philosophy in high esteem, found themselves bewildered by the seeming contradictions in logic that characterized so many passages in the Bible. These Jews envied the apparent success of the Moslem theologians, particularly Avicenna, in reconciling Mohammed with Aristotle. Already a great expert in applying logic to the Scriptures and Talmud, the Rambam now sought a definitive reconciliation (or rather, a unification) of Greek reason with Jewish faith. There need be no apology in this quest, he maintained, for there was intrinsically nothing foreign for Jews in the ancient Greek philosophy. Indeed, Maimonides was pleased to play on the concept that Hellas had borrowed much of its metaphysics from Israel.

"Those passages in the Bible which, in their literal sense, contain statements that can be refuted by proof must and can be interpreted otherwise," the Rambam explained. By this, he did not mean that there is anything in the Book that is false. On the contrary, everything in it is true on one level or another. But because God's Word is addressed to everyone, it must, according to Maimonides (whom no one ever accused of loosening himself from millennia of Jewish sexism), speak the language of "the young, of women, and of the common people," as well as the language of those fortunate few men grounded in philosophy. "Employ your reason," the Rambam implored, "and you will be able to discern what is said allegorically, figuratively, and hyperbolically, and what is meant literally."

A central problem in scriptural interpretation derives from God's anthropomorphic features. The Hebrew Bible depicts Jehovah in human form, with organs of sense and speech that He freely uses. This was taken by Islamic authors as proof of the superiority of the Koran, since that book, by contrast, attributes no corporal features to Allah and has all spoken words coming from Gabriel. But the Rambam, through intriguing argumentation, explained that the functions of acting, seeing, hearing, and speaking are intellectual perfections in man. In the Bible, man invested God with these functions as a way of asserting His perfection, although He in fact presides over the highest sphere of *immaterial* things. The Rambam went on to argue that no positive definitions of God are possible but only negative definitions of what He is not. True, there are theoretically an infinite number of such nonattributes; yet, by a process of exclusion, the more of these one can rationally assign to God, the closer one comes to knowledge of Him.

Only two years after his arrival in Cairo, an event took place in Moses Maimonides' life, that, as tragic as it was for him personally, was to have an immensely positive impact on the history of medicine. The Rambam held a strongly principled belief that Jewish spiritual leaders should earn their livelihood not from their religious activities but from worldly sources. So for the first decade or so of his adult life he worked as the stay-at-home partner in the precious stone trade while his brother David regularly traveled down the Nile, crossed the desert by caravan to the Red Sea, and then set sail for the East. One day in 1167 word reached Cairo that David's ship had sunk in the Indian Ocean. Not only was this event emotionally devastating for Maimonides (even years later he would write to a friend, "This is the heaviest evil that has befallen me. . . . I should have died in my affliction but for the Law, which is my delight"), it was also a double financial blow. The family's capital of precious stones was lost at sea and Maimonides now had to assume responsibility for his widowed sister-in-law and his niece. The Rambam took up, alongside his religious and communal activities, the full-time duties of medical practitioner and writer. Soon he would earn an undisputed reputation as the greatest physician of his age.

If the healing profession was new to Maimonides, the subject of medicine surely was not, though precious few details about his medical education have been preserved. The Medieval Spanish scholar Judah ben Samuel ibn Abbas wrote of the great importance given to the natural sciences by the Jews of Spain—an importance second only to the study of the Bible, the Talmud, and the ethical teachings. Medicine topped the scientific hierarchy, followed by mathematics, logic, astronomy, physics, and metaphysics. There was a long tradition of Spanish-Jewish spiritual leaders being prominent physicians. The Rambam's contemporary, the Islamic scholar Ibn Rusud (better known by his Latinized name, Averroes), was, like Maimonides, a native of Cordoba, and also like Maimonides a physician and philosopher. (He advocated the use of Aristotilean logic for interpreting passages in the Koran allegorically rather than literally.) It has sometimes been suggested that he was Maimonides' teacher, but in view of the fact that the family of Maimon was uprooted from Cordoba when Moses was only 13 and Averroes only 22, it seems more likely that the former became acquainted with the latter only in later life and then quite possibly only through books. Maimonides does, however, make reference in his medical writings to personal contact with Abu Bakr, court physician and vizier to the caliph of Seville, and son of the famed court physician Avenzoar (ibn Zuhr), whose treatise Al-Teisir was later translated into Hebrew and subsequently into Latin, and who was renowned for his clinical observations and for introducing such techniques as stomach intubation. The Rambam also made passing reference in his writings to medical observations he made during his stay in Morocco.

The more practical medical skills of Spain and the Magreb, which Maimonides brought with him to the Eastern Caliphate, along with perhaps some influences from Christian Europe, could serve as a bit of a brake on the beautiful but dubious dialectical speculations of the worshipers of Avicenna. According to an account written some thirty years after the Rambam's death by the Arab historian Alkopto, when Maimonides sojourned in Alexandria—before his move to Fostat and the death of his brother David—his reputation in medical matters was already so great that the physicians there invited him to address their medical study group on a regular basis.

In many parts of the Islamic world at the zenith of its intellectual and scientific glory around the turn of the second millenium, the number of physicians as a proportion of the population exceeded that of the West at the turn of the third millenium. True, some of these practitioners were to be found, rather undignified, hawking their services in the oriental bazaar like any craftsman or merchant. But other doctors occupied the top rungs of the social ladder. By the twelfth century, however, the Islamic World was experiencing a sharp increase in tension between medical science and religion. The mystical Sufi movement emphasized the role of Allah alone in determining illness and health. Prominent Sufi thinkers such as al-Ghazali furthermore denied the scientific principles of causality, thus undermining the basis of the Hippocratic and Galenic worldview. On the other hand, the influential Hanabali theologian Ibn al-Jawzi countered the Sufis by viewing medicine as a charitable and praiseworthy pursuit sanctioned by Mohammed himself.

A somewhat parallel schism over medicine was taking place in the Jewish community due to the Karaites, a branch of Judaism that had emerged in the eighth century and opposed the talmudic commentaries of the rabbis in favor of reliance on the Torah alone. The most important founder of Karaitism, Anon ben David, citing the Old Testament passage "I am Hashem Who heals you," had forbidden any intervention by a physician as a usurping of the healing power of the Almighty. In Maimonides' time the Karaite movement was centered in Cairo and counted many of the wealthiest Jews among its adherents. It was looked on with more favor by the Shiite rulers of Egypt, who similarly opposed the Sunna, the explanations and commentaries on the Koran made by their great rival sect, the Sunnis. The rabbi-doctor Maimonides took up his pen against the Karaites and in favor of the talmudists, arguing among other things that the Karaites, too, indulged in scriptural interpretation (how, indeed, could they do otherwise?). Drawing a parallel between a man seeking medical treatment and a man who "is hungry and partakes of food for the purpose of curing himself of hunger," the Rambam argued that the former was showing no more a loss of faith than the latter. And just as one says prayers of thanks before a meal, so might one thank God for the drugs He has provided as cure for disease. Maimonides' brilliant polemics, aided by the ascent to the throne of Saladin, a Sunni, and therefore less scripture-bound Moslem, served to turn the tide of Karaitism. Even when, years later, Judaism experienced a reaction against Greek science, the rabbis would explicitly exclude medicine from their ban. In fact, throughout the High Middle Ages and far beyond, the leaders of the Jewish community in Egypt and the neighboring lands would almost all be physicians. (The Karaite movement, incidentally, has never died out completely. Today there are a few thousand Karaites in Lithuania and the Crimea—during the Second World War they had the good fortune of not being considered Jews by the Nazis—and perhaps 2,000 in Israel.)

The Jewish tradition of viewing the body as a useful servant, to be well-maintained for higher ends, is clearly reflected in the Rambam's writings.

"The purpose of keeping his body healthy is that his soul will have a healthy, complete vessel with which to acquire wisdom and good character trait," Maimonides declared in his *Commentary*. "It is impossible to understand and gaze at the teachings of wisdom when one is hungry or ill or if any of one's limbs ache." In his *Mishneh Torah* the Rambam wrote: "Since when the body is healthy and sound [one tends] in the ways of the Lord, it being impossible to understand or know anything of the knowledge of the Creator when one is sick, it is obligatory upon man to avoid things which are detrimental to the body and acclimate himself to things which heal and fortify it."

Although Maimonides never lost sight of the great moral virtue of curbing one's base desires, he was not averse to introducing Hippocratic and Galenic concepts to show that some of the biblical commandments and injunctions had a medical basis aside from their religious, ethical, and so-cial-cohesive origins. So, in the *Guide for the Perplexed,* when discussing the prohibition against the eating of pork, the Rambam went beyond the arguments about the pig's inherent uncleanliness and expounded on how swine meat contained an excess of moisture and how fat not only interrupted digestion but produced cold and thick blood. (It is at least true, we now know, that high fat diets tend to produce fat in the blood, with greater risk of arteriosclerosis.)

What of the practice of circumcision, which on the face of it seems barbaric? This custom, too, was a medical blessing, according to Maimonides, for it restricted the loss of vital energy that might otherwise occur through excessive sexual activity. In the *Mishneh Torah* he had written: "Semen is the strength of the body and its life, and is the light of the eyes. Whenever too much is ejaculated, the body decays, its strength is spent, and its life destroyed. As Solomon said in his wisdom: 'Do not give your strength to women, and your years to that which destroys kings.'" A man should therefore not have sexual intercourse merely when he felt like it, but when his body required it as shown by physical signs: "a heaviness in his loins and below, as if the cords of the testicles were drawn out, and his flesh is hot." "Such a man," Maimonides allowed, "needs to have sexual intercourse and his medicine is to have sexual intercourse." With a view toward limiting the expenditure of seed to what was required to maintain bodily equilibrium and procreate, the purpose of circumcision, Maimonides maintained in the *Guide for the Perplexed,* was to "weaken the organ of generation as far as possible and thus cause men to be moderate." Maimonides further explained that the removal of the foreskin "simply counteracts excessive lust, for there is no doubt that circumcision weakens the power of sexual excitement, and sometimes lessens the natural enjoyment; the organ necessarily becomes weak when it loses blood and is deprived of its covering from the beginning."

Maimonides was not alone in seeking scientific justification for Jewish customs. Even the mystical Spanish-born rabbi Nachmonides would claim, a century later, that swine milk induced leprosy and that unclean birds led to melancholy. Such medical rationalizations would not, however, go unchallenged by other Jewish authorities, such as the fifteenth-century Spanish rabbi-philosopher Isaac Arama, who wrote: "The dietary laws are not, as some have thought, motivated by therapeutic considerations. God forbid! If that were so the Torah would be lowered to the status of a second-hand medical tract or even worse!"

The previous passages of Maimonides reflect to some extent the Hippocratic-Galenic conception of the four humors and their four body organs, to which he strongly subscribed. In the case of what we would today call endocrinal disorders, the global principle of the humors is right on the mark. It, of course, almost inevitably erred in its specific details as to description of the secretions, their functions, and the organs that produce them. Maimonides was apparently describing diabetes when he wrote in his *Medical Aphorisms of Moses:* "Individuals in whom sweet white (humor) occurs are very somnolent. To those who have an excess of sour white (humor), hunger occurs, then they will become extremely thirsty. When this white liquid will be neutralized, then the thirst will disappear." While the specifics are open to interpretation (is the somnolence to be taken as a symptom of hypoglycemia?), we see here the quite valid principle of interacting or antagonistic humors, something on which the Rambam commented in other contexts as well. In fact, the pancreas secretes two hormones, insulin and glucagon, and disorders in their production are the cause of diabetes mellitus. Antagonistic "humors" are also found in the secretions involved in the sympathetic and parasympathetic nervous systems, and their opposing effects on heart rate and other body functions. As we shall see, Jewish endocrinologists would be instrumental in elucidating the workings of insulin and neurotransmitters, but not before the dawn of modern physiology and biochemistry, some seven centuries after Maimonides.

The whole concept of the four bodily humors and their ideal equilibrium naturally led to the question of the etiology of their imbalance in illness. Maimonides devoted much of his writings to what we today call preventative medicine. "Be cognizant of [the fact] that medicine is a very essential wisdom for man at any time and at any place," he wrote, "not only during illness but even so in full health." Improper food intake causes bodily disharmony, and the concepts of a "balanced diet" and preventative medicine were laudable features of the Rambam's writings, even if some of his specific recommendations seem odd in the light of present-day knowledge. (For example: "A man should always restrain himself from eating the fruit of trees. He should not eat much of them even when they are dried and, needless to say, when they are fresh.")

Even when diet is theoretically perfectly balanced, human flesh is still heir to all manner of insult. Sometimes the offending factor is obvious, as when venom is introduced into the body due to an unfortunate encounter with an animal or to malicious activities by humans. At the request of the Grand Vizier al-Fadil, Maimonides wrote a treatise *Poisons and Antidotes,* which understandably enjoyed much popularity in the Medieval world of court intrigues. The Rambam followed Galen in dividing poisons into theoretically hot (a quality shared by the yellow bile and blood humors) and cold (a quality shared by the black bile and phlegm humors). The former—as, for example, viper venom—was said to produce fever and psychic excitement. By contrast, cold poisons such as scorpion venom resulted in cooling and depression. This division foreshadowed the modern classification of poisons according to their hemolytic action (rupturing of red blood cells) or neurocytolytic action (attacking of nerve cells). For Maimonides, rabies, too, was transmitted by a venom. His description of the disease was excellent: "Symptoms do not generally appear until after eight days have passed, sometimes much later. . . . All cases are to be treated for forty days during which the wound is to be kept open." But until the invention of the microscope (and even, as we shall see, for centuries thereafter), there would never be more than an inkling that the "venom" involved in the transmission of a disease such as rabies was in fact a microorganism.

Ignorance of living, reproducing microbes was a great hindrance to the understanding of illnesses caused and transmitted in more subtle or complex ways than by snake bites or poisoned wine. Medieval Islamic doctors placed much emphasis on the ancient Greek concept of miasmata: kinds of noxious disturbances in the atmosphere caused by climatic conditions, by the positions of the stars and planets, or by unsanitary human activities. From his readings, Maimonides was undoubtedly aware that Galen had specifically mentioned Egypt as a country with intemperate climate and thus not conducive to a good bodily constitution. Earlier, Hippocrates had written about Egypt in his *Air, Waters and Places,* on which Galen commented. (The original passages have been lost to us but may have been known to Maimonides.) Compounding the climatic situation were some unhealthy habits in Fostat. As Maimonides' predecessor, the influential eleventh-century Islamic physician Ibn Ridwan wrote:

> One of the practices of the people of Fostat is to throw into the streets and alleys everything that dies in their houses: cats, dogs and other domestic animals of that kind. They rot there, and this putrescence spreads through the air. Another of their habits is to throw into the Nile, whose water they drink, the remains of the corpses of their animals. The latrines empty into the Nile and sometimes obstruct the flow of the water. They thus drink this putrid matter mixed with their water.

To this description the Rambam added: "City air is stagnant, turbid and thick, the natural result of its big buildings, narrow streets, and refuse of its inhabitants. . . . The concern for clean air is the foremost rule in preserving the health of one's body and soul." Indeed, Maimonides lost his baby daughter to what seemed to be a miasmic illness emanating from the Nile; his son Avraham likewise became deathly ill but survived.

If, whatever the etiology, illness is an imbalance of the humors, then restoration of health comes from reestablishing a proper equilibrium. Maimonides' fame as a physician rested in large measure on his knowledge and transmission of Greco-Roman science. Yet the Rambam's enduring contribution to medicine lay also in his moderation of some ancient excesses. One traditional manner of restoring the proper equilibrium was by withdrawing from the body a supposedly superabundant humor. We have seen how the Greeks, and not the least Galen, saw an excess of the blood humor in particular as the cause of many ills—a misconception that was stimulated by observations of wound inflammation. We have also seen how the Talmud often referred to prophylactic and therapeutic venesection, and not just in the case of a plethora of blood at a local site. Although Maimonides did not reject bloodletting, he urged great restraint in its practice: "A man should not accustom himself to have blood let continually; he should not have blood let unless there is an extraordinary need. . . . After age 50, he should not have blood let at all." (Lest there be any doubt for the need for such a warning, consider the case some six centuries later of the 67-year-old George Washington suffering from what was probably the flu. His physicians, trained at the prestigious medical faculty of Edinburgh, bled him of some four and a half pints and thus, at the very least, contributed to his demise. This happened only weeks before the dawn of the nineteenth century, which would finally see the end of bloodletting.) Yet if the Rambam was cautious about extracting blood, he very much shared the concerns of his talmudic predecessors about the necessity of evacuating the contents of the intestines and bladder. "A man should try to keep his bowels loose and a bit close to diarrhea," he wrote. "Whenever he needs to urinate or defecate, he should do so at once; he should not delay for even a single moment." "Anyone . . . whose intestines are constipated . . . —all his days will be painful ones and his strength will wane." (As we shall see, this would become a veritable obsession to another great Jewish medical man, Eli Metchnikoff, some seven centuries later.)

Aside from the passive removal of supposedly superabundant humors or other matter, the Medieval physicians had recourse to the Galenic principle of *contraria contrariis,* that is, fighting off an illness by administering drugs of opposite qualities to the presumed pathogenic agent (excess humor or poison). Thus, a hot poison such as viper venom was to be countered by mild, quieting remedies. A cold poison such as scorpion venom called for stimulants. Galen was so fond of using multiple drugs, often as many as fifty in one prescription, that in the early twentieth century such polypharmaceutical cocktails would still be known as "Galenics." Furthermore, his doses were often "heroic" in their strength. Galen's whole concept of a massive, combined frontal assault on disease was perhaps influenced by the zeitgeist of the Roman Empire at the height of its military power.

Living in a different age and coming from a different culture than that of the mighty Roman legions, Maimonides took a more placid approach to drugs. Although accepting the *contraria contrariis* approach in principle, he also sounded a note of caution, especially in the case of diseases that are (to use a modern term) self-limiting. "Sometimes a man will find a change in his digestion or he will experience some heaviness in his head, or some pain in one part of his body," wrote the Rambam. In such cases he advised his students: "Be very careful and do refrain from treating these symptoms and from hurrying to use medicines.""A physician should begin with simple treatment, trying to cure by diet before he administers drugs." There was the seed of such a restrained approach two centuries earlier in the writings of Isaac Judaeus and, in turn, Avicenna, but this achieved its strongest expression when Maimonides wrote: "The physician has to find out which are the diseases requiring prompt assault and control, and discern diseases in which no action at all is indicated and in which he shall first rely on the working of nature." The polyglot Maimonides went on to compile his *Glossary of Drug Names*, denoting over 400 vegetable, animal, and mineral substances (many of which are still to be found in Middle Eastern bazaars and some of which have entered the modern medical pharmacopoeia) not only by their Arabic names, but also by their names in Greek, Syriac, Persian, Berber, and Spanish. Thus the Rambam helped to bring order to what was threatening to become a terminological chaos in medicine.

As for recourse to surgery, this took very much a back seat to medicine among the ancient Islamic doctors. Yet Maimonides allowed that "At times surgical and at times medicinal treatment will be more praiseworthy," and he offered some tips on the surgical art that are as valid today as they were eight centuries ago. Regarding cancer, for example: "Cut out the whole of the growth till you reach a healthy place." Credit is also due Maimonides for explaining the techniques and use of ligature of the blood vessels to prevent hemorrhaging—a procedure that has more than once been lost and revived in the course of the centuries.

As a great spiritual leader, Maimonides understandably devoted much of his writings to mental health or what we today call the specialization of psychiatry. Notwithstanding his deep religious beliefs, the Rambam, like a modern psychiatrist, sought the etiology of mental disturbances in a mix of hereditary and physical, as well as cultural and psychological, factors. The treatment correspondingly involved the reestablishment of equilibrium according to the Galenic concept of *contraria contrariis*, but again without Galen's rush to treat with drugs. The Rambam's recognition of a certain mind-body isomorphism is evident in his prescribing of a "psychological" treatment for a presumed disequilibrium of bodily humors (what we would today call a psycho-endocrinal disorder): "If the humor of *black bile* agitates him, he should make it cease by listening to songs and various kinds of melodies, by walking in gardens and fine buildings, by sitting before beautiful forms, and by things like this which delight the soul and make the disturbance of the black bile disappear from it." (Indeed, modern research has pointed to the effects of psychological stress in generating hormonal changes that can depress the immune system—another demonstration that the psychosomatic humoral concept was on the mark, even if black bile itself has proven to be fictitious.)

The demarcation line between medical-psychiatric and ethical-behavioral matters has never been clear. In his chapter "On Medical Treatment for the Diseases of the Soul" in the *Mishneh Torah*, Maimonides quite openly advocated the application of Aristotle's principle of the Golden Mean to problems of character, a principle that was analogous to the Greco-Roman physiological concept of humoral balance. As we have seen in a previous chapter, the Golden Mean demanded that one be liberal rather than either miserly or extravagant, courageous rather than either rash or cowardly, witty rather than either buffoon-like or dull, moderate rather than either lustful or insensible, generous rather than either prodigal or stingy, humble rather than either haughty or self-abasing, content rather than either greedy or lazy, gentle rather than either irascible or servile, modest rather than either impudent or shy, and so on. In line with the *contraria contrariis* principle, Maimonides prescribed: "Should [a person's] soul become sick, he must follow the same course of treating it as in the medical treatment for bodies. For when the body gets out of equilibrium, we look to which side it inclines in becoming unbalanced, and then oppose it with its contrary until it returns to equilibrium." Thus, if a person was miserly, the course of treatment would start by having him repeatedly act not in a liberal but in an extravagant manner. Only when he came close to acquiring an extravagant disposition would the treatment switch to having him perform merely liberal acts.

Yet the version of the Golden Mean principle propounded by Maimonides contained a certain bias toward one of the two given poles. He deemed it easier for a man to turn from extravagance to liberality than from miserliness to liberality; from insensibility to moderation than from lust to moderation; from rashness to courage than from cowardice to courage; from self-abasement to humility than from haughtiness to humility; and so on. Conversely, it was easier for a man to slip into miserliness than into extravagance, and so forth. So, as a kind of prophylactic measure, Maimonides advocated deviating slightly from the mean, in favor of extravagance, insensibility, rashness, and so on. "This is the rule for the medical treatment of moral habits, so memorize it," he commanded his disciples.

So great was Maimonides' fame as a physician that the two opposing leaders in the Wars of the Crusades—the Moslem Saladin and the Christian Richard the Lion-Hearted—bid for his services as court physician. The Rambam's loyalty lay with Saladin, who was far more tolerant of the Jews than was his Crusader adversary. At the 4,000-room Eastern Palace in the fortified city of Cairo, the caliph maintained a retinue of over 20,000, not a few of whom were doctors. Yet, although a Jew, Maimonides rose to the position of chief physician. As such, while unpaid for his services, he was able to influence policy in favor of his coreligionists, particularly in regard to the plight of the Yemeni Jews, who had been hard-pressed by decrees of the Shiite rulers. Yet on at least one occasion, court intrigues and the jealousy of the Moslem physicians almost cost the Rambam his life, as he was accused of having converted to Islam in Morocco and then lapsing back into Judaism (a capital offense under Koranic law). Fortunately, the vizier took a lenient view of the matter.

The hectic pace of Maimonides' practice foreshadowed by several centuries the busy medical schedule of modern physicians. After attending every morning to the sultan and his family in their palace in Cairo and to any royal officers who fell ill, Maimonides would return to his practice in Fostat in the afternoon. As he wrote to Samuel, the son of Judah ibn Tibbon: "I find the antechamber filled with people, both Jews and gentiles, nobles and common people, judges and bailiffs, friends and foes—a mixed multitude who await the time of my return. . . . I partake of some slight refreshment, the only meal I take in twenty-four hours. Then I go forth to my patients, write prescriptions and directions for their several ailments. Patients go in and out until nightfall, and sometimes even, I assure you, until two hours and more during the night. I converse with and prescribe for them while lying down from sheer fatigue."

This doctoring schedule had obvious consequences for the Rambam's philosophical and rabbinical activities, since, as he explained, "no Israelite can have any private interview with me, except on the Sabbath." That day was consequently hardly less busy than the rest of the week, with morning services, instructions to the congregation about their proceedings for the rest of the week, afternoon services and then readings and studying with some members, and finally evening prayers. Nevertheless, the Rambam continued his impressive writing on both religious and medical matters, authoring along with the three already mentioned medical works another seven (perhaps even more, which have not survived).

The original works of Galen and Hippocrates lost something in the process of translation in the sixth through tenth centuries, as the Syrian Christian monks and the Nestorians in Baghdad rendered the Greek texts in Syriac and subsequently in Arabic. But if something was lost, then much was gained, though not always in a favorable sense. Galen himself was notoriously prone to interspersing his clinical and theoretical concepts with verbose polemical arguments. Successive compilers, among whom was Avicenna, added their own commentaries and observations, thus rendering Galen's works in Arabic all the more heavy, unwieldy, and unsystematized. This was the situation that Maimonides, the physician, sought to remedy.

The Rambam brought to this task the same abilities that made him renowned for his great systematization and codification of Jewish law: a comprehensive knowledge, a philosophical spirit, and the fact that he "never forgot anything." From Maimonides' pen came three general medical books. His *Extracts from Galen* distilled the most important pronouncements from the more than 100 books by the great doctor. Next, Maimonides' *Commentary on the Aphorisms of Hippocrates* elucidated a previous Arabic translation, which was in turn based on Galen's commentaries on Hippocrates, rather than on Hippocrates himself. Most important of all was the aforementioned *Medical Aphorisms of Moses.* Although the aphorisms in question were 1,500 in number, this book was short enough—about 250 pages—to be carried around by the physician. Only a few of the aphorisms were original with Moses (i.e., Maimonides). The rest, as he explained in the introduction, were selected by him from the writings of Galen and Hippocrates, and occasionally of Rhazes, Ibn Zuhr, and other Islamic physicians, and presented in such a way as to be easily comprehended and memorizable. Not the least of the Rambam's contributions to medicine were to be found in his commentaries and addenda in the *Aphorisms,* and in the last chapter, entitled "Dubious Sayings of Galen." "No one is without fault save the Prophets," wrote Maimonides, so even Galen was subject to some cautious modification.

In the course of his service to the various sultans and caliphs, Maimonides specialized in some ills to which the flesh of the royal family was particularly heir. Thus the Rambam came to write his *Treatise on Hemorrhoids* (in which he preferred, where possible, a nonsurgical approach), a *Treatise on Asthma* (in which he recommended travel to suitably dry climates over recourse to powerful drugs), a *Regimen of Health* (much of which dealt with psychosomatic afflictions), and a *Discourse on Fits* (which went into detail on how to establish a healthy day-to-day lifestyle). For Saladin's debauched nephew, the Sultan al Muzaffar Omar ibn Ad-Din, Maimonides wrote the *Treatise on Sexual Intercourse,* in which he obligingly listed supposedly aphrodisiac foods and drugs, but warned of the presumed deleterious effects of overindulgence and so also provided a list of anti-aphrodisiacs.

Although his father Maimon believed in angels and the importance of miracles, the Rambam was more the rationally minded monotheist, ever on guard against idolatry. Thus he distinguished between science and superstition in healing. Maimonides did not necessarily forbid irrational treatment. The reciting of a superstitious incantation over, say, a scorpion bite might be allowed if it helped ease the patient's mental anxiety. But when it came to desecrating the Sabbath, the Rambam's distinction between science and superstition became crucial. When the patient's life is in possible jeopardy on the Sabbath, the carrying out of medical procedures was not only allowed but mandated. (Here, Jewish practice was more flexible than that of strict Islamists, who, for example, ruled for a seriously ill patient deemed by medical authority to be in need of therapeutic doses of wine: "Wine is forbidden to us by Allah. If it is the patient's fate to recover, he will recover even without wine.") But Sabbath desecration was justified in Maimonides' eyes only when the therapy was based on rational theories of cause and effect. Success did not necessarily have to be assured beforehand; there had only to be a reasonable chance. As for would-be cures lacking even the pretense of a natural causal basis—"all imaginary and foolishness which attract only those who are deficient in knowledge"—the Rambam sweepingly condemned them, and he certainly would not permit the Sabbath to be desecrated by them.

In the framework of the Rambam's dichotomy of science versus pseudoscience, his attitude toward the influence of the heavenly spheres on human life and destiny is of particular interest. The long association of Jews with astronomy, which began on the nighttime Babylonian plains and was nurtured in Hellenic Alexandria, blossomed when the light of learning passed to the Islamic world. Jewish astronomers were the great transmitters and developers of this ancient knowledge, including the astrological aspect. Arabic mathematical astrology in fact began with the establishment by the Jew Jacob ben Tarik of a school of astrology in Baghdad under the auspices of the caliph Al-Mansur in the eighth century. We have seen that Hasdai ibn Shaprut was astronomer as well as physician to the caliph of Cordoba in the tenth century. Maimon, the father of the Rambam, was likewise an accomplished astronomer, and astronomy formed an integral part of the education of his son, who is said to have read every book ever written on the subject. Indeed, while still in Spain Maimonides wrote a lucid book called *Maamar Ha'ibbur* (essay on intercalation) about the heavenly spheres, the division of the year into seasons, the calculation of the new moon, and the interpolation of leap years. Maimonides was not averse to contradicting earlier talmudic pronouncements on astronomy since "at the time mathematics was imperfect." All the more did he oppose astrology, even when grounded in earlier Jewish thought.

Maimonides subscribed to the broad Greek concept of the heavenly bodies as movers of the four elements on the terrestrial level: "The sphere of the moon moves the water, the sphere of the sun the fire, while the sphere of the other planets moves the air. . . . The sphere of the fixed stars moves the earth." And in as much as he adhered to the doctrine that the four physical elements had their counterpart in the four body humors, the Rambam also saw the celestial objects as having a pronounced effect on the human organism and, in line with his mind-body isomorphism, on man's temperament and behavior as well. But acceptance of this supposed influence was not tantamount to accepting complete determinism. Strict determinism was as a matter of principle traditionally distasteful to the Jewish theologians. One way of reconciling celestial influence with God's mastery over the universe was to grant Him the power of veto, as did the twelfth-century rabbi Abraham Bar Hiyya of Barcelona, who declared: "At any time the Holy One, blessed be He, wishes, He can overturn their sovereignty [of the power of the stars and constellations] or cancel their decrees." But aside from the will of God, most great Jewish thinkers—not least of whom were the physician-philosophers Maimonides and ha-Levi— assumed also that humans had free will.

But even if, for the sake of argument, human determinism were accepted, the presumptions of the astrologers to have so thoroughly understood the influence of the heavenly bodies upon the human mind so as to predict in detail the interactions among men and among nations on any given day in the future was the height of preposterousness. Indeed, the tendency of the Arabic scholars was to concern themselves not with the fortune-telling aspects of astrology—opposed by the great Avicenna—but rather with the more reasonable concept of "elections," that is, the determining of the ideal moment for executing life's tasks, such as starting a journey or, for the physician, carrying out some medical procedure. So it was that Maimonides, the greatest scholar of the twelfth-century Arabic world, wrote in response to an inquiry from the Jewish community of southern France: "Notice your faith in astrology and the planets' influence on human destiny. You should give up such notions. Clear your minds as one washes dirty clothes! Experienced scientists refuse to allow any truth in this knowledge. Its claims can be disproved by irrefutable evidence on rational grounds." Yet, as we shall see in later chapters, the influence of astrology in the lives of the Jews and Jewish doctors, particularly in France, by no means ended with the Rambam's admonition.

It is appropriate that a philosopher and spiritual leader of Maimonides' towering stature should also turn his pen to the composing of ethical prayers. It is ironic that the one that has by far become most associated with Maimonides' name, the "Physician's Prayer," is generally attributed by scholars to a more recent author. No one, however, disputes that the prayer fully reflects the Rambam's spirit and the Jewish tradition in medical ethics he did so much to transmit and refine. So, just as the Hippocratic Oath, which may not have been penned by Hippocrates himself, is forever bound to his name, so the following text will ever be known as "Maimonides' Physician's Prayer":

Supreme God in heaven: Before I begin my holy work, to heal the human beings whom Your hands formed, I pour out my entreaty before Your throne of glory, that You grant me the strength of spirit and great courage to do my work faithfully, and that the ambition to amass riches or goodness shall not

blind my eyes from seeing rightly. Give me the merit to regard every suffering person who comes to ask my advice as a human being, without my
distinction between rich and poor, friend and foe, good person and bad.
When a person is in distress, show me only the human being. If physicians
with greater understanding than mine wish to teach me understanding, give
me the desire to learn from them, because there is no limit to the learning
of medicine. But when fools insult me, I pray: Let my love of the profession
strengthen my spirit, without any regard for the advanced age of the scorners
and their prestige. Let the truth alone be a lamp to my feet, for every yielding in my profession can lead to perdition or illness for a human being whom
Your hands formed. I pray You, compassionate and gracious Lord, strengthen
and fortify me in body and soul, and implant an intact spirit within me.

So beloved was Maimonides by both Moslems and Jews that when he died
in 1204, three days of mourning were declared in Fostat. The Rambam's
fame in the spheres of ethics and psychology, as well as medicine, was such
that the poet and patient Said ben Sana Almulk could permit himself more
than a bit of hyperbole when he poeticized:

Galen's art heals only the body,
But Abu Amram's [the Arabic name for Maimonides] heals the
    body and soul.
His knowledge has made him the physician of the century.
With his wisdom, he could heal the sickness of ignorance.
Were he to attend the moon,
He would free her of her spots when she was full,
He would heal her of her periodic defects,
And at the time of her weakness save her from waning.

If Maimonides could metaphorically stop the moon from waning, still not
even his great contributions to philosophy and medicine were enough to
prevent the eclipsing of the crescent of Islam. The Rambam's fame remained
so great that for hundreds of years, even in the twentieth century, sick
persons in search of a cure went to sleep in the Synagogue of Maimonides
in Cairo or journeyed to his gavesite in Tiberias in Palestine.

But while the spirit of the great rabbi-physician continued to dwell in the Islamic World and the Holy Land, the torch of medical and scientific learning was being passed to Christian Europe. It was the Jewish doctors formerly from the House of Islam who carried it.

Chapter 4
A Tale of Two Peninsulas

The faithlessness of the Jews whom the Lord of the world has created must be rejected, and the stubbornness of their unbelief must be crushed . . . nevertheless their preservation is useful and necessary to Christians in certain respects, specially such as are well trained in medical art and who show themselves helpful in restoring Christians to their former health.

—Senate of Rome

Jews are universally entrusted by the great with the care of their health. Nor is the Church free from this abomination, for nearly every monastery has its Jewish physician. The custom is accursed.

—Raymond Lully

When the fourteenth century was only a few months old and Christianity had been the dominant religion of Europe for almost a millennium, Arnold of Villanova, a prominent gentile physician who lost no love on his Jewish colleagues, journeyed to Rome to present a deep grievance to Pope Boniface VIII. "We remember to have heard in the sermons of the clergy," Arnold told the Pontiff, "that every Christian who entrusts his body to the medical treatment of Jews merits excommunication and is guilty of a capital crime." Indeed, as both Arnold and Boniface well knew, back in the year 692 the Quintisext Oecumenical Council held in Constantinople had decreed: "No Christian whether layman or cleric may eat the unleavened bread of the Jews, have confidential intercourse with Jews, receive medicine from them or bathe with them. The cleric who does so is deposed, the layman is excommunicated." Such prohibitions were repeated at many other councils. In the eleventh and twelfth centuries they were incorporated into the decretals of Saint Ivo and Gratian (the "father of canon law," whom Dante placed in Paradise). But it was especially in the thirteenth century that the doctors among the Jews were targeted. At the synod of Albi in 1254 it was resolved that "all Christians who, when sick, put themselves in the care of Jews will be excommunicated."

The bigoted Arnold was naturally delighted with these decrees. So what was his grievance? "We see however," he bemoaned to Pope Boniface, "that in general no physician enters either a convent or a monastery except a Jew." Arnold accordingly beseeched His Holiness to take action. Boniface, however, equivocated, as well he might. For the pontiff had placed his own mortal body in the hands of Maestro Gajo (Isaac ben Mordecai), a distinguished rabbi as well as court physician. And Boniface well knew that he was hardly unique in this regard. Popes Martin IV and Nicholas IV before him had retained Jewish court physicians, as would many of his successors. So, too, did kings and princes throughout Europe, some of whom banned all other Jews from their realms. And so did less eminent persons, clerical and lay, noble and commoner.

One supposed justification for the prohibition on Christians consulting a Jewish physician was that he would secretly cause their demise. As the council of Valladolid put it in 1322, Jewish physicians "under guise of medicine, surgery, or apothecary commit treachery with much ardor and kill Christian folk when administering medicine to them." And then there was the assumption that the Jew, always looking to lead Christian souls to perdition, would seek to obstruct his gravely ill patient from obtaining the last rites. Add to this the disturbing image of the passive patient and the powerful doctor when the former was a worshiper of Christ and the latter his betrayer. As one Church council lamented: "The servile status of these Jews [physicians] is inflated and elevated beyond their boundaries." Yet, as the bigoted Arnold knew, Jews were in such demand as doctors that, although they constituted only about 1 percent of Europe's population, they accounted for half of Europe's medical profession.

From where did the Jewish doctor get his medical knowledge and powers, which induced sick Medieval Christians to risk intentional poisoning in order to consult him? What motivated gravely ill Christians to chance excommunication and perdition in the next world in the hope of obtaining from a rabbi-physician a lease on life in the present? The Jewish doctor's sources were mostly heathen or non-Christian. They derived from the pagan physicians Hippocrates and Galen, with some Old Testament traditions and talmudic insights—always transmitted and enhanced by Islamic civilization in its Golden Age with its great Jewish and Mohammedan doctors.

It is hardly coincidental that when Christian Europe began to grope its way out of the Dark Ages, medical learning should have flourished first in precisely those two regions of Europe that for centuries had been under Islamic domination and influence: Iberia (more about which later) and southern Italy. And it was particularly fitting that, according to legend, when Christian Europe established its first medical school at the turn of the tenth century, it was a Jew, Elinus, together with a Greek, an Arab, and a Roman, who served as founding father. No less fitting was the site: Salerno.

Already in the mid-seventh century, even before their incursion into Spain, the armies of the Prophet jumped over from Tunesia in North Africa to begin their raids on Sicily. The whole island came under the domain of Islam with the fall of Palermo in 831, whereupon the Moslems began extending their influence to the boot of Italy proper. Within the next two decades they established themselves in Bari, made their appearance around Naples, and conducted raids farther to the north in Italy, perhaps even through the Alpine passes into Switzerland.

The Islamic presence in Italy was more tenuous than the Arab hold on Spain. Christian forces recaptured Bari and the rest of the Italian heel from the Mohammedans by the end of the ninth century. In the eleventh century the Norman Roger I completed the reconquest of Sicily. But although the cross replaced the crescent, the influence of Islamic civilization in southern Italy was enduring. The Norman monarchs especially surrounded themselves with Arab scholars, including physicians, and even adopted oriental dress. Under these "baptized sultans," southern Italy continued to serve as a conduit of learning from the Middle East and North Africa to the rest of Europe. Fortunate for southern Italy was also the fact that through the Dark Ages many ancient manuscripts had been preserved in cloisters such as Monte Cassino, whose sanctity was respected even by marauders, fearful as they were of the wrath of God. Furthermore, Salerno, to the south of Naples and hardly seventy-five miles from Monte Cassino, had been a Greek colony and then a popular health resort in Galen's time, and subsequently a Benedictine *hospitale* (hostel-hotel-hospital), offering shelter to the traveler and care and comfort to the sick. Lay as well as clerical practitioners tended to the infirm and formally transferred knowledge to students.

The legend of the founding of the Salerno medical school by Elinus the Jew, together with a Greek, a Roman, and an Arab, may be apocryphal, but the symbolism is apt. Even in ancient Roman times Salerno had been home to a community of Jewish physicians. Now as the second millennium approached, the Jews and Arabs were the great bearers of the learning of Hippocrates and Galen back to Europe, elaborated and commented on by the likes of Maimonides and Avicenna. Prominent as a channel between the ancient world, the House of Islam, and Christendom in the tenth century was the Jew Achimaaz, born near Salerno, and a friend of the Egyptian ruler Al-Mansur. The eleventh century brought to the medical school of Salerno Constantine the African, the most prolific translator of the age. In between his birth in Carthage and death at the monastery of Monte Cassino, Constantine spent decades wandering through Babylon, India, and Ethiopia. When accused of witchcraft upon his return to Carthage, he fled to the Christendom of Italy. Constantine taught at Salerno, where his multilingualism in Greek, Arabic, Latin, and other tongues made him a one-man bridge spanning most of the civilized world. In an age when the transfer of information in Europe otherwise proceeded very haltingly, if at all, Constantine's membership in the Benedictine order expedited the distribution of his works among the monasteries, with the encouragement of Pope Victor II. Yet for all this, Constantine was himself a convert to Christianity, probably from Judaism or else from Islam. Certain is that he translated many works of Jewish origin, including those of Isaac Judaeus (see Chapter 3).

In the first half of the thirteenth century, the Holy Roman Emperor Frederick II, a "baptized sultan" and king of Sicily (which included southern Italy and Salerno), invited Rabbi Jacob Anatoli to Naples, where he translated the physician-philosopher Averroes from Arabic into Hebrew. Such medical translations into Hebrew from other Eastern languages were not necessarily only for the benefit of Jewish physicians and scholars. Many monks were literate in Hebrew, and, subsequently, Rabbi Jacob's Hebrew version of Averroes was rendered into Latin. But the multilingual Jews also translated directly into Latin, as when later in the thirteenth century Charles of Anjou, king of Naples and Sicily, employed the Jew Faraj ben Salim of

Girgenti to produce a Latin version, the *Liber continens,* of Rhazes' enormous works. When Charles realized that the Jewish medical scholar Moses of Palermo lacked the necessary Latin, he commanded him to be instructed in that language so that he could then translate from Arabic a supposedly lost work of Hippocrates on equine diseases, which became a foundation stone of veterinary medicine for centuries to come.

Already in the twelfth century, the curriculum followed by aspiring physicians at Salerno had been codified to include three years of humanities followed by five years of medical studies proper, culminating in a stringent exam. (Consider that in the United States throughout the nineteenth century the M.D. degree was regularly granted following two years of postsecondary school study.) It was at Salerno that the academic title "doctor," deservedly awarded after such a lengthy study, first came to be associated with medical practitioners. Also probably originating from the School of Salerno was the name *physicus* (physician), which emphasized the integration of medicine with the natural sciences.

So many years of academic study were a dauntingly expensive investment, even for members of the small middle class that arose in the Middle Ages. This was true whether at the medical school of Salerno or at the medical faculty of Bologna in northern Italy, Europe's first university, founded in the eleventh century. The Church had the means to subsidize such education for the members of its orders, but there were objections in principle. As the Council of Clermont lamented in 1130: "We understand that an evil and detestable habit has taken root, one according to which monks and regular canons, after having received the habit and made profession [of faith], engage in the study of jurisprudence and medicine, despite the rule of Saints Benedict and Augustine: and this they do for the sake of temporal gain." A prohibition against clergy purging bodies when they should be purging souls was reiterated at five other councils within the next 100 years. Although, like anti-Jewish regulations, such bans were often honored in the breech, the canon had a substantial effect in limiting clerical participation in medicine. This left the profession all the more open to the Jews, and not least to rabbis, who saw no ethical problem in attending to both Jewish and Christian medical needs as they attended to Jewish spiritual needs.

In the late Middle Ages, however, the number of university-trained doctors, Jewish or Christian, comprised but a small part of the overall medical profession. Italian records show the annual number of medical graduates from any given university varying on average from less than one to at most ten or so per year. Furthermore, of the three Medieval Italian universities—Bologna, Padua, and Pisa, founded in the eleventh, thirteenth, and fourteenth centuries, respectively—only Padua regularly admitted Jews (more about which shortly). Admission to what would today be called the medical board exams was, however, possible also for those who acquired their knowledge through non-university study, and in many cases Israelite candidates were tested by their coreligionists. ("Jewish and Saracen physicians should be examined by physicians of their own law or sect, if any are available," stated an Aragonese regulation, which, however, also stipulated that "one Christian physician should nevertheless assist in the examination.") Some of the required medical theory may have been offered as part of the curricula at the yeshivas (the Jewish schools of higher education), which, as we shall soon see, were fountains of ancient learning drawing from the flow of Jews from Iberia. But most Medieval Jewish physicians probably acquired their esoteric knowledge as apprentices to established Jewish doctors. This customarily came at a price (albeit at a far lesser one than for university study), except, of course, in the case of the numerous father-son medical dynasties or when knowledge was transmitted from father to son-in-law as part of the dowry agreement.

Understandably, in the century when an irate Arnold of Villanova visited the equivocating Pope Boniface VIII to complain about the gross and blatant violation of ecclesiastic law committed by all those Christians—clerical and lay—who couldn't resist consulting Jewish doctors, it seemed judicious for the powers-that-be to incorporate a few loopholes into their anti-Jewish prohibitions. Thus, when the Synod of Prigueux reiterated the ban in the fourteenth century, it allowed exceptions "in case of necessity." Similarly, the Roman Senate, while declaring that "the faithlessness of the Jews whom the Lord of the world has created must be rejected, and the stubbornness of their unbelief must be crushed," further decreed that "nevertheless their preservation is useful and necessary to Christians in certain respects, specially such as are well trained in medical art and who show themselves helpful in restoring Christians to their former health." Other loopholes allowed, for example, recourse to a Jewish doctor when "imminent danger to the patient exists."

So it was that when the Jews were expelled from Venice in 1397, physicians were exempted. Elsewhere, secular legislation against Jewish doctors was suspended or repealed outright within a couple of years or even months of its promulgation, as when severe ordinances in Provence were revoked on the grounds of public utility. Backtracking authorities might also lamely claim that contact with Christians would lead the Jewish doctor to the Light. Furthermore, when in the beginning of the thirteenth century ecumenical laws were enacted requiring Jews to wear special badges and pointed caps, the Jewish physicians were often exempted and permitted to don the same professional garb as their Christian colleagues. The Roman Senate would occasionally even relieve some prominent Jewish doctors, such as Maestro Manuele and his son, of the special tax placed on Jews, "because of their great experience in their profession and the valuable services they had rendered and were daily rendering through their art to the citizens of Rome."

The language of the Senate's declaration pales before the hyperbole of the papal decree of Boniface IX around the turn of the fifteenth century, in which he appointed his "beloved son" Angelo as his court physician:

> Since you are adorned with the jewels of honesty, justice, and virtue, as we are convinced by careful experience, and since you are desirous of devoting yourself even more intensely to our service and that of the Roman Church as you have done so worthily in the past, and since we have become sensible of your fame for probity, we are graciously attached to your person and are willing to advance you in accordance with your service by a more worthy title and by our grace, therefore, we appoint you by these presents as physician and familiar to us and to the Apostolic Chair under the protection of the sainted apostles Peter and Paul and of us and of the above mentioned Chair and make you one of the number of physicians reckoned as familiar to us and to the Chair. With this intent that you enjoy through the preferment more richly the Apostolic Grace, and that you shall truly enjoy as it is our desire all the privileges, honors, immunities, indulgences, liberties, and exemptions as well as all other marks of grace now belonging to or in

future to be bestowed upon our familiars, other Apostolic Constitutions or
contrary edicts notwithstanding. May you so devote yourself to the culture
of virtue as we call upon you to win for yourself still greater favor.

Among Boniface's more immediate successors in the Holy See, Alexander
VI, Julius II, Leo X, Julius III, Clement VII, and Paul III were served by the
Jewish physicians Samuel, Simon and Isaac Zarfati, Bonet de Lattes,
Emmanuel ben Jacob Lattes, Jacob Mantino, and Vitale Alatino, on whom
honors were often bestowed in language not much less bombastic than that
reserved for Angelo. The fifteenth-century Master Elia served Popes Martin V and Eugenius IV and was one of the first European Jewish knights (a
distinction bestowed by the duke of Milan). And, of course, lesser princes
of the church—cardinals and archbishops—were often served by erudite,
if slightly less illustrious, Jewish physicians. So, too, were such diverse Italian nobility as the duke of Medina Sidonica and the grand duke of Tuscany.

The mid-sixteenth century, however, marked a reversal in fortune for the
Jews and their relation with the Holy See. In 1555 the bitterly anti-Jewish
Paul IV became pontiff, an event celebrated the following year by an auto-
da-fé in Ancona in which twenty-four Jews perished. Ignoring the honors
his predecessors bestowed upon their Jewish physicians, Paul reinstated not
only a special garb and residence restrictions for all Jews, but also a ban—
to be reiterated later in the century by Pius V and Gregory XIII—on the
consulting of Jewish physicians by Christians.

These unfortunate developments motivated the doctor David de Pomis—
who traced his family's roots in Italy back a millennium and a half to a
prisoner brought by Titus from Jerusalem—to write *De Medico Hebraeo
Enarratio Apologica,* a vindication of Jews in the medical profession. Drawing upon Christian as well as Jewish scriptures, de Pomis stressed the common origins of the two faiths and their belief in the same God: "The eternal, unchangeable and fundamental commandments are accepted by both,"
he wrote, and he cited passages in Leviticus that he interpreted as meaning
that "whoever of the gentiles fulfilled the Law may be regarded as is a High
Priest, and, at his own level, acquires eternal salvation." De Pomis went on
to paraphrase commentaries by Rabbi Nissim as enjoining Jews to "sorrow
at the deaths among other peoples and console the relatives of the dead."
Also cited by de Pomis was the Jewish daily prayer to God to "bring forth

the dew and the rain, as a blessing for the surface of the earth, and pour Thy blessing upon the world," this being proof of the Jew's concern for all mankind. Then, de Pomis went on, there is the Sabbath prayer enjoining "He who giveth salvation unto kings and dominion unto princes, etc., [to] preserve in life, guard and deliver him [the sovereign] from all trouble and sorrow"—a show of the allegiance of the Jews to the ruler who affords them protection.

These universalistic Jewish ethical principles apply all the more in the practice of medicine, de Pomis declared. He knew all too well of the Jewish court doctors who came to grief due to accusations of poisoning. In the eighth, ninth, and tenth centuries, the Jewish physicians to Carloman (Charlemagne's brother and likewise king of the Franks), Charles the Bald (Holy Roman Emperor), and Hugh Capet (founder of the Capetian dynasty, which endured until the French Revolution) had all met inglorious ends. More recently, in the late fifteenth century, the Italian-Jewish physician Leo, who had been brought to the royal court in St. Petersburg to treat Ivan III's son for gout, was executed when the boy expired (although this punishment may have been due to the czar's anger at Leo's overconfidence as much to suspicions of wrongdoing). Countering the libel on poisoning, de Pomis declared: "No one has ever witnessed any crime by a Jewish physician and no one has received reliable information of such. It is only because of common prejudice that we are accused and suffer injury. When Christians accept falsehood for truth, they harm themselves more than us, for this is completely contrary to the teachings of Christ."

Understandably in the hostile climate of the early Renaissance, the temptation was considerable for ambitious Jewish doctors to be baptized and thus to be able to serve as physicians to the Holy See as their unconverted ancestors had done in a more tolerant age. Among the most noted of the seventeenth-century papal doctors of Jewish descent who espoused Catholicism (at least in public) was the Marrano Gabriel da Fonesca, professor of philosophy and medicine in Pisa and Rome, who served Popes Gregory XV, Urban VIII, and Innocent X. The conversion ceremonies at the Vatican were often accompanied by great festivities.

But in this age of increasing intolerance toward Jews and Jewish physicians in Rome and the rest of Italy, one institution stood out as a beacon of toleration. This was the University of Padua, which had come into being back in 1222, as the medical school at Salerno, having fulfilled its role as the transmitter of ancient knowledge through the last centuries of the Dark Ages in Europe, was expiring. Like the first European university, Bologna, Padua was a church institution. But unlike Bologna (and unlike the University of Pisa), Padua gained a reputation for religious tolerance. It was to Padua that Jews aspiring to an academic education in medicine would look for centuries to come. True, a university statute stipulated that "the Jews shall not in any manner be admitted to the 'primatus' or public examination, and may not be given the doctorate or have the insignia of any other dignity, or obtain from the Sacred College any authorization whatsoever to practice medicine." To show they weren't kidding, the academic powers-that-be added that "this injunction we mean to be so fixed and immutable that except on unanimous vote, it may not be abolished even once or annulled in the slightest particular." Nevertheless, from 1517 to 1816 some 250 Jewish students received the degree of Doctor of Medicine, sometimes, though not always, under direct papal dispensation, as when in 1555 Julius III, just before his death and succession by the bigoted Paul IV, commanded the university to examine a Jewish candidate. Furthermore, in at least some cases, the wording of the diplomas issued to Jews showed quite a bit of tolerance in taking their religious sensitivities into account. The salutation would then begin: "In Nomine Dei aeterni, Amen," instead of the usual "In Christi Nomine, Amen," and the year would be given as "Currente anno" rather than the traditional "Anno a partu Virginis" or "Anno a Christi Nativitate." Aside from the privilege of practicing medicine, the M.D. degree from Padua also granted Jews exemption from having to wear the "Jew's hat." (Some different accommodations were made at Padua for Protestants and Anglicans. To the latter sect belonged, presumably, William Harvey, the great discoverer of the circulation of the blood, who graduated from Padua early in the seventeenth century.)

Such toleration notwithstanding, Padua was not free of discrimination. Jewish students were required to pay higher tuition. And since they did not have their own "corporation" (student body), they had to join one of another nationality, usually the German, which meant additional monetary discrimination. As a Christian German medical student wrote home: "Here at the University there are 22 various nations, Jews and Turks among them. A Jew desiring to become a doctor has to pay to the University 20 pounds of sweetmeats, of which ten pounds the German nation takes for itself, to be distributed among its members. . . . This is an old custom, and so, to a Jew, the privilege of becoming a doctor is more costly than for a German, who has to pay less than one fourth of that amount." Fortunately, Jewish medical students at Padua were often subsidized by the aristocrats of their respective countries, particularly Poland and Hungary, with the understanding that they would then return to serve as personal physicians for a specified time period.

The rise of the towns in late Middle Ages and early Renaissance, though a sign of economic advance out of the Dark Ages, brought with it problems of public health unique to urban environments. The late Medieval towns did have privies, cesspools, drainage pipes, and public latrines, but the street sewers remained open. The wealthier homes had privies built into jutting bays, such that the deposit fell into a moat or river. Other well-to-do homes had backyard cesspools, supposedly at a regulated distance from well water sources, but often in fact quite capable of causing contamination.

Conditions were no better a few centuries later even in the very center of the Renaissance. A report of the Sanitation Office of the Magistracy of Florence ran:

> Things are very badly arranged because the [chamber] pots, all inadequately set just below the commodes, let the waste run out through gaps in the walls and fall into certain alleys between the houses in which [the inhabitants] throw all the dirt and rubbish from their houses. The result is that so much stuff accumulates in these alleys that even when it rains the rainwater is not sufficient to carry it out to the ditches designed for that purpose; and the small proportion which does come out gets stuck in certain ditches next to the walls. The result is a stench and filth so awful that it is quite impossible to live there.

It was in such an environment, when baths and a change of clothes were luxuries, that the perfumes and incenses of Arabia traded by the Jews since biblical times attained the value of precious stones, likewise a typical Jewish trading commodity.

Bad as sanitary provisions may have been in many gentile quarters, for the Jews of Italy, as elsewhere in most of Christendom, the late Middle Ages and Renaissance were a time of ghettoization under increasingly congested conditions (more about which later). The Israelites were blessed, however, as always, with their ancient hygienic regulations, which had the force of divine ordinance and served as prophylactic measures. They also had perhaps developed some stronger genetic resistance to disease by natural selection in past centuries of urban life. But when patients got sick or an epidemic struck the crowded ghetto, there was little of value even their most brilliant and learned doctor with all his rigmarole could provide.

One example of Jewish medical thought, caught between moribund medieval academic learning, ancient Jewish tradition, ghetto superstitions, and the new scientific awakening of the Renaissance, is provided by the career of Abraham Yagel, who lived in northern Italy from the mid-sixteenth until well into the seventeenth century. Galenism still very much dominated academic medicine. In Yagel's writings on the epidemiology of the plague we find mention of humoral imbalances that cause some people to be more vulnerable to venomous air. This was particularly so during certain astral conjunctions or moon phases. Jewish religious writings were of course traditionally replete with astronomical and astrological passages, and although Yagel was familiar with Galileo's astronomical observations with the newly invented telescope, he was reluctant to challenge the sanctified Jewish texts on the matter. In keeping with the more ancient beliefs, Yagel was prone to prescribe as protection against the plague a lunar seal of gold inlaid with precious stones. On the one hand, this was merely a means to counteract the supposed negative astral forces, a concept that, although false, was not in and of itself unscientific. But so as not to neglect the purely spiritual aspects, the lunar seal was also engraved with magic words in Aramaic. (This was not considered idolatrous, whereas a talisman with a human figure might be.)

Most interesting with regard to Yagel's position between the worlds of ancient and modern rationalism and the world of the spirits was his attitude toward demons—beings that for millennia had haunted the more superstitious Jewish manuscripts. For Yagel, belief in a demonic aspect of disease etiology was combinable with aspects of Galenic theory: "As long as the [given] humor increases in a human body and is left to magnify its strength, and no one hastens to cure it, then according to its nature and constitution, a spirit will attach itself to it that matches it, for one type finds its same type." The new trends in natural science also influenced Yagel's thinking. Just as the earth was assumed to be able to generate insect and perhaps even animal life *de novo,* so Yagel speculated, the air could perhaps likewise spontaneously generate spirit life. The first assumption, though quite mistaken, was by no means irrational and was in fact based on observations, however faulty. So, in line with the prevailing zeitgeist, Yagel and his like-minded Jewish contemporaries endeavored through observation to determine the place of demons and other occult phenomena in the natural, rather than supernatural, order of things.

All this was in keeping with the spirit of the Kabbalah, which combined belief in the occult with a kind of scientific drive to understand all nature by empirical means. But already in Yagel's day, with the increased isolation of the Jewish community from the Renaissance—the Jewish doctors being an exception—the Kabbalah and modern science went their own ways. The Kabbalah became increasingly ritualistic and superstitious and in this regard was at least able to offer some much-needed spiritual comfort to the ghettoized Jews.

Iberia and Italy shared much history in common. Integral parts of the Roman Empire that retained their Romance vernacular through the barbarian invasions and chaos of Dark Ages, the two Mediterranean peninsulas took on an Arabic cultural overlay after the advent of Islam. For much of late Middle Ages, parts of Iberia and Italy formed a single kingdom under a Christian monarch. And both lands were home to a substantial Jewish population, including, of course, Jewish doctors, whose fortunes were subjected to the vicissitudes of the rulers and clerics, Islamic and Catholic.

From the Christian perspective, the five centuries leading up to the climactic year 1492 were the period of *Reconquista,* when from a small unconquered Christian corner of northeast Spain, the defenders of Christ retook the peninsula piece by piece. With the advent of an independent Christian Kingdom of Castile in north-central Spain in the mid-twelfth century, the relative toleration the Jews had enjoyed for much of the Islamic era was placed in jeopardy. The Castilian Alfonso VII, who briefly reigned as emperor over all the Christian states of northern Iberia, was quick to restrict the freedom of the Jews. Some of his Castilian successors followed suit, as when Alfonso X ("the Wise") a century later adopted into the "Seven Codes," some of the Church's most intolerant laws. For Jewish physicians in particular, prohibition followed prohibition, from royal, ecclesiastic, and local authorities. Already in the mid-thirteenth century, laws prohibited Christians from taking "medicines or purges from the hands of Jews unless prescribed by a learned Jew and (prepared) by the hand of a Christian who knows and understands the substances contained." Early in the fourteenth century the Church council of Zamora and the municipal council of Valladolid placed a general ban on the employing of Jewish physicians by Christians. This, in turn, influenced the legislation of the Cortes (Assembly) of all Catholic Spain.

For their part, Jewish leaders in this era of increasing marginalization reacted with a certain spiritual withdrawal. Scholarship turned inward and increasing attention was paid to the less worldly aspects of the Talmud. The pious and mystic Kabbalah, influential among the Ashkenazim, found a receptive audience in Iberia. Five years into the fourteenth century the great Barcelona rabbi Solomon issued a sweeping prohibition, declaring that "Every man with his censer in hand offers incense before the Greeks and Arabs. Therefore have we decreed for our community that for the next fifty years, under threat of the ban, no man under twenty-five shall study the books which the Greeks have written on religious philosophy and the natural sciences."

Fortunately for our story, Rabbi Solomon hastened to add: "Medicine, though one of the natural sciences, has not been included in our general prohibition, because the Torah permits the Jewish physician to heal." So it was that, despite the ecclesiastic anti-Jewish restrictions and the corresponding insularity of the rabbinical authorities, virtually every Castilian Christian monarch, right up to Queen Isabella in 1492, entrusted their temporal bodies to Jewish physicians. Telling is that even the previously mentioned Alfonso the Wise had to be reproached by Pope Nicholas III for showing preference to Jews. (It was Alfonso's wisdom to initiate a new wave of medical translations from Arabic into the vernacular using a team of Jewish scholars, most notably his physician-astrologer Don Judah ben Moses ha-Kohen.)

A virtually unique exception to the royal hypocrisy in Castile was Enrique III, a bigot who practiced what he preached and had no Jews in his entourage. Nevertheless, upon Enrique's death a Jewish doctor was accused of having somehow poisoned him and was barbarously executed. This led Enrique's son Juan II to promulgate some of the harshest anti-Jewish economic and dress legislation and to prohibit Jews from practicing medicine and surgery. But unlike his father, Juan prudently exempted the royal household from such ordinances, and he in fact surrounded himself with Jewish court physicians, most prominent of whom was Joseph ibn Shem-tob, philosopher and financial expert as well as medical doctor. From the period of the *Reconquista* are also records of Jewish doctors accompanying their sovereigns on military campaigns, as when the royal physician El'azar took part in King Pedro's war against Majorca.

Neighboring Aragon to the east likewise had a long tradition of Jews in medicine, extending from the Moorish through the Christian eras. Notwithstanding the frequent spates of anti-Jewish regulations, a virtually unbroken line of Aragon kings—whose domains often extended to Sicily and parts of southern Italy—retained Jewish physicians at court, and often Jewish astronomers, poets, interpreters, and diplomats as well. Especially notable were the court physicians to Jaime I in the mid-thirteenth century. These included the doctor cum satiric poet Joseph ben Meir Zabara. At Jaime's request, Dr. Isaac of Barcelona received dispensations from Pope Honorius III, who wrote: "Although we could not heed the prayers in his favor in every respect, nevertheless we have granted whatever seemed proper, and in view of your intercession we caused to be extended to him the shelter of our protection." So, too, was a dispensation granted to Dr. Isaac Benveniste, distinguished as "Nasi" (prince), who furthermore managed to have the papal order for the wearing of Jew-badges rescinded in Aragon. Honorius's successor, Clement IV, tried in vain to get Jaime to remove the Jews from court. The Jew-baiters in Aragon had a short-lived victory when at the close of the fourteenth century Queen Maria, declaring that "the perfidious Jews are thirsty for Christian blood," proclaimed that "no Jew, in any case of a Christian's infirmity, should dare to exercise his office of medicine unless a Christian doctor will take part in the cure." But when her consort, King Martino, returned from his journey to Sicily, he immediately countermanded the order, as well he would, having entrusted his corporal being to the Jewish physician Bonsenyor Asday.

One can almost sympathize with Raymond Lully—the famed Christian physician, alchemist, and Jew-baiter in the court of Jaime II of Aragon—who lamented around the turn of the fourteenth century: "Jews are universally entrusted by the great with the care of their health. Nor is the Church free from this abomination, for nearly every monastery has its Jewish physician. The custom is accursed." Telling was the petition sent to the monarch by a crown representative requesting on behalf of the city of Barcelona an order restraining a Jewish doctor, Benvenisti Ismael, from leaving town, thus in effect prohibiting him from *not* practicing. And Lully had no reason to be happier about the situation in Navarre, the small country sandwiched between Castile and Aragon. Its monarchs, too, had been treated by Jewish court physicians through the ages. Perhaps the most telling comment from a Navarrese monarch came from the ailing Queen Juana, who justified her sending for Maestre Salamo of Tuledo, with the words: "[T]he excellent cures that he has brought about in Navarre have led us to place such hopes in him that we should feel restored as soon as we saw him."

The influence of the Jewish royal physician and other court Jews, particularly the financial advisers and tax collectors, helped ensure some crown protection for their coreligionists. As another Jew-baiter complained: "[H]ardly one of them [temporal lord or ecclesiastic prelate] is to be found who does not harbor some devil of a Jewish doctor and consequently the Jews obtain privileges in that kingdom, even in the royal palace, and there is one big official or many to act as their advocate and defender whenever anyone accuses them." But this royal patronage counted for precious little in times of popular panic and breakdown of authority. In 1348, when the Black Death was ravaging Spain and most of Europe, the Jewish physician Balovignus in the German town of Neustadt confessed while being broken on the rack that the chief rabbi of Toledo had sent him a poisoned powder that he was ordered, under threat of excommunication, to put in the wells, but not, of course, before warning his fellow Jews. When word of this reached Iberia, such slaughters took place that by the time, two years later, the plague subsided and central authority was restored, Iberian Jewry had been reduced to perhaps a quarter of their previous numbers. Yet even in the absence of the Black Death, the Jews, diminished in population though they were, were the targets of religious hatred and economic envy. Before the fourteenth century was out, rioters with swords and torches were again rampaging through the streets of Seville, shouting "Death or the cross." Some Jews choose the former alternative, many more (at least nominally) the latter. Fanned by the petty clergy, the flames of unrest engulfed all of Andalusia and then spread to Aragon and Castile. With the restoration of law and order came official rather than mob pressure on the Jews. In the second decade of the new century, hordes of barefoot flagellant monks were allowed to storm the synagogues in an effort to convert the Jews "voluntarily."

A far worse disaster—one of the greatest in Jewish history—came a century later. In 1479, wishing to create a unified Christian Spain, Queen Isabella of Castile and King Ferdinand II of Aragon tied the royal knot. This did not necessarily auger unfavorably toward their Jewish subjects. Indeed, like so many of their predecessors, both Catholic monarchs had their Jewish physicians, Thomas and Rodrig da Veiga. As Ferdinand remarked, "Just as it is necessary to refute misbelievers with the Catholic cult of the Christians and to repulse them, so it is not absurd to accept them in many things, especially in those in which without injury to our faith they may be useful to us, not doing harm to the healthfulness of our soul, but aiding us in the condition of our body." But when, with the reconquest of the last Moorish stronghold at Granada in 1492, Ferdinand and Isabella found themselves ruling over all Spain, whatever Jewish influence there was at court was not enough to avert the coming catastrophe. To solidify the homogeneity of the new state, the Catholic monarchs ordered that all non-Christians either convert or be expelled—the latter group to forfeit their considerable wealth to strengthen the newly united crown. Apart from the disastrous consequences this action would have for culture and industry in Spain for centuries to come, the most immediate impact was on the medical profession. So, for example, we find a pleading document in the archives of the city of Vitoria reading: "Knowing the want of physicians the city, its territory, and vicinity experience from the departure and absence of the Jews and the physicians of the said city and its neighborhood, they agree to request, and hereby request, the licentiate Doctor Antonio de Tournay, physician, to remain and reside in said city, there to practice his profession and art. . . ."

Neighboring Portugal had at times been united with Spain but was an independent kingdom in the late fifteenth century. Through much of its history its monarchs, too, had prominent Jews at court, most notably as physicians but also as treasurers and other officials. While a Portuguese monarch might enforce anti-Jewish regulations even while entrusting his or her health to a Jewish doctor, more often the influence of the Jews at court worked positively for their coreligionists. In 1391 Rabbi Moses Navarro, the physician to João I, prevailed upon the king to offer protection to Jews fleeing the mobs raging through Spain.

A century and a year later, when the Spanish expulsion order was issued, the Portuguese king João II was likewise served by Jewish doctors and courtiers, including his top physicians Leo and Joseph Vecinho. Now, for a price (poll tax), the monarch agreed to offer limited sanctuary to some 100,000 of their coreligionists from Spain. Manuel I, who succeeded his father João to the Portuguese throne in 1495, was initially sympathetic to the Jews, perhaps due in part to the influence of his renowned astronomer-physician Abraham Zacuto. But two years later, desiring to unify the whole Iberian peninsula by marrying the daughter of Ferdinand and Isabella, Manuel acceded to the Spanish monarchs' demands that all Jews in Portugal, too, be converted or expelled.

Large numbers of Jews chose the harder alternative of exile (more about them shortly). But at every step in the increasing persecution in both Spain and Portugal, many accepted baptism instead. Quite a few of the New Christians, or at least their descendants, genuinely embraced the Catholic faith. A new world of opportunity initially opened up to these *conversos* (or "Marranos," meaning "pigs," a contemptuous term originally applied to them by Jews who had chosen exile). They could now study at the flourishing universities and achieve prominence in the civil service and even among the clergy and in the ranks of the nobility, as well as, of course, in the traditional fields of commerce and medicine. Marrano physicians would serve the Iberian royal courts for centuries to come. In Spain, particular mention should be made of Ferdinando Mendez and Francisco Lopez de Villalobos, doctors to the monarchs Carlos II and Carlos V. It was telling that, although the authorities, doubtful of the strength of faith in Christ among the former Jews, forbade them to possess any books in Hebrew, an exception was made for New Christian physicians and surgeons, who were allowed to keep and use their Hebrew medical books.

Many *conversos* were in fact not Christians to the depths of their souls. A Spanish doctor, using the anatomical metaphor, told a contemporary Englishman in confidence "that his complyance was only the work of his Nerves and Muscles, and that his Anatomy told him nothing of the heart was therein concerned." As we have seen, the phenomenon of the "crypto-Jew," who accepted nominal conversion above martyrdom, slavery, or exile but secretly remained true to Judaism, was not a new phenomenon in Spain. It had occurred under the Catholic Visigoths some nine centuries earlier and under the Almohade Moslem fanatics in the time of Maimonides. But the previous persecutions had been haphazard or temporary. The Holy Inquisition, brought to Spain by Ferdinand and Isabella as a powerful tool for entrenching their absolute rule, was something different. It became an efficient and durable Spanish institution, tracking down Judiazers (secret adherents of the Jewish religion) for generations to come. The first descendants of forced converts may have passed on such customs as changing into clean linen on Saturday, eschewing pork, and observing Passover instead of Easter. (Circumcision, that hitherto unbroken link with Abraham, was probably too deadly a potential give-away to be continued.) But in the absence of any rabbis or Hebrew literature, and with increasing intermarriage with Old Christians, especially of the professional and mercantile classes, remnants of the Mosaic religion became scarcer. The rabbis outside Iberia themselves debated the legal and religious status of those converted under extreme duress. For the Church, however, the status of the *conversos* was clear. Although canon law did not condone forced conversion, baptism under whatever circumstances was absolutely binding, and any reversion was a serious crime.

The post-expulsion situation in Portugal was at first more favorable than in Spain but was later to take an especially pernicious turn. Although it was obvious that much of the mass conversion of 1497 was in name only, King Manuel—who, like his predecessors, was served by Marrano physicians, Drs. Diogo Avar and Rodrigo da Veiga—forbade by edict any inquiry into the genuineness of the faith of the New Christians or discrimination against them. But some three decades into the new century, his successor, King João III, allowed the Holy See to bring the Inquisition to Portugal. As might be expected, João himself had a Marrano physician—Thomas Rodrigo da Veiga, the son of João's father's doctor, a philosopher, first professor of medicine at the University of Coimbra, and elucidator of problematical passages in Galen's works. So would a long string of later Portuguese royalty. These included Kings Sebastiao, Felipe II, and Felipe III and various dukes and cardinals. Among their distinguished doctors were Ludovicus Mercatus, first professor of medicine at Valladolid, and the Montpellier-educated Drs. Jacob Hebraeus Rosales and Fernando Mendez. When in the mid-seventeenth century the Infanta Catherine of Braganza journeyed to England for her marriage to Charles II, she brought with her, along with Bombay and Tangier (her dowry), the converso physician Antonio Ferreiro. When the widowed Catherine returned to Portugal thirty years later and was taken ill by an attack of erysipelas, the Marrano Dr. Antonio Mendeze, first professor of medicine at the University of Coimbra and physician to the king, was summoned.

Old Christian burghers were all the more jealous of their new brethren in Christ, whose economic and social advancement was now unencumbered by religious restrictions. This led, for the first time in European history, to "racial" as opposed to purely religious hatred of people of Jewish ancestry. The crown, for its part, coveted the potentially confiscable wealth of this economically powerful segment of the bourgeoisie and so was not averse to seeing Judiazers even where there weren't any. Bans were introduced systematically excluding those even of only partial Jewish "blood" from ecclesiastic, military, and administrative posts and from teaching at the university. The descendants of the royal physicians Thomas and Rodrigo da Veiga may have gained exemption due to a breve issued by Pope Sixtus V in 1585, ennobling all their male descendants (thus according them the title "Dom"), opening all military and ecclesiastic orders to them, freeing them from all taxes imposed on New Christians, and granting them the use of the Pontiff's family arms. But hundreds of other "racially" Jewish doctors were not so fortunate and were persecuted by the Holy Inquisition like so many other Marranos. (Indeed, if anything good ever came from the Inquisition, it was its archives showing us that even centuries after the expulsion, people of Jewish descent still dominated the medical profession.) From the late 1400s to well into the eighteenth century, some 200 to 300 Marrano Iberian physicians were hauled before the court. Along with the usual accusations of secret Judaizing went charges of poisoning. (The record goes to Dr. Garcia Lopes, who "confessed" to murdering 150 Christians, including many noblemen; but the prize for ingenuity goes to the Marrano doctor who concealed under his fingernails a poison so potent that he could contaminate household medicines just by touching them.)

In one case, at least, the tables were turned on the inquisitors. A Marrano doctor, "a very good Catholic" by reputation, confessed under torture to secret Judaizing. However, his patient, a prominent nobleman more fearful of disease than of the Inquisition, seized the inquisitor and extracted from him the same confession by the same means, thus saving the physician. But exculpation was otherwise rare. If the judges showed leniency and the accused was not executed, he was subjected to confiscation of all property, whipping, incarceration, wearing of the *sambenito* (Jew costume), condemnation to the galleys, and exile to such places as Angola. Most commonly, the accused was burned at the stake, a practice not ended until the mid-eighteenth century. A few, more fortunate, of these victims were already dead, having been granted the mercy of strangulation first as reward for re-embracing Christianity. Some who had already died of other causes were exhumed and burned anyhow. The luckiest of all were burnt in effigy, having escaped abroad. Understandably, it was Jewish doctors who in the sixteenth and seventeenth centuries went to Rome as representatives of their people to implore the pope to curb the Inquisition's excesses. But the Portuguese racial edicts would not be officially lifted until 1773. By then, this concept of *limpeza de sangue* (purity of blood), as opposed to simply religious Jew-baiting, had established a deadly precedent for the twentieth century.

The religious oppression in the Iberian and Italian peninsulas produced a constant flow—sometimes a trickle, sometimes a flood—of medical and scientific knowledge northward over the Pyrenees and Alps, borne in the minds and books of the Jews. It is to southern France that we will likewise be journeying in Chapter 6. But the centuries before and after 1492 were also an era when East met West—when peoples who had previously been largely or totally unaware of one another's existence came into contact—sometimes for commerce, sometimes for slaughter, plunder, or enslavement. It was also a period when a channel was opened for the flow of medical knowledge and lore between Orient and Occident, as the supposed lost tribes of Israel whose home was thousands of miles to the east of Europe encountered once more their Western brethren.

Chapter 5
The Fifth Element from the Orient

Physician An Cheng in the nineteenth year of the Yong Le period of Emperor Cheng Zu, was presented with ceremonial incense and authorized by the Prince of Zhou . . . to rebuild the synagogue. . . . [H]is merits were reported to the throne, and he was rewarded . . . by designating him a Major of the Brocaded Robe Security Corps, and later raising him to Lieutenant Governor of the Military Area of Zhejiang Province.
— Fifteenth-century inscription

The year 1241 was one of extreme peril for the people of Christian Europe. At the battle of Liegnitz to the west of Breslau (Wroclaw), near the present-day border between Germany and Poland, a combined German-Polish army was annihilated by a force of mounted archers whose homeland lay some 5,000 miles to the east, in a region beyond the European's ken. Scarcely three decades earlier these nomadic Mongol people had burst out of their traditional habitat, breached the Great Wall, and begun their conquest of China. They then struck westward, conquering all the Islamic countries of Asia outside the Arabian peninsula, and then began their assault on Europe.

As was traditional in times of peril or upheaval, the panicky Christians blamed the Jews for their plight. In this case the presumption was that the Mongols were a lost tribe of Israel—the descendants of the Jews who in the eighth century B.C.E. had been taken by the Assyrians to Babylonia, never to return to Israel—and that the Jewish merchants of Europe were their collaborators, smuggling arms to their long-lost brethren. Accordingly, the Christians in the border region slaughtered the Jews. This apparently did the trick, for with Europe defenseless before them, the Mongols suddenly turned south toward the Adriatic and then withdrew through the Balkans to consolidate their gains.

That the Mongols were a lost tribe of Israel was, of course, nonsense. The miracle that saved Christian Europe was not the timely massacre of supposed Jewish fifth-columnists but the sudden death of the great Khan Ogedei and the dispute in the Mongol ranks over the succession. Yet there would turn out to be more than a grain of truth in the tale of almond-eyed, yellow-complexioned Jews thousands of miles east of Europe and in Mongol Khans who venerated Moses.

Although the sweep of the Mongol Golden Horde through the Eurasian land mass had been accompanied by massacres and devastation bordering on genocide, when things settled down there followed decades of Pax Mongolica. Needing to administer their far-flung domains and encourage the commerce from which they could derive tribute, the Mongols adapted to civilization and established safe and speedy routes along the Russian Steppes. The legendary Italian adventurer Marco Polo took daring advantage of the Pax Mongolica and traveled in the late thirteenth century to the courts of China to witness at firsthand an ancient culture that for over 1,000 years had deliberately maintained its isolation from the Western barbarians and had been known in Europe only through tidbits of usually inaccurate information.

Being of a cultured Venetian merchant family of the late Middle Ages, Marco was likely familiar with the Hippocratic and especially Galenic doctrines that still very much dominated European medicine. In his memoirs Marco would tell of how during two decades of travels through the Far East, he encountered physicians at the courts of Kublai Khan in Peking, Cachar Modun, and Su-chau in China, as well as in the Indian subcontinent.

To the extent Marco delved into the ancient medical lore of China, he was no doubt struck by exotic concepts without much equivalent in the West. Yin, the dark, moist female force in the universe mingled with yang, the bright, dry masculine. Illness was seen as resulting from a person's deviation from the Tao (the "way"), causing a dearth or overabundance of either of these forces. Diagnostic techniques included a pulse-taking ritual so complex that it could require hours and yield any of hundreds of possible bits of information about the patient's status. Therapy commonly included acupuncture, whereby excess energy was drained off by pins inserted at several of the 365 (or 600) points along a system of bodily meridians that in Marco's time, as in our own, had almost no correspondence with any anatomical system known to Western medicine. By means of another technique, ignipuncture (or moxibustion), a small cone of powdered mugwort leaves burned on a specific part of the skin raised a blister and thus rekindled the fiery yang as a remedy for an excess of yin.

Yet overlaying or underlying this exotic Oriental cosmos and the corresponding healing arts, Marco also found in China a metaphysical and medical system whose similarities to that of the ancient and medieval European were far more striking than the differences. The Chinese universe, like the Greek, was built up of a few basic elements (five, rather than the Greek four). Among them were the earth, water, and fire of the Hellenic philosophers. (The fourth and fifth Chinese elements were metal and wood, rather than the Greek air.) Each element was associated with a particular organ, among which were the heart, liver, and spleen, which the Greek physicians saw as producing three of their four humors. (For their fourth and fifth organs, the Chinese had the lungs and kidneys in lieu of the Greek brain.) As in Galenic theory, each of the Chinese elements in the human body was also related to a particular flavor. (Each Chinese element furthermore had its own color and geographic direction, rather than its own season and portion of the day as the Greco-Roman medicine had it.)

Such resemblances of the Chinese macro- and microcosm to that of the Greek philosophers and physicians might be put down to coincidence in view of the long history of virtually total ignorance of China in Europe, and the Chinese contempt for barbarians, not least of all those said to live beyond the headache mountains far to the West. Yet jade axes have appeared among the archaeological ruins of the ancient Greek city of Troy. The Hippocratic texts made mention of cinnamon. The Romans adored their silk garments, even if they knew virtually nothing of the land they called Seres from which the fabric originated. And if there was anything resembling a balance of trade and payments, the Chinese must have been receiving something in return. Evidently, in ancient as well as in more recent times, there must have been some people with one foot in the West and another in the East. And if they were passing tangible goods along the vast expanses of land and water, perhaps they were transmitting some ideas as well.

Marco's reminiscences of his decades of travel abound with encounters with strange and exotic peoples. Yet one ethnic group was quite familiar to him from his native Italy and throughout the Mediterranean. From Tiflis at the gates of Asia Major, to Malabar on the coast of India, to Abyssinia on the Horn of Africa, and all the way to the courts of the great Khans in China, Marco Polo encountered Jews. He might have been less surprised, had he read the *Itineraries* of the globe-trotting Rabbi Benjamin of Tudela. Although Benjamin would come to be dubbed the "Marco Polo of the Jews," he had in fact journeyed from his Spanish home through southern Europe, the Middle East, India, and up to the borders of China in the late twelfth century, a hundred years or so *before* Marco. Benjamin told of coming across Jewish communities everywhere he went. And although he didn't penetrate into China proper—this was still before the Pax Mongolica—he was aware of their presence there as well. When Marco encountered them in the 1270s, the Jews in Peking and Hangzhou were specialized in, among other things, the manufacture, dyeing, and pattern printing of cotton fabrics. They were obviously no newcomers to the Orient, for in Kaifeng—the capital of China during the European High Middle Ages and the site of the most important Jewish community—the Jews were *re*building their synagogue.

For how long had the Jews already been in China? And when did they leave their ancient homeland on their eastward Odyssey? As always, one thinks first of the great Diaspora of the whole Jewish nation in the wake of the destruction of the Second Temple by Roman forces in 70 C.E. and the suppression of the Bar Kochba revolt in 135. This did indeed produce a steady eastward migration of thousands of Jews, first to Persia and Arabia, and then north into Afghanistan. Some probably continued along the old Silk Road, making their way via Balkh, Samarkand, and Bokhara to Chinese Turkestan and then into northern China. Other Persian and Arabian Jews migrated along a southerly coastal route to Indian ports on the Arabian Sea. From there, Jewish merchants traveled on Arab, Persian, and Chinese vessels to southeastern Chinese ports, there perhaps encountering other Jewish merchants plying the long route from Persia via the Red Sea and Persian Gulf.

Yet Jewish history even before the great Diaspora was one of intermittent forced dispersion, as well as voluntary travel and migration for purposes of trade. So perhaps ancestors of the Chinese Jews whom Marco encountered had already left the Holy Land centuries before the destruction of the Temple by the Romans. Here's where the Lost Tribe hypothesis comes in. Strongly advocated by the seventeenth-century Amsterdam rabbi-physician Menasseh ben Israel (more about whom in a later chapter), this theory has it that after being taken off in captivity by the Assyrians in the eighth century B.C.E., some of the Israelites continued in a slow eastward migration, eventually arriving in China during the Zhou dynasty (which endured until the mid-third century B.C.E.). Among the circumstantial evidence mustered in support of this theory is the passage in Isaiah (49:12) prophesying the return of the Jews, with the words "Look, they are coming from afar, from the north and from the west, and from the land of *Sinim*," supposedly a reference to China. Also, it is claimed that in Kaifeng the Jews were in fact originally quite unfamiliar with the term "Jew" (*Zhuhu*) but called themselves Israelites (*Yicileye*), which linked them to the lands north of Judah from which the lost tribes hailed.

But scholars have noted that the Kaifeng Israelites venerated Ezra as their "second law-giver" (the first being Moses) and that they possessed a few verses of Daniel and the complete verses of the "Great Mother" Esther—all of which refer to events *after* the taking into captivity of the ten tribes. On the other hand, the Kaifeng Israelites seemed to be unfamiliar with Hanukkah, the festival of lights that commemorates the Maccabee uprising and the restoration of national independence. These facts would place their departure from the Holy Land after the fifth century B.C.E. but before the middle of the second. In any case, the Chinese Jews burned incense in their temples, were unfamiliar with the rabbinical system, and seemed not to know of Jesus—all of which suggests that their eastward migration must have begun before the great Diaspora of their coreligionists in the wake of the destruction of the Second Temple in 70 C.E.

One might think that the surviving texts of the Kaifeng Jews would decide the issue. Indeed, the oldest written record, an inscription from 1489 entitled "A Record of Rebuilding of the Purity and Truth Synagogue," would appear to do just that. It reads in part:

> Our religion was transmitted to China from Tianzhu. We settled in Kaifeng by imperial command. More than seventy clans . . . arrived during the Northern Song dynasty [969–1127 C.E.], bringing entry tribute of Western cloth. The Emperor said, "You have come to our Central Plain. Preserve your ancient customs and settle in Bianliang [Kaifeng]." In the first year of

the Long Xing period [1163] of Song emperor Xiao Zong, when *wusida* [rabbi] Liewei was the leader of our faithful, the *andula* [supervisor] commenced the building of our synagogue. It was rebuilt in the 6th year of the Zhi Yuan period [1279] of Kublai Khan.

Unfortunately, this inscription was not the final word on the matter. Succeeding generations of Kaifeng Jews had the curious tendency of extending the history of their people in China further back in the past. A 1512 inscription tells of their arrival during the Han dynasty (206 B.C.E.–220 C.E.), while a 1663 inscription traces their roots in China back to the Zhou dynasty (1066 B.C.E.–256 B.C.E.).

However long their history in the Orient, in the thirteenth century the Jews encountered by Marco Polo in the eastern reaches of Europe and across the vast Asian land mass were (except for India and Arabia) under the rule of the Mongols. This was not without consequence for the physicians among them and for the history of Jews and medicine. The almost genocidal massacres carried out by the conquering hordes against whole cities were military measures that did not reflect a religious or cultural hatred. The Mongols were in fact known for their tolerance, or else simple indifference, toward the beliefs of their subject peoples. As Edward Gibbon wrote in his famous *Decline and Fall of the Roman Empire,* "The Catholic inquisitors of Europe, who defended nonsense by cruelty, might have been confounded by the example of a barbarian, who anticipated the lessons of philosophy and established by his laws a system of pure theism and perfect toleration." This somewhat exaggerated the theological and intellectual sophistication of the khans. But, practically speaking, they were heir to a long-standing tradition of the exercise of different religions among the various nomadic tribes of the steppes. "We believe there is only one God," said Mangu Khan, Genghis's grandson and successor, to the Franciscan traveler William of Ruysbroek in the mid-thirteenth century. "But just as God has given the hand a variety of fingers, so has He given mankind a variety of ways."

The Mongols themselves originally held shamanistic beliefs revolving around myths and ancestors from the past and this-worldly concerns in the present. But the Mongols were intrigued by the otherworldly aspects of the peoples with whom they came in contact and later conquered. Hedging their bets in their relations with the divine powers-that-be, the Mongols venerated various prophets, including Moses. As Kublai Khan, another Genghis grandson, who succeeded Mangu, said to Marco: "There are four prophets who are worshiped and to whom all the world does reverence. The Christians say that their God [sic] was Jesus Christ, the Saracens Mahomet, the Jews Moses, and the idolaters Sakyamuni Burkhan. . . . I do honor and reverence to all four, so that I may be sure of doing it to him who is greatest in heaven and truest; and to him I pray for aid." In China the Mongols adopted the dominant religion of Buddhism, in Persia the dominant faith of Islam. While the Mongols didn't convert to the minority religions in their realms, they far surpassed the Europeans in their tolerance of the Nestors, who were condemned as heretics by their European brothers in Christ, and the Jews. In the Islamic lands that came under their rule, the Mongols relieved the Jews and Nestor Christians of the special tax on non-Muslims (*jizyah*).

In their desire to establish efficient administration of their vast subject territories so as to derive long-term revenues rather than simple plunder, the Mongols were inclined to permit local administrations to continue and to draw upon talented administrators, including Jews. So, for instance, in the aftermath of initial mismanagement in the Persian part of the empire, the khan Arghun appointed as vizier in 1289 the Jewish physician-scholar Sa'd al-Dawla, who, by all accounts, instituted impressive reforms.

More interesting from the point of view of medical history was the role of the Jewish-Persian physician Rashid al-Din, the son of an apothecary in Tabriz, who for twenty years, beginning at the end of the thirteenth century, served as chief minister of the Mongol Ilkhanate, the kingdom encompassing present-day Iran and Iraq. Medicine in the Eastern part of the Mongol Empire was still dominated by Taoist concepts. Several decades earlier Genghis had vainly sought from a Taoist sage a medicine for immortality. (The sage could only advise the khan to give up hunting and to sleep alone from time to time.) Perhaps in the hope of reigning longer than his grandfather Genghis, Kublai Khan, the first of the Yan emperors of China, initiated a project to translate the corpus of Chinese-based Tibetan medical writings (back) into Chinese. But at the western end of the khan's vast territory in the early fourteenth century, Rashid al-Din represented Jewish-Arabic medicine and its Greco-Roman inheritance. A prolific writer and theologian as well as physician, Rashid's knowledge was so vast that he was entrusted by his overlords to write the history of the whole world, which included the "History of the Children of Israel," as well as of the Mongol Empire. At a time of safe and reliable travel along the Mongol-controlled roads, with an imperial courier service going from the courts of the Middle East to those of China in a couple of weeks, Rashid and his contemporaries were probably the first physicians in the West to have had a direct influence in the Orient.

Rashid's further career incidentally provides a rather extreme example of the potential perils facing Jewish physicians who, as was so often the case, were also high government officials and as such found themselves caught up in political intrigues. On one occasion, Rachid's enemies produced a letter in Hebrew, supposedly instructing a fellow physician to poison the khan. Rashid was able to prove it to be a forgery, but when six years later, in 1318, his enemies accused him of deliberately prescribing a purgative that worsened instead of improved the khan's condition, the charge was accepted. Rashid, although over 70 years old, was mutilated and decapitated. Even though he had earlier conveniently converted to Islam, his head was paraded around Tabriz for several days, amid cries of "This is the head of the Jew who abused the name of God; may God's curse be upon him!" So enduring was the animosity that a century later the demented ruler ordered Rashid's tomb destroyed and his bones reburied in the Jewish cemetery.

As great as was the devastation initially wrought by the khan's Golden Horde on the peoples of the Near East and much of Europe, this paled almost into insignificance when compared to the loss of millions of lives—a third or more of the European population—that came later as an inadvertent and ironic consequence of the Pax Mongolica. The bringers of death were not the Mongol arrows and torches but invisible microorganisms, *Yersinia pestis,* of which neither the khan's horsemen nor virtually anyone else could have any conception for centuries to come.

A description of the plague's course was provided by the Islamic writer Ibn al-Wardi before he himself succumbed to the pestilence in 1349 in Aleppo, an ancient Syrian trading center that was then part of the Mongol domain. According to al-Wardi, the plague originated in the "Land of Darkness," spread northward through Asia, and then invaded the civilized world, passing through China and then through India into the House of Islam. The Land of Darkness may in fact refer to Yunnan-Burma, which, about a century earlier, the Mongol horsemen of the great khan had begun to penetrate and where the plague bacillus was endemic in the rats and fleas.

Along the Steppe roads established between East and West under the Pax Mongolica, ordinary caravan traffic could cover at least twenty-five miles a day. Mounted couriers could, when necessary, move from post station to post station almost ten times as fast. It was probably the soldiers, messengers, and caravans along these routes that brought the rats and fleas with *Yersinia pestis* across rivers and other natural obstacles, to the burrowing rodents of the Russian grasslands. From there, the bacillus was ready to begin its devastating assault on the Mediterranean basin and Europe. This was greatly facilitated by the burgeoning trade of the late Middle Ages. By 1347 the plague had reached the Black Sea port of Kaffa at the mouth of the River Don and before the year was out had ravaged several port areas between there and Genoa, including Constantinople, Crete, Greece, Sicily, and Sardinia. By the end of 1349, shipborne rats and their fleas had spread the Black Death through the coastal areas not only of the Near East, North Africa, the Balkans, Spain, and France, but also via the Atlantic route to England, Ireland, and Scandinavia. From 1350 to 1352 the pestilence followed an inland and river route, decimating the populations of Germany, Poland, and northern Russia, thus coming almost full circle. Moslems accused the Christians of deliberately spreading the disease, the Christians in turn accused the Moslems. Both Christians and Moslems (but particularly the former) naturally accused the Jews, and as we shall see in later chapters, the Black Death would have a powerful influence on the Jewish demography and population shifts in Europe and thus on the history of Jews in medicine.

In 1368, a little more than a decade after the plague burned itself out in Europe, the Pax Mongolica came to an end. The khans in Peking were overthrown and replaced by an ethnically Chinese dynasty, the Mings. This had no adverse consequences for the Jews of China, for they were long esteemed by the Chinese not only for their manufacturing and mercantile talents, but also for beliefs and a way of life quite compatible with what the Chinese held dear. As an early sixteenth-century inscription reads: "Wherever they [the Jews] are met with, they all, without exception, honor the sacred writings and venerate Eternal Reason in the same manner as the

Chinese, shunning superstitious practices and image worship. Differing little from our laws, they [the Jewish sacred books] are summed up in the worship of heaven, the honor of parents, and the veneration of ancestors."

As elsewhere in the world, prominent Jewish physicians in China were often important leaders of their communities. Most notable in the post-Mongol era was An Cheng. In the late fourteenth and early fifteenth centuries, Zhu Su, who was the prince of Zhou and younger brother of the Ming emperor Chen Zu, served as governor of the Kaifeng prefecture. Being also a medical man, Zhu actively worked on two treatises on healing, *Jin Huang Ben Cao* (Materia Medica for Epidemic Diseases) and *Pu Ji Fang* (Prescriptions for Common Ailments). It was in this labor that he was likely aided by the medical knowledge of his Jewish physician An Cheng, perhaps acquired in part from contacts with An's coreligionists to the west.

Zhu bestowed favor on An and the Jewish community in general, as recorded in the inscribed tablets of the Purity and Truth Synagogue:

> Physician An Cheng in the nineteenth year of the Yong Le period [1421] of Emperor Cheng Zu, was presented with ceremonial incense [money] and authorized by the Prince of Zhou . . . to rebuild the synagogue. An Cheng erected a plaque therein wishing "Long Life to the Emperor of the Great Ming Dynasty." In the twenty-first year of the Yong Le period [1423] his merits were reported to the throne, and he was rewarded . . . by designating him a Major of the Brocaded Robe Security Corps, and later raising him to Lieutenant Governor of the Military Area of Zhejiang Province.

Prior to the passing of the Pax Mongolica, the ruling khans in China had encouraged maritime commerce across the Indian Ocean and the Arabian Sea, as well as overland trade. This policy was at first continued by the Mings. Giant four-masted Chinese junks, containing four decks to accommodate a crew of hundreds, dwarfed the ships of all other nations. The emperor's mariners commanded further respect for their navigation skills and their weaponry, both the magnetic compass and gunpowder being Chinese inventions. But in 1424 the traditional ethnocentrism and xenophobia of the Chinese reasserted itself. Convinced that more might be lost than gained by trade and other contact with the barbarians, the emperor severely curtailed and then banned all long-distance voyages and even the building of ocean vessels. This left the less formidable but still quite efficient Arab *dhows* to dominate the trade in spices, medicines, and silk across the Indian ocean and Arabian Sea. It also left the Europeans doubly and triply dependent on the enemies of Christ—for the cargos of drugs, spices, and silk always had to be discharged at Arabian ports before being transshipped to Europe, often with Jews, the traditional bridge between Christendom and the House of Islam, serving as middlemen. Fortunately for Christian Europe, there was still the overland route from China to the Black Sea ports of the Crimea, even if these had become less safe and reliable with the end of the Pax Mongolica. But this passage, too, came under the control of the Infidel when in 1453 the Islamized Turks captured Constantinople and with it the access to the Black Sea.

By now, however, Europe, having a few centuries earlier awakened from the Dark Ages, was feeling a burst of intellectual and cultural energy and a drive toward expansion that would culminate in the Renaissance and the Age of Exploration. The time seemed ripe for European vessels, particularly those of the sea-faring Portuguese, to venture directly into the Eastern waters. But the Portuguese mariners, inspired by Prince Henry the Navigator, had no firsthand knowledge of India and the Indian Ocean. Here again, the Jews, as a bridge between East and West, proved invaluable. In the late fourteenth century on the island of Majorca off the Spanish coast in the Mediterranean, the Jewish cartographer Abraham Crescas—designated by Juan of Aragon as "Master of Maps and Compasses"—had produced the beautiful Catalan Atlas, depicting all the known world with unprecedented accuracy. In this endeavor, Crescas drew not only from Arab sources and Marco Polo, but particularly from the Jew Joseph the Physician (Yuceff Faquin), said to have been the world's most traveled man.

Missing from the Catalan Atlas, however, was any description of the southern half of Africa. It was around the southern tip that the Portuguese vessels would have to sail if they were ever to enter the Eastern waters. Yet there was no record of any such voyage or any knowledge of whether the seas converged. But fortunately, there was the physician-astronomer Abraham Zacuto, one of the most prominent of the Zacuto scientific and medical dynasty, who after being expelled from Spain in 1492 became Astronomer Royal to the Portuguese kings João II and Manuel. Abraham's favorable advice to the royal court ("in this province there are great riches and merchandise which are conveyed to many parts of the world . . . . Sire, your planet is high under your Royal device"), perhaps encouraged by reports from Jews in Cairo that Africa did indeed have a southern tip, led to Vasco da Gama rounding the Cape of Good Hope, as the jubilant Portuguese named it.

However, Vasco da Gama's debt to the Jewish physician-astronomers in general and to Zacuto in particular involved much more than just this favorable advice, for they were the great developers of celestial navigation devices. We have seen how Jewish astronomer-astrologers were prominent in the Islamic world in the eighth and ninth centuries. Most notable was Mashallah of Egypt, the author of (as it was known in the Latin translation from the Arabic) *De Scientia Motus Orbis,* on which he based his construction of astrolabes. In southern France the scholar-philosopher (and probably physician) Levi ben Gershon, also known as Gersonides, developed the quadrant, or "Jacob's staff," for measuring visual angles. In the fourteenth century, the physician-astronomer Isaac Nafuci, the favorite of King Pedro IV of Aragon, perfected extremely accurate clocks and quadrants on the island of Majorca. Abraham Zacuto improved the astrolabe and wrote an almanac—invaluable aids to navigation as well as for medical indications (determining the days on which to carry out or refrain from phlebotomy) and the calculation of holidays for the Jewish calendar. As King Manuel later wrote: "In those days of maritime exploration there is no knowing how many voyages were indebted to the scientific work of Zacuto; certain it is, however, that Vasco da Gama, the first navigator who made the voyage to the East Indies by the Cape of Good Hope, utilized Zacuto's *Almanach Perpetuum* as an aid to navigation."

Da Gama departed Lisbon in July 1497. Already seven months earlier, King João, bowing to the wishes of his prospective parents-in-law, Ferdinand and Isabella of Spain, had ordered all Jews to convert or leave Portugal within a year. Many Jews and Jewish physicians accepted nominal conversion. These were to play a continuing role in medicine as Portugal expanded east and west. Zacuto's descendants underwent nominal baptism and were able to remain in Portugal until the screws of the Holy Inquisition tightened. In a later chapter, we will encounter his great-grandson Abraham Zacutus Lusitanius IV, one of the most renowned physicians of the early seventeenth century, as a refugee in Amsterdam. It was, however, in the House of Islam that the fleeing Iberian Jews and their doctors first sought sanctuary. The elder Zacuto himself escaped to North Africa and eventually died in Damascus. Other refugee Jewish doctors would serve at the courts of the beys of Tunis and Tripoli and the pasha of Egypt.

Most of all, fleeing Iberian Jews were drawn to the tolerant realm of the Ottoman Turks. The Turks were a people of central Asian nomadic origin akin to the Mongols, who like the Mongols converted to Islam as they expanded westward. In the twelfth through fourteenth centuries they overran Asia Minor (renamed Turkey) and in 1453 they captured Constantinople (called Istanbul in Turkish). The Ottomans then spent the next hundred years or so establishing a sizable empire that encompassed Egypt, the Holy Land and the Arabian coast in the Middle East, and Greece, the Balkans, and the Crimea in Europe. In the twelfth century Benjamin of Tudela had written of how the Jews of Constantinople, then under Greek Orthodox rule, although fairly prosperous, had been subjected to various humiliations. (For example, no Jew was permitted to ride a horse—the sole exception being, of course, the emperor's physician, Rabbi Solomon Hamistri.) But three centuries later the Jews fleeing the Inquisition in Iberia found a welcome under the tolerant Islamic Turkish sultan Bayezid II.

That the settling of the exiled Jews in the Ottoman Empire went hand in hand with Turkey's rise to great power status was not entirely coincidental. "You call Ferdinand a wise king, he who impoverishes his country and enriches our own!" exclaimed Bayezid, with reference to the refugees. That Spain's loss was indeed Turkey's gain is attested to by an account given by a Spanish Christian visitor: "Here at Constantinople are many Jews, descendants of those whom the Catholic King Don Ferdinand ordered to be driven forth of Spain, and would that it had pleased God that they be drowned in the sea coming hither! For they taught our enemies the most of what they know of the villainies of war, such as the use of the brass ordinance and of firelocks." This quite accurate assessment of the Turkish Jews would be falsely extended to their coreligionists in Austria, Bohemia, Hungary, and elsewhere in Europe proper, whom the Christians accused of abetting the Turkish invasion.

Aside from contributing to the Ottoman Empire's military power, the Jews of Turkey were, of course, also instrumental in their country's commercial and economic expansion. Yet it was in two other areas that the Jewish refugees from Christendom left their most distinctive mark. One of these was printing, which was previously unknown in Turkey. The highly literate Jewish immigrants brought with them from Spain their Medieval Castilian language, which would come to be called Ladino—the Sephardic counterpart of Yiddish, likewise written with Hebrew script—and which they would maintain on Ottoman soil for centuries to come. The Jews soon set up presses for their own literature, but when it came to printing Turkish texts, they were restricted by the authorities from using the traditional Arabic characters, as this would in theory defile the holy script and in practice infringe upon the vested interests of the scribes and calligraphers. So, until the ban was lifted some 200 years later, Turks could read their own printed works only in Roman or Hebrew script, printed mostly by Jews. (It was, incidentally, not until the twentieth century that Turkish officially switched from the Arabic script to Roman letters.)

The other great contribution of the Jews to the Ottoman Empire was, of course, medicine. Distinguished physicians such as the notable philosopher Moses Hamon and his sons served at the court of Bayezid II and his successors. But the historically most important of the exiled Iberian physicians to find refuge under Turkish rule was Juan Rodrigo, better known as Amatus Lusitanius, born in Castello Branco, Portugal, in 1511. When the new Portuguese king followed the Spanish example and brought the Inquisition to his country, Amatus fled to Antwerp, where he established a flourishing practice. Such was his renown that, at the age of 29, Amatus was invited by the Italian duke Hercules d'Este II to occupy the chair of medicine in Ferrara. Among his distinguished patients was Pope Julius III and his extended family. But in 1555 a new, vehemently anti-Jewish pope, Julius IV, ascended to the Holy See. Jewish real estate was auctioned off, ghettos established, the yellow badge ordered, and the ban on the treatment of Christian patients by Jewish doctors reinstated.

The Holy Inquisition in Italy now moved vigorously to determine the sincerity of the Christian convictions of the supposedly Catholic Jews there. Amatus was attacked by envious rivals as a false convert: "For as you now pretend to adhere to our faith (so I learn), and then give yourself over to Jewish laws and superstitions and thus insult not only your fellow beings, but also God, the Almighty . . . so in truth you are completely blind to medical art which you unworthily profess." After twenty-four Jews were burned at the stake in 1556 and Amatus's home was broken into and his books and manuscripts confiscated, the doctor joined many of his coreligionists in fleeing to the hospitable realm of Sultan Bayezid, there to openly re-espouse the Jewish faith. The Ottoman Empire encompassed the ancient Greek cradle of medicine—Hippocrates's Isle of Cos, and the Greek mainland, where Aristotle and the other Hellenic philosophers had developed their theories of elements and biology—as well as Galen's Pergamon in Asia Minor. Thus Amatus, steeped in traditional Greco-Roman medicine, was physically returning to his medical roots.

In the decade before he apparently succumbed to the plague that ravaged the Ottoman port of Salonica in Greece in 1568, Amatus completed his *Centuriae* series, so called because each of the seven books contained 100 medical case histories with commentaries and discussions. At a time when syphilis was ravaging Europe, Amatus, a skilled botanist, wrote of the therapeutic use of sarsaparilla, guaiacum, and the China root, brought by Portuguese sailors from the Far East and the New World. For other (gynecological) problems of the reproductive system, Amatus recommended the topical use of the arsenical compound auripigment—some three and a half centuries before Paul Ehrlich's development of the safe arsenic Salvarsan. One of the most important points in Amatus's writings was his recommendation (based on trials with corpses) of the proper place between the lower ribs for drainage of a patient suffering from empyema. His medical curiosa included cases of hermaphroditism (change at puberty from male to female predominant sexual characteristics, or vice versa). Amatus furthermore voiced his opposition to superstition, including reliance on lunar phases, and he once helped acquit a woman of charges of witchcraft by showing that her supposed victim became deaf due to syphilis rather than to a hex.

In historical retrospect, however, by far the most important of Amatus's works involved his reference—the first ever to appear in print—to the valves of the veins, in particular the azygos vein at the juncture where it feeds into the vena cava (the great vein that carries the circulated blood back to the heart). Not content merely with passive postmortem observations, Amatus conducted a long series of experiments with corpses by which he blew compressed air into veins above and below the azygos valve juncture and noted how the veins at either side of the valve did or didn't bulge.

This kind of experimentation was very much in the spirit of the Renaissance. But although Amatus was not so subservient to Galen as never to contradict him (for example, Amatus did correctly point out that, unlike what Galen believed, the optic nerves aren't hollow and the human uterus cavity isn't divided), Amatus was, like his contemporaries, still very much under the sway of the ancient master, especially in so important a matter as the cardiovascular system. This influenced Amatus's observations and his interpretations of them, and led him not to dispute Galen's doctrine that blood sloshes back and forth from the heart through the same veins. The valves, Amatus reasoned, must be merely slight hindrances to the flow of blood away from the heart. Perhaps this was intended—so speculated a few decades later the famed professor of anatomy at Padua, Hieronymus Fabricus, who may or may not have known of Amatus's previous publications—to prevent the extremities from receiving too much blood at the expense of the vital upper portions of the body. It was left to one of Fabricus's students, the great William Harvey early in the seventeenth century, to finally break out of the Galenic mind-set and correctly perceive the one-way function of the valves of the veins, which he then used as a powerful argument for the circulation, rather than ebb and flow, of the blood.

Like many other Jewish physicians, Amatus addressed the ethical as well as the scientific side of medicine. Among the lines in his *Oath* were the declarations: "I swear by God the Almighty and Eternal . . . I have given my services in equal manner to all, to Hebrews, Christians, and Moslems [and that] I have published my medical works not to satisfy ambition, but that I might, in some measure, contribute to the furtherance of the health of mankind. . . ." In such esteem was Amatus held that when he succumbed to the plague he was combating, the poet Didacus Pyrrhus composed an epitaph that reads (in translation):

He who so often halted the spirit fleeing from the dying body,
now he has been summoned to the waters of Lethe;
He who showed loving kindness equally to the people and to the
great—here he lies. Dying Amatus embraces this earth.
Lusitania was his home: His lonely grave finds its place in the
Macedonian earth, far from his fatherland,
For his great day, his day of death, came and the fatal hour and
led him to the Stygian river; the way goes forward directly
to the other world.

Other Portuguese Jews and Jewish physicians forced to convert to Christianity and hoping to evade the Inquisition were attracted to reaches of the Portuguese Empire far to the east of the Turkish sultan's realms. Among the Portuguese sailing to India was the New Christian physician and professor of logic at the University of Lisbon Garcia d'Orta. The Inquisition in Portugal persecuted his family and executed his sister in an auto-da-fé on charges of continuing to practice Judaism secretly. Garcia would himself be condemned posthumously, his bones dug up and burned. But while he lived, Dr. Garcia was hailed as the most important contributor to pharmacology since the fall of Rome. The records of the Inquisition, even as late as the eighteenth century, show that he was by no means the only Marrano physician in Goa and elsewhere in India to be charged with secret Judaizing, and that he was in fact lucky to be dead when he was burned at the stake.

When the Portuguese first reached the shores of India around the turn of the sixteenth century, they encountered, among other things, a system of medicine with orally transmitted, and later written, texts dating back to the Sanskrit *Vedas* of the Aryans who invaded the subcontinent some three millennia earlier. Situated between East and West, the Indian physicians knew a medical system similar to the four elements of the Greeks and also identified a variety of health-points on the body (*marmas*) with resemblance to Chinese theory. All this was heavily overlaid with religious incantations and supernatural portents. But on a practical level, the Indian physicians excelled in surgery and had an impressive pharmacopoeia at their disposal.

Although the Portuguese Jews, like all Portuguese, were newcomers to India, other Jews had in fact already been settled there for at least five centuries. Indeed, throughout the Middle Ages Jews from Europe and the Near East who had been plying the Arabian Sea in order to bring the delicacies of India to the West were aided by their coreligionists living in the Indian coastal cities. Perhaps the indigenous Jews of India also aided in the transmission of medical knowledge to their new-found coreligionist Garcia d'Orta, whose *Coloquio dos simples e drogas,* published in Goa in 1563, was the first scientific work in the Portuguese language and the highlight of the Portuguese Renaissance. In it d'Orta provided not only an extensive classification of Indian medicinal plants but also first-rate descriptions of Eastern diseases such as Asiatic cholera. D'Orta's work was carried on by another Marrano physician, Cristoval Acosta, known as "the African." The years of travel and research by this botanist and surgeon in India and other tropical countries achieved fruition in 1578 with the publication of his *Tractado de las drogas* ("Treatise on the Drugs and Medicines of India"), in a sense an update of d'Orta's work of the previous decade.

Meanwhile, another Marrano doctor, Luis d'Almeida, was making his mark at the farthest reaches of the Asian continent. D'Almeida was born in Lisbon around 1525, the son of forcibly converted Jewish parents, at a time when the era of acceptance of the New Christians as the equals in Christ of the Old Christians was drawing to a close. D'Almeida set sail for the Orient, where he engaged in trade at the easternmost ports of Portugal's new seaborne empire. He also engaged in the study of medicine and in 1552 entered the Jesuit order in Yamaguchi, Japan, as an *irmo* (brother). At the time there existed among the Buddhists and Shintoists a community of Japanese converts to Christianity. A quite wealthy man, d'Almeida is said to have donated his worldly fortune to the activities of the financially hard-pressed order.

The Japanese physicians, who had imported the Chinese system of medicine from the mainland when an epidemic struck their islands some 1,000 years earlier, were at a stage of development, or rather underdevelopment, comparable to that of their European colleagues. At least, as d'Ameida remarked in his letters, the Japanese—certainly the nobles and the wealthy—were characterized by an "exquisite cleanliness," which had definite hygienic benefits. The lower and needy classes, however, lacked medical care. Then there was the Japanese practice euphemistically referred to as *mabiki* (thinning our seedlings), but in fact meaning abortion, infanticide, and exposure to get rid of unwanted children. All this appalled d'Almeida, who in 1556 established a foundling hospital at Funai (present-day Oita), where he also taught medicine. D'Almeida soon raised funds to expand it with a hospital for lepers and syphilitics, and he saw to the pharmacy being supplied with herbs and other medicines from the Portuguese colony of Macao. Being a unique institution of its kind in Japan, the hospital was attracting some 200 patients from near and far within three years of its opening.

The last decades of the sixteenth century marked an end to the previous toleration by the Jesuits of padres of Jewish descent in their ranks. But

soon their intolerance was repaid in kind by the Japanese rulers, who instituted a crackdown on Christianity and a kind of reverse Inquisition.
Foreigners, including, of course, Marranos, were expelled *en masse* and Japan
kept its doors to the outside world virtually shut for the next two and a
half centuries.

As for the Jews in China, in succeeding generations many would rise to
prominence as An Cheng had. These included the eighteenth-century physician Ai Yinggui, who was also a distinguished man of letters. The Xiangfu
Gazette records his fame as an expert in the art of pulse-taking and a curer
of many ailments—talents he passed on to his physician son Xiansheng.
However, the ancient Chinese-Jewish community was already on its slow
but inexorable course to extinction. Mao tse-Tung would have a Jewish
physician, yet this was not a Chinese but a Soviet Jew (who, incidentally,
was arrested on Stalin's orders for supposedly being involved in the so-
called Doctors' Plot). The necessity for the Jewish pioneer men in the Far
East to intermarry with Han (ethnic Chinese) women had not only made
the faces of the Chinese Jews hardly distinguishable from those of their
neighbors but had weakened their older clan ties. Furthermore, for aspiring Chinese-Jewish professionals and bureaucrats, there were the State
examinations to be passed, which required long years memorizing the
Confucian classics at the expense of Jewish education. Today, little more
remains than some Chinese with the family name Li to whom some vague
awareness has been transmitted that centuries ago they were of the clan
Lie Wei (Levi). And there are Moslem Chinese who wear caps of blue rather
than the usual white—quite possibly a relic from the days before their Jewish
ancestors, no longer numerous enough to conduct their own services, began
to frequent the much larger mosques, seeing Islam as the closest alternative to their own religion.

In Turkey, by contrast, there remains to this day a small number of Jews
who have resisted conversion to Islam and immigration to America or Israel. But their glory days in medicine, as in other fields, have long since
passed. From the time of Bayezid II onward, a long series of Turkish sultans—Sulaiman I, Mahmud II, Selim II, Sulaiman II (the Magnificent),
Ahmad III, and Murad IV, to name but a few—employed as their court
physicians refugees from Iberia and their descendants. But in due course
the intellectual and commercial fervor of the Turkish Jews began to wane.
As a French visitor remarked:

Little by little . . . the taste for study and letters was lost among the Jews of Turkey. When the Greeks, following their example, began to study the languages of Europe, the fear of being supplanted by them, instead of stimulating their ardor, struck [the Jews] with a kind of apathy, and they saw themselves gradually dispossessed of their position as interpreters and other lucrative functions which they had occupied at the Sublime Porte and in the chanceries. . . . While the other communities, Christian and Muslim, familiarized themselves more and more with the languages and affairs of Europe, [the Jews] continued to remain stationary, and, with apparent indifference, saw their riches pass into the hands of their rivals.

So it was that when in the mid-nineteenth century Sultan Abd al-Hamid sought a Marrano-descendant to be his court physician, he had to import Dr. Jacques de Castro from France. For across the mountain ranges to southern France had flowed for centuries the enormous medical knowledge of Italy and Iberia, carried in the books and minds of Jewish doctors who were sometimes merely travelers, but more often refugees fleeing for their lives. It is to them that we now turn.

Chapter 6
The Stars across the Pyrenees

The great King abandoned by the Physicians,
By fate not the Jew's art he remains alive,
He and his kindred pushed high in the realm,
Pardon given to the race which denies Christ.

—Nostradamus, *The Centuries*

Credulous France, what are you doing, hanging on the words of Nostradamus? What
sort of Jewish sorcery restrains your anger?

—Jules-César Scaliger

A poor miser, of Jewish race, a great charlatan, meager in science, rich in chemical
and pharmaceutical knavery (who) assassinated various persons.

—critic of Antoine d'Aquin, *premier médecin* to Louis XIV

*T*he marble portals that stand before the University of Montpellier attest to the historical greatness of that institution, founded around the turn of the thirteenth century on the French Mediterranean coast, not far from the border with Spain. To be seen to this day inscribed in the portals are the names of the Medieval medical scholars Isaac ben Abraham, Meschulam, and Shem Tov ben Isaac. The irony is that, being Jews, they probably were barred from official faculty posts. At most, they may have taught informally at the university's medical school. Yet no one questions the appropriateness of the inscription or its symbolic importance. For it was the Jews from the south—from Italy, but particularly the refugees from religious persecution in Iberia—who contributed so much to the rise of

France as a center of medical learning in the Late Middle Ages and the Renaissance.

Already in the twelfth century, when Iberia was still largely under the hitherto relatively tolerant crescent of Islam, a hemorrhaging of Jewish medical knowledge occurred when the fanatical Moslem Almohade sect swept to power in Spain and demanded conversion to Islam. Many Jews fled across the Pyrenees to Provence and Langedoc. Maimonides, as we have seen, sought refuge in North Africa and the Middle East. Yet he maintained contact with his French brethren and was particularly laudatory of their religious fervor. "You, members of the congregation of Lunel, and of neighboring towns, stand alone in raising aloft the banner of Moses," he wrote. "You apply yourselves to the study of the Talmud, and also cherish wisdom. But in the East the Jews are dead to spiritual aims. . . . Thus it remains to you alone to be a strong support to our religion. Therefore be firm and of good courage, and be united in it." Indeed, the refugees in France were quick to found religious academies in Beziers and Montpellier, as well as in Lunel.

But more important to our story than the religious fervor of the Provençal Jews was the scientific learning they brought with them over the Pyrenees. The independent Jewish schools in Provence also taught medicine and produced many of southern France's finest physicians. A student of Rabbi Albon of Narbonne wrote the anonymous *Book of Medicine,* highly prized at Montpellier. Rabbi Benjamin of Tudela, the "Marco Polo of the Jews" whom we met in the previous chapter, made particularly mention of the Spanish exile Dr. Judah ibn Tibbon, the "father of translators" and teacher at Lunel and Montpellier.

Ibn Tibbon's translating activities were, of course, a continuation of a centuries-old tradition among the multi-literate Jews. But there also emerged a crucial shift, reflecting the new situation in Christian Europe. Throughout the hundreds of years that formed the Golden Age and Twilight of Islamic civilization, Arabic had been the universal language among Jews as well as Moslems from Spain to Persia, the scientific medium of the likes of Isaac Israeli and Maimonides. But whereas the Jewish refugees from the fanatical Almohades were highly literate in Arabic, this was to be less and less so with each succeeding generation of their descendants in France. All Jews, whether in the Christian or Moslem worlds, were, however, literate in Hebrew. As the scientific center of gravity shifted northward, the scientific language of the Jews shifted from Arabic to Hebrew. Refugee scholars such as Judah ibn Tibbon were particularly suitable for the huge and urgent task of translating the great works from the one Semitic language to the other, and Judah also saw to it that his son Samuel remained literate in Arabic so as to continue this work. In this way the works of Averroes, Rhazes, Avenzoar, Avencinna, and, of course, the Jewish Arabic writers such as Isaac Israeli and Maimonides, all became available in Hebrew.

The rise of Hebrew as a scientific lingua franca among the Jews soon meant that ancient Greek and Latin works of Hippocrates and Galen as well were translated into the holy language. So, too, were the contemporary Latin texts of Christian medical writers such as Guy de Chauliac and Roger of Palermo, although not without some misgivings. ("The Christians are not completely lacking in science!" declared the thirteenth-century Jewish translator Judah ben Moses, better known as Judah Romano, by way of apology.) This was followed by Hebrew editions of vernacular Spanish, French, and Italian medical texts. The process, of course, also afforded the Jewish translator the opportunity to add his comments, especially on texts directly concerning his coreligionists. The fourteenth-century *Lilium Medicinae* by Bernard de Gordon included the passage:

> The Jews suffer greatly from hemorrhoids for three reasons: first, because they are generally sedentary and therefore the excessive melancholy humors collect; secondly, because they are usually in fear and anxiety and therefore the melancholy blood becomes increased, besides (according to Hippocrates) fear and faint-heartedness, should they last a long time, produce the melancholy humor; and thirdly, it is divine vengeance against them (as written in Psalms 78:66): and "he smote his enemies in the hinder parts, he put them to a perpetual reproach."

This was duly translated into Hebrew, but not without the commentary: "What is written is a lie, and they who believe it lie." (This disclaimer referred more to the etiological than to the epidemiological part of Gordon's statement. Indeed, even centuries later Yiddish-speaking Jews would declare: *A yiddische yerusche is a guldene uder* [a Jewish inheritance is a golden vein] and *Vas yirushene Yidn? Tsurus en meriden!* [What do Jews inherit? Worries and hemorrhoids!].)

Even in Moslem Spain, some original scientific texts had been written in Hebrew. But now in the Christian world, the ancient tongue of the Jews became a full-fledged international medium for new learning, not least in medicine. Already in the thirteenth century, the great English philosopher-scientist Roger Bacon urged his fellow Christian scholars to learn Hebrew as the key to a storehouse of scientific and medical, as well as theological and philosophical, wisdom. ("Teachers are not wanting," he wrote, "for everywhere there are Hebrews, and their tongue is substantially one with Arabic and Chaldean, though different in manner.") The new tendency would gather such momentum that in time original Hebrew texts on such diverse subjects as dietetics, hemorrhoids, psychology, syphilis, and the Black Death were published from Venice to Amsterdam to Constantinople. Telling is the oration delivered by the rector of the University of Leipzig, Mosellanus, in the sixteenth century, urging Christians to penetrate the medical secrets of the Jews by learning their ancient and revitalized language. Mosellanus (speaking Latin) first bemoaned, yet found totally understandable, the fact that monarchs and popes sooner entrusted their health to Jewish than to Christian physicians. He then declared:

> There lies hidden in the libraries of the Jews a treasure of medical lore so great that it seems incapable of being surpassed by the books in any other language. . . . What prevents our Christian youths of quick intelligence, who are destined for this profession (medicine), from learning this language (Hebrew), in a few years, or if they have a burning desire for study, in a few months, up to a point necessary for comprehending and understanding it?

Previously among the Christians, only some monks and other clerics had knowledge of Hebrew, but around the turn of the sixteenth century, chairs of Hebrew were established at the universities of Bologna, Rome, Louvain, and Paris. Indeed, in history's most important book of anatomy, *De Humani Corporis Fabrica,* which in the mid-sixteenth century finally freed medical science from slavish repetition of Galen's errors by relying on direct observations of dissected corpses, the Belgian-born gentile Andreas Vesalius took care to supply Hebrew equivalents to the various Greek terms.

Although Jews may have been barred from official positions on Montpellier's medical faculty, apparently some Israelites were admitted as students. A proposal that "no one of an alien sect, such as a Jew or Saracen, or anyone else of whatever alien sect he may be, be given instruction by any doctor, master, licentiate, bachelor, scholar, publicly or privately in grammar, logic, philosophy medicine or law or other science" was *rejected* by the university council. The rigorous medical curriculum followed by Jew and gentile at Montpellier was similar to that of Salerno. Much emphasis was placed on acquiring a sound foundation in the liberal arts, considered a necessity for becoming a physician. As a contemporary wrote, "If the doctors have not learned geometry, astronomy, dialectic, nor any other good discipline, soon the leather workers, carpenters, and skinners will quit their own occupations and become doctors."

As for the medical part of the curriculum, up to the publication of Vesalius's *Fabrica* in the mid-sixteenth century, the teaching consistently downplayed the visual in favor of the power of the written word. Even textbooks were typically devoid of anatomical diagrams, a kind of reversal of the proverb of one picture being worth a thousand words. But the medical faculty at Montpellier prided itself on not neglecting the practical side of medicine. "The Parisian and northern physicians study a great deal in order to have a knowledge of the universal, but they do not care to have a particular and experiential knowledge," wrote a critic. "Thus, I remember seeing one who was outstanding in the arts, an excellent naturalist, logician, and theoretician. In medicine, however, he did not know how to apply a clyster or any particular treatment, and he knew hardly how to treat a daily fever."

It was in keeping with the more down-to-earth aspect of the Montpellier curriculum that in 1340 the chancellor of the university was placed "under sworn obligation" to provide the medical faculty with a cadaver for dissection no less than every other year, "because experience is the best teacher." (Although by this time Bologna may have known dissections, this was a century before the Parisian students would see the inside of a body.) The dissections became an annual event when in 1376 King Louis of Anjou ordered that the body of an executed criminal be delivered to the medical faculty each year. Thus the Catholic Church's taboo against the spilling of blood was gradually broken.

In the course of time, dissection would become strongly identified with medical education, as attested to the modern joke "What's the definition of a lawyer?" Answer: "A Jewish boy who couldn't stand the sight of blood." Although the Jewish religion didn't share the Church's general taboos regarding dissections (talmudic prohibitions applied only to Jewish corpses), the dissecting room was to create a problem for Jewish boys who are *kohanim*—that is, descendants of the priestly class of ancient Israel. Leviticus 21:1–3 states: "And the Lord said unto Moses: Speak unto the priests the sons of Aaron, and say unto them: There shall none defile himself for the dead among his people; except for his kin that is near unto him. . . ." For centuries, rabbis would debate whether this precluded a *kohen* from studying medicine. The more lenient authorities would come up with several loopholes, not least of which is the overriding consideration of the (future) physician's ability to save lives.

Even before the close of the eleventh century, the Catholic Church in France had made a major contribution to anti-Jewish legislation when Bishop Ivo of Chartres—also known as Saint Ivo, the patron of lawyers—drew up his decretum incorporating prohibitions on Christian-Jewish interaction and specifically a ban on the faithful taking medicines from Israelite physicians. Three centuries later one of the statutes of Valladolid stated: "It is decreed that there should not be among them (the Jews) a physician." To this, the Hebrew translator added the line "except a physician to the king," an ironic recognition of the fact that royalty throughout Europe were ill-inclined to practice what their faith commanded. The kings and princes of France were no exceptions, and they were in particular awe of the Ibero-Jewish doctors. Thus the viciously anti-Jewish prince Alphonse of Poitier, brother of Louis IX, sought the aid of a Jewish physician, Abraham of Aragon, for his blindness and in fact seems to have plotted to abduct him if need be. A curious and telling incident took place in the mid-sixteenth century, when the long-ailing French king Francis I explicitly requested from Spain's Charles V the aid of that country's best Jewish doctor. There were, officially, no Jews in Spain, but Charles obliged by sending a Marrano. When Francis asked him whether he wasn't tired of waiting for the Messiah, the doctor (whether sincerely or wary of a trap) replied that the Messiah had already come a millennium and a half earlier. The despairing Francis immediately dismissed him and sent to Constantinople for a "real" Jewish doctor, who apparently cured the king with a diet of ass's milk. Not without reason did a contemporary bigot lament: "One trusts a single Jew more than a thousand Christians."

The thirteenth and fourteenth centuries in Christian Europe were an era of the medicalization of society, as the physician's services were sought not only by the secular nobles and the princes of the church, but also by the growing middle class, with their increasing accumulation of wealth from commerce. Medical services to non-clergy commoners, once the exclusive domain of Christian charity, were provided more and more by private practitioners who could expect to be suitably remunerated by their bourgeois patients. This had consequences for the theory and practice of medicine and for the Jews who participated in it. Once, only kings, popes, sultans, or other nobles would be put on physician's diets, or *regimina sanitatis,* in which food intake and other activity would be prescribed only after careful account was taken of "climate"—that is, the specific socio-physical surroundings in which the distinguished patient lived—and his individual *complexio* (constitution or temperament). The less illustrious, unable to command such time-consuming and costly medical procedures, had had to settle for more drastic and dramatic options in the form of powerful drugs. But now in the fourteenth century, as middle-class patients strove to emulate the nobility, the Jewish physicians of Montpellier, Israel ben Joseph Caslari and Joseph ben Judah ha-Sefardi, were motivated to translate into Hebrew the *Regimen sanitatis* of the aforementioned Arnold of Villanova and to add some insightful commentaries of their own. Villanova's diet was custom-made for King Jaume II of Aragon. But the Hebrew translators suggested that by a process of "experimental reasoning," those aspects in medical treatment could be found that were most universal and least dependent on the specific "climate" and the individual's *complexio,* thus providing an affordable if less exclusive regimen. Although the term *experimental* meant "by experience" rather than the systematic manipulation of variables, these proposals by the Jewish doctors indicated a transition to modern medical thinking.

The medicalization of society even extended to the poor. Towns appointed municipal doctors to serve the public health needs of the population at large. This often meant the doctor's analyzing all flasks of urine brought to his office and his advising on proper diet. Doctors were also increasingly called upon by civil authorities to render expert opinions in judicial matters. Despite, or because of, prejudice, the post of municipal physician often went to a Jew. The Jewish doctor's accepting of a lower salary from the town fathers was often regarded by his Christian colleagues as his way of undercutting the going rates while he engaged in other economic activities such as money-lending on the side. More charitable Christians, however, recognized the simple fact that discriminatory measures meant lower pay for Jews. Such was the medicalization of society that by the fourteenth century, many regions of Europe, most particularly Southern France, had a physician-to-population ratio of around 1:500, a figure comparable to that of industrialized nations in the late twentieth century. On average, about half of these Medieval doctors were Jews, even though Jews constituted only about 5 percent of the inhabitants of most cities and towns and only about 1 percent of the European population in general.

If the Jewish doctors were traditionally held in awe for the centuries of medical knowledge to which they were heir, they were also feared for their supposed eternal hatred of Christ and their need to do away with his servants. Even the Jewish doctor's medicinal wine was suspect. A Provençal regulation stipulated that "a Jewish surgeon has to taste from the same wine given to sick ones" and warned against the clever Jew's ruse of claiming the wine was not kosher and therefore forbidden for him to drink. In point of fact, drugs and dosages being such a tricky matter in those days, Jewish doctors *did* poison Christian patients. So, too, did Christian doctors poison Christian patients. And, so did Jewish doctors poison Jewish patients. The latter is attested to by cases in Medieval court records of the venerable Jewish tradition of malpractice suits and countersuits. So, for instance, we find the Jewess Blanqueta in mid-fifteenth century Provence suing Master Vitalis Salves for causing the death of her father, whereupon the Jewish doctor retaliated with a suit charging Blanqueta with having the *chutzpah* of defaming him in the synagogue—on the Day of Atonement, no less.

Jewish doctors were well aware that religious bigotry, which even when not manifest was always lying just beneath the surface, required that they be overachievers and particularly scrupulous. As stated in a late Medieval Hebrew manuscript: "We Jewish doctors in the Diaspora have to possess extraordinary knowledge, for the Christian doctors envy us and challenge us. . . . And if they discover any ignorance on our part they say, 'He kills gentiles.'" Added to this was the fear and awe of the Jew—and all the more, the Jewish doctor—as sexual stranger. Courts in Provence and elsewhere in the late Middle Ages heard accusations about the seduction of Christian women patients. Fortunately, the doctor's medical services were often considered so invaluable that, even if found guilty, the punishment for his supposed transgressions might be commuted, as when a Provençal Jewish physician condemned to "lose his member" got off by paying a fine.

⁓

The awe in which Christian Europe—and, not least of all, France—held the Jewish physician derived not just from his ancient scientific learning but also from his presumed occult powers. This has to be seen in the context of the Christian Church's attitude toward magic in general. When the Roman Empire officially adopted Christianity, the Church Father Augustine declared his opposition to the occult arts. The practices continued, however, and in the ensuing centuries the Church's attitude wavered. As long as the rationalist view of magic as a baseless—and therefore harmless—superstition prevailed among the Church Fathers, magic practices, although perhaps frowned upon, didn't call for active suppression. A contrary view, which gained the upper hand in the late Middle Ages, held that there was real power in sorcery and that this was derived from the devil and his minions. Yet even so, the measures to suppress it were often half-hearted, the assumption being that the Satan's power in Europe had been virtually destroyed by Christianity anyhow. The schism brought about by Protestantism (more about which later) led to a new shift in the Catholic Church's attitude toward the black arts, such that the persecution of sorcerers in league with Satan became as much a part of the Holy Inquisition's brief as the ferreting out of heretics and Judaizers. Yet the Church's efforts may have had the unintended affect of convincing the populace that magic powers were indeed real and worth tapping into.

Especially, in matters of life and death, many a Christian in the Middle Ages and beyond would make recourse to the Jewish doctor's supposed supernatural power, without inquiring too deeply into its source. As we have seen, an aura of mystique already surrounded the Jewish *magi* in pagan Rome. This was carried over by the Christians of the empire as their religion gained ascendancy. The third-century Church Father Origen spoke of magic as a Jewish calling par excellence. Chrysostom of Antioch decried the strange attraction that Christians felt for the power of Judaism and particularly for Jewish charms and amulets. In the early sixth century—some 200 years after the conversion of the Roman Empire to Christianity—we find the Byzantine emperor Justinian resorting to Jewish diviners, this despite the condemnation of *superstitio* and *magia* by St. Augustin and Justinian's own promulgation of anti-Jewish legislation.

In the weltanschauung of the Middle Ages and even beyond, the Jew—

and not least, the Jewish physician—was seen as being in league with the devil and his minions and was assumed to have access to those powers of which a true Christian (and true Christian doctor) should remain innocent. Furthermore, as in the case of the Jewish doctor's access to ancient scientific works, it was assumed that access to the most potent magic required literacy and learnedness, matters in which the Jews in general far outdistanced their Christian neighbors. Faced with a potentially fatal ailment and lacking confidence in the potency of the Church's "good" magic—the figurines, relics, and appeals to saints and martyrs—to save his body in this life rather than his soul in the next, a Catholic king, prince, merchant, or even pope would summon the Jewish physician. The Jew's eternal soul was already lost to heaven, due to his rejection of Christ. While he was on earth, one might as well make use of his occult powers. If need be, these supposed Hebrew powers could themselves serve as a clever excuse for consulting the Jewish doctor, as when two women, accused of violating the Church's prohibition, claimed that the Jewish physician had bewitched them so that they could consult no other practitioner.

But what of the attitude of the Jews themselves to magic powers, whatever their source? The Jews as a whole were, of course, by no means free from beliefs today regarded as occult or superstitious. Yet skepticism toward the concept of black magic was long part of the Jewish tradition, even in the Middle Ages, particularly in the more enlightened Mediterranean area. This tendency was especially noteworthy among Jewish physicians. In his *Guide for the Perplexed* back in the twelfth century, Maimonides had taken to task those who "believed that by means of these arts they could perform wonderful things . . . although no analogy and no reasoning can discover any relation between these performances of the witches and promised result. . . . Great is the number of these stupid and mad things." Such rationalistic views were also found among the community of Jewish physicians who crossed the Pyrenees, as when in the thirteenth century the French Jewish doctor Leo ben Gershon, otherwise known as Leo Hebraeus or Gershonides, attributed the biblical account of Saul's witchcraft to a mental disturbance.

Interesting in this regard are the writings of the famed sixteenth-century French humanist and skeptic Michel de Montaigne, whose mother was of Marrano descent. Montaigne's scathing satires on the medical profession were motivated not just by personal experience but also by family memory—perhaps significantly through his *paternal* line. "The antipathy I have for their [the doctors'] art is hereditary with me. My father lived seventy-four years, my grandfather sixty-nine, my great-grandfather nearly eighty, without having tasted any sort of medicine." Having long suffered from a bladder stone, for which the pompous doctors with their pretentious theories gave contrary and (at best) useless advice, Montaigne wrote:

> No one, I see, falls sick so often and takes so long to recover as those enthralled by the rules of medicine. Their very health is weakened and injured by their diets and precautions. Doctors are not satisfied to deal with the sick; but they are forever meddling with the well, in order that no one shall escape from under their thumbs. I have been sick often enough that I can endure my disease (and have had a taste of all sorts) and get rid of it as nicely as anyone else, and without adding to it the vileness of their prescriptions.

About the kindest thing Montaigne could say about doctors was that "If they do no other good, they do at least this, that they prepare their patients early in life for death, undermining little by little and cutting off their enjoyment of life." Yet Montaigne's skeptical worldview pertained no less to superstitious nonsense as to the pseudoscience of Renaissance medicine. Thus witchcraft, too, became the target of his scathing pen.

Also in sixteenth-century France, Montaigne's fellow Marrano descendant Dr. Andres a Laguna provided an especially important case history regarding sorcery. Although a devout Catholic and physician to Popes Paul III and Julius III, the Spanish-born Laguna was probably influenced by previous Jewish thinking on witches. As municipal physician in the French town of Metz he was called to the bedside of the fatally ill Duke of Lorraine, who believed that an old couple had bewitched him—an accusation to which the couple themselves, who were rumored to be sorcerers, admitted and even supplied all sorts of details of their pact with the devil. Laguna fully believed in the devil and his works, in line with Catholic dogma. But perhaps as a result of his Jewish heritage, he took a rather rationalist position in this matter, maintaining that Satan "cannot work except through natural causes." In this particular case, it meant the devil duping the would-be witches to anoint themselves with an unguent composed of ingredients—cicuta, nightshade, henbane, and mandrake—that according to Galenic theory, had a strong cooling effect. This induced not only sleep but also hallucinations, in which the dreamers committed the most fantastic and devilish deeds, which they fully believed upon awakening, even though (as Laguna empirically showed) "neither in spirit nor in body do they ever quit the spot where they fall overcome with sleep."

Such was Laguna's fame—he is even mentioned by Cervantes in *Don Quixote*—that his writings could not but carry weight in the early Renaissance. Yet strong popular and judicial belief in witchcraft continued through the seventeenth century, causing hundreds of thousands of victims to perish at the stake. Of these, some were probably genuine participants in witch cults. Others belonged to outgrowths of earlier heretical sects forced underground. Still others were people afflicted with mass hysteria brought about by the spirit of the times and the often miserable health conditions. Many were, of course, the unfortunate victims of other people's imagination or deliberate malice.

Somewhere between religion, superstition, pseudoscience, and what we today recognize as genuine science, there is a Twilight Zone whose borders have continually shifted throughout the centuries. One of these was the Great Art of alchemy, the other, the even Greater Art of astrology. In both of these the Jews excelled, though more so and for far longer in the latter.

The very word *alchemy*—derived from an Arabic definite article added on to a Greek noun—attests to the fact that the Great Art was transmitted in a similar way as was Hippocratic and Galenic medicine. And as in the case of medicine, the Jews were prominent in alchemy—so much so, in fact, that not a few Christian alchemists peppered their texts with Hebrew words and even wrote under Jewish pseudonyms. The Jews of fourteenth- and fifteenth-century Europe had all the more motivation to excel in the Great Art, as a shortage of mined gold combined with a very unfavorable balance of trade with the East to produce a money famine. For the Jewish community, which by circumstances depended so much on money-lending and trade for its economic survival, the drying up of coinage was of particular concern. Hopefully, it could be alleviated by the realization of the age-old alchemist dream of transmuting base metals into gold.

Most Jewish alchemists were physicians, often court doctors esteemed by the sovereign for their alchemical wizardry as well as for their healing skills. The connection between alchemist and physician was by no means fortuitous. The alchemical doctrines taught that gold was the perfect substance, all other metals suffering from some illness. Silver, for example, although having achieved a degree of perfection, was leprous but capable of being turned into gold if "cured" of its leprosy by the alchemist. In a similar vein, practitioners of the Great Art sought to discover the elixir of life, which would restore health and youth to the human body. Not surprising, perhaps, in view of the age-old association between Jews and medicine, the writings of the Jewish alchemists were particularly strong on the medical aspects, although, of course, gold-making was by no means ignored.

The pseudoscientific aspects of alchemy would, in the course of centuries, be replaced by the solid principles of the science of chemistry. There, too, the Jews would play a wildly disproportionate role and, as we shall see, not in the least in the application of chemistry to modern medicine. The advent of the atomic theory would show the vanity of attempting by any chemical reaction to "cure" one element and thus change it into another. Jewish chemical wizards would fashion magic bullets capable, if not of curing sick silver into the perfect substance gold, then of transforming disease-ridden men into healthy beings. With astrology and medicine, however, there would be no parallel modern developments. For centuries the relationship of the stars to healing was especially intimate and flowered, as we shall see, in Southern France. But when astronomy divested itself of its pseudoscientific aspects, so, too, did it almost entirely divorce itself from modern medicine.

In chapter upon chapter we have seen how involved the Jews were in the science of the heavens. In biblical times the Hebrews were exposed to the astronomy and astrology of the Babylonians, who divided the moon's yearly migration through the heavens into twelve zodiac signs, each with the domain of one lunar cycle. Daniel, instructed in the language and learning of the Chaldean soothsayers under orders of King Nebuchadrezzar, became "ten times better than all the magicians and astrologers that were in all his realm" (Daniel 1:20).

Traditional Jewish life could truly be said to have been determined by the heavenly bodies, though not necessarily in the astrological sense. The calendar the Jews adopted was meticulously based on the positions of the celestial objects, which, in combination with various regulations, determined the exact dates and times of the Sabbath, holy days, and monthly prayer days. Its drawing up called for highly skilled calculations of positions of the heavenly bodies for months or years into the future. Hardly surprisingly, the Jews of Alexandria gladly absorbed the astronomical theories and methods of the Greeks—so much so that they even entertained a myth that their stargazing patriarch Abraham was the true originator of Ptolemy's theory of concentric celestial spheres. And we have seen how Jews of the talmudic period were adept in astronomy, most particularly the Babylonian physician Mar Samuel, who was "as familiar with the paths of heaven as with the streets of Nehardea," could "make a calendar [of leap years] for the whole Diaspora" and could calculate the intercalation of months sixty decades ahead.

The Jewish expertise in the science of the heavens blossomed during the Golden Age of Islamic civilization, particularly in Iberia, where Israelites were favored as court astronomers. As the peninsula reverted to Christian rule, Jewish translators such as Johannes of Seville and Master Abraham (the latter under the auspices of Alfonso the Wise) conveyed to Christian Spain much of the astronomical and astrological science of the shrinking Moslem world. When Spain and Portugal prepared to burst out of the confines of their peninsula, the Jewish court astronomers (who, like the great Abraham Zacuto and Gershonides, were often also court physicians) were indispensable for the astrolabes, almanacs, quadrants, clocks, and other navigational aids they provided. But persecutions, first by the fanatical Islamic Almohades in the thirteenth century and then by the Catholic monarchs and the Holy Catholic Inquisition in the sixteenth, forced thousands of Jews, along with their vast knowledge of heavenly as well as human bodies, to flee across the Pyrenees.

Thus did Southern France, and particularly Montpellier, become the great new center of celestial learning. Already in the thirteenth century under the auspices of Robert of Anjou, physician-astronomer Maestro Calo (Kalonymos ben Kalonymos) translated the works on the stations of the moon by the great Arab astronomer al-Kindi, just as he translated into Hebrew various works of Galen. Highly prominent at the University of Montpellier in the late thirteenth and early fourteenth centuries was the Jewish astronomer Profatius Judaeus (Jacob ben Mahir ibn Tibbon, a descendant of Judah ibn Tibbon, whom we met at the beginning of this chapter). It was he who translated into Provençal (he was not proficient enough in Latin) the astronomical tables of al-Zarqali, known as *Saphea*. In 1288 Profatius wrote an astronomy tract in Hebrew, which a mere two years later appeared in Latin and soon became known as *Quadrans novus*. Likewise speedily translated into Latin was the set of astronomical charts, the *Almanach*, that Profatius drew up for the longitude of Montpellier for the year 1300, and his treatise on the phases of the moon.

Along with their centuries of knowledge of the science of astronomy, the Jews of Southern France brought from Spain a certain measure of belief in the pseudoscience of astrology. It was the aforementioned Calo who, in his ethical tractate *Even Bochan* (The Touchstone), interpreted the talmudic line "the best of physicians is destined for Gehenna (hell)" as referring not to genuine doctors, but to quacks, since "their art is lying and deception; all their boasting is empty falsehood; their hearts are turned away from God and their hands are covered in blood." Yet Calo no doubt considered astrology anything but deceptive, at least when practiced by those competent in it. Among the great Spanish physician-astronomers was Abraham ben Meir ibn Ezra (also known as Abraham Judaeus), who traveled through France, as well as Italy and England, and was influential among Christians and Jews alike. As the Amsterdam Rabbi Menasseh ben Israel, a refugee from Iberia, would later declare: "And now, since the God-given Torah and the words of our rabbis prove the truth of this science, who can deny it? In all periods there have been great astrologers among our people, and most notable in the land of Spain." Jews in France as elsewhere continued to consult the stars to determine such things as when to marry, when to engage in trade, when to undertake a journey, and when to (as it were) be born. By 1500 there were an estimated 250 or more practicing Jewish astronomers, most of whom dabbled in astrology as well. Telling is that the Hebrew word *mazel*, which to this day is used colloquially by Jews in whatever language they speak, originally meant "star" as well as "luck."

Yet of all the peoples of the earth, the Jews were rather unique in having a long tradition of skepticism toward astrology. As noted in earlier chapters, the biblical Jews, with their monotheistic aversion to idolatry, rejected the Babylonian view of the planets as gods or even, in the watered-down version, as being controlled by their respective deities. (Zephenia: "I will cut off the remnant of Baal from this place . . . and them that worship the host of heaven upon the housetops." Jeremiah [10:2]: "Do not dread the signs of heaven, like the heathens, who fear them.") Josephus and Tacticus wrote of astrology's relative lack of appeal to the Jews at a time when the Roman Empire was obsessed by oracles. Mar Samuel exempted the Jews from planetary influences, in accordance with the talmudic legend that quotes Abraham as saying: "I have seen in the stars that I will have only one son," to which God retorted: "Leave your astrology; for Israel there are no stars" (Nedarim 32a).

This Jewish hard-headedness was reinforced in the Middle Ages by Maimonides, particularly in his response to a query from the Jewish community of Southern France. "It is true," the Rambam conceded, "that you will find stray utterances in the rabbinical literature which imply a belief in the potency of the stars. But," he hastened to add in the spirit of his *Guide for the Perplexed,* "no one is justified in surrendering his own rational opinions because this or that sage erred, or because an allegorical remark is expressed literally. A man must never cast his own judgment behind him; the eyes are set in front, not in the back." "Know, my masters, that no man should believe anything which is not attested by one of these three sanctions: rational proof, as in mathematical science; the perception of the senses; or tradition from prophets and the righteous." Astrology—as opposed to astronomy—failed on all three points. Worse yet, it verged on idolatry and, by its implication of a foreordained future, robbed life of its purpose.

In his opinion, the Rambam was supported by his otherwise philosophical opponent Moses of Tachau, who took to task "those men to whom the spirit of the Torah is foreign, who busy themselves with astrology and believe in it and make it their creed, and thereby bring harm to others." Even those Medieval Jews who believed in astrology tended to be dissuaded by their religious traditions from an overly fatalistic interpretation. If the stars were created by God to serve a special function, then the extent of their power was subject to His will. And this could be influenced by human actions such as repentance, prayer, and good works.

That the great Jewish stargazers of the Middle Ages were typically also physicians was hardly coincidental. For so long as medicine was stuck with the false, though rational, Greco-Roman formulations about humors and their properties, so the equally false, though rational, concepts of what might be called astro-medicine could continue to exert their influence. Medieval Jewish physicians such as Eleazar of Worms expounded on Ptolemy's notion of the stars and planets, as well as the Sun and Moon, moving the four Greek elements on Earth and the corresponding four humors in the human body, producing the respective properties of heat, cold, dryness, and moistness. Astronomical data such as Profatius's table of Moon phases was considered vital for physicians for the prognostic information it gave about the critical days such as those determining the duration of fevers. Isaac Judaeus's *Tractactus de febribus* was prominent on the required reading list at the University of Montpellier. At the end of the fifteenth century, the physician to Pope Alexander VI, Bonet de Lates (Rabbi Jacob ben Immanuel Proviniale), invented the astronomical ringdial, which he dedicated in the pontiff.

Still more important to the Medieval physician, for whom bloodletting was a staple of medical treatment, was the presumed influence of the heavenly bodies on the blood humor. Certain so-called Egyptian days were deemed unfavorable for phlebotomy. Jewish doctors in particular shied away from bleeding on the eve of a holiday or on Hoshana Rabbah and they took account of other supposed do-not-bleed periods such as the first day of Iyar, Elul, and Tebet when these fell on a Monday or Wednesday; the entire months of Tamuz, Ab, Elul, and Shebat; and/or the period between Passover and Lag B'omer. Medieval illuminated manuscripts written in Hebrew showed the various zodiac signs superimposed upon diverse parts of a human body. Scorpio, for example, appears superimposed on the genitals, with its tail extending down the length of the (circumcised) penis. The illustration guided the doctor in determining the most effective times for bloodletting and other medical or surgical treatment. In his classic work on the concordance of medicine and astrology, the sixteenth-century Marrano physician Hieronymous de Chaves, cosmographer to the king of Spain and professor of cosmography in Seville, made particular reference to the critical days for bleeding, purging, and surgery.

As great as was the involvement of the Medieval and Renaissance Jewish physicians in the arcane sciences of the heavens, their names are all but forgotten except to a few historians. There is, however, one exception to this: a Provençal medical doctor of pure Jewish descent who would become broadly synonymous with astrological prophecy for centuries to come and who bore the improbable family name of Our Lady—or in its Latinate version, Nostradamus.

For several centuries, Jews in the area of Provence, straddling the Mediterranean from the east of Montpellier to the Italian march, had been living in relative tolerance—although they did feel the effects of the Christians' wrath during the crusade against the Albigensian heretics in the thirteenth century and during the visitation of the plague a century later. Toleration was particularly evident in the fifteenth century under Count René, fittingly known as the Good. By his edict of 1454 Jews were not only completely free to practice their religion but could also engage in commerce, the arts, finance, and, of course, medicine.

However, in the wake of the death of René in 1480 and of the only other male descendant of the House of Anjou six years later, Provence reverted to the king of France, Charles VIII, who soon ordered all Jews to be baptized. This command, which preceded by a few years a similar edict by Ferdinand and Isabella of Spain, was at first not stringently enforced. But in 1501, at the urging of the Vatican, Charles's successor, Louis XII, issued an uncompromising edict whereby all Jews of Provence were given three months in which to convert to Christianity or face confiscation of their property and expulsion. Confronted with the same dilemma as their Iberian Spanish coreligionists, some Jews accepted conversion, at least for public purposes. One of these was a Monsieur Guy de Gassonet of the town of St. Rémy, who then adopted the very Christian name Pierre de Notredame (or Nostredame in the Provençal language). This was the grandfather of Michel de Nostradamus.

In his own writings, Nostradamus told how his grandfather Pierre had been personal physician to Count René. Furthermore, the family was supposedly descendant from the Hebrew tribe of Issachar, which according to some Jewish analysts of the Bible was particularly skilled at calculating the dates of holy feasts and interpreting heavenly signs. If this lineage wasn't illustrious enough, Nostradamus further related how his maternal grandfather, Jean de St. Rémy, another converted Jew, likewise held the post of personal physician at Count René's court. It was at the latter's home that young Michel was raised for several years, where he was tutored in mathematics, Latin, Greek, and Hebrew and was first exposed to the celestial science of astrology.

Research of old civil records by twentieth-century historians would cast doubt on Nostradamus's account of his ancestry. If Jean de Rémy had indeed been a physician, then he was a failed one, who turned to collecting taxes for the king's treasury instead of attending to his body. And Pierre de Notredame and his son Jacques, Nostradamus's father, may have been grain dealers. Even if so, such a lineage is, particularly in retrospect, nothing for a Jewish doctor to be ashamed of. As we shall see in a later chapter, the ancestors of arguably the greatest of all Jewish physicians, Paul Ehrlich, were likewise in the grain business. (Nostradamus, if he really could look centuries into the future, should have known this.) What is not in doubt is that Nostradamus himself became a medical doctor, and a very successful one. On the advice of his grandfather, the 19-year-old Michel, having completed his preliminary liberal arts education in Avignon, was sent by his parents in 1522 to pursue his medical studies at the Univesity of Montpellier.

Just as Nostradamus was licensed as a physician in 1525, the plague once again struck Southern France. This was around the time when a new twist to the well-poisoning libel made the rounds: Jews were accused of kidnapping redheaded Christians—the hair color was apparently important here—stinging them with adders, collecting their saliva during their death-throes, and concocting from this a highly virulent yet invisible unguent to be smeared on Christian doorknockers. To potentiate the effect of the poison, the doctor could also mutter in Hebrew the curse: "In the name of Satan and so many other devils, kill him."

Baptized in the Catholic faith, Michel de Nostradamus was spared such suspicion. In fact even those who consider Nostradamus to be a charlatan in the field of astrological predictions generally concede that he was remarkable among physicians of his day—be they Jew or gentile—in adhering to the first commandment of medicine: Do no harm. In particular, Nostradamus appears to have opposed the widespread practice of bloodletting and purging, based (as we have seen) on an extreme interpretation of the concept of the four humors. If Nostradamus did no harm, it did not necessarily follow that he did much good. It was probably in 1525 that he began concocting his rose pills, which he would also use in outbreaks of the plague in subsequent decades. These were compounded of sawdust of green cyprus wood, iris of Florence, cloves, odorated calamus, and lign aloes, all ground into a base made of red roses, which had to be plucked before dawn and then pulverized. Some of these ingredients, particularly clove oil, may have antiseptic properties, but this was unlikely to be of much use in combating the plague.

As is still very much the case in most countries, though not in the United States, physicians are not doctors in the academic sense unless they go on to pursue the higher degree, usually by writing and defending a dissertation. Nostradamus returned to Montpellier, where one of his fellow med students was a former monk named François Rabelais, destined for a place in the French literary pantheon with his bawdy satires. For his dissertation, Nostradamus had to elucidate and defend his unorthodox remedies. Having done so successfully, he was awarded, along with the doctorate, a gold ring, the book of Hippocrates, and the distinctive four-sided hat by which he has become familiar to generations of his followers through the centuries. Although we have been referring to Pierre de No(s)tredame as Nostradamus, it was only at this point that he followed the custom of using the prestigious Latin version of his name that appeared on his doctoral diploma.

While continuing his practice of medicine, particularly in combating revisitations of the plague, Nostradamus devoted himself to the work for which he would forever be known, the book of prophecy called the *Centuries*. The title is fully misleading when taken, as it so often is, as referring to periods of 100 years. The centuries, in fact, refer to collections of a 100 verses each, with an explicit disclaimer of any chronological parallel. In consequence, one is free to relate virtually any of the 1,000 verses of Nostradamus's ten centuries to *any* event in history from his time onward. Nostradamus was extremely wise in this regard, for in the few instances in his writings where he did dare give some time specification, future events showed him to be woefully off the mark.

Of interest to our medical story are the 37 of the 1,000 verses that make direct mention of plague and pestilence, usually in connection with other calamities such as famine, war, and fire. For almost a half millennium, these have regularly been seen as fulfilled predictions of some epidemic, most recently AIDS. One verse is, however, sometimes seen as heralding the modern age of medicine:

Lost, found, hidden for so long a time,
Pastor [*Pasteur*] will be honored as a demigod:
Before the Moon finishes its full period
will be dishonored by other winds. (I:25)

In the nineteenth century, a *Pasteur,* named Louis, would indeed be honored, although how the last two lines of the verse might relate to this is unclear. More interesting from the specific point of view of the Jewish history of medicine is the following verse. It is one of the few making explicit reference to the Jews, but is otherwise typical of Nostradamus's very cryptic style:

> The great King abandoned by the Physicians,
> By fate not the Jew's art he remains alive,
> He and his kindred pushed high in the realm,
> Pardon given to the race which denies Christ. (VI:18)

As is often the case with Nostradamus, there seems sooner to be a (somewhat fanciful) reference to events past rather than things to come: in this case the benevolence bestowed by René the Good upon the Jews of Provence, in part as gratitude for the services of the Jewish court physicians—presumably Nostradamus's two grandfathers—even if it was fate that saved the king. But if one will, one can see this as a prophecy by a physician, well aware of his Jewish roots, of very real Jewish accomplishments in medicine to come several centuries later.

The matter of Nostradamus's true religious convictions remains to this day uncertain. Being only a generation or two removed from Judaism, he had to tread cautiously. He may not have been particularly pleased to see his works appear in Hebrew, such as his *Ein Mishpat* (Eye of the Law) translated by Moses Botarel in 1561. At opportune times Nostradamus loudly proclaimed his Catholic piety, as when, in 1563, with the Protestant Reformation causing a religious fissure right across the European continent, his predictions for that year contained not just quite favorable prophecies for the Church against its enemies, but also a paean to Pope Pius IV, whom Nostradamus termed "truly pious in name and deed."

Yet letters unearthed in the Bibliotèque Nationale in Paris, purportedly from Nostradamus to the German Protestant Lorenz Tubbe, express strong sympathies for Luther, distinguishing his followers as "Christians," in contrast to the "Papists." In secret, this doctor descendant of Israelite physicians and bearing the name Our Lady may have been neither Jewish nor Catholic but Protestant. Yet whatever his genuine religious convictions, Nostradamus's Jewish roots were no secret and were sometimes brought up in attacks against him. So it was that a one-time friend and collaborator, the physician, astrologer, and scholar Jules-César Scaliger (de l'Escalle), jealously railed against the success of Nostradamus's publications with the words: "Credulous France, what are you doing, hanging on the words of Nostradamus? What sort of Jewish sorcery restrains your anger?"

Nostradamus died in 1566. Six years later some 20,000 Protestant Hugue-nots were massacred on St. Bartholomew's Day as part of the drive to create a unitary France ruled by a centralized authority in Paris under a Catholic absolute monarch. But many Protestants held out, particularly in the West and South. By the Edict of Nantes, issued two years before the turn of the seventeenth century by King Henry IV (himself a convert from Protestant-ism to Catholicism), the Huguenots were granted freedom of conscience, given limited freedom of worship, and allowed to maintain fortified strong-holds, albeit within a unified French state. Henry's reluctant toleration did not extend to Judaism, a religion whose exercise he forbad throughout his realm, even in regions such as Provence that had once been hospitable to Jews. Yet during Henry's reign in the early seventeenth century, there was an openly practicing Jew in France, and he fulfilled his religious obligations right in the middle of the royal court.

When once passing through Paris, the exiled Portuguese doctor, Philotheus Montalto, author of the book on vision *Optica* and physician to Grand Duke Ferdinand in Florence, so impressed the court with a cure that Henry's wife, Queen Marie de' Medici, sought his permanent services. Montalto was not the first Jewish doctor to serve the Medicis. Previously, Catherine de' Medici had employed the famed Marrano physician Luis Nuñez (Nonnius), and Marie's own retinue already included the Marrano-descendants Drs. François Alverez, André du Lauentiu, and François Vautier (later physician to Cardinal Mazarin and King Louis XIV). But if these physicians continued to practice Judaism, they were discreet about it. Montalto, however, was adamant that he be allowed freedom of worship as a condition for his service. King Henry objected to the prospect of Montalto's open insult to Christianity, but Marie nevertheless successfully petitioned the pope for a dispensation.

To Montalto goes credit not just for his successful opposition to bigotry. In the Jewish rationalist tradition, he also countered superstition and sor-cery with regard to mental illness, even if he based his arguments on old-fashioned doctrines. Melancholy, Montalto wrote, "should not be attributed to the Devil, as some do, who imagine that such insanity is caused by his direct injurious influence, but, on the contrary, it is to be explained by the peculiar nature of the melancholy humor, its quantity and quality, associated with the temperament of the subject. This was evidently also the view of Aristotle."

Although Montalto was exceptional in openly practicing Judaism at the French court, the role of royal physicians of Jewish descent by no means ended with him. Another of Marie de' Medici's trusted physicians was Louis d'Aquin, a biblical and talmudic scholar and son of a converted professor of Hebrew, Mordicai (Philippe) d'Aquin of the University of Paris. Later in the seventeenth century, Louis's Montpellier-educated son Antoine d'Aquin in turn served as *premier médecin* (chief physician) at the court of the great Louis XIV. There he was involved in one of the most notable incidents in the history of pre-modern medicine.

What made the medical situation of Louis XIV particularly interesting for historians, aside from the importance of the great monarch at the pinnacle of European power, was his *Journal de la Santé du Roi*. Meticulously maintained by court physicians throughout the second half of the seventeenth century and the first decade of the eighteenth and preserved for posterity, the *Journal* chronicles not just the king's health and his physicians' ministrations but an important transition in French medicine. For while *le Roi-Soleil* (Sun King, as Louis was known) was conducting a series of wars for twenty-seven of his fifty-four years on the throne, the French medical profession was engaged in conflicts of its own. The University of Paris battled against the provincial universities, especially Montpellier, while the physicians, as men of learning, strove to retain their superiority over the surgeons, who were, after all, manual workers. Affairs at the royal court, and not the least those involved in Antoine d'Aquin's rise and fall, played a central role in the evolution of these conflicts.

Among the entries in the *Journal* are references to Louis's insomnia, venereal disease, smallpox, tapeworm, gout, indigestion, headaches, chronic fevers, anthrax, melancholy, urinary difficulties, night sweats, vertigo, colic, typhoid fever, measles, bile, toothache, and rheumatism. That the Grand Monarch survived all these real or imaginary afflictions and died just short of his 78th birthday (a gangrenous leg finally doing him in) was in almost all instances not thanks to but in spite of the retinue of physicians he had at his disposal. Being a gluttonous eater, Louis was subjected to many hundreds of enemas and an estimated 2,000 purges in his lifetime (in some cases, as often as seven times in one day). The royal evacuations were duly analyzed, and on occasion the royal physician in attendance was not satisfied until the purges produced bloody stools. However, bleeding by means of phlebotomy was the usual prescription, as often as eight times for one illness. In at least one instance the *Journal* tells that "the blood came out with such violence that we had trouble stopping it."

In 1671 the position of *premier médecin* went to the Antoine d'Aquin, who beat out other Jewish-descendant court physicians, most notably the previously mentioned François Vautier, who was also doctor to Cardinal Mazarin, the prime minister and second most powerful man in France. With the office of *premier médecin* came various privileges such as the authority to appoint city coroners, jurisdiction over many aspects of French medicine and pharmacy, superintendence of the Jardin des Plantes, and even control of the mineral waters. Perhaps most important, particularly to the likes of d'Aquin, was the measure of social acceptance granted the doctors by the nobles, something rarely extended to those of bourgeois origin other than the clergy. The jockeying for social position and the professional rivalry at court were tinged with anti-Semitism. D'Aquin was, in the words of another court physician, "a poor miser, of Jewish race, a great charlatan, meager in science, rich in chemical and pharmaceutical knavery (who) assassinated various persons."

Yet in retrospect, something positive can be said about d'Aquin's practice. Although by no means opposed to bloodletting, d'Aquin brought with him the tendency of his Montpellier alma mater to rely on chemical and botanical specifics. For the professors of the University of Paris, neglecting bloodletting as a basic remedy bordered on charlatanism and only went to prove the inferiority of the provincial medical faculties. But Louis himself had developed an understandable aversion to bloodletting, and d'Aquin as *premier médecin* was quite willing to acquiesce to the monarch. Even when Louis dislocated an arm, d'Aquin refrained from carrying out the almost obligatory phlebotomy, out of concern for the "cruel vapors which this remedy excites in the king."

It was however d'Aquin's helplessness in the year 1686, referred to in official state documents as *l'anneé de la fistule*, that caused him and the whole French medical profession—Parisian and provincial—much loss of face.

The *Roi-Soleil* had long complained of an anal fistula (fissure in the wall of the rectum). D'Aquin and the lesser court physicians tried various medicinal waters and laxatives, but to no avail. Finally, they had to deign to consult the *premier chirurgien* (chief surgeon), Charles-François Félix. This came at a time when the medical doctors were having increasingly difficulty keeping the surgeons in their place. The fine work of the Frenchman Ambroise Paré, the "father of modern surgery," in the previous century had given many of the barber-surgeons aspirations of rising above haircutting, wart-removing, bloodletting, and occasional tooth-extracting to become the equals of the physicians. The medical faculty of the University of Paris accordingly tried to keep the surgeons in the same guild with the barbers and also to maintain control over the training and licensing of those surgeons (always a small minority) who were academically trained at the independent Collège de Saint-Côme.

Premier chirurgien Félix, who had never before treated an anal fistula, perfected a long, narrow surgical knife (bistoury), made of silver and modeled on one described by Galen. He then tested it—with what results, we do not know—on various patients in the charity wards of Parisian hospitals before cutting into the royal rectum. The success of *la grande opération* meant elevation to the nobility for Félix and a rise in status for the whole surgical profession. Indeed, court members and sycophants now sought the prestige of having fistula operations performed on themselves, even if they were suffering merely from hemorrhoids or from nothing at all.

Louis's fistula was not, however, what led to d'Aquin's fall. In fact, he was given 100,000 livres by the relieved king simply for having been in attendance at the operation. Rather, according to the court chronicler Saint-Simon, d'Aquin got too caught up in court politics at the magnificent new palace at Versailles. As the protegé of Louis's *maîtresse en permanence,* Mme. de Montespan, d'Aquin was naturally resented by her successor Mme. de Maintenon, the most influential of the king's mistresses. She began a long-term campaign to undermine the authority of the Hebrew *premier médecin.* But d'Aquin himself, never known for his lack of ambition or greed, played a role in his own fall from grace with his scheming. When d'Aquin had the *chutzpah* to try to manipulate his son into the archbishop's chair at Tours, Louis dismissed him from the court.

D'Aquin's successor, a gentile graduate of the University of Paris, reinstituted with a vengeance the policy of bleeding. This included an annual spring bleeding *(saignée de précaution),* even if the king wasn't ill. The ministrations of the court doctors when a mysterious fatal disease struck Versailles almost extinguished the Bourbon line. Fortunately, the wise dutchess of Ventadour locked herself and the future Louis XV in a room, refused to see any doctors, and put the infant on a diet of mother's milk. Thus she ensured that there would yet be a Bourbon to be beheaded a century later in the French Revolution. As for d'Aquin, unlike Louis's ill-fated superintendent of finance, Nicolas Fouquet, he did not go to prison after his fall from royal grace but was in fact granted a pension of 6,000 livres. Jettisoned from the world of Catholic royalty, however, the social-climbing one-time Hebrew physician soon expired. "With him died his family," wrote Saint-Simon, "which relapsed into nothingness."

Le Roi-Soleil presided over economic expansion and great achievements in science, the arts, and architecture, as exemplified by the palace he built at Versailles. Yet by means of one simple act, his revocation in 1685 of the Edict of Nantes, which for nine decades had guaranteed freedom of worship to the Protestant Huguenots, Louis in the long run impoverished France far more than his greatest achievements enriched it. The tiny number of Protestants who remained in France would in centuries to come produce scientific accomplishments wildly out of proportion to their numbers, not least in the field of medicine. This was particularly evidenced in the heyday of the mid- and late nineteenth century by the work of the neurologist Paul Broca, the physiologist Charles Edouard Brown-Séquard, and the medical classicist Emile Littré. One can only wonder about the additional contribution to French industry, science, and medicine that might have been made had not the vast majority of Huguenots—half a million in number—been forced to flee for their lives in the late seventeenth century.

Catholic Europe's loss was Protestant Europe's gain. The expulsion of the Huguenots was one factor shifting the focus of medicine in the modern era northward. But there were more reasons. Not least of these was the fact that when the Huguenots arrived at their havens, they encountered other refugees. Although these exiles, too, had fled from the fanaticism of Catholic monarchs, they were not Protestants or even Christians. They had fled to towns of northern Germany, particularly Danish-administered Altona, near the port city of Hamburg. But most of all they had found refuge behind the dunes and dikes of a small country with a big soul.

Chapter 7
The Sage of Amsterdam

I am a Jew and a stranger who fled from Portugal and my beloved and most lovely birthplace Lisbon, tossed hither and thither by severe misfortune and the storms of life. I have allowed no day [in Holland] to pass—as Seneca says—without writing a line in which I showed my love for the Republic of Medicine.
— Abraham Zacutus Lusitanius IV

This is the end I aim at: to acquire knowledge of the Union of the mind with the whole of Nature. . . . [B]ecause health is no small means to achieving this end, the whole of medicine must be worked out.
— Baruch Spinoza

The dark Portuguese and Spanish eyes that look out from so many of the portraits painted by Rembrandt van Rijn in the seventeenth century bear testimony to the new home that thousands of Jewish refugees from the Iberian Inquisition found in the hospitable Netherlands. This migration and the Dutch Golden Age in the arts, sciences, and commerce coincided—but they were hardly coincidental.

References to Jews in the Netherlands prior to the Golden Age were few and far between. And, of course, they typically involved physicians. One of the earliest works in the history of Dutch literature, the thirteenth-century satire in fable form *Van de Vos Reynaerde* (Reynard the Fox), tells of the physician Master Abrioen, who, as the wisest Jew in the world, knew "all manner of herbs and stones" and was adept at deciphering mysterious illegible inscriptions. A note found among some ancient accounts tells of a journey undertaken by the Jewish physician Simon from Cologne to Zutphen in 1404 at the request of the duke of Gelderland in order to treat the local *Jonkheer* (lord). Simon and his servant, observing the Jewish dietary regulations, partook of "none but sweet beer, for they refused to drink either wine or hops." It was also in Zutphen in the Late Middle Ages that the burghers pleaded to keep their Jewish doctor in the face of anti-Jewish regulations promulgated by the Catholic Church.

While exceptions might be made for physicians, the climate in the Low Lands remained inhospitable to all other Jews up to the sixteenth century, the area being under repressive Burgundian and Habsburg rule. With the rise of Protestantism, the staunchly Catholic regent of the Netherlands, Margaret of Palma, was glad to accuse the Jews of "attempting to foster new sects, to the detriment and obscuration of our holy Christian faith, hoping thereby to extol their own law." Even Erasmus of Rotterdam, the great Catholic humanist, admitted early in the sixteenth century: "If it is Christian to hate the Jews, then we are all of us outstanding Christians."

The situation changed dramatically, however, when in the 1560s the Dutch under the leadership of the Protestant prince of Orange, William the Silent, rose in revolt against their Catholic overlord, the Habsburg Philip II. The grandson of Ferdinand and Isabella, Philip had his power base in Iberia and maintained holdings in the Low Lands, France, and Italy. The Spanish army of occupation under the notorious duke of Alba did not flinch from wholesale massacres of the civilian population in the Netherlands in order to attain Philip's political and religious goals, in a war that lasted until 1648, broken only by a twelve-year truce early in the century. In the course of the seventeenth century, the Netherlands offered sanctuary to Flemish and Walloon Protestants from the southern Low Lands, dissenters from England, and tens of thousands of Huguenots fleeing France, who included a disproportionate number of the best and the brightest of French society. Subsequently, Holland would likewise provide refuge to Mennonites from Switzerland and Lutherans from Austria.

Unlike all these groups, the Iberian Jews, who were also in search of a new home in the seventeenth century, were not Protestants. But having themselves so suffered from the expulsion and the Holy Catholic Inquisition under the kings of Spain, the Jews were regarded sympathetically by the Netherlanders. Furthermore, as a trading nation, the Dutch were more aware than most of the potential economic benefits to be derived for their country from the international network of Jewish mercantile contacts. And, of course, there were the Iberian-Jewish doctors, the world's most renowned. So it was that Hugo Grotius, the great Dutch jurist and author of the international law of the seas, wrote of the Jews: "Plainly, God desires them to live somewhere. Why then not here rather than elsewhere?"

Enshrined in the Union of Utrecht—the document that in 1579 united the seven northern, predominantly Protestant, provinces of the Netherlands—is the principle that "every individual should remain free in his religion, and that no man should be molested or questioned on the subject of divine worship." In practice, however, there were restrictions. These applied more to the Dutch Catholic minority, whose religion was identified with the Inquisition and the hated Spaniards, than to the Jewish newcomers, who had fled from Spanish tyranny. The Jews were, however, expressly prohibited from propagandizing and from marrying Christians (neither of which stipulations caused the rabbis much loss of sleep). There were also economic restrictions, more about which shortly. Moreover, for a while the individual municipalities could decide whether to admit Jews at all, and if so, how many. Yet nowhere in the Netherlands were Jews forced to wear any distinguishing badges. And although they naturally tended to congregate in certain neighborhoods, there were no restrictions as to which parts of town they could reside in. So it was that Rembrandt and other Christians inhabited Amsterdam's Jodenbreestraat (Jews' Broad Street) and other lanes of the Jewish Quarter, while wealthy Jewish merchants were to be found living in fancy canal houses throughout the city.

The gratitude of the Iberian refugees was given poignant expression by one of Rembrandt's subjects, Rabbi Menasseh ben Israel. This "Divine and Doctor of Physick" or, as he was also known in Latin, *Medicus Hebraeus,* owed his international fame less to his medical skills, impressive though they may have been, than to his diplomatic and publishing activities. (We shall meet Menasseh again in a later chapter, negotiating with Oliver Cromwell for the re-admission of Jews to England.) An accomplished orator, Manasseh waxed poetically on the occasion of the visit to the synagogue by Prince Hendrik in 1642, the first in a tradition of courtesy calls by members of the House of Orange:

> We no longer look upon Castile and Portugal, but upon Holland as our Fatherland; we no longer wait upon the Spanish or Portuguese King, but upon Their Excellencies the States-General and upon Your Highness as our Masters, by whose blessed arms we are protected, and by whose swords we

are defended. Hence no one need wonder that we say daily prayers for Their Excellencies the States-General and Your Highness, and for the noble governors of this world-renowned city.

Not surprisingly, contemporaries tell that the dedication of the magnificent new Portuguese Synagogue in Amsterdam in 1675 was marked by such festivities and fanfare that one would have thought it to be the rebuilt Second Temple.

Such a beckoning light was Amsterdam, the "Jerusalem of the West," to the Sephardim that at least one Marrano doctor made his way there in death. This was the aforementioned Philotheus Montalto, court physician to Queen Marie de'Medici and the only openly practicing Jew in all France. When he died accompanying the royal family to Tours in 1616, Queen Marie arranged for Montalto to find his last resting place in Amsterdam's Jewish cemetery, where a few decades later the famed landscape painter Ruysdael would capture his tomb on canvas.

Understandably, the Netherlands also began attracting Ashkenazi Jews from Germany and Poland, who soon outnumbered the Sephardim. Although far poorer and less cultured than their Iberian brethren, and thus less respected by both the Christians and Sephardim, the Ashkenazim at least had the advantage of not having lived for generations as uncircumcised crypto-Jews. They were thus closer to their ancient roots—so much so, that Ashkenazi rabbis were sometimes called upon to re-instruct the early Sephardic arrivals in the religion of their forefathers. That the sentiments of both branches of Jewry toward their new home were very similar can be seen from the prayer offered by the Parnas Zodak Perelsheim at the opening of the Ashkenazim's own Great Shul in the same decade as the building of the Portuguese Synagogue: "Blessed art thou, O Lord God, Who hast shown us Thy wonderful mercy in the city of Amsterdam, the praiseworthy."

For the whole of the seventeenth century, as the economy of the rest of Europe stagnated or even declined, that of the Netherlands underwent an unprecedented boom. The prosperous Dutch population increased by half and became the most urbanized and industrialized in the world. The Dutch fleet of some 15,000 vessels outnumbered the English by four or five times for much of the century and maintained an almost monopoly position. Dutch ships transported grain, iron, hemp, and wood from the Baltic, and salt, wine, spices, and precious metals from France, Spain, and Portugal. Beyond Europe, the fleets of Dutch East and West India Companies plied the seas to the far-flung empire in Indonesia, the Caribbean, and South Africa, while Dutch privateers preyed upon the enemy Spanish ships carrying silver from the New World. The Amsterdam exchange bank, established at the beginning of the century, made that city the word's financial center. In these commercial activities the Jews of Holland played a role far out of proportion to their numbers, as they once had in Spain, now a misgoverned country facing centuries of continual decline as a European power.

But as mentioned earlier, the rights and freedoms granted the Dutch Jewish community did not necessarily extend to all fields of endeavor. A 1632 ordinance of the city of Amsterdam stipulated "that Jews be granted citizenship solely for the purposes of trade . . . but not a license to become shopkeepers." More important for the story of Jews in medicine was the power of the guilds. One exception to the generally exclusionary policies of the guilds toward the Jews was the printing industry. Amsterdam soon overtook Venice as the center of Jewish publishing, so much so that books printed elsewhere often bore the deliberately misleading Hebrew inscription "printed as in Amsterdam." It was there that Abraham Elsevier and the Querido family established publishing houses that today, three centuries later, still rank among of the most prestigious in the world, not least in the field of medical publications.

As was customary throughout Europe until into the nineteenth century, the surgeons, being manual workers, occupied a far lower rung in the medical hierarchy than did the physicians, especially the academically trained doctors. The surgeons of Amsterdam had their own guild, and Jews were generally excluded from it. There were exceptions, however. Such was the prestige of Portuguese-born Samuel Leon Benavente, renowned for his skill in kidney stone cutting and for his *Libello aureo da difficultade de ourinar* (Golden booklet on the difficulties in urinating), that he was received as full member of the surgeons guild, although not without having to pay double dues. His less illustrious coreligionist Abraham Abarbanel passed his exam for the surgeons guild, got off with paying only the regular dues, but was restricted to the lower "barbering" activities, which included toothpulling and bloodletting alongside hair-cutting.

Among the Rembrandt etchings that have come down to us are *The Doctor on the Stairs* and a closer portrait of the same gentleman, Dr. Ephraim Hezekia Bueno. The physicians, being an educated elite, were independent professionals rather than guild members, and this was much to the advantage of the Portuguese immigrants such as Bueno. Born in Castello-Rodrigo in northern Portugal in 1599, Ephraim was taken by his father, Joseph, to France when the Inquisition began hounding them. In Bordeaux both father and son received their medical education before moving to Holland. Such was the elder Bueno's reputation in the Netherlands that in 1625 he was summoned to treat the fatally ill Prince Maurits, son of William the Silent, and for decades head of state of the Dutch Republic and leader in the war against Spain. But Ephraim outshone his father, if not necessarily as a physician, then in other spheres. As a man of letters, Ephraim Bueno wrote poetry in Spanish and edited hymn books, including the first Hebrew book to be printed in Amsterdam. As a scholar, he was co-founder of the Or Torah scientific academy in 1656. When Rembrandt painted his portrait, Ephraim had also been bestowed the status of Freeman of the City of Amsterdam by the town fathers.

By the mid-seventeenth century, there were some 40 learned physicians among the 400 or so families that comprised Amsterdam's Jewish congregation. This being the height of Holland's Golden Age, many of the doctors were, like Bueno, also involved in cultural and scientific activities. Several were poets in the Portuguese and Spanish languages, and occasionally in Hebrew and Latin. Others published works on astronomy-astrology, mathematics, and the tides. Almost all the Jewish doctors were prominent in religious affairs, as cofounders, board members, and occasionally presidents of the various synagogues—this in line with the long tradition of physicians as leaders of the Jewish community in the Islamic world. Not a few Jewish physicians were in fact rabbis and distinguished themselves as religious scholars.

But, of course, the greatest literary output of the Jewish doctors was in the field of medicine proper. Spanish-born Dr. Benjamin Mussafia wrote *De Auro Potibili Epistola* on the healing properties of gold, and *Sacro-medicae sententiae ex Biblis*, perhaps the first work by a Jewish author on medicine in the Old Testament. From the pen of Lisbon-born and Montpellier-educated Jacob Rosales came the treatise "Armatura Medica sive Modus Addiscendi Medicinam." Dr. Zachariah da Silva edited and wrote the preface to William Harvey's classic on the circulation of the blood, *De Motu Cordis.* Da Silva's preface was important enough to soon appear in English, in which language he was known as Zachariah Wood, the literal translation of his family name. Benedict de Castro authored "Flaellum callumniantum seu apoligia," an apology for the physician, which three centuries later would likewise be published in English.

The most prolific of the Dutch-Jewish medical writers was Dr. Abraham Zacutus Lusitanius IV, the great-grandson of the physician-astronomer Abraham Zacuto, whom we met in a previous chapter as adviser on astronomical matters to the Portuguese kings in the late fifteenth century. Born in 1575 in Lisbon (whence the Latin appendage "Lusitanius") and educated at the Universities of Coimbra and Salamanca, Zacutus, at the age of 50, was forced by the Inquisition to abandon his flourishing practice—which included service to the poor as well as to the royal court—and seek refuge in Amsterdam. Although he had never before published anything, Zacutus's decades of extensive reading and observations were now, in his last dozen years, to culminate in an outpouring of printed works. "I am a Jew and a stranger who fled from Portugal and my beloved and most lovely birthplace Lisbon, tossed hither and thither by severe misfortune and the storms of life," wrote Zacutus, now safe in Holland. "I have allowed no day to pass— as Seneca says—without writing a line in which I showed my love for the Republic of Medicine."

Zacutus's observations on disease, which he compared and contrasted with those of other physicians, earlier and contemporary, appeared in his six-volume *De Medicorum Principum Historia.* His support of the ancient Hippocratic and Galenic doctrines are evident in his *De Praxis Medica Admiranda,* which encompassed another three volumes. In his *Introitus Medici ad Praxim Necnon Pharmacopoea Elegantissima,* Zacutus presented an important code of ethics as well as a manual for the practitioner. Always the proper gentleman, Zacutus gained the trust of his Christian clientele—especially the women—by having a gentile interpreter present when doing his examinations.

In the year of Zacuto's death, 1642, the first part of his oeuvre, encompassing thousands of pages, saw the light of day. Its title, *Opera Omnia* (Complete Works), was short and sweet. Its subtitle ran: "The History of the Great Physicians, being all the medical histories of internal diseases, which are found scattered in the works of the foremost physicians, most carefully arranged in proper order and supplied with explanatory notes and commentaries; together with (a review of) questions and matters of doubt."Two years later Part 2 appeared posthumously, bearing the no less impressive title: "The Practice of Cases—in which the treatment of all internal diseases is explained according to the views of leading physicians; serious doubts are discussed and resolved; and finally many practical observations are interspersed in their proper places. With an introduction of the physicians into practice, together with a most eloquent pharmacopoeia. To which are added extraordinary medical cases by the very same author, fully and newly enriched, in which rare, wonderful, monstrous cases are presented together with their hidden causes, signs, courses and treatments."

A strong defender of the moribund Galenism though he was, Zacutus nevertheless relied on autopsies for his anatomical observations on plague, heart disease, malignant tumors, renal and vesical calculi, and the like— this in an age when postmortems were rare. Zacutus's contacts with Portuguese and Dutch navigators gained him access to drugs from the far corners of the globe unknown to the ancients. And although Zacutus could not free himself from Galen's description of the heart and blood flow, he wrote sympathetically of Harvey's theory that blood circulates. The last of the line of the great Zacutus dynasty, Abraham Zacutus Lusitanius was by no means the least in his contributions to medicine and science. In the words of the Count Palatine Rosales (Immanuel Bocarro), a friend of Galileo and likewise an exiled physician, who contributed to one of Zacutus's books, Abraham was "the one who has replenished anew the ancient glory of medicine, enabling her again to celebrate triumph."

One of Rembrandt's best-known paintings, *The Anatomy Lesson of Dr. Tulp*, symbolizes the scientific prestige that grew around the medical faculty of the recently founded University of Leiden. In 1574, the town of Leiden had for months been under siege by the Spanish forces led by the dreaded duke of Alba, when William the Silent opened the sluices some twenty miles away in the hope that the water, carried by the winds and tide, would flood the countryside and spare Leiden from the massacres to which other Dutch cities had been subjected. From May to the beginning of October many of the burghers succumbed to plague and famine as relieving troops waded through mud and water to get some barges with provisions through. When the Spanish siege lifted, William, in recognition of Leiden's gallant resistance, offered the burgers the choice of freedom from taxation for ten years or the establishment of a university. The good citizens opted for the latter and the doors of Holland's first university opened the following year. Prince William presented the library with its first book, a copy of the Hebrew Bible.

Prominent from the very beginning was the medical faculty, under the direction of Professor Gerard de Bondt (Bontius). The university's reputation rapidly rose, thanks to its outstanding clinicians and anatomists. Foremost among the clinicians was Francis de la Boë (Sylvius), a chemically oriented doctor who introduced bedside teaching. "I have led my students daily to visit the sick of the public hospital," wrote Sylvius. "There I have put the symptoms of disease before their eyes; have let them hear the complaints of the patients . . . and have asked them their opinions in each case. . . . Then I have given my own judgment on each point." On the anatomical side, Renier de Graaf, while still a student under Sylvius, was the first to study pancreatic secretions in animals and humans. Although the theoretical basis of his interpretation was still very much in keeping with the misconceptions of his day, he was in a sense a forerunner of the modern insulin researchers. On display to this day in Leiden are body parts whose structures were preserved and distinguished through the injection of colored preparations by Frederick Ruysch in the seventeenth century. Ruysch's colleagues Boekelman and Six used a similar technique and injected solidifying liquids into the heart and thereby revealed the structure of its finer blood vessels.

And, of course, among the anatomists there was Rembrandt's Dr. Nicolas Tulp himself, who among other things wrote a classic description of beriberi, a disease prevalent in the Dutch colonies in far-off Indonesia (and whose precise etiology as a vitamin deficiency would be identified by a Polish-Jewish biochemist in London in the early twentieth century). Being also an eminent clinician, Tulp was Rembrandt's own doctor, as well as friend and subject, and on one occasion had to relieve the great painter of the notion that "his bones were like jelly," an idea probably put into Rembrandt's head by one of the medical books that were increasingly written in Dutch and therefore accessible to a broader public. (Such popularization was strongly opposed by Tulp, who considered a little knowledge to be a dangerous thing and therefore championed the continued use of Latin.) That medicine was a popular subject and that its practice was not limited to the university-educated can be seen from the paintings not only by Rembrandt but by other great artists of the Golden Age. While Caspar Netscher portrayed the doctor clad in academic robes solemnly examining the color of urine in a flask, artists like Jan Steen and Jan de Bray became better known for their hilarious paintings of barber-surgeons and out-and-out quacks.

Obviously, medical practitioners preferred to belong to the university-educated class, and not least of all the Jews. While the only other university in the Low Countries, Louvain, required that its students sign a Catholic "declaratio fidei" upon matriculating, Leiden, although a Protestant institution, made no corresponding demands. So whereas the refugees from the Inquisition had received their education on the Iberian Peninsula, a dozen or so first-generation Dutch-Jewish physicians would graduate from Leiden. The Universities of Groningen and Utrecht, founded early in the seventeenth century and following the nondiscriminatory practice, likewise attracted Jewish med students. "De Phthisi," "De Phrenitide," "De Asthmate," "De Diabete," "De Syncope," "De Apoplexia," "De Pleuritis," "De Dysentaria Vera" were among the early Jewish M.D. dissertation titles. But although the climate of tolerance at the Dutch universities was almost unique in all the world, the Jewish student might be wise not to test its limits, as did Philip Levi, a follower of the messianic Zionist Shabbetai Zevi. Levi's defense of his M.D. dissertation, "De Pleuritide," in Leiden in 1683 received highest honors from the university senate but also a reprimand, since Levi had the *chutzpah* to close the proceedings with a prayer in Hebrew, which the Senate took to be insulting to Jesus.

Such was the reputation of the Dutch Jewish doctors that many of them were in demand as court physicians outside the Netherlands. Benedict de Castro was personal physician to Queen Christina of Sweden. Dr. Benjamin Mussafia served at the court of King Christian IV of Denmark. On Jacob Rosales was bestowed the title Count Palantine by the grateful Holy Roman Emperor Ferdinand III. Dr. Isaac Henrique Sequeira, while he remained in Holland, held the honorary post of personal physician to the prince regent of Portugal. Farther east, Antonio Sanchez was personal physician to Czarinas Anna Ivanovna, Elizabeth Petrovna, and Catherine II of Russia, and a fellow Jewish Leiden graduate served at the court of the king of Poland.

Among the many depictions by Rembrandt of anonymous subjects is his *Portrait of a Young Student*. Tradition, however, has it that the dark-haired teenage scholar with large drooping eyes, clad in Mediterranean garb, is Baruch Spinoza.

Born in Amsterdam to Portuguese refugees in 1632, the precocious young Baruch quickly absorbed the Torah and the Talmud, which were part of the traditional Jewish studies. Among his teachers was the distinguished rabbi-physician Menasseh ben Israel, who probably considered him a prime candidate for the rabbinate. But in the Amsterdam of Holland's Golden Age there was more for a first-generation Dutch Jew to learn than was conveyed by the Hebrew literature. At the home of the Christian medical doctor Frans van den Ende, the young Spinoza received instruction in Latin and in the physical sciences. Knowledge of Latin opened up to Spinoza the medical books of Dr. Nicholaas Tulp and it was probably the language in which he conversed with Tulp himself. But aside from the intellectual cross-currents from the gentile world influencing the thinking of the young Spinoza, there were to be found brewing within the Jewish immigrant community itself some rather unorthodox tendencies that would impact Baruch. Here, too, the Jewish physicians played a central role, particularly one of Spinoza's friends, the Spanish exile Dr. Juan de Prado.

Growing up as a Catholic in Spain in the first half of the seventeenth century, Juan de Prado had been able to pursue academic studies in philosophy and medicine, first at the University of Alcal de Henares and later at the University of Toledo. But although he was a few generations removed from official Judaism, he secretly espoused the faith of his ancestors and in fact was militant in his covert attempts to draw other New Christians back to the Jewish fold. As one of his reconverted *conversos*, who fell into the hands of the Inquisition, confessed under torture: "Dr. Prado's words moved me especially because he said that he was one of the most learned people in Alcal, and since he himself practiced the Law of Moses, so could I. Prado said that no one had taught him this Law. He had learnt by himself, through his books and his university education."

Yet while Prado was risking his life as a secret proselytizer for the ancient religion of Judaism, there were some quite nontraditional ideas gestating in his mind. This is shown by the Inquisition files of the testimony extracted from another secret Jew, Balthasar (Isaac) Orobio de Castro, who was likewise a physician. Like Prado, Orobio had first studied philosophy at the University of Alcal de Henares. He then taught metaphysics at the University of Salamanca before turning to the study of medicine. Dr. Orobio had a very successful practice in Seville, where he was professor at the university, and he served as the personal physician to the duke of Medina Celi. Then Orobio got trapped by the Inquisition as a secret Jew. Orobio told his tormentors how Prado considered all religions—be they Judaism, Christianity, or Islam—to be fundamentally equal. The purpose of religious laws, whatever the creed, was political and derived from the law of Nature, the First Cause posited by Aristotle. Prado further claimed, Orobio told the inquisitors, that all religions seek the same objective, "namely to know God, and this suffices for salvation."

This confession might have spelled the end for both Prado and Orobio, but in fact the two physicians would eventually meet again in Amsterdam. Prado, knowing the Inquisition was closing in, escaped from Iberia apparently by traveling along with a Spanish cardinal to Rome and then fled to Holland. Orobio in Spain was made to wear the sambenito for two years, after which the inquisitors graciously burned Orobio's effigy rather than Orobio, whom they merely banished. Once more concealing his still-cherished Jewish faith, Orobio became professor of pharmacy in Toulouse, France, but was exposed and fled again, this time to the Netherlands. A literary man, Dr. Orobio was elected president of Amsterdam's Academia de los Floridos, a Spanish poetry circle. In theological matters, he became known for his debates with the Protestant minister and professor Philip van Limborch, published in 1687 in Limborch's book *Friendly Discussions with a Learned Jew.* The first word of the title reflects the tolerant nature of the Dutch environment and the freedom of the Jews to publicly defend their religion. Indeed, as the great French philosopher Voltaire would write, "This is perhaps the first dispute between two theologians in which no insults are traded; on the contrary the two adversaries treat each other with respect."

But if Dr. Orobio's relations with the Protestant minister were cordial, his feelings toward freethinking Jews, particularly his erstwhile mentor Prado, were decidedly intolerant. In Spain, Prado had been quite willing to risk life and limb in the cause of a somewhat nebulous spirit of Judaism. True, his life as a Christian on the outside and a Jew on the inside—combined with a this-worldly spirit, which permeated certain Marrano literary circles—led Prado to nurture some freethinking and universalist concepts. But these were mostly suppressed for the sake of the higher cause of keeping the flickering flame of Judaism alive in Spain. Now in the freedom of the Netherlands, when confronted with all the detailed ritualistic and doctrinaire aspects of Judaism, Dr. Prado found his more skeptical and rationalist, even deistic, tendencies coming to the fore. Whereas in Spain he had apparently entertained the thought that all religions were equally good in the quest for knowledge of God or the First Cause, he now seemed to be suggesting that they were all equally *bad* in doing so. Worse still, from the point of view of his fellow Jews, Prado wouldn't keep his ideas to himself.

But whereas Dr. Prado's freethinking was unsystematic and vacillating, that of his brilliant young friend Baruch Spinoza was taking on a cool geometric rationality that was absolutely shockingly to the seventeenth-century European, still caught in the Medieval mind-set. The Jewish philosopher Philo, who lived in Alexandria around the time of Jesus, had set the stage for over a millennium and a half of Jewish, Christian, and Islamic philosophizing by taking the rationalistic principles of Aristotle and other Greeks and applying them to explicate the divinely revealed Scriptures. Maimonides, Aquinas, and Avicenna were perhaps the most brilliant followers of this tradition in their respective faiths. Now young Spinoza was refusing to accept in his philosophizing any scriptures as emanating from God—or at least, from any God as thitherto conceived.

At a time when the Iberian Jewish community in the Netherlands was struggling to rebuild itself and re-establish its ancestral religion after having lived for generations as uncircumcised Christians, the rabbis and other Jewish leaders were hardly open to freethinking from Prado or Spinoza. Furthermore, there was probably a worry that the tolerance that the Dutch powers-that-be had shown toward Judaism might be jeopardized by the presence of such heretics in their ranks. Some Jewish physicians, being prominent intellectuals in their community, were particularly outspoken in their condemnation. Dr. Orobio wrote in his "Epistola Invectiva contra Prado": "It is only to you that it so happened, to be a fake Christian and a true Jew where you could not be a Jew, and to be a fake Jew where (finally) you could be truly Jewish." In Orobio's eyes Prado (and also his fellow free-thinking Marrano doctor Juan Piero) was "a man of very limited

204 Jews and Medicine: An Epic Saga

judgment, a small philosopher and even less of a physician, mad in his reasoning, dauntless in his talk, the friend of novelties, solicitor of paradoxes,
and what is worse, abominable in his morals."

If Prado was a "small" philosopher, Spinoza was a gargantuan one. Yet
Orobio dubiously damned the former, with his limited intellect, for supposedly having corrupted the latter, who was of almost unbounded intelligence: "The whole miserable precipice had its origin in the ignorance of
one student or physician [Prado] whose pride did not allow him to understand the divine antidote [to be found] in the doctrine of our ancient and
contemporary Sages and Doctors. . . . [S]omeone [Spinoza], to the great
scandal of our nation, arrived by this path at his extreme ruin and contaminated others who, outside Judaism, gave credit to him and to his foolish
sophisms. . . ." Another physician, the Brazilian-born Dr. Jacob d'Andrade
Velosino, who fled to Amsterdam when the Portuguese conquered Brazil
from the Dutch, circulated a polemic pamphlet, "Theologo Religioso contra o Theologo Politico de (E)spinoza."

In 1656 Spinoza was excommunicated from the Jewish community. This
fate was shared the following year by Dr. Prado, who soon moved to
Antwerp and was more or less forgotten by his contemporaries and by
history. But Spinoza, while keeping a discreetly low profile in the town of
Rijnsburg and then in The Hague, spent the next two decades developing
a philosophy so new and powerful that two centuries later the famed Jewish poet Heinrich Heine would write: "All our contemporary philosophers,
perhaps without knowing it, are looking through the eyeglasses that Baruch
Spinoza polished."

Heine's quote alludes to the fact that Spinoza earned his livelihood by
grinding lenses. Herein lies one of Spinoza's connections to our larger story,
optometry being one of medicine's allied fields. Whereas the young man
Spinoza had first earned his daily bread as partner with his brother in the
fruit import-export firm of Bento y Gabriel d'Espinosa, the excommunication meant a severing of ties not only with the Jewish community in
general, but with his family in particular, and hence the necessity to seek
another livelihood. The latter part of the seventeenth century was a time
of major theoretical advances in the field of optics. Christiaan Huygens,
the greatest scientist of Holland's Golden Age, crossed swords with Sir Isaac
Newton as to whether light is made up of waves, as Huygens believed, or
corpuscles, as Newton maintained (an issue that would be resolved in a

bizarre manner with the introduction of the concept of quantum duality some two centuries later). Spinoza himself was stimulated to write a mathematical treatise on the refraction and reflection of light through tiny water droplets that give rise to the rainbow. A more down-to-earth application of the laws of optics was to be found in the grinding of lenses for improved vision. Spectacles were a rather recent invention. There is no reliable mention of such prostheses in the Talmud (or other old Jewish writings), although Rabbi Gamliel is said to have had a tube with which he could see for a distance of some 2,000 cubits, perhaps a primitive telescope. Be this as it may, eyeglasses, once invented, were of particular value to Jews with the ocular *tsuris*. Indeed, perhaps already in Spinoza's time, certainly in ours, the name *brillejood* ("four-eyes," literally "spectacles-Jew") is applied by nasty Dutch children to anyone wearing glasses.

As important as eyeglasses were in compensating for one of man's physical frailties, the young science of optics in Holland's Golden Age produced an instrument whose role in alleviating humanity's sufferings would, eventually, be truly incalculable. In the town of Delft, hardly five miles from Spinoza's home in The Hague, lived Antoni van Leeuwenhoek, a draper and janitor of the townhall. Born in the same year as Spinoza (1632), largely self-educated, and likewise interested in the new field of optics, van Leeuwenhoek began shaping lenses in such a way as to reveal to him, the first in human history, the corpuscles of blood, the sperm of semen, the striations (stripes) of voluntary muscles, and much more. But all this paled before van Leeuwenhoek's shocking discovery of the "wretched beasties"— the veritable zoo, never before seen by human eyes or conceived of by the most feverish human imagination, now to be observed in droplets of stagnant water from Delft's canals, the scrapings from his teeth, and the intestines of frogs. "They stop, they stand still as 'twere upon a point and then turn themselves round with that swiftness, as we see a top turn round, the circumference they make being no bigger than that of a fine grain of sand," wrote van Leeuwenhoek in Dutch to the Royal Society in London, whose enthralled members made him a fellow, despite his illiteracy in Latin.

Van Leeuwenhoek was a brilliant observer but was not given to profound philosophizing, being content to accept life forms large and small as manifestations of God's desires and purpose, often beyond the grasp of human understanding. By contrast, Spinoza in the nearby Hague could not conceive of God desiring anything. How could He? To believe this was to believe that God (or Nature) was imperfect, a logical absurdity in Spinoza's system. Although making do with less efficient magnification instruments (van Leeuwenhoek would not divulge the secrets of his lenses to a soul), Spinoza set for himself the overall philosophical quest of understanding "the relation of every part of nature to the whole and how each part relates to the others." "The human body," Spinoza declared, "is composed of a number of individual parts, of diverse nature, each one of which is in itself extremely complex." Important in elucidating the relationships of the body to the whole of Nature was a knowledge of "the movement of particles of the lymph, the chyle, and the blood."

Spinoza's most important contribution to anatomy involved his dispute with the great French philosopher René Descartes over the importance of the pineal gland, the little pinecone-shaped body tucked inside the cerebrum. Descartes, who lived in Amsterdam when Baruch was very young and whose writings strongly attracted Spinoza as he grew up, was also an accomplished physiologist. Endeavoring to resolve the ancient mind-body problem in philosophy, he conceived of the soul as having its seat in the pineal gland, from which it communicated with the physical body. "[T]he slightest movement on the part of this gland may alter greatly the course of these [gas-like] spirits [traveling down the nerves]," Descartes declared, "and conversely any change, however slight, in the flow of spirits may do much to change the movements of the gland." Spinoza was not content with this explanation. "I should very much like to know how many degrees of motion the mind can give to that pineal gland, and how great a force is required to hold it in suspense," he declared. "For I do not know whether this gland is driven about more slowly by the mind than by the animal spirits, or more quickly; nor do I know whether the motions of the passions which we have joined closely to firm judgments can be separated from them again by bodily causes." Spinoza's objection had little to do with Descartes's particular choice of the pineal gland rather than some other locus in the brain, but rather with his placing of some ghost in the machine in a philosophically untenable way.

Spinoza had his own solution, of sorts, to the mind-body question. His all-embracing philosophy conceived of God or the whole of Nature as possessing two attributes—thought and extension—which are merely aspects of the same substance. This applies no less to each human being as a part of Nature. "The mind and the body are one and the same individual which is conceived now under the attribute of thought, now under the attribute of extension," Spinoza declared in his greatest philosophical work, *The Ethics*. Centuries later, in the information age, some writers would draw a cautious analogy with software and hardware aspects of processing by computers, or with functionalist and neurophysiological descriptions of mental processes in living organisms.

Another of Spinoza's contemporaries in the philosophical pantheon, the German Gottfried Leibnitz, addressed him as "Médecin très célèbre et philosophe très profond" (very famous physician and very profound philosopher). Spinoza was in fact not a medical doctor and he never treated a patient in his life. Yet he declared: "This is the end I aim at: to acquire knowledge of the Union of the mind with the whole of Nature. . . . [B]ecause health is no small means to achieving this end, the whole of medicine must be worked out." Spinoza was apparently planning an outline of the science of medicine, but if such was ever drafted, it has been lost to posterity. However, from *The Ethics* one can deduce something of his principles of medicine. Most essentially, Spinoza conceived that the ideal situation for the body was for it to persist without any violent fluctuations from external causes. In the absence of great transfers of energy either to the body from its surroundings or vice versa, the mind is freer and can therefore also be more active.

But even given this peaceful existence of the body within its environment, still "a way must be conceived by which the intellect can be cured (*medendi*)." Spinoza's endeavor to provide a means for doing just that made him perhaps the greatest thinker in the field of psychology and psychiatry up to the dawn of the twentieth century. His definitions in *The Ethics* of the emotions of love and hate, pleasure and pain, hope and fear, and a host of other mental states so commonly spoken of but never before rigorously defined, were so lucid that in Germany almost two centuries later, Johannes Müller, a pioneer of modern medicine and physiological psychology (more of whom in a later chapter), would declare: "With regard to the relation of the passions to one another, it is impossible to supply anything better than what Spinoza professed with unsurpassed mastery." Spinoza proceeded to justify what many in his day and ours would consider some of the noblest of the Old and New Testament commandments, but on the basis of reason rather than by recourse to any supernatural authority, promise of rewards or punishment in this life or the next, or even appeals to sentiment. It was by pure geometric deduction that Spinoza derived, for example, the proposition that: "He who lives under the guidance of reason endeavors as far as possible to render back love or kindness for other men's hatred, anger, contempt, etc. for him."

Essential for the cure of the intellect was the intellect's becoming aware of its own thought processes. Here some of the propositions in *The Ethics* offered insights into the workings of the human mind that foreshadowed the depth psychologists of the twentieth century. For example, regarding the phenomenon of what would later become known as repression, Spinoza wrote: "The psyche tries as much as it is capable to become aware of those things which increase the power of the body." Its corollary: "The psyche is bent not to become aware of those things which decrease the power of the body."

From the Golden Age up to the Second World War, the Netherlands would be home to 700 or so Jewish physicians. Two of them, Barend Gompertz and Antonio Sanchez, were influential disciples of Herman Boerhaave, Leiden's brilliant clinician and bedside teacher who in the first half of the eighteenth century strove to free medical education from the dry scholastic books of the ancient and Medieval writers (Hippocrates, whose genuine writings he regarded as analogous to the uncorrupted Holy Scriptures, was an important exception) and to unify medicine with the emerging sciences of chemistry and botany. (It is said that as a student Boerhaave was forced to switch from divinity to medicine when an incautious remark he made led to his being branded as a Spinozist.) At the end of the eighteenth century, when Amsterdam's Jews numbered over 23,000, more than twice that of any other city in the world except Constantinople, Jewish physicians were prominent in introducing to the Netherlands the principles of vaccination against smallpox developed by the English physician Edward Jenner. (Such interference with God's works was not taken kindly to in some religious Christian circles.) Dr. Lion Davids translated Jenner's work into Dutch. Immanuel Capadoce, physician in ordinary to King Louis Napoleon, used his influence at court to further the cause. Dr. Hartog Lemon insisted on vaccinating the populace for free, and Dr. Ezechiel Goldsmit rallied the rabbis in support of the campaign. (Only one Jewish physician, Abraham Capadoce, was a vehement opponent of vaccination on religious grounds. He later converted to Christianity.) Still other Jewish doctors, influenced by the social consequences of the industrial revolution, were active as reformers in the field of public health and industrial medicine.

In the late nineteenth century Samuel Rosenstein, the German-born professor of internal medicine in Groningen and Leiden, was perhaps the most important pioneer and propagator of the germ theory in the Netherlands. Barend Joseph Stokvis, professor of pharmacodynamics and internal medicine in Utrecht and most illustrious of Holland's preeminent medical dynasty, pioneered the field of chemical physiology and chemotherapy. In all, the Dutch doctors up to the Second World War counted in their ranks some two dozen full professors (four of whom also served as Rectores Magnifici, or university presidents), five generals in the Dutch army, seven physicians to the royal family, and dozens of heads of hospitals, clinics, and institutes. Together, they wrote more than twenty textbooks that were authoritative for their respective periods.

Yet arguably, the historically most influential Dutch Jewish physician—a student and protegée of Rosenstein and Stokvis—was not a medical man, but a medical woman. For it was Aletta Jacobs, the daughter of a provincial doctor, who broke the gender barrier in medicine and went on to pioneer birth control and women's rights and to work for international peace as the confidant of presidents, princes, and popes.

As for Spinoza, the time would come when the concept of a nonbelieving Jew—once as great a *contradictio in termines* as a nonbelieving Catholic or nonbelieving Protestant—would become a meaningful label, worn with pride. The Sage of Amsterdam, the excommunicated heretic born centuries before his time, would come to be looked upon and admired by masses of Jewish intellectuals as the first of the breed. His philosophy would inspire some of nonbelieving Jewry's greatest thinkers, including physicians. Nowhere was this more so than in the Germanic lands to the east of Holland. There, as the nineteenth century progressed, medicine's most dramatic triumphs would be played out in breathtakingly rapid order. But as we shall see in the next chapter, the Enlightenment among Jew and gentile that preceded them was slow in dawning.

Chapter 8
Enlightenment under the
North German Sun

The practice of medicine is fraught with perils, and I am a man and of no under-
standing, fearing lest I grope at noonday as the blind grope in the dark.
—Physician's prayer of rabbi-doctor Jacob Zahalon (eighteenth century)

[Wishing you] especially good light in wintertime.
—1836 New Year's greeting to microscopist Jacob Henle

Contagion is a matter endowed with individual life which reproduces itself in the
manner of animals and plants, which can multiply by assimilating organic material
and can exist parasitically on the sick body.

—Jacob Henle (1840)

Whereas the Jews of the Mediterranean region called themselves
Sephardim, after the Hebrew name for Spain, those who after the
destruction of the Second Temple in 70 C.E. followed the route through
Northern Europe called themselves Ashkenazim, after the Hebrew name
for Germany. As Spain was for some 1,000 years the focal point of Mediterranean Jewish life, so was Germany the center of Jewish culture in Northern and Eastern Europe—in fact, for a far longer, if more intermittent,
period. And just as after the expulsion from Spain an old form of Spanish
(Ladino) remained the language of many thousands of Sephardic Jews, so
Germany provided an old form of her language (Yiddish), which up to the
advent of Hitler remained the mother tongue and lingua franca of millions

211

of Jews from Poland to the Russian Steppes, whose ancestors had fled from Germany centuries earlier.

Already during the Roman Empire there were Latin records of Jews living in Colonia, today's Cologne. And this area of settlement probably extended to other Roman towns on the Rhine and Moselle Rivers, such as Confluentes (Coblenz), Treveri (Trier), and Mogontiacum (Mainz). This was in an era when the main population in the region was not yet even German but Celtic. Indeed, when some 2,000 years later a Jewish doctor named Sigmund Freud was being harassed by the Pan-Germanism of the Nazis, he would point with pride to the Jews having already been settled on the Rhine when the Teutonic tribes were still pushing their way there from the east.

The Dark Ages left many gaps in the historical record of Germany in general and the German Jews in particular. But documents dating from before the close of the first millennium attest to Jewish communities engaged in trade in the very same Rhineland areas they had inhabited in Roman times. In fact, Freud would again point with pride to a Medieval fresco painter named "Freud of Cologne," whom he liked to think of as a distant ancestor.

Being far removed from the Enlightenment radiating from the Medieval Islamic world, the science of the Jews of Germany, and not least their medicine, for centuries lagged far behind that of their southern coreligionists. The views on disease among German Jews were permeated by what we today would call outright superstition rather than such pseudosciences as alchemy and astrology. The Jewish medical lore thus differed little from that of their gentile neighbors and in fact drew much from it, as well as from specifically Jewish sources such as talmudic passages. Demons, widely accepted among the general population of Medieval Germany as agents of disease, were similarly viewed by many German Jews. Jewish adults as well as children feared the "neck-twister" spirit, which attacked the young. The demons inhabiting the moon-shadows of the *Judengasse*, consisting as they did of fire and hail, afflicted their victims alternatively with fever and chills. Even the quite valid concept of contagion was couched in supernatural terms in Medieval Jewish texts: "One should not drink another's leavings," warns the *Nishatmat ayim*, "because if the first man has a disease a spirit goes out of his liquid; it is mortal danger to drink it." The unhealthiness of places like malarial marshes were similarly ascribed in some Jewish texts to demons that supposedly haunted them.

If the etiology of diseases was supernatural among the German Jews, so their treatment was commonly based on folk remedies that were correspondingly irrational (at least, by modern standards), whether borrowed from the German gentiles or derived from more specifically Jewish sources. Even the court physician to the secretary of Pope Martin IV—one of the relatively few Medieval German-Jewish doctors of note—readily conceded in the thirteenth century: "I have seen illnesses upon which the greatest medicines had no effect, cured by spells and charms." Based on prohibitions in the Bible and fear of idolatry, orthodox Judaism, particularly as influenced by the great Maimonides, remained in principle opposed to anything smacking of magic. Yet, no doubt in response to pressure from the common people, loopholes were sought. Some rabbis permitted the use of amulets inscribed with holy names and passages only for prophylactic purposes. But others, citing the dictum that a danger to life overrides even the prohibition on desecrating the Sabbath, permitted their supposedly curative use.

Indeed, two prominent and often disagreeing authorities of the *Gemara*, Abaye and Raba, found themselves in agreement that "nothing done for purposes of healing is to be forbidden as superstitious." Rabbi Israel Isserlein concurred when he advised a correspondent: "Regarding your question as to whether an invalid may consult a magician, know that we have found no explicit prohibition of such a course, for the biblical strictures against sorcerers do not apply in this case." The Talmud is not without its fair share of wounds and diseases being treated with charms. And although the Talmud prohibits the use of the word of God for healing, it was customary among the Medieval Ashkenazim to lay a scroll upon the body of a sick person and to recite various biblical selections as remedies for specific ailments. Certain charms had to be repeated nine times, according to the *Sefer Hasidim*— a concession to German gentile custom.

A curious Medieval German institution was the *Dreck-apotheke*, or dirt pharmacy. As the subtitle of a prominent drug book assured its readers, one could maintain one's health and even recover from otherwise incurable diseases through the use of "urine, behind and ear filth, spittle, and other natural little remedies." Other delectable ingredients included sweat, nails, afterbirth, and semen. Such recipes were by no means limited to Germans and gentiles. The use of excrement and other disgusting substances was not entirely unknown in the ancient Middle East, and the Talmud makes mention—albeit only briefly—of forty-day-old urine as treatment for wasp and scorpion stings, children's feces for scurvy, and white dog excrement for pleuritis. Rabbi Israel Isserlein used urine to relieve his gout. But it was in medieval Germany that the *Dreck-apotheke* particularly flourished. One rationale for such remedies within the framework of the Medieval weltanschauung may be sought in the concept of expelling the pathogenic spirits from the body by making life uncomfortable for them. (Shades of this view seem to have survived into the modern era, with the feeling among some patients that terrible tasting medicines are more effective.) Where the Medieval Jewish and gentile filth recipes tended to part company was in the matter of blood as an ingredient. Whereas the gentile *Dreck-apotheke* included such prized ingredients as menstrual secretions, the age-old Jewish prohibition on the consumption of any and all blood forbade its internal use, and even references to topical applications are exceedingly rare in Jewish texts.

By contrast, the widespread belief among German gentiles that water possessed curative properties at certain times of the year presented no problem to the Jews. In their own adaptation, they drew upon a midrashic legend of miraculous water from "Miriam's well," which moved through rivers and sources at the end of the Sabbath. "Anyone who is ill, and is fortunate enough to get some of that healing water and drink it, even though his body be wholly broken out with sores, will," so the Jewish texts assures us, "be immediately cured." Alternatively, the Talmud tells us, a fever could be transferred from the body of the patient into a body of water.

A more particularly Jewish healing custom in Medieval Germany was that of changing the name of the seriously or chronically ill patient, in the hope of allowing him or her to escape the fate that had already, as it were, been entered in some divine book of orders. An apparent assumption of German Jews was that God, omnipotent and omniscient though He Himself was, entrusted the execution of His orders to an angelic bureaucracy, who, like their none-too-bright earthly counterparts attempting to serve a warrant, might be confused by an alias. The Talmud—while, of course, recommending prayer, change of conduct, and almsgiving in an attempt to commute a divine sentence (diseases being still viewed as the wages of sin)—allowed such name-changing as symbolic of a changed person. New names such as Hayim ("life"), Alte ("old one"), and Zeide ("grandfather") were particularly in vogue for their connotations of longevity. After reciting a prescribed formula while holding the Torah before an assembly of ten persons, the reader would advise the heavenly powers-that-be that the renamed sufferer "is another man, like unto a newborn creature, an infant who has just been born into a long and good life."

If many Medieval Jewish healing practices derived much from gentile folk medicine, the influence also flowed in the other direction, the Christians often being in awe of the supposed healing power contained in Jewish lore. Such attitudes were not limited to Germany. When the famed sixteenth-century sculptor and goldsmith Benvenuto Cellini wrote of sorcerers in Rome uttering their "awful invocations, calling by name on multitudes of demons . . . in phrases of Hebrew," he was not necessarily referring to Jews. For gentile magicians were fond of using Hebrew or pseudo-Hebrew abracadabras for their effect.

It was among the Jewish communities in the Rhineland that the hasidic movement took root in the twelfth and thirteenth centuries, particularly in the towns of Speyer, Mainz, and Worms. In the latter town, Eleazar ben Jehudah, the most zealous of the *hasidim*, wrote the books *Sefer Raziel* and *Ha-Rokeah* around 1230. Late in the same century in Spain, the mystic Moses de Leon wrote the kabbalistic "Book of Splendor," the *Zohar.* The expulsion of the Sefardim from Spain and the migration of many Ashkenazim eastward from Germany was a reason why in later centuries the hasidic movement would find its strongest expression not in those countries but, after some further development in the Holy Land, in Eastern Europe. Among the medical lore of the *hasidim* was the concept that each of the 248 positive commandments of Judaism corresponded to one of the 248 bones of the human body (as reckoned by the anatomists in the Talmud) and to one of the 248 lunar days of the year (as reckoned by the astronomers in the Talmud). The 365 negative commandments corresponded to the solar days of the year. Anyone violating a commandment risked an affliction in the corresponding anatomical region or *schlim Mazel* (bad luck) on the corresponding day. *Hasidim* have traditionally eschewed any form of non-Jewish higher education, including medical school. Thus any doctors they consult need be from outside their community, even if orthodox Jewish. From Medieval times into the age of nuclear medicine, the rebbe of any given hasidic *Hoyf* (court) has had the authority, based on his otherworldly insights, to override the diagnoses and treatments of the doctors with respect to his congregants. Hasidic lore is also replete with stories of rebbes performing miraculous cures, though not promiscuously but in subtle ways.

The visitation of the Black Death in the mid-fourteenth century, a medical disaster for all Europe, was no less a political catastrophe for so many Jewish communities, especially those in the Rhineland of Germany and Switzerland. Jean Froisart, who chronicled the plague years on the Continent, wrote how the contempt for the human body so evident among the early Christians erupted with a vengeance in 1348:

> The penitents went around, coming first out of Germany. They were men who did public penance and scourged themselves with whips of hard knotted leather with little iron spikes. Some made themselves bleed very badly between the shoulder blades and some foolish women had cloths ready to catch the blood and smear it on their eyes, saying it was miraculous blood. While they were doing penance, they sang very mournful songs about nativity and the passion of Our Lord. The object of this penance was to put a stop to the mortality, for in that time . . . at least a third of all the people in the world died.

In the beginning, at least, the flagellants usually had enthusiastic support from the local population and the town authorities, who saw them as martyrs atoning for the sins of the world that had brought the plague. This was particularly unfortunate for the Jews, for the flagellants preached anti-Semitism. Due to their age-old concern with hygiene, Jews in some localities in Europe were accustomed to drawing water from streams rather than from wells they considered to be contaminated by "bad, noxious moistures and vapors." Now this rather quirky but otherwise harmless practice became highly suspicious to the gentile population. In the Rhineland, where central political authority was particularly lacking during the plague years, the Jews were at the mercy of the whims of the local government and populace.

Another chronicler of the Black Death, Jean de Venette, the Carmelite friar and master of theology from the University of Paris, wrote of events in the Rhineland in the 1340s:

The Jews were suddenly and violently charged with infecting the wells and water, and corrupting the air. The whole world rose up against them cruelly on this account. In Germany . . . they were massacred and slaughtered by Christians, and many thousands were burned everywhere, indisciminantly. The unshaken if fatuous constancy of the (Jewish) men and their wives was remarkable. For mothers hurled their children first into the fire that they might not be baptized, and then leapt in after them to burn with their husbands and children.

In 1348 all the Jews of Basel were gathered on an island on the Rhine to perish in a conflagration. The town council then banned Jews from settling in the city for the somewhat arbitrary period of 200 years. A similar genocidal fate awaited the 2,000 Jews of Strassburg the following year, when the merchants guild forced out the more tolerant town council and replaced it with violent anti-Semites. After the fires, citizens were allowed to sift through the ashes in search of valuables not consumed by the flames. Comparable scenes recurred up and down the Rhine and in adjacent regions, resulting in the destruction of the Jews of Frankfurt, Cologne, and Mainz (in the latter case, also costing the lives of some 200 Christians when the Jews fought back). At Speyer the Jewish bodies were placed in wine caskets and floated down the Rhine.

By 1349 flagellantism was threatening to get out of control and yet was losing some of the initial enthusiasm of the population, since the plague had not abated. Pope Clement VI sought advice from the theologians at the University of Paris, while its prestigious medical faculty, together with that of Montpellier, investigated the accusations of Jewish culpability in causing the plague. The gentile medical men, even if prejudiced against Jews, were not inclined to accept the well-poisoning libel. Most Jewish communities partook of the same water as their Christian neighbors. And in any case, the prevailing theory of the causation of the plague (correctly) excluded well water as a vector. The pestilence was instead attributed (incorrectly) to an inauspicious alignment of the planets, causing earthquakes and the release of noxious vapors (miasmas) into the atmosphere, something beyond even the devilish power of the Jews to bring about. Furthermore, the Jews suffered a death rate from the plague comparable that of the Christians. (As Shakespeare's Shylock would later plead: Aren't we Jews "subject to the same diseases, healed by the same means?"). In fact, survivors in many hard-pressed Jewish communities had to acquire additional cemeteries to cope with the tragedy.

Pope Clement accordingly issued a bull condemning the flagellant movement and urging protection of the Jews, since "most of the (flagellants) or their followers, beneath an appearance of piety, set their hands to cruel and impious works, shedding the blood of Jews, whom Christian piety accepts and sustains." But by then, there were not many Jews left along the Rhine for the Christians to accept. More than 350 massacres on top of the mortalities from the plague had wiped out some 60 major and 150 smaller Jewish communities. Many survivors fled to Eastern Europe, where two centuries earlier other German Jews has sought refuge from the Crusades. Along with them went their Medieval Rhenish German, which would become known as Yiddish and undergo its own natural evolution, although remaining to the present day in some respects more conservative than the German of Germany.

Yet even as Jews were blamed for the Black Death, the magical or demonic powers contained in the symbols of their ancient religion and in their ancestral language were seen as offering protection from the pestilence. Many charms and amulets inscribed in Hebrew and once thought of as Jewish are now known to have been produced by and for Christians. Popular as neckwear in the sixteenth century were the Old Testament—inspired plague medallions and thalers. These amulets, minted in Joachimsthal and other places, depicted Moses and the brass serpent, but also—to hedge one's bets—displayed the crucified Jesus on the flip side. (Interestingly, in Austria around the turn of the twentieth century, when a new age of scientific, rational medicine had finally come into being, we find supposedly "galvanic" medals being sold to gullible rheumatic patients shaped like a cross, or, alternatively, like a star of David above a crescent. The latter version was probably not for Jews but instead owed its popularity to a legacy of the power of Semitic signs among Christians.)

The mysterious forces that were associated with Judaism in the gentile German mind adhered, of course, to the Jewish physician, both before and after the visitation of the plague. This added to the patients' awe of his book learning, by which the ancient and Medieval Islamic medical lore continued to be transmitted, and also their appreciation of his practical skills in physical manipulations (something the learned gentile doctor shunned). Even back in the ninth century the Holy Roman emperor Charles the Bald had a Jewish personal physician, Zedekias. In the high and late Middle Ages Jewish physicians graced the courts of various German dukes and electors as well as the palaces of emperors such as Frederick III, who entrusted his health to Jakob Loans. Frederick specifically exempted certain Jewish physicians in his realm from the burden of taxation, as did other temporal rulers.

The princes of the Church, for their part, were not about to deprive themselves of Jewish medicine, all the ecclesiastic bans notwithstanding. So, for example, the twelfth-century archbishop of Trier, Bruno I, retained Josua as his personal physician, and 200 years later we find the physician Simon attending Bruno's successor, Boermund II. Also, commoners in Germany who could avail themselves of medical services tended to prefer Jewish to Christian physicians. Jewish doctors were likely to be exempt from having to live on the *Judengasse*, and the Jewish *Wanderärtze* (traveling physicians) were in demand in towns far away from the ghetto. So great was the awe of the Jewish medical art that when the plague struck again in the fifteenth century, rumor had it that a Jewish doctor had a secret cure. The rumor-mongers were right, only they were about half a millennium premature. For, as we shall see in due course, at the dawn of the twentieth century a Jewish bacteriologist would develop the first prophylactic vaccine for the plague. And a few decades later another Jewish biologist would discover antibiotics to virtually eradicate the age-old scourge. They were Yiddish-speaking descendants of the German Jews driven eastward by the irrational slaughter carried out by their plague-stricken Christian neighbors.

If the visitations of the plague were a political catastrophe for the Jews of Germany and Western Europe, they were in the long run secondary to the political tribulations to befall the Jews as a result of the schisms and heresies that afflicted the Catholic Church a few centuries into the new millennium. After the brutal suppression of the Albergensians, Hussites, and other Christian rebels by the Catholic Church, the early sixteenth century saw the success of Martin Luther. Some ecclesiastic powers-that-be were glad to attribute the rise of Protestantism to Jewish machinations and branded the Lutherans "Jews." In point of fact young man Luther was initially quite well disposed toward the Jewish people. As part of his opposition to the rituals of the Roman clergy, Luther advocated a return to the "true faith" and encouraged the study of Hebrew. The general Protestant derision of superstition and magical practice was instrumental in the waning of the Medieval ritual murder charges against the Jews in particular (more about which in a later chapter), and Luther hoped to convert Israel to his new faith. "The Jews are our kith and kin and brothers-in-blood of our Savior," he wrote. "If we are going to boast about the virtues of race, Christ belongs more to them than to us. To no other people has God shown such favor in entrusting them with His Holy Word."

In time, however, old man Luther, having despaired of winning the Jews over to Protestantism with kind words, would turn against them with a vengeance and even imply that Jews—including those well disposed toward his new religion—were intrinsically incapable of becoming Christians. Although he derided the blood libel as superstition, Luther believed in the power of certain Hebrew incantations and other magical practices in Jewish folk medicine. (So, for example, when he fell ill sometime after passing through a Jewish village, he reasoned that this was due to Jews blowing at his wagon.) As for the Jewish physicians, Luther was all the more in awe of their powers, both supernatural ("The devil can do much!" he conceded) and scientific, and he took for granted that these were used for evil ends. "If [the Jews] could kill us all, they would gladly do so, aye, and often do it, especially those who profess to be physicians," wrote Luther. "They know all that is known about medicine in Germany; they can give poison to a man of which he will die in an hour, or in ten or twenty years; they thoroughly understand this art." Indeed, Luther's contemporary Johannes Eck, author of *Ains Judenbüchlein,* recounted how "When they [Jewish physicians] come together at their festivals, each boasts of the number of Christians he has killed with his medicine; and the one who has killed the most is honored."

The great schism in Christianity and the consolidation of the modern nation states heralded the ghettoization of the Jews and their marginalization from wider intellectual life. This occurred in Protestant northern Europe, where, with a certain irony, Luther had lumped Catholics with Jews as the enemies of Christ, just as it did in the Catholic realms to the south, where the Counterreformation struck back at what it perceived as "Jewish" Lutheranism. In the seventeenth century the Frankfurt clergy declared to the city council: "Sooner sick at God's will than healed through forbidden means. To employ Jewish doctors means nothing else than to cuddle serpents in our boson and to raise wolves in our homes." Similarly, the clergy at Halle decreed: "It is better to die with Christ than to be healed by a Jew doctor with Satan."

As his coreligionist colleague David de Pomis had done in Catholic Italy in the late sixteenth century, so now deep in Lutheran northern Germany in the seventeenth century the Jewish physician Benedict de Castro wrote an impassioned *Apologia*. Benedict was the son of the physician Rodrigo de Castro, a doctor from the University of Salamanca, who was among the Iberian refugees to settle in the Free City of Hamburg. Especially renowned for his book on gynecology entitled *De Universa Mulierum Medicina,* Rodrigo was a figure at the courts of the king of Denmark, the archbishop of Bremen, the dukes of Holstein and Mecklenburg, and the Landgrave of Hessen. His son Benedict would in turn be appointed physician-in-waiting to Queen Christina of Sweden. In 1631 Benedict published a Latin work whose title reads in translation: "The Scourge of Calumniators or Apology in which the malicious charges of an anonymous author are refuted, the lust for lying of this person is disclosed, and the legitimate method of the most famous Portuguese physicians is commended, while the ignorance and temerity of empiric quacks are condemned as injurious to the commonwealth."

Germany in the first century of Lutheranism was indeed a place where Jewish physicians were the target of various polemic tracts. In 1631, the same year that Benedict de Castro published his retort to an anonymous hatemonger, the Frankfurt physician Lodovicus von Hoernigk issued his *Medicaster Apella oder Juden Artzt*—400 pages of vehement religious, medical, and social condemnation of Jewish doctors.

Most interesting of all was the case of the enormously influential German-Swiss Renaissance physician Philipp Auroelus Theophrastus Bombastus von Hohenheim. Although he took the name Paracelsus, meaning the equal of the ancient Roman doctor Celsus, he also became known in his lifetime as *Lutherus medicorum* (Luther of the physicians) for the way he overthrew much of the medical establishment. Like Luther, Paracelsus used the German vernacular rather than scholarly Latin as his written and spoken vehicle, and did not shy from punctuating his diatribes with vulgar biological metaphors in order to drive home some angry point. During his *Wanderjahre* early in the sixteenth century, Paracelsus traveled over Western Europe, the Middle East, Russia, and Turkey, searching for medical truths from whatever sources he could obtain them, high or low. Settling down in Basel, he commenced his brief tenure as university lecturer by publicly burning the works of Galen and Avicenna, stating, "Gentlemen, let's begin once more at the beginning." Paracelsus's wrath was no less directed at contemporary physicians, especially those who "have learned so much that their learning has driven out their common sense." "When I saw that nothing resulted from their practice but killing and laming, . . . I determined to abandon such a miserable art and seek truth elsewhere."

Apart from his merely undermining the old systems, which were admittedly of questionable value, Paracelsus made some positive contributions to medicine. Growing up at the Carinthian mines (where his father was physician to the workers of the powerful Fugger company), Paracelsus developed a lifelong interest in metallurgy. Disgusted with the Galenic compounds of fifty or more ingredients in a single prescription, Paracelsus sought the vital quintessence or arcanum of simple metals and was later influential in introducing lead, sulpher, iron, arsenic, copper sulfate, and potassium sulfate into the pharmacopoeia. For him, the human body was sooner a collection of chemicals than of muscles and sinew. Although in that age, his drugs, like those of the Galenists, might well have done more harm than good, Paracelsus is rightly seen as one of the first iatrochemists, the chemically based physicians who would be much in vogue in the seventeenth century. More important, he was, in a sense, the herald of chemotherapy, which would become so important in the twentieth century.

If Paracelsus was critical of the poisoners and purgers in general, who "care a great deal more for their own profit than for the health of their patients," he made sure to save some of his nastiest invective for the Jews in particular. In this way, too, he lived up to his title of *Lutherus medicorum*. In his *Labyrithus Medicorum Errantium,* published posthumously in 1553, Paracelsus wrote:

> As regards medicine the Jews of old boasted greatly, and they still do, and they are not ashamed of falsehood. They claim that they are the oldest and first physicians. And indeed they are the foremost among all nations, the foremost rascals, that is. . . . God himself and his only Son they have rejected, and not recognized, and then they should know the works and powers of nature? God has snatched from them and taken away from their hands

the art of medicine, condemning them and their children for all eternity and casting them away at the same time . . . and yet they vindicate for themselves all praise of medicine. Let us pay no attention to all that. . . . For they are not born for medicine, nor are they educated in it. From the very beginning of the world it has been their task to wait for the divine Messiah . . . and whatever they have tried beyond this has been foreign to them and false. Medicine has been given to the gentiles.

In light of this polemic, it seems at first sight extremely odd to find in the Paracelsean corpus lavish praise for the Jew Techellus, whom he calls "a great teacher in Israel and true naturalist," a practitioner of the "Highest Art, Magica and Cabalia," whose wondrous work was ignored by "inexperienced and wanton sophists," primarily because Techellus was a Jew. Techellus, known elsewhere as Zethel, Zachel, or Zael, may also be identical with Sahl ibn Bishr, a ninth-century Jewish astrologer. Techellus apparently knew the secrets of *gamahei*, stones with images that appear to be carved but in fact have grown naturally by God's ordinance. Their images convey, according to Paracelsus, a "great prophetic message," understood by "magi and chiromantici."

All this says much about the spirituality of Paracelsus and explains his apparent attraction to the occult Kabbalah. Although in a sense the forerunner of modern chemotherapy, Paracelsus's chemistry was in fact Medieval alchemy, bound up in mysticism. His quest for "signatures" in nature—divine signs of healing power in stones and metals—was part of the Great Mystery. The *Lutherus medicorum*, for whom God and Nature met in Man, was not really a Lutheran in the religious sense, being far too involved with his own esoteric spiritual quest to take sides on denominational issues.

In much of the German-speaking lands of Germany, Austria, and Bohemia, from the sixteenth century onward, the traditional *Judenstädte* turned into official ghettos, increasingly isolated from the broader society. So, for example, in the city of Prague, where Jews had once engaged in the learned professions, as well as more mundane occupations, legislation reduced them predominantly to peddling and petty shopkeeping by the close of the eighteenth century. Interesting is the popular book of health tips written in seventeenth-century Prague by one Issachar Teller. That the book was written in Yiddish and that Teller was a lowly barber-surgeon, not a physician (although he did receive instruction from a distinguished Jewish doctor from Padua, who had himself been a pupil of Galileo) was indicative of the increasing isolation and downward mobility of the Jews. Nevertheless, there were still Jewish *Stadtsärzte* (municipal physicians) serving the population at large in German towns, and the Jewish *Hofärzte* (court physicians) and even an occasional *Hofzahnarzt* (court dentist) were still deemed indispensable by the various German princes. These were not the only *Hofjuden* (court Jews) enjoying privileged positions. Drawing upon centuries of experience in international monetary and commercial dealings, Jewish finance ministers were instrumental in transforming the feudal economies into modern capitalistic systems. As the ghettoized Jews labored under increasing restrictions, the *Hofjuden* endeavored to ease the lot of their coreligionists but seldom with much success. Their numbers dwindling in Western Europe, ghettoized in Central Europe, and living in backwater *städtls* in Eastern Europe, the Jews in the sixteenth through eighteenth centuries went through a period of retrenchment and retreat into their own religious and cultural world, as particularly exemplified by the influence of the mysticism of the Kabbalah, and later the growth of the hasidic movement.

In this comparative low point in the Jewish history of medicine, the Jews had their fair share of the pseudoscience and outright quackery that was so widespread in the healing arts, cashing in on the awe with which the mysterious Israelites have traditionally been held by the gentiles. A prototypical example of the combination of supposedly brilliant medical ability and uncanny alchemical (and financial) wizardry at the courts of eighteenth-century Germany is found in the person of Dr. Hayyim Sh'muel Falck, the "famous Prince and Grand Priest of the Jews." Having first demonstrated his medical magic by "cur[ing] the daughter of a court Jew who had suffered almost daily attacks of the falling sickness," Dr. Falck offered to increase the treasury of a German prince by 4 million écus if he be allowed the freedom of the principality for forty days in order to conduct alchemical work. The prince refused, fearful of some Satanic connection, even though Dr. Falck had proposed to let his work be "examined by such theologians as the prince deemed reliable to ensure that he did nothing except with the help of God." Dr. Falck, who also made a name for himself in London society under the name of Dr. Falkon, was such a magnificent conjurer that he was banned from several German states because he "performed things that were above the prodigies that one could relate."

Not all Jewish mountebanks were so highly placed. The apologist Benedict de Castro, while admitting in the seventeenth century that "Jewish quacksalvers, . . . though rare, are still to be found in Germany," hastened to add that "these are forced by hunger to resort to quackery, for they are not permitted to become mechanics and thus they seek their livelihood." Having the disadvantage of being Jews as well as quacks, the Jewish mountebanks also were the focus of anti-Jewish feeling, which their gentile counterparts were spared. An etching published at the turn of the eighteenth century bore the title "Unscrupulous Jew doctor in which is represented with irrefutable cause from religious and secular law firstly the true counterfeit of a Christian physician and his indispensable science as well as his conscientious practice, secondly however the horrible appearance of the Jew doctor as well as his unfitness for learning and the doctorate, and the harmful service to the patients."

The intellectual and physical isolation of the Jews was, ironically, taking place at a time of great scientific advances outside the ghetto walls. Fortunately, the Jewish physicians could serve as conduits to their community of the scientific and intellectual developments in larger European society. This special position was due in part to the fact that just about the only university-educated Jews were found in the medical profession, a circumstance that arose from factors on both sides of the religious divide. Through the eighteenth century and later, German universities (Frankfurt an der Oder, Halle, Giessen, and Marburg, in that chronological order) tended to allow Jewish students to matriculate but only in medicine. As a result, inquisitive young Jews who might otherwise have preferred to go for a degree in natural philosophy or the like nevertheless took up the healing arts. The rabbis, for their part, were suspicious of the new spirit of free inquiry into the natural sciences but willing to grant dispensations for medical students. As Rabbi Leo Modena of Venice wrote in the seventeenth century: "Some study philosophy and the natural sciences, but only with the intention of being better able to understand the Holy Scriptures; otherwise they would consider the study pernicious, unless someone intends to qualify in medicine: in that case he is allowed to do otherwise." This situation no doubt contributed to the identification—already strong among the gentiles—of "doc-

tor" with "physician," the medical man being just about the only academically trained person whom the population at large had occasion to deal
with. Yet even so, the spirit of the age was such that the period up to the
end of the eighteenth century remained a comparative ebb in the great
history of Jewish medicine.

The caution with which even a highly eminent Jewish doctor approached
the new developments in the natural sciences is illustrated by the career of
Tobias Cohn. The son and grandson of physicians in Eastern Europe, Cohn
gained admittance to the medical faculty of the University of Frankfurt an
der Oder despite his religion, thanks to the good offices of the grand elec-
tor of Brandenburg. (This was in 1677, a mere three decades after the first
admission of a Jew to a German medical school, in Köningsburg.) Cohn
was, however, obliged to participate in public discussions concerning his
faith and was furthermore barred from actually taking the degree in Frankfurt. This was in strict compliance with the twenty-fourth canon of the
Council of Basel in 1434, which in fact forbade Jews from receiving any
academic diploma. So Cohn had to go to the more tolerant University of
Padua in Italy in order to graduate. Dr. Cohn went on to become the court
physician to five successive Turkish sultans and to publish in 1708 his en-
cyclopedic work in Hebrew *Ma'aseh Tobiyyah,* which dealt mostly with
medicine but included some theology, astronomy, cosmology, and botany,
as well as a discourse on the four Greco-Roman elements.

Cohn's fellow Jewish physician Isaac Cardozo declared in justification of
the scientific zeitgeist that "we shall investigate nature and its founder, so
that from the world and its multitude of things, as if by a ladder, with
enlightened and instructed mind, we may be lifted to God its maker; for
His creatures are the ladder by which we ascend to God, the organ with
which we praise God, and the school in which we learn God." But Cohn
himself was generally wary of anything smacking of deism or pantheism.
When the study of Creation and its principles becomes a goal in and of
itself, one tends to ignore or reject the Creator and His law: "There exist,"
Cohn wrote, "weak-minded men of deficient intelligence and understanding not only from among the Gentile nations who never observed the light
of the Torah but also among the members of our people, the nation that
walks in the darkness of the exile and the light of the Torah . . . and they
think that the world has no originator or creator or leader but only that

everything is determined by nature and its custom." Cohn's writings showed him to be conversant with René Descartes's mechanics and with Marin Mersenne's experiments on air pressure. But if the new science threatened to conflict with ancient religious authority, the latter won out in Cohn's thinking. So although he seems to have been impressed by the eloquence and simplicity of Nicholas Copernicus's arguments for a heliocentric universe, he rejected them on biblical grounds, declaring rather lamely: "The counterarguments are easily confusing [even] to one who understands [them]: thus I will not dwell on them anymore."

In the field of medicine, however, Cohn was more a child of the new age of science. He shared Paracelsus's opposition to many aspects of Galenism. He spoke of "a new medicine which dwells in the bosom of the physicians of our time" and referred favorably to the chemical approach. He was well versed in the teachings of Leiden's leading clinician and iatrochemist Sylvius, who explained disease in terms of an excess of acid or alkali. Cohn furthermore accepted the hypothesis of the English physician Thomas Willis of five principles, rather than the traditional four elements of nature: three active ones (spirit, sulfur, and salt) and two passive ones (water and earth). Cohn also shared Willis's belief that the most frequent changes in nature are due to fermentation. Modest yet hopeful regarding these new approaches, Cohn wrote: "I do not wish, beloved reader, to force you to follow in a rigorous way my teachings, . . . but it is true that the method which modern physicians use with such constancy and reflective analysis has led them to new discoveries. . . ."

Cohn was certainly more upbeat than his near-contemporary colleague, the Italian rabbi-doctor Jacob Zahalon, who beseeched the Lord's help in his physician's prayer, declaring: "The practice of medicine is fraught with perils, and I am a man and of no understanding, fearing lest I grope at noonday as the blind grope in the dark." Certainly, no light of knowledge was shed by the burning torch of tar Zahalon carried that was supposed to "purify the air" when he visited plague victims. But it was possibly Zahalon's good fortune that the impregnation of his clothes with these tar fumes made them inhospitable to the fleas carrying the plague microbe *Yersinia pestis,* of whose existence he had no conception. What neither Jacob Zahalon nor Tobias Cohn could have known was that a century and a half later, another Dr. Cohn would focus the sunlight of the mirror of his microscope on the invisible microorganisms and help bring about the greatest breakthrough in medical history, rendering obsolete most of the work of Tobias's "modern" contemporaries.

The beginning of the end of the groping in the dark that Jacob Zahalon so lamented in his physician's prayer came with the *Aufklärung*, the German Enlightenment (or Elucidation). Not coincidentally, this period also marked the beginning of the emancipation of the Jews and their enthusiastic participation in the wider world of science, literature, and philosophy in Germany. In 1743, a 14-year-old named Moses Mendelsohn hitchhiked from his ghetto in Dessau to the Prussian capital, Berlin. There, in the course of time, his reputation as philosopher and art and literary critic made him the prototypical salon Jew. Mendelsohn became a personal friend of the philosopher Emmanuel Kant and was further inspired by the writings of the *philosophes* Rousseau and Voltaire in France. The German Socrates, as Mendelsohn came to be known, also had contacts with the Jewish medical circles in the capital, and particularly with Abraham Hirsch, the hospital physician of Berlin's Poor and Sick House of the Jewish Community. Up until his death in 1786, Mendelsohn endeavored to bring to the ghetto the light of the new German *Aufklärung*. Judaism should now focus on interpretation according to eternal truths and the social contract (though not excluding God), rather than subservience to the ritual details that had characterized ghetto life for centuries. Jews should read and write in German, a language that was now the vehicle for a flourishing science and philosophy. So impressed was the great playwright Gotthold Lessing by the philosophy of his friend Mendelsohn that he modeled around him the title character in his sensational play *Nathan the Wise*, which included lines such as: Friar: "Nathan! You are a Christian, by God, you are a Christian!" Nathan: "So be it! For that which makes me a Christian in your eyes, makes you a Jew in mine!"

Yet in the field of medicine, the first decades of 1800s in Germany gave no hint of the veritable explosion of knowledge that the German doctors—Jewish and gentile, working hand in hand—would bring about later in the century. The continuing impotence of mainstream medicine understandably encouraged various fringe movements. Historically, the most important was homeopathy, as it alone would endure into the age of nuclear medicine and laser surgery. The gentile German physician Dr. Samuel

Hahnemann, who founded homeopathy in the late eighteenth century, took to heart Hippocrates' first commandment, "Do no harm." Eschewing the powerful purgatives and poisons with which the orthodox doctors attempted a frontal assault on diseases that they usually didn't understand, Hahnemann opted for infinitesimal doses of substances that, if administered at full strength to healthy persons, would cause the same symptoms as the disease being combated.

Jews participated in the homeopathic movement. In Hahnemann's time the Marburg-educated doctor Carl August (né Sekkin Amscel) Metz authored several books on homeopathy for physicians and laymen. Metz was no doubt aware of traditional Jewish remedies seemingly based on some such *similia similibus curantur* (like cures like) principle. For example, in the Mishnah the lobe of the liver of the animal that bit you was mentioned as a cure for rabies. A *Midrash* story told of a certain herb that blinded a sighted person but restored sight to his blind companion. Medieval Jewish manuscripts also recommended for staunching bleeding: "Take some blood which has been shed, parch it in a pan over the fire until it becomes dry and powdery and place it on the wound." (Yet we also read in the old scriptures: "Every cure is the natural contrary of the ailment," this being the classical *contraria contrariis curantur* [opposites cure opposites] approach.) Dr. Hahnemann evidently had cordial relations with his Jewish disciples, as attested to by his letter to Duke Ferdinand of Anhalt-Köthen, to whom Hahnemann was *Hofrat* (court councilor), petitioning His Serene Highness for permission for a disciple, Dr. Ludwig Meyer, to establish a practice in the town of Lindau. "I would not speak for him if I did not know him personally," wrote Hahnemann. "He seems to me to possess good ability for becoming a useful homeopathic physician, and is a capable physician, which is so rarely the case with the younger doctors." In the event, the duke's decision was unfavorable. "Dr. Meyer is also said to be an Israelite," His Serene Highness wrote back, "which fact I have also found worth considering in my reply."

Meanwhile, mainstream medicine in Germany fell under the influence of *Naturphilosophie*. An elaboration and interpretation of the philosophy of Mendelsohn's friend Emmanuel Kant and his disciples, *Naturphilosophie* took various forms and dominated German thought around the turn of the century. In the "land of philosophers and poets," as Germany became known, Friedrich Schelling and Georg Hegel represented the philosophical side of

Naturphilosophie as the great Goethe embodied the poetic. The *Naturphilosophen* endeavored to construct romantic and metaphysical systems by which the problems of science could be solved, if need be by adapting their observations to fit their preconceived worldviews. In this way they sought to establish the assigned roles for which each being (animate or inanimate) was created and the purpose it fulfills by its individuation of that role.

The views of the *Naturphilosophen* toward epidemic illness are particularly relevant here. Disease, being in their view a parasitic being or life process, might be capable of being transmitted, perhaps even by means of seeds or germs. But the assumption was that this occurred if and when the given parasitic life process reached a high point in its vigor and thus became procreative. The contagious agents, if seeds or germs, were not the disease entity or being itself—just as, say, dandelion seeds aren't dandelions and wheat germ isn't wheat stalks. At the dawn of the nineteenth century, the Jews, constituting some 10 percent of the student body of the Berlin medical faculty and about a quarter of the med students in Frankfurt an der Oder and Königsberg, absorbed this aesthetically attractive, but medically fairly useless, philosophy.

Germany after the Napoleonic Wars, as before, was a patchwork of sovereign kingdoms and principalities. The Germanic Confederation, established in 1815 in the wake of Napoleon's final exile, was a loose one, represented by an assembly of ambassadors at the Diet in Frankfurt. Yet even though not all of Prussia was within the borders of the Confederation, it was that kingdom, with its capital in Berlin, that would take the lead in German affairs—scientific and educational, as well as political and military—as the century wore on, eventually culminating in unification. The years after the Napoleonic Wars were a time of sweeping overhaul of the Prussian gymnasium and university system. Nationalistic scholars such as Alexander von Humboldt, still reeling from the humiliation of Prussia's swift and total defeat by Napoleon at Jena in 1806, perceived a malaise in German society that had to be countered by educational reforms. The concept of practical, professional education, the so-called bread-and-butter studies (*Brotstudium*) were to be downgraded in favor of intellectual, aesthetic and ethical cultivation (*Bildung*). Attached to this was the ideal of science (*Wissenschaft*). This originally signified the quest for an all-embracing unified knowledge but came more and more to represent rigorous and detailed research and scholarship in specific fields, as typified by massive, heavily footnoted tomes on even the most obscure subspecialty, preferably with *Ur* (primeval) prefixed to the key word in the title.

Such an idealistic approach worked well enough in the university departments of humanities, mathematics, philosophy, and the natural sciences, whose graduates, if they didn't go on to teach, would typically enter the prestigious civil service where they could acquire the necessary practical skills on the job. But the place of medicine in the new educational scheme of things was problematic, the art and science of healing being by nature a very practical matter. A resolution of sorts was achieved by the incorporation into the medical curriculum of the basic sciences of physiology, chemistry, physics, zoology, and botany, which were to be included in the state exam. This covering of the future physician's practical training with the mantle of *Wissenschaft* laid the foundations for a century of German preeminence in the basic medical sciences. So it was that romantic concepts such as "vital force," as prevalent at the turn of the nineteenth century as it had been in ancient Greece, soon gave way to purely physicochemical processes such as the irritability of protoplasm (the essential content of the living cell) in the motions of plants.

In no other branch of medicine would the breakthrough brought about by this new approach, particularly by German Jews, be as dramatic as in the field of communicable disease. We have seen how in biblical times the Hebrews had strict rules for the isolation of lepers. In the Middle Ages various ports had quarantine regulations (from Italian *quarantana* or forty, the number of days a ship had to remain at anchor before docking in Ragusa [Dubrovnik] and Venice so that its crew and passengers could be observed for outbreaks of the plague). But the manner by which a supposedly communicable disease was in fact transferred from one individual to another remained a mystery and a source of endless speculation. Already in the first century B.C.E., the Roman scholar Marcus Terentius Varro suggested (and perhaps even he wasn't the first to do so) that "certain minute animals, invisible to the eye, breed . . . and borne of the air reach the inside of the body by way of the mouth and the nose and there cause serious disease." In the sixteenth century Girolamo Fracastoro in Verona speculated that epidemic diseases were transmitted by germs (*seminaria*), perhaps living entities, that had the power to multiply in the body of the patient. An obvious problem with such a concept was the invisibility of the hypothesized agents. Anything smaller than the itchmite of scabies—just visible to the naked eye as a white dot and recognized by Islamic physicians as parasitic—remained in the realm of sheer speculation.

The situation might have changed in the seventeenth century when, as mentioned in the previous chapter, the Dutchman Antoni van Leeuwenhoek developed the first microscope, bringing bacteria into the range of human vision. Among the many objects of his obversation were his own bodily discharges, and he seems to have been particularly impressed by the swarms of animalcula he found when he was "troubled by a looseness." Yet by then, Fracastoro's suggestion of subvisible creatures as the cause of disease, in so far as it had ever enjoyed any currency, was largely forgotten.

Although each of van Leeuwenhoek's microscopes contained but a single lens, the spectacle-maker brothers Hans and Zacharias Janssen in the Dutch town of Middelburg had decades earlier aligned concave and convex lenses to produce what was probably the world's first prototype of a compound microscope. Nevertheless, until well into the nineteenth century, poor optical quality was apt to combine with the overheated imagination of the observers to produce reports of fantastic subvisible creatures aside from the baffling array of genuine sightings. Under these confusing circumstances, it could hardly dawn on anyone that specific microbes might be linked with some specific diseases. The Italian Agostino Bassi, who around the turn of the nineteenth century connected a disease of silkworms to a fungal parasite (*Botrytis paradoxa*) and even suggested that diseases of humans might be caused by microorganisms, was merely an exception that proved the rule.

In his essay "Israel and Medicine," the gentile William Osler, whom we will meet again in a later chapter as one of the great initiators of the American Century in medicine, wrote: "In estimating the position of Israel in the human values we must remember that the quest for righteousness is oriental, the quest for knowledge occidental. With the great prophets of the East—Moses, Isaiah, Mohamet—the word was 'Thus saith the Lord'; with the great seers of the West, from Thales and Aristotle to Archimedes and Lucretius, it was 'What says Nature?'" Osler was no doubt being a bit too dichotomous in the presumed influence of the ancient Semites and ancient Europeans upon later generations of Jews and gentiles. Yet it is true that up to the early nineteenth century the Jewish doctors—great bearers that they were of ancient Greek and Roman medical knowledge, which had almost Scriptural authority—produced no seekers after new medical truths of the stature of Harvey, Vesalius, or van Leeuwenhoek. But now, as the ghetto walls fell, the Jews of Germany—whether adhering to the older religious orthodoxy, the modern Reform movement, or even (by way of the baptismal font) to Christianity—were swept up by the force of the German *Aufklärung* and the Jewish equivalent, the *Haskalah*.

So it was that the greatest contribution of the first half of the nineteenth century to the elucidation of the true nature of contagion and the establishment of the germ theory came from the grandson of a rabbi. Jacob Henle was born in 1809 in Fürth, Bavaria, a prosperous town composed largely of refugees from anti-Jewish persecutions in nearby Nuremberg. His father was a businessman and purveyor to the army; his mother, the daughter of the rabbi of Baiersdorf. After studying medicine at the universities of Heidelberg and Bonn (where, as everywhere else, the curriculum still included bloodletting), Henle qualified as a physician. He subsequently obtained his M.D. degree with a dissertation on the membrana pupillaris of the eye, and he wrote his *Habilitation* thesis (for qualification as a university lecturer) on epithelial tissues, which cover and line the internal and external surfaces of the body, including the vessels.

Henle became prosector at the laboratory of Johannes Müller in Berlin, who, despite the medical faculty's strong objections to his advocacy of pure research, had recently been appointed to the chair of anatomy and physiology. Soon Henle became managing editor of the influential new scientific journal *Müller's Archiv* and he later launched the *Zeitschrift für rationelle Medizin,* whose name indicates the goal of reducing normal and pathological processes to underlying physical and chemical events. This great dawn of pure academic research in the basic medical sciences did not take place under idyllic conditions, as far as facilities and equipment were concerned. As thirsty as Henle and his colleagues were for knowledge of the subvisible world, it could not be said that even the most fanatical of them worked day and night. Microscopes were not yet equipped with light condensers. Gas illumination, which in those decades was just coming into general use, was insufficient for microscopy. For the time being, the scientific Enlightenment could only come from the erratic north German sun. This fact of life was reflected by Müller's New Year's greetings to Henle and his fellow young anatomists, wishing them all the best and "especially good light in winter-time." As Henle later wrote:

> I recollect the working place of what was called, euphemistically, the ana-tomical laboratory behind the Garisonkirche, where we stayed with our kind chief Johannes Müller till late in the afternoon. So as not to miss the light hours, each of us took his main meal according to the English custom, and at noontime we used to gather in the director's room for a second breakfast. For this the janitor's wife supplied the food, and we, each outdo-ing the other, supplied the wine and the good sense of humor.

The Spartan conditions notwithstanding, Henle's discoveries were such that in 1839, at the young age of 31 he was called to the chair of anatomy at the University of Zürich. Within a year, in 1840, his *Pathologische Untersuchungen* (Pathological Research) was published. This classic book covered a broad range of medical fields, yet its greatest impact on the course of medical science was made by its first chapter, "Von der Miasmen und Kontagien" (Concerning Miasmata and Contagions). These were the pages that set the stage for the victory of the germ theory. Henle had himself looked for microorganisms in such places as the corpses of typhoid vic-tims, smallpox pustules, and scabs of scarlet fever. But the limited state of the art in microscopy guaranteed that the search, whether by Henle or anyone else, would be largely futile for decades to come (and in the case of viruses, until the invention of the electron microscope a century later). Yet scattered through the literature on disease patterns, pathological symp-toms, and microscopic observations—including veterinary studies—pro-duced in the previous twenty years or so by German, and to a lesser extent French and other scientists, were bits and pieces of information, which Henle sifted and analyzed. From these far-from-unitary writings and his own observations, deductions, and intuitions, he produced a document decades ahead of its time.

"Contagion," Henle declared, "is a matter endowed with individual life which reproduces itself in the manner of animals and plants, which can multiply by assimilating organic material and can exist parasitically on the sick body." Unlike the transmission of snake or insect venom, the spread of epidemic disease could not be chemical in nature, since "the ability to multiply by assimilating foreign materials is known to us only in living organic beings. No dead chemical substance, not even an organic one, multiplies at the expense of any other." Furthermore, there was the incubation, or latency period: "At first, during the *stadium latentis contagii,* the parasites do not give rise to any perceptible symptoms," Henle wrote. "Either they remain undeveloped during this period, or some time is necessary until they have multiplied in such quantity as to make themselves felt in the body in which they live."

Henle saw the recently elucidated role of microscopic yeast plants in the fermenting of beer as parallel to the role he believed other microorganisms play in the infecting of animals and humans. "This comparison is very apt," wrote Henle, who especially noted that, just as in the case of fermentation, "the quantity of the effect is in no relation to the quantity of ferment used, [so] a needle dipped in diluted chicken-pox material (a grain of chicken pox material having been mixed with half a dram of water) is still capable of infecting." Similarly, as became known in the late 1830s, a tiny plant parasite could infect entire silkworm colonies with muscadine disease, and a small favus fungus could spread over the scalp and body. So it is that, although Maimonides and other medical theoreticians classified the foam of a rabid dog as venom just like the poison of a viper, when sufficiently diluted the latter becomes harmless whereas the former may still be deadly.

Henle helped break the influence of the *Naturphilosophen,* even of those among them who speculated on the transmittabilty of disease by means of some living germs. True, dandelion seeds aren't dandelions, and wheat germ isn't wheat stalks; but the germs of, say, cholera are cholera. They may perhaps undergo transmutations in form, but they do not grow into a cholera entity the way a dandelion seed grows into a dandelion. The germs multiply greatly, but they remain individual germs.

In his 1840 work, Jacob Henle anticipated by a quarter to a half century the discoveries and innovations of some of the greatest names in the history of medicine—including Louis Pasteur and Joseph Lister. "Organic substances can neither ferment nor putrefy, nor become moldy, even in atmospheric air, if they are boiled, and the air which is conducted to them is heated thoroughly," Henle declared. In the 1860s Pasteur would report a series of—as it were—airtight experiments proving this thesis. Henle specifically stated that "an example of putrefaction caused by locally acting contagion is furnished by hospital gangrene," and he pointed to the disinfecting power of strong acids, and particularly of vinegar, in combating the scourge that so often rendered the most brilliant operation worse than useless. Today, we can only guess as to the precise bacterial nature of this hospital gangrene, for it is now mercifully extinct. A quarter century after Henle's book appeared, the Englishman Joseph Lister, later Lord Lister, a.k.a. the Prince of Surgeons, took a cue from Pasteur's experiments and speculated that postsurgical putrefaction and blood poisoning were, like fermentation, the result of contamination by microorganisms. Lister experimented with solutions of carbolic and nitric acid in the treatment of wounds and potentially gangrenous bedsores and also brought the antiseptic principle into the operating theater. (He would later place increasing emphasis on asepsis rather than antisepsis—keeping sources of pathological microbes away from the patient to begin with.)

Jacob Henle returned to Germany in 1844 to occupy the chair of anatomy at Heidelberg. Having converted in the *Taufepidemie* (baptismal epidemic), which claimed thousands of ambitious German Jews early in the century, Henle was not hindered in his advancement by the faith of his fathers. Nevertheless, his Jewish birth would affect him in curious ways. It was the distinguished professor of anatomy Tiedemann who brought Henle to Heidelberg. Yet the aging professor soon openly cursed his protégé as a "shameless Jew" when the two of them fell out over the architectural plans for the new Anatomical Institute. Henle resigned in protest and considered immigrating to America. But then the Ministry of Education made the soon-to-retire Tiedemann apologize in writing. Yet Henle remained dissatisfied with the scientific climate in Heidelberg. "I am still somewhat strange here, and hope to remain so unless new elements appear," he wrote in a letter.

> To feel at home among these boresome antique university-pigtails would . . . be for us a degradation. Here nothing remains but to allow the old to die out and to found a new colony . . . [T]he faculty utilizes Heidelberg's reputation and its wonderful location to fatten in comfortable calm and lock themselves in from intruders. . . . But the students are already beginning to see that something new, something capable of development, is offered them.

They are full of enthusiasm for our rational medicine, and consequently enraged at the backwardness of affairs here.

The rage not only of the students of Heidelberg, but of much of the population of Europe, boiled over in 1848 (more about which later). The immediate result was a crackdown by the Bavarian government. Henle, who held the title of *Hofrat*, was not accused of any political wrongdoing. But he nevertheless grabbed the offer of a chair at Göttingen University in the state of Hannover "in order to live among scientific colleagues and under a government to whom one does not become objectionable because of one's justified ambition for one's intuition." He was soon called to an audience with the blind Hannoverian king Georg, who, although well apprised of Henle's scientific accomplishments, seems to have been misled as to his religious zeal. As the baptized Jew wrote: "The King received me with the statement that he felt it a necessity to inform me how much he congratulated himself upon the acquisition of a teacher whose reputation as a scientist was combined with that of a strictly Christian mind. The poor deluded man . . . So I stood face to face with him as a brother in Christ."

Henle remained at Göttingen until his death in 1885. His wide-ranging contributions to the whole of medicine are represented by his *Systematic Anatomy,* published in three volumes between 1855 and 1871, which reexamined the emerging specialisms of osteology (bones and their disorders), syndesmology (ligaments), myology (muscles), splanchnology (viscera), and neurology (nervous system). Henle's *Atlas,* published from 1874 to 1877, was a definitive contribution to the science of anatomy. The eponyms bearing his name attest to both the quantity and diversity of his discoveries: Henle's loop, Henle's membrane, Henle's fibrous layer, Henle's stratum nerveum, Henle's warts, Henle's layer, Henle's spine, Henle's fissures, Henle's ligaments, Henle's ampulla, Henle's cells, Henle's fibrin, Henle's internal cremaster, Henle's sphincter, the canal of Henle, and the trachoma glands of Henle.

Yet it was Henle's pioneering of the germ theory that was to have the greatest ramifications for medical science. This was aided by chance circumstances that no one could have anticipated when he moved to Göttingen in 1848. For, as we shall see in the next chapter, among Henle's pupils would be a gentile med student from nearby Clausthal named Robert Koch.

His destiny to be one of the greatest figures in the history of medicine would probably never have been fulfilled without the concepts implanted in him by his teacher Henle, as well as the selfless patronage given him by another Jewish professor, Ferdinand Cohn.

A germ theory that maintained simply that microorganisms are the culprits in the transmission of communicable diseases would have been only half complete. For it still need not have followed that every sufferer had been infected by someone before, in an endless chain of transmission. Already ages before humans ever imagined the existence of microscopic life forms, there was widespread belief in the spontaneous generation (or, to use the Latin term, *generatio aequivoca*) of at least some visible creatures. Casual observations led to the commonsense conclusion that maggots are produced by putrefying meat and vermin by dung (as Aristotle held). Fracastoro, who had speculated about subvisible seeds of contagion in the sixteenth century, had felt that these *seminaria* might first arise spontaneously in individuals or from air, earth, or water, thence to flourish and be transmitted from host to host. In Henle's time, as in ours, the concept of parasitic-like seeds apparently developing spontaneously at some organic site and spreading out to other sites, there to grow, was quite consistent with medical observations, at least *within the same body.* Among Henle's masterful disquisitions in his 1840 book was his consideration of cancers (which, being *neoplasms,* are by definition seemingly formed *de novo*) and the metastasis of their seeds to other parts of the body along the veins and lymph vessels. The tubercles of tuberculosis were likewise known to travel from the lungs to colonize other organs in the same body, as well as to give off some sort of seeds capable of infecting other people. How, then, to determine if such tubercles did not first develop spontaneously in the lungs of at least some patients before spreading out and colonizing others?

The question of spontaneous generation had potential religious overtones for European scientists in the context of the story of Genesis. In the eighteenth century, Lazarro Spallanzani, the Italian priest and professor at the University of Pavia, took a cue from the experiments of Francesco Redi a century earlier, which systematically demonstrated that no maggots can form on meat that has been screened from flies. Focusing now on the subvisible world, Spallanzani similarly showed that jars of broth and air remain free of microscopic life if they are first sufficiently heated and then kept tightly sealed. Life comes only from life, and Spallanzani, systematically following up the casual observations of the Swiss Nicholas de Saussure, went on to show how microbe reproduction takes place: by division rather than by the sexual means common to visible life forms.

In all this, Spallanzani is said to have been gratified that his research confirmed that God had indeed limited His creation of life to the first six days of the biblical account. Two centuries later, the devoutly Catholic Pasteur would similarly see his own demonstrations against spontaneous generation as a victory over cold materialism and in favor of the original divine creation. However, this strict Genesis-based view did not necessarily enjoy favor among all pious Christians. Spallanzani's foremost adversary was the English naturalist John Turberville Needham, himself a Catholic priest. For a long time, before being finally refuted by Father Spallanzani's more meticulous research, Father Needham claimed that his experiments proved that *generatio aequivoca* could take place in mutton gravy. He attributed this to a Vegetative Force, which could be seen as one of the greatest powers emanating from God and hence not explicable by the laws of chemistry and physics.

The matter of the generation of life, with its religious connotations, was broadened in the early nineteenth century when more sophisticated microscopes and microscopists began to reveal that all living entities—whether infinitesimal or gigantic—are composed of cells. The word *cell* in the biological context actually had its origin much earlier, with the seventeenth-century English naturalist Robert Hooke, who was particularly impressed by the structures of cork and elder pith as seen under his rather crude microscope. But the very idea of a cellular structure conjures up an image of a cloister containing more or less empty rooms, and Hooke did not suspect the existence of very different kinds of cells far beyond the range of his primitive instrument. When the nineteenth century dawned, it was, in fact, the textile industry and not the monasteries that supplied the metaphor for the building blocks of life: various basic *fibers* were woven together by nature into assorted structures called *tissues*.

A scientist of apparently Jewish descent was instrumental in establishing the cell, once and for all, as the basic unit in biology, comparable to the atom in chemistry. Born in Hamburg in 1804, Matthias Jacob Schleiden was the son of a physician from Schleswig-Holstein. But at the University of Heidelberg young Schleiden made the initial mistake of pursuing a career in that other stereotypically Jewish profession, law. Returning to Hamburg, he became deeply discouraged with his legal practice and in 1831 shot himself in the head. His failure to do more than cause a slight wound may have been responsible for a sudden interest in anatomy and he went on to study medicine at the University of Göttingen and then in Berlin.

Schleiden had a physiologist uncle in the Prussian capital, Johann Horkel, who was particularly skilled as a botanist. Under his influence, Schleiden was drawn especially to the microscopic study of plants and their structures. This was at a time when German thinking in the biological sciences had not yet broken free of the speculations of the *Naturphilosophen*. Botanical and zoological scholarship was still dominated by dry classification according to dubious systems rather than by research into dynamic processes. Now came Schleiden who, on the basis of his observations, was the first to forcefully advance the idea that all plant life consists of cells, with each cell in turn containing a nucleus (cytoblast). More important, he voiced the opinion that new plant cells were formed and built up within other plant cells, similar to the way an embryo is formed within the uterus.

In Berlin, Schleiden had a devoutly Catholic friend and neighbor named Theodor Schwann, a young researcher at Johannes Müller's lab. It was Schleiden, during their frequent after-dinner conversations, who inspired in Schwann the idea, which he confirmed by his microscopic studies, that not only plant life but *all* life consists of cells. Schwann was particularly impressed by the discovery of his fellow researcher Henle that the epithelial layer, which Henle showed to line all internal body surfaces, is composed of cells. But as to how new cells came into being, Schwann dissented from his friend Schleiden's idea that they were formed within parent cells. Instead, Schwann theorized that new cells derived by means of a sort of crystallization around a matrix or "cytoblastem" from unorganized, noncellular body fluid, the supposed mother liquor. This was, in its way, a holdover from the ancient tradition of Hippocrates and Galen, which viewed humors as the basis of everything organic. Schwann's concepts were contained in the landmark book *Microscopic Investigations of the Similarities in Structure and Development in Animals and Plants,* which he published in 1839, but not before first submitting the draft to his bishop for assurance that this kind of spontaneous generation did not seriously violate the Church's

dogma. Even Jacob Henle—who, when it came to the origin of pathogenic microorganisms, chose as a working principle "to manage without
generatio aequivoca, which we would like to avoid as long as possible"—
accepted that new body cells of humans and animals, be they normal or
malignant, came into being through such a crystallization process.

The question of the origin of cells, and therefore of all life—whether animal
or plant, visible or microscopic, beneficial or pathogenic—was finally settled
by the Polish-German Jew Robert Remak. Born in 1815 in Posen (Posnan),
Remak was the son of a cigar store owner and lottery agent and nephew
(or cousin) of a physician. They were, in turn, descendants of the sixteenth-
century rabbi Mose ben Jakob Cordovero, whose book on kabbalistic concepts is said to have influenced Spinoza and from whose Hebrew initials
(ReMaK) the family's name derived. It was in the year of Robert Remak's
birth that, in the wake of Napoleon's defeat, the Congress of Vienna re-
drew the map of Europe. There was no place on it for an independent
Poland. Parts of the country were placed under Russian and Austrian authority, and the western part, Posen, was governed by Prussia.

Robert received his elementary education at the German Bürgerschule
but attended for his secondary education the Polish Royal Gymnasium.
Granted Prussian citizenship in 1833, the year of his graduation, Remak
went to Berlin to pursue his university studies. Yet his high school days also
instilled in him, even though he was a Jew, a sympathy for the suppressed
Polish nationalists as well as gratitude toward the Polish aristocrats who
were subsidizing his university education. For the defense of his M.D. thesis, *Observationes anatomicae et microscopicae de systematis nervosi structura*—
based on research carried out in Johannes Müller's lab, where he worked
along with Henle and Schwann—Remak accorded to three Poles, rather
than Germans, the honor of being his formal opponents. Yet Remak would
remain in Berlin until his death in 1865, and his short but extremely productive life would be bound up with the dramatic developments in German science and politics in those decades.

Although starting up a medical practice, Dr. Robert Remak continued
to do research, unremunerated, in Müller's lab. The greater part of his most
important early contributions to medicine were in the field of neurology.
Most notably, Remak's microscopic investigation of different nerve fibers,
along with his clinical observations, led to a paper in 1840 in which he

described an "organic nervous system" as distinct from the "animalistic nervous system." The former's function was to influence the movement of involuntary muscles and the secretion of hormones by glands everywhere in the body. Decades ahead of its time, Remak's concept of the organic nervous system and its functions was only rediscovered early in the twentieth century, to be rechristened the "autonomic nervous system."

But to return to the matter of spontaneous generation: Remak was familiar with his colleague Schwann's concept of formation of new cells from some sort of crystallization of a mother liquor in the body and also with Schleiden's idea that new cells are formed inside old cells, like a fetus in a uterus. Remak rejected both hypotheses. Already in 1841 he reported the production of new cells by *division* of old cells in his observations of red blood corpuscles in animal embryos. In ensuing years he reported on cell division in muscles and elsewhere and observed that embryonic development likewise starts with the division of a (fertilized) cell. Remak further observed that pathological growths such as cancer can arise only from other body cells and never spontaneously outside the cells. Thus the concept of *generatio aequivica* gave way to the principle to become known as *omnis cellula e cellula*. Cells can only come into being from cells of a similar kind. And this applied to microorganisms as it did to all other life forms.

By any standards, Remak's achievements would have entitled him to a university lectureship and even a professor's chair. But something more was still required—the abandonment of his ancestral faith. The French Revolution, with its ideals of Liberty, Equality, and Fraternity, had culminated in the National Assembly granting full citizenship and equal rights to French Jews in 1791. In the ensuing Napoleonic Wars these same ideals were imposed on the German principalities that came under Bonaparte's rule. When Prussia, divided and humiliated, rose up against French hegemony, its king, Friedrich Wilhelm II, needing the support of all his subjects, promised the Prussian Jews many rights granted by the French. By the edict of March 1, 1812, the Israelites were accorded Prussian citizenship. The provisions included freedom of trade, movement, and residence. And although eligibility for state office was not granted, there were paragraphs explicitly permitting Jews to hold teaching posts at the Prussian universities (all of which were state institutions).

The Jewish-Prussian patriotism engendered by these developments was captured in the painting *The Return of the Volunteer*, by the distinguished premed-student-turned-artist Moritz Oppenheim, which depicted a wounded but smiling Jewish Prussian soldier being given a hero's homecoming by loving parents and younger siblings. Aside from the Jewish soldiers, Jewish wound-physicians and surgeons had been active in the campaigns, and ten of them earned distinctions for their service by the Prussian state. But with the retreat of the French, the Jews found they were still second-class citizens in many respects. For decades thereafter the Prussian Army would not allow Jews to become military doctors, and even when it finally did, they were barred from officer rank. (There were exceptions in other German states, as when the teenage Jewish wound-surgeons in the Napoleonic Wars, Johanas Meyer Hoffa and Joel Fiorino, went on to pursue distinguished careers as medical doctors in the army of the Principality of Hesse.)

Similarly at the universities, virtually no unbaptized Jew in all of Prussia was admitted to a teaching post in the decade after the emancipation edict. In Berlin in 1816 the Breslau-born Jew Dr. David Ferdinand Koreff, follower of Antoine Mesmer's concept of animal magnetism and friend of the poet E. T. A. Hoffmann (Koreff was later immortalized in Jacques Offenbach's *Tales of Hoffmann*), was appointed to the professor's chair. This was due to the influence of his powerful patient Prince Hardenberg, who conveniently neglected to mention Koreff's unconverted status to King Friedrich Wilhelm III. When the Berlin medical faculty brought this to the monarch's attention, Koreff was forced into the indignity of an overnight baptism to save his appointment. In 1822 Friederich Wilhelm reconciled the law with the established practice at the universities by simply revoking the pertinent provisions of the tolerance edict. Henle and (presumably) Schleiden, having been born Jewish but later baptized, had no problem pursuing academic careers. (Indeed, Schleiden soon became professor extraordinarius in Jena and later full professor in Dorpat.) Henle and Schleiden were, of course, not the only ones to follow this path in the era of Enlightenment but only partial emancipation. Also, talented Jews like Abraham Mendelsohn—the son of Moses and the father of the great composer Felix—were willing to view religion as a form of ethics, whose ceremonial garb could be provided well enough by Christianity, especially when conversion meant the opening up of career opportunities.

It was the age of the German *Aufklärung* and the Jewish *Haskalah* that gave rise to the Reform movement in Judaism. This current, which gained particular momentum in Germany in the 1840s at rabbinical conferences held in Braunschweig, Frankfurt, and Breslau, preferred to view Judaism as evolving and adapting in the course of history, according to time and place. It consequently challenged the eternal validity of past codifications of Jewish law and ritual, such as those found in the Talmud and Medieval scriptures. Remak was one of the many German Jews to move away from the strict orthodoxy of their parents. But for Remak this liberalization stopped well short of conversion to Christianity.

In 1843 Remak addressed to Friedrich Wilhelm IV, who three years earlier had succeeded his conservative father to the Prussian throne, a petition for permission to assume a university teaching post in Berlin. Emphasizing the communality rather than differences between German Jews and German Christians in the new age of Enlightenment and deghettoization, Remak declared "respectfully and solemnly that my education and my feelings are intimately connected with those views rooted in Christianity which penetrate the life of science and of the state." But he went on to lament that "I find myself deprived of the opportunity to devote all my power to science and to the state to which I both belong and am fervently devoted." Remak beseeched the king not to insist on conversion—even if only nominal—as a requirement for full participation. "The condition of having fewer political rights takes away from a decision [to convert] first its necessary, external freedom" and thereby demeans the act. Rather than follow this path, Remak felt in himself "the obligation of each individual to endeavor to help to advance the community given to him by nature, instead of entering another community." If the king would consent to his request to be allowed to teach at the university, Remak avowed that "I shall prove my gratitude through the most conscientious fulfillment of my duties to the honor of God, to the advantage of the State, and to the progress of Science."

Remak's petition was supported by the 74-year-old Alexander von Humboldt, who in many ways embodied the spirit of German science and enlightenment. Explorer, scientist, educational reformer, and member of the king's inner circle, Humboldt was in the habit of helping Jewish scientists who were facing intolerance. In the 1830s, when Jacob Henle was sentenced to six years imprisonment and banned from all civil service (including university) posts for supposedly having belonged to a radical student organization in Heidelberg, Humboldt managed to get the sentence nullified. In 1842, as president of the prestigious Berlin Academy of Science, Humboldt secured the king's confirmation of the academy's election of its first unbaptized Jewish member, the distinguished physicist Dr. Peter Theophil Riess, famed for his work on electricity. In Remak's case, however, Humboldt was less successful, for Friedrich Wilhelm turned the petition over to his bigoted minister, who replied unfavorably.

Robert Remak lived until 1865 and continued to do pioneering work in the field of embryology, neuritis, and rational galvanotherapy. He lived long enough to see a change for the better in the legal status of the Jews, although he himself was never accorded the full professorship he merited. Remak also lived to see the dawn of general acceptance of his theory of cell division and the twilight of the concept of spontaneous generation. Yet in 1865, despite the triumph of the cell, the nature of just what was transmitted in communicable disease remained in doubt. The germ theory was still adhered to by only a minority of medical men. The concept of "dyscrasia"—that even epidemic diseases were produced by the wrong mixture of body fluids—remained a persistent holdover of the millennia-old humoral view. But at the time of Remak's death, the stage for the final vindication of the germ theory and the ensuing victory of man over microbe was being set—by Jews in the southeastern corner of what was soon to become the Second German Reich.

Chapter 9
The Subvisible Botanist of Breslau

These little forms are of the very greatest moment, since they, with invisible, yet ir-
resistible power, govern the most important processes of animate and inanimate na-
ture; and even seize on the being of man secretly, but at the same time fatally.
—Ferdinand Cohn, *Bacteria, the Smallest Living Organism* (1872)

Since the end of the Second World War, the region of Silesia—as well as those of Posen and Pomerania—has been ethnically almost exclusively Polish and governed by Polish rulers. Such was also the case a millennium or so ago. But during the intervening centuries, the situation was more complex. In the thirteenth century Germans from the West, among them Jews, were invited by the Polish princes to settle peacefully in Lower Silesia, a country that was then still heavily forested and sparsely populated and in need of improved agriculture and new towns and cities. Although the countryside would forever remain ethnically Polish and although political authority may still have resided in a Polish territorial prince, the members of this merchant class were consciously German by nationality and usually lived under a German legal code. Indeed, in these areas, *German* became an economic term, referring to those who earned their livelihood by trade, handicraft, small industry, or shopkeeping. It was the Germans who in the wake of the Mongol devastation of 1242 rebuilt Breslau, (Polish, Wroclaw), a city that six centuries later would figure prominently in the history of the Jewish contribution to medicine.

The Jews in the towns of Lower Silesia spoke the same language as their German neighbors and often, especially in later centuries, shared their national consciousness. This was less so with those Jews who settled far-

ther to the Polish east. Some of them had on occasion been driven out of
Silesia and found protection under Polish nobles, who valued the Jews as
money-lenders and tradesmen. Others had been driven out of Germany
proper, particularly the Rhineland, during the Crusades and the hysteria of
the Black Death. In cultural isolation from gentile Germans, their Rhenish
dialect became the particularly Jewish lingua franca, Yiddish.

As pioneers in sparsely inhabited woods in the eastern marches, the Jews
encountered different diseases and were not above combining religion and
outright superstition in hopes of protection: "When you build houses in
the forest you find the inhabitants stricken with plague since the place is
haunted by spirits," states the *Sefer Hasidim.* "They asked the sage what they
should do; he answered: Take the Ten Commandments and a Torah Scroll
and stretch out a cord the length of the ground, and bring the Torah Scroll
to the cord . . . and then at the end say: 'Before God, before the Torah, and
before Israel its guardians, may no demon nor she-demon come to this
place from today and forever.'"

Although the peasantry was largely Polish, the German influence in Silesia
was such that for centuries the region was politically bound not to the Polish
principalities to the east, but to the German principalities to the west and
then to Austria to the south. In the 1740s, in the wake of the War of Austrian Succession, Silesia was ceded to Prussia. The number of Jews permitted to reside in the Silesia's main city of Breslau was long restricted by law,
so Jewish communities grew up in nearby towns, particularly in Dyhrenfurth
(today Brzeg Dolny) some twenty miles northwest on the Oder.
Dyhrenfurth had, besides the region's main Jewish cemetery, also a prominent Hebrew printing house, which published prayer books and other literature. It was there around the turn of the nineteenth century that one
Jacob Cohn worked, and it was in Dyhrenfurth that his son Isaac was born
before the family removed to Breslau.

Isaac Cohn proved to be a gifted pupil at the local Jewish grammar school
and he later went to study at the rabbinical *Hochschule,* the Jewish equivalent of a university, in Ratwitsch just across the provincial border in Posen.
Financial circumstances were, however, generally unfavorable among the
Silesian Jews in the era before industrialization, and the Cohn family was
no exception. Father Jacob was a sub-collector for the Prussian state lottery, and Isaac's mother had a stall where she sold cotton and linen. Forced
to cut his studies short and return to Breslau, Isaac borrowed money to

open a rape-oil store and then married, at the age of 21, the 16-year-old daughter of another lottery agent.

The southeast corner of old Breslau, between the moat and the Ohle branch of the Oder, was still known as the Jewish Ghetto in the early nineteenth century. Although it was no longer shut off by gates or walls, most Jews by historical tradition continued to maintain their homes and businesses on its streets and alleys. Being an old crossroad between East and West Europe, Breslau's Jewish quarter was home to many bearded, kaftan-clad eastern Polish Jews who clung to the ancient customs. But from the west the *Aufklärung* affecting the weltanschauung of the Christians was also penetrating the former ghetto and instilling in many of its inhabitants the feeling of being Germans and a longing to participate in wider German society. Indeed, among the books printed at Jacob Cohn's publishing house at Dyhrenfurth were the works of Moses Mendelsohn. It was in this new German-Jewish spirit that young Isaac Cohn and his wife, Amalie, relocated to the Ohlauerstrasse near the center of town. So it was that in 1828 their son Ferdinand was one of the first Breslau Jews to be born outside the old ghetto walls.

The second French revolution, in 1830, two years after Ferdinand's birth, gave a jolt to liberal sentiment in the German states even as far away as Breslau. But more influential was the economic revolution that was getting under way. In 1834 the German Customs Union was established, abolishing trade restrictions between the various kingdoms and principalities. The beginning of the next decade saw the laying of the railway, which opened up the world's markets for the coal, iron, zinc, and other natural resources of the Silesian hills. The business instincts of the Jews had hitherto evolved mostly from small-time peddling. But they were now extraordinarily quick to see the potential in the dramatic economic developments. Jewish banking houses opened in Breslau, and the upper floors of many a patrician dwelling in the city's ring came to be inhabited by Jews, while the ground floor became a upscale shop or office. So it was that Isaac Cohn's business prospered. And so it was that a world of academic opportunities that had been denied to him would be opened up to his son Ferdinand, the first of his seven children.

An extraordinarily gifted child even by Jewish standards—he was already reading at age 2—Ferdinand suffered the alienation that all too often accompanies such precociousness. Entering school at a much younger age than usual, and being as weak and poorly developed physically as he was power-ful mentally, he had no school friends and was often mistreated by his class-mates. Ferdinand's feeling of social isolation was much compounded by a hearing disability resulting from an accident, which none of the thousand remedies he resorted to, orthodox and fringe, could alleviate. The handi-cap also slowed down his rapid advancement through school. The endless hours of school lectures at the St. Maria Magdalena *Gymnasium* became largely meaningless for the young student and resulted in a certain absent-mindedness that would later help to make him the stereotypical professor.

Yet so intellectually precocious was Ferdinand that while still in second-ary school, he delivered a public lecture—on creation myths and creation history—to a large meeting of the Jewish Teaching and Lecture Society. It was not only greeted by loud applause but was also given coverage in the Breslau and Silesian press. At home, in the spirit of the *Aufklärung*, there were discussions about democracy, pantheism, and the possibility of rec-onciling science and religion. The German authors Schiller and Goethe exercised a particular fascination for Ferdinand, who turned his own hand to poetry. This new interest went well with the Romanticism and patrio-tism for Silesia, which he shared with many other Christians and Jews in the region. A frequent hiker through the Riesengebirge range, the 18-year-old wrote in his diary: "free and happy, wonderful blissful moments in the mountains and in the valleys; moments which I never will forget."

Ferdinand Cohn was accompanied in these expeditions by his "very lovable friend," Leopold Auerbach, who in decades to come would make a name for himself in the field of microscopy. His most notable accomplishments include his demonstration of the one-celled nature of amoebas, his descrip-tions of the process of nucleus division in the fertilized egg, his determin-ing that capillary walls are formed of flat nucleated cells, and his surprising discovery of a network of nerves ("Auerbach's plexus") in between the various layers of the intestinal muscles, which appeared to be under the functional control of what we today call the autonomic nervous system. Auerbach would carry out most of this research with less-than-ideal equip-ment purchased from his modest earnings as a practicing physician with a family to support. Any potential academic career in a university lab was made difficult by his Jewish religion, and he would never become more than a private lecturer (*Privatdozent*).

Ferdinand Cohn was well aware that he, too, would face such problems if he were to seek an academic career, and so he was likewise drawn to the study of medicine and a possible future as a practicing physician. But Ferdinand was handicapped by his hearing disability, as well as by his religion, and was concerned about the effect the former would have in his dealing with patients. Many other careers, especially in the civil service, were restricted for members of the Mosaic faith, posing a problem not only for Ferdinand but also for his four younger brothers. (His three sisters had, of course, no career choice to make in those days.) Brother Richard was—like many an academically minded young Jew in those days—drawn to chemistry, and would eventually go on to receive a Ph.D. in this subject but would die soon after. The youngest brother, Max, would take his degree in law. The two other brothers—under some pressure from their father—went into the family's flourishing business. But Ferdinand, with his love of the flora and fauna of Silesia, decided to go for a doctorate in the natural science curriculum and hope in the future to pursue an academic career despite his religion.

At the University of Breslau, the young student integrated better into the social life of his peers than in previous years. His diary tells that wine and song—if not women—were part of his student activities. The natural science curriculum was broadly based and included astronomy, physics, chemistry, and even philosophy—the Ph.D. title was not yet an anachronism—as well as Ferdinand's beloved botany and zoology. Yet so extraordinary were Ferdinand's abilities that he mastered all the subjects after only a year or so of study, and it became time to set a date for the doctoral examination. The academic statutes, however, prohibited Jews from sitting for the Ph.D. examination in Breslau, and Cohn's petition for exemption was turned down by the minister. Two subsequent petitions on Ferdinand's behalf by the Breslau faculty, which voted to give its unanimous backing, were subsequently vetoed by the ministry, and a fourth petition from his father was likewise to no avail.

So Ferdinand Cohn went to the University of Berlin, where no such religious restrictions existed. Being a nature-lover at heart, the young Jew did not take to the hustle and bustle of the Prussian capital, which was already home and workplace to almost half a million people and growing rapidly. Berlin did, however, boast a botanical garden, and the whole Potsdamer Strasse that led to it was alive with exotic plants and trees. There were also frequent field trips outside the city, when Ferdinand would exercise his talent for drawing and painting—important assets for a naturalist. It was during one of these excursions that he discovered a plant that came to be called *Cohnia floribunda,* the first of several life forms to bear his name.

But the blessing in disguise for the science of medicine that came from Ferdinand Cohn's exile from Silesia derived from the Berlin faculty's expanding interest in microscopy—a still quite unusual subject in a university natural science curriculum. Botany was traditionally concerned with the visible morphology of plants and was even more under the influence of the old *Naturphilosophie* than were the other sciences. But the University of Berlin was home to Johannes Müller, who was then rector, and also to Christian G. Ehrenberg, another pioneer of bacteriology and protozoology. For them, the cell was the building block of all life, and so a key to the understanding of more complex plant and animal forms might be gained by studying the simplest unicellular creatures. Ferdinand became so enthralled with the world of invisible life forms that he prevailed upon his father to provide him, at the exorbitant cost of 312 guilders, a Viennese microscope—an instrument so large that one could only use it standing. In 1847 Ferdinand Cohn successfully defended his doctoral thesis, "Laboratoria phytophysiologica in hortis botanicis instituenda censeo." He was 19 years old.

In the same year in Berlin, the Prussian Diet—a legislative body of limited power based on a restrictive franchise—began debate over possibly extending further equality to the Jews and, in particular, admitting Jews to teaching posts at universities. Among those queried as part of this deliberation were all the full professors in Prussia. Perhaps most interesting was the opinion of Johann Evangelista Purkinje at Ferdinand Cohn's alma mater in Breslau. Purkinje—a distinguished anatomist, microscopist, and physiologist, whose name has come down to us in the eponym of the fibers responsible for conduction of impulses in the heart—was a fervent Czech nationalist from Bohemia. He knew what it was like to be an outsider in Germany and the target of professional envy. Purkinje was also very conscious of the suppression of Czech culture in Bohemia under the dominance of German-speaking Austria. As such, he might also have been expected to feel sympathy for the Jewish minority, both in Prussia and in Bohemia. Yet in his advice to the Prussian Diet, Purkinje would deny the Jews what he so ardently wished for his Czech minority. In his view, the Jews "should give up their own racial and national peculiarities and amalgamate with us entirely as one people." Until that happens, he added, "I find it neither permissible nor proper to depart from the present [i.e., restrictive] constitution."

Curiously, Purkinje had close and cordial relations with Jewish pupils and knew firsthand the barriers placed in their way. Most notable was the case of his pupil Gabriel Gustav Valentin, a native of Breslau, who received his M.D. degree there in 1832 with a dissertation on microscopic embryology. Valentin's work in that field—especially his stress on comparative embryology and histogeny (the development of tissue)—soon won him the prestigious Grand Prix des Sciences Physiques from the Institut de France. So meteoric was his rise that at the age of 25 he received offers from the medical faculties of both the University of Dorpat and the University of Köningsberg to occupy a full professor's chair. The only condition was that he first be baptized, and this he refused. When a similar offer came from Bern in Switzerland, Valentin inquired as to the baptismal requirements and was given the ambiguous reply that "religion will be no obstacle in the mind of any enlightened personality," *but* since apparently not everyone is enlightened, it would be better to be baptized before accepting the post. To this, Valentin replied that "such a step, if connected with the attainment of any worldly goal, becomes despicable and discreditable. It means yielding to old prejudices, abandoning one's own people because one desires to join the group of better human beings."

The university and the Bern government decided not to press the issue, and so Valentin became the first unbaptized Jewish full professor at a German-speaking university. He was later also naturalized as a *Bürger* of Bern— the Breslau authorities had revoked his citizenship when he accepted the Swiss professorship—and, as such, was perhaps the first unbaptized Jewish citizen of Switzerland. He quickly did his adopted country proud with his pioneering work in integrating physics, and particularly mathematics, into medicine; his discovery of new parasites (although he initially believed them to be the product of spontaneous generation); his research on the two nervous systems regulating the heart; his elucidation of Siamese-twin embryology; and his discovery of the function of the pancreas and its secretions in food digestion. Much of this was already incorporated into the first edition of Valentin's *Lehrbuch der Physiologie des Menschen,* published in 1844 and translated into various foreign languages.

Young Dr. Cohn himself might have been hoping for some academic opportunity abroad when the slow deliberations of the Prussian Diet over Jewish emancipation were overtaken by dramatic events. The year 1848 was marked by revolution all over Europe. Paris, Vienna, and Berlin, the capitals of the three triangular powers, were in an uproar. German intellectuals, perceiving the chance to bring important changes to their country, met in Frankfurt, the site, since the Congress of Vienna, of the weak All-German Federal Diet, and also, with its ancient former ghetto, the main Jewish town in Germany and already an important financial center thanks to the Rothschilds. At the St. Paul's Church the delegates formed a National Assembly to replace the insignificant Diet. They proposed an all-German constitution that would truly unite Prussia, Bavaria, and the various petty principalities. (A hope of including Austria was soon abandoned, due to that country's special ties to the Habsburg monarchy and its rather separate historical traditions.) The goals of the revolution were patriotic in its glorification of German culture as well as its striving for German unity; politically democratic in its advocating election by universal suffrage; socially liberal in its wishing to abolish aristocratic and other class privileges, as well as clerical authority and religious restrictions; and economically liberal in its demanding of freedom of commerce and industry, and minimal government interference. (In the latter sense this European concept of liberalism should be kept distinct from the "L-word" in America, which has long been identified with governmental economic controls, higher taxation, and increased spending on state welfare programs.)

Of the 586 representatives returned by the first election to the National Assembly, the vast majority were from the university-educated middle class. Although these included eighteen physicians, it was understandably the magistrates, lawyers, higher civil servants, and university and *Gymnasium* teachers who were particularly well represented. Only seven of the delegates were Jewish, but the role of the Jews and Jewish doctors in the events of 1848 was out of proportion to this number. A Jewish lawyer from Köningsberg, Eduard Simon, was elected president of the National Assembly. Many Germans, both Jewish and Christian, were inspired by the eloquent words of the Köningsberg physician Dr. Johann Jacobi: "I myself am a Jew as well as a German," he wrote. "The Jew in me cannot be free without the German. The German in me cannot be free without the Jew." Jacobi was especially known for formulating the "Four Questions Answered by an East Prussian." In this work he pleaded that the German people had demonstrated their political maturity and that all free citizens should have legally secured participation in the affairs of the state, not as a favor, but as a right.

In Berlin the General Assembly of the Physicians played a role in the upheavals. Robert Remak was one of its most active members, proclaiming his support for the Constitutional Assembly, pushing for reform of the bureaucracy and the reorganization of medical instruction and teaching, and meeting with the Prussian king Friedrich Wilhelm IV on behalf of some imprisoned Poles. For his part, young Dr. Cohn joined the Manual Workers' Association in order to be among the people and played a more physical role. Singing "The people rise up. The storm breaks forth," he manned the barricades against the feared crackdown by the authorities and went on night patrol sporting a dragoon's saber and the black, red, and gold colors of a united Germany.

In the Assembly's hope of harnessing the political and military strength of Prussia for the stability of the proposed union, Eduard Simons offered Friedrich Wilhelm the imperial crown of all Germany in the Knight's Hall of the Royal Palace in Berlin in 1849. When the king hesitated and then decided that he would accept the crown only from the princes of the various petty German states and not from the German people, the forces of reaction in the form of Prussian bayonets took over in both Frankfurt and Berlin. Ferdinand Cohn entered in his diary: "Today, as I write, there sound the uninterrupted crackle of guns, the thunder of cannon, and the screams and cries for revenge of the people around me. We're now in the midst of a revolution, and it's a matter of life and death. . . . All burghers and workers, young and old, rich and poor, are burning with rage and vengeance. . . . Long live liberty!" When Prussian troops opened fire, 230 citizens—21 of them Jewish—died at the barricades. "When I look to the future, I dread the thought," wrote Cohn in his diary. "The present torn with hate and passion with its madness and blindness. What shall the future bring? Civil war! My beautiful Germany! . . . That it should seem impossible for mankind to make freedom its own, impossible after 6,000 years of history— that's a terrible thought."

But not only the guns of the soldiers claimed the lives of the people around Ferdinand Cohn. An outbreak of cholera carried off four residents in his building and many more in the rest of the neighborhood. Hospitals received the ill and dying, but there was no effective treatment. When Cohn himself developed the body aches that he feared to be cholera, he stayed in bed, applied hot water bottles, and drank black coffee. Although he had long known bouts of pessimism and melancholy, the year of revolution had been a year of hope in which Cohn wrapped himself in politics and hardly had time for science. Now, with his hopes for the Fatherland dashed, he wrote grimly: "Germany dead, . . . Freedom, unity, equality dead; Faith, love, hope dead;—and cholera and the court-martial undying. I withdrew from the unfriendly world outside, burying myself in my books and studies."

With the failure of the revolution of 1848 went the chance to establish a democratic tradition on German soil—a missed opportunity that was to have disastrous consequences for all Europe for a century to come. It also caused a flood of some four million immigrants—many of the best of the Germans—to seek in the United States the freedom they had failed to obtain for Germany. Among these were many Jews. Dr. Abraham Jacobi, having been imprisoned after the revolution and then escaping to New York, was appointed to the first American chair of pediatrics, at Columbia University's College of Physicians and Surgeons in 1860, and later became president of the American Medical Association.

Another loss for German medical science due to the suppression of the 1848 uprising was Moritz Schiff. Born to a Jewish family in 1823 in Frankfurt am Main, Schiff received his M.D. from the University of Göttingen twenty-one years later. This was at a time when leadership in medical science had not yet passed from France to Germany, and like many new German graduates Schiff was delighted at the opportunity to do some postdoctoral study in Paris. There he studied brain physiology under the famed experimentalist François Magendie, while also spending much of his time among the animal specimens at the Jardin des Plantes. Returning to Germany, Schiff began churning out the first of his more than 200 publications, beginning with his "Contributions to the Knowledge of the Motoric Influence of the Structures United in the Thalamus," "On the Nerves of the Heart," and "Concerning Changes in the Lungs after Severing of the

Tenth Nerve"—the latter in support of observations made by Jacob Henle. At the same time that he was breaking new ground in the field of neurology, Schiff served as head of the ornithological collection of the Senkenberg Institute and was responsible for the determination and cataloging of the Institute's more obscure bird specimens.

When the revolution broke out, the 25-year-old Dr. Schiff—together with his friends Tiedemann, the son of the distinguished anatomist professor, and Carl Vogt, physician and future naturalist—enlisted in the revolutionary army, where he served as military surgeon. The three were eventually captured and condemned to death by court martial. But although Tiedemann was executed, Schiff and Vogt managed to escape. Vogt would go on to become distinguished in his own right, most notably from the point of view of the present history as the author of *Lectures on Man,* published in 1864. In that book he was, perhaps, the first to point to important biological distinctions between the Ashkenazim and the Sephardim, and he held that these were due to mixing with non-Jews. (More on this subject in a later chapter.)

For his part, Moritz Schiff, likewise immersing himself in his work, published in the next five years a pile of articles on the neurology of the tongue, eyes, spinal column, heart, lungs, bones, and whiskers; the distinction between smooth (involuntary) and striped (voluntary) muscles; the digestive process and intestinal muscles; and much more, while also continuing to catalogue his birds. Schiff's immense output would ordinarily have easily qualified him for at least a position as *Privatdozent* at Göttingen. But despite the hearty approval of his application by the faculty, the Hannovarian government refused to confirm his appointment, apparently due to his part in the ill-fated revolution and their concern that his teaching could affect politically susceptible young minds.

So Moritz Schiff, declaring his love of Germany but animosity toward authoritarianism, joined the millions of Germans who emigrated in the 1850s. An especially prominent branch of the Schiff family was establishing itself in America, which would include the well-known investment banker philanthropist Jacob H. Schiff, a second cousin to Moritz. But Moritz accepted a professorship in microscopic anatomy and pathology at Berne, Switzerland, where he stayed for eight years before moving on to the University of Florence, where his brother Hugo was professor of chemistry. In 1876 he returned to Switzerland, this time to the medical faculty of the University of Geneva, where he would serve as professor of pathology until his death twenty years later.

It was during this period that Schiff made his vital discoveries in endo-crinology, in particular the consequences and treatment of an inactive or overactive thyroid gland, especially with relation to cretinism. A stereo-typical workaholic, whose idea of relaxation was to switch from one form of work to another, Schiff drove his assistants almost as hard as he drove himself. Yet he was also known for his joviality, witticisms, and extreme modesty. A somewhat comic figure with his diminutive stature, flowing white beard, and hair that had never known the inside of a barber's shop, Schiff murmured and hummed through the pipe perpetually clenched between his teeth. A target of attacks by the Antivivisection Society, Schiff in fact consistently anesthetized the animals he experimented on in an age when this wasn't standard practice. His pockets were always full of bis-cuits, pieces of cake, drumsticks, and other leftovers from his meals, all of which he handed out to his lab animals. So wrapped up was Schiff in his labwork that when his assistant found him carrying out an experiment on the first of January and offered his best wishes, the puzzled Schiff, always oblivious to Sundays and holidays, naively posed the traditional Passover question: "Why is this day different from all other days?"

Schiff's disregard of the calendar apparently applied to the Jewish new year as well and to all other Jewish holidays, for he was quite irreligious. But a vast number of the students at the Swiss universities were Russian Jews, who were denied educational opportunities in their native land. Schiff, who proudly proclaimed his own Jewish origins, felt a deep contempt for persecutors and a corresponding sympathy for the young Jews who were among his protégés. One of them was the Russian émigré Waldemar Haffkine, the future developer of the cholera and plague vaccines, about whom we will hear more in a later chapter.

Meanwhile, back with Ferdinand Cohn in Germany, as the political revolt largely failed, a far more successful revolution was brewing in the field of medicine. Whereas German Jews had played merely a disproportionate role in the political revolution, their part in the medical upheaval would be truly staggering. And here, too, as we shall see in later chapters, the cities of Frankfurt and Berlin would be the locale of some of the most dramatic phases. But for Ferdinand Cohn, the developments would be played out in his beloved Silesia, to which he returned after the ill-fated revolution and where he would remain until his death a half century later. His great medical breakthrough would be years in coming. For Cohn was, after all, a botanist, not a physician or bacteriologist, and his first love was the plants of his native region.

Silesia had the distinction of being the first German country to have its local flora registered in the remarkable Renaissance botanical book of Caspar Schwenkfeld. This categorization was meticulously carried on in the eighteenth and nineteenth centuries with regard to flowering plants, or phanerogams. Now Ferdinand Cohn dedicated himself to making Silesia also the first country with a registry of flowerless plants, cryptogams. This and much other research into macroscopic botanical life would be revealed in, among other publications, Cohn's famous book *Die Pflanze* (*Plants*). The political solidarity Ferdinand Cohn felt with the people was now also sublimated into a popular-scientific bond. Breslau, the capital of Silesia, was home to a rather unique institute, the Silesian Society for Fatherland Culture, which sponsored lectures open to the general public. It was there that, beginning in 1849, Cohn often gave Sunday afternoon talks on such diverse popular-scientific—or, more precisely, popular-botanical—subjects as the effect of lightning on trees and the dates of blossoming. His popularity as a speaker was augmented by his use of demonstrations and preparations. On the occasion of his *Habilitation* (qualification as a university lecturer) in 1850, he once more showed his feeling of closeness to the people, by choosing as his inaugural address "Mankind and the World of Plants," a popular botanical-cultural study.

Yet even in Cohn's popular-scientific lectures, there was a hint of the dramatic bacteriological·developments to come, as his focus shifted from the visible to the microscopic world. Some of his early observations had a Jewish connection of sorts. Since the dogmatization in the early thirteenth century of the doctrine of transubstantiation (the turning of the consecrated wafer into the body of Christ), the occasional appearance of bloodlike spots on the communion bread had been interpreted in a variety of ways. Some Christians saw it as miraculous proof of the presence of Jesus, while the more pessimistic considered it a bad omen. The latter it certainly was for the Jews in the Middle Ages, for the finding of a bleeding piece of bread near the Jewish quarter led to accusations of stealing and torturing the host. (The logical assumption here is that the Jews in fact recognized the divinity of Jesus—why else would they take the risk of stealing and then abusing a piece of bread?—but had thrown their lot in with Satan against him.) In the thirteenth century at Belitz, near Berlin, all the town's Jews, accused of host desecration, were burned on the spot, which then became known as the Judenberg. Such incidents would continue to take place sporadically in Germany and elsewhere for another four centuries. But in Cohn's laboratory it was shown that blood-like spots seeming to grow from nowhere on bread—be it the consecrated wafer or some profane morsel—were due to red spherical bacteria (*Micrococcus prodigiosus*) that feed on and decompose the bread's albumen.

Another of Cohn's important observations, communicated at a lecture in 1853, can, in a sense, likewise be seen as relating to an age-old anti-Jewish libel: the accusation of well-poisoning. With the return of a cholera epidemic, Cohn suggested to his audience that microscopic vegetation was the culprit, polluting wells he suspected of spreading the disease. This preceded by a year the case—almost legendary in the annals of medicine— of Dr. John Snow and the "pump on Broad Street"! (When cholera struck London in 1854, a small area in the Soho section was particularly devastated. Snow correctly deduced that the water from the local pump, though tasty and sparkling clear, was somehow responsible, and he persuaded the authorities to remove the handle. Yet unlike Cohn, Dr. Snow speculated about some "cholera poison" in the water and not living microscopic organisms.)

His young age notwithstanding—in the mid-1850s, he was not yet 30— Cohn's considerable accomplishments would ordinarily have put him in line for a professorship. But the obstacles to Jews that prevented him from obtaining his doctorate in Breslau now hindered his advancement at the university. During a visit to Berlin, Cohn made representations to the Prussian Minister of Education (on whom all professorial appointments were dependent) and was told: "As long as I'm Minister, you will not become a professor in Prussia." Under the circumstances, Cohn might have been advised to seek a chair in one of the other German lands. But alongside Cohn's all-German patriotism, so evident in his diaries and letters in 1848–1849, there was the particular hold that the Silesian province, in the far-flung southeast corner of Germany, had on her children.

Fortunately for the story of medicine, the hostile minister wasn't minister for much longer, and Cohn received his appointment as *professor extraordinarius* in Breslau in 1859. But it wasn't until 1866 that Cohn was provided with the facilities—a corridor and a few rooms on the second floor of a former convent—that enabled him to establish the world's first institute for plant physiology. There Professor Cohn taught from live plants from the botanical gardens and from specially molded artificial models, rather than from the pressed specimens that traditionally made the subject of botany literally and figuratively dry for its students. In the same year, Breslau was again struck by a cholera epidemic. Those who could, fled to the towns and spas in the nearby mountains, where—if Cohn's theories were to be believed—the water might be free of microscopic vegetable pathogens. It was at one of these spas, Salzbrunn, that Ferdinand Cohn proposed to his future wife, Pauline, the daughter of a cultured Jewish merchant, who was likewise a temporary refugee from the epidemic raging in Breslau. The dining room in their new home would become a focal point for scientific discussion and heated debates among the faculty and students of Breslau and for guests from as far away as Russia and America.

Whereas Cohn's earlier interest in minute and potentially pathogenic life forms had mostly focused on algae and fungi, his attention was shifting to bacteria. Cohn was of the opinion that these creatures, too, were the domain of the botanist rather than the zoologist. The behavior of bacteria, and especially their lack of volition, set them apart from the animal kingdom. And their method of reproduction, Cohn observed, is also quite unlike what is typical of animals: "The bacterium grows till it has reached perhaps double its original size, then constricts itself in the middle like a figure eight, and breaks into two new individuals."

Although the proper classification of various microorganisms as plants, animals, or something else would long provide topics for debate among biologists, the fact that the botanist Ferdinand Cohn focused his attention on bacteria in the 1860s was a blessing for the advancement of medicine. For despite the discoveries of Jacob Henle, Matthias Schleiden, Theodor Schwann, and Robert Remak earlier in the century, and the impressive work by Louis Pasteur and Joseph Lister on asepsis and antisepsis in the 1860s, the germ theory was in an uncertain state and faced an uphill battle for acceptance by the medical community. The complicity of microbes in the spread of epidemics was generally recognized for, at most, only a few diseases. And even then, the concept of spontaneous generation of pathogenic germs within an already ill body seemed to fit what available data there was, suggesting that germs were—initially, at least— the effect of disease rather than the cause. Furthermore, there was the widespread belief among medical men that once an ill body generated and then spread to other people the germs of a certain disease, these same germs could metamorphose into germs of some different disease (pleomorphism).

One of the strongest opponents of those attempting to put germs center stage as the culprits in epidemic diseases was Florence Nightingale. The voice of this Angel of Mercy carried much weight, for she had drastically slashed the mortality rate among British soldiers during the Crimean War in the mid-1850s by introducing improved nutrition, strict cleanliness, and other sanitary measures to the military hospitals. Having demonstrated the miracles wrought by proper hygiene, Miss Nightingale went on to found the modern science of nursing and resisted with a certain moral indignation the concept of microbes as pathogenic agents in general and of specific germs causing specific illnesses in particular.

Miss Nightingale no doubt took comfort from previous triumphs of British military medicine. A century earlier, the scourge of scurvy aboard ship (today known to be non-transmissible and caused by lack of vitamin C) had been eliminated when sailors, henceforth to be called limeys, were issued citrus juice to supplement their miserably unbalanced rations. Meanwhile, typhus (today known to be caused and transmitted by louse-borne bacteria) had been successfully combated by baking the clothes of newly recruited sailors. The shipboard epidemiological patterns presented by the two diseases were not so very dissimilar. What point was there for any new-fangled germ theory to make a fundamental distinction between the two, when both obviously arose from improper hygiene? As Miss Nightingale asked rhetorically even late in the nineteenth century: "Is it not living in a continual mistake to look upon diseases, as we do now, as separate things, like dogs and cats? instead of looking upon them as conditions, like a dirty and clean condition, and just as much under our own control; or rather as reactions of a kindly nature against the conditions in which we have placed ourselves." Dogs did not change into cats; but given unsanitary conditions, Miss Nightingale maintained, the stagnant air is "ripe" for breeding small-pox and in turn scarlet fever, diphtheria, "or anything else you please." In Germany, such an attitude was shared by much of the medical establishment, most notably by the famed Munich hygienist Max von Pettenkofer, who, if he admitted that microorganisms played a part at all in epidemic diseases, saw them not as causative agents but as reacting with the soil to produce a cholera infectious material, which was itself not composed of living organisms.

Of course, in a practical sense, the hygienists were quite right. The latter part of the nineteenth century in Germany and elsewhere saw dramatic improvements in life expectancy that were in large measure independent of discoveries taking place in the medical labs but had much to do with rapid economic advances and their effect on urban living conditions, such as diet and sanitation. A middle-sized German town that, for example, used to open its moat once every Saturday so that the water, aided by women with wicker brooms, could roll down the slightly inclined streets and carry away the human and other waste, now found itself able to afford the construction of an underground sewer system for the first time in its centuries of existence.

Of the hundreds of people who read Jacob Henle's textbook in the 1840s and who attended Ferdinand Cohn's lectures in the following decade, virtually all of them had at some time probably been parasitized by the tuberculosis bacillus (whose existence was yet to be established), and many continued to harbor it. Yet few had ever shown any clinical symptoms. Among the determinants of whether a person falls ill to a contagious disease are nutrition, hereditary constitution, psychosomatic factors, the quality of the environment, and weakening of resistance due to other diseases. Yet, as we now know, though it still had to be proven in the late nineteenth century, even the most adverse combination of all such factors could never cause tuberculosis in a host in the absence of the tuberculosis bacillus. Furthermore, this bacillus cannot arise spontaneously or mutate from, say, a cholera microbe but must be introduced into the body from an external source. This was the principle of specific etiology, combined with rejection of the concept of spontaneous generation.

Yet even Jacob Henle, who, as we have seen, chose "to manage without *generatio aequivoca* ... for as long as possible," was stumped by his observations of certain intestinal worms that, he conceded, seemed to develop *de novo*. Henle did, however, append an extensive footnote pointing to mounting evidence of the almost incredible life cycle of certain flukes, and he

suggested that when all the pieces of the puzzle would one day be supplied, spontaneous generation would yet prove an unnecessary hypothesis.
But if there were still so many gaps in man's knowledge of the complex life
cycle of a large parasite such as the intestinal worm, could there be any
realistic hope of gaining a true understanding of the lives of infinitesimal
pathogens?

Much pioneering descriptive research on microbes was carried out in
Paris around mid-century by the Hungarian-born Jewish doctor, David
Gruby. Gruby described mold diseases, termed by him "maladies parasitique
végetales ou phyto-parasitiques," and drew excellent pictures of the pathogenic fungi, including that of favus. He also described trypanosomes (the
kind of microorganism that causes African sleeping sickness) in frog blood,
microfilia (the larval form of ringworm) in canine blood, and the acarus
mite, which caused erythema autumnale in dogs. (Refusing a professorship
from his alma mater, the University of Vienna, which was conditioned on
his first accepting baptism, Gruby did his experiments as a private practitioner in Paris, where his patients included Heinrich Heine, Frédéric
Chopin, Alphonse Lamartine, Georges Sand, and Alexandre Dumas, père
et fils.)

The bacteriological work of Gruby and other microscopists was, however,
dramatically eclipsed in 1872. That year saw the appearance of a great landmark in the field of medicine, arguably the most important publication in
the history of bacteriology. The book—actually, a thirty-page booklet—
entitled *Bacteria, the Smallest Living Organisms,* was the culmination of a decade
of meticulous microscopic observations by Ferdinand Cohn. (In the same
year, incidentally, he was finally granted *professor ordinarius* status.) Its opening
page ran:

> The smallest, and at the same time the simplest and lowest of all living forms,
> we call *Bacteria.* They form the boundary line of life; beyond them life does
> not exist, so far at least as our present microscopic expedients reach. . . .
> [The] smallest bacteria may be compared with man about as a grain of sand
> to Mont Blanc. . . . These little forms are of the very greatest moment,
> since they, with invisible, yet irresistible power, govern the most important
> processes of animate and inanimate nature; and even seize on the being of
> man secretly, but at the same time fatally.

Although he lacked the sophisticated techniques of staining and fixation that would be available to the coming generations of microbe hunters, Cohn's painstaking observations provided a classification system in the bewildering world of microscopic shapes. "According to their form," he wrote, "we can distinguish ball, rod, fiber and screw bacteria." Cohn specified six genera: micrococcus, bacterium, bacillus, vibrio, spirillum, and spirochaete. For these, he provided not only drawings but vivid descriptions of their activity. For example,

> When the wavy-formed vibrios and the screw-formed spirilla turn themselves quickly on their axes, they give rise to a curious delusion, as if they possess an eel-like motion, although they are in reality perfectly rigid. They often, meteor-like dart here and there through the water, so that the observer is scarcely conscious of their presence, or they roll rapidly through the field of vision; sometimes they fasten themselves by one end, and move the other end in a circle exactly like a sling around a cord.

But Cohn also knew that there was more to the classification of bacteria than meets the eye, even with the aid of the most powerful microscope then available. "We are able to discern nothing about the internal structure of bacteria," he conceded. But there were other ways of telling even look-alike microorganisms apart. We have seen how in Cohn's laboratory it was shown that the growing blood-like spot that forms on bread (and sacred wafers) was due to red spherical bacteria (*Micrococcus prodigiosus*). By decomposing the albumen of the bread, these microorganisms produce a substance related to aniline dyes (which, as we shall see in the next chapter, were so important to the German textile industries in which the Jews were playing a central role). Now, one of Cohn's students, Joseph Schroeter, carried on from there and observed that similar-looking bacteria colonies produced different colors. This became an important supplementary tool for distinguishing one type of bacterium from its look-alike cousin.

Cohn's meticulous observations of the life cycles and reproductive manner of microorganisms lent much authority to those who rejected the whole concept of spontaneous generation. Once, in the case of a mysterious infection deep in the body of the housefly, Cohn wondered if he had found a possible exception, but some further detective work showed that even these microorganisms had entered the fly from outside. Now he concluded: "Bacteria are not the chance companions, but the cause of putre-faction. *Putrefaction is a chemical process excited by bacteria.* Death does not, as is commonly supposed, cause putrefaction, but rather it is caused by the life of these invisible organisms."

Perhaps Cohn's most important single contribution to bacteriology was his rejection of the concept of pleomorphism:

> Within the last few years, a theory has caused some sensation by seeking to account for the origin of bacteria by saying that the ordinary mould-fungus will, under certain conditions bring forth moving germs of extraordinary minuteness; which germs are capable of developing into bacteria, into yeast, and finally again into mould. When bacteria are found in the blood or other organs in certain diseases, the authors of this theory are satisfied that the spores of common mould or blight fungus germinate in the human body; that these germs first swarm as bacteria, but under suitable culture may be nourished into different kinds of mould. However, unprejudiced research has not given the slightest proof that bacteria stand in any connection with the history of the development of yeast, blight, or mould fungus. They always originate, as far as we know at present, from germs of the same kind.

Yet the principle of specific etiology—that each infectious disease was due to parasitism by colonies of a specific microorganism—still had an uphill fight against the concept of pleomorphistic etiology. Despite the work of Henle, Cohn, and others, so few microorganisms had been convincingly shown to be in a one-to-one relationship with specific diseases. Further, many microorganisms do indeed undergo dramatic physical transformations. In the absence of stronger proof, who was to say that one species of pathogen couldn't change into another? In Vienna Theodor Billroth, one of the most innovative surgeons and influential medical men of the day, remained skeptical of many aspects of the germ theory and publicly maintained on the basis of his inadequate observations that all bacterial forms are developmental stages of a single species, capable of metamorphosing at will and causing a spectrum of ills.

Furthermore, many diseases today known to be microbial presented to the late nineteenth-century medical men an epidemiological pattern seemingly irreconcilable with the germ theory. Malaria provided one of the greatest puzzles. Even Henle doubted a bacteriological etiology and conceded a probable miasmatic origin in accordance with the ancient view (*mal' aria* being Italian for "bad air"). For the disease appeared only in certain geographic areas characterized by swamps and dank air, and it so readily infected visitors from elsewhere, even when they had no apparent contact with other people or animals. Furthermore, no malaria sufferer coming to a nonmalarial region ever seemed to infect anyone. Yellow fever (also believed by Henle to be miasmatic), anthrax, and a host of other diseases today known to have a microbial etiology similarly defied explication, according to the principles of the germ theory, so long as so many aspects of the life cycles and vectors of the responsible microorganisms remained a mystery. Yet the last quarter of the nineteenth century was to be the heyday of the microbe hunters, as one transmissible disease after another was forced to reveal the secrets of its living agent and manner of spreading.

Much of this triumph was due not just to the foundation in microbiology laid by Ferdinand Cohn, but also to the way he chose to reply to a letter sent to him in the spring of 1876 from the town of Wollstein, some eighty miles to the northwest of Breslau, just across the Silesian border in the predominantly Polish province of Posnen. "I have found your work on bacteria, published in the *Beiträge zur Biologie der Pflanzen,* very exciting," the letter began. I have been working for some time on the contagion of anthrax. After many futile attempts I have finally succeeded in discovering the complete life cycle of the *Bacillus anthracis.* I am certain, now, as a result of a large number of experiments, that my conclusions are correct. However, before I publish my work, I would like to request, honored professor, that you, as the best expert on bacteria, examine my results and give me your judgment on their validity. . . . If this request is agreeable to you, perhaps you might inform me of a suitable time that I should come to Breslau.

Although some tentative identification of the microorganism of anthrax, a disease of cattle and sometimes of humans, had been made in mid-century, the mystery of its life cycle and means of transmission cast doubt on the concept of specific etiology and even seemed to provide arguments for spontaneous generation. The letter writer, a 33-year-old physician of Protestant background named Robert Koch, was unknown to Cohn. Indeed, outside the environs of Wollstein, where he served as regional medical doctor, he was hardly known to anyone.

An important exception was his former teacher Jacob Henle in Göttingen. Henle's classic textbook *Pathologische Untersuchungen* contained the crucial passage: "If it could be possible to prove that a contagion can be cultured outside the body . . . then such a contagion could only be a plant or animal." Henle further specified that separating the "living, mobile animals or distinct plants" from the contagious material or fluid (e.g., pus) in which they occur and observing their power independently would, hopefully, prove them to be the active agent of contagion rather than chance by-products forming in the nonliving component of the contagious material spontaneously or by accidental contamination from contact with the air. Furthermore, Henle taught: "One knows how long the fixed contagia retain their infectious power, even when dried. If one assumes that the contagious agent of an epidemic remains in such a state of latent animation after the conditions for its extension cease to exist, then the disease could again arise years later under favorable conditions, apparently miasmatically, actually by contagion." As Henle's student in the 1860s, Robert Koch took all these pioneering concepts to heart. He now believed himself to have isolated, along Henle's principles, the causative agent of anthrax and elucidated the latency period in its life cycle.

Through the years Cohn had received similar letters from dilettantes, whose works had typically failed to deliver what they promised. Nevertheless, the professor invited the country doctor Koch to visit Breslau the following week. "Within a matter of hours," Cohn later wrote, "I recognized in him an unrivaled master of scientific research." Koch methodically demonstrated how the active *Bacillus anthracis* could temporarily transform itself into almost lifeless encapsulated spores. Cohn himself had recently described a similar phenomenon, for a nonpathogenic bacteria called *Bacillus subtilis.* But here, Koch had provided a missing link in the life cycle of a very deadly microorganism, whose extraordinarily tough spores were capable of waiting patiently in the soil for years—indeed, for decades—in order to enter a new host and revert back to its virulent form.

Koch's results were soon published in Cohn's journal, *Beiträge zur Biologie der Pflanzen,* and the professor began selflessly advancing the young country doctor's career, first by informing scientists in Germany and abroad, and then by intervening with the medical faculty and municipal health authorities in Breslau, and with the minister of education and Imperial Health Office in Berlin in order to secure for him a suitable position. So it was that Robert Koch could go on to isolate the bacillus of tuberculosis, discover the vibrio of cholera (about which his patron had only been able to speculate), and elaborate his former teacher Henle's principles into "Koch's postulates," the laboratory protocol that would be used for the definitive identification of countless other specific disease agents.

Robert Koch's meeting with Ferdinand Cohn was one of the great events in medical history, yet it was not Koch's only important encounter in Breslau in those spring days in 1876. Among those in attendance at Koch's demonstration at the botanical department were Professor Julius Cohnheim of the medical faculty and his up-and-coming pathologist assistant Karl Weigert. Impressed by the country doctor, the two Jewish scientists invited him to tour their Institute of Pathology. Pausing in one of the labs, Cohnheim introduced Weigert's cousin, a medical student from the nearby town of Strehlen, whose table and lab coat were covered with multicolored blotches of dyes. "This is our little Ehrlich," Cohnheim told Koch. "He's very good at staining, but he'll never pass his exams."

Chapter 10

The Molecular Locksmith
from Strehlen

It must be assumed that this ability to combine with antitoxin is attributable to the presence in the toxin complex of a specific group of atoms with a maximum specific affinity to another group of atoms in the antitoxin complex, the first fitting the second easily, as a key does a lock.

—Paul Ehrlich

For hundreds of years before the nineteenth century, Jews in both the Christian and Moslem worlds had played a vital role in the clothing and textile industry and in the search for ever more attractive dyes for their fabrics. Maimonides knew well the Jewish dyers' quarter in Fez, where the plant extracts saffron, poppy, and indigo were used to color fabrics yellow, red, and blue. In Medieval Europe, Jewish dyers in southern Italy and Greece were especially prominent. Indeed, the dye-house formed, along with the synagogue, the center of the Jewish quarter in many a Mediterranean town.

But it was in nineteenth-century Germany—particularly in Silesia—that the Jews would effect the greatest advances in the textile and dyeing industry, bringing much wealth to that country. In 1841, the Jewish textile merchant Meyer Kauffmann and his wife, Philippine, opened a draper's establishment in Breslau, having expanded from the little shop in Schweidnitz that they had begun two decades earlier. Inspired by machines of the industrial revolution he had seen at the London Exposition of 1851, Kauffmann bought 200 mechanical looms and started a textile factory. "It soon became clear," wrote Kauffmann, "that the sale of goods to printers and finishers did not yield sufficient return; for that reason, we decided to bleach and dye our own cotton fabrics and to sell the products, together with hand-made goods, at fairs and through traveling salesmen, to the retail trade." Such innovations brought misery to the Silesian hand weavers. Their revolution in the 1840s (immortalized in the song "Die schlesischen Weber") was unsuccessful; but in the long run the Industrial Revolution they could not stop provided all of society with a previously undreamt of abundance of goods.

Up to the middle of the nineteenth century, all dyes, whether based on secret recipes or not, were derived from natural sources. But now, with the rise of the science of chemistry and the rapid industrialization of the textile industry, the color spectrum was about to be greatly broadened. In 1855 came news from England of mauve, the world's first synthetic dye. This was created by the oxidation of a commercial aniline, a substance chemists had extracted a decade earlier from coal tar naphtha, which has the same nitrogenous base as the natural dye indigo. This British discovery was accidental. But now the Germans, and particularly the German Jews, lost no time in creating other aniline dyes. To *Geheimrat* (Privy Councilor to the Emperor) Heinrich Caro, the Jewish president of a great industrial concern Badische Analin- und Soda-Fabrik (BASF), goes the credit for discovering, among other dyes, aniline red, induline, eosine, Manchester brown, and Victoria blue. In later years, the Jewish chemist Otto Wallach, a pioneer in the field of acrylics and the perfection of aniline dyes, would receive the Nobel Prize for Chemistry, as would the half-Jewish Adolf von Baeyer, the synthesizer of, among other tints, artificial indigo.

Predictably, these anilines were a blessing to textile manufacturing and to the general advance of industrialization. Less predictable was the boon they were to indirectly provide for suffering humanity. This was thanks to the genius of the Silesian Jewish physician Paul Ehrlich and the childlike fascination with the coloring properties of chemicals that he maintained throughout his life.

The Ehrlich family's Silesian roots extended back for countless generations. Records from the turn of the eighteenth century list them as stocking manufacturers, innkeepers, and grain merchants. In the latter capacity, they were familiar faces on the large Prussian estates and served also as financial advisers to the nobility. But it was particularly in the distillery business that the family rose in both wealth and social status. Whereas Paul's great-grandfather Simon Ehrlich hardly eked out a living as a merchant, his son Heymann became a supplier to the Prussian Army at the front during the Napoleonic Wars and then went into the production of brandy. This business was not uncommon among Jews in the region, although very little of the spirits was for their own consumption. More than half the inns in Silesia were in Jewish hands and perhaps half of Silesia's Jews were involved in the inn trade. This naturally encouraged their coreligionists to go into the manufacture of spirits, the lifeblood of the innkeepers.

But Heymann Ehrlich also had extensive noncommercial pursuits. He took a keen intellectual interest in the scientific work of his contemporary Alexander von Humboldt, whom he is said to have physically resembled. The Ehrlichs began a tradition of free thinking, a product of the Age of Reason that since the end of the eighteenth century had influenced both the German Christian and German Jewish communities of central Silesia. The salon of the Ehrlich home on the market square in Strehlen, ten miles south of Breslau, became an intellectual meeting point for Jew and gentile, noble and commoner. Paul Ehrlich would himself attribute much of his scientific gifts to grandfather Heymann, who at the age of 90 delivered popular scientific lectures and also had them printed.

The social status of the Ehrlich family rose further with Paul's father, Ismar, who attended the *Gymnasium,* where he was educated in Greek and Latin, as well as German. Like Heymann, he was well read and had many interests, although he perhaps lacked the old man's originality and imagination. Ismar acquired, alongside the prosperous distillery, the office of collector for the Royal Prussian State Lottery, a position that was otherwise almost exclusively awarded to retired military officers. For years up to his death at age 80, Ismar Ehrlich was looked upon as a leader of the Strehlen Jewish community.

Although Heymann and Ismar lived to a ripe old age, the longevity of the Ehrlich men had in fact been decreasing even as the family grew more prosperous. In 1843, Paul's great-grandfather Simon was paid homage at the town hall on the occasion of his 100th birthday. This milestone was extraordinary even for the Jews, whose ancient hygienic regulations may have afforded them on average a higher life expectancy than their gentile neighbors. Simon would live yet another three years, just short of the birth of his great-grandson Paul, during whose comparatively brief life the Ehrlich name would become immortalized.

What of Paul's maternal line? The Weigert family, hailing from the ethnically more Polish than German region of Upper Silesia, was less affected by the West European Enlightenment and remained religiously more conservative. Yet there must have been powerful potential scientific talent in the Weigert genes, as attested to by Paul's slightly older cousin Karl. This somewhat inbred product of a marriage between two Weigert cousins would in his own right become a pioneer in modern pathology and bacteriology. No less important is the fact that Paul's maternal grandfather, Abraham Weigert, was, aside from being a brewer and distiller, also involved in textile manufacture and dyeing.

Paul Ehrlich was born in Strehlen in 1854. Growing up so close to the textile center of Breslau in which his mother's relatives were active, Paul was naturally somewhat dye-conscious. Even the alcohol-distilling business of Paul's nuclear family was directly affected by developments in the dying industry. A tradition among Silesian distilleries was to introduce onto the market new brandies with variations in color and taste. This applied also to the important side-line of the distilleries, the manufacture of candy. The older aniline dyes had been notorious for their toxicity and therefore unconsumable. But now, among the hundreds of new dyes coming onto the market were some touted as nonpoisonous. Already at a young age, Paul had turned an unused kitchen in the family home into a laboratory for concocting recipes for new sweets.

It was, however, his contact with his older cousin Karl Weigert, at the time a medical student at the University of Breslau, that inspired Paul to steer his fascination with dyes in the biological direction. Strehlen would always be remembered affectionately by Paul Ehrlich (indeed, a half century later, he would leave a generous sum of money to the town in his will); but it had no secondary school. So in 1866 Paul joined Karl in nearby Breslau, already Germany's third largest city with a population of over 200,000 and increasing so rapidly that it would more than double by the end of the century. There Paul attended the St. Maria Magdalena Gymnasium, where Ferdinand Cohn had studied two decades earlier and where there now happened to be another Jewish boy, Albert Neisser, who like Paul Ehrlich would one day strike a great blow in the fight against venereal disease.

At the time, Karl the medical student was already taking advantage of the new anilines developed by Caro and others for preparing his microscope slides. Drawings in modern textbooks of anatomy invariably give the layman a misleading impression of contrasting colors in the human and animal body. Cardiac illustrations, for example, are apt to show a pinkish heart, a scarlet aorta, light blue veins, and yellow-green nerves. As beginning medical students quickly learn to their dismay when confronted with a mass of indistinguishable tissue in the dissecting room, such color coding is a vast exaggeration of what in reality are often at best extremely subtle differences in hue. The differentiation between types of tissue and organs so evident in our textbooks had literally and figuratively to be teased from nature in the course of hundreds of years. Such having been the case on the gross anatomical level, one can imagine how much the microscope photographs in modern textbooks, produced by such techniques as florescent staining and false color photography, belie the situation faced by the medical scientists when in the nineteenth century they focused their imperfect microscopes on the subvisible fabric of the human body.

Staining was not part of the *Gymnasium* science curriculum. But having heard of some experiments by the famed French physiologist Claude Bernard in dyeing organisms from the inside out, young Paul tried his hand at some independent research and added massive quantities of anilines to the feed of his family's pet doves. Two of the birds, the favorites of his sister Elise (Paul was the only son, among four daughters), indeed turned blue but then walked around in circles and keeled over dead. This unfortunate incident made a lasting impression on young Paul, who in years to come would be confronted with an ethical problem never faced by previous generations of scientists: the deliberate infecting, poisoning, and dissecting of not a few, but tens of thousands of laboratory animals as sacrifices for the advancement of medicine.

A half century later, Nazi politicians, who often espoused antivivisectionism (and were typically also nature-lovers and sometimes, like Hitler, vegetarians), would denounce animal experimentation as "Jewish." Paul Ehrlich, although not a strict follower of Jewish customs and rules, remained all his life true to Judaism and, as his grandson, exiled to America by the Nazis would later attest, "identified with deep and warm feeling with our people." Paul is said to have been influenced by the biblical story of Abraham, whom God instructed to offer an animal in place of a human sacrifice. Paul's lifelong principle would be that the wholesale sacrifice of laboratory animals could be justified only if—unlike the frivolous case of the blue doves—it served the preservation of human life and the amelioration of human suffering.

Very much a child of the revolution in biological thinking, Paul Ehrlich listened intently as cousin Karl told him: "Medical science has to start with precise observations of nature. The human body is subject to no other laws and shows no other compositions than those of animals and plants." So it happened that when for the final exam in German language and literature Paul's class was asked to write an essay on the topic "Life Is a Dream," he wrote: "Life rests on normal oxidations. Dreams are an activity of the brain and the activities of the brain are only oxidations . . . dreams are a sort of phosphorescence of the brain!" His teacher was unamused by this extension of the revolt against romanticism to the liberal arts, but Paul graduated nonetheless.

Now came the question of what he should study at the university. Organic chemistry or pharmacy were obvious possibilities, with a view toward a career in commerce or industry. But Paul seemed never to have inherited any business acumen from his ancestors. Medicine, then? Unfortunately, Paul had always been shy with both his peers and older people, and the thought of having someday to start a practice had no appeal to him. But cousin Karl assured him that he himself intended to be a physician-researcher and convinced Paul to follow his lead.

Paul Ehrlich's freshman year at the University of Breslau, as recollected by one of his professors, the famed neuroanatomist Heinrich von Waldeyer, seemed to set the tone for a method in madness that was to characterize the rest of his life: "Gradually his bench became covered with stains in all colors. One day, when I saw him sitting there again, I went across and asked him what he was doing that made his bench gleam in all the colors of the rainbow. Whereupon [he] just answered, 'I'm experimenting.' 'Well,' I replied, giving him a friendly nod, 'then just stick with it.' . . . In Ehrlich I had an unusually gifted student. He seldom asked for advice but worked almost entirely independently right from the start." Similar accounts abound, including one from the visiting American doctor William Henry Welch (more about whom in a later chapter), who would recall "the brilliant eccentric wandering around the laboratory with hands that looked as though they had been thrust into innumerable paint pots up to the wrists."

Still, when Professor Cohnheim told the visiting Robert Koch that "our little Ehrlich is very good at staining," he himself probably did not yet realize just how good. The staining of microscope specimens, which by then was no longer a novelty, was recognized as a very practical technique, especially in combination with the ever increasing precision of the microscopes being produced by Zeiss and Schott at Jena, with their achromatic and, later, oil-immersion lenses. But any consideration of the molecular processes involved in staining was generally felt to be needless speculation for a physician. Yet how else were fundamental advances to be made, if not by a physician-chemist? Chemists in the dyeing industry needed to concern themselves with the characteristics of only a few fiber varieties, such as wool, cotton, and silk, which furthermore did not necessarily demand an exceptional degree of dye purity. The industrial chemists could hardly be expected to care about the far more refined techniques needed for staining the cells of animal tissues, muscles, bones, glands, blood, and the like, or, more subtle still, for differentiating the various parts of individual cells. But here in Paul Ehrlich was a physician whose first love was chemistry. Although unprepossessing by nature, Ehrlich, when asked, admitted of himself, "I can see the structural formula and the benzene rings with my mind's eye, and my chemical imagination has developed so rapidly that sometimes I am able to foresee things recognized only much later by the disciples of systematic chemistry." Add to this a love of colors, and one has the basis for great advances in anatomical staining.

After qualifying as a physician, Ehrlich moved on to Leipzig where in 1878 he obtained his doctorate on a dissertation entitled "Contributions to the Theory and Practice of Histological Staining." He introduced the technique of counterstaining, whereby the washing of a stained specimen with a second, acidic chemical removes the color from only specific cells or parts of cells and thus permits far greater differentiation. Young Dr. Ehrlich next went on to pioneer the field of dynamic vital staining. We have already noted Paul's smart-aleck essay in his German class that even dreaming is a process of oxidation. But how much oxygen does the brain or any other organ of man and beast consume, when sleeping, waking, or whatever? By developing dyes that vary in color according to their oxygen content, Ehrlich was able to determine from the hue how much oxygen a living tissue contains and how much it is absorbing. From this would come one of the earliest of his more than 150 publications, "The Organism's Oxygen Requirement."

What Paul Ehrlich would later call "the most gripping experience of my scientific life" took place on March 24, 1882, when he met Robert Koch for the second time. As a physician at the Charité—the renowned Berlin hospital founded in the early eighteenth century as a plague house by the father of Frederick the Great—Ehrlich was among the audience of the Physiological Society when Koch announced his discovery of the tuberculosis bacillus. With it came the hope that the scourge would soon be eradicated. One of the reasons for young Dr. Ehrlich's excitement was that during his own staining activities, he had in fact seen the same TB rods before Koch ever laid eyes on them but had mistaken them for crystals. Ehrlich showed Koch his own ingenious way to stain the mycobacteria, only to find out later (when he happened to look through a microscope at his sputum) that in his microbe-hunting enthusiasm he had seriously infected himself. Very reluctantly, Ehrlich went on leave to Egypt. In those days the only way to treat TB was by resting and hoping that the body would marshal enough of its own resources to beat off the infection. Millions of people (including, indirectly, later generations of TB patients) would owe their lives to the fact that Paul Ehrlich won his bout with consumption and could return to his work in Berlin.

As a resident at the Charité, Ehrlich inevitably had his share of clinical responsibilities. Colleagues would later speak of him as being conscientious in his duties and kind to his patients. But it was no secret that medical practice was not much to his liking. Paul Ehrlich would look at patients and dream of curing them not with his bedside manner or by hoping that their bodies would somehow gain the upper hand. The proven effective drugs, such as quinine for malaria, opium for pain, and digitalis for cardiac insufficiency, discovered by chance in the course of millennia, were of little comfort to him. There were so few of them and their modes of action were still pretty much a mystery.

A breakthrough in Ehrlich's thinking came from an obscure article, ignored by everyone else, on the subject of lead toxicity. The author showed that certain body organs more than others tended to absorb lead and thus be poisoned by it. An important point here is that lead is not a dye and the absorption cannot in fact be seen. Yet the selective nature of lead poisoning was similar to the way certain stains color only specific body tissues. So it was that an idea germinating in the mind of Paul Ehrlich began to take shape: that not only poisoning but even the ravage of infectious illness was the result of chemical attachment of invading foreign material to protoplasm, the essential constituent of the body's cells. Although Paul had disdained the Latin and Greek terms that his professors pretentiously spouted, as if the learned vocabulary itself could effect a cure, he was not above coining a classical phrase himself. *Corpora non agunt nisi fixata* became his battle cry, by which he meant that it is only by such chemical interactions of their cells that living organisms—be they microbes or men—are affected for good or ill.

At the Charité, Ehrlich used this principle of chemistry to develop the so-called diazo-reaction urine test. Uroscopy had been around since at least the Middle Ages. The thirteenth-century writer Shem Tov Falaquera of Navarre described the scene in the office of a Jewish doctor

sitting on a chair with much dignity and magnificence covered with his ceremonial gown, which he put on to cover his cloak. Each person presented then his flask containing urine. The doctor took them and looked at them and examined their appearance and aspect. He observed the urine's appearance, noting whether or not it was cloudy or if there were any irregularities about it. To one of his patients he said, "This urine indicates a serious illness of the liver, a weakness of the stomach as well as the constipation of the liver. If it is not dealt with at its very inception it will end fatally. And this other flask indicates high and strong health, while that one coldness."

So closely was uroscopy identified with medicine that for centuries, the urine bottle painted on a wrought iron shield was the traditional sign to be hung outside a doctor's house for the benefit of the illiterate.

It wasn't until after the invention of the stethoscope by the French physician René Laënnec early in the nineteenth century that doctors became identified with a more dignified tool of their trade. Yet no sooner did this occur than Jewish physician-chemists started bringing uroscopy back, in a scientific form. In the 1820s Dr. Gustav Wetzlar, who had just graduated in medicine in Marburg and was already on his way to making a name for himself in the fields of metallurgy and electrochemistry, published two papers on the chemical properties of human urine and the reaction of borax to uric acid. Now, a half century later, Paul Ehrlich was demonstrating how when urine is added to a test tube of "Ehrlich's reagent" (a mixture of sulphanilic acid, nitric acid, and acidified sodium nitrate) and then covered with ammonia, there appears a spectrum of colors undreamt of by the physicians of old. The concoction either turns deep yellow, or it becomes dark brown and then changes to brilliant red-violet, or else it starts as pale yellow and then turns one of various shades of red. Let the mixture stand a while and a precipitate may form at the bottom, ranging in color from brilliant green to violet. In each case, the diagnosis was different: liver disease, heart ailments, pneumonia, typhus and the like.

But diagnosing isn't the same as curing, and Paul Ehrlich cherished a dream of rationally bringing about chemical reactions not just in the test tube or urine flask, but inside the body of his patients and so defeating the age-old scourges of mankind. Such a vision could not be accomplished by a physician who had to earn his living as a full-time clinician. It was Paul Ehrlich's father-in-law who helped free him for a few years from the obligations of medical practice. In 1883 the 29-year-old doctor married Hedwig Pinkus, a pretty 19-year-old daughter of an Upper Silesian industrialist who had, appropriately enough, made his fortune in the textile industry. "Everywhere in the world I go, I find the tables set with my linen, even on ocean liners," Paul's father-in-law would say with pride. As was the custom in those days, the couple's meeting had been discreetly arranged by their parents, who saw in them an ideal match. Hedwig had, aside from her good looks and her family's wealth, a keen intelligence and an interest in language and literature that had been cultivated at the girls' secondary school in the Pinkus's hometown, Neustadt. Paul, for his part, had even at his young age already earned a reputation in the world of medicine and there was the promise of much more to come. But aside from such social considerations, there quickly formed an affectionate bond between the couple. Hedwig, despite her literary interests, was by nature quite practical and level-headed—precisely the type of partner needed by the otherworldly young medical scientist.

The wedding took place at the synagogue in Neustadt and was soon followed by the birth of two daughters, Stephanie and Marianne. The financial obligations of parenthood notwithstanding, Paul was still determined to dedicate his life to research. So father-in-law Pinkus financed a small laboratory in a few rooms of a building near the young couple's home. "I can also work in a barn," declared Paul. "All I need is a test tube and a flame." The space, however, belonged not to a farmer but to a locksmith, and this was to Paul Ehrlich's advantage, for he was constantly forgetting his keys and otherwise living up to the stereotype of the absent-minded professor. (The title of professor was granted to him at age 30, a great honor in German society, especially for someone so young.) But more important, the concept of a lock and key was becoming a powerful metaphor in Paul Ehrlich's medico-chemical thinking, and in particular in explaining how a body fights off the germs and toxins of diseases, and why it is that, once having survived an attack, the body is often to a greater degree invulnerable to the same illness. A rational explanation of resistance and immunity had been eluding humanity since time immemorial.

As we have seen, in the universe of the primitives, often inhabited by malevolent spirits or unfriendly fellow humans with magic powers, falling ill to a disease was commonly viewed as the entrance into the victim's body of a demon or some pathogenic magical object, both of which could be protected against by the appropriate amulets or reversed by the suitable magical countermeasures or exorcism rituals. Alternatively, the sickness had its etiology in some offense to the gods or the breaking of taboos, in which case confession, atonement, and ritual sacrifices were in order. It was especially this latter notion that dominated in early Judeo-Christian thinking. A person's being passed over by an epidemic was a sign of being free of sin. If one got sick and then recovered, this indicated that the sin was purged, as alluded to in the Psalm of David: "Bless the Lord ... who forgiveth all thine iniquities; who healeth all thy diseases" (Psalms 103:1–3). This view gained particular force among Christians and Moslems and vied for centuries with the scientific concepts of Hippocrates and Galen.

The Greco-Roman approach, rational though it was, had difficulty in explaining why some folks didn't get sick while other folks did, and why some of the latter died while for others the disease proved to be self-limiting—resulting in recovery or at least a stable condition. It was assumed within the framework of the concept of the four humors that imbalances could arise in the bodies of a large segment of the population in a given geographic area due to climatic conditions—air, waters, winds, vapors, and the angle of the sun and even the alignment of the nocturnal heavenly bodies. Individual variations could be accounted for by variations in regimen, diet, and perhaps natural constitution, all of which could make the body more or less vulnerable to climatic disruption. When imbalance and blockages did occur, *physis*—the healing power of nature—and *pepsis*—internal concoction—strove to restore the balance, and could theoretically be aided by the physician's prescription of a specific diet, his administration of a counteracting drug, or his purging of an excess humor.

The Renaissance brought a hint of the germ theory—though on a purely speculative level. With regard to immunity and self-limiting disease, Girolamo Fracastoro mused in the sixteenth century that the various kinds of minuscule seeds (*seminaria*) that can sow diseases each had a particular affinity for certain plants, animals, and people, and also for specific organs, tissues and humors. When an attack resulted in a depleting of a particular body humor needed by the seeds in question, then they could no longer flourish and the disease couldn't progress.

In the latter half of the nineteenth century, as the germ theory of infectious disease began to triumph, the concept of transmittable disease as self-limiting due to nutritional depletion was taken up by Louis Pasteur, who observed how initial multiplication of bacteria in a test tube was followed by abrupt termination. David Gruby, the pioneering Hungarian-Jewish bacteriologist in Paris, showed how microbes in the infected blood of one species (say, a dog) usually fared well for a while when injected into a new host of the same species (another dog) though often not in a new host of a different species (say, a rabbit or frog), which could hypothetically be attributed to differences in the nutritional resources each host species offered the given pathogen. Ferdinand Cohn was particularly impressed by the lightning speed at which microorganisms multiply. Dividing once an hour or even more often, "the bacteria which spring from one germ would in less than five days fill the whole world's seas completely full," he calculated. That nothing of the sort happens in reality Cohn attributed partly to nutritional depletion—but he also speculated on an additional factor: mutual destruction among different species of microorganisms competing for the same limited resources. One had to further assume that individual host variables helped determined whether some attacks would have a fatal outcome before the germs ran out of nutrients while in other cases the host would survive.

Such speculations might have been sufficient—at least in principle—to explain a patient's recovery from a first attack of a given disease. But the theory would then have to accommodate the well established fact of acquired immunity, where recovery from certain diseases gave the patient long term, even life-long, invulnerability to the same disease. Acquired immunity was particularly noticeable in the case of smallpox, for the disease left as a token of its first visitation pock-marks that seemed to guarantee protection from subsequent revisitations of smallpox epidemics.

In the religious scheme of things—pagan, Jewish, Christian, or Islamic—it was probably assumed that the first attack of a disease succeeded in purging the transgressor of his sins, so no second attack was necessary (provided, of course, that he didn't commit more transgressions in the interim). As for the specificity of the phenomenon (the smallpox survivor acquired no particular immunity to, say, the plague)—well, maybe specific transgressions were linked to particular afflictions.

Explanation within the rationalistic system of medicine was more problematical. Acquired immunity was well known to Hippocrates and the ancient Greeks. As the historian Thucydides wrote when an epidemic revisted Athens: "Those who had [once] recovered from the disease ... had now no fear for themselves; for the same man was never attacked twice—never at least fatally." The classical physicians could only assume that recovery somehow provided a certain enhanced and specific humoral stability. It wasn't until the tenth century that the Islamic physician Rhazes came up with some more impressive, though nevertheless false, explanations, at least with regard to smallpox. The disease, Rhazes speculated, "arises when the blood putrefies and ferments, so that superfluous vapors are thrown out of it and it is changed from the blood of infants, which is like must [grape juice] into the blood of young men, which is perfectly ripened [like wine]." In later life the blood becomes drier and sourer, but since the vapors have been expelled at a young age, smallpox does not recur.

Fracastoro combined his germ concept with similar speculation six centuries later. If the seeds of contagion of a specific disease had an affinity for a certain body humor (in the case of smallpox, the supposed humor was assumed to be traces of menstrual blood that contaminated the child during the birth process), and this humor was spoiled or purged in the course of the illness, then that disease would be denied a site for a renewed infection in the future. As one of the adherents to this theory put it: "Its seeds were sown in an exhausted Soil." Such a concept was taken up by Jacob Henle at the dawn of the modern era of medicine. In his 1840 classic on infectious diseases, Henle asked rhetorically: "Couldn't one express it [acquired immunity] as follows: that one species of these beings [microbes] has destroyed the disposition for the reproduction or the nutrition of the same species? At least there is a striking analogy with many epidemic diseases, which spare the body in which they had once appeared, for the duration of the epidemic and often during its entire life." (Interestingly, fever played a role in this process, according to Henle, since "without the general action [of fever] on the blood, the disease would not exist in its fullest development and for that reason would not protect against falling ill anew through the same contagion.")

An alternative but complementary theory making the rounds in the eighth and ninth decades of the nineteenth century was that a given strain of invading bacterium produced various substances as by-products of its own metabolism, such as phenols and phenylacetate, whose accumulation eventually inhibited its growth and afforded the host a measure of protection against future attack.

The nutrient depletion and microbe self-poisoning hypotheses could theoretically also supply the basis for the protective effect of vaccination, such as Jenner developed for smallpox and Pasteur for rabies. In the former case, the relatively harmless cowpox microorganism with which the subject was prophylactically inoculated could be assumed to have similar nutritional requirements to its virulent smallpox cousin—but first come, first served. In the case of the rabies vaccine, although the virulently pathogenic microorganism had been deliberately weakened by exposure to air or chemicals before inoculation, it apparently still metabolized and thus exhausted the nutrients and denied an infection site to a nonattenuated rabies microorganism. Both forms of microbes could also be assumed to be poisoning themselves and related strains in their own exudes.

But soon there arose an insurmountable theoretical hurdle. For in the mid-1880s David E. Salmon and Theobold Smith demonstrated that effective vaccination against various diseases was possible by inoculation of killed bacteria, which, being dead, consumed no nutrients and did not metabolize or exude anything.

Clearly the body must be *actively* defending itself. But how?

Paul Ehrlich was a medical doctor with a passion for chemistry, who was born in the right time and place to provide the foundation for the emerging discipline of immunology. A century earlier the iatrochemists (physician-chemists) had been particularly in vogue but had, for all their beautiful theorizing, produced virtually nothing of therapeutic worth. True, the late eighteenth century had heralded the birth of organic chemistry. Independently of one another, Joseph Priestly in England, Antoine Lavoisier in France, Carl Scheele in Sweden, and Mikhail Lomonosov in Russia discovered the secret of combustion and oxygenation. Lavoisier went on to determine the exact composition of carbon dioxide and then study the combustion processes in living organisms by which food is transformed into energy. Yet, ironically, these early breakthroughs sooner had a negative effect on the advancement of medical science, as doctors, on the basis of the impressive but still woefully inadequate advances in chemistry, sought to explain epidemics in terms of biochemical atmospheric disturbances (miasmas), to the detriment of the germ theory.

The state of the art in chemistry in general and organic chemistry in particular would, however, advance dramatically in the course of the nineteenth century. In 1824, Justus von Liebig established at the University of Giessen the first laboratory for the systematic teaching of chemistry. Liebig introduced the concept of the compound radical, a substance whose atoms can combine with atoms of other compound radicals and yield new combinations (he joined various atoms to produce chloral and chloroform in his lab) but that in the final analysis retains its identity. Turning his attention to foodstuffs, Liebig divided these into respiratory foods (sugars and fats) and tissue-building foods (proteins and substances containing nitrogen). Early in the second half of the century, the German organic chemist Friedrich August Kekulé elucidated the manner in which carbon atoms combine into chains and described the structure of the benzene ring. In Russia Dimitri Mendeleev published his periodic table, demonstrating that the elements when arranged in the order of their atomic weights, showed certain recurring properties (rather like musical octaves), particularly in their ability to combine with other elements.

Louis Pasteur was a chemist, not a physician, and he began by making important discoveries about left- and right-facets of crystals and then about the left- and right-turning molecular asymmetry of organic matter acted upon by fungi. This eventually led him to studies of the role of microorganisms in the fermentation of wine and beer, and from there to the germ theory of disease in living beings and his development of protective vaccination. But now, relying as he did on stimulating the body to do the work of healing, Pasteur had less and less reason to engage in detailed theorization about the role of molecular structures in the processes of infection, defense, and immunization. However, the German chemist Emil Fischer took up where Pasteur, as a chemist, had left off decades earlier. Fischer elucidated the stereochemical (three-dimensional) structures of organic compounds, such as isomeric sugars, purines, and polypeptides, and explained the mechanism of nitrogen metabolism. It was Fischer who coined the term *side-chains*, referring to the appendage structures by means of which organic molecules react with other compounds.

Enter Professor Ehrlich, who adopted as his principle that: "What the microscope can and has done for us is now reaching its limits." To know what goes on beyond the visible range, we would have to "break up the finest chemical activities of the life of the cell into a great number of specific partial functions." By nature, this would be speculation, and speculate is what Ehrlich did. "Progress in science can proceed only from a theoretical approach," he stated. "Therefore even an incorrect theory can turn out to be more fruitful than pure experiences which are registered without further explanation." Yet, in fact, the theory that arose from Paul Ehrlich's fertile imagination, far from being incorrect, was uncannily close to the mark. A compulsive doodler, Professor Ehrlich considered no surface inviolable for the chalk and colored pencils he always carried in his pockets. He drew sketches of his imaginary models of cells on tabletops, floors, restaurant menus, and even, we are told, on the shirtboards of visitors if they didn't dodge quickly enough. As for the consequences for the tablecloths in his home, Frau Professor Ehrlich was particularly thankful to be the daughter of a great linen manufacturer.

Paul Ehrlich attached Emil Fischer's side-chains to cells and called them receptors, each of which is capable of joining with only one form of chemical molecule, as—to use Ehrlich's favorite metaphor—a lock fits with a specific key. He then further classified them as chemo-ceptors, nutri-ceptors, ambo-ceptors, and the like, according to their presumed function for the life processes of the cell, and he doodled for each of them some fanciful shape. Ehrlich assumed there were certain types of cells that specialized in actively defending the body against toxins and other pathogens. In an intriguing bit of speculation, he suggested that such a cell does its work as a matter of self-interest, so to speak. For instance, when its nutro-ceptor is latched onto by a toxin (or pathogen) and it is thus prevented from obtaining nourishment, rather than just starving it has recourse to a mechanism, developed during eons of evolution, by which it sprouts more nutro-ceptors. These would in turn be latched onto by other toxin molecules, and so it goes. This was the kernel of Paul Ehrlich's principle of hyperregeneration of antibodies, inspired in part by the general phenomenon of overcompensation that cousin Karl Weigert had observed in various pathological cases.

The first great triumph that Ehrlich's biomolecular theory helped bring about—even as it was still germinating in his mind—involved the concept of transferred immunity (technically, and somewhat confusingly, called passive immunity). In ages passed, such a concept had been expressed in only the vaguest of terms, as when the famed Herman Boerhaave of Leiden stated early in the eighteenth century that "people who have smallpox must have something remaining in [rather than, as the nutrient depletion theory would have it, removed from] their body which overcomes subsequent contagious infection." This notion was derided by a contemporary of Boerhaave, Legard Sparham, who remarked: "Unless we could suppose some singular Virtue to remain in the Blood as a proper Antagonist, it would be absurd to think them secure from a second Infection, any more than that the Transfusion of the Blood or Matter of a venereal pocky Person into a sound Habit, should secure him from any future Amour with Impunity."

Yet in the late nineteenth century this ridiculed concept of transferable immunity turned out to be very much a reality for several diseases. Paul Ehrlich showed that when a plant poison such as ricin or abrin—or an insect or snake venom—was introduced into the body, the host formed antitoxins that rendered it harmless. How about the just as lethal toxins generated by diphtheria and tetanus bacteria when they invade the body? Paul

Ehrlich's friend Emil von Behring showed that in the case of such diseases the doctor could harness the antitoxins in the serum—the clear, watery component of blood after coagulation—generated by a guinea pig that has been exposed to nonlethal doses of the toxin in question. When injected into another guinea pig this antitoxin-rich serum would produce in it, for a limited time, immunity from attack from diphtheria or tetanus. Such a serum could also tip the balance in favor of a host already under attack by toxin-producing microbes by augmenting the antitoxins generated by its own system. (Incidentally, although he himself wasn't Jewish, Behring was the son-in-law of *Geheimrat* Spinola, the Jewish co-director of the Charité Hospital.)

The next step was to cultivate on a large scale such antitoxin-rich sera in order to save human lives. One of Paul Ehrlich's vital contributions to Behring's breakthrough lay in his meticulous calculations and his quantifications of the minimal lethal dose and the units of immunity in relation to body weight. Thus he was able to specify the gradually increasing doses of diphtheria toxin that could be administered to the serum-producing animal—preferably a strapping stallion—allowing its body's immune system to bring forth the maximum amount of antitoxin without itself succumbing to the disease. Here Ehrlich's locksmith metaphor came in handy again. "A molecule of toxin combines with a definite and unalterable quantity of anti[toxin]," he wrote. "It must be assumed that this ability to combine with antitoxin is attributable to the presence in the toxin complex of a specific group of atoms with a maximum specific affinity to another group of atoms in the antitoxin complex, the first fitting the second easily, as a key does a lock."

Only some pathogenic microorganisms are toxin-producing. Viral infection, we now know, occurs when viruses enter certain body cells, commandeer them from within in order to replicate, and (in clinical manifestations) cause their widespread destruction. Pathogenic fungi grow on internal and external body surfaces to such an extent that they cause dysfunction. Some protozoa may invade red blood cells and destroy them from within as part of their life cycle. Intestinal worms, fastened to the gut and sometimes growing to ten meters in length, may cause debilitation by their blood sucking. Other worms infect internal organs and cause dysfunction by their encystation. Paul Ehrlich was convinced that in all such cases the host's immune system mobilizes a counter-assault—not necessarily with antitoxins to neutralize the toxins, for there needn't be any, but with antibodies against the parasitic invaders themselves. If the counterattack is mounted quickly and efficiently enough, it results not only in the host's victory, but, at the end of the day in a tremendous overkill, which leaves enormous quantities of antitoxin or antibodies in the host's system for some time to come.

By 1900 Paul Ehrlich was ready to give full artistic rendering to his fanciful concepts. In a lecture presented in England, he produced a series of drawings, complete with shading to give a three-dimensional effect, showing a defense cell's side-chains (receptors) of specific molecular shapes being attacked and latched on to by toxins or other pathogens (termed antigens, that is, leading to the *gen*eration of *anti*bodies) of reciprocal molecular shapes. The cell responds by hyperregenerating vast numbers of the same side-chains and releasing them into the bloodstream as free antitoxins or antibodies, thus neutralizing the attack and providing immunity from future attack for as long as they remained active. Others of his diagrams showed the intermediary role of complements. These are free, noncellular chemical components in the blood that contribute to the host's defense by directly weakening the membrane of the pathogens or else helping to target them and mediating their neutralization by the antibodies. (This was a vestige of the ancient humoral view and, as it turned out, a quite valid one.)

Critics of Paul Ehrlich—and these were never in short supply—called him "Dr. Phantastus" and objected to the images of toxins, receptors, and complements fitting one another like keys in locks. Ehrlich himself knew that he was giving somewhat arbitrary visual form to processes occurring in a sort of twilight zone between the chemical, biological, and physical. "Those dumb people think I really conceive of it that way!" was his reaction to the critics. Nevertheless, it is of almost symbolic significance that Ehrlich's revolutionary use of visualizations appeared at the very dawn of the century in which powerful computers would later generate three-dimensional images of molecular structures showing that Ehrlich's models were uncannily prescient as first approximations.

Yet for much of the first half of the twentieth century, an important aspect of Ehrlich's model would fall into disrepute. This was largely due to demonstrations by Karl Landsteiner (we will learn more about him in a later chapter) that the host can form antibodies to a virtually unlimited variety of antigens—even to synthetic substances that do not exist in nature but are created artificially in the chemist's lab. That an immune response could be evoked in a human body, when neither the person himself nor the countless generations of *Homo sapiens* before him could ever have encountered the antigen in question, seemed to call for a more flexible model than one with preformed key and lock shapes. Ehrlich had stated that "the formation of antibodies does not represent the creation of new types of atomic grouping but is the reproduction of normal cell performance. In the organism or its cells there must be physiological analogues of the antibody group with specific linkage." Put more simply: there are only a limited number of substances that body cells encounter in nature and that can interact with the cells and, if toxic or pathogenic, adversely affect them; so the variety of defense cells a body needs is correspondingly limited. But in view of Landsteiner's discovery that the body can produce an immune response even to new artificial toxins, Ehrlich's original model came to be superseded by a so-called instructional version, whereby—to continue the key-and-lock metaphor—the receptor-locks on the defense cells are wax-like in their malleability so that the antigen encountering them, of whatever conceivable shape, can make a complementary impression that then hyperregenerates in a vast number of locks of the same kind.

Only in the second half of the twentieth century, with the great advance of molecular biology and genetics, was it shown that hyperregeneration is a cloning process using the DNA at the nucleus of the defense cell, and that this DNA cannot be altered by any supposed changes in the cell's receptors as the instructional model would have it. Thus, surprisingly, Ehrlich's original version proved to be more correct. In his model he erred in that he placed various shapes of hyperregeneratable receptors on the same defense cell, rather than having each type of shape on a different defense cell. (Each cell can have only one DNA nucleus and can therefore clone only one type of receptor.) And, as we have said, he underestimated the variety of receptors that the body's immune system can hyperregenerate. The problem of reconciling a finite number of defense cells in the body with their ability to produce an almost infinite variety of antibodies to counter an almost infinite variety of possible antigens had to wait until late in the twentieth century for a solution. Thus would the processes of multiple genes, somatic mutation, and somatic recombination within defense cells and specialized memory cells—concepts beyond even Paul Ehrlich's fertile imagination—be incorporated into his model.

Of all the dyes Paul Ehrlich discussed in his 1878 M.D. dissertation, the one he appreciated most was Bismarck brown, whose high tinctural strength made it particularly suitable for histological staining. That the German dye manufacturers should have honored Count Otto von Bismarck in such a way is understandable, for it was under his chancellorship of Prussia and then of a united Germany that the most rapid scientific and industrial developments took place. A staunch opponent of the revolution of 1848, Bismarck was fifteen years later appointed chancellor of Prussia by King Wilhelm I in order to break the constitutional impasse caused by the refusal of the Prussian parliament—weak and less-than-democratic though it was—to approve the crown's army budget. Bismarck was a member of the Junker class, the holders of large Prussian estates. Aristocratic, though culturally rather rustic, the Junkers supplied the army's officers and as such also constituted a military caste. In the first seven years of his chancellorship Bismarck brought about the unification of Germany, in his famous words, by "blood and iron." In 1864 Bismarck's armies drove the Danes out of the provinces of Holstein and Schleswig, whose mixed German and Danish population had hitherto lived under the Danish crown. This was followed in 1870 by his provoking of the Franco-Prussian War. Bismarck's victory resulted not only in the takeover of Alsace and parts of Lorraine from France, but also the uniting, the following year, of the Prussian-dominated North German Confederation with the southern German states, which had contributed their troops to the fight in fulfillment of their treaty obligations.

Bismarck's chancellorship of the new, centralized Reich was not without apparent contradictions. The Prussian and later the unified German government was renowned for the priority it gave to funding its scientific establishment, particularly under the education minister Friedrich Althoff. (By contrast, the Institut Pasteur in Paris had to be funded by public subscription and the sale of antitoxin.) This in turn enhanced the pride of the German scientists in their preeminence in medicine and other fields and their enthusiasm for the unified state. Yet the funds were more the product of a late but extraordinarily rapid industrialization than of unification per se. (When earlier in the century Prussia acquired the sleepy Ruhr far removed to the west, no one could have predicted that its coal reserves would form the basis of an explosion of heavy industry.) Although Bismarck presided over this process, there is an almost sad story of the aging Iron Chancellor on a visit to Hamburg in 1895, viewing the massive steamships and huge cranes and feeling rather bewildered. For Otto von Bismarck was ever conscious of his agrarian roots as a Prussian Junker. Considerations of regional and traditional class divisions competed with feelings of national or ethnic solidarity. The partial restructuring of German society due to the wealth generated by the onslaught of industrial capitalism not only perplexed the artisans and small shopkeepers but was viewed with some disdain by the warrior-agrarian Junker class, for whom blood, honor, and virtue—not money—determined rank. Much of Bismarck's policy was aimed at increasing the power of Junker Prussia over the rest of Germany, without becoming submerged in it. Although Hitler named an ill-fated battleship after him, Bismarck was in fact far from the dedicated Pan-Germanist the Nazis later cracked him up to be. In 1866 he had initiated a war against Austria to determine that Prussia and not Austria would lead Germany. Bismarck's swift victory ensured that Hitler would be born an Austrian rather than a German, and that until the Nazi reign of terror a half century later, Austria would be excluded from the Reich and its affairs.

A factor in Bismarck's animosity toward Austria was its almost exclusively Catholic population. He and his Junkers were, after all, Lutherans, striving to maintain domination over the nationalist aspirations of the Polish Catholic peasant majorities in East Prussia. While Bismarck somewhat reluctantly accepted into the Reich the large Catholic population of Bavaria ("The Bavarians," he is quoted as saying, "are the missing link between the Austrians and the human race"), he knew that the incorporation of the Austrian lands would reduce the Protestants to a minority. For much of the 1870s, the Iron Chancellor was engaged in the *Kulturkampf*—literally, the struggle of civilizations—against the Catholics, which began with the abrogation of certain traditional rights of the church, particularly in matters of marriage and education. Later, however, Bismarck saw the political advantage of reconciliation with the large Catholic Center Party, which in nonreligious affairs had few hard and fast principles.

What, then, was Bismarck's attitude toward the Jews during his rule? It was sometimes wavering but never hostile. In the deliberations on Jewish equality a year before the ill-fated 1848 revolution, he had told the Prussian United Assembly: "I am no enemy of the Jews: indeed I love them under certain conditions. I would also like them to have every conceivable right." But then he hastened to add: "except [the right] to an administrative post in a Christian nation." Yet it was during Bismarck's chancellorship of the North German Confederation that, in 1869, the Jews were granted full legal equality. This was on the eve of the Franco-Prussian War. Prussian Jewish soldiers, now the *de jure* equals of their Christian comrades, fought as Germans, just as their coreligionists on the opposite side, having enjoyed civic equality since the French Revolution, fought as Frenchmen. Among the Prussian-Jewish soldiers were army physicians, including Paul Ehrlich's cousin Karl Weigert. In a shell-pocked house at the Metz battlefield a contingent of Prussia's 2,500 Jewish soldiers celebrated Yom Kippur while their Christian comrades stood guard. More than 80 of them would receive the Iron Cross, and Prussian Jewish women were decorated for their nursing of the wounded.

With the uniting of North and South Germany as a consequence of the war, religious equality became the law of the whole Second Reich. As Reich chancellor, Bismarck relied heavily on the advice of the ennobled Jewish banker Gerson von Bleichröder, one of his few close friends; and suffering as he did from migraine, gout, insomnia, hemorrhoids, neuralgia, gallstone, varicose veins, constipation, and other afflictions often associated with overeating, excessive drinking, and an enervating life at the pinnacle of European power, Bismarck, of course, sought relief from a Jewish physician, Dr. Cohn. ("Physicians still retain something of their priestly origin: they would gladly do what they forbid," was Bismarck's comment on the medical profession in general.) The Iron Chancellor spoke positively of the results of union between the "gentile stallion with the Jewish mare," although for tactical reasons he was not above accepting support from anti-Semitic factions in his political battles against the leftists. His left-wing political opponents, of course, numbered more than their fair share of Jews. For although the Jews as a group had achieved a very prosperous status in Wilhelmine, Germany, they were most conspicuously active in the leadership of the Social Democratic Party. Still, there was no shortage of conservative, nationalistic, even chauvinistic Jews. And even of those on the left,

Bismarck was careful to remark: "In their opposition to me, the Jews have never been as base as my Christian adversaries."

One Christian opponent who was a particularly troublesome thorn in Bismarck's side deserves special mention in our story. In 1848, on the eve of the ill-fated revolution, a 27-year-old Pomeranian German, Dr. Rudolf Virchow, served as medical officer to the Prussian government commission sent to Upper Silesia to investigate a typhus epidemic and concurrent famine in that region. Virchow not only presented his report to the government but also published it in his journal *Medicinische Reform* for everyone to read. The document included a scathing indictment of the Prussian authorities for misgoverning the ethnically largely Polish province. It also contained a plea for local self-rule and the providing of proper education, roads, agricultural improvements, and stimulation of industry, the withholding of which had contributed so much to the present public health disaster. Not surprisingly, Virchow found himself at the barricades in Berlin when the revolution broke out.

The failure of the revolt encouraged Rudolf Virchow, as it did Ferdinand Cohn, to withdraw from politics and immerse himself in medical science. The next ten years of meticulous research were crowned by the publication, in 1858, of his *Cellular Pathology,* one of the most important books in the history of medicine, marking as it did the definitive shift of medical science from the visible to the microscopic level. Yet Virchow himself never fully accepted the germ theory of contagious disease, preferring instead to emphasize public health measures, preventative medicine, and the influence of supposed miasmas under conditions of poverty. Inevitably, in view of his concern with public health, Virchow was eventually drawn back into politics. In autocratic Prussia, and later in a united autocratic Germany, the decks were stacked against the popularly elected parliament and in favor of the monarch and his chancellor. It has in fact been suggested that one of the reasons for Germany's formidable achievements in science and industry was that talented people, who might otherwise have gone into politics despaired of the system of government and channeled their energies elsewhere. But such was the drive and talent of Rudolf Virchow that for more than three decades he served as representative of the German Progressive Party in the Prussian House of Deputies and then in the all-German Reichstag, all the while continuing his great contributions to medical science. It was in 1865 that Virchow, as chairman of the finance committee, disputed Bismarck's honesty and managed to block an appropriation for naval expansion. This was too much for the Iron Chancellor, who challenged Virchow to a duel, a not very courageous act for a Prussian of the military caste, skilled in the art of pistols and swords. The frail little professor was able to ridicule Bismarck by accepting the challenge under the condition that he be allowed the choice of weapons: scalpels and syringes. Yet despite their obviously antagonistic views and the anti-socialist legislation the Iron Chancellor pushed through the Reichstag, it was Bismarck who, in yet another apparent contradiction, "stole the Socialists' thunder" (his words) by also introducing legislation for comprehensive social security. This was the world's first such system and, of course, had consequences for the development of the medical profession. "Laws are like medicine," Bismarck declared. "They generally cure an evil by a lesser or a passing evil."

Rudolf Virchow's antimilitarism did not prevent him from heading the first hospital train to go to the front in the Franco-Prussian War of 1870. This campaign had ramifications that brought political and nationalistic conflicts into the realm of medical science, which eventually drew Virchow in. After the siege of Paris by Prussian troops, the great Louis Pasteur, who two years earlier had received an honorary M.D. degree from the University of Bonn, returned the diploma with a note declaring: "Now the sight of that parchment is odious to me, and I feel offended at seeing my name . . . placed under a name which is henceforth an object of execration to my country, that of Rex Gulielmus [King Wilhelm]." The president of the Bonn medical faculty in turn replied with an "expression of utter contempt" for this "insult which you have dared to offer to the German nation in the sacred person of its august Emperor." Soon Pasteur patriotically turned his microscope to the subvisible organisms in beer, hoping to make the French product superior to that of the Germans and thereby also help pay off the huge indemnity the Prussian victors had placed on his country. But it was an instance of French-German bitterness resulting from the 1870 war involving Virchow rather than Pasteur that is more directly relevant for the Jewish history of medicine. After the shelling of the Natural History Museum in Paris and the burning of the library at Strassburg, French journalists, understandably incensed by these demonstrations of *Schadefreude*, took up the claim of the anthropologist Armand de Quatrefages that the Prussians— the driving force behind German unification—were of barbarian Finno-

Mongol descent. Rudolf Virchow happened to be, aside from a great medical man *and* a prominent politician, *also* one of the world's leading anthropologists, who had dug up ancient skulls all over North Central Europe. He decided to investigate the French claim scientifically.

Virchow initiated a ten-year study measuring the physical characteristics of some seven million German school children. This showed that inhabitants of the Prussian regions were on average blonder than those of other parts of Germany, thus largely disproving the accusation of the Prussians were of Mongol descent. (For the enduring epithet "Hun," the Germans can thank their own Kaiser, who at the turn of the twentieth century told his troops as they marched off to crush the Boxer Rebellion in China to "comport yourselves like the Huns of Attila.") But at the same time, Virchow's study also put to rest—or should have—the concept of Teutonic racial purity among the newly united Germans. Fewer than one third of the gentile children displayed the supposed pure Teutonic racial strain. More than one in five of the others were decidedly of the "nonGermanic" type. (This was the national average; in Bavaria, which would later be a hotbed of Nazism, the pure brunette children in fact far outnumbered the pure blonds.) The remaining gentile children, the majority, scored intermediately as mongrelized, and even the blond children tended to see their hair darken with age. In any event, Virchow considered the matter of supposed racial descent irrelevant. To de Quatrefages' claim that German unification was "an anthropological error," Virchow replied, "Ought we, as we construct our state, ask everyone what their ancestry and racial origins are? No, Monsieur de Quatrefages, we will not undertake such policies."

Virchow was a patriotic German, particularly in his pride in German science. His attitude toward the pseudoscientific Teutonic racial myths were quite another matter, and their disproval was not unwelcome to him. All the more since, like many Germans from Pomerania, most of which region lies in present-day Poland, he had a Slavic family name and was also Slavic in appearance. Virchow even referred to himself as a Slav-German, feeling that this made him no less patriotic toward Germany than a fourth-generation German-American might be toward America. In fact, Virchow's 80th birthday, just after the turn of the century, would be celebrated as a national holiday throughout Germany—an indication of his status as one of the greatest living Germans and of the great esteem in which his research was held.

As far as is known, Virchow, who was baptized and raised as a Christian (and soon became agnostic), had no Jewish ancestors. But as one of the greatest medical men in his own right, he was all the more aware of the enormous Jewish contributions to medicine past and present. So he derived a certain satisfaction when analyzing the separate record he kept of the Jewish school children in his survey. This revealed that more than one in ten was of pure Teutonic appearance, while the majority of the rest variously fell into the mixed-features category. All in all, the Jewish German figures showed a vast degree of overlap with those of the gentile Germans. (This brings to mind the story of the pilgrimage of the renowned German-Jewish philosopher Ernst Cassirer to the house of the great poet Goethe in Weimar. When he noticed a guard staring at him, he inquired why and was told that that Cassirer's handsome, tall, blond appearance seemed like Goethe reincarnated.)

In Virchow's era of obsessive skull measuring—of the excavated remains of prehistoric peoples as well as of their presumed present-day descendants—the question, of course, was posed of how such Teutonic traits arose in such a substantial percentage of Jews. Environmental factors such as occupational and dietary habits were sometimes accepted as influencing the Jewish constitution and physique, predisposing Jewish groups to some diseases while making them more resistant to others. But in the new age of Darwinian genetics it was generally agreed that these factors as well as climatic conditions were unlikely, even within the space of a 100 generations, to have substantially affected the Ashkenazi gene pool when it came to skull shape, hair, and eye color.

Of the studies and theories on the genealogy of the European Jews published late in the nineteenth century, the most important were those of the Russian Jew Samuel Weissenberg. Like most racial anthropologists, Weissenberg was a medical doctor, having qualified at the University of Heidelberg in Germany in 1890. Although his doctoral dissertation was on the little understood phenomenon of dyslexia and as such was a pioneering work in the field, he soon turned to the ancestry of the Jews. With a stipend from the Rudolf Virchow Foundation, he took his skull-measuring devices to the Middle East and adjoining regions and came to the conclusion that the vast majority of European Jews—certainly, the Ashkanazim—owed most of their ancestry to peoples of the Caucasus who had been Judaized by northward migrating Hebrews before the destruction of the

First Temple in 586 B.C.E. A devoutly orthodox man, Weissenberg saw the greatness of Judaism not in the racial, but in the intellectual and cultural traits of its people and in a religion that promoted both reason and good health. Interestingly, Weissenberg was outdone in his theory of ancient admixture by the German gentile anthropologist Felix von Luschan, who speculated that even the biblical Hebrews themselves, although they spoke a Semitic language, were largely descendant from the "Aryan" Hittites, the people who had introduced the Indo-European chariot to the Middle East.

Whatever the ancient origin of the Jews, recent studies have shown that the longer a Jewish community has resided in a particular country, the more they have come to physically resemble their gentile neighbors, apparently due to a slow but sure influx of gentile genes through conversions, inter-marriage, concubinage, or illicit relations, plus the influence of a common geographic environment and similar food sources. Even in the days of the Roman Empire, large numbers of pagans converted to Judaism, especially after the destruction of the Second Temple, as attested to by Josephus and other Latin writers. And communities of these Roman Jews existed on that most German of rivers, the Rhine, before there were any Germans there. But such indications of Jewish hybridization—whether suggested by Jews or gentiles—have not necessarily been welcomed by all Jews, and least of all by the German-Jewish physician Eias Auerbach, a contemporary of Weissenberg and pioneer of the Zionist movement, who pointed with pride to the supposed racial integrity of the Jews from Biblical times through the present.

Of course, by any reasonable standard, all such anthropological studies of the ancestry of the Jews should have been of purely academic interest, on a par with, say, the philological study of the evolution and distribution of intervocalic consonant sounds among the speakers of various North and South German dialects. But in late nineteenth-century Germany, just at the time when religious restrictions were removed from the law, a shift was taking place among opponents of the Jews, from religious anti-Juda-ism to the ultimately more deadly concept of racial anti-Semitism. Eupho-ria over the victory over France and the building of a unified German state combined with envy of the meteoric rise of people of Jewish descent in business, finance, journalism, the arts, and of course, the sciences, to pro-duce in some circles, especially among students, the opinion that, try as he might, a Jew could never be a German. As one medical folklorist wrote: "Even when he (the Jew) adopts the language, dress, habits, and customs of the people among whom he lives, he still remains everywhere the same. All he adopts is but the cloak, under which the eternal Hebrew survives; he is the same in his facial features, in the structure of his body, his temperament, his character." Worse still: whereas previous generations of Jew-baiters had merely despised the Jews, the new anti-Semites also feared them and suspected a mortal conspiracy among all those of Jewish blood.

Medicine, the traditional source of Jewish eminence, was, of course, part of this conspiracy. In his 1890 diatribe "The Desperate Struggle of the Aryan Peoples with Jewry," the anti-Semite Hermann Ahlwardt—who saw the malfeasance and conniving of the Jews behind the stock market scandals—turned his venom on the Jewish doctor. Of all areas of endeavor, "medicine is the one most penetrated by Jewry. Already Jewish physicians everywhere dominate the field," he lamented. This preeminence was due not to merit but to the Jewish *Schwindelgeist* (cheating spirit) and a conspiracy involving the Judaized press. "What kinds of physicians are they who publicize themselves day in and day out in the newspapers?" Ahlwardt asked rhetorically. "Jews, without exception. The fame of Jewish doctors who happened once to be consulted for the treatment of whatever notable person resounds again and again in all the Jewish (-controlled) newspapers, and probably nets the latter a nice chunk of money."

These currents of hatred were painfully evident to Rudolf Virchow, who, in his capacity as rector of the University of Berlin, proclaimed: "Our time, so sure of itself and of victory by reason of its scientific consciousness, is as apt as former ages to underestimate the strength of the mythic impulses with which the soul of the nation is infected by single adventurers. Even now, it is standing baffled before the enigma of anti-Semitism, whose appearance in this time of the equality of right is inexplicable to everybody, yet which in spite of its mysteriousness, or perhaps because of it, fascinates even our cultured youth." Exquisitely aware of the contributions to the field by his Jewish confrères, Virchow, in an address to the International Medical Congress held in Rome, praised the "zeal and learning of Jewish physicians of early Medieval times (who) were active in the preservation and advancement of medicine," and "the hereditary talent of the Jews, which has contributed so much that is great to science down to the present times."

Yet even Rudolf Virchow couldn't have known that what was perhaps the greatest single Jewish contribution to medicine was at the moment still in the making. For as the new century dawned, a blond-haired gray-eyed German Jew named Paul Ehrlich, encouraged by his blond-haired, blue-eyed German-Jewish wife, Hedwig, was losing interest in the natural process of immunization he had so brilliantly pioneered and elucidated and was dreaming of magic bullets—man-made chemical compounds to be shot directly into the patient's bloodstream, there to target and destroy the microscopic scourges of mankind against which the natural defenses of the body, even when stimulated by vaccination and the like, are woefully inadequate.

We shall rejoin Paul Ehrlich later. But the story of the great Jewish breakthrough in the emerging science of immunology is still far from complete. For when Paul Ehrlich journeyed to Stockholm to receive the Nobel prize for medicine, he shared it with an eccentric Russian half-Jew, who identified strongly with his Jewish heritage and came up with a different theory of immunity—one even more fantastic than Paul Ehrlich's and just as uncannily on the mark.

Chapter 11
A Russian's Amoebae
to the Defense

I remained alone with my microscope, observing the life in the [amoeboid] mobile cells of a transparent star-fish larva, when a new thought suddenly flashed across my brain. It struck me that similar cells might serve in the defense of the organism against intruders.

—Eli Metchnikoff

In the tenth century, some startling news reached the Jewish court physician Hasdai ibn Shaprut in Spain concerning a far-off Kingdom of Khazaria, bordered roughly by the Volga River and the Black and Caspian Seas. The Khazar king, Joseph, and his people were reported to have blue eyes, red hair, and white complexions; speak a Turkic language; and practice the Jewish religion. According to tradition, Doctor Hisdai sent Joseph a missive, asking for more information: "Is there a Jewish kingdom anywhere on earth? In what way did the conversion of the Khazars come about? Where does the king live and to what tribe does he belong? What is the method of procession to his place of worship? Does war abrogate the Sabbath?" King Joseph is said to have replied with the story about one of his predecessors, King Bulan, in the eighth century, when the Khazars still held shamanist beliefs and were being pressed upon by Christian missionaries from the west and proselytizing Moslems to the south, and also contained communities of Jewish refugees. Bulan, so the story goes, set up a debate between representatives of the three monotheistic religions and was won over to Judaism. Under King Obadiah, Joseph further related, synagogues were built and schools were organized in which the foundations of rabbinical Judaism—including the Torah and Talmud—were taught.

For a few centuries after the presumed exchange of letters between Doctor Hisdai and King Joseph, the Khazar kingdom survived somewhat precariously despite Russian raids from the north. During this time, it is speculated, some Khazar migrants formed Jewish communities in Eastern Europe. The devastation wrought by the Mongol invasions of the thirteenth century brought an end to the Khazar state and drove the survivors westward through Russia into Poland, where the red-bearded inheritors of their genes would be found inhabiting the *städtls* and ghettos for hundreds of years to come. But, even assuming the validity of this story, the Khazars were by far not the only Jews drawn to Slavic lands, for masses of their coreligionists were fleeing eastward from Germany.

As we have seen, the genocidal massacres in the Rhineland in the fourteenth century were a direct result of the social upheaval wrought by the Black Death. In Poland, however, only about a quarter of the population succumbed to the pestilence, a figure far lower than in Germany and France. This was perhaps because the disease in its travels to the Hansiatic Baltic ports had assumed a somewhat attenuated form; less virulent strains tend to spread more easily, and thus beat out the more virulent ones. Furthermore, the geographic distribution of people and rats in Poland was less conducive to the plague's transmission. Hysteria in the east was therefore less than in the west, and King Casimir III (known as "the Great" or "the Charlemagne of Poland"), was in a better position to offer the Jews sanctuary. In return, the Jews contributed their commercial and intellectual skills to help bring Poland out of its feudal past. Thanks to Jewish management, a market-oriented agriculture arose in the Vistula and Nieman valleys.

But no such welcome was extended to the Jews farther to the east, in Russia. The traditional suspiciousness of the Russian rulers made them inhospitable to foreigners in general, and the Jews, of course, had the disadvantage of not even being Christians. Among the various brutalities committed by Ivan the Terrible in the sixteenth century was his order that the Jews of the newly annexed town of Pskov either convert or be drowned in the river. His successors repeatedly issued decrees banning Jews from their realms. This suggests that Jewish merchants, either legally (with special authorization) or otherwise, regularly penetrated Russia by plying their trade. Issuing yet another order expelling the few Jews living in Russia, the eighteenth-century Czarina Elizabeth Petrovna replied to Russian critics of the economic consequences of her actions with the words: "I do not want any benefit from the enemies of Christ." Catherine II ("the Great") considered reversing her predecessor's edict but backed down in the face of hostility from her subjects.

Of course, the bigoted Elizabeth herself had a Jewish court doctor, at least for a while. He was Antonio Ribeiro Sanchez, a Portuguese exile, who studied medicine in Leiden under Herman Boerhaave. At Boerhaave's recommendation, Elizabeth's predecessor, the Empress Ivanova, had brought Sanchez to the royal court in St. Petersburg in 1731. There he quickly rose to chief physician of the cadets, collected a large body of medical literature (later to form an important part of the Imperial Library), and was elected a member of the Imperial Academy of Science. Although Elizabeth, upon ascending to the throne, replaced much of the old guard, she retained Sanchez, whose medical skills she praised, and even appointed him councilor of state. In 1757, however, Sanchez was ordered to resign and leave St. Petersburg, perhaps due to his religious practices. The doctor moved to Paris, where he treated the poor and advocated the use of Russian vapor baths. With Sanchez's finances in decline, Elizabeth's successor, Catherine the Great, who credited him with having saved her from a dangerous illness as a child, granted the doctor a lifetime pension of 1,000 rubles a year.

In view of the fact that legal restrictions on the settlement of Jews in Russia were reiterated under every monarch, it is not a little surprising that in the nineteenth century about half the world's Jewish population was living under czarist rule. This historical irony was the result of the long and slow expansion of the Grand Duchy of Moscow, from the fourteenth century onward, to encompass such diverse ethnic peoples as the Ukrainians, Georgians, Tartars, and Balts. As a consequence of the treaty of Vienna in the wake of the Napoleonic Wars, the czars found themselves ruling over most of the Poles as well.

The plight of the Jews within the shifting borders of Eastern Europe is highlighted by the life story of the ophthalmologist Lazar Ludwik Zamenhof, better known as "Dr. Esperanto" after the artificial language he created in the decades spanning the turn of the twentieth century. Born in 1859 in the town of Bialystok, now in Poland but then in the Lithuanian part of the Russian Empire, Zamenhof later wrote (here translated from Esperanto): "The population consisted of four diverse elements: Russians, Poles, Germans, and Jews; each spoke a different language and was hostile to the other elements." But the Jews were the particular target of hostility. "Had I not been a Jew from the ghetto," Zamenhof wrote, "the idea of uniting humanity would either never have come into my head or, if it did, would never have become a lifetime preoccupation. No one can feel the misery of barriers among people as strongly as a ghetto Jew." Indeed, even Jews who, on the model of their enlightened German brethren, wished to consider Judaism as a religion and not a nationality would have a hard time deciding into which nationality to assimilate in such a multi-ethnic environment. "My Jewishness," Zamenhof emphasized, "has been the main reason why, from earliest childhood, I have given my all for a single great idea, a single dream—the dream of the unity of humankind."

Zamenhof's experiences as a university student and doctor only reinforced the feelings he had acquired in childhood. After first studying medicine in Moscow, he completed his degree in Warsaw, where he set up practice and was all the more conscious of the anti-Semitism of the majority Polish population. Unlike the situation in Bialystok, Poles were overwhelmingly the largest ethnic group in the Polish part of the Russian Empire. But as a Catholic Slavic people lorded over by Russian Orthodox Slavs to the East and Lutheran Prussians to the West, the nationalism of the Poles became as much identified with their religion as with their language and culture. And here in their own midst were Yiddish-speakers, adhering to an alien faith toward which the Polish priests had long expressed a strong intolerance—an intolerance that the czarist rulers in turn were glad to encourage if this would deflect the discontent of the Poles from their Russian overlords.

The second half of the nineteenth century was a time of increasing urbanization among the Eastern European Jews. Previously, the Jews had long occupied a niche not in the cities but as cogs in the farm economy: as intermediaries between the land-owning gentry and the peasants, brewers and distillers of alcoholic beverages, innkeepers, small artisans, and, of course, merchants, traders, and sometime money-lenders. Now, with the advent, however belatedly, of a capitalist economy and the Jewish migration to the cities, there also came increasing secularization among the Jews of Russian Poland as the enlightenment ideas from the neighboring German Reich spread to the larger towns. Warsaw in particular was a whirlpool of diverse and often opposing currents. Assimilationists pointed with pride to the role of Jewish-Polish patriots in the ill-fated uprising against the czars in 1863 and advocated, along the German model, the concept of loyal Poles of the Jewish faith (or, for the more secular, of Jewish heritage), with Polish as their common language. For some well-to-do Jews, this eventually led all the way to the baptismal font, opening the path to titles of nobility. Other Jews pointed to the unique cultural and linguistic, as well as religious, traditions of the Jews and sought a national Jewish renaissance on Polish soil, with Yiddish elevated from its previous status as a jargon to a literary language. The Bundists—Jewish socialists—were likewise advocates of *Yiddishkeit* but saw the future in collaboration with other socialist parties for the building of a democratic socialist Poland. Jews further to the left were lured by the internationalism of Marxism, with its secular messianic goals. Meanwhile, the Zionists, despairing of the pervasive anti-Semitism of the nationalistic Poles and the economic resentment of much of the Polish middle class, advocated a return to the Holy Land and a revival of the ancient Hebrew language.

As elsewhere, the Jews in Poland were traditionally associated with medicine, all the more so due to the general illiteracy of the rest of the Polish population compared to the book-loving Jews, and the eschewing of scholarly activities even by the Polish gentry. From the fifteenth century onward, Polish royalty had their Jewish court physicians. These included the Marranos Jacob Isaac, Solomon Calahora, Daniel Luna, and Astruc, who served Kings Sygmunt I, Sygmunt August, and Jan III, and Prince Stanislas, respectively. The gentry, often sympathetic to "their" Jews, would sometimes subsidize the medical education of a promising Jewish student, as in the case of Tobias Cohn in the late seventeenth century and Robert Remak early in the nineteenth. Failing such opportunities, a large number of Jews in Poland traditionally found themselves in the ranks of the barber-surgeons.

In the atmosphere of late nineteenth-century Russian Poland, the Jewish doctor in particular was caught up in conflicting currents in the urban centers. Indeed, the main characters of two important contemporary novels by gentile Polish authors, *Lalka* (The Doll) by Bolesaw Prus and *Ludzie bezdomni* (The Homeless) by Stefan Zermonski, are Jewish physicians who, leaving their Jewish past basically behind them, react to their experiences in entering the Polish milieu with varying measures of idealism, cynicism, rationalization, and bitterness.

Such were the conflicting multilingual and multicultural environments in which Dr. Lazar Zamenhof was seized with the idea of solving not only Eastern Europe's problem, but all humanity's, by creating an artificial language linked to an almost millennial worldview. As a young student in the 1870s Zamenhof had drafted his first effort at Esperanto. His notes were, however, destroyed by his father, who feared that their discovery by the czarist secret police would fuel accusations of conspiracies in a secret code. Now, Dr. Zamenhof's ophthalmology practice, although not lucrative (he moved several times before establishing himself in a working-class district of Warsaw), gave him some financial resources to propagandize for his new language.

Esperanto was by no means the first artificial international language. But it had certain advantages over the others, in its particularly user-friendly structure and in its vocabulary drawn mostly (though by no means exclusively) from Latin and Romance roots familiar to educated speakers of even Germanic and Slavic languages. But most important to the relative success of Esperanto was its association with a non-linguistic ideal with a distinctly Jewish-messianic flavor. As Zamenhof wrote in his pamphlets with reference to Rabbi Hillel (Jesus' contemporary and possible inspiration, best known for his summary of the scriptures: "What is hateful to you, do not do to your neighbor. This is the entire Torah. All the rest is commentary"): "This plan (which I call 'Hillelism') involves the creation of a moral bridge by which to unify in brotherhood all peoples and religions, without creating any newly formulated dogmas and without the need for any people to throw out their traditional religion." Zamenhof, who himself was active in the Zionist movement when he developed Esperanto, further declared: "Hillelism is a doctrine that, without separating a person from his native country, or language, or religion, gives him the possibility of avoiding all untruths and antagonisms in the principles of his national religion and of communicating with people of all languages and religions on a basis that is neutrally human, on principles of common brotherhood, equality and justice." (Hitler would, of course, explicitly point to Esperanto as another instrument of Jewish world domination.) Thus was Zamelhof's plan for harmony among the various peoples and religions of the world, and in the lands under the domain of the Russian czar in particular.

It was as a consequence of the czar's gaining control of most of Poland when that country was partitioned in the wake of the Napoleonic Wars that the Jewish grandfather of one of the greatest figures in the history of medicine, Eli Metchnikoff, came to be a Russian subject. A highly cultivated man, Leo Nevahovitch, while serving as farmer-general for tobacco in Poland, also contributed literary newspaper articles defending his fellow Jews against persecution. When at the beginning of the Polish Revolution of 1830, Leo received word that his house was to be sacked, he moved his family from Warsaw to St. Petersburg. In the Imperial capital, Nevahovitch dedicated the rest of his life to literary work, translating German philosophical books and becoming friends with Pushkin. One of his sons became editor of a popular caricature newspaper—journalism in Russia, as elsewhere, being a profession strongly associated with the Jews. But St. Petersburg was beyond the pale of settlement (the areas where Jews could legally live), so Leo followed the advice of Czar Alexander I and let his family be baptized. His daughter Emilia Lvovna Nevahovna married an officer (later general) in the czar's Imperial Guard. These were the parents of Eli Metchnikoff.

It was in the land of Panassovka in the Kharkov Province of Russia—a boundless and fertile, if not particularly scenic, country of steppes and hillocks covered with low grasses and wild wormwood—that Eli was born in 1845. The name on his birth certificate was Ilia, the Russian form of Elijah, but he is better known by the Westernized version. Eli and his four older siblings grew up at their father's ancestral estate. Mother Emilia saw to the development of the children, their father being rather aloof and often away. So it was that a certain intellectual tradition was transmitted to the young boy. "I ascribe my love for science to my descent from the Jewish race," Eli Metchnikoff would unequivocally declare after becoming one of the world's most celebrated scientists.

Yet the gentile branch of Eli Metchnikoff's family tree was not without at least one luminary—the seventeenth-century Moldavian Nicholas Milescu, known as Spartar (Romanian for "sword-bearer"). Already as a young man, Spartar was admired for his great erudition, acquired in his studies of theology, history, philosophy, and languages in Constantinople, and natural sciences and mathematics in Italy. His talents got him the posts of interpreter at the court of Czar Alexis Michailovitch and first tutor to his son, the future Peter the Great. Spartar became involved in various intrigues, both foreign and domestic, and gained further fame for his diplomatic missions to China. While conducting negotiations, he acquired linguistic and geographic knowledge of the East, which he set down on paper. This was but one work in a vast literary output, which included articles on theology, arithmetic, art, archaeology and history, the compilation of a Greco-Latin-Russian dictionary, and the translation of the New Testament from Greek into Romanian. It was by the literal translation of "sword-bearer" into Russian that the family name Metchnikoff was derived.

Young Eli Metchnikoff was naturally influenced not only by his family traditions but also by the broader intellectual climate in Russia in the second half of the nineteenth century. The hard regime of Czar Nicholas I had given way to the liberalism of Alexander II, who peaceably freed the serfs in 1861, the same year the United States got itself into a civil war over a similar issue. Physical and natural science were in the ascendancy. Like Ferdinand Cohn in Silesia, young Eli was drawn to the flora of his native region—collecting flowers and even using his pocket money to bribe his siblings to listen to his botanical discourses. While a pupil at the Kharkov Lycée and still in his early teens, Eli attended lectures at the university and authored a visionary article on infusoria (a class of protozoa microorganisms with hair-like appendages for movement), which was accepted by the *Bulletin of the Moscow Society of Naturalists,* only to be withdrawn by Eli himself when he began having doubts about his conclusions. As a consequence, it wasn't until the following year, when he had already reached the world-wise age of 16, that Eli's first publication appeared, a review of a geology textbook for the *Journal de Moscou.*

Most important of the classes Eli attended at Kharkov University while still a Lycée pupil were those on physiology and anatomy. As his future wife and biographer, Olga would write many decades later: "Fired with a passionate desire to produce something personal in medical science, and attracted by Virchow's cellular theory, he dreamt that he might create a general theory of his own in medicine." But when Eli had to choose the course of study that would determine his career, his mother warned him: "You are too sensitive. You could not bear the constant sight of human suffering." It's a rare Jewish mother, indeed, who discourages her son from becoming a doctor, but Emilia Nevahovna Metchnikoff was probably right in her assessment. So upon graduation from the Lycée, Eli went to Kharkov University's Natural Science Faculty, where he would be spared the sight of blood.

The rationalist roots on both sides of Eli Metchnikoff's genealogical tree—particularly his mother's family, whose conversion of convenience seems to have reflected an agnosticism toward all religion—were nurtured by skeptical currents among the Russian intelligentsia and from the West. In Eli Metchnikoff these factors produced a mind whose worshiping of science went with such an outspoken rejection of religion that his fellow students nicknamed him "God-is-not." The passing years would only deepen Metchnikoff's commitment to rationalism and science, which he viewed as an almost messianic deliverer for suffering humanity. His thinking was encouraged by his contact with a fellow student named Bogomoloff, whose father was a dye-manufacturer and whose brothers were chemistry students at Kharkov University who would bring back from their travels abroad materialistic books banned by the Russian censors.

The Bogomoloffs were apparently Jewish, and Metchnikoff identified and sympathized with the Jews—whether religious or freethinking—especially when they were subjected to bigotry. But Metchnikoff himself, having been baptized, was generally immune from such intolerance. However prejudiced in religious or cultural matters, the Russians were rather tolerant when it came to race, viewing themselves as admixtures of pre-Indo-European ("Ural-Altic") Finns, Aryan Slavs, Mongol invaders, and other strains. Nevertheless, ethnic bias may have disrupted Eli's academic plans. Wishing to study under the eminent German embryologist Rudolf von Koelliker at the University of Würzburg, he arrived a few weeks early and sought out the company of his fellow Russian students. Metchnikoff was given the cold shoulder, which, it has been suggested, he took as a sign (real or imagined) of anti-Semitism. This was enough to throw the always sensitive and melancholia-prone Metchnikoff into one of his many depressions. Eventually, Ferdinand Cohn, who a decade later would play a pivotal role in advancing the career of Robert Koch, came to Eli's aid by directing him to the University of Giessen to begin his doctoral research. Subsequent wanderings to various institutes in Germany and Italy, eventually brought him back to Mother Russia to receive his doctorate from the University of St. Petersburg.

It was soon after his arrival in Germany that Eli acquired a copy of Darwin's *Origin of Species*. Under its profound influence, Metchnikoff became convinced that certain disharmonies in human life are the consequences of biological aspects unique to the evolution of *Homo sapiens*. "Man appeared," Eli wrote, "as the result of a one-sided, but not total, improvement of the organism." Such ideas would later be publicized in his books *Education from the Anthropological Point of View* and *The Time for Marriage*. Metchnikoff was particularly distressed by the appearance of certain biological instincts long before the lengthy process of maturation of the child's brain into its adult form has been completed. This disharmony, he reasoned, has been exacerbated by the advance of culture and civilization, which has steadily widened the gap between the onset of puberty and the entering into marriage.

In his books, Metchnikoff viewed proper education as a means of rectifying this situation. When he became enamored with a 13-year-old daughter of a professor, he saw his chance to put his pedagogical concepts into practice by spending a few prenuptial years training her to become his wife. Metchnikoff soon ended up marrying a somewhat older friend, Ludmilla Fedorovitch, instead. But tragedy was on the cards, for the bride was already consumptive and had to be carried into the church for the wedding ceremony.

Young Eli Metchnikoff had already known what it meant to have people near him carried away by the scourge of infectious disease. During a stay in Naples where he was studying marine biology, a cholera epidemic struck the port, and Eli's sensitive soul was witness to the processions of hooded penitents bearing torches through the streets to the sound of tolling church bells. The pestilence soon hit closer to home when a lady of Eli's circle suddenly failed to appear at the *trattoria* for dinner and was found dead the next day. Unhinged, Eli fled from Italy. But now the suffering of his new bride unraveled the sensitive Metchnikoff far more. When she died, he couldn't even bring himself to attend the funeral.

Some days later Eli was walking over a bridge on the Rhone in Geneva, about to make his second suicide attempt. (The first one, earlier in the day, had miscarried when he swallowed a dose of morphia so great that he quickly vomited it up with little ill effect.) Suddenly, his attention was diverted by a swarm of insects hovering around a street lantern and he found himself puzzled by a curious aspect of their existence that seemed to defy the principles of natural selection. Unwilling to depart this life with such riddles unsolved, Eli Metchnikoff gave up his suicide plans and redirected his intellect to the science of biology. In so doing, he would contribute greatly to the elimination of all infectious diseases, such as the one that had claimed the life of his young bride. Yet the road which led him there was a long and winding one.

Metchnikoff somehow became fascinated by the two distinct food absorption processes found in primitive organisms—intercellular and intracellular digestion—both of which date back almost to the very origin of multicellular life on earth. The German biologist Ernst Haeckel had speculated that in the beginning there were unicellular creatures that evolved into organisms comprised of multicellular colonies, whose structure more or less resembled a hollow rubber ball. All the cells of the organism had part of their coat along the exterior wall and were thus in direct contact with the external environment from which they received their nutrients. In the course of evolution, the size of this food-absorbing surface area was, Haeckel suggested, topologically optimized by its evolving into a vessel-like shape. This so-called invagination process resembled the making of a very deep dent in the hollow rubber ball by pushing in the top of the surface and stretching it downward. The overall dimensions of the ball were not increased, but the surface area, part of which was now folded over to form the inside of the vessel, was much greater. Thus was laid the basis for what would later evolve into an internal digestive tract.

But Metchnikoff speculated that even prior to the development of such vessel-like gastrulae in the course of evolution, some of the cells of the colonies that constituted the primitive organism had broken away from the inner surface of the rubber ball and begun migrating to the previously cell-free interior. These freelancers led an existence similar to that of their cousins, the wandering one-celled amoebae in ponds, except that the former fed not upon external nutrients but predominantly upon nutrients that entered their host's body from outside. Their descendants, comparatively little changed, are today found in abundance, even inside organisms with the most advanced digestive and blood circulation systems, such as man. It was this speculation—interesting, but without any apparent practical significance—that would eventually lead Eli Metchnikoff to one of the profoundest insights in the history of medicine.

In 1875 Metchnikoff married again, to Olga, the daughter of a landowner in Little Russia. Although a few years later she would have a near-fatal brush with typhus, Olga would outlive Eli and go on to write his biography. In the autumn of their lives, their age difference would be inconsequential; but at the time of their marriage he was 30 and she still in secondary school. (Under pressure from Olga's father, Eli was obliged to modify his ideal of training a future wife and then marrying her. He wed Olga first and then set about educating her.) From Olga's perhaps slightly biased account, we learn that Eli's appearance was "not unlike a figure of Christ; his pale face was illuminated by the light in his kindly eyes, which at times looked absolutely inspired." Yet Metchnikoff could tolerate no criticism of any of his strongly held scientific ideas and was apt to become overly combative. He was also so highly strung that a seemingly small distraction could send him into a rage; once in Naples he poured a bucket of water on serenaders under his balcony who were disturbing his concentration.

Wrapped up as he was in science, Metchnikoff was not naturally inclined to get emotional about politics. But in the turbulent 1880s he could hardly avoid the political developments in society at large and their ramifications for the University of Odessa, where he held the post of professor. When in 1881 the relatively liberal Czar Alexander II was assassinated by an anarchist, a wave of repression swept the land under his ultra-reactionary and Jew-baiting son, Alexander III. Having been baptized, Metchnikoff was not affected by religious bigotry. But there were other forms of intolerance to be feared under the autocratic régime. Although the University of Odessa was theoretically autonomous, in practice the Ministry in the capital, St. Petersburg, had a veto power, which it exercised to block the appointment to professorships of any but the most reactionary nominees, regardless of scientific merit. Metchnikoff did not look favorably upon the revolutionary and socialist doctrines that were gaining in popularity in academic circles. Seeing collectivism as stifling personal initiative and individuality, he coined for himself the political label "progressive evolutionist" and placed his hopes in the advancement of culture and science. His outspoken views at the meetings of the university council were in any case to little avail as long as any but reactionary resolutions would be quashed by the Ministry. His nerves frayed, Metchnikoff eventually tendered his resignation.

Fortunately, the landholdings of Eli's and Olga's families allowed him for the time being a degree of financial independence. It was during his wandering through Europe as an unemployed intellectual that Eli Metchnikoff found himself on the beach at Messina, on the northeast corner of Sicily. While musing about the intracellular digestive processes, he was suddenly inspired to go out into the garden, pluck a rose thorn, stick it into a starfish egg, and observe the effects under his microscope. Never before or since has such a simple and offhand experiment had such a radical influence on medical science. For this marked the beginning of the solution to a riddle as old as rational medicine, namely the origin and nature—good or bad—of pus.

The not unreasonable concept of illness as something within the body that must be expelled was already prevalent in prehistoric times, as it still is today among many primitive people. As we have seen in the first chapter, one widespread version of this concept was that the etiological agent was an evil spirit that needed to be exorcised. But even within the magico-religious framework, often something more tangible than a spirit was held responsible for the disease. Such a concept may have developed hand in hand with the perceived necessity to remove the arrowheads that had been physically introduced into the body in warfare. (Indeed, in Metchnikoff's day, a German surgeon remarked that "The public still thinks the bullet (after having lodged in the body) most dangerous; the soldier is happy when you put into his hand the bullet which you have cut out." He was commenting on the case of President Garfield, who apparently died not from an assassin's bullet, but from the doctors' attempts to remove it under unsterile conditions, despite the increasing acceptance of the germ theory.) Even today, among some primitive people the shaman, in treating what is obviously (to us) an infectious or endocrinal disease, may feel obliged to produce by slight of hand an arrowhead or other tangible pathogenic object that he has supposedly sucked out of the patient's body. For centuries until the dawn of modern medicine, physicians relied on cupping, vomitives, emetics, and, of course, bloodletting, in an attempt to physically remove the disease from the patient, although in fact more likely hastening his demise by causing dehydration or additional infection.

It was to this overall treat-by-removal concept that one of medicine's most enduring misconceptions—that of "laudable pus"—owed its long career. Already in the Smith papyrus from Egypt in the third millennium B.C.E. there is reference to the desirability of suppuration (pus formation) and the duty of the physician to encourage it. "It is good for a wound to rot a little," the hieroglyphs tell us. "Some wounds may close too early, while there is still rot inside. Therefore, put something on the wound that will get the rot out." Of course, when there already is suppuration, then the draining of pus from the wound is indeed desirable. But the implication in the papyrus is that suppuration itself is to be encouraged.

The ancient Greeks, for their part, saw pus in the framework of their theory of the four elements and four body humors. The blood that collected around the wound, as part of the process of inflammation and reddening, ripened or concocted and apparently stagnated there. The Greeks, too, considered the appearance of pus favorable—at least in its "laudable" white form, if not in its putrefying yellow variety—for this purged what they saw as an excess form of blood humor. Conceivably, some Greeks also reasoned that, since a dead or—to use our modern term—immunosuppressed body was incapable of producing pus around a wound, suppuration was a vital sign. So, once again the classical theories, being rational, contained kernels of truth among their useless chaff. The Greeks were at least correct in preferring the appearance of white pus to the putrid yellow kind and they were also right in theorizing that pus had something to do with the blood. But their almost always detrimental preference for the exuding of white pus to no pus at all was based on a fundamental misconception that retained its pernicious influence for 2,000 years.

In Vienna in the late 1830s—as the microscopic cell was coming to be recognized as the building block of all biological tissue—the Hungarian Jew David Gruby, the pioneer of the germ theory we met in Chapter 9, submitted his M.D. dissertation in which he extended the cellular principle to body fluids as well, particularly the blood. The existence of red blood corpuscles had already been known to van Leeuwenhoek in the seventeenth century. Now Gruby dramatically advanced the field of hematology by producing charts with counts of white blood cells—called by him *globuli*—under normal and pathological conditions. More important, he wrote of how some blood corpuscle parts *(moleculi minimi)* seemed to leave the dilated capillaries in a stream of fluid, subsequently to re-enter the bloodstream after having formed some sort of pathological secretions. Gruby's descriptions were as vague as they were groundbreaking. The true meaning of the processes he described remained obscure for decades.

In the 1870s, while Gruby's dissertation was gathering dust, the brilliant German-Jewish researcher Julius Cohnheim, experimenting on frogs, discovered the process by which white blood corpuscles—now called leukocytes (Greek for "white cells")—from inside the capillaries emigrate through the capillary wall to the site of a wound, there to collect into pus. Cohnheim's visual observations of this phenomenon, termed extravasation, disproved a then widely held hypothesis that pus was the product of cell-division of the local tissue at the wound site. But Cohnheim, like so many of his contemporaries in this new age of medicine, was appalled by the whole concept of laudable pus, which for centuries had exerted such a disastrous effect on medicine. In an overreaction against the discredited old concept, he considered the whole extravasation process to be ipso facto unlaudable, something that should be suppressed, if possible.

As fate would have it, Eli Metchnikoff—who was no doubt more interested in frogs than in medicine—happened to attend a reading of Cohnheim's "Lectures on General Pathology." A novel interpretation of the extravasation process began to germinate in his head. As he later wrote: "[I] was struck by his [Cohnheim's] description of the facts and his theory of inflammation. The former, especially his description of the diapedesis [oozing] of the white corpuscles through the vessel wall, seemed to be of momentous importance." But why? Somewhere in Eli Metchnikoff's mind—without his being quite conscious of it—a connection was being made between the behavior of white blood corpuscles and the free-ranging amoeba-like creatures that (as he had speculated a few years earlier) had in the early course of the evolution of multicellular organisms detached themselves from the interior of the creature's wall in order to wander around its insides.

Then came the momentous afternoon in the autumn of 1882 on the Sicilian beach, far away from the political and academic woes of Mother Russia. As Metchnikoff later related:

> I was resting from the shock of the events which provoked my resignation from the University [of Odessa] and indulging enthusiastically in researches at the splendid setting of the Straits of Messina. . . . One day when the whole family had gone to a circus to see some extraordinary performing apes, I remained alone with my microscope, observing the life in the mobile cells of a transparent star-fish larva, when a new thought suddenly flashed across my brain. It struck me that similar cells might serve in the defense of the organism against intruders. Feeling that there was in this something of surpassing interest, I felt so excited that I began striding up and down the room and even went to the seashore in order to collect my thoughts. I said to myself that, if my supposition was true, a splinter introduced into the body of a star-fish larva, devoid of blood vessels or of a nervous system, should soon be surrounded by mobile cells as is to be observed in a man who runs a splinter into his finger. This was no sooner said than done.

Metchnikoff ran out and fetched a few rose thorns from the garden and stuck them under the skin of a star-fish egg. His account continues: "I was too excited to sleep that night in the expectation of the result of my experiment, and very early the next morning I ascertained that it had fully succeeded. That experiment formed the basis of the phagocyte theory, to the development of which I devoted the next twenty-five years of my life."

Metchnikoff went on to observe that when yeast is introduced into water fleas (which like star-fish larvae are transparent), the wandering cells similarly devour the intruding microscopic fungi. He soon published his findings in his article "Research on the Intracellular Digestion of Invertebrates." This rather dull and general title belies Metchnikoff's conviction of having established the basis of active immunity to every transmittable disease for all visible living organisms, including man. The same kinds of amoeboid cells that hundreds of millions of years ago served the purpose of digesting nutrients that enter the intracellar spaces of simple organisms now serve instead the purpose of defense within even the most evolved complex creatures in the phylogenetic tree. Metchnikoff distinguished these special types of leukocytes with the name phagocytes ("devouring cells").

The fact that white blood cells may be seen moving around the body with pathogenic germs inside them was already known to other medical men. But previous to Metchnikoff, it had generally been supposed that blood pressure forced the microbes and other foreign material through the leukocyte membranes, which were assumed to be highly permeable and elastic. These white cells were thought to be passive receptacles rather than active predators. True, in 1871 the German (and, by his name, probably Jewish) physiologist Solomon Stricker described in his *Manual of Human and Animal Histology* the devouring (*fressende*) activity of some leukocytes. But this view generated little interest. And in any case, neither Stricker himself nor virtually anyone else saw this activity as defending the host. In fact, there was a widespread belief in the medical community that leukocytes, far from fighting pathogenic microorganisms, provided a nutritive medium for their multiplication. Worse still, those leukocytes that were observed to contain microbes were thought, in view of their motility, to be culprits in the spread of disease from one body site to another.

It was Metchnikoff alone who focused on the defensive role of his phagocytes and fought tirelessly for his theory, while also setting up a whole research paradigm for further investigating the phenomenon. In due course he got the medical world to believe him, beginning with his first convert, Joseph Lister, the Prince of Surgeons, famed for his introduction of antisepsis to the operating room. But perhaps no less important than Metchnikoff's phagocyte theory was his broader anti-holistic and anti-romantic concept of how a complex organism can evolve without necessarily always maintaining sovereignty over its component parts. Eli Metchnikoff's devouring leukocytes—similar in behavior to the external, independently feeding amoebae found in ponds—were envisaged by him as having developed a symbiotic existence with the rest of the human body, but not always sharing the same agenda with it. This was perhaps the reason why, in searching for a new home outside of reactionary Russia, Metchnikoff was given a rather cool reception by Robert Koch in Berlin. The concept of the body being defended not by a disciplined army with unity of purpose, but by a horde of freebooters who coincidentally happened to be serving a higher good, could hardly have appealed to the newly united and militaristic Germans.

There was no such problem in the French mentality, certainly not in the thinking of the grand old man of the microbe-hunters, Louis Pasteur. He told Metchnikoff, "I at once placed myself on your side, for I have for many years been struck by the struggle between the diverse micro-organisms which I have had occasion to observe. I believe you are on the right road." Pasteur was busy setting up a new Institute on the Rue Dutot in Paris and it was there, in 1888, that the wandering Eli Metchnikoff settled down for good. The new building was financed in part by the Russian czar, for recently Pasteur and his new rabies vaccine had saved the lives of sixteen *moujiks* who had been savaged by a mad wolf. The grateful Alexander III sent Pasteur the diamond cross of St. Anne and a contribution of 100,000 francs. But this Russian connection notwithstanding, the contrast between Metchnikoff's old and new home could hardly have been greater. As he later wrote: "It was in Paris that I succeeded at last in practicing pure science apart from all politics. . . . That dream could not have been realized in Russia because of obstacles from above, from below, and from all sides." Further musing on the situation in his native land, Metchnikoff added: "One might think that the hour of science in Russia has not yet struck. I do not believe that. I think, on the contrary, that scientific work is indispensable to Russia, and I wish from my heart that future conditions may become more favorable. . . ."

Aside from his general liberal sympathies, Metchnikoff was also ever conscious of his Jewish origins and the lot of his Jewish countrymen. "The Russians have the mind, but the Russian Jews have in addition to that vivacity and energy to a remarkable degree," he declared. "Russia has lost many great talents by persecuting the Jews." Indeed, as we shall see shortly, several important figures around Metchnikoff in Paris were émigré Jewish scientists who were denied opportunities to develop in Russia. Nevertheless, an overtly optimistic Metchnikoff declared: "I feel quite certain that . . . the Russian Government will realize its errors and will improve the condition of the Jewish people, for its own sake, if for no other reason."

The situation of the Jews of France was dramatically different, at least since the revolution a century earlier. We have seen how Jews fleeing Islamic and then Christian persecutions in Spain found refuge across the border in southwestern France in the late Middle Ages and early Renaissance. But we have also seen how in the ensuing centuries in the centralized absolute monarchy of the Bourbons, the Jewish religion was severely repressed.

With the Enlightenment of the French philosophes and the rise of a prosperous bourgeoisie came the ideals of the Rights of Man. Voltaire, with his wisdom and satiric wit, encouraged free inquiry, human dignity and equality, and freedom of conscience and was instrumental in producing not revolutionary masses but an ungovernable middle class that would carry out the revolution a decade after his death. Sarcastic of orthodox religion in general, Voltaire reserved some especially biting comments for the Jews past and contemporary and their supposed Old Testament fanaticism. His intolerance of intolerance led him, ironically, to deride the Jews just as he did the Spanish Inquisition. But some Jews merited Voltaire's highest praise, particularly Spinoza. And, of course, Voltaire had a Jewish doctor. This was Jean-Baptiste Silva, the son of a Marrano refugee physician, who served as court physician to Louis XV and other European royalty. In an age when the play Le médecin malgré lui (Doctor Despite Himself) of Voltaire's fellow satirist Molière enjoyed great popularity, Voltaire called Dr. Silva "one of those physicians whom Molière neither could nor dared to make ridiculous."

In the late 1770s, in the last years of the Ancien Régime, a gentile physician, Dr. Le Jau, reported to the Société Royale de Médecine on the health of the Jews in Phalsbourg, a town in Lorraine in Northeastern France. The report was in the context of the Society's general mandate to study the health of France's various population groups and make recommendations for their improvement. Le Jau had good things to say about the health habits of the Jews he studied. "Jewish morals s are unarguably better than those of Christians; it is a rare thing for them to indulge in the debaucheries and excesses of our young people." He further suggested that "observance of the law of Moses and of the Talmud benefits the Jews because of their frugality and their choice of meats and drink."

Yet, Le Jau went on to note, the lot of the Jews, even in the prosperous section of the community, was not happy: "Their separation from other citizens contributes unfailingly to the gloom and melancholy that is seen among most of them. Indeed, how can their souls not be affected by their withdrawn and anxious lives, and the humiliation to which they are reduced in spite of their wealth and money?" Furthermore, being restricted in their professional activities by the laws of the realm, the Jews were heavily dependent upon commerce, whose ups and downs were deleterious to their well-being: "Since trade is subject to one abrupt change after another, which constitutes a source of endless anxiety for men hungry for profit, it is not a surprise to find them gloomy, musing, fearful, preoccupied, mistrustful; and if their efforts succeed, their excitability increases sometimes to transports of joy and to hopes for a happy future; these fond hopes cannot fail to be thwarted by inevitable reverses in trade."

In Alsace, where most of the Jews lived and where every head of cattle and every Jew was subject to a cloven-foot toll at each customs post, Louis XVI granted exemption to the latter in 1784. The monarch subsequently issued letters of patent to end some other abusive practices, but such reforms were completely overtaken by the dramatic events of the French Revolution and its ideals of Liberty, Equality, and Fraternity. In January 1790, six months after the storming of the Bastille, the Jews of Bayonne, Bordeaux, and the former papal state of Avignon—Sephardim who presented themselves as French Jewry's cultured élite—were granted full rights and citizenship by the National Assembly. Twenty months and much heated debate later, this was extended to all of France's 70,000 Jews, most notably, the large concentration of Ashkinazim in Alsace-Lorraine. The pattern of modern Jewish social and political life was set in motion with the advent to power of Napoleon Bonaparte, who assumed the role of leader after the revolution degenerated into chaos and foreign forces threatened the country. In 1807 Napoleon convened the first Sanhedrin (Jewish Grand Council) to be held for about a millennium and a half. Drawn from the length and breadth of the Empire that Napoleon had conquered in what had started out as a defensive war, the eighty delegates, about half of whom were rabbis, declared that Jews owed their allegiance to their respective countries. The Medieval concept of a Jewish corporate state within a state was abolished. The laws of the country took precedence in secular matters (including marriage), the Mosaic laws being limited to religious affairs.

The legal equality of the French Jews was extended by Napoleon to the many countries under his domain. The retreat of the French armies often meant a rolling back of these legal advances, frequently leaving in their place an overt or smoldering resentment toward the Jewish beneficiaries, most notably, in the Germany states. But in France itself, even with the restoration of the monarchy, the ideal of Liberty, Equality, and Fraternity continued to encompass the Jews. Even the discriminatory rules promulgated, ironically enough, by Napoleon himself—the most restrictive of which prohibited Jewish settlement in northeastern France—were repealed in due course.

A sign of French religious toleration, or indifference, can be seen from the eyewitness description by the great German-Jewish poet Heinrich Heine of events during the cholera epidemic in Paris in 1832. Panic followed a rumor that the disease was in fact the result of deliberate poisoning of vegetables, meats, and wine. As Heine (who survived the epidemic to die of syphilis two decades later) wrote:

> There is no more dreadful sight than such popular anger thirsting for blood and throttling its defenseless victims. . . . In the Rue Vaugirard, where two men were killed who had white powders on them, I saw one of these unfortunates when he was still breathing and the old hags were just pulling the wooden shoes from their feet and beating him on the head with them till he was dead. . . . [O]ne ruffian tied a rope to the feet of the corpse and dragged it through the streets, shouting constantly, "*Voilá le Cholera-morbus!*" A very beautiful female, pale with rage, with bare breasts and bloody hands, stood by and kicked the corpse as it came near her.

How was this a sign of French enlightenment? In neither Heine's account nor anyone else's was there any indication that Jews or Jewish doctors were singled out for such treatment.

Whereas when Metchnikoff left Odessa, the Jews in the Russian Empire already numbered some four million, in his new home France there were only about 75,000, or between one-tenth and two-tenths of 1 percent of the whole population. Even in Paris, where most of the Jews lived, they constituted but a small minority. This, coupled with the great prestige of French culture, was an important factor leading to their assimilation. Yet the Jews of France were conspicuous in other ways, especially in the age of modernism. The philosopher Henri Louis Bergson was famed for his writings on time, duration, consciousness, and memory. Paris resounded with the melodies from the operettas and comic operas of Jacques

Offenbach, "the Mozart of the Champs-Elysées." Émile Durkheim was the founding force in the new discipline of sociology. Other Jews were prominent in government, politics and finance. (Social tensions resulting from such Jewish preeminence would boil up with the Dreyfus affair in the 1890s.) Marcel Proust, half Jewish, frequently considered the theme of Jewish identity in his novels. He had his share to say about the medical science of his day. (His father, although not Jewish, was a physician.) "Medicine being a compendium of the successive and contradictory mistakes of medical practitioners, when we summon the wisest of them to our aid, the chances are that we may be relying on a scientific truth the error of which will be recognized in a few years' time. So that to believe in medicine would be the height of folly," Proust concluded, but then added: "if not to believe in it were not greater folly still, for from this mass of errors there have emerged in the course of time many truths."

To the relief of the cultured native Jews of Paris, they were spared the embarrassment felt by their counterparts in Berlin and Vienna at the hordes of traditional Yiddish-speakers migrating from the Russian Empire. The Eastern Jews who made it to Paris numbered hardly 10,000 and tended to congregate in the *Plätzl* (little square). For its part, the Pasteur Institute on the Rue Dutot had its share of Russian Jews, though hardly of the kaftan-clad variety. Among the outstanding researchers to gather around Eli Metchnikoff were Alexander Besredko and M. Weinberg. But the greatest of the Russian-Jewish émigrés was Waldemar Mordecai Haffkine.

Born in Odessa in 1860 to a Jewish merchant family, Haffkine was a student at the Faculty of Natural Science at Odessa University when he was caught up in the events of the early 1880s following the assassination of Czar Alexander II. In the crackdown that ensued under the reactionary Alexander III, any hostility toward the Jews was aided and abetted by the authorities. As a member of a League for Self-Defense, Haffkine, while trying to protect a Jewish home under attack by a group of military cadets, was wounded in the head, arrested, and placed on trial. Fortunately, young Haffkine was a student of Professor Metchnikoff, who had taken him on zoological field trips and who, thanks to his growing scientific reputation, was not without influence among the powers-that-be. Metchnikoff's favorable testimony as a defense witness spared Haffkine from execution or exile to Siberia—the fate of many other student activists. But although able to complete his doctorate, the young Jew, like millions of his coreligionists, saw no future in Russia. Along with the *numerus clausus* restricting the admission of Jewish students to the university, there was a virtual ban on unbaptized Jews occupying a professor's chair.

So in 1888 Haffkine went to work for a year with Moritz Schiff in Geneva and then followed his teacher Metchnikoff to Paris. Haffkine commenced his research at the Pasteur Institute with valuable observations of microorganisms and particularly on the way the rod-shaped bacteria of typhoid fever adapt to various media. But Haffkine's great contributions to medicine began in earnest in 1893 when the brother of the king of Siam visited the Rue Dutot to beseech Pasteur, the discoverer of attenuated vaccines, to do something about cholera, the everlasting scourge of Asia. Pasteur turned the job over to his rising young star, Haffkine.

Some ten years earlier Robert Koch had already isolated the comma-shaped bacterium *Vibrio cholerae* and had succeeded in breeding a pure culture. But producing a prophylactic was another matter. A cholera vaccine developed by a Spanish bacteriologist, first thought to be effective, later proved to be of dubious value and, furthermore, met with opposition on principle from the Catholic Church. Haffkine had been brought up without much religious education, although he would later in life become a practicing orthodox Jew with a rationalist, or rationalizing, bent. (For example, he pointed to the kosher drainage of blood from meat as depriving pathogens of a natural medium for multiplication and infection.) Either way, Haffkine had no theological problems with vaccination.

Haffkine took a highly virulent culture of cholera bacteria and cultured it further at precisely 39 degrees Celsius. This was the temperature, Haffkine determined, at which the *Vibrio cholerae* would keep multiplying, but only in an attenuated—that is, less virulent—form. When inoculated subcutaneously into a human or animal host, these tamed vibrios continued to replicate but caused just a rather harmless infection, which conferred a high measure of immunity to any subsequent all-out attack from the virulent strain. Haffkine went to India, where he would spend most of the rest of his life, and began inoculating the first of millions, reducing their mortality from cholera by some three-quarters. Haffkine himself was stricken by malaria, and it was also rumored that suspicious Moslems in East Bengal tried to poison him with snake venom. As the prestigious *British Medical Journal* wrote in tribute in 1895: "He has given many of the best years of his life to . . . life-saving purposes without fee or reward other than his own conscience, his love of humanity, and his scientific devotion." Yet this was only a prelude to a more dramatic triumph on the subcontinent.

Around the turn of the twentieth century over a million Indians were annually falling victim to the bacterium *Yersinia pestis,* which a few years earlier had, in time-honored fashion, once again found its way there from Yunnan in Southeast Asia. This bacterium was the same one that in the fourteenth century had caused the Black Death, which swept away a third of the population of Europe and sowed such panic among the Christians in the German Rhineland that they massacred the Jews and drove Haffkine's ancestors eastward. Since then, the Black Death had been visiting its devastation upon Europe at fairly regular intervals. Now, borne by steamships, it was again beating at the doors of Europe, as well as of the New World, South Africa, and Australia. Haffkine went to its epicenter in Bombay to stop it.

Waldemar Haffkine was among the first to suspect the rat-borne flea as an integral link in the plague's chain of transmission. But its elimination in the Indian subcontinent would be impractical, largely because of the religious customs of the Jains, whose admirable respect for all living things even led them to deliberately nourish the fleas. Alexandre Yersin of the Pasteur Institute, who a few years earlier had isolated the plague microorganism that bears his name, had tried, unsuccessfully, to develop a curative antiplague serum. Haffkine, for his part, placed his hopes in developing a preventative vaccine. Because each disease has its own particular pathology and pathogens, different diseases require different kinds of vaccines. Haffkine hit on the method of growing plague cultures in a broth containing layers of coconut fat, shaken from time to time like a deadly piña colada. An attenuated vaccine, so effective for cholera, seemed too risky in the case of the plague, so Haffkine killed his bacteria by subjecting them to up to 90 degrees (C) of heat for an hour and then exposing them to carbolic acid. Fortunately, what was left proved capable of triggering a strong immune response when inoculated in sufficient dosage.

The mortality from plague soon dropped by a staggering 85–90 percent. A grateful Queen Victoria conferred on Haffkine the Order of the Indian Empire, and his Plague Institute in Bombay was renamed the Haffkine Institute in his honor. Although Haffkine, who died in 1930, would not live to see it, his institute would play an important part in the successful testing of the antibiotic streptomycin against the plague, developed by his fellow Russian-Jewish émigré Selman Waksman (more about whom in a later chapter). But in Haffkine's native land, where Jewish doctors were long suspected of poisoning the populace, the reception accorded to Haffkine's vaccine was more cautious. As the great Russian playwright Anton Chekhov wrote sarcastically to the anti-Semitic editor of the reactionary newspaper *Novoe Vremia* around the turn of the century: "You ask whether the plague will reach us. . . . There is some hope in the vaccine of Haffkine, but unfortunately, Haffkine is not very popular in Russia: 'Christians must beware of him since he is a Jew.'"

While Haffkine was off battling cholera and the plague in India, Eli Metchnikoff continued to mind the fort in the laboratories of the Pasteur Institute in Paris. For years he fought to establish the phagocyte theory of immunity in a skeptical medical world. Then the mercurial half-Jew half-Russian went overboard. He maintained that his devouring white blood cells were responsible not for just some, but for *all* aspects of host defense. "There is but one permanent element in natural and acquired immunity," he stated flatly, "and that is phagocytosis." This was at a time when Paul Ehrlich's models of hyperregenerating side-chains were promising to account adequately for all the known facts about immunity. But for Metchnikoff, Ehrlich was engaged in just some fanciful theorizing. How to explain the active immunizing effects of vaccination such as the kinds developed by Haffkine? Well, Metchnikoff reasoned, a phagocyte's dining habits involve something of an acquired taste. So once a phagocyte ingests a given strain of bacteria—whether virulent, attenuated, or killed—it tends to seek out and devour the same invaders all the more quickly and effectively in the future.

But what, then, of the workings of passive immunization developed by von Behring and Ehrlich, who had convincingly demonstrated that when in the case of certain diseases the serum (the clear part of the blood after coagulation) from an immunized animal is injected into a non-immunized animal, the former's immunity is transferred to the later? The serum itself is cell-free, and as such contains no phagocytes (or any other leukocytes) and no bacteria. Metchnikoff suggested that phagocytes excreted or leaked bactericidal juices into the blood fluid after they've devoured the invading bacteria or toxins. Later he updated his explanation of both active and passive immunization by postulating that when the phagocytes devour a certain microbe, they also release a targeting fixator into the host's blood fluid. There it circulates, ready to bind to any new intruders of the same strain, thereby marking them for quicker annihilation by homing-in phagocytes. This process, Metchnikoff reasoned, would work as well when the fixators in the serum of one animal are transferred to another.

Well, then how could he explain the phenomenon of lysis, whereby the red cells of transfused blood are seen to be destroyed by the ambient humors of the host blood and not by the phagocytes (if, as we now know, the blood is of an incompatible group)? This was apparent proof of a defensive biochemical property of the blood fluid proper. But not for Metchnikoff, who dismissed this as a last hangover from the ancient humoral theory. Blood-cell lysis by the serum just had to be the result of a phagocyte-mediated phenomenon similar to the one he envisaged for antimicrobial defense. Digestive juices from the host's phagocytes leak into the serum and attack the foreign blood cells. As for defense against poisons—be it snake venom introduced directly into the body or the toxins excreted by invading microorganisms such as diphtheria or tetanus—and the partial immunity against future poisoning that results if the victim survives, Metchnikoff argued that each phagocyte developed an ever greater tolerance for absorbing increasing amounts of the poison in question. (This was in addition to the antitoxins the phagocytes supposedly exuded into the blood fluids as part of their digestive process.)

Eli Metchnikoff was brilliantly right in his concept of amoeba-like phagocytes serving in the defense of the body as they feed themselves. In many ways he was also on the right track in his description of fixators and antitoxins released into the blood. But as we now know, it is not the phagocytes that fulfill these functions, but other leukocytes, which are not amoeba-like and do not devour. So in a way it was fitting that Eli Metchnikoff was awarded half the Nobel Prize in 1908. Symbolically, he stood at the podium in Stockholm together with Paul Ehrlich, whose fertile imagination had envisaged very different kinds of cells hyperregenerating side-chains of antibodies and antitoxins to defeat foreign invaders in the body.

But already long before receiving the Nobel for his work on immunity, Eli Metchnikoff had embarked on a new mission, which was so great that it even dwarfed his phagocyte hypothesis in his own mind. As the new century loomed, he returned to his old preoccupation with the disharmonies in human life due to an evolutionary mismatch of man's biology and his mental development. But now rather than concerning himself with marriage and the sexual instincts of youth as he had decades earlier, the middle-aged Metchnikoff addressed the problems of the declining years.

There is a natural human death instinct, Metchnikoff speculated, and this has a proper place in man's life cycle. Metchnikoff's death instinct was somewhat more reasonable than the one that Freud would come up with in 1920 in his *Beyond the Pleasure Principle*. Metchnikoff saw the fear of death that typically characterizes the human condition as due to a mismatch between the death instinct and man's life span, the latter being cut short, often long before the appropriate tenth or eleventh decade. A man who has reached his proper age of 90 or 100 no longer fears death but welcomes it instinctively, just as one welcomes sleep at the end of a long day. The sleep analogy particularly appealed to Metchnikoff, for in the late nineteenth century the prominent German physiologist Wilhelm Preyer theorized that the increasing desire for sleep arose from the accumulation of substances in the blood in the course of the day. Similarly, Metchnikoff hypothesized, the welcoming of death should naturally arise from the accumulation of certain substances in the course of, ideally, a century or so. The biblical prophets who expired satiated with life provided good examples of this.

Famine, pestilence, war—the dreaded horsemen of the apocalypse—can all lead to our premature demise. So could what Metchnikoff called "the poisons generated by evil temper and emotional excess over non-essentials." But Metchnikoff was convinced that even given an inner and outer state of tranquillity, man's life is cut short by autointoxication—toxins secreted by harmful microorganisms in the large intestines. These toxins attack and thus enfeeble body cells that would otherwise be healthy. In this process, too, phagocytes play a role, though not a happy one. Metchnikoff noted that the phagocyte army was responsible not only for the defense of the body against foreign invaders but also, for example, for the scavenging of injured cells of the body itself. When phagocytes devour a tadpole's tail in its metamorphosis to a frog after the tail cells have been weakened by internal biochemical processes, this was very much the natural order of things in the frog's life cycle. But Metchnikoff assumed that phagocytosis can also occur insidiously by attacking and scavenging all those body cells that would have been healthy if they hadn't been weakened by autointoxication from the bowels, the bane of mankind.

Metchnikoff reasoned that—unlike the case of man and other land animals—those birds and bats fortunate enough not to be killed by predators, accidents, famine, or infectious disease live out a full life cycle not cut short by autointoxication. This he attributed to the necessarily lighter weight and therefore smaller bowel size of flying creatures, which as a consequence are continually relieving themselves. By contrast, humans and other land animals, with their large intestines, have the evolutionary advantage of being able to flee from predators over long distances without the necessity of pausing for calls of nature. But in the case of humans, at least, predators are seldom any longer a threat, and in modern times, according to Metchnikoff, the price paid for man's ability to avoid the inconvenience of constantly evacuating himself is a truncated lifetime of slow poisoning by toxins released by the microorganisms of the bowels. These toxins even weaken the hair pigments, which in turn caused phagocytes to scavenge them and turn hair white.

People wrote to Metchnikoff, pointing out the obvious lack of any negative linear correlation between bowel size and longevity among mammals. Humans outlive other mammals with proportionately more modest intestines; and elephants with their giant intestines outlive them all. But Metchnikoff was unconvinced. For him, the Egyptians some 4,000 years earlier had been quite right in their dread of disease caused by rot and decay in the bowels and had been wise to constantly purge themselves. Right, too, were the Jewish sages, especially Maimonides, who insisted that the heeding of the call of nature not be delayed even a minute longer than necessary. But, of course, this commandment was inevitably constrained by the demands of social propriety. Not everyone was as fortunate as Rabbi Judah ben Illay of the Talmud, who had twenty-four lavatories along the route between his house and his place of study.

By a combination of empirical observation and theoretical deduction, Eli Metchnikoff hit on a solution to this evolutionary dilemma. He had heard reports of whole communities of Bulgarian peasants living into their tenth or eleventh decades on diets containing large amounts of yogurt. As Pasteur had shown in the 1850s, milk fermentation occurs when bacteria (in the case of yogurt, *Lactobacillus bulgaricus*) convert lactose into lactic acid. The fermented milk then keeps rather well, due to its bacteriostatic acidity. Similarly, the bowels of the Bulgarian yogurt-eater become acidic and supposedly form a most inhospitable environment for the flora that would otherwise, according to Metchnikoff, produce toxins leading to arteriosclerosis, senility, and atrophy.

But perhaps there was also a hidden reason for Eli Metchnikoff's great fondness for yogurt, having specifically to do with his Jewish origin. For untold prehistoric millennia, bands of hunter-gatherers drank only human milk, and then only as babies. It is therefore not surprising that in the course of evolution the ability of humans to produce lactase (the enzyme that breaks down lactose [milk sugar] into digestible sucrose and galactose) should, as with all other animals, cease at the end of infancy. With the dawning of civilization in the Middle East some 12,000 years ago came the domestication of milk animals. But before the milk could be stomached by most weaned children and adults, the breakdown of lactose had to first be accomplished by fermentation. The loss of lactose, however, also meant that the milk's calcium content was less readily absorbed by the body. But for the Jews and other peoples of the Middle East there were abundant green leafy vegetables for calcium and also ocean fish and sea mammals for providing vitamin D, which aids in calcium digestion.

The Northern climes, however, were poor in such natural resources. So when, millennia before the Common Era, dairying spread northward from the Middle East, anyone who happened to possess a mutant gene that allowed for the production of lactase in later childhood and adulthood had a decided Darwinian advantage. The ability to digest cupfuls of unfermented, and therefore lactose-rich, milk went hand in hand with a lower incidence of calcium deficiency diseases such as rickets and osteomalacia in the misty north. So the lactase-producing genes spread slowly but surely to most of the non-Mediterranean population in the course of some five millennia, whereas in the gene pool of the Middle East no such mutation was needed or occurred. The Jews were relative latecomers to the northern climes— at least to the extent modern Jews are genetic descendants of the ancient Israelites—and as such they still had a few thousand years of evolutionary catching up to do when it comes to the digestion of nonfermented milk. And so it perhaps was that Eli Metchnikoff inherited through his mother an ancient Middle East taste for sour milk and yogurt.

Metchnikoff's concepts of bowel-toxin aging and its yogurt antidote were, as presented, inherently no more absurd than his theory that free-ranging descendants of amoeba-like creatures inside the body were responsible for defending it against foreign invaders. But whereas in the latter case he was mostly on the mark, in the former case he was farther off. As far as is known today, weakening due to toxins from intestinal microorganisms and the scavenging by phagocytes have nothing to do with turning hair white or most other aging processes. Yet Metchnikoff's bowel-toxin concept contains some genuine insights, in that intestinal bacteria have been implicated in colon cancer. More generally, there was at least a kernel of truth in Metchnikoff's obsession as it relates to the concept of autoimmunity, a condition in which the defense system, rather than defending the host against foreign invaders, attacks the host's own cells.

Paul Ehrlich was perhaps the first to come up with the notion of autoimmunity and to coin the term. However, while allowing that self-destructive antibodies and antitoxins could in principle be produced by the host's immune system, he assumed that they would in fact immediately be rendered harmless. "The organism possesses certain contrivances by means of which the immunity reaction, so easily produced by all kinds of cells, is prevented from acting against the organism's own elements and so give rise to autotoxins," wrote Ehrlich. "So," he added, "we might be justified in speaking of a *horror autotoxicus* of the organism. The contrivances are naturally of the highest importance to the individual."

Ehrlich's fertile mind was once more on target in suggesting the theoretical possibility of autoimmunity, and he was also quite correct in the corollary importance he assigned to the biological mechanisms preventing this from actually occurring. He erred, however, in assuming that since such safeguards were so crucial, they must always operate flawlessly. It has now been established that some of the worst afflictions of old age—although not necessarily the aging process itself—are due to the ideally finely tuned immune system becoming unregulated in the course of the decades. The host defenses not only become less effective against foreign microbes and home-grown cancers but, as if to add injury to insult, sometimes attack the body's own healthy tissue. Eli Metchnikoff's phagocytes have been clearly implicated—as well as an array of other types of immune processes (in which the stubborn Russian, even were he alive today, might still refuse to believe as a matter of principle). Late in the twentieth century, it became increasingly evident that rheumatoid arthritis results from the body's defense system attacking the lining of joints. And with half the deaths in the industrialized world now being caused by cardiovascular disease, researchers have come to suspect an important secondary role of autoimmunity in hardening of the arteries.

Despite the quarts of yogurt with which he daily filled his intestines, the middle-aged Eli Metchnikoff could not be sure that leaking bacterial poisons and wayward phagocytes would not cut his life short. Concerned as he was for the future of the Pasteur Institute, it being so dependent on private contributions, he was able to rest more easily knowing that he was instrumental, in a rather bizarre way, in obtaining for it a grant of tens of millions of francs. Here Metchnikoff's Jewish connection played a role, in the form of a banker of the French *haute finance,* Daniel Iffla, who sooner conformed to the stereotype of the wealthy miserly Scotsman than of the wealthy ostentatious Jew. (Among other things, he used candles instead of electricity in his home for the sake of economy.) Iffla dabbled in archaeology, collected Egyptian relics, and had recently changed his name to Osiris, after the ancient Egyptian god of light and health. Yet this did not prevent him from falling terminally ill at the not-so-young age of 82. He complained of the costliness of the food his doctors were prescribing (three portions of ice cream per diem: cholesterol was apparently a good thing in those days). Yet he had some forty million francs at his disposal, which, presumably, he couldn't take with him. Osiris decided to donate the entire amount to the Pasteur Institute, with the proviso that Eli Metchnikoff visit him every day for the duration of his illness. (Whether Osiris entertained visions of a miracle cure that his Egyptian artifacts could not give him or simply wanted the company of the great scientist in his last days—or perhaps was motivated by the cheaper price of yogurt compared to ice cream—has not been recorded.)

At the time when the Great War was ravaging Europe, Eli Metchnikoff himself fell ill with what he realized would be his last illness. His impending death in no way modified his atheistic beliefs. To the end Metchnikoff remained true to his student nickname, "God-is-not," and maintained an almost religious faith in science and its universal potential. "If an ideal is possible, capable of uniting men in a sort of religion of the future, it can only be based on scientific principles," he wrote. "And if it is true, as is so often affirmed, that it is impossible to live without faith, that faith must be faith in the power of science." Rather than look to an afterlife, Metchnikoff expressed an almost messianic vision of creating some heaven on earth. He maintained this faith in the future even as Europe was being torn asunder. "Let those who will have preserved the combative instinct direct it toward a struggle, not against human beings but against the innumerable microbes, visible or invisible, which threaten us on all sides and prevent us from accomplishing the normal and complete cycle of our existence." More generally, Metchnikoff believed that "with the help of science, man can correct the imperfections of his nature." Morals must consist "not in rules of conduct adapted to our present defective human nature, but on conduct based upon human nature modified, according to the ideal of human happiness." True, modern biology has revealed the laws of the struggle for existence and the survival of the fittest, but man himself is not obliged to live by them. Rather, he can use the benefits derived from other scientific laws—such as immunology—to counterbalance the cruel and harmful effects of the natural world. "Just as, in order to satisfy his aesthetic need, man revolts against the laws of nature which creates races of sterile and fragile flowers, he does not hesitate to defend the weak against the laws of natural selection."

In 1916, having attained the age of 71, Eli Metchnikoff succumbed to complications caused by cardiac insufficiency. He passed away in the former apartment of Louis Pasteur, which had been provided by the Institute in the hope that the spaciousness and the soul of the place would brighten his last days. Metchnikoff survived the non-yogurt-eating Pasteur by twenty-one years, but failed by nineteen months to outlive him. (He did, however, outlive by ten years and survive by eleven months the twenty-five-cigar-a-day Paul Ehrlich, to whom we shall be returning in the next chapter.) Such had been the appeal of France to this Russian half-Jew that when receiving offers of more lucrative jobs from abroad, he declared that the only place for which he would leave the Pasteur Institute was the neighboring cemetery of Montparnasse. In the event, however, he would not leave the Rue Dutot even in death. For the Pasteur Institute remains to this day home to Eli Metchnikoff's ashes, as well as to his great spirit.

Chapter 12
The Magic Bullet in Frankfurt

The antibodies are magic bullets that find their targets by themselves.—Paul Ehrlich

[I]nitially, chemotherapy was a "chromotherapy"—Paul Ehrlich

arbenfabriken Bayer, Farbenwerke Hoechst . . . *Farben* is the German word for "dyes," and the origins of some great pharmaceutical houses in the rather mundane field of synthetic textile coloring is reflected in their old names. Not surprisingly, therefore, the gigantic conglomerate that for decades controlled Bayer, Hoechst, and every other German pharmaceutical house, as well as virtually all other branches of the German chemical industry, was named Interessegemeinschaft (I. G.) Farben. Yet there is a touch of irony in the fact that Germany's pharmaceutical, and particularly chemotherapeutic, sector, which was unrivaled in all the world in the late nineteenth and early twentieth centuries, had *its* origins in synthetic dyeing and staining. For, in fact, it was a student trying to synthesize a drug who, by accident, gave birth to the artificial dye industry. And he was English, not German.

One of the precious few drugs of any proven value to the early nineteenth-century physician was quinine. This is said to have been introduced into the Western *materia medica* by Dr. Juan Lopez da Vega, who was apparently of the da Vega dynasty of Jewish physicians we met in Portugal. As physician to the duchess of Cinchón, the wife of the viceroy of Peru, de Vega is credited with prescribing for the febrile viceroy a native Indian remedy, the bark of the fever tree, in 1638. Originally called "cinchona," quinine suppresses aches and fever and, as we now know, disrupts the life cycle of the malaria parasite, *plasmodium vivax*, within the host. Brought back to Europe by the Jesuits, cinchona was greeted with skepticism, for it went counter to the Galenic concept that malaria was due to an excess humor that had to be purged. Furthermore, the Puritan Oliver Cromwell, Lord Protector of the Commonwealth, was suspicious of this "Jesuits' bark" and chose to die of malaria rather than take it. Yet the drug quickly proved its worth.

In 1855, in what was once Cromwell's London, a 17-year-old student at the Royal College of Chemistry, William Henry Perkin, was told to try to produce synthetic quinine. For this assignment he was given a specimen of commercial aniline. This is a substance that chemists a decade earlier had extracted from coal tar naphtha and that happens to be of the same nitrogenous base as the natural dye indigo. Oxidizing the aniline with potassium dichromate, Perkin obtained some dark sediment that, although quite unlike quinine, seemed worthy of further analysis and manipulation. The result was the world's first synthetic dye, called mauve.

As we have seen, the German chemists—most particularly, the German Jewish chemists, whose coreligionists were so involved with the rapidly industrializing textile industry—quickly gained a worldwide lead in developing a spectrum of new synthetic dyes. The immediate spin-off for medical science was the application of these new compounds for microscopic staining techniques in order to tease from nature the secrets of life at the microscopic and cellular levels. Perhaps the greatest stainer—certainly the most compulsive—was Paul Ehrlich.

We take up the life of Professor Ehrlich at the dawn of the new century. In 1899, he had been appointed director of the Institute of Experimental Therapy, situated in Frankfurt am Main, near the great dye factories like Hoechst and Casella. Now he was seized by a new vision: Since it was possible for a chemical stain to react so selectively with a particular strain of pathogenic germ on a microscope slide, would it not be possible to develop similar compounds—whether with or without dyeing properties—in order to poison such microbes in a human while leaving his body cells basically unaffected? This was Paul Ehrlich's dream of a magic bullet. The expression had been used earlier by him in reference to natural immune processes he did so much to elucidate. "The antibodies," he wrote, "are magic bullets that find their targets by themselves." But in view of the fact that for so many diseases, neither acquired immunity in the form of vaccination-induced antibodies nor transferred immunity of antibodies in transfused serum seemed to be possible, it became Ehrlich's dream to create artificial magic bullets in the test tube, just as a few decades earlier chemists had created artificial dyes.

The term *magic bullet* smacks of ancient alchemy. Indeed, the concept of a particular drug for a particular disease was strongly identified with the early Renaissance physician-alchemist Paracelsus and his search for "specifics." But in the first half of the nineteenth century, such ideas were long in disrepute. Doctors treated a disease according to its stage and the symptoms it manifested, thus using the same drug for a variety of diseases and different drugs in the course of the same disease. It was, after all, an era when the medical profession widely believed that, for example, any disease of the bowels could transform itself into cholera, given among other things a patient's intemperate lifestyle. As one prominent contemporary physician wrote: "The search for a specific for cholera in all its stages would be as vain as that of the ancient alchemists for the philosopher's stone, or any of the visionary enterprises of the knight of La Mancha. It is humbug resorted to alone by designing charlatans who would batten on the ignorance and credulity of the people." But the triumph in the second half of the nineteenth century of the concept of specific etiology—that a particular microbe causes a particular disease—placed the idea of a specific remedy in a new light.

The class of protozoa known as trypanosomes is characterized by an elongated, somewhat spindly shape and a whip-like tail or flagellum. They typically live in bloodsucking insects, leeches, or ticks, whence they pass into the bloodstream of man and beast. Since time immemorial two species of this family, *Trypanosoma gambiense* and *Trypanosoma rhodesiense,* have been the bane of humankind in tropical Africa. For, transmitted by the tsetse fly, they cause the debilitating sleeping sickness and employ particularly devious—quite literally, turncoat—methods in order to evade the host's immune system. In terms of Ehrlich's side-chain model: the receptors of defense cells may bind to the surface of a trypanosome and then hyperregenerate an army of antibodies to wipe them out, but by then the antibodies find themselves confronting swarms of trypanosomes with a changed coat that they cannot target and bind to. For this reason, no serum therapy or prophylactic vaccination is effective, and the disease, even if one could rid oneself of it, confers no immunity to a new attack. Yet the trypanosomes were vulnerable in one sense: they are relatively large and easy

338 ~~ Jews and Medicine: An Epic Saga

to see through the microscope. As such, Paul Ehrlich opined, they would make good targets to shoot with chemical magic bullets.

Ehrlich had always had the talent, perhaps acquired from the rabbis and religious scholars in the Weigert branch of his family tree, for digesting vast amounts of reading material. His new office became notorious for the stacks of books and journals piled on every table, chair, and windowsill. "Please be seated," he would tell his distinguished guests from all over the world, but there was never any available surface. Yet there was a method in this seeming disarray. Already in his student days Paul had developed a technique of scanning enormous numbers of pages of medical and scientific texts diagonally from the upper left-hand corner to the lower right-hand corner until some words connected with some essential idea in his head. Then, as if by a modern day computer, the text would be flagged for careful analysis.

So it was that Ehrlich was aware of all the work in his field and was particularly interested in the attempts of the French scientist Alphonse Laveran, the discoverer of the malaria microbe, to find arsenical compounds to combat trypanosomal diseases. Laveran was experimenting on a cousin of *Trypanosoma gambiense* called *Trypanosoma equinum,* the causative agent of mal de Caderas, an affliction of the hindquarters of horses. Laveran had found that arsenic killed many of the trypanosomes, but that all his guinea pigs would die anyhow. That was as far as he got.

Acquiring a mal de Caderas guinea pig from the Pasteur Institute in Paris, Ehrlich transferred the infection to some 10,000 mice and rats. Together with his superbly methodical Japanese assistant Kiyoshi Shiga and a team of expert chemists and lab-workers, he tried with nearly 500 dye compounds to selectively stain the trypanosomes in the rodent blood. But Ehrlich could make no substantial improvement on Laveran. Among the unsuccessful types of dyes was benzopurpin. Ehrlich suggested to his chemists that they add something of the sulfa group to the dye in order to allow it to dissolve better in the rodent blood. The product was called Trypan red. Thanks to it, 1903 went down in medical history as the first year in which a mouse infected by trypanosomes survived them. But some other mice weren't cured by Trypan red, while some others lived on for two months, only to suffer a fatal relapse. Worse still, the real targets of Ehrlich's research, the trypanosome cousins of mal de Caderas that cause sleeping sickness and nanga, seemed to be completely uninhibited by Trypan. And in any case, what worked on rodents might fail on humans. Clearly, much more research had to be done, but where was the extra money to come from?

Frankfurt was home to many wealthy Jews, famous for their public spirit. Among them was the influential banker Georg Speyer, patron of many charities. In 1901, Speyer was deeply touched by the death from spinal cancer of the Dowager Empress Victoria, the daughter of Britain's Queen Victoria and mother of the present kaiser, Wilhelm II. "Vicky's" suffering had not been helped by the confrontations at the sick-bed between English and German doctors over the proper morphine dose. Speyer also well remembered how thirteen years earlier, the Dowager had been widowed when Kaiser Friedrich III had likewise succumbed to cancer, after a painful reign of just ninety-nine days on the imperial throne, during which similar recriminations had flown between the German and English consultant doctors. Speyer got together with other Jewish citizens of Frankfurt and contributed in Vicky's memory some 100,000 marks for cancer research at Ehrlich's Royal Institute for Experimental Therapy. In time, the Institute's experiments on mice would yield important data on the body's immunological response to home-grown and transplanted tumors. In the spring of the following year, however, Georg Speyer himself died of cancer. Left with a large fortune, his widow, Frau Franziska Speyer, wished to continue his good works in the medical field, and so Ehrlich suggested using two million gold marks to enshrine her late husband's name in a Georg-Speyer-Haus. This would stand next door to the Royal Institute for Experimental Therapy but be an independent institution dedicated very specifically to the Ehrlich dream of developing safe and rational chemotherapeutic agents.

With these new facilities at his disposal, Paul Ehrlich was drawn to study an arsenical compound called Atoxyl, which in trials at the London School of Tropical Medicine had cleansed some mice of sleeping sickness. The name, meant to suggest that the drug was nonpoisonous, was overly optimistic. For even in moderate doses it had killed many of the London rodents, including those in the control group that were not even infected with sleeping sickness to begin with. And when Atoxyl was rashly tried out on African patients, it led to some of them becoming blind and still infected by the trypanosomes.

Arsenic was nothing new in the *materia medica* of the physician, Jew or gentile. Back in the sixteenth century, for example, the author of the alchemical-kabbalistic treatise *Esh M'saref*, declaring that "I should not desist from the good and right way until I find the best medicine," detailed an alchemical process that would yield "a white matter, which is the *materia prima*, the dyeing arsenic, the living water of metals, which all philosophers call dry water, and its vinegar." What distinguished the deadly poison of the murderer from the supposedly life-saving drug of the physician was too often merely the intended use to which the substance was put—not the actual outcome. (Napoleon, whose hair samples are said to show abnormal levels of arsenic, may have been deliberately murdered or he may have been unintentionally poisoned by large doses of arsenic-laced Fowler's solution, prescribed by well-meaning doctors. Then again, perhaps he was done in by arsenic wallpaper pigments released by mold into the air.)

But the new age of chemistry offered insights into the structure of arsenical compounds and the hope of developing a safe and therapeutic drug. Atoxyl, it was known, was made up of a benzene ring (six atoms of carbon in a circle with four atoms of hydrogen) plus some ammonia and oxide of arsenic. Antoine Béchamp, the French chemist who had first developed it in the 1860s, had been certain that the nature of its structure prohibited it from being changed without spoiling the benzene-arsenic combination. Now, forty years later, all chemists seemed to agree with him; but Paul Ehrlich was convinced otherwise. Always with his pockets full of colored pencils and chalk, he would doodle diagrams everywhere of fanciful molecular structures—again, no surface was safe from him—in an attempt to convince the doubters that Atoxyl could be varied in hundreds of ways.

Kindly Paul Ehrlich was capable of occasional arguments and outbursts when things went wrong at the lab, although a half hour later he would be slapping the back of the object of his anger, having genuinely forgotten the incident. But on one occasion, a discussion on chemical theory at the Georg-Speyer-Haus got so heated that a parting of the ways took place before there could be reconciliation. Ehrlich's trusted secretary, Martha Marquardt, recorded for posterity his yelling at his three top chemists:

"Atoxyl is *not* an arsenic acid anilide—it contains free amino groups. I produced and investigated the relevant arsenic-containing azo dyes some time ago. The need to reduce the Atoxyl is apparent from my work, and I consider hydrosulphite most suitable for the purpose."

One of the chemists, Dr. von Braun, unconvinced, retorted: "On the basis of the biological facts I'm deliberately having the simplest compounds produced first. Afterwards I'd like you to . . ."

"You can't judge the correctness of this procedure," Ehrlich interrupted.

"We can't recognize your instructions," von Braun retorted. "We must work in accordance with the classical Béchamp formula."

"I adhere to my instructions and leave you to take the consequences!" insisted Ehrlich, walking away.

Von Braun and another of Ehrlich's senior chemists changed from labcoats to topcoats and walked out, never to return. The third chemist, Dr. Alfred Bertheim (himself Jewish, as the others may or may not have been), was about to join them but hesitated, saying, "Perhaps he *is* right."

Bertheim stayed, and it was good that he did. For as it turned out, Paul Ehrlich was indeed right; the Atoxyl molecule could be varied. But the road to the magic bullet was not easy. Some of the new compounds could in fact get rid of the mal de Caderas trypanosomes, but the mice died anyhow of jaundice caused by the cure. The compound's "parasitropy must be made stronger, but its organotropy less," declared Ehrlich. One arsacetine variation caused the mice to dance around endlessly, apparently due to the sensitivity of their auditory nerves. As Ehrlich, unperturbed, wrote, "It is very interesting that the only [!] change to the mice is that they become dancing mice. Those who visit my laboratory must be impressed by the great number of dancing mice it entertains." He tried to get around such obstacles by administering many little doses instead of one large, dangerous one. But there arose the problem of arsenic fastness—that trypanosome strains developed that were immune to the compound. In Ehrlich's terms, side chains of succeeding generations of the microorganisms had time to mutate spontaneously and, true to the Darwinian scheme of things, those trypanosomes survived that no longer had a chemical affinity to the drug.

Sleeping sickness, the curse of Africa, is confined to that continent. The distribution of most of the other, less notorious, trypanosomal diseases were similarly limited to the tropics. By 1905 Paul Ehrlich may have been wondering whether it was worth additional investment of time, effort, and golden Reichmarks in a perhaps vain attempt to find a magic bullet to combat them. Then he was struck by a journal article about the discovery by the German protozoologist Fritz Schaudinn of a spirochete microbe called *Treponema pallidum*. Its description and the accompanying drawings showed it to be a ghostly pale and corkscrew shaped. On the basis of morphological similarity, Schaudinn took the dubious liberty of relating it to the trypanosomes, which meant that it should be susceptible to similar chemotherapeutic agents. Here were microbes far more important than those of sleeping sickness as targets for Paul Ehrlich's magic bullets. For *Treponema pallidum* is the cause of the disease of the loathsome name, the age-old, worldwide scourge of syphilis.

The soaring temples, raised gardens, and intricate canals of fifteenth-century Tenochtitlán, the Aztec capital, bore witness to a sophisticated civilization in which architecture, astronomy, mathematics, and gold-working flourished. The very size of the city, several times that of contemporary London, attested to the military and economic might of the Aztec empire, which encompassed tens of millions of people throughout present-day Mexico and whose armies were in the habit of raiding still farther to obtain prisoners for massive human sacrifices. At first sight, it seems totally incomprehensible that not long after the arrival of Columbus in the New World, the Aztec empire should have been overpowered by mounted bands of Spanish conquistadors numbering only in the hundreds and armed with nothing more technologically advanced than blunderbusses and a few cannons.

Historians traditionally pointed to the political circumstances of the Aztec empire, which had already passed its zenith and was now in decline. It is also quite true that the Spanish were skillful in allying themselves with rebellious tribes under Aztec subjugation. Religion, too, is said to have played a crucial role, particularly some prophesy of the return of the god Quetzalcoatl, whom the Spanish leader Cortès was first thought to be. Sincere Christians, of course, see the wholesale abandonment of the native religions and the mass conversion to the Christianity of the Spanish missionaries as proof of the power of Jesus' word. Indeed, many factors played a part in the rapid conquest. But they were all probably secondary to the epidemiological catastrophe that befell the American Indians, far and away the greatest in all medical history.

In 1521 Cortès's band stood distraught before the Aztec capital of

Tenochtitlán (present-day Mexico City), having been beaten back several times by the defenders. The Spaniards were girding themselves for an Aztec counteroffensive, but this never came. Soon the besiegers were able to enter the capital, to find that some other power had accomplished what their muskets and swords never could have. "I solemnly swear that all the houses and stockades in the lake were full of heads and corpses," wrote Bernal Díaz, the Spanish chronicler."It was the same in the streets and courts. . . . We could not walk without treading on the bodies and heads of dead Indians. . . . The stench was so bad that no one could endure it . . . and even Cortès was ill from the odors which assailed his nostrils."

The stage for Cortès's conquest was in fact being set on the microscopic level for the previous ten millennia. From the inundation of the Bering land bridge between Siberia and Alaska after the great global thaw around 8,000 B.C.E. up to the arrival of Columbus, America was very much an island unto itself, whose people, animals, plants, and microorganisms were isolated from the rest of the world. Even if the Asian ancestors of the American Indians had known diseases such as smallpox and measles, they migrated across the Bering Strait to the New World in numbers too small for the diseases, which can be sustained only in large crowds, to be carried along. Whatever natural, genetically transmitted immunity they once had to the causative microorganisms was lost in the course of countless generations.

In the Old World, by contrast, there was always some chain of contact between populations across the vast Eurasian land mass and also with the African continent, a stone's throw away. A certain amount of communal immunity was therefore kept active. True, diseases transported from far away places could wreak demographic havoc, as did the plague when brought to Europe by the Mongol invasions. But the significance of this paled in comparison to the almost total extinction visited on the native Americans by Old World microorganisms unwittingly carried by the Europeans. Mexico alone was quickly reduced from an estimated thirty million inhabitants to about a tenth that number. (And because the Indians fell victim to not one but several European diseases in the course of time, it would be centuries before the population recovered.) Yet even these staggering figures represent a survival rate perhaps twice as favorable as in most other places in the Americas. As one missionary put it, "The Indians die so easily, that the bare look and smell of a Spaniard causes them to give up the ghost." In fact, communication among the native Americans was at such an advanced level that the pestilence preceded the Spaniards. By the time the conquistador Francisco Pizarro reached the great empire of the Incas, which extended from present-day Ecuador to Chile, most of the royal family had already succumbed to the European microorganisms, and the rest of the decimated population were engaged in a civil war over succession.

Given the generally dismal state of Western medical knowledge up until the dawn of the modern era, Aztec and Inca medicine was probably no less effective than that of the Europeans. The New World pharmacopoeia included drugs gratefully adopted by Western medicine and still in use today, such as quinine, cocaine, curare, and atropine. But in their basic underlying philosophy toward disease, the inhabitants of the New World had never achieved the sophistication of the ancient Greeks. Ailments were of divine or otherwise supernatural origin, and the roles of priest and physician were intertwined. With their traditional social structures largely destroyed by depopulation, and the priest-physicians totally helpless if not dead, it was little wonder that the survivors also abandoned their own gods for the Christian God, who was obviously sparing the Spaniards this divine wrath.

Divine will aside, the biological laws of nature and evolution were clearly favoring the white man. But perhaps not entirely. For at exactly the same time as the American Indians were being decimated by European microorganisms, something very unwelcome was suddenly ravaging Europe.

> It was a pestilence ne'er to be found at all
> In verse or in prose, in science or in story,
> So evil and perverse and cruel past control,
> Exceedingly contagious, and in filth so prodigal,
> So strong to hold its own, there is little got in glory;
> And it makes one dark in feature and obscure in countenance,
> Hunchback'd and indisposed, and seldom much at ease,
> And it makes one pained and crippled in such sort as never was,
> A scoundrel sort of thing, which also doth commence
> In the rascalliest place that man has.

So runs (in translation) just one of the seventy-four stanzas that make up the poem *Tratado sobre las Pestiferas Bubas,* published in 1498. Its author was Franscisco Lopez de Villalobos, the son and grandson of eminent Jewish physicians. At the time he was still a medical student at the University of Salamanca. But within ten years he would be court physician to King Ferdinand of Spain (and later to the Italian Charles V and his successor Philip II, having been hounded out of Spain by the Inquisition). Villalobos said of this ravaging disease, *"no vista jamas"* "never seen before," and pointed out that he could find nothing comparable in all the extant works of Avicenna.

Five years earlier, in 1493, a prominent Barcelona physician, Dr. Ruy Diaz de Isla, had reported treating the local inhabitants for a hitherto unknown *morbo sepentino* ("It is a grave malady which ulcerates and cor-rupts the flesh, breaks and destroys the bones, and cuts and shrinks the tendons, and for all these reasons I give it this name"), which he was con-vinced Columbus's crew had just brought back from the New World. But a debate rages to this day among medical historians as to whether the dis-ease may in fact have been present in the Old World all along. Villalobos himself termed the new disease the Egyptian scab, "because it is as awful as the scab which God sent to punish us and make us repent." ("The Lord shall smite thee with the botch of Egypt, and with the emerods, and with the scab, and with the itch, whereof thou canst not be healed. The Lord shall smite thee with madness, and blindness . . ." Deuteronomy 28:27–28.) Descriptions of afflictions found in Leviticus and the Book of Job (ulcers accompanied by pains in the bones at night) likewise suggest that the 1493 pestilence was not an American import. A compromise view is that yaws, which is caused by *Treponema pertenue* very similar to the microorganism discovered by Schaudinn, had long been present in the Old World and had already evolved as a milder form of syphilis when Columbus brought back its deadly relative.

We have noted that, contrary to the popular conception, it is often not in the parasitic microorganism's evolutionary "interest" to quickly kill or seriously disable its host. A milder form or mutation of the germ, which infects the host while still permitting him or her to be active, will tend to be spread among far more people. And to the extent one strain confers immunity against related strains, the more fatal variety gets edged out. But Columbus quite possibly brought back from the New World a particularly virulent *treponema* against which the Europeans, despite their previous contact with yaws, would for generations to come have far less communal immunity than the Indians.

All this unfortunately coincided with increased movement of traders and armies as Europe awoke to the Renaissance. The year after Columbus's return, Charles VIII of France crossed the Alps into Italy at the head of a multinational force of 36,000 mercenaries and 800 *puellæpublicae* (ladies of easy virtue), including Spaniards who had been to the New World. The conquering army lay siege to Naples but was soon decimated and in full retreat, not before enemy arms but before a ravaging scourge. The survivors disbanded to all corners of Europe and brought the disease with them. It manifested itself in Rome and the Vatican, where in the course of history it would strike at least three popes as well as an assortment of lesser clergy. It made its appearance in the Low Lands with the arrival of Spanish troops in 1496 and was prevalent from Scotland to Russia by the following year. The pandemic would claim some 100,000 victims and continue in its often rapidly fatal form for another fifty years or so. Already in 1496 we find Albrecht Dürer producing a woodcut of one of its victims, while a six-teenth-century representation of the disease depicts the "high and mighty Queen of the Fountain of Love" as vanquisher of whole armies.

Since no country particularly wanted to take credit for the scourge, the English called it the "French disease," the French the "Italian disease," the Dutch the "Spanish pox," and the Italians, somewhat undecidely, the "French disease" *and* the "Spanish disease." For their part, the Spanish called it (rather more accurately, if one accepts the Columbus hypothesis) the "disease of Hispaniola." As it spread eastward, the Poles christened it the "German sickness," and the Muscovites the "Polish disease." This naming process would continue all the way to the Pacific, where the Japanese called it the "Chinese ulcer."

In time-honored tradition, the Jews, too, were accused of spreading the new disease. It was their *schlimazel* to have been expelled from Spain in the very year Columbus's soldiers and sailors presumably were acquiring the *Treponema pallidum* microorganism. The infected Spanish mercenaries and their *puellae publicae* were therefore roving across Europe at the very time the Jewish exiles were migrating in search of a new home. So the scourge also became known as the "peste of the Marranos." Yet at least one contemporary medical observer, the Spanish exile Isaac Abravanel who settled in Italy, stated unequivocally that the disease "is not found among the Jews." It may at least be fairly said that the advent of scientific statistics in later centuries has shown the generally quite lower incidence of venereal disease among Jewish populations.

The doctors, whatever their nationality or prejudices, felt they needed a more learned-sounding term with which to impress their patients. It was, somewhat ironically, a French physician, Jacques de Bethencourt, who coined the term *morbus Gallicus* (Latin for "French disease"), apparently since the army that besieged Naples, though international in composition, marched under the banner of the French king Charles VIII. In 1530 Girolamo Fracastoro—the physician who speculated on the existence of invisible pathogenic germs—turned his hand to poetry and composed an epic in which a vengeful sun god strikes down a shepherd called Syphilis with a disease that in the future would bear his name. In the course of time, however, "syphilis" came to have such an ominous ring that doctors avoided its use in the presence of patients in favor of a more neutral Latin term, *lues*, meaning simply "pestilence," but that in fact was a shortened form of *lues venerea* (venereal pestilence).

Naming the disease was one thing. Figuring out what caused it was something else. Unlike many other illnesses, the transmission process of syphilis did not in most cases present any missing links, for its venereal nature was readily apparent to physicians and laymen alike. But exactly *what* was transmitted to cause the disease? Within the framework of the ancient concept of the four humors, Renaissance doctors assumed the transfer of a venom that "infects the substance of the blood and the natural spirits and is transmitted to all parts by the corruption of the humors, giving rise to a multitude of bad qualities in them." Also to be considered were "some particular circumstances, such as heat, rubbing, coition at an inopportune moment, venereal orgasm, contact between impure humors, the special virulence of a courtesan's menses, etc." (As for astrological factors—exemplified by the zodiac signs appearing above the head of the syphilis sufferer in Dürer's woodcut—we find Villalobos warning that "when we wish to consummate the act of Venus and Mars, we should ensure that Saturn, who is an unlucky companion, is absent.")

Although, as we have seen, the germ theory of contagious disease did not gain general acceptance until late in the nineteenth century, and the pathogen of syphilis was not discovered until early in the twentieth, there were some antecedents. Early in the eighteenth century, after a professor of chemistry at the University of Montpellier had speculated about "tiny living worms which produce eggs by copulating and can multiply readily," trustworthy surgeons told of seeing minuscule vermicular creatures teeming on syphilitic chancres. Beginning with the French microscopist Donné in 1837, there were some reported sightings of a spiral-like microbe in syphilitic lesions, which might seem to deserve some special credence, since this is indeed the shape of the syphilis pathogen. But as Jacob Henle pointed out in his classic paper on contagion, Donné's vibrio microbe was known to appear in some nonsyphilitic ulcers and pus and to be absent in syphilitic lesions when kept clean. In 1841 and 1842, the three Jewish physician-microscopists, Gabriel Valentin, Robert Remak, and David Gruby independently reported seeing peculiar corkscrew-shaped microorganisms in the blood of frogs and fish, to which Gruby gave the name *Trypanosoma*, and which, as we have noted, have a morphology similar to the *Treponema* of syphilis discovered by Schaudinn in 1905. At the time, however, before the rise of the germ theory, the prevailing opinion was that these trypanosomes were not contagious pathogens but rather sperm-like creatures produced by the host's own body.

As varied as were the doctors' theories of the etiology of syphilis through the centuries, their treatment of choice remained surprisingly constant, for it was on the alchemist's staple, mercury, that generation after generation relied. Its origins are somewhat obscure. In 1615 Miguel Cervantes wrote sarcastically in *Don Quixote* that "Virgil forgot to tell us who was the first man in the world to have a cold in the head or the first to take inunctions for the French disease." In Fracastoro's epic poem on syphilis, which pretends to draw from ancient mythology, a character is cured by bathing three times in a stream of quicksilver poured over him by a nymph. In reality, however, it seems that mercury was known to Galen and, although he discredited it, was used by the Arabs for dermatoses and even leprosy. In 1363 Guy de Chauliac at the University of Montpellier concocted an ointment of gum-resin, yellow lead oxide, extract of wild dephinium, old pig's fat, and about 10 percent mercury for scabies. And so it was not illogical at the end of the next century for a Heidelberg professor, Konrad Schelling, to propose the use of mercury for the dermatological sores of syphilis. This was to remain the basic treatment for the next 400 years—to be sure, with certain refinements, beginning with the discovery by a contemporary physician, Giovanni de Vigo, that the addition of live frogs supposedly improved the quality of the quicksilver ointment.

The use of mercury was not limited to topical application. When in 1537 a notorious Algerian pirate called Barbarossa heard that Francis I of France had acquired *morbus Gallicus,* he sent the king a present of pills made of mercury plus rhubarb, amber, musk, and flour. With Francis's royal endorsement, the tablets became all the rage. Also in use from the sixteenth century onward was the smoke closet, in which the patient inhaled steaming mercury vapor and sweat profusely. This method was still standard treatment 200 years later, with Herman Boerhaave of Leiden prescribing that his syphilitic patients produce three liters of sweat and saliva a day. And it would endure for two centuries more. The early eighteenth century saw the introduction by the English physician Thomas Dover of orally administered mercury in its metallic form. The rationale was that since the globules were defecated unchanged, the patient was spared the unpleasant physical side effects although somehow, supposedly, the healing power would still be maintained. There were, in any case, unpleasant social side effects. In one instance, the gentleman partner of a lady at a dance, thinking she had dropped her necklace, reached down only to find to his confusion and her embarrassment that the "pearls" were globules of voided metallic mercury. With the introduction of syringes early in the nineteenth century, the liquid metal was injected subcutaneously. That the treatment, in whatever form, was never a short affair is indicated by the old quip, "You spend one night with Venus and six months with Mercury."

To the extent there was theory underlying these remedies, it was based on the restoration of the balance among the four humors. The sweating process purged the body of an excess humor and hence, of the disease. Furthermore, in the context of the overlay of Medieval astrology and alchemy, mercury was of particular significance. In reality, quicksilver may have had a certain power to combat dermatological lesions. But since the local manifestations of primary syphilis often clear up spontaneously within a few weeks, the fact that they also disappeared under mercury treatment is unimpressive. Certainly, this could not be taken as proof that lues had actually been purged from the body as a whole. Furthermore, the treatment was often worse than the disease itself, the presumed healing dose being much too close to the lethal dose. Centuries earlier, the Islamic physician Rhazes had shown by tests on his pet monkey the poisonous effects of mercury, including (short of death) abdominal pains and teeth falling out. The famed sixteenth-century French writer (and sometime physician) Rabelais expressed the plight of mercury patients thus: "Their teeth dance like the jacks of little pairs of organs or virginals when they are played upon, and they foam with their very throats like a boar which the mongrel mastiff-hounds have driven in."

On balance, one may pretty much agree with the writer who stated: "The use of mercury treatment of syphilis may have been the most colossal hoax ever perpetrated in the history of a profession which has never been free of hoaxes." Indeed, syphilis can be said to have helped fulfill the ancient alchemist's dream of turning a rather common metal (mercury) into gold. It also bequeathed to the English language the enduring term "quack," from "quacksalver," someone who rubs in quicksilver salve. A story is told of a barber-surgeon in Paris who was found praying before the statue of Charles VIII, the leader of the 1494 siege of Naples. When taken to task because the statue was not that of a saint, the medic replied that the king was nevertheless holy to him, since "this man has given me an income of seven thousand lire." One may take some comfort from the fact that at least the members of this lower caste of barber-surgeons, who were charged with the actual rubbing in of the ointment, suffered as much as their patients from diarrhea, colic, and other effects of mercury poisoning.

Other concoctions were tried that, if not more effective, were at least less harmful. These were commonly drawn from the folk medicine accumulated through the ages by indigenous peoples around the world. Remedies from the Americas, the presumed original source of the scourge, were particularly popular, perhaps due to the religious belief that where disease naturally occurs, the Lord also provides natural sources of cure. In 1519, the German humanist Ulrich von Hutten introduced the bark of the West Indian tree *gauiacum* as the wonder drug for syphilis since, taken internally, it induced heavy sweating in the patient without his having to undergo the ordeal of the smoke closet. Its use was encouraged by certain of the clergy, who called it *lignum sanctum* (holy wood). The powerful Fugger banking house, which had a monopoly on the import of the bark from the New World, is said to have used its influence to censor a vicious attack on the wood by Paracelsus. The pro-*gauiacum* lobby could take little comfort, however, from the fact that von Hutten himself died of syphilis at the age of 35, and the Fuggers wisely hedged their bets by also gaining control of the Spanish mercury mines.

The sixteenth century also saw introduced into the antisyphilis pharmacopoeia sarsaparilla from America and the "China root" (smilax sinesis) brought from Goa by the Portuguese. A later wonder drug, publicized in the authoritative British medical journal *The Lancet*, was potassium oxide, which supposedly had mercury's power to combat the dermatological symptoms without its often lethal side-effects. A look at the medical journals and the popular press of the nineteenth century reveals advertisements by drug companies (many of whose names are familiar to us today as highly respected and reputable) offering tonics with exotic names like "Berberis aquiform" and "Iodia" from places ranging from California to the East Indies, promising relief from the ravages of syphilitic infection. As microbe-hunting came into fashion, one French quack, adept at slight-of-hand and the switching of slides, gave demonstrations through the microscope of what we today call antibodies, supposedly tracking down and destroying syphilis animalcules in the blood.

All these breakthroughs notwithstanding, syphilis kept claiming its toll of human lives, and it has been estimated that in the nineteenth century as much as 10 percent of the overall European population was syphilitic—with an even higher proportion in the cities. Among the many famous men to succumb to lues in the eighteenth and nineteenth centuries were the musician Schumann; the writers Heine, Baudlaire, Flaubert, and Dostoevski; the painter Manet; and the philosopher Nietzsche. The last case is a classic example of a terminal stage of syphilis—*dementia praecox*—which can lead to delusion, paralysis, amnesia, and finally madness. A particularly unfortunate case involved the London surgeon John Hunter. In 1786, following in the tradition set a century before by his great compatriot Thomas Sydenham of distinguishing the various diseases and detailing their clinical course, Hunter courageously infected himself with the pus of a gonorrhea patient to test his hypothesis that syphilis and gonorrhea were two manifestationsof the same disease. Unfortunately, the patient happened also to be suffering from lues. Hunter indeed contracted both diseases at once and published his observations. Thus his bold experiment set venereology back several decades. In 1832 the French physician Phillipe Ricord clearly established the distinctness of syphilis and gonorrhea through a series of, it is said, 1,626 inoculations (prudently never on himself).

Few of the physicians mentioned up to now in the story of syphilis were Jewish. But with the dramatic explosion in medical science in the second half of the nineteenth century, particularly in Germany, Jews were in the forefront of the fight against venereal disease. One reason for this was that venereology fell under the domain of dermatology—one of the more marginal specialisms into which Jews were channeled, due to obstacles placed in their way in the mainstream fields of internal medicine and surgery. In venereology, as in the broader field of dermatology, the Jews could at least take pride in a medical heritage extending back thousands of years. Leviticus (15:2) describes gonorrhea, stating that "Everyman, from whose flesh [penis] there issues a flux, is unclean," and prescribes various disinfection measures and isolation (yet, oddly enough, doesn't prohibit coitus). Further descriptions and regulations were provided in the Midrash. Now, scores of generations later, Albert Neisser, who had been Paul Ehrlich's secondary school classmate in Breslau, described the whole genus of paired spherical (diplococcus) bacteria that came to be called *Neisseria*, most species of which are harmless, but certainly not *Neisseria gonorrhoeae,* which he isolated in 1879. In the first years of the twentieth century, August Wassermann devised a complement fixation test for the detection of syphilis even in asymptomatic patients. The scion of a prominent Jewish banking family in Bamberg, Wassermann was financially independent enough to work unremunerated for ten years at Robert Koch's Institute of Infectious Diseases in Berlin, before finally receiving an appointment as head of the serum department. The general principles of complement fixation, though not the syphilis test itself, were first discovered by the gentile physician Jules Bordet of the Pasteur Institute in Brussels. As a legacy of the Franco-Prussian War and the Pasteur-Koch rivalry, the French to this day call the test Bordet-Wassermann. The Germans, for their part, not only named the test after Wassermann alone but soon ennobled him, Jew though he was, and placed him—now August *von* Wassermann—at the head of the new Kaiser Wilhelm Institute of Experimental Therapy in Dalhem.

But as for curing or eradicating syphilis, the early twentieth-century physicians remained just as helpless as their Renaissance colleagues, despite all the breakthroughs in medical science of the preceding decades. Pasteur's principle of vaccination with attenuated or killed microbes was of no use. In fact, even someone who has completely recovered from a full-blown case of syphilis has no immunity against contracting the disease at his very next sexual encounter. Unlike diphtheria, the syphilis microbe does not produce toxins, so there can be no antitoxin serums with which to combat it. And unlike the plague, anthrax, childbed fever,and the like, there have never been missing links in the chain of transmission needing to be discovered. It had taken the Renaissance physicians very little time to determine the predominantly venereal means by which syphilis was passed from person to person. The disease is said to have brought an abrupt end to the bath culture that had flourished in the Middle Ages. But warnings to refrain from illicit sex as a preventative measure, beginning with a strong admonition by the great theologian and humanist Erasmus of Rotterdam around 1500 ("If it were up to me, in the interests of the State I would let them marry and then I would have them burned," declares a personage in one of his works with regard to a syphilitic couple) were not well heeded, least of all by the clergy, and it is said that Erasmus himself was stricken by lues. With the failure of biological methods for the prevention or cure of syphilis, other means would have to be sought. If mercury, in all its variations, did not work, or if this cure was worse than the disease itself; then perhaps some other chemotherapeutic agent would lift the scourge.

Paul Ehrlich, though not a venereologist or dermatologist, was well aware of the four centuries of failure to tame syphilis with the poisonous heavy metal mercury. Yet he was now seized by a dream of transforming the poisonous heavy metal arsenic from the traditional weapon of murderers into an assassin of the spirochetes of syphilis. Always a workaholic, Ehrlich now outdid even himself. Smoking twenty-five of his imported black cigars a day (and complaining that his salary was hardly enough to pay for them), he kept on drawing for his skeptical staff of expert chemists fantastic diagrams of imaginary arsenical remedies. A happy optimist, even when he was running around the laboratory cursing the negative results and yelling Latin phrases at his staff, Ehrlich also became more and more the absent-minded professor, especially in his perception of time. He'd mail a letter to a drug company one evening and send a telegram the next morning asking why he hadn't yet received a reply. He'd send postcards to *himself* in an attempt to remember those upcoming social commitments that he couldn't avoid.

The early marriage of his two daughters at the ages of 19 and 20 was something Ehrlich did not oppose—in fact, he is said to have encouraged it—since this would free him from some social obligations. But the honors that were being constantly heaped upon him brought other commitments in line with proper etiquette. Aside from the Nobel and other prizes, there were five honorary doctorates and professorships (including ones from the University of Chicago and from Oxford) and honorary memberships in a dozen learned associations such as the Royal Society in London. Then there came the highest Prussian decoration, carrying with it the title Medical Privy Councilor and the custom of being addressed as "Your Excellency." It is said that Paul Ehrlich carried his medals around in a box, never knowing which ones to wear on what occasion. Given the choice, if he had to relax, His Excellency preferred a few *Seidels* of beer with visitors and colleagues and, before dropping off to sleep at night, a few pages from the novels of the Frenchmen Dumas, de Balzac, Anatole France, and de Maupassant, the last of whom had died of syphilis in an insane asylum a decade earlier.

Paul Ehrlich knew that the Pasteur Institute in Paris and the Rockefeller Institute in New York were working along lines similar to his own. From France came Trypan blue, an improvement on Trypan red, and from America Tryparsamide, which Ehrlich had to admit was quite superior to Atoxyl. One obvious problem for Ehrlich was a meager working budget of only 100,000 marks a year. The Georg-Speyer-Haus would in time receive far greater funds from Jewish philanthropists such as Mathilde de Rothschild, the Stern family, and the New York Schiffs of newspaper publishing fame (relatives of the 1848 revolutionary, Dr. Moritz Schiff). But at the time, the Rockefeller and Pasteur Institutes were far better funded, the latter by the Jews Daniel Osiris Iffla and Mme. Furtado Heine of the French "haute finance."

Yet in one of those ironies in the history of science, it appears that the restricted financial circumstances of the Georg-Speyer-Haus—combined with Paul Ehrlich's optimistic fanaticism and the role of chance—led to the development of the first cure for syphilis. In 1907, one of Ehrlich's associates, Dr. Ludwig Benda, had produced at Ehrlich's direction a certain nitrophenylarsenic acid compound, but due to the lack of the necessary vacuum apparatus for reducing the compound, it could not undergo the proper testing against mal de Caderas. If such apparatus had been available and the tests carried out, the compound might well have proved ineffective against the trypanosomes of mal de Caderas and have been discarded, never to be tried against the *treponemata* of syphilis. But as Benda's compound had never been tested, it was more or less rediscovered in 1909, reduced with newly acquired vacuum apparatus, and prepared for trial.

On August 31 of that year, Ehrlich and another super-methodical Japanese co-worker, the bacteriologist Sahachiro Hata, stood before the cage of a rabbit infected with large syphilitic sores on its scrotum. Into the rodent's ear vein went an injection of this drug 606 (its name derived from the fact that it was the six-hundred-sixth compound tested). By the next day no trace of syphilis spirochetes was to be found in the rabbit's blood, and the sores were already drying up and healing. Wrote Ehrlich, "It is evident from these experiments that, if a large enough dose is given, the spirochetes can be destroyed absolutely and immediately with a single injection!"

But as Ehrlich's assistants remarked, "It is still a long way to the sick bed." It wasn't until the end of the year that Ehrlich felt himself far enough to write to his friend Dr. Konrad Alt in Uchtspringe, with the request, "Will you be so good as to try this new preparation, 606, in human beings with syphilis?" When Alt reported miraculous results, there followed something then unprecedented in the history of pharmacology: a clinical trial not with tens but with tens of thousands of patients. The Georg-Speyer-Haus produced 65,000 doses of Salvarsan—"safe" or "healing arsenic," the trade name for 606 that Ehrlich thought up together with the management of his sponsor, Farbenwerke Hoechst—under extraordinarily strict conditions. (Not only was there the constant danger of explosion from the vapors, but the least trace of contamination from the air could oxidize the safe arsenic back into a form hardly less poisonous than that traditionally used by murderers.) These doses were supplied free of charge to clinics and hospitals in Germany, while the team at the Georg-Speyer-Haus waited in suspense for feedback.

At the 82nd Congress of German Physicists and Physicians in Königsberg, reports were presented—to the thunderous applause of the participants—of long-term bedridden patients who were up and about only hours after a shot of Salvarsan; of a man with syphilis of the throat, previously fed on liquid food, who received a shot of Salvarsan at two o'clock in the afternoon and was able to eat a sausage for supper; of emaciated syphilis sufferers who gained thirty pounds after Salvarsan treatment; of a woman who after years of morphine every night to ease the pain of syphilis in her bones was now able to sleep unsedated.

While the medical community was ecstatic, certain religious groups were less kindly disposed. If any disease in recent centuries was still viewed according to the primeval and biblical concept of punishment for sin, then it was syphilis. Shortly after Columbus's return from the New World, the Holy Roman Emperor and King of Germany Maximillian I issued an edict declaring the new pestilence to be divine retribution. In the American Colonies in the early eighteenth century, the firebrand preacher Cotton Mather, who was broadminded enough to advocate inoculation against smallpox, declared syphilis "the Just Judgment of God . . . reserved for our late Ages." Now, with a cure in sight, a highly conservative Russian newspaper wrote sarcastically, "No more danger! Down with the family! No need to toil in the sweat of one's brow to support it! Long live prostitution—the like of which has not been seen since the downfall of Rome!" Some such protests had anti-Semitic overtones. But these voices were very much on the fringe. Almost all the German and international press reported the taming of the four-century-old scourge with the greatest of superlatives: "A real miracle!;" "Astounding results!;" "Unbelievable cure!;" "A great blessing!" One German newspaper went so far as to write, "The Jewish people have brought forth two great men: Christ and Ehrlich."

Such praise would only be embarrassing to the shy little professor who (as one contemporary account put it) "slight, hardly noticeable, awkward in his demeanor as he is, seems more like a lyrical poet." Furthermore, Ehrlich was soon preoccupied with the fact that for every couple of thousand miraculous cures, there came a report of the magic bullet backfiring. A patient injected from the identical batch of ampoules that had cured so many other people would experience kidney blockage, stiffening of legs, convulsions, and even death. Another two years were spent producing over 300 more manipulations of the 606 formula. Then in 1911 compound 914, christened Neosalvarsan, was arrived at—more soluble and more easily injectable than 606, with twice the curative power and yet a lower arsenic content. But even 914 was not quite the *therapia magna sterilans* Paul Ehrlich hoped for. Repeated injections were often required, and there was still some risk of side effects, such as liver and kidney dysfunction and the occasional fatal shock reactions. Yet it became the sovereign treatment of syphilis for a generation, slashing within a decade the scourge's incidence in England and France by half; in the Netherlands, Belgium, Sweden, and Denmark by three-quarters and more, and showing promise of combating yaws and relapsing fever—diseases caused by spirochete cousins of *Treponema pallidum.*

In the classic novel *Arrowsmith,* published in 1925, Sinclair Lewis has young Dr. Martin Arrowsmith telling his fiancée, Leora: "Up to the present, even in the work of Ehrlich, most research has been largely a matter of trial and error, the empirical method, which is the opposite of the scientific method, by which one seeks to establish a general law governing a group of phenomena so that he may predict what will happen." Indeed, with regard to the Salvarsan miracle, Ehrlich himself once replied to a worshiping admirer: "Ach, my dear colleague, for seven years of misfortune, I had one moment of good luck." Yet, as Martin Arrowsmith's remark implies, it was Paul Ehrlich, more than anyone else, who set the stage for the breathtakingly rapid advances in medical science later in the twentieth century—advances that Ehrlich himself would soon no longer be around to witness. Suffering from diabetes, smoking twenty-five cigars a day, and allowing himself no rest, it was clear that Paul would not achieve the longevity for which previous Ehrlichs had been renowned and that his 60th birthday might be his last. On that occasion, the Frankfurt post office had to hire extra help to cope with the flood of telegrams to be delivered to the Georg-Speyer-Haus on the recently renamed Paul-Ehrlich-Strasse.

It was around this time that Paul Ehrlich, who had done so much for all humanity, undertook to do something special for the Jewish people. The occasion was a visit from Dr. Chaim Weizmann, the future first president of the State of Israel. Weizmann was himself a great chemist and there was much overlap between his scientific work and that of Ehrlich. Weizmann's doctoral dissertation some fifteen years earlier had in fact been on research into dyestuffs, and since then he had harnessed the process of bacterial fermentation for the production of synthetic rubber. But the intended purpose of Weizmann's meeting with Ehrlich had nothing to do with anilines or polymers. Weizmann was working for the establishment of a Hebrew University in Jerusalem, and Baron Edmond de Rothschild in Paris was prepared to back the plan, on condition that Paul Ehrlich be recruited to head the university committee. Through his contacts with Ehrlich's son-in-law, Weizmann was sandwiched in between Ehrlich's many other interviews. As Weizmann relates, Ehrlich's one-track mind, together with his qualities of the absent-minded professor, made for a humorous if somewhat delicate situation:

> Ehrlich was then at the height of his phenomenal career, and utterly unapproachable by ordinary mortals. I had heard, moreover, that he took little interest in Jewish matters, and indeed in any matters outside the scope of his medical research. . . . Ehrlich knew that I was a chemist, but he did not know what I was coming to see him about. He therefore plunged at once into the subject of his research. . . . It was fascinating; but it would have been more so if I had not been wondering how I could switch the conversation to the purpose of my visit. I listened respectfully while he unfolded part of his theory of chemistry—for he was a great chemist as well as a great medical man. He spoke of chemistry as a weapon with which one could shoot at diseases. . . . At last I took my courage in my hands, and steered the conversation cautiously in my direction. . . . He listened for a few moments and then exclaimed: "But why [in] Jerusalem?" . . . Somehow I had caught his interest, and my excitement rose as I saw that he was following my argument with increasing attention.

The interview, which was scheduled to last only ten minutes or so, went on for an hour at the Institute and then continued over dinner at the Ehrlich home. A few days later Ehrlich went to Paris to meet with Baron de Rothschild and wired Weizmann a Passover telegram conveying his acceptance of the chairmanship of the university committee. Today, a Paul Ehrlich Pavilion, established by the government of the Federal German Republic, stands at the Weizmann Institute of Science in Rehovoth as a fitting reminder of the collaboration of these two great chemists in the cause of the future State of Israel. A plaque there bears a quote from Weizmann: "The name of Ehrlich will now be inscribed in letters of gold in the history of our people, as it fights for better days." It is dated April 1914, the month of their meeting. Soon after, however, world events would dramatically disrupt their plans.

Whereas Bismarck's initial policies were overtly aggressive, after the humiliating of Austria, the annexation of some Danish and French territory, and the unifying of Germany, the Iron Chancellor turned to a *Realpolitik* and worked through alliances, diplomatic maneuvering, and some blustering to maintain the status quo of a continent under Germany hegemony.

But the ascension of Kaiser Wilhelm II to the German throne in 1888 and the resignation by a disgruntled Bismarck two years later marked a change in course. The constitution of the German Reich vested substantial power in the monarch and allowed much influence to be exerted on German foreign and domestic affairs by forces outside the democratically elected Reichstag, particularly the military. While all Germany was justly proud of its great scientific and industrial accomplishments, elements around the Kaiser sought to establish the Fatherland as an even more powerful political and military force. Envious of the British and French overseas empires, Germany belatedly acquired colonies in West, East, and Southern Africa and a collection of islands in the South Pacific (all of which, predictably, drained vastly more money from the German economy than they ever contributed). With an overseas empire of its own, Germany, the traditional land power, now hastily built a large naval fleet to outdo the French and even challenge British supremacy on the high seas.

In August of 1914, a few months after Paul Ehrlich's acceptance of Weizmann's invitation to head the committee of the proposed Hebrew University, Austrian Archduke Franz Ferdinand was assassinated by a lone Serbian nationalist in Serajevo, part of the Austro-Hungarian Dual Monarchy. The German leaders encouraged their Austrian ally to make harsh demands on the neighboring independent Serbian Republic, confident that if and when Russia came to the aid of their Serbian friends, Germany could demonstrate once and for all to the Russians and their treaty-bound French allies who the master of Europe was. When the German forces invaded neutral Belgium in their unsuccessful attempt to deal a first-round knock-out blow to the French, England honored her international commitments and joined the Allied side. (So great, incidentally, was Germany's lead in synthetic dyestuffs that Britain, the country where the process was first discovered, had to resort to buying German khaki dyes for its uniforms via neutral Switzerland.)

Paul Ehrlich found it hard to believe that such a thing could actually occur. "But this war is pure madness," he exclaimed upon first hearing the news. "No good can come of it!" To him, only waging war on pathogenic germs made sense. And he probably had his doubts about the claims of the German state secretary to justify the declaration of war on France that "a French physician with the aid of two disguised officers attempted to infect the wells of Metz with cholera bacilli." (At least, there was no mention of the well-poisoner in this old canard being Jewish.) As Ehrlich remarked to his friend and fellow Jewish microbe hunter August von Wassermann, "If a person is not decent by nature, then he ought to be for the sake of common sense," and this applied to statesmen as well. Only months before the outbreak of war, Ehrlich had been lionized at the seventeenth International Congress of Medicine in London. He, in turn, had spoken of the "outstanding and eminent position England has taken and still holds in the fight against infectious diseases," and noted with adulation the past British medical greats Edward Jenner and Lord Lister, as well as the more recent microbe hunters, Sir Donald Ross and Sir David Bruce, and Ehrlich's personal friend and former student, Almroth Wright. He had ended his address by applauding the "thousands [who] have come from all corners of the world to bear witness that in science all boundaries between nations have fallen"

Yet with the war now a fait accompli, Ehrlich was touched by the patriotism felt by so many German Jews. In his private correspondence he stated, "Germany has a clear conscience," and in public he was among the distinguished German scientists who signed the "Manifesto to the Civilized World," which sought to clear the Fatherland of blame for starting the war. True, the manifesto conceded, Germany had been the first power to declare war, but hadn't the Russian hordes been the first to mobilize? As for the violation of neutral Belgium—well, it would have been military suicide to have done otherwise. (Ehrlich's fellow German-Jewish venereologist Albert Neisser went considerably further than anything stated in the manifesto and advocated the Pan-Germanist aim of annexation of conquered territory.)

As the international tragedy unfolded, the fragile health of the chainsmoking, diabetic workaholic, Paul Ehrlich, declined. Now, disheartened by the war, he succumbed on August 20, 1915, to coronary sclerosis. Such was his greatness that across the hostile North Sea the *Times* of London declared, "The vast number of problems he set himself bear witness to the strength of his imagination. He opened new doors to the unknown, and the whole world at this hour is his debtor." Dr. Lewis H. Marcks of the United States, which two years later would likewise face Germany on the battlefield, eulogized at the funeral at the Jewish cemetery in Frankfurt, "I feel I'm acting in the spirit of the entire American world of medicine when in this place I give expression to the feelings of veneration and gratitude for Paul Ehrlich with which America's physicians are filled."

Standing before the gravestone of marble from Paul Ehlich's native Silesia, flanked by columns bearing the star of David and the staff of Aesculapius, the rabbi Dr. Lazarus spoke:

The German fatherland looks with pride on this man who spread the fame of Germany throughout the rest of the world. And yet, the man's achievements and successes are crowned by that most German of strengths: loyalty. In this virtue, above all others, the German meets the Jew. Paul Ehrlich was loyal because he was a German. Paul Ehrlich was loyal because he was—and remained—a Jew. For this reason German Jewry honors him as one who, by his influence and character, by his achievements and life, helped to root many millennia of Jewish loyalty firmly in the soil of German culture. As the Scriptures say, "A man of loyalty, rich in blessings." That is how Paul Ehrlich lived. No, that is how he lives in our memory. And so he will continue to live in the memory of every age and nation.

Such was once the spirit of German Jewry.

Chapter 13
Vienna, City of Dreams

Why did it [psychoanalysis] have to wait for an absolutely irreligious Jew?
—Sigmund Freud.

*T*he swift defeat of the Austrians by Bismarck's Prussian army at the battle of Sadowa in 1866 and his excluding them from the unified Reich four years later left Austria very much part of the Habsburg Dual Monarchy with Hungary. This supranational state, which would endure until its breakup in the aftermath of World War I, had decided advantages for Jews both within and outside of Austria proper. The free trade across the whole empire encouraged commerce, a traditional forte of the Jews, and led to their upward mobility in the course of the nineteenth century. Jews everywhere in the Austro-Hungarian Empire—including the large Slavic regions of Czechoslovakia, Croatia, and southern Poland—also enjoyed the benevolent protection of Franz Josef I (Ferencz Joszef to the Hungarians; *der Judenkaiser* or "Jew Emperor" to anti-Semites).

Vienna, being the capital of an Austria not submerged in the German Reich, attained its greatest intellectual, cultural, and architectural splendor in the second half of the nineteenth century. Franz Josef personally saw to the building of a new Imperial Palace facing two new museums, plus a Reichstag Building, an Imperial Theater, and an Imperial Opera House. The great industrial expansion brought new wealth and prominence to the bourgeoisie. The capital broke through its former city walls, which were demolished to make way for the magnificent tree-lined boulevard, the Ringstrasse.

This was the Vienna in which Sigmund Freud grew up. In 1867, in the wake of Austria's defeat at the hands of Prussia, a new constitution was adopted that ushered in the *Bürgerministerium*. The liberal government (in the European, rather than American, sense), elected by a franchise based among other things on the amount of taxes paid, was drawn largely from the powerful new middle class (whence came the name *Bürger*, or "bourgeois") and included some Jewish ministers. In his *Interpretation of Dreams,* Freud would later tell the story of how in the late '60s, when he was 11 or 12 years old, a street poet at Vienna's famous amusement park the Prater composed a verse declaring that Sigmund was destined for a cabinet post. Such a prediction would have been quite absurd a decade or so earlier, but not now when the portraits of the *Bürger* cabinet ministers were gracing the walls of the Freud home.

But the political climate soured in the decades following the stockmarket crash of 1873, for which liberal capitalism was blamed. On the left there emerged the Social Democratic Party of Viktor Adler, an apostate Jewish medical doctor whose practice had given him firsthand experience of the effects of rapid industrialization and urbanization on Vienna's workers. A former liberal, Dr. Adler continued in the liberal tradition of belief in reason and progress, as he used his personal wealth and his gift for oratory to establish discussion groups, adult-education programs, libraries, and newspapers to prepare the proletariat for their supposedly inevitable takeover of the reigns of power.

As the stockmarket fell, anti-Semitism rose, a sentiment to which the *fin-de-siècle* mayor of Vienna, Karl Lueger, was happy to appeal. Originally a liberal himself, albeit of the left-wing variety, Lueger attained prominence in the Christian Social Movement by exposing corruption, profiteering, and mismanagement, with particular emphasis on the wrongdoings of Jewish capitalists and Jewish liberal deputies. It was from the "little man" of Vienna—the petty bourgeois shopkeeper, artisan, and minor civil servant—that demagogic Lueger drew his greatest support, appealing to their worries about being squeezed out by big business and capital from the one side and organized labor from the other. And, of course, for the gentile shopkeeper there was always concern about competition from the Jews down the block.

In an age when the tradition of anticlericalism inherited from liberalism remained strong across much of the Austrian political spectrum, the word *Christian* in the name of Lueger's organization sooner signified anti-

Jewishness rather than a particularly strong orientation toward Christianity per se. Yet Jews who converted were spared the hostility of the Movement. Indeed, some Christian Socials were themselves apostate Jews and it is said that Lueger's own family tree included a Jewess who during a pogrom in the fifteenth century had accepted baptism over martyrdom. Lueger's famous quote, *"Wer Jude ist, das bestimme ich"* (I decide who's a Jew), was his way of saying that the Jews from whom he frequently accepted dinner invitations were in his eyes at least not offensively Jewish Jews. Indeed, although Lueger declared his antipathy toward the Hungarian Jews to be even stronger than his dislike of the Hungarian gentiles—it was he who coined the nickname "Judapest" for the Hungarian capital—he graciously conceded on at least one occasion that "our Viennese Jews are not so bad and we can't do without them." In turn, quite a few Jews shared the widespread admiration of their fellow Viennese for the program of public works initiated by *der schöne Karl* (handsome Karl, as Lueger was popularly known).

If some Jews were ambivalent toward Lueger, they hardly entertained such mixed feelings about Georg Ritter von Schönerer. Originally also a liberal, Schönerer went on to combine elements of liberalism with socialism, anti-Semitism, and (in contrast to Lueger, whose loyalty was to Austria, not Germany) pan-German nationalism. A central point of Schönerer's German National Union was that: "The removal of Jewish influence from all sections of public life is indispensable for carrying out the reforms aimed at." In overwhelmingly Catholic Austria, Schönerer embraced Lutheranism, the religion of the Prussians, and mixed it with a kind of Germanic paganism. Although he never had much success at the polls, Schönerer enjoyed a large following among professors, university students, and professionals resentful of Jewish successes. The young drifter in Vienna, Adolf Hitler, although certainly not a professional nor even a student (he had twice failed to gain admittance to the Academy of Art), would later write in *Mein Kampf* that his admiration for Schönerer even surpassed his admiration of Lueger.

One of the *bêtes noires* of anti-Semites was the "Judaized" Viennese press. Journalism, like medicine, was indeed a Jewish profession par excellence, in the German-speaking metropolises of Europe. In Vienna, Jews accounted for about half of all journalists. A violent attack by Schönerer and his stick-wielding followers on a Jewish-owned newspaper got him a jail sentence and the cancellation of the family's patent of nobility earned by his father.

At the time, one of Vienna's most distinguished Jewish journalists was Theodor Herzl, the editor of the prestigious *feuilleton* section of the *Neue Freie Presse* and later that paper's foreign correspondent in Paris. Although born in Budapest, his family was German-speaking and in his early days he was drawn to German nationalism and the mythologies of Richard Wagner. But the soured cultural and political climate eventually convinced this basically nonreligious man that he and his fellow Jews were intruders, or at best guests, in Europe and would be better served by joining together in a new exodus. Compounding the Jewish question was the matter of the several other non-German ethnic groups in the Austro-Hungary Empire. Lueger had it in for Hungarians in particular, and Schönerer played on the German Austrian's fear of encirclement by the Czechs, Slovenes, Serbs, Croats, and other Slavs, who constituted a decided majority in the Austrian half of the dual monarchy of Austro-Hungary. Many Jews in the predominantly Slavic and Hungarian parts of the empire were members of the German-speaking minority, and this made them a target for local anti-German, as well as anti-Jewish, feeling. Some Jews opted for assimilation to the majority ethnic communities in their regions—the remarkable contributions of Jews to Hungarian literature and culture in the late nineteenth and early twentieth centuries are a particular case in point. But in the Slavic regions, many Jewish schools were German-medium, and they even received aid from the Deutsche Schulverein, an organization supporting German schools in areas threatened by de-Germanization. And, of course, in German-speaking Austria proper, many Jews were enamored with German literature and culture and were even drawn to German nationalism—which led to their acute embarrassment at the many *Ostjuden* migrants in Vienna, who, although counted as fellow German-speakers for census purposes (Yiddish being a variety of German), seemed so backward in their idioms and customs.

All these factors—supranationalism, Austrian nationalism, pan-Germanism, Jewish Germanism, *Yiddishkeit*, and anti-Semitism—affected not only Viennese Jews in general, but Viennese Jewish doctors and med students in particular. Not the least of these was Sigmund Freud.

There had, of course, long been Jewish doctors in Vienna, especially in high places. In the sixteenth and seventeenth centuries the Austrian archdukes were served by the Jewish physicians Alvarez Nunez (Alvarez Nonnius

Hispanus) and Dr. Henriques, whose names tell of their Iberian origins. The archdukes may or may not have been relieved by a report from the medical faculty of the University of Vienna early in the seventeenth century that—contrary to what some radical Jew-baiters believed—Jewish physicians were not under religious obligation to hasten the death of each and every Christian patient they reasonably could, but merely one in ten.

Since Christian physicians were under no religious obligations to poison their patients, conversion to Catholicism had its perks for the Jewish doctor. This is well illustrated by the career of the seventeenth-century doctor Paul Weidner. After studying medicine in Padua, where Jews were more readily admitted, and then practicing in Udine and Venice, Weidner was called to serve as national physician in Carinthia (in present-day Austria)—quite an accomplishment in a region from which Jews had been barred since the previous century. But to further advance his career, Paul had himself and his family baptized by the bishop of Vienna in St. Stefan's Cathedral, an event that drew a massive crowd. This act gained Paul imperial protection and access to Emperor Ferdinand, who supported the publication of his works and elevated him to the nobility. Serving as professor at Vienna's medical faculty, Paul—now bearing the noble family name of von Billerburg—was thrice elected *rector magnificus* (president) of the university.

In the mid-eighteenth century, medicine at the University of Vienna experienced a period of minor glory under Dutch influence, as Gerard van Swieten, one of Herman Boerhaave's pupils brought to the Austrian royal court by Empress Maria Theresa, proceeded to reform the medical faculty along the model of Leiden and gathered around him another Boerhaave pupil, Anton de Haen, a pioneer in methodology, as well as the pharmacologist Anton Stoerck, the epidemiologist Maximillian Stoll, and the dermatologist Joseph von Plenck. Unbaptized Jews, however, were excluded. Only with the promulgation of the Tolerance Act by Emperor Josef II in 1781 was the way opened for Jews to study at the University of Vienna, and even then academic posts were restricted. An early nineteenth-century gentile ophthalmologist, as unhappy at such toleration as he was with the Jewish success in commerce and banking, declared the Jews to be "so identified with the spirit of capitalism [that they had] a much greater tendency to be quacks." But even if there was any truth to this, in an age when Viennese medicine had fallen under the spell of German *Naturphilosophie*, with its propensity to spin beautiful hypotheses on the basis of little or no data, the distinction between quack and mainstream doctor was an academic rather than practical matter. This was all the more so after Josef's successor, Leopold II, arbitrarily banned the use of microscopes in the university's anatomy curriculum.

But as in neighboring Germany, the advance of medical science in Austria would become dramatic as the nineteenth century progressed. As the main intellectual center of the Habsburg Empire, Vienna had the advantage over its German counterparts of also drawing the best and the brightest from the emperor's Czech and Hungarian domains. The most heroic of these met the tragic fate that so often awaits those who make their appearance too early on the stage of history. Vienna's rising eminence in medicine rested in large measure on meticulous postmortem dissections conducted at the university's teaching hospital, the Allgemeine Krankenhaus. In the 1840s a young Hungarian doctor at the hospital's maternity ward, Ignaz Semmelweis, using statistical compilations, reached the ironic conclusion that these very autopsies were inadvertently responsible for the postpartem deaths of countless mothers, whose wombs were contaminated by the examining hands of doctors and students coming directly from the dissecting room. Instituting a ritual of handwashing in a solution of lime chloride, Semmelweis dramatically reduced the number of deaths from childbed fever in the wards. Yet even though Jacob Henle had inaugurated the decade with his masterful publication on the role of microorganisms in contagion, the germ theory was still an obscure concept, and Semmelweis merely speculated about some indeterminate "putrid particles" as the possible culprits. Having no clear theory and being caught up in personal antagonisms with his superiors, Semmelweis was driven back to Hungary, where he eventually died in a lunatic asylum, still cursing the murderers who had rejected his reforms. (Semmelweis's non-Hungarian, rather Jewish-sounding name has led to some speculation about a non-Christian origin. But one must resist assuming that such a great and tragic medical figure just *had* to be Jewish.)

Fate was kinder to three Czech professors at the University of Vienna—Carl Rokitansky, Josef Skoda, and Ferdinand von Hebra (the last of whom was Jewish)—who were instrumental in elevating Vienna's medical faculty to world-class status. This process was given a boost by the revolution that swept Europe in 1848 and stirred up the med students and faculty to demand the implementation of reforms that up to then had existed only on paper.

Rokitansky, the master of the postmortem, compiled reams of data from the autopsy rooms at the Allgemeine Krankenhaus and thus elucidated the dynamics of disease processes. In an era that was seeing the beginnings of medical specialization, Rokitansky assembled data in the fields of dermatology, ophthalmology, otology, obstetrics, and gynecology. In the good old Germanic philosophical tradition of hypothesis spinning, he speculated that changes or abnormalities in blood proteins (crasis) were the etiology of transmittable disease, a hold-over from the ancient humoral theory. But this didn't hinder him from supporting Semmelweis's ill-fated struggle with the medical establishment. In the thoracic field, Vienna's great specialist was Skoda, a master diagnostician, who made important contributions to the art and science of auscultation and percussion, establishing the distinctions between heart sounds and murmurs.

As elsewhere in the German-speaking lands in the era of emerging specialisms, Jews were often marginalized by the prejudiced establishment into less mainstream fields. The most common of these was dermatology, so much so that it was sarcastically referred to as *Judenhaut* (Jew-skin). Yet at least the marginalized Jewish doctors in this field could draw upon a heritage extending back to biblical times. As we have seen, the ancient Hebrews were experts on analyzing the colors, textures, and changes of the various dermatological manifestations that fell under the collective term of *leprosy* (*tzaraath*). Similarly, the Midrash described the five dermatological scourges of man preordained at the time of creation: boils, scabs, bright spots, risings, and burnings. Now at the dawn of the age of modern medicine, the Jew Ferdinand von Hebra subjected various rashes to his microscopic scrutiny. He produced dermatology atlases that came into use all over the world and he described several new skin diseases, such as *erythema multiforme* and *dermatitis exfoliativa*. Hebra's pupil and son-in-law Mortiz Kaposi (né Kohn in the village of Kaposvar, from which he derived his new name) a *privatdozent* at the University of Vienna, distinguished, among other dermatological malignancies, the skin sarcoma that bears his name and would become well-known a century later with the AIDS epidemic.

Kaposi's dermatological writings were long on etiology and differential diagnosis but short and skeptical as to treatment. His talmudic forebears recommended smearing the skin patient with the juice of roasted Arzanian wheat stalks or else rubbing him with a concoction of cooked white and black snakes. Since then, whole arsenals of other skin remedies had been added to the *materia medica*. But Kaposi subscribed to the new Vienna's therapeutic nihilism—the opposition to the gratuitous prescribing of drugs whose effectiveness had never been proven. This approach contributed to the international fame of Vienna's medical faculty, which attracted physicians from many countries in the latter part of the nineteenth century, most notably from the United States, where the training for the degree of doctor of medicine was generally of a very low standard. It was many of the American doctors returning from that Vienna who laid the foundation for the preeminence of American medicine in the twentieth century. The therapeutic nihilism they acquired in Vienna found expression in Oliver Wendell Holmes's declaration in 1860, that "if the whole of the *materia medica* as now used could be sunk in the bottom of the sea, it would be all the better for mankind—and all the worse for the fishes."

Another marginal area into which the Jewish doctors of Vienna were channeled in the age of specialization was ophthalmology. It was in this field that one of the greatest Viennese-Jewish medical breakthroughs would come—a contribution second, perhaps, only to Freud's psychoanalysis—and one in which, oddly enough, Freud would play a pivotal role.

Interest in things ocular is well rooted in Jewish medical tradition. Leviticus (21:20) prohibits a high priest from serving in the temple if he "hath a blemish in his eye." In this connection much ink was used by the talmudic scholars in describing cloudings of the cornea and the pigmentations and positions of cataracts in human eyes—and also in the eyes of animals whose blemishes might render them unfit for sacrifice in the temple. Superstition mingled with wisdom as to the etiology of ocular afflictions in the Talmud. On the one hand, we learn that water at night contained demons that could cause blindness in the heedless drinker. On the other hand, there were prescriptions by the likes of Mar Samuel as to proper care of the head and the pronouncement of Rabbi Muna that "the unwashed hand that touches the eye in the morning is worthy of being cut off, for it causes blindness." Treatment was correspondingly superstitious or rational. The blindness caused by a demon could be transferred to a dog's eye through a ritual involving raw meat, a cord of hair, and a dung pile. On the other hand, there were various eye salves, such as the collyrium solutions recommended by Mar Samuel and compresses of bread dipped in wine. As for the use of the spittle of a fasting person as an eye medication, this apparently superstitious practice may have had some rational basis in the antibacterial properties of saliva. In the age of Islamic medicine, Jewish physicians wrote treatises on vision and specialized in ocular diseases and operations.

In Christian Europe in the late Middle Ages, Jewish doctors gained particular renown for their operations on cataracts. After a successful cataract removal by the Jewish oculist Cresque in the fifteenth century, King Juan II of Aragon wrote in a letter to his cousin the duchess of Milan of how "God Himself, the One and glorious Ruler of all, has put an end to all this misfortune, for He has provided such a most able man through whose skill and industry we are restored [in sight]. . . . [We shall not fail] to offer prayers to our Redeemer for so great loving kindness bestowed upon our person, so long afflicted by terrible suffering. . . . " (Let it be added, however, that not all Jewish oculists were as fortunate and well rewarded by the sovereigns. After being treated unsuccessfully by an apparently Jewish eye doctor from France in the fourteenth century, King John of Bohemia baptized the hapless physician by tossing him into the river, tied up in a bag.)

As for the eyes of the Jews themselves, their disproportionately high literacy, at least among men, no doubt brought with it particular ocular *tsuris*. God may have intended Jewish boys to read as they and their eyeballs are still growing, but eons of pre-biblical evolution in hunter-gatherer societies, where distant-viewing was crucial, had laid down a program for ocular development less compatible with literacy. The Jewish girls and women, for their part, apparently suffered adverse consequences from a different source during the period of ghettoization in the sixteenth through eighteenth centuries. Witness this passage from *De morbis artificum,* the first book on occupational diseases, written by the Italian gentile clinician Bernardini Ramazzini in 1700:

> The [Jewish] women, the girls and even the young brides seek a living for themselves by plying their needles. . . . This work demands great concentration of the eyes, on account of which all the Jewish women engaged in seaming during the whole day and often until late at night by the dim rays of a lamp or a light pale as the sepulchral lanterns, undergo not only all the inconveniences of a sedentary life but also with the passage of time they

work with such gradual weakening of the vision that about when they reach
their fortieth year they go forth nearsighted or totally blind.

Understandably, when the Jews enjoyed a measure of emancipation in
the nineteenth century but the Jewish doctors found themselves nevertheless marginalized from mainstream internal medicine and surgery, they
gravitated to the specialization of ophthalmology. Jews occupied chairs of
ophthalmology at the German and Austrian universities of Berlin,
Köningsberg, Breslau, Freiburg, Strassburg, Rostock, Vienna, and Innsbruck,
as well as in Hungary, France, and even Russia. Jews founded eye hospitals
and wrote atlases of ophthalmoscopy and definitive works on such afflictions as astigmatism. They researched phenomena such as the actions of
atropine and strychnine on the pupil. Even in far-off American—still a
scientific backwater—the Jewish father and son ophthalmologists Isaac
Hayes and Isaac Minis Hayes gained fame at the Wills Hospital and as editors of the textbooks *Ophthalmic Surgery* and *Diseases of the Eye* in the decades spanning mid-century.

A career in general surgery in Vienna in the 1880s was something to
which few Jewish doctors could aspire. Professor Theodor Billroth was
perhaps the world's most eminent and innovative surgeon, known especially for his stringent training program at the Allgemeine Krankenhaus.
Billroth was also known as being prejudiced against Jews. Some Jewish
surgeons nevertheless trained under Billroth. Most eminent was Anton
Wölfler, who introduced Lister's antiseptic techniques to Vienna and was
the first to perform a gastroenterostomy, a procedure whereby the stomach is surgically joined directly to the small intestine so as to bypass a
constriction of the lower stomach orifice due to ulceration or a carcinoma.
Wölfler's later accomplishments included studies on the thyroid gland and
the development of suturing techniques on the inside of the intestines. These
advances gained him professorships at Graz and Prague.

In general it was easier for a Jew to enter the more marginal field of eye
surgery, particularly on cataracts. This was the track chosen by young Dr.
Carl Koller, a contemporary and friend of Sigmund Freud. As an eye surgeon, Koller was painfully aware that for all the advances in ophthalmology, the removal of cataracts was a terrible ordeal for the patient. For even
though general anesthesia with ether, nitrous oxide (laughing gas), or chloroform had already been around for half a century, these were not usable

for the highly delicate ophthalmological operations. General anesthesia could induce retching at a critical moment; furthermore, the patient's conscious cooperation was often required. Yet there was no effective local anesthetic. The consequences for the surgeon were bad, but for the patient far worse. As an old Dortshire man described his cataract operation to Thomas Hardy: "It was like a red-hot needle in yer eye whilst he was doing it. But he wasn't long about it. Oh no. If he had been long, I couldn't ha' beared it. He wasn't a minute more than three quarters of an hour at the outside." Soon Koller would bring salvation, from an unlikely source.

In 1884, Freud was planning a trip to Hamburg to visit Martha Bernays, to whom he had become engaged two years earlier but whom, due to lack of money, he hadn't seen in over a year. Understandably, he dreamed of making some get-rich-quick discovery that would permit them to marry in the not-too-distant future. Freud vested his hope in cocaine, which he saw as a cure-all for a whole range of ills, from diabetes and consumption to seasickness and sexual inadequacy—this despite the fact that the drug, which had already been available in pharmacies for some time, was given hardly any notice in the standard medical textbooks. Before leaving for Germany, Freud asked his friend and colleague Koller to help him test cocaine by chewing on the drug and seeing if his muscular strength increased. But Koller's mind had long been, in Freud's words, "exclusively focused on one central interest," the eye. So it was that Koller paid little attention to cocaine's heightening of his physical prowess and was struck instead by the drug's numbing of the mucous membranes of his tongue and lips. Koller began immediately to wonder if the mucous membrane of the eye would be similarly affected by direct application of cocaine.

Just before departing for Martha in Hamburg, Freud had dashed off to a publisher with his paper *Über Coca,* suggesting many uses for the drug. But its application as a local anesthetic was mentioned only in passing, with no specific reference to ophthalmology. Upon his return to Vienna, Freud found his friend Koller the center of a sensation, due to his successful tests of cocaine for painless eye surgery. Seldom before or since has the application of a new medical discovery spread with such rapidity, hopping across borders and oceans. The previously mentioned Jewish assistant of Billroth, Anton Wölfler, was also quick to test cocaine as a local anesthetic agent in general surgery. In virtually all other aspects, however, cocaine would prove useless or too dangerous. This may have rankled Freud, who, having missed a great chance, would have to seek his fame and fortune in a different direction. Indeed, a decade later the Koller affair contributed to Freud's dream of the botanical monograph, which he eventually published with a lengthy analysis in *The Interpretation of Dreams.*

But any conscious resentment Freud may have felt toward "Coca-Koller"—this was the nickname he gave his friend in 1885, unaware that in Atlanta in distant America a cocaine-based soft drink with a similar name would be introduced onto the market the following year—was neutralized by an incident that caused a sensation at the Allgemeine Krankenhaus, particularly among the Jewish doctors. A disagreement about the bandage on a patient's finger in the admitting room led a gentile doctor to hurl an anti-Semitic epithet at Koller, whereupon Koller, never known for his composure, responded with a blow. The colleague soon sent two seconds challenging Koller to a duel (at the time, not at all a common practice among the Viennese bourgeoisie once they graduated from the university). Although never having fenced before, Koller agreed to duel with foils. This prompted Freud, who in his letters to Martha complained of the "general bitterness" of the sectarian tensions in the hospital, to send his friend a bottle of expensive wine to fortify him for the contest, from which he emerged triumphant and unscathed. (His anti-Semitic opponent received substantial, though not fatal, gashes.) Freud was moved by this incident to propose in a letter to Koller that they henceforth address one another with the casual *du,* instead of *Sie,* a particular mark of friendship in those formal times. (Martha was one of the few other persons Freud addressed as *du,* and even this didn't come until after a year or two of courting.)

While awaiting a court judgment on the legal consequences of the duel (he was eventually pardoned), Koller saw a slogan painted on the side of a house: "*Die Religion ist uns einerlei / In der Rasse liegt die Schweinerei,*" which might be freely translated as "No matter the creed, theirs or mine / As a race they're a bunch of swine." Like Freud, Koller proudly identified with the Jewish people despite having grown up and lived without any religious education or ritual observance. Unlike Freud, Koller in later years would speak with some sadness about the loss of religious meaning in modern life. But throughout his years in Vienna, Koller had at least consoled himself with the thought that anti-Jewish sentiment was basically a religious and social problem that would resolve itself with the increasing secularization of society in general. Yet here, quite literally, was the writing on the wall.

His great discovery notwithstanding, Koller despaired of obtaining an appropriate university position in Vienna. In 1885, when the capital's Jewish population numbered at most 10 percent (the percentage for all Austria was, of course, far lower still), over 40 percent of the university's medical students were Jewish, and over 60 percent of the Viennese physicians. But at the medical faculty, appointments were deliberately restricted. Even Jewish department heads were reluctant to appoint other Jews, no matter how highly qualified, for fear of being accused of turning the faculty into a *Judenschul* (Jew-school, a contemptuous term for synagogue). Koller traveled around for a while, spending some time in Utrecht in the hospitable Netherlands. All the while, Freud remained in correspondence with his *du-Freund* and advised him on his next career move. "That you should come home now does not seem very sensible to me," Freud wrote. "You get into bad situations too easily in Vienna and you have nothing to come back for. . . . When you are ready, go confidently to America."

So Coca-Koller went to the land of Coca-Cola. He eventually established himself as one of New York's leading ophthalmologists and by his death in 1944 had amassed various honors and gold medals. In a sense the most significant distinction had come ten years earlier, in 1934, on the occasion of the fiftieth anniversary of Koller's discovery, which also coincided with the jubilee of the founding of the German Ophthalmological Society. In a sadly rare gesture of scientific independence, the society's president delivered an address at the jubilee congress, expressing the profession's enduring gratitude to Koller, the "benefactor of mankind"—all this after the very same president had opened the congress with the obligatory pledge of fidelity to Hitler and the ideals of New Order.

If ophthalmology and dermatology were particularly common fields for German and Austrian Jews in the new era of specialization, so were psychiatry and neurology, and for similar reasons. The nineteenth-century alienist occupied a lower rung in the medical hierarchy than did the mainstream internist or surgeon, who, due to established prejudice, was more likely to be a Christian. But, aside from this, there was a centuries-long tradition of writings by talmudic scholars on the definitions of insanity and mental incompetence and by Diaspora Jewish physicians and philosophers on the means of attaining well-being within the framework of the age-old religious ethical values. This was perhaps a more pressing concern for the Jewish doctors than for their Christian and Moslem colleagues, in view of the unique situation of the Jewish communities as islands in a usually hostile sea of humanity.

In the late nineteenth century, there was discussion in the medical community of a particular Jewish vulnerability toward certain psychiatric afflictions. The presumed deleterious effect of inbreeding was offered as a physiological substratum for mental disorder. For his part, the influential psychiatrist Richard von Krafft-Ebing wrote of Jews in his *Text-Book of Insanity:* "Very often excessive religious inclination is itself a symptom of an originally abnormal character or actual disease, and not infrequently, concealed under a veil of religious enthusiasm there is abnormally intensified sensuality and sexual excitement that lead to sexual errors that are of etiological significance." But most writers emphasized the mental conflicts of the Jews as arising from their being loosened from their traditional religious and cultural moorings in an age of modernity that they themselves were doing so much to shape. The Italian anthropologist-psychiatrist Cesare Lombroso (we will learn more about him in a later chapter) attributed the high rates of insanity among his fellow Jews to "intellectual overactivity," and a German-Jewish doctor similarly pointed to Jews being "more addicted to head work than to manual labor" and to many of them being "of a rather nervous temperament." In his book *Le Suicide: Étude de Sociologie,* which virtually established the discipline of sociology at the close of the nineteenth century, the French Jew Émile Durkheim noted the lower-than-average suicide rates among observant Jews. But fewer and fewer West and Central European Jews retained the orthodoxy of their fathers. And nowhere was the Jewish contribution to modernity greater than in Vienna as the twentieth century approached. While Gustav Mahler, influenced by Bruckner and Wagner, composed ten lengthy symphonies for huge orchestras, Arnold Schönberg began daring experiments with atonal *Lieder.* Josef Popper-Lynkeus was expounding the concept of the aesthetic beauty of technology for its own sake, and the mind of the young Ludwig Wittgenstein was forming a philosophy of science to be known as logical positivism.

In no Viennese was the conflict around one's Jewish identity combined with a greater intellectual overdrive, in a rapidly evolving yet still traditionally hostile world, than in the person of the *Nervenarzt,* Sigmund Freud.

At a dinner party at the Parisian home of the renowned neurologist Jean-Marie Charcot, young Dr. Freud, still in his twenties, snorted a bit of his beloved cocaine as an antidote to ennui and then found himself in conversation with fellow neurologist Georges Giles de la Tourette (who several years later would describe the "foul-mouth syndrome" that bears his name). Freud, who was looked upon as a Jew in Austria, was seen as a German in France. Tourette, bitter about the loss of Alsace-Lorraine in the Franco-Prussian War sixteen years earlier, warned Freud of a greater war to come. As Freud wrote to his fiancée, Martha, in Hamburg, "I promptly explained that I am a Jew, adhering neither to Germany nor Austria." But, the letter immediately continued, "such conversations are always very embarrassing to me, for I feel stirring in me something German which I long ago decided to suppress."

Indeed, Freud, like so many of his Austrian and German brethren, would spend the next half century feeling ambivalent about both his Jewishness and his Germanness. He was a great admirer of the German *Aufklärung*, which came and then went. As Freud's friend, the Berlin novelist and playwright Arnold Zweig, wrote to him with reference to the age of Goethe: "We certainly have our Germanness in common—only it's a Germanness of the past, it seems to me." In his later years, Freud would write in retrospect, "My language is German. My culture, my attainments are German. I considered myself German intellectually, until I noticed the growth of anti-Semitic prejudice in Germany and German Austria. Since that time, I prefer to call myself a Jew."

But what did it mean to Freud when he, by choice, attached the label "Jew" to himself? Freud's fiancée, Martha, was the granddaughter of the chief rabbi of Hamburg, Isaac Bernays, who in the 1830s had stubbornly opposed reform innovations in the prayer ritual. Martha in turn was raised in a deeply pious home. Her brother Michael, however, accepted baptism as the price for obtaining a professorship, causing his family to sit *shiva*, the mourning for the dead. Conversion was something Freud would never consider for himself. "A Jew," he wrote, "ought not to get himself baptized and attempt to turn Christian, because it is essentially dishonest." Yet the disingenuousness in question could hardly have been a matter of faith for the man who declared that "[T]he Christian religion is every bit as bad as the Jewish" and that "Jew and Christian ought to meet on the common ground of irreligion and humanity." Not surprisingly, Freud insisted that his future wife abandon the traditional Jewish rituals of her upbringing. Yet he assured her that "even if the form in which the old Jews were happy no longer affords us any shelter, something of the core, of the essence of this meaningful and life-affirming Judaism will not be absent from our home."

The reveries that form the empirical basis of Freud's *Interpretation of Dreams* date from the mid-1890s and were perhaps physiologically influenced by his use of cocaine or, more accurately, his discontinuation of it. (Although cocaine distorts the sleep architecture and suppresses the quantity of REM, the recurring physiological sleep phase that we now know to be most associated with vivid dreaming, withdrawal from the drug can cause a rebound effect.) Content-wise, Freud discovered during this period that— ultimately, on a deeper, latent level—the driving force behind his dreams (and therefore, he assumed, behind everybody's dreams) were unconscious Oedipal and other complexes stemming from earliest childhood. Yet a perusal of Freud's dreams and his own interpretations of them leaves no doubt that some tribulations surrounding Freud's Jewish identity in the City of Dreams, as Vienna was called—tribulations of which he was all too conscious—were a powerful motivating force in the generation of his nightly scenarios.

In 1895 Karl Lueger, with his opportunistic anti-Semitic rhetoric, was elected mayor of Vienna. When Franz Josef exercised his imperial prerogative of not sanctioning Lueger's election, Freud, who was trying to break his addiction to tobacco as well as to cocaine, lit up a cigar in celebration. But when Lueger was elected for the fifth time two years later, the emperor relented. Lueger maintained that the teaching profession in general should be in the hands of believing Catholics. At various points, when the time seemed opportune, he directed his populist rhetoric against the Jews of the university medical faculty in particular. The Jewish doctors were engaging in inhumane animal vivisection, which inured them to the suffering of their Catholic patients on whom they likewise carried out irresponsible experiments. And when a poor Christian patient expired, the Jews gladly dissected him and were sure to turn a profit by trafficking in his skeleton. "When at last Jewish corpses are dissected, perhaps the doctors will then learn still more than they can from dissecting ours," Lueger railed. "Christian professors . . . laid the foundation for the medical school's fame of the University of Vienna. But as soon as the Jews got in, the fame of this

school in Vienna sank low . . . . The medical school will thrive again and
the hospitals once more become places of refuge, whether for rich or poor,
when the principle—out with the Jews from the university and the hospitals—is enforced, so that we Christians can be humanely treated." (Needless to say, many a Viennese anti-Semite was a complete hypocrite when it
came to his own medical care. So, for example, in the same decade the
pan-German firebrand Karl Türk was publicly embarrassed when it was
revealed in Parliament that in between his anti-Semitic diatribes, he and
his family were treated by a Jewish doctor.)

It was in this political and academic climate that we find Freud dreaming (albeit in a rather indirect way, and therefore more acceptable to his
conscience, even when dormant) that two of his fellow Jewish *privatdozente*
(lecturers) at the medical faculty have made academic fools of themselves.
Superficially, this may seem rather paradoxical for someone with a strong
core of ethnic pride—why not let a couple of Christian lecturers show
their incompetence? The 40-something Freud knew that on the basis of his
accomplishments, he would already have long been granted the title of
professor if he had been a Christian. Instead, he found himself as third in
line on the much more restricted and competitive list of Jewish candidates.
But now, at least in his dreamworld, Freud's two more senior Jewish colleagues had revealed their lack of competence, thus clearing the way for
Freud to rise to the top of the Jew list.

In the same period, Freud paid a visit to a mental institution in Siena in
neighboring Italy and learned of a Jewish fellow psychiatrist who had been
forced to resign as director. The exact reasons were unclear, but the implication was that religious factors played a role. Back in Vienna Freud went
to see a play about the Jewish question entitled *The New Ghetto*, and found
himself bemoaning the fact that he couldn't somehow bequeath to his
children their own country in which to live. The Siena incident and the
biblical lament of exile ("By the waters of Babylon, there we sat down, and
yea we wept when we remembered Zion") were reverberating in his mind
when he dreamed:

[I]t had become necessary to remove the children to safety, and this was
done. The scene was then in front of a gateway, double doors in the ancient
style (the "Porta Romana" at Siena, as I was aware during the dream itself).
I was sitting on the edge of a fountain and was greatly depressed and almost

in tears. A female figure—an attendant or nun—brought two boys out and handed them over to their father, who was not myself. The elder of the two was clearly my eldest son; I did not see the other one's face. The woman who brought out the boy asked him to kiss her good-bye. She was notice-able for having a red nose. The boy refused to kiss her, but holding out his hand in farewell, said *"Auf Geseres"* to her, and then *"Auf Ungeseres"* to the two of us (or to one of us). I had a notion that this last phrase denoted a pref-erence.

The root of the neologism *"Auf Ungeseres,"* which appeared in place of the usual *"Auf Wiedersehen,"* could be traced, according to Freud's analysis, to a Hebrew verb, *goyser,* with the meaning "imposed suffering." Contrib-uting to this was the German word for leavened (*gesaüert*) bread, which the Jews have to forgo as part of the Passover ritual when they eat their unleavened (*ungesaüert*) matzohs. Of course, Freud's professional and so-cial burdens could be relieved in a day with a splash of baptismal water from a Catholic priest. This was the path taken by his brother-in-law. All the roads may lead to Rome, as the saying goes, but Freud himself had never come closer to entering the Eternal City, either literally or spiritu-ally, than the Porta Romana (the gateway to Rome) in Siena, some hun-dred miles to the north.

In his youth, with the rise of anti-Semitism, Freud had been an admirer of Hannibal, the brilliant Semitic general who almost conquered Rome (albeit in the pre-Christian era). But on the other hand, Freud was, no less than Heinrich Heine, deeply in love with Europe's classical antiquity, as well as the modern forms of European civilization, and felt marginalized as a Semite. Consciously wanting to go to Rome but not daring to, he almost got there in three of his dreams, though not quite:

I dreamt once that I was looking out of a railway-carriage window at the Tiber and the Ponte Sant'Angelo. The train began to move off, and it oc-curred to me that I had not so much as set foot in the city. . . . Another time someone led me to the top of a hill and showed me Rome half-shrouded in mist; it was so far away that I was surprised at my view of it being so clear. . . . In the third dream I had at last got to Rome, as the dream in-formed me; but I was disappointed to find that the scenery was far from being of an urban character. There was a narrow stream of dark water; on one side of it were black cliffs and on the other meadows with big white flowers. I noticed a Herr Zucker (whom I knew slightly) and determined to ask him the way to the city.

Who was Herr Zucker in the un-Roman Rome of Freud's dream? This not uncommon Jewish family name means "sugar" in German, and it required of Freud only a minimum of free-association to find a connection in his mind with *Zuckerkrankheit*, "diabetes." In Freud's day this was also known as "the Jewish disease," due to the presumed susceptibility of Jews to it. In the case of some other supposedly Jewish infirmities, there was talk among Jews and gentiles of the possibilty of prevention by abandoning some presumably deleterious ancient religious rituals and adapting to modern life. So it was that in 1866, ten years after Sigmund Freud was circumcised, a group of sixty-six Viennese Jewish physicians submitted a brief to the capital's Jewish Community Board, rejecting the rite as, among other things, sapping the physical strength of the Jews and condemning them to a shorter lifespan. But diabetes was an inherent constitutional ailment of the Jews. So, too, Freud's web of associations implied, was Judaism itself.

Freud was by no means the first Jew to see Judaism as such, consciously or unconsciously. Already at the close of the fifteenth century a forced convert from Judaism told the Portuguese monarch in his book *Shevet Yehudah* (The Scepter of Judah), "And what will it profit our lord and king to pour holy water on the Jews, calling them . . . Pedro or Pablo, while they keep their faith like Akiba or Tarfon? . . . Know, Sire, that Judaism is one of the incurable diseases." Some three centuries later, Heinrich Heine poeticized in *Das neue Israelitische Hospital zu Hamburg:* "A hospital for sick and needy Jews/ For those poor mortals who are triply wretched/ With three great maladies afflicted:/ With poverty and pain and Jewishness/ The worst of these three evils is the last one/ . . . No treatment/ By vapor bath or douche can help to heal it/ No surgery, nor all the medications/ This hospital can offer its patients."

Freud acknowledged that his dreams and his dream theory owed much to his being Jewish. His Jewishness evoked anti-Semitism, and this did more than just contribute some of the stuff of which his dreams were made. It strengthened his resolve in the face of opposition to the more daring—even shocking—assertions of his theory of the mind in sleep and wakefulness, in particular the role of child sexuality and the traces it leaves in the adult unconscious. "As a Jew," he told his lodge of the B'nai B'rith in retrospect, "I was prepared to join the opposition and to do without agreement with the 'compact majority.'" But apart from anti-Semitism and his reaction to it, Freud attributed to Judaism—or at least to the kind of Judaism he had come to be familiar and comfortable with—a tradition of rationality and freedom of thought without which the science of psychoanalysis could not have developed. "Because I was a Jew, I found myself free from many prejudices which restricted others in the use of their intellect," he told his B'nai B'rith lodge. "We Jews, dear Brothers, stand more open to the world, that is the metaphysical world, than do the Christians, especially the Catholics. This is a result of our education, especially our religious education, and the atmosphere in which we are raised. We are not constrained by dogma."

So it was that in the years of struggle of the psychoanalytic movement in the first decade of the twentieth century, virtually all of Freud's followers were free-thinking Jews. One important exception was the British psychiatrist Ernest Jones, who was of Christian background although likewise a free-thinker. The greater exception was the young Swiss psychiatrist Carl Gustav Jung. A Protestant pastor's son, Jung in fact felt a strong attraction to mysticism (we will learn more about this in the next chapter). Yet Freud, fearful that his movement was turning into a "Jewish national affair," urged tolerance of what he perceived as Jung's *goyische* characteristics. As Freud wrote to his colleague Karl Abraham in 1908: "Please be tolerant and do not forget that it is really easier for you than it is for Jung to follow my ideas, for . . . you are closer to my intellectual constitution because of racial kinship, while he as a Christian and a pastor's son finds his way to me only against great inner resistances. . . . On the whole it is easier for us Jews, as we lack the mystical element."

At this time in Zürich, Jung had a young physicist from the Federal Institute of Technology as an occasional guest in his home. Like Freud, he was a totally nonobservant Jew, whose radical concepts would greatly permeate the whole zeitgeist of the new century. His discussions with Jung were not particularly fruitful, although this was perhaps more due to the differences in their respective fields than to the Jewish rational tradition as opposed to Christian mysticism. As Jung later recalled: "I am not gifted in mathematics and you should have seen all the trouble the poor man had to explain relativity to me. He did not know how to do it. I went fourteen feet deep into the floor and felt quite small when I saw how he was troubled. But one day he asked me something about psychology. Then I had my revenge."

Although Yeshiva University in 1953 named its new School of Medicine in the Bronx after him, Albert Einstein's contributions to medicine were indirect. Shortly before the First World War, the Danish physicist Niels Bohr (who, a quarter century later, would have to flee Nazi-occupied Denmark because of his Jewish ancestry) developed the principle of spontaneous emission of discrete bursts of light quanta, or photon particles, when an electron orbiting the nucleus of an atom drops from a high level to a lower one. In Berlin during the war, Einstein (German-born, but jealously maintaining his naturalized citizenship of neutral Switzerland) took a short break from constructing the monumental General Theory of Relativity to give some thought to Bohr's model. Einstein proposed the idea that if an atom with an electron in a high orbit is struck by a photon of a certain wavelength and vector, the atom will deflect it, but at the same time the electron will drop to a lower orbit and, in so doing, fire off a photon of its own of the same wavelength of the deflected photon. This stimulated—as opposed to spontaneous—photon emission was, in a sense, a way of getting a double beam of light of a specific color for the price of one.

It wasn't until 1960, five years after Einstein's death, that his principles were developed into the first laser, an acronym for light amplification by stimulated emission of radiation. Once this happened, three Jewish doctors—at the Cincinnati University College of Medicine, Stanford University, and Créteil, near Paris—were quick to see the potetial medical applications. The laser scalpel came to rival the steel knife, particularly in the fields of ophthalmology, oncology, and cardiovascular surgery, thanks to its painlessness, reduced risk of infection, minimal hemorrhaging, and great precision. It was in regard to the latter that Paul Ehrlich's principle of chromotherapy unexpectedly found a whole new spectrum of possibilities. Generated to order at a given wavelength, Einstein's monochromatic (single color) laser beams are absorbed preferentially by substances of the same color. Now in the age of Star Wars technology, various dyes (including the same methylene blue that had caused countless blotches on Paul Ehrlich's old labcoat) have been used to stain malignant tumors, arterial plaque, and discolored superficial skin vessels, thus targeting them for selective annihilation by magic bullets in the form of like-colored laser pulses.

Yet Einstein, who did so much to pioneer the quantum theory, even a decade before his discovery of the principle of stimulated light emission—the whole concept of light behaving like quanta, or photon particles, derives in fact from his 1905 paper—would part company intellectually with his friend Bohr and remain estranged from the new generation of quantum physicists until his death in 1955. In the late 1920s, Bohr described the unpredictablility of the actions of a subatomic particle in a way superficially similar to the description of the erratic movement of a tiny particle of pollen in water (the so-called Brownian movement) that Einstein presented in another paper published in 1905. A crucial underlying difference, however, was that although the pollen particle's movement is random in practice, it is predictable in principle if one only had information on the precise movement of each and every one of the much smaller water molecules whose collisions with the pollen determine its seemingly random motion. But according to Bohr and the new quantum physicists, the behavior of subatomic particles was completely causeless and truly random. "God doesn't play dice," Einstein protested. "Stop telling God what to do!" was Bohr's reply. But Einstein would not stop, for he based his opinion on a book that was the highest authority he was ever willing to recognize. That book unambiguously stated: "Nothing in the universe is contingent (i.e., by chance), but all things are conditioned to exist and operate in a particular manner by the necessity of divine nature." Its title was *The Ethics,* and its author was Baruch Spinoza, whom Einstein called "one of the deepest and purest souls our Jewish people have ever produced."

Created, as we have seen in Chapter 7, in an era when the concept of a nonbelieving Jew made as little sense as that of a nonbelieving Christian or Moslem, Spinoza's philosophy had to wait some two and a half centuries to provide the atmosphere for a community of rationalist Jews numbering in the millions, of whom Einstein and Freud were the most prominent. "I believe in Spinoza's God, Who reveals Himself in the orderly harmony of all that exists," declared Einstein publicly. "[A] belief bound up with a deep feeling in a superior mind, which reveals itself in the world of experience, represents my concept of God. In common parlance, this may be described as 'pantheistic.'" "I have not found a better expression than 'religious' . . . to describe [my] emotional and psychological attitude which shows itself most clearly in Spinoza."

Einstein, let it be recalled, dealt with all existence, from the behavior of the most infinitesimal subatomic particles to the shape of the entire cosmos; from the genesis of everything with the *creatio ex nihilo* of the Big Bang some ten or twenty billion years ago, to the ultimate fate of the universe many billion years from now—perhaps in a gravitational collapse of burnt-out galaxies, which one may, with a bit of imagination, read into Jesus's prophecy of the last days ("the sun shall be darkened . . . and the stars of heaven shall fall" [Mark 14:24-25]). Having shown with his powerful equations that the markings on yardsticks are convertible into the ticks of a clock and that both are mere shadows of a spacetime reality, Einstein gained a glimpse of a higher-dimensional universe *sub species aeternalis.* As such, he has a taste of Spinoza's "third kind of knowledge," the *amor Dei intellectualiis* (intellectual love of God), which is the most difficult to attain and has sometimes been described as an (intellectual, rationalistic) equivalent of an ultimate Buddhist mystical experience.

Although Einstein used divine terms to express his awe and love for the universe and its mysteries, the God of Spinoza Whom he worshiped was defined by Einstein as much by contrast to the traditional biblical God as by similarity. "Judaism is not a creed," Einstein wrote. "The Jewish God is simply a negation of superstition, an imaginary result of its elimination." The Jehovah of the Old Testament represented for Einstein "a regrettable and discreditable attempt to base the moral law on fear." But, he added, "the strong moral tradition of the Jewish nation has to a large extent shaken itself from this fear." And while Einstein declared that "the idea of a personal God . . . a God Who concerns Himself with the fates and actions of human beings . . . is an anthropological concept which I cannot take seriously," he never neglected this moral aspect of Judaism. Science in and of itself "pursues one single goal: the establishment of that which exists in reality." But Einstein, citing Spinoza and his *Ethics,* continually emphasized "the moral side of our nature," "the determination of that which *should* be."

In an age of waning belief in God-given shalts and shalt-nots, the determination of the moral life required—alongside the belief in the power of

386 ～ Jews and Medicine: An Epic Saga

human reason bequeathed by the French Enlightenment, the German *Aufklärung*, and the Jewish *Haskalah*—some improved knowledge of the darker recesses of the human mind. In 1888, the great historian of Judaism, Heinrich Graetz, wrote in retrospect of Spinoza: "the Jewish race once more brought a deep thinker into the world, one who was radically to heal the human mind of its rooted perversions and errors, and to prescribe a new direction for it, that it might better comprehend the connection between heaven and earth, between mind and matter." Graetz wrote this just as Freud was moving away from his neurological studies on the substance of the brain and toward a depth-psychology model of man based on mental constructs. A new generation was to repeat Graetz's comment virtually word-for-word, only now with reference to an Austrian rather than Dutch Jew.

Freud himself was well aware of the intellectual heritage bequeathed to him by the Sage of Amsterdam, albeit in a more amorphous way than Einstein:" *I most readily admit my dependence on Spinoza's doctrine. . . . I conceived my hypotheses from the atmosphere created by him.*" And again: "Throughout my long life I [timidly] sustained an extraordinary high respect for the person as well as the mental achievements of the great philosopher Spinoza." Freud may or may not have actually studied Spinoza's *Ethics,* but some lines from his essay on that great Renaissance thinker Leonardo da Vinci are almost perfect summations of the Dutchman's writings: "One has no right to love or hate anything if one has not acquired a thorough knowledge of its nature." Leonardo "did not love and hate, but asked himself about the origin and significance of what he was to love and hate. . . . For in truth, great love springs from great knowledge, and if you know it but little you will be able to love it only a little or not at all." Freud also shared Spinoza's and Einstein's concern with defining and living the ethical life. "In his inner being the Jew, the true Jew, feels only one eternal guide, one lawgiver, one law," Freud told his B'nai B'rith brethren. "That is morality."

Although perhaps no less a genius than Einstein, Freud, in focusing his scientific attention not on all of creation but on the workings of the human mind, did not feel the same religious-like ecstasy experienced by Einstein and Spinoza. Nor did his patients. For the limited purposes of liberation from neuroses, the psychoanalytic technique relies not on the rarely obtainable *amor Dei intellectualis* but on (in the words of Israeli philosopher

Yirmiyahu Yovel) *amor medici imaginarius,* or "the imaginary love for the physician." By this is meant the process of transference whereby the patient displaces onto the psychoanalyst (whose job includes deliberately remaining detached throughout) the emotions and feelings derived from earlier experiences with others, particularly with the patient's childhood parents. "Finally every conflict has to be fought out in the sphere of transference," wrote Freud. In the absence of this cornerstone of Freudian technique, all other forms of psychotherapy (including self-analysis), no matter how insightful, lack effectiveness. That the psychoanalyst in Freud's day was always a medical doctor—poking around in the less respectable recesses of the mind, just as his more physically oriented colleague probed the hidden recesses of the body, which he could even cut open—no doubt greatly added to the affective charge that could be transferred to him by the patient. As psychoanalyst Ernst van den Haag has pointed out, as a giver and maintainer of life and also the emissary and accompanier of death, the medical doctor resembled the patient's childhood father, at least in the Freudian unconscious with its Oedipal complex. That the psychoanalyst was also almost invariably a Jewish medical doctor, and as such a living representative of the "father religion," of course only increased the emotional charge that attached to him in the various layers of the minds of gentile patients.

As a rationalist in an age that had seen the complete discrediting of vitalism in the biological sciences, Freud first sought a neurological basis for his emerging discipline of psychoanalysis. The nineteenth century in Vienna had in fact begun rather inauspiciously for the science of neurology, as Franz Gall was driven out of the capital by the Catholic Church. An accomplished brain physiologist by the standards of his age, Gall believed not only that various character traits and abilities were each located in a specific region of the brain but also that these could be read in any individual by palpating the skull and determining which areas bulged or dipped. Gall had to flee Vienna not because his phrenology was a pseudoscience (as indeed we now know it to be), but because it was seen by the Catholic Church as being materialistic, which is another matter altogether. Yet later in the century, a materialistic approach to the mind would bear much scientific fruit at the

University of Vienna's medical faculty where Freud trained. Ernst Brücke, under whose supervision the student Freud carried out significant research on the nervous system of lower animals, was a firm advocate of applying to neurology the laws of physics and chemistry rather than some spiritual concept of a vital force. Another prominent teacher of Freud's, Theodor Meynert, endeavored to connect various mental diseases with histopathic characteristics at various brain sites.

But it was only in the last decade of the nineteenth century that the neuron was established as the basic building block of the nervous system, including the brain. For decades, despite important microscopic observations by, among others, Gabriel Valentin and Robert Remak, it had eluded positive identification due to its size, forms, and hue. The establishment of the universality of these nerve cells represented the crowning triumph of the cellular theory begun by Schwann and Schleiden early in the century. The neurologist Freud made use of the new concepts in some significant research he did on aphasia (loss of speech as sequel to cerebral trauma), drawing on the groundbreaking work of the Jewish neurologist Adolf Pick. Freud then went on to pioneer the neuron theory by making the nerve cell and its interconnecting synapses the building block of his first general model of the mind in wakefulness and sleep.

With regard to dreaming, Freud assumed that at night a flow of particularly large and uncontrolled endogenous neural energy caused some neurons, and the ideas they represented, to link up in such as way as to result in condensations (fusion of images or ideas) and displacements (one idea or image being suppressed but represented by a different one along the web of associations)—phenomena that would be pathological in waking cognition. In the absence of incoming stimuli from the outside world during sleep, the neural energy flows retrogressively to the perceptual areas of the brain, resulting in the condensed and displaced images and ideas being hallucinated as elements of a dream story. Since the neural pathways along which the nocturnal neural energy flows are the well-worn canals associated with ancient gratification of a basic kind, the dream is also of a wish-fulfilling nature. Freud termed these dream phenomena the "primary processes," for he assumed that these were also characteristic of the normal infantile way of thinking before being superseded in the course of ontogenetic development by the logical "secondary processes" typical of normal adult cognition.

Jewish as well as Christian views on the genesis of dreams in the Middle Ages and beyond recognized a physiological component, as when the sevententh-century Amsterdam rabbi Menasseh ben Israel spoke of various physical stimuli. "When one is overheated at night," he wrote, "he may dream that he is warming himself before a fire, or enjoying a hot bath; if he is cold, he dreams of ice and sleet and snow." Also found in Jewish and gentile writings were physiological theories derived from the ancient Greeks, by which, for example, the vapors of rich and heavy foods consumed before bedtime were thought to rise to the brain and evoke fantastic images. Presumably for this reason, a Medieval Jewish sage suggested giving greater credence to dreams of the early morning, after the digestion process has been completed.

Many a sage in the Talmud looked upon dreams as being (in the words of Rabbi Abahu) "of no value and of no harm." They were deemed nonadmissible in cases before the Jewish court. For his part, Spinoza in his *Ethics* and *Theologico-Politcal Tractate*, found it hardly worthwhile to comment at all on dreams; when he did, he compared them with delusions caused "by fever and other bodily ailments," similar to the way his gentile fellow philosopher Thomas Hobbes attributed dreams to the "distemper of inward parts." In young Freud's day the hard-headed neurologists were just as dismissive of dreams. An influential theory assumed that certain toxins that accumulated during the day had to be oxidized during sleep; this supposedly resulted in an ischemic (oxygen-deprived) cortex at night apt to producing senseless hallucinations and thought processes.

On the face of it, Freud's neurologically based theory of dreams as the product of a nightly regression to the infantile primary processes was in keeping with these views of the fundamental weak-mindedness of the sleeping brain and the meaninglessness of dreams. But, of course, it was Freud who declared dreams to be the "royal road to knowledge of the unconscious," the conveyers of important though hidden meaning. Through his brilliant writings Freud made the practice of dream analysis respectable even among the highly educated for most of the twentieth century. But in so doing, he was forced to give up his earlier attempts to explain the workings of the dreaming brain on the basis of nerve cells, synapses, and neuronal energy. The psychological discoveries Freud made—particularly with regard to the suppression of early childhood events into the unconscious—were beyond the descriptive power of the state-of-the-art in neurology in his day, although he never abandoned the hope that someday even the most subtle manifestations of the Oedipus complex would be explicable in neurological terms.

As a proud product of the rationalist tendencies in Judaism and the German *Aufklärung*, Freud maintained that his new psychological discoveries were derived from empirical data he gathered and analyzed, notably his own dreams and those of his patients. Freud's long introductory chapter in *The Interpretation of Dreams,* which concerns the previous literature on the subject, gives not the slightest hint of Jewish and talmudic antecedents to his dream theory. The book, although published in 1899, bore the date 1900, a deliberate allusion to the new century rather than to times past. But the question arises of whether Freud the dreamer was as totally a child of the modern rationalistic current of Judaism as he believed—or as he wanted the rest of the world to believe.

Freud's forebears had begun the nineteenth century not in Austria, but in Lithuania and Poland, where they had lived for many generations after presumably having been driven out of Germany at the time of the Crusades and the Black Death. Sigmund's father came from Galicia, in the eastern, Polish, reaches of the Habsburg Empire and grew up in a hasidic milieu. Sigmund himself was born in Moravia, a predominately Czech region of Franz Josef's realm, today part of the Czech Republic. In this sense Freud, like Skoda, Rokitansky, and von Hebra, was a Czech. He even acquired some knowledge of the language very early in life, which he completely forgot until it came back to him forty years later during his self-analysis. The Freud family's home language was, however, German. This, along with their Jewishness, did not endear them to the Czech nationalists. Furthermore, in their town, Freiburg, the economic conditions were becoming less favorable for father Jakob's wool business. So in 1859, when Sigmund was three years old, the family moved to the great political and cultural center of Vienna. Yet this last leg of the westward migration of generations of Freuds could hardly be said to have cut them off from their East European roots, for the Austrian capital was also receiving a wave of rather backward Yiddish-speaking *Ostjuden* immigrants.

Thus Freud the rationalist had a cultural link to a more mystical Jewish tradition of dream interpretation extending back over 2,000 years. Oneiromancy was already ancient in the Middle East when the Jews made their entrance onto the stage of history. The Bible attests to the particular talent of the Jews as oneirocritics, perhaps most noticeably in Joseph's interpretation of the pharaoh's dream as signifying seven fat years followed by seven lean ones. In the time of the Roman Empire, we find Juvenal quipping: "The Jews sell at cut prices as many dreams as you may wish." The reputation of the Jewish oneirocritics remained strong throughout the Middle Ages, although in fact the theory and practice of dream interpretation among the Jews largely overlapped those of the Christians.

"A dream uninterpreted is like a letter unopened," says the Talmud. The *Berakhot* tells that the fulfillment of a dream depends on the suggestion of the interpreter, and that in this way, a single dream can be interpreted by the twenty-four oneirocritics in Jerusalem in twenty-four different ways— all of them correct. Medieval Jews, like their Christian neighbors, regularly resorted to books of dream symbols after awakening in order to know of future events. To incubate pertinent revelations in dreams, Jews commonly practiced certain bedtime rituals. "Oh, Supreme King, great, mighty, and revered God, guardian of the covenant and fount of grace," beseeched the Medieval rabbi Jacob Halevi, in a typical incantation, "preserve Thy covenant and Thy grace for us, and command Thy holy angels who are appointed over the replies to dream questions to give a true and proper answer, unqualified and specific, to the question which I shall ask before Thy glory."

So great was the credence given to the clairvoyant power of dreams in Medieval Jewry that when a dream event was symbolically interpreted as a portent of future disaster, some Jews followed the curious practice of trying to avert the foretold calamity by seeing to it that the literal dream event would come to pass instead. So, for example, when someone dreamed that a bird he was carrying in his bosom flew away—which, according to the dream books, portended disaster—he was well advised to make this dream come literally true the following day by clasping a real bird to his bosom and then letting it loose. This, combined with charity to the poor and fasting, would hopefully change the course of a personal destiny not yet etched in stone. But in the Middle Ages, dreams could have an important influence far beyond one's own life if the dreamer was a political or religious leader. Rulings and responsa of various rabbis came to them in dreams, as when Efraim ben Isaac of Regensburg felt obliged by a dream revelation to reverse his previous decision, which had pronounced sturgeon to be kosher. Interesting in this history of medicine was the case of Gershon ben Hiskiya, who, imprisoned in France in the fifteenth century, was inspired by a dream to write a medical book (similar, incidentally, to the way, a millennium and a half earlier, the seventeen-year-old pagan Galen took up the study of medicine due to a dream).

Relevant in the framework of the development of psychoanalysis was the concept, prominent among Jews and Christians in the Middle Ages and beyond, that dreams could originate from demonic rather than the divine sources typical of the Bible. Martin Luther had such difficulty in distinguishing the two that he beseeched the Lord not to communicate with him via dreams. Jewish writings similarly allowed such demonic, as opposed to divine, origins of dreams, as when the *Sefer Hasidim* stated: "When a man suddenly beholds in his sleep a woman with whom he has never had relations, and whom he may not even have consciously desired, such a dream is caused by a demon or spirit. . . . The demon does not actually penetrate his thoughts but whispers into the depths of his aural cavity." Freud clearly decided in favor of the underworld as the dream source—albeit not some theological inferno but the subterranean id.

But although manifest instinctual gratification of dreams like the one alluded to previously would be prized by Freud, he maintained that few dreams so blatantly displayed their true colors. A dream, Freud wrote, "seems like a transcript of the [underlying] dream-thoughts into another mode of expression, whose characters and laws it is our business to discover. . . . The dream-content is expressed as it were in pictographic script. . . ." Here, too, he shared the opinion of his Medieval ancestors. As the *Sefer Hasidim* stated: "What is shown a man in a dream is as though he were to find himself in the midst of a strange people whose tongue he doesn't understand, so that they can only suggest things to each other in sign language, as one does with a deaf person."

Much dream symbolism in the Medieval Jewish dream books was based on a universal semiotic language. For example, the thirteenth-century *Ez Hayim* (Tree of Life) stated that "if he (the dreamer) is on a roof, he will achieve greatness; if he is descending, he will be humbled." In a similar vein, Eleazar of Worms suggested that dreams of dividing up meat portend quarreling. But for the rabbis of the Middle Ages, as for Freud at the turn of the twentieth century, dream symbols were usually not so transparent. Most interpretations in the Medieval dream dictionaries were so unrelated to their respective dream symbols that whatever connections there were had likely derived from plays on words in some long dead language. So when, for example, Eleazar of Worms in Medieval Germany warned that the common dream of a tooth falling out portended the death of a son or relative, he unknowingly derived his interpretation from a play on words based on old Egyptian sound similarities between the words for "falling out" and for the "pharaoh's subordinates," and also between "mouth" and "house door."

Hebrew, by contrast, was still a living language in the sense of being forever read and prayed in, and occasionally even written and spoken, by the Diaspora Jews. As such, it continued as a source of word-plays by which dreams could be interpreted. So when in the *Berakhot* (one of the less legalistic books of the Talmud) a dreamer reported: "I dreamt that you told me, 'You will die in the month Adar and therefore not see the month Nisan,'" the interpreter answered, "'You will die in all honor' [*adrutha* in Hebrew] and not be led into temptation [*nisayon*].'" Similarly, a camel (*gamal*) in a dream suggested that the dreamer would escape impending death, for similarly sounding words appear in the comforting line from Genesis (46:4): "I will go down with thee into Egypt, and I will surely bring thee up again [*gam 'aloh*]." Such word games are not uncommon in Freud's *Interpretation of Dreams*. For example, a woman patient dreamed, as Freud himself was wont to, of a trip to Italy. In her case, however, analysis revealed that it had nothing to do with an inner conflict of a socio-religious nature but to a sexual one: "to Italy" is *gen Italien* (genitals) in poetic German.

In at least some of the old Jewish dream books, the interpretation was apparently the opposite of what was dreamed. "If he dreams he has lost his property, an inheritance will soon come his way," assured *Ez Hayim*. Eleazar of Worms, for his part, told that a dream of snow in summer portended fire and that if the dreamer saw a groom or attended a wedding ceremony, she would soon be in mourning. One could especially seek opposite meanings to things seen or experienced in dreams if some transmutation of the Hebrew letters produced a contrary word. Thus pleasure (*oneg* in Hebrew) in a dream could also signify pain (*yagon*), while king (*melach*) could stand for fool (*lemach*). This recalls Freud's assertion that in dreams any object or event may simply stand for itself but may alternatively stand for its exact opposite. For example, when one of his middle-aged patients dreamed that she dove into a swimming-pool, Freud interpreted this as harking back to the birth trauma (coming *out* of the amniotic fluid). Or when a young patient dreamed that she stood before a closed meat shop, this was interpreted by him as meaning an *open* meat shop and, as such, was laden with sexual significance due to associations with a vulgar Viennese slang expression for "open fly."

All in all, when Freud stated that only a Jew could have created psycho-analysis, there was perhaps more to this declaration than he cared to recognize or admit. His minority status in a Christian society may, indeed, have encouraged his independence of thought. Anti-Semitism may have supplied much of the stuff of which his dreams were made, as well as fostered a defiant attitude toward the establishment. And the rational branch in Judaism may have provided him with much of his scientific philosophy—all of which he acknowledged. But perhaps more mystic currents of the Jewish tradition made a contribution to his thinking as well.

If, indeed, only a Jew could have created psychoanalysis, perhaps only a Jew could have created individual psychology, the alternative model of the mind and corresponding therapeutic technique developed by Freud's fellow Viennese and one-time disciple Alfred Adler, which had as its core the inferiority complex and a compensatory upward striving. Adler's parents hailed from Burgenland, a buffer area between Hungary and Austria that, although predominantly German-speaking, was in the Hungarian part of the dual monarchy. Growing up in Vienna, Alfred was therefore doubly a minority member, being Jewish and legally Hungarian. Eventually, he officially changed both statuses. Adler acquired Austrian citizenship in 1911. Already five years earlier, despite having married within the faith, he had converted to Protestantism. This move, Adler declared, was not motivated by any inferiority feelings concerning his Jewishness. Rather, Adler said he preferred a religion that was universal and not restricted to an ethnic group. In support of this it may be said that his family, coming from liberal Burgenland where Jews were fairly well tolerated and prosperous, had relatively little experience with anti-Semitism. But, on the other hand, the situation they encountered in Vienna was by no means so friendly.

Like many Jews, whether baptized or not, Adler embraced socialism and he devoted much of his medical practice to helping the underprivileged workers of Vienna. As a physician, Adler was familiar with the physiological phenomenon of compensation, by which the body makes good for the inferiority of one part by producing superiority of another. Insufficiency of heart valves can be offset by overdevelopment (hypertrophy) of the cardiac muscles. Damage to one of the lungs or kidneys can to a certain extent be made good by the extra activity of the healthy one. When one area of the cerebral cortex suffers impairment, its function can often be taken over by another part, and all the more readily when this occurs at an early age. Freud's pre-psychoanalytic monograph *On Aphasia* in fact contributed to this concept as it relates to loss of speech caused by trauma to the cortex. "In pathological cases," he wrote, "the (cerebral) center which has suffered least is the one whose assistance is sought first." Indeed, as we have seen, Karl Weigert in Germany showed how compensatory mechanisms can overcompensate, and Paul Ehrlich's model of immunity was based on hyperregeneration by defense cells. Adler endeavored to carry these principles over to the field of psychology.

Adler's concepts were reflected in the title of his 1907 book *A Study of Organic Inferiority and Its Psychical Compensation*. Adler was at the time a prominent member of Freud's fledging Vienna Psychoanalytic Society. The master accepted Adler's ideas as an interesting contribution to psychoanalytic theory. Indeed, Freud himself was fond of pointing to the German Kaiser Wilhelm, whose withered arm seemed to be a factor in his belligerent attitude in European affairs. But Adler sought to generalize his theory to encompass all humanity by virtue of the common helplessness all people have experienced to a greater or lesser degree as infants and children within the family constellation. Thus the inferiority complex displaced the Freudian Oedipus and Electra complexes as the principle forces shaping a normal or neurotic character in Adler's model of the mind. Furthermore, Adler's "will to power" (a term borrowed from the philosopher Nietzche; Adler later preferred to modify the concept as a "striving for superiority," and finally a "striving for perfection," or "upward striving") displaced Freud's libido as the driving force in human behavior. Overcompensation, retreat into neurotic fantasy, or passive-aggression were, in Adler's scheme of things, the less favorable coping strategies. Adler saw socialist values as a means of establishing a community in which such aberrant lifestyles would be less likely to be resorted to.

In 1911, amid growing acrimony with Freud and his more orthodox adherents, Adler and a group of his followers seceded from the Vienna Psychoanalytic Society, of which he was president, to form their own Society for Individual Psychology. Their new therapy involved more of a common sense approach, with friendly face-to-face chats rather than free association and a distant therapist. Whereas Freud's mission was to shed light on the unconscious, Alder saw only the need to eliminate some blind spots. This was sooner accomplished by the therapist's simply pointing things out to his patients rather than having them spend years free-associating and developing an *amor medici imaginariius*

As for dreams, they occupied a far less important place in Adler's model of the mind than in Freud's. Adler's writings on the subject were correspondingly less extensive, and then also less well thought out and somewhat self-contradictory. In line with his overall theory about striving, Adler wrote:

> In a dream the individual's goal of achievement remains the same as in waking life, but a dream impels him toward the goal with increased emotional power. . . . In dreams we produce the pictures which will arouse the feelings and emotions which we need for our purposes—that is, for solving the problems confronting us at the time of the dream, in accordance with a particular style of life which is ours. . . . [E]very dream state has an exogenous factor. This, of course, means something more than and something different from Freud's "day residue." The significance consists in that a person is put to the test and is seeking a solution. This seeking of a solution contains the "forward to the goal" and the "whither" of individual psychology in contrast to Freud's regression and fulfillment of infantile wishes. It points to the upward tendency in evolution.

At best, Adler's statement was a sweeping generalization based on a few quite special dreams. Even in the examples of his own dreams, which he furnished to illustrate his point, the supposed solutions were in fact delusional, oversimplified, or opposed to common sense. And although stories are told, and then endlessly repeated, of great discoveries supposedly made in dreams, these are often apocryphal. The aforementioned Niels Bohr, for example, is still often said to have literally dreamed up the planetary structure of the atom. Yet when he himself was once asked about it, he pointed out that the planetary model was due more to Lord Ernest Rutherford than to himself, and added that as far as he knew, he had never had a useful dream in all his life.

Yet in at least one important instance, Adler's upward-striving, problem-solving function of dreams has been well documented, namely with regard to his and Freud's fellow Austrian-Jewish medical doctor Otto Loewi. Like Freud in his pre-psychoanalytic days, Loewi was drawn to the investigation of the nervous system. We have seen how in 1840 Robert Remak had distinguished an organic nervous system that influences the movement of the involuntary muscles and the secretion of glands. Early in the twentieth century, Remak's concept, now called the autonomic nervous system, was rediscovered. Loewi wondered in general how this system manages to act upon the cardiovascular system, digestive tract, kidneys, stomach, liver, sweat glands, and the like. More specifically, Loewi pondered how the vagus nerve, when stimulated, exerts its inhibiting effect on the heart muscles. (Being part of the parasympathetic subsystem, as we now term it, the vagus nerve commands the heart muscles to slow down; but Loewi's question applied as well to the means by which nerves of the opposite, so-called sympathetic system command the heart muscles to speed up.) Loewi was among the first to suspect that this process involved the release by the nerves of minute quantities of chemicals that affect the muscles. But the limited refinement of the measuring techniques in the early years of the twentieth century seemed to render his hypothesis unverifiable.

When Loewi, now professor of pharmacology at the University of Graz, returned to the problem after World War I, techniques of chemical analysis were still too insensitive to detect the tiny quantity of chemicals he suspected were released by the nerves. But one night in 1920 Loewi awakened from a dream, knowing that some other experimental solution to his problem had been presented but not remembering the details. The following evening Loewi tried to incubate the dream anew by concentrating on the problem before retiring. In the middle of the night he awoke with a dream of a so-called crossed-heart perfusion experiment. This involved electrically stimulating the vagus nerve of one frog's heart and then transfusing its blood to another frog's heart in the hope that it would then slow down, even though its vagus nerve had not been stimulated. Rushing off to his lab, Loewi performed this experiment and obtained the hoped-for results. By a similar method he later showed the same effect regarding the nerves that speed up the heart, thus confirming the existence of chemical messengers—today called neurotransmitters—by which both the sympathetic and parasympathetic subsystems of the autonomic nervous system act upon the body organs it regulates.

For his discovery Loewi shared the Nobel Prize for Physiology and Medicine in 1936. The following year Alfred Adler died while on a lecture tour in Scotland. For Freud, who abandoned all religion but never his Jewish identity, Adler's conversion from Judaism and his defection from Freud's movement made him doubly a turncoat. Upon hearing the news from a sad Stefan Zweig, Freud wrote back unsympathetically: "For a Jewboy out of a Viennese suburb a death in Aberdeen is an unheard-of career in itself and a proof of how far he had got on. The world really rewarded him richly for his service in having contradicted psychoanalysis."

Adler was gone, but Freud and Loewi were still very much alive and productive in Austria. Yet soon, in the wake of the *Anschluss* with Germany, they would have to flee for their lives as their fellow Austrians strove with a vengeance to outdo the German Nazis in anti-Semitic hatred.

Chapter 14
Blood, Germs, and Genes in the Third Reich

I wish to separate myself from those who attach the blood groups to the mystique of race.

—Ludwik Hirszfeld

All great cultures of the past perished only because the originally creative race died out from blood poisoning.

—Adolf Hitler

Should another Moses arise and preach a Semitic exodus from Germany, and should he prevail, they would leave the land impoverished far more than was ancient Egypt by the loss of the "jewels of gold and jewels of silver of which the people are spilled." . . . [T]here is not a profession which would not suffer the serious loss of its most brilliant ornaments, and in none more so than our own [medicine]."
     —Sir William Osler, "Letters from Berlin" (1884)

$\mathcal{A}$ t the harbor on the island of Cos there stands today a deserted synagogue, a stone's throw away from the tree under which, according to legend, Hippocrates some twenty-five centuries ago taught his pupils the ethics, as well as the art and science, of medicine. The first and most sacred rule for his disciple physicians: Do no harm. In the summer of 1944, under the German occupation of the island, the Jews of Cos were deported to Auschwitz. Before being sent to the gas chambers, each of these 120 souls, like millions of their coreligionists, was duly examined and certified for destruction by a fully licensed doctor of medicine wearing a white tunic and a military cap, decorated with a perverted version of the staff of

Asklepios and the double lightning strokes of the SS. Germans have traditionally been sticklers for propriety. The Nazis wished to ensure that the
"final solution" was a proper medical procedure.

If in the eyes of the world the M.D.s of the SS engaged in the most
unthinkable perversion of medicine, their actions were far less aberrant
within the general framework of the German medical community at the
time. Willingly purged of its once glorious Jewish component, seized partly
by envy, partly by ideology, the German medical profession lent, proportionately, perhaps more support to the Nazi movement and the Hitler
regime than did any other segment of German society.

In the medically oriented anti-Semitic ideology and propaganda of the
National Socialists and the complicity of the German physicians, as well as
much of German society in general, lies one of the greatest ironies of history, an irony that goes virtually unnoticed in all the vast literature on the
Holocaust. It was the German Jewish medical men who pioneered the germ
theory and then proceeded to eradicate the great scourges, thus saving
millions of men, women, and children in the Fatherland and untold millions more beyond. Yet the Nazis gleefully adopted and propagated the
metaphor of the Jewish bacillus and targeted the Jews themselves for eradication. Jewish doctors were the great pioneers in the field of hematology.
More particularly, the whole concept of blood group classification, to which
countless transfused patients, gentile and Jew, in war and peace, owed their
very lives, was developed by medical men who were of Jewish descent. As
such, even if they were faithful Christians, they were deemed to be, quite
literally, of pure Jewish "blood," according to the perverted pseudoscience
of the Nazis, and were slated for extermination along with all others of
Jewish descent. To this, one may add the significant, though more minor,
contributions of German Jewish doctors to the field of eugenics and their
concern that the best and the brightest—of whatever religion or ethnic
background—were too often neglecting to make their genetic contribution to the next generation. In the twisted Nazified concept of racial hygiene, however, eugenics meant death to the "genetically unfit," a category
to which each and every person with more than two Jewish grandparents
belonged by definition.

We have seen how in Medieval Germany and elsewhere, visitations of the
plague brought the wrath of the Christians down upon the alleged well-

poisoners, the Jews. In the late nineteenth century there were still echoes of such defamations, now with reference to pathogenic microorganisms rather than poisons. So when a cholera epidemic struck the port city of Hamburg, a newspaper of the small but vociferous anti-Semitic movement published a series of articles on "the corrupting bacillus of Judaism." Having it both ways, the paper, on the one hand, attacked the "Jewish-patrician interests," which supposedly ruled Hamburg only for profit, to the neglect of public health. On the other hand, the paper blamed the epidemic on "the mass arrival of Jewish emigrants," often quite poor, and the consequent "impurity of the Hamburg water mains." Yet even at the height of the health crisis, the anti-Semitic parties in Hamburg gained hardly more than 7 percent of the vote in elections to the Reichstag.

But the same period, the age of the great microbe-hunters, saw the introduction into the German body politic of the Jew more as a metaphoric, rather than literal, pathogenic agent. It began, perhaps, with the anti-modernist prophet of German cultural despair Paul de LaGarde, who wrote around 1880 regarding the Jews: "With trichinae and bacilli one does not negotiate, nor are trichinae and bacilli subject to education; they are exterminated as quickly and thoroughly as possible." The metaphor went through an interbellum period when, for example, a racial hygiene journal wrote: "Ethnobiologically, Judaism plays the role of certain septic bacteria; whoever doesn't realize this is beyond help." It attained a particular ominousness and viciousness during the 1930s when, for example, *Der Stürmer* informed its readers that: "The mobilization of the German people's will to destroy the bacillus lodged in its body is a declaration of war on all Jews throughout the world. . . . Bacteria, vermin, and pest cannot be tolerated. For reasons of cleanliness and hygiene we must make them harmless by killing them off." And it reached its climax when Hitler, who called the Jew a "pernicious bacillus spread[ing] over wider and wider areas," had the power to make good on his ranting: "How many diseases have their origin in the Jewish virus! We shall regain our health only by eliminating the Jew."

Within months of Hitler's appointment as chancellor in January 1933, some 800 university professors and lecturers were dismissed from their posts. Even more (those temporarily exempt) would follow later. But the figures alone don't tell the whole story of the scientific disaster Germany brought upon itself. For a disproportionate number of the dismissed Jews were from the very top echelons of their professions. These included no fewer than fifteen past or future Nobel Prize winners, particularly in physics, Einstein being, of course, the most prominent.

There then arose the question of what science the Aryans, few of whom either resigned in protest or were dismissed, should be allowed to practice. In the wake of Hitler's coming to power, Hans Schemm, the leader of the National Socialist Teachers League and newly appointed Bavarian minster of education and culture, stated ominously before a meeting of Munich university professors: "From now on, the question for you is not to determine whether something is true, but to determine whether it is in the spirit of the National Socialist revolution." In the ensuing years some confused and even self-contradictory attempts were made by Nazi scientist-ideologues to define a proper Aryan (or Nordic, or Germanic) physics. On the one hand, there was a movement emphasizing observation and experimentation in the "real" world, in opposition to the "Jewish" penchant for theory and mathematical abstraction, exemplified by relativity and quantum physics. This Nazi view drew inspiration from the *Foundations of the Nineteenth Century,* the racial interpretation of history by the fanatical Germanophile H. S. Chamberlain, son-in-law of Richard Wagner. But on the other hand, there was a strong current among the Nazi scientist-ideologues harking back to the century-old romantic rejection of materialism and rationalism (likewise considered to be Jewish traits) in favor of the mystery and subjectivity of the natural world. The National Socialist opinions on applied science were similarly confusing. Some Nazi professors saw the vaunted technology of the Germans as proof of their superiority, while others, in the romantic tradition, longed for a return to the Germanic past before the Jews, in their disrespect for nature and their lust for profit, overindustrialized the country.

Such mixed-up ideas found no acceptance on the part of the vast majority of scientists still in Germany, and after years of lower level discussion, the powers-that-be in Berlin shelved the issue. In the end, what mattered to the Reich Ministry of Education was that, whatever the scientific theory or discovery, when the originator was Jewish (as was often the case) this simply had to go unmentioned; or, if possible, the theory should be ascribed to an Aryan. Aside from this, it was sufficient that the scientists be politically correct (or at least apolitical) and, later, that their science be perceived as somehow aiding the war effort.

The situation in the field of medicine in some ways reflected the overall situation in the sciences, but in other ways did not. "The only Jew fit to live" was the way Hitler is reported to have retrospectively characterized the early twentieth-century self-hater Otto Weininger, who wrote: "The present turn of medical science is largely due to the influence of the Jews, who in such numbers have embraced the medical profession. From the earliest times, until the dominance of the Jews, medicine was closely allied with religion. But now they make it a matter of drugs, a mere administration of chemicals. . . . The chemical interpretation of organisms sets these on a level with their own dead ashes." (Though fit to live in Hitler's eyes, Weininger committed suicide in 1903 at age 21, unable to live with the Jewishness he despised but couldn't purge himself of.) Not a few Nazi ideologues similarly decried as Jewish (or, more specifically, as Jewish-capitalist or Jewish-socialist) the proliferation of laboratory techniques and the mechanistic or physiochemical way in which organs of the body were viewed and treated. The increase of impersonal specialization in medicine was seen as one more unfortunate result of the industrialization of society. As one Nazi professor of medicine wrote: "The Jew [anti-Semites have traditionally preferred to speak of *the* Jew, rather than 'some Jews,' or even 'a Jew' or just 'Jews'] always has the tendency to split up and divide everything into its atoms, thereby making everything complicated and incomprehensible. . . . The healthy non-Jew, in contrast, thinks simply, organically, creatively. He unifies, builds up! He thinks in terms of wholes."

Attracted by the concept of *Blut und Bodem* (blood and soil), such Nazi ideologues romanticized the holistic folk remedies of their Teutonic and supposed Aryan forebears. The traditional remedies of the *Kräutenweiblein* (herbalist woman) had a pride of place here, along with the homeopathy of the early nineteenth-century German physician Samuel Hahnemann and the half-scientific, half-mystical concepts of the seventeenth-century German-Swiss Paracelsus. Yet even before the advent of the Nazis, alternative forms of folk healing, mostly unregulated and unlicensed, had long been rife, particularly in rural areas. It was now the declared intention of the Reich Committee for the New German Science of Healing to unite all the alternative schools and "bridge the gap that separates academic medicine from the feeling and desires of the people." As things turned out, however, pragmatism again prevailed among the powers-that-be, and whatever plans there were for the marriage of folk and scientific medicine were shelved. By the outbreak of the war, the schools for natural healers had in fact been disbanded, although coordinated operations were conducted under government auspices to supplement the diet of the wartime population with rosehips, health-promoting herbs and medicinal teas.

A major reason for the failure of a particularly Aryan or Germanic folk healing to take root in the Third Reich was the strong opposition from most of the regular medical community. But unlike in the case of the physicists, this opposition was seldom motivated by ideological antipathy toward the Nazis. Germany's physicians belonged, of course, to the middle class, the social stratum from which the Nazis drew so much of their support. Like the rest of the bourgeoisie, they were hit hard by the run of hyperinflation in the early '20s and made further insecure by the great economic depression at the end of the decade, which threatened yet more social dislocation, particularly in the form of left-wing radicalism. But there were reasons for the appeal of the Nazis to the medical profession in particular.

In his personal life, Hitler's attitude to doctors and medicine was ambivalent. A presumed crucial point in his psychopathological development was the death of his mother from breast cancer in 1907 when he was 18. This was after a heroic and painful, but ultimately futile, course of iodine treatment, administered by the Hitler family's kindly Jewish GP, Dr. Eduard Bloch, who extended the family credit in order to carry out the costly therapy. Hitler, at the time an unsuccessful would-be artist in Vienna, subsequently sent Bloch hand-painted picture postcards signed, "Your eternally grateful patient." (Dr. Bloch would himself later attribute his being able to leave the Reich around the outbreak of the Second World War to a residue of that gratitude.) Whatever the possible unconscious Oedipal ramifications of this adolescent experience for Hitler's attitude toward the Jews and Jewish doctors, it may also have resulted in his hypochondria—he discouraged any discussion about dying in his presence—and some peculiar attitudes toward medicine in general. Hitler's vegetarianism, which began early in the '30s, indicated a tendency toward nonorthodox approaches to health and he furthermore consumed a vast array of vitamins and other supposed health preparations. The body physician he most trusted tended to quackery and continuously injected Hitler with hormones. And although he had as many as five doctors at a time on standby, the Führer apparently never allowed any of them to give him a full check-up or to x-ray him.

In public, however, Hitler and the Nazis, with their obsession with genetics and racial hygiene (we will learn more about this shortly), made use of the medical metaphor in relation to Germany's problems and appealed directly to the doctors. The same Minister Hans Schemm, who openly declared that not truth but ideology mattered in science, also defined National Socialism as "applied biology." When addressing the National Socialist Physicians League, Hitler, whom some of his medical followers called "the physician to the German people," declared that he could, if need be, get along without lawyers and engineers, but that "you, you National Socialist doctors, I cannot do without you for a single day, not a single hour. If not for you, if you fail me, then all is lost. For what good are our struggles if the health of our people is in danger?"

As for Hitler's anti-Semitism, this in itself may not have appealed to many Germans. And even mild or moderate anti-Semites might have been turned off by the sheer vulgarity of his hatred, especially as expressed in his biological metaphors, assuming they bothered to read *Mein Kampf* at all. At first thought, German physicians as a group might have been expected to have a particular immunity toward anti-Semitism, for they could not but be aware of the great contribution of their Jewish colleagues to their country's scientific glory, particularly in the fields of bacteriology, venereology, and public hygiene. Nevertheless, there were reasons why many doctors were not about to object to the injection of a dose of anti-Semitism into the German body politic.

The last quarter of the nineteenth century had already seen a doubling of the number of physicians in Germany to some 28,000, considerably more than the market could bear. By the end of the First World War, their numbers had again increased by more than half, and over 20,000 demobilized doctors (another 1,000 of their colleagues never returned from the front) were faced with a saturated job market. Already in Ehrlich's day, almost one in every six German physicians was Jewish and in the capital, Berlin, about one in every three (eventually to increase to over half)—this from an ethnic group comprising but 1 percent of the German population. Furthermore, hundreds of Russian Jewish doctors fleeing the czarist pogroms or the revolutionary upheavals arrived on German soil. The economic and social uncertainties of the German physicians were further heightened by the establishment of rationalized medical insurance companies and impersonal, business-like clinics (both of which were perceived as Jewish).

Even before Hitler's appointment as chancellor in 1933, physicians were among his most ardent supporters, including nine Nazi doctors elected to the German Parliament, the Reichstag. The National Socialist Physicians League, founded four years earlier, already boasted close to 3,000 members (or 6 percent of all doctors, far higher than in other Nazi professional organizations). Within months of Hitler's electoral victory, the number quadrupled and would eventually rise to at least 40,000, some half of the whole medical profession. Physicians were also greatly overrepresented in the SA (Storm Troopers, the Nazi party's private army) and the SS (the élite special units, originally formed as Hitler's bodyguards).

The Nazis made good in their pledge to eliminate Jews from medicine and to free up jobs for Aryans. The dismissal of most Jews in the civil service at the beginning of the Nazi regime applied to the physicians at the universities and government or government-funded research and public heath facilities. At Berlin's Charité Hospital, where Paul Ehrlich had begun his great work, 138 doctors were eliminated the first year. The medical university faculties, being even more heavily Jewish than those of physics and chemistry, were also the hardest hit. Well over 400 German-Jewish professors and lecturers in medicine were dismissed, a greater number in fact than in all the other sciences combined. In the first year of the Third Reich, university admissions quotas were set so that Jews, no matter how highly gifted or qualified, would not exceed 1 percent of the student body. (Within a few years they would be excluded altogether.)

Jewish physicians were forced out of the social insurance programs, which meant that patients could pay for them only out of their own pockets. Subsequent laws prohibited Jewish doctors from treating Aryan patients (or even performing autopsies on Aryan cadavers), and in 1938 their medical licenses were revoked outright. Job advertisements in German medical journals often ran: "Aryan doctor wanted to fill position recently vacated by Jew." With the Anschluss in 1938 the Austrian Jewish doctors came in for the same treatment. Although many Jewish physicians hoped in vain to weather the storm, thousands saw the writing on the wall and emigrated when they could find a country of refuge. Those driven from

Greater Germany included four past or future Nobel Prize winners in medicine.

As with physics and the other sciences, it was not enough that medicine be purged of Jewish practitioners and researchers, but also that past medical discoveries, regardless of how famous or important, no longer be ascribed to Jews. This applied not just to the academic world but to all spheres of life in Nazi Germany. By a government decree of July 27, 1938, all streets named after Jews had to be renamed. Thus was the Paul-Ehrlich-Strasse wiped off the map of Frankfurt. Censorship of books meant more eradication, with shades of Orwell's *1984*. For example, a popular biography of Robert Koch published in Germany in 1929 contained a lengthy chapter on the crucial role played by Professor Cohn in gaining attention for Koch's discoveries and advancing his career. In later reprintings (including the revised Dutch version in Nazi-occupied Holland) there appeared page after page about "the Breslau professor" or "the Institute's director" without his name ever being mentioned. As for Paul Ehrlich and Julius Cohnheim, they were vaporized from the book's pages without leaving even an indirect trace.

Yet occasionally, the powers-that-be in the Nazi hierarchy could be whimsical in deciding which doctor qualified as a Jew, especially when Hitler's hypochondria was involved. In 1935 the Führer had a polyp removed from his nose. Hitler fretted that the cancer that had carried off his mother would do him in, too, before he could established his 1,000-year Reich. Germany's foremost cancer researcher happened to be Otto Warburg, whose name was indissoluably linked with what was perhaps the world's most prominent Jewish banking family and as such the particular target of anti-Semites in the Third Reich.

The Warburgs owed their financial ascendancy to an early seventeenth-century ancestor, Jacob Samuel Warburg, who as banker to the Margrave of Hesse-Cassel withstood pressure to convert and instead moved to Altona-Hamburg, which was then under the comparatively tolerant and liberal Danish crown. It was there that the banking house of M. M. Warburg was incorporated later in the next century. An important branch of the family subsequently grew in England, where Warburgs were distinguished not just as financiers, but as academics, publishers, philanthropists, and civil servants. In America, too, they made their mark on the financial and social

scene beginning late in the nineteenth century. But the main, most imposing branch of the family tree remained close to its Germany roots up until
Kristallnacht.

In the late nineteenth century, a German Warburg, Emil, was professor
at the Universities of Freiburg and Berlin and was one of the country's
most eminent physicists. He married a gentile woman from a distinguished
Southern German family, who bore his son Otto in Freiburg in 1883. Otto
Warburg received his doctorate in chemistry in Berlin and then went on to
obtain an M.D. degree in Heidelberg with a dissertation on oxygen consumption. At Heidelberg, young Warburg authored some thirty major papers
on the energetics of living cells and their growth. His guiding principle,
still far from taken for granted at the time, was that life processes obey the
laws of physics and chemistry.

In 1913, Otto Warburg's achievements gained him, at age 30, an appointment as member of the Kaiser-Wilhelm-Gesellschaft, which meant
his heading his own biological research department. But while his new lab
was being completed in Berlin, the war broke out. Warburg enlisted, was
wounded on the Russian front, and was decorated with the Iron Cross,
first class. In the last months of the conflict, with the carnage continuing
even though the cause was lost to Germany, Warburg received notification
that his transfer back to his research lab could be arranged. Albert Einstein,
a friend of Otto's father and director of the Physics Institute of the Kaiser-
Wilhelm-Gesellschaft, wrote a pleading letter to Otto implying that a
disaster would befall postwar German physiology if he didn't survive. Never
one to be accused of false modesty, Warburg concurred with this assessment. Having already been decorated for his services on the battlefield, he
agreed to the transfer.

Through the 1920s, using various ingenious contraptions and techniques
he devised, Warburg solved the riddle of how a living cell "breathes," that
is, the riddle of the chemical processes, involving iron and catalyzations,
by means of which the cell absorbs and burns oxygen from its surroundings and thus keeps alive. He further determined the gases and processes
involved in photosynthesis and alcohol fermentation and also elucidated
the production of lactic acid by animal tissues. In 1929 the Rockefeller
Foundation provided Warburg with over 1.2 million marks for the establishing of a new Institute of Cell Physiology under Kaiser-Wilhelm-
Gesellschaft auspices.

Having demonstrated much about the chemical and physical processes by which normal cells breathe, take in energy, and grow in a regulated manner, Otto Warburg turned to a problem that had held his interest since his student days: the unchecked growth of abnormal, cancerous cells. Warburg showed that multiplying cancer cells apparently draw much energy through a conversion of glucose into lactate that is abnormally high, even when compared to the correspondingly rapid growth of (normal) cells in an embryo. This conversion takes place in the presence of oxygen, although the oxygen consumption is not higher than in normal cells.

The German-Jewish medical doctor Otto Meyerhof, with whom Warburg collaborated in Heidelberg before the war, had elucidated the chemical processes involved in muscle contraction and relaxation. For this work he shared the Nobel Prize for Medicine and Physiology in 1922. Of particular interest to Warburg was Meyerhof's demonstrating that when, in various action phases, muscle tissue takes up oxygen, there is a mechanism that sees to it that not all glucose is converted to lactate. Warburg found similar control mechanisms in other normal tissue and concluded that a crucial defect of cancerous cells was the malfunctioning of this mechanism, resulting in defective respiration, abnormal fermentation, and unchecked growth. For his elucidation of normal and cancerous cellular processes, Warburg received the Nobel Prize for Medicine and Physiology for 1931. This was at a time when the Nazis were experiencing a meteoric rise in their popularity at the polls. Among the staple bogeymen of the Nazis was the Warburg family.

In the first three decades of the twentieth century, the Warburgs were the premier family of Hamburg and one of the most eminent in all Germany. They were renowned not only for their banking and business achievements but also for their public spirit, including their role in the founding of Hamburg University. In the last days of World War One, Max Warburg, with his access to the highest echelons of political power, urged the German army to hold out for another two weeks, not in any hope of turning the tide but to strengthen Germany's hand at the peace talks. This proposal was rejected by the exhausted generals Hindenburg and Ludendorff. At the ensuing negotiations at Versailles, Warburg, the most important financier in the German delegation, consistently bargained for less harshly punitive economic reparations and urged the new German government to reject the Allied terms. When it didn't, Warburg resigned rather than put his signature to the treaty. In the postwar years he was active in the conservative Deutsche Volkspartei. Max's naturalized American brother, the powerful financier Paul M. Warburg, a confidant of presidents and prime mover behind the creation of the Federal Reserve System, joined with the celebrated British economist John Maynard Keynes in authoring a declaration, subsequently signed by many luminaries, warning in vain of the potentially dire consequences of too harsh a reparations policy. It was the Warburgs who, during the Roaring Twenties, served as an essential conduit of Wall Sreet dollars to the hard-pressed German economy. They rebuilt Hamburg's merchant marine while continuing to lobby Washington for reduction in reparations.

Reality, however, was never allowed to cloud Nazi mythology. The Warburg Elders of Zion were the force behind the "November criminals," who stabbed a potentially victorious German army in the back and then bargained away the Fatherland's future at Versailles while financing a Bolshevik revolution. The intermarriages of the Warburgs with the scions of other Jewish banking houses were ipso facto proof of the international Jewish conspiracy. Max Warburg, the "Chief of Staff of World Jewry," was the "Secret Kaiser" pulling the strings in German politics. The Warburgs were regularly featured on the pages of the viciously anti-Semitic *Der Stürmer*.

In 1935, Jewish heads of research institutes, hitherto temporarily enjoying exemption from the mass dismissals two year earlier, were given the axe. But Hitler was concerned that his next nasal tumor might be cancerous and not be removed in time. The Jewish doctor Bloch had been unsuccessful in treating his mother's cancer with iodine a quarter century earlier, but now there was a Warburg, who as department head of the Institute for Cell Biology was busy discovering the abnormal metabolic processes of cancerous cell growth and offering hope that they could one day be controlled. And Otto Warburg had something more that may have appealed to the cancer-fearing Hitler. In his laboratory, Warburg had shown that normal cells could be turned cancerous by means of radiation and other assaults from the outside, even by an increase in oxygen pressure. Warburg, who never denied his eccentric nature, became fearful of additives in food and avoided all bread sold in shops, preferring to have loaves baked specially for him at home. He maintained a large garden where his vegetables could be grown organically. The only dairy products he trusted came from a special herd at the School of Agriculture, whose milk he centrifuged in his lab. And, of course, he despised smoking. Warburg's finickiness resonated with Hitler, a vegetarian (and staunch nonsmoker and teetotaler), who is quoted as speculating that personal and cultural decadence "had its origin in the abdomen—chronic constipation, poisoning of the juices, . . ."

So it was that when Reichsmarschall Hermann Göring conducted a search of the Warburg family tree, he conveniently discovered that Otto Warburg's father, Emil, was in fact half Aryan. This made Otto, the son of a gentile mother, only a quarter Jewish and as such exempt from most anti-Semitic legislation, even as his erstwhile colleague Meyerhof and so many other fellow Nobel laureates were driven into exile. (Meyerhof, along with the painter Marc Chagall and some 2,000 other refugees, was eventually smuggled out of occupied France through an underground network organized by a gentile American socialite-heiress in Paris.)

Otto Warburg was, then and later, criticized by anti-Nazis for reaching this false accommodation with the Hitler regime. To the extent Warburg had political feelings, these were anti-Nazi, as attested to by his remarks reported by informants to the Gestapo (and conveniently overlooked by order of higher authority). But Warburg's vision was narrowly focused on science and on the cancer breakthrough he, too, believed was around the corner (in retrospect, a rather vain hope in the absence of knowledge of the deviant gene expression that, as we now know, underlies the abnormal metabolic cell processes Warburg discovered). Voluntarily abandoning the research team and facilities he had built up in Berlin was as unthinkable as eating store-bought bread.

As for the financier Max Warburg, for the first five years of Nazi rule his reputation along with his international financial relations, still important for Germany's foreign trade, gave him access to high non-Nazi government bureaucrats. This allowed him to hang on and serve as leader of the hard-pressed Hamburg Jewish community, torn between the prospect of exile and the hope that the anti-Semitic storm would yet abate. The illusion came to an end in the wake of the *Kristallnacht* pogrom in 1938, when the Warburg Bank was Aryanized and the family assets virtually confiscated, Hitler having apparently decided that it would soon be time to conquer the rest of Europe rather than trade with it. An irony was that, whereas the Jewish

Warburgs then fled, the baptized branch of the family, having so distanced themselves from Judaism, felt safe in remaining in Germany and perished in the Final Solution.

The diverse religious affiliations and mixed genealogies of the various Warburgs were typical of so many German families of Jewish origin. This highlights the lunacy of the Nazi concept of the eternal Jews sinisterly allied to one another in their life-and-death struggle against the Aryans for world domination. The fact was that already for decades before the advent of Hitler, the German Jews had been following a voluntary path to extinction, through conversion, intermarriage, and low birth rates.

Already in 1911 there appeared an important study entitled "The Demise of the German Jews," which showed that they were freely disappearing, even while the Jewish population in other countries was increasing. Its author was the medical doctor Felix Aaron Theilhaber, son of the distinguished gynecologist researcher Adolf Theilhaber, professor at the University of Munich. Like many Jewish doctors, Felix Theilhaber specialized in dermatology and he built up a prominent practice in Berlin. His involvement in the traditional dermatological subspecialism of venereology led him, by extension, to concern himself with matters of reproduction and demography.

Theilhaber noted that, having survived brilliantly for thousands of years in a sea of enemies, the Jews seemed now, in post-emancipation Germany, to be placing severe restrictions on their future numbers. This was, to be sure, not a uniquely Jewish phenomenon but part of a larger trend among the educated and commercial urbanized classes, as they turned away from traditional religious values and rustic customs. The tendency was especially evident in the German capital, and Theilhaber's subsequent book, *Sterile Berlin,* drew particular interest from eugenicists concerned not with Aryan mythology but with the decline in the best and the brightest of whatever ethnic or religious background. The Jews, belonging as they did in disproportionately far greater numbers to the middle class, were most drastically affected as a population group. Jewish achievements in industry building and the professions came at the expense of family life. Jews married later, if at all (twice as many Jews as gentiles never wed), and had fewer children. The Jewish birth rate, which already in 1880 had been considerably below the national average, plunged to almost half by 1910. Twelve of the German states registered an absolute decline in their Jewish populations. But compounding all this was the rate of intermarriage and conversion of a people who no longer considered themselves a Jewish nation but as Germans adhering—ever more loosely—to the Mosaic religion. Already around the turn of the century, one out of every six German Jews was marrying outside the faith and their children were usually lost to Judaism. On the eve of Hitler's coming to power, this had risen to an incredible 60 percent.

The concern of some Jews with their declining birth rate and unfavorable demographics coincided with the growth of the field of *Rassenhygiene* following German unification. Despite its now ominous ring, racial hygiene did not have overtly evil beginnings. Nationalistic Germans in the late nineteenth century, concerned with maintaining Germany's military and economic dominance in Europe, were initially troubled by a declining birth rate and by the potentially fatal pediatric diseases facing babies and young children (given expression in the *Kindertotenlieder* of the Jewish composer Gustav Mahler at the turn of the century). But the dramatic advances in medicine that were reducing the child mortality from diseases such as diphtheria gave rise to a complementary concern in German minds about the quality rather than the mere quantity of the population and the potential weakening of the genetic stock through interference with Darwinian natural selection. Experiments on changing the constitution of egg cells and sperm, and microscope observations of the behavior of chromosomes during fertilization and cell division, offered at least the theoretical prospect of someday countering the unfavorable technological interference in the quality of the stock with favorable technological interference through direct genetic manipulation. But the discovery of the secrets of DNA was still a long way off. Racial hygienists accordingly placed the collective well-being of society and the improving of the genetic stock of future generations above the rights of the individual in the here and now, including the right to have children. But although anthropology and racial concepts (in, for example, matters of physique and immunity) were incorporated into the medical curriculum in Wilhelmine Germany and the Weimar Republic, racial hygiene did not necessarily carry connotations of anti-Semitism or Aryanism, except among fringe groups such as the National Socialists.

In fact, the eugenics movement drew much from the influential theories of, in Sigmund Freud's proud words, "a man of my race—the great Lombroso." A professor of legal medicine and criminal anthropology at the University of Turin, the Italian Jew Cesare Lombroso had earlier served as a military surgeon and then specialized in psychiatry. His book *l'Uomo Delinquente,* published in 1876, gained fame for its controversial studies on the inheritability of criminal traits and (more dubiously) of corresponding physical features or stigmata, as signs of an evolutionary throwback. (Somewhat the antipode of the delinquent man was profiled in another of Lombroso's books, *Man of Genius.*) Remarking upon criminality among his coreligionists, Lombroso reported: "the percentage of crimes among Jews is always lower than that of the surrounding population . . . murder is extremely rare." But, he conceded: "there is a prevalence of certain forms of offenses, often hereditary, such as fraud, forgery, libel, and chief of all, traffic in prostitution."

Socialists disputed Lombroso's emphasis on heredity and questioned the validity of his findings. Preferring the term *social hygiene* to *racial hygiene,* they were more inclined toward effecting environmental rather than genetic improvements. They also placed greater emphasis on health and welfare from the cradle all the way to the grave, rather than just to the barracks. (Even Lombroso embraced socialism and advocated improvement in living conditions.) But the social hygienists and the racial hygienists had quite similar goals, and these were strongly conditioned by the German tendency toward authoritarianism and respect for a (hopefully beneficent) *Machtstaat.* Civil servants, grand or petty, were fond of parading around in military-style uniforms, complete with swords, and thus competing with the army officers for public awe, a mentality so much in contrast with the spirit of liberalism, democracy, and personal freedom in the English-speaking countries. The recent triumph of the germ theory served in Germany as a justification for greater state intervention in health matters—central government being better able to wage war on the infective agent. Indeed, it has been suggested that—Louis Pasteur notwithstanding—the development of the pathogenic germ concept in France in the previous century was impeded by the spirit of French liberalism. ("The interests of humanity, science, and commerce will not be sacrificed to the systematic views of the government's advisers on sanitary measures," declared a prominent

French anticontagionist during a cholera epidemic.) In turn-of-the-century German medicine, by contrast, military and police metaphors were gladly used, not the least Paul Ehrlich's "magic bullet."

If the First World War was a disaster for Germany, it was a double tragedy for the German Jews in particular. The immediate loss to the Jewish community were the 12,000 soldiers who gave their lives for the Fatherland. Compounding this was the ironic fact that, just as the victory of 1870 and the building of a unified German state had led to the rise of anti-Semitism in some circles, now the defeat of Germany encouraged an ever more vicious anti-Semitism among certain groups, despite the Jewish front-line sacrifices and the fact that 25,000 German-Jewish soldiers had been decorated. This occurred against a background of political and social upheaval and the threat of starvation in the war's aftermath, which led many Germans to feel that, whereas once they were engaged merely in the quest for German preeminence, they were now locked in a struggle for national survival.

Although the postwar Weimar constitution provided for individual human rights, the collectivist mentality dominated in matters of health and welfare, most notably in clause 119, which provided for the protection of the health of the family and of future generations. That some demobilized soldiers were infected with syphilis raised the specter of sterile marriages or children with congenital defects. With the availability of Ehrlich's Salvarsan, legislation for compulsory screening and treatment was enacted, which, while fairly innocuous in itself, represented a further step in the role of the physician as state policeman. The Reich Ministry of the Interior also gave the genealogical department of the German Psychiatry Institute in Munich widespread authority in its compilation of a "total register of the biological population," with access to state and criminal records.

So when in the 1920s Hitler wrote in *Mein Kampf* that "We must do away with the concept that the treatment of the body is the affair of every individual," this was hardly out of step with the ingrained German awe of state authority. But whereas the Weimar constitution had made various provisions for individual rights in the field of health as in the social and political spheres, the Nazis, drawing a physiological analogy, declared the whole new German state to be *biologisch* (organic). Social or political dissent was prohibited, since no part of the organism must be allowed to battle another.

The first year of Nazi rule saw the German birth rate jump by almost a quarter. Subsequent laws relegated unmarried women to the same legal status as Jews: *Staatsangehöriger* (subjects) as opposed to *Bürger* (citizens). Contraception was curtailed and abortion carried a potential death penalty—but not for the Jews. For them, the restriction was gladly waived by the justices (if one may used such a term) of the Third Reich. This pro-choice exemption, on the face of it a not unwelcome option, was a prelude to far less liberal measures to reduce and eventually annihilate the Jewish population. "[We] must make certain," Hitler ranted, "that in our country, at least, the world enemy [the Jew] is recognized and that the fight against him becomes a gleaming symbol of brighter days to show other nations the way to the salvation of an embattled Aryan humanity."

Hitler was undoubtedly unaware of the irony that the term *Aryan* he so proudly bandied about had been introduced into popular usage by the son-in-law of Moses Mendelsohn, the eighteenth century "German Socrates," who, as we have seen, interpreted Judaism in the spirit of the German Enlightenment and paved the way for Jewish intellectual participation in the wider society. Like Mendelsohn, his Christian son-in-law Friedrich Schlegel, a Romantic novelist, historian, and diplomat, campaigned for Jewish emancipation. But whereas previously the Germans, like all Christians, had sought a biblical origin for themselves (from Adam to Noah to Jepheth to Ashkenaz) and had speculated that German and all tongues derived somehow from Hebrew, studies carried out by Schlegel and others pointed, quite correctly, to a special relation of most ancient and modern European languages to the Persian of Iran and the Sanskrit of India. Perceiving in particular a kinship between the Persian and Sanskrit root *ari* (noble), the German *Ehre* (honor), the Irish-Celtic *aire* (free, ruling class), and cognates in other European languages, Schlegel placed the origins of the Europeans not in the biblical Middle East, but beyond Eden, on the Roof of the World in Northern India, from which the noble Aryans of the ancient Vedic texts marched westward, carrying their civilization with them. Although such speculation offered, along with the linguistic differentiation, a presumed biological distinction between speakers of Aryan and non-Aryan languages (among which the Semitic group), Schlegel himself was no racist, as shown by his marriage into the Mendelsohn family.

Today the term *Indo-European*, which indicates the geographic spread of this family of languages in the Old World has replaced the name Aryan, which is properly confined to the Persian-Indian branch of the family (as indeed is reflected in the modern name for Persia: "Iran"). But Schlegel's term remained current for some 150 years. In the second half of the nineteenth century, with the rise of the sciences of biology, geology, and archaeology, Old Testament truths were further brought into question, not least with regard to the age of the earth and the origins of man and the various branches of mankind. Particularly influential in the zeitgeist of the late twentieth century were the Darwinian concepts of the struggle for existence and the survival of the fittest, extrapolated from the animal kingdom to human ethnic groups. But whatever the pseudoscientific veneer, the new anti-Semitic diatribes of the nationalist Germans, particularly the fringe groups, tended to revert to blatant occultism. The number three and a tripartite division were seen as genetically inherent in Aryan thought. This gave the Christian Trinity, and perhaps even Christ himself, Aryan rather than Semitic credentials. Adam, for his part, was turned into an Aryan sun-worshiper.

Although *Aryan* became part and parcel of the vocabulary of German (and of most other European languages), German nationalists in the latter decades of the nineteenth century, particularly in the wake of unification, were disinclined to accept an Indian origin of their *Volk*. This was also a time when the *Blut und Bodemromane* (blood and soil novels, later contracted by the Nazi regime to the homely term *Blubos*) were highly popular among the reading public, particularly those of the middle class who were averse to the currents of modernism, such as the stock exchange, department stores, mass marketing, advertising, and avant-garde art and theater—all considered to be so very Jewish. Nationalist elements, harking back with particular pride to the description by the first-century Roman historian Tacticus (wholly speculative though it was) of the Teutons as being indigenous to Germany and of pure race, sought the cradle of Aryanism closer to home, in Eastern Europe, Southern Scandinavia, the Baltic Coast, or (best of all) in Germany itself.

With all this went the assumption that the original Aryans were blue-eyed blonds, that the modern Germans were the purest of their descendants—though needing to be bred purer still—and that German was the most Aryan of all the Indo-European languages. Actually, on the basis of present-day linguistic and archaeological evidence, the prime candidate for the ancestral home of the first speakers of Indo-European are the Caucasus and the Caspian Sea area of the former USSR, straddling the border with Asia. They seem to have been pastoralists who were the first people to domesticate the horse and one of the first to use wheeled vehicles, which aided the expansion of their language and culture to peoples west and east of them, beginning some 5,000 years ago. In this process, over thirty separate languages and many more dialects developed, of which German can by no means claim to be the most like the original. (On balance, that honor goes to Lithuanian, which derives from a quite un-Germanic branch of Indo-European.)

Needless to say, this identification of language with "race" was among the more confused aspects of National Socialist ideology, particularly as it applied to Jews. No Jew had had Hebrew as a mother tongue for some 2,000 years. In fact, for centuries the great majority of European Jews—many of whom, as Virchow systematically showed, had fair hair and light eyes—spoke German as their native language: either the standard language of Germany, or one of its dialects, particularly Yiddish, the Rhineland German they had brought with them to Eastern Europe in Medieval times. Thorstein Veblen, the famed turn-of-the-century Swedish-American social scientist whose study of the Jews we have mentioned in the introduction, wrote plausibly that the blond race was a biological mutation arising among some darker-haired northward-migrating Mediterraneans who spoke non-Indo-European languages and to whom the Indo-European languages were later brought by brunette invaders from the East. Indeed, the Finns and Estonians, who have always spoken a totally non-Indo-European mother tongue and have never been "Aryanized," probably conform on average better to the Nordic ideal than do the Germans. Then there are the Georgians, to whom we owe the very term *Caucasian* as exemplar of the white race. (The founder of modern anthropology, the German Johann Friedrich Blumenbach, wrote around the turn of the nineteenth century: "I have taken the name of this variety from Mount Caucasus, both because its neighborhood, and especially its southern slope, produces the most beautiful race of men, I mean the Georgians.") Although living in the presumed Indo-European cradle, the Georgians speak a language that is totally unrelated to Indo-European, let alone to its Aryan (that is to say, Irano-Indian) branch.

Strictly speaking, in fact, the European people with the best claim to the Aryan title on linguistic grounds are the Gypsies. Their language, derived from ancient Sanskrit, which they brought from India to Europe in their migrations centuries ago and maintained for countless generations, truly belongs to the Irano-Indian branch of the Indo-European family. Yet it became Nazi policy to destroy Europe's only group of Aryan-speakers, albeit more as an afterthought than as a consequence of a long history of demonization, as was the case with the Jews.

If Nazi ideologues merely downgraded Jewish achievements in medicine in general as not being of much value to the Aryan body, they vehemently attacked Jewish accomplishments in psychiatry as destructive to the Aryan soul. In his so-called "Manual of the Jewish Question," circulated in the Third Reich, Theodor Fritsch concluded that "the Volk would be shielded from much harm if the corrupting influence of Jewish medical science or pseudoscience could be restrained." Very begrudgingly, even he had to recognize some positive contributions of the great Jewish doctors. But, like all other Jewish intellectual and cultural achievements, these were derived in an almost parasitic manner from the work of others. To be weighed against these positive contributions were the deleterious effects of Jewish thought. In particular, "the most calamitous influence wrought by the Jews has been in their pet field, sexology. The Jew simply has a different sexuality from the Teutons; he can't and won't understand them. And when he tries to transfer his own attitudes to the Germans, this can lead to the destruction of the German soul," Fritsch railed. "A typical example of the inner dishar-mony between the spiritual life of the Jews and that of the Germans is represented by Freudian psychoanalysis."

That psychoanalysis should be branded a Jew science poisonous to the Teuton's psyche is all that could be expected from a raving German anti-Semite such as Fritsch. Yet in what was one of the most bizarre episodes in the history of psychiatry—indeed in the whole history of medicine—his racist rantings found a voice of support from a hitherto respected source in Switzerland, Freud's erstwhile "crown prince," Carl Gustav Jung.

As we have seen, the rationalistic, "absolutely Godless Jew" Freud felt toward his people "a miraculous thing in common, which—inaccessible to analysis so far—makes the Jew." The old Freud, musing on Judaism in his

Moses and Monotheism, even showed a hint of Lamarckism—the concept, rejected by virtually all biologists since the ascendancy of Darwin's theory of natural selection, that the effects or memories of events experienced during the lifetime of individuals can be transmitted genetically to future generations, including to the descendants of Moses and Aaron. But such occasional flirtations with spirituality and pseudoscience in Freud's thinking were insignificant compared to Carl Jung, who made mysticism the cornerstone of his brand of depth psychology.

Initially drawn to the psychoanalytic movement due to Freud's pioneering exploration of the unconscious, Jung soon complained that Freud had stopped prematurely at the level that Jung termed the "personal unconscious." For Jung, this was still a rather shallow layer of the proverbial iceberg of the psyche. Jung went on to posit that at the profoundest level, all individual psyches meet in a collective unconscious common to all humanity. Jung populated this collective unconscious with numinous archetypes with names such as the Spirit, the Trickster, the Hero, the Anima (in men), the Animus (in women), the Shadow, and the Wise Old Man. By definition, the archetypes, like religious symbols for the faithful, were not subject to rational analysis. Whereas Freud sought phallic symbols in art and dreams, Jung was of the opinion that even an undisguised representation of the penis was itself a phallic symbol, standing for something numinous and inherently unanalyzable in the collective unconscious. As for Oedipal incest fantasies, these symbolized for Jung an archetypal longing for the Rebirth of the Spirit through contact with the Maternal Soil. Jung was furthermore convinced of the realities of paranormal events and the role played in them by archetypal symbols. Particularly dear to his heart was the paranormal phenomenon he termed *synchronicity*, a sort of short-circuiting of the spacetime continuum (to borrow a term from Einsteinian physics) via the collective unconscious.

Most relevant to the present episode of the history of Jews and medicine was Jung's positing of an additional layer, between the individual unconscious and the collective unconscious, the so-called racial unconscious. At this level of one's psyche, archetypes have taken on a form molded in a Lamarckian manner by the experiences of one's racial ancestors through the ages, even, hypothetically, in the absence of any conscious cultural transmission.

Already early in their relationship in the first decade of the twentieth century, Freud was troubled by Jung's mystical tendencies. But Freud was more concerned with the prospect of psychoanalysis becoming, in his words, a "Jewish national affair." Freud's dream was that when the day would come for him to be succeeded, a more mature and rational Jung would bring psychoanalysis to the wider world. So, as we saw in the previous chapter, Freud was prepared to overlook temporarily some of Jung's more objectionable *goyische* traits, in the hope that the pastor's son would yet overcome his "great inner resistances" and "find his way to me."

As it turned out, Jung was never able to divest himself of his mysticism. The inevitable break came in 1913 and was preceded by an exchange of letters that bordered on the hilarious. When Freud wrote that Jung "without intending it, has solved the riddle of all mysticism, showing it to be based on the symbolic utilization of complexes that have outlived their function," an angry Jung accused Freud of never having lost his neurosis since at one of their mutual dream interpretation sessions he (Freud) had not submitted to a full analysis out of fear of losing his paternal authority. Jung contrasted his own Swiss bluntness with Freud's "depreciating Viennese criterion of egoistic striving for power or for heaven-knows-what other insinuation from the father complex." He went on to accuse Freud's followers of "misusing psychoanalysis for the purpose of devaluating others." Particularly annoying to Jung was the rumor supposedly making the rounds in psychoanalytic circles that his objections to Freudian theory were the product of his anal eroticism.

Later, however, a vacillating Jung professed his continued loyalty to Freud. Alfred Alder and his group had recently seceded from the psychoanalytic movement, but Jung assured Freud that "even Adler's cronies do not consider me one of theirs." Unfortunately, Jung made the mistake of capitalizing the German word for "theirs" (*ihrigen* in German) so that it came out "yours" (*Ihrigen*) instead. Freud replied by pointing out to Jung this Freudian slip and, in a witty frame of mind, signed the letter "Yours nevertheless." Jung, apparently not amused, accused Freud of "sniffing out all the symptomatic actions in your vicinity, thus reducing everyone to the level of sons and daughters who blushingly admit their fault." Soon afterward, all contact ceased.

Not long after, Freud, desiring to set the record straight as he saw it, wrote the *History of the Psychoanalytic Movement*. There he stated that Adler's concepts of the inferiority complex and the compensatory will to power, though radically false, were at least characterized by a certain consistency and coherence and were founded on a theory of the instincts. Jung's concepts, on the other hand, were "mystifying and incomprehensible to wise men and fools alike." Freud further stated that at the beginning of their relationship Jung had been prepared to "give up for my sake certain race prejudices." What exactly Freud based this assumption on is not clear. But the "Viennese" characteristics Jung derided may have been a code word for "Jewish." (As Freud wrote in another context: "[T]he reproach of being a citizen of Vienna is only a euphemistic substitute for another reproach which no one would care to put forth openly." "Between the lines you can further read that we Viennese are not only swine but also Jews. But that does not appear in print.")

Jung, for his part, was far more traumatized by the break and went through, as he would later call it, "a state of disorientation." Twice on a train trip Jung lost consciousness and had frightening visions of a tidal wave of blood sweeping from the North Sea to the base of the Swiss Alps, and he feared that this might herald a schizophrenic episode. But not long afterward a tangible wave of blood in the form of World War One did indeed drench Europe, thereby shocking Jung back to reality and allowing him to attribute his visions to an archetypal prescience.

There was only one more exchange of letters between the two psychiatrists. In 1923, ten years after the break, Jung felt obliged to refer one of his patients to Freud —a thoroughly assimilated Jew and well-to-do diplomat—since this man was so impressed by Freud's writings that he had even begun to dream of him. But (so one of Jung's pupils later related) the patient's analysis in Vienna turned out to be of little use and he returned to Jung in Zürich. The diplomat then had a dream of trying to reach a light source beyond an impasse, where an old woman told him, "Only a Jew can get through!" The diplomat's acceptance of his Jewish identity supposedly marked the beginning of the cure for his neurosis.

In the next ten years, Jung, with his prolific writing, continued to build up a respectable following in the field of psychotherapy. But it was the old master who not only had by far the greater number of adherents in the medical profession, but whose ideas were permeating the general weltanschauung of the age. This was nowhere truer than in the Weimar

Republic. And as the Austrian Freud had suggested to the Swiss Jung long before (and Jung had agreed), "the future of psychotherapy will be decided in Germany." But the game was not yet over, for there were violent forces emerging totally outside the scientific and cultural spheres that would radically alter the rules.

When Hitler came to power in January 1933, Jung was serving as vice-president of Germany's General Medical Society for Psychotherapy (GMSP). A few months later, its president, the distinguished professor of psychiatry Ernst Kretschmer, resigned. Kretschmer wasn't Jewish but objected to the Nazis' plan to make the GMSP conform to Hitler's ideology. Jung, although a Swiss, took over the presidency of the society and the editorship of its journal, the *Zentralblatt für Psychotherapie*. Within a week, Jung appeared on Berlin Radio and was introduced by the interviewer, his former pupil Dr. Adolf Weizsäcker, with comments that the Germans were tired of the Freudian manner of continually probing and dissecting the mind along intellectual lines. Jung heartily agreed and stressed the "hostility toward life" of Freudian reductionism (the view that higher human aspirations originally developed from more primitive, asocial drives), which doesn't take into account "one of the privileges of the German mind, to let the whole of creation work upon it."

In response to other questions, Jung spoke positively of the youthful element in the Nazi revolution for "seizing the helm, because they alone have the daring and drive and sense of adventure." He went on to say that "only in times of aimless quiescence does the aimless conversation of parliamentary deliberations drone on." Jung found it perfectly natural that "a leader should stand at the head of an élite, which in earlier centuries was formed by the nobility . . . which believed in the law of the blood and the exclusiveness of the race."

By year's end, the first edition of the *Zentralblatt* under Jung's editorship appeared. This was introduced by a signed editorial that, although not mentioning Freud by name, derided the "one-sided and mutually exclusive observations [that] have exerted too far-reaching an influence not only on specialized medical opinion, but also on the psychological views of many intelligent laymen." Jung went on to say that "the differences which actually do exist between Germanic and Jewish psychology . . . are no longer to be glossed over, and this can only be beneficial to science." The editorial was immediately followed by a manifesto by Dr. Matthias Göring, the *Reichsführer* of the German section of the society and cousin of the notorious air marshal Hermann Göring. In it he stated that "the Society expects all its author and speaker members to have worked through Adolf Hitler's fundamental book *Mein Kampf* in all scientific seriousness and recognize it as their foundation."

In the next issue, in 1934, Jung contributed a lengthy and rather confused article on "The State of Psychotherapy Today." In it he branded as Jewish the psychology of Adler. (The fact that Adler was, by conscious choice, a Christian when he formulated his theories was apparently as irrelevant to Jung as it was to the Nazis.) But this was incidental to Jung's venomous attack on his erstwhile Jewish mentor. Freud's theory was a "dirty joke psychology," which only revealed "the adolescent smutty-mindedness of the explainer." Freudian psychoanalysis was criminal in its search for "unnatural dirt" behind the "natural purity" of people who are not cheaters. Using the mercantile metaphor, Jung derided the reductionist view of the psyche as comparable to a trader's attempt to bring down the price of some item by claiming it is "nothing but. . . ." Then Jung went on to pay a compliment of sorts to Freud: one is at heart only as base or noble as the psychological theory that one constructs or to which one subscribes. Freudian psychoanalysis therefore *does* have validity, but only for Freud and "all those who are similarly constituted."

Not many editors of a scientific journal would allow themselves to engage in such self-serving ad hominem diatribes. This is especially so since Jung—even as negatively fixated as he was on the sexual aspect of psychoanalysis, which had played a large part in the traumatic break with Freud two decades earlier—could not but have been aware of the broader scope of Freud's thinking. But far more disturbing were Jung's statements about those whose personalities he supposed to be "similarly constituted" to Freud's. "In my opinion," he continued, "it has been a grave error in medical psychology up to now to apply Jewish categories . . . indiscriminately to German and Slavic Christians." Perhaps still annoyed at the supposed rumors among the Viennese psychoanalysts concerning his anal eroticism, Jung stated that "the Jews have this in common with women: being physically weaker they have to aim at the chinks in the armor of their adversary." He explained that because of their civilization, more than twice as ancient as ours, they are vastly more conscious than we of human weaknesses, of the Shadow-side of things, and hence in this respect are much less vulnerable than we are. It is also their ancient culture which they have to thank for their ability to live with their own vices fully consciously and even in the most benevolent, friendly and tolerant surroundings, whereas we are still too young not to have "illusions" about ourselves.

For good measure, Jung threw in that "the Jew, who is something of a cultural nomad, has never yet created a cultural form of his own and as far as we can see, never will." (This old theme would be used again the following year by Hitler in his first speech at the Nuremberg rallies as a prelude to the introduction of his notorious racial legislation.)

Neither Freud nor his misled gentile followers understood the Aryan and particularly the German psyche, wrote Jung, who then asked rhetorically: "Has the formidable phenomenon of National Socialism, on which the world gazes with astonished eyes, taught them any better? Where was that unparalleled tension and energy when as yet no National Socialism existed? Deep in the Germanic psyche, in a pit that is anything but a garbage-bin of unrealized infantile wishes and unresolved family resentments."

Jung's gloating over events in Germany as somehow vindicating his own psychological theories could only have pleased the Nazis. All the more since, according to depth and social psychologists less mystically inclined than Jung, infantilism *was* a powerful factor in the Nazi movement. Psychoanalysts have pointed to, among other things, the particularly authoritarian structure of the German lower-middle-class family, and especially the father's repression of the sexual drive in the name of morality. The resulting ambiguous fear and love of authority could easily be transferred into masochistic obedience to and identification with the Führer. Furthermore, Hitler, with uncanny insight drawn from his own particularly disturbed family background, was singularly adept at channeling the Germans' repressed hostility and drive toward overcompensation into the breaking down of an older authoritarian hierarchy and the creation of a new one. The Jews—living representations of the Father religion that would not accept the Son religion of Christianity—made ideal targets for the projection of the negative side of the paternal image, an image reinforced for centuries in Medieval Germanic folklore by tales of old bearded Jews bleeding to death young Christian boys (never girls) as part of the Passover ritual.

This is not to say that the psychoanalytic explanations in themselves disproved Jung's semi-religious concepts, which sought the roots of Nazism in numinous archetypes of Fathers, Saviors, and twisted Crosses at a level deeper than childhood—namely, in the archaic racial and collective unconscious—especially under circumstances when more traditional religious outlets were on the wane. Only that Jung's gloating over the triumphs of the Nazi movement as invalidating Freudian psychoanalysis and validating his own archetypal depth psychology was scientifically questionable as well as ethically. In any event, Freud and Jung held at least one tenet in common: that times of great social stress (the Black Death in Medieval Germany, the defeat and economic crisis in the Weimar Republic) were apt to cause one form or another of mass susceptibility to unconscious forces, as individuals formed into mobs.

Understandably, Jung's Jewish followers—these were, in fact, some of the most prominent Jungians—were dismayed by his diatribe. So, too, were Jung's gentile colleagues in Switzerland, where the anti-Semitism of the Nazis across the border found little resonance. Jung was openly criticized on the pages of the *Neuer Zürcher Zeitung*. He soon ceased any further polemics about Jewish-Freudian psychology and eventually became disillusioned with the Nazis in general. (Even if Freud hadn't been Jewish, Jung would still have had this original amiable interest. For at the time he felt that an archetypal image like the cross—even when given a leftward [literally, "sinister"] twist to form a swastika—contained highly creative and healing forces as well as destructive ones. Furthermore, Jung doubted the workability of parliamentary democracies with populations far more massive that than of Switzerland. Yet the course of events in Germany increasingly convinced him that only the consciousness of each individual could discriminate between the creative and destructive extremes and effectively channel the energy, and that this became impossible when the individual was part of a spellbound mob.)

But no admission of wrongdoing was forthcoming from Jung. For the rest of his life (he died in 1961), Jung was periodically called to account for his actions of 1933–1934. He invariably resorted to rationalizations of the type he no doubt would have deemed highly disingenuous or (more kindly) self-

deceiving, if coming from one of his patients. In taking over the chairmanship of the GMSP, Jung had been motivated by pure altruism, wishing not
to leave "the people clinging to me in the lurch." He sacrificed his "egotis-
tic comfort" so as to "preserve a spirit of scientific cooperation and save
psychotherapy" in Germany "for humanity's sake." Göring's *Mein Kampf*
manifesto had appeared in Jung's *Zentrallblatt* due to a misunderstanding.
As for his diatribe on Jewish versus Aryan psychology, much was taken out
of context or mistranslated into other languages. And besides, why were
the Jews so "ridiculously hypersensitive" with their "paranoid attitude"? Jung
pleaded his "total inability to understand why it should be a crime to speak
of 'Jewish psychology,' when no-one objects to discussing the differences
between French and German psychology." Would he himself be so offended
if accused of "Swiss wooden-headedness?" (It did not seem to matter to
this great depth psychologist that, unlike the Swiss, the "ridiculously hypersensitive" and "paranoid" Jews were at the time being beaten and humiliated on the streets of Germany and facing eventual extermination due
to their supposed inherent spiritual differences—a fate already foretold in
Mein Kampf, a book that, for whatever reason, was accorded official status
in Jung's journal.)

And what of Jung's diatribe against Freud's Jewish psychoanalysis? Well,
"surely the individual [Freud] is not the people," Jung declared. While Freud
may indeed have recognized his own Jewishness, his error was to view
psychoanalysis as applicable to a broader humanity. In fact, it is "not even
binding on all Jews," but only on those who fit Freud's own type—those
who have a "materialistic, intellectual and irreligious attitude." "Silence" on
the part of Jews not openly opposing Freud, "may be taken as consensus."
For the Jews willing to recognize their roots (and such recognition is a
prime step in the Jungian process of so-called individuation, as we have
seen in the 1923 case of the assimilated Jewish diplomat), any outcry against
Jung's remarks was misplaced. Indeed, Jung personally intervened with
the Nazi regime in order to help German Jews sympathetic to his own
philosophy. Religious Jews in particular should "summon up the courage
to distinguish themselves clearly from Freud," and especially from that
"damnable capacity of the Jew, as exemplified by Freud, to deny his own
nature," even when he still knows he is a Jew.

Jung's attempts at exculpation for his deeds during the first year of the
Third Reich were as tortuous as they were self-serving. One might ask why

he did not instead plead that he had been temporarily swept up in a *partici-pation mystique* in the Nazi movement, including its anti-Semitic aspects. This would have been in accordance with his own theories of the psyche and particularly the collective unconscious. As a physician Jung could have explained by analogy that even the greatest bacteriologist or epidemiolo-gist is not necessarily immune from contagion by the disease of his exper-tise. Alternatively, if he could muster the *chutzpah,* Jung might have pleaded, as did his friend and biographer Laurens Van der Post on his behalf, "how profoundly engaged he was in another dimension of reality." The answer would seem to be that Jung, although emotionally overcharged in 1933–34, was fully conscious of his motives in his opportunistic appeal to anti-Semitism in his dispute with Freud. "The next thing that's now going to be made up about me is that I suffer from a complete lack of conviction and that I'm neither an anti-Semite nor a Nazi," Jung bewailed in response to his critics. This "made up" charge is in fact close to the mark. For Jung was only mildly influenced by anti-Semitism, if at all, and only briefly infatu-ated with Nazism. But he was shameless in using politics and bigotry to settle a score with his erstwhile mentor and father-figure. Indeed, in a letter written during the '30s Jung revealed perhaps more than he intended when he declared that if Freud—even with his "soulless materialism"—had been "more tolerant of the ideas of others, I would be standing at his side today." Unabashed, Jung challenged the Jewish intellectuals to distance themselves from Freud and thus "*prove that spirit is stronger than blood.*"

Blood had long played an important part in anti-Jewish persecution and prejudices in many lands, but nowhere more so than in Germany. This was based in large measure on interpretations of events in the New Testament. In the Middle Ages and beyond, myths abounded that Jews, being the de-scendants of those who taunted and martyred Jesus, were at certain times of the year afflicted with bloody wounds on their hands, feet, and crown. Hemorrhoids were likewise part of their punishment, and Christians—perhaps in awe of the bloody circumcision ritual—also believed that Jew-ish men menstruated. A complementary myth had it that Jews needed Christian blood as an antidote to these afflictions, which for good measure was also a supposed cure-all for a range of other maladies such as painful childbirth and blindness. These medical applications were, of course, supplemental to the sheer religious ecstasy the Jews' felt when slowly extracting blood from innocent Christians.

As we have noted, the actors in the archetypal blood libel drama were elderly bearded Jews bleeding to death a young Christian boy. Although the myth of the medicinal power of young blood did not originate with the blood libel, this scene was particularly emotive in psychoanalytic terms, with the elderly adherents of the Father religion drawing the stream of life from the prepubescent representative of the Son religion. While Jewish *physicians* were not in particular implicated in such acts, suspicion was aroused that they relied on their "therapeutic" bleeding of gentile patients in order to augment the synagogue's Christian blood supply. This was especially so around Passover-Easter time, when it was in strong demand as an essential ingredient in matzoh—the Seder being, of course, as much a rejoicing in the crucifixion of Jesus as a celebration of the Exodus from Egypt. Blood drawn surreptitiously by doctors from adult gentile patients was perhaps less coveted than the blood rabbis obtained by slowly martyring a young Christian boy; but its use was still preferable to having to dilute the latter with tomato extract, as was sometimes necessary when supplies ran low.

Of course, as we have seen, in the long centuries before the dawn of modern medicine, some Jewish doctors *did* bleed Christian (as well as their fellow Jewish) patients to death or, more accurately, inadvertently hastened their demise by letting their blood. Yet the Jewish physicians were, if anything, less likely to do this than their Christian colleagues, thanks to Maimonides' cautious warnings about bloodletting. A greater irony of the blood-matzoh libel is that—even if one accepts the Freudian analysis that the Oedipal associations and the awe of the symbolic castration of the circumcision ritual invested the myth with particular power in the unconscious of the Christian accusers—this libel should be directed against the very people who for over 3,000 years were conditioned to abhor the consumption of any and all blood, even that of the most kosher of animals. ("And whatsoever man there be of the house of Israel, or of the strangers that sojourn among you, that eateth any manner of blood; I will even set my face against that soul that eateth blood, and will cut him off from among his people" [Leviticus 17:10).]

As we have noted in previous chapters, the blood libel in its quite literal manifestations accompanied the eastward migration of the German Jews to the Slavic lands, where it endured into the twentieth century. In Germany itself the libel became dormant, due in part to Luther's general opposition to superstition (anti-Jewish though he otherwise was) and, of course, the influence of the *Aufklärung*. But the concept lingered in the German folk memory. With the rise of anti-Semitism, it lent itself metaphorically to the image of, in Hitler's words, the "eternal blood-sucker": the Jewish financiers and merchants under the command of the Elders of Zion, who went around bleeding a country white and diverting its pecuniary life-blood to sinister activities.

But "blood" and "bloodlines" have, of course, traditionally been used in another metaphoric sense: to connote biological inheritance through family, ethnic, or racial ancestry. This has been the case in many cultures. The Germans, however, happen to be traditionally concerned with their blood—the power of the soul, according to the Nibelungenlied epics—as the seat of their weal and woe, in the way the French are preoccupied with their livers, the Americans with their hearts, and the English with their bowels. So perhaps not surprisingly, when Hitler wrote in *Mein Kampf* that "All great cultures of the past perished only because the originally creative race died out from blood poisoning," he was being more than just metaphorical. The popular health magazines that proliferated under Nazi auspices contained articles on the determining of Jewish ancestry by blood test. "Think what it might mean," wrote one expert, "if we could identify non-Aryans in the test tube!" When in 1935 a member of the SA "brownshirts" was injured in a traffic accident and was taken to a nearby Jewish hospital where his life was saved by a transfusion of blood from a Jew, the question came before the SA court as to whether this now disqualified him from membership. Fortunately for the Nazi, a loophole of sorts was found when the Jew turned out also to be a front-line World War One veteran who had been exempted from the 1933 anti-Semitic civil service laws at the insistence of the aged president Paul von Hindenburg. But the former field marshal had recently died, and the Nazis now moved to eliminate all such exemptions and turn all Jews into pariahs by enacting the notorious Nuremberg laws. At the Nuremberg rallies, Dr. Goebbels ranted on, applying an array of traditional biological metaphors to the Jews ("the parasite among the peoples, the son of Chaos, the incarnation of evil, the ferment of decomposition"). But when the Nazis officially called the statutes promulgated at Nuremburg the Law for the Protection of German Blood and German Honor, they took themselves literally.

Once again, the Third Reich not only enacted a criminal law but also committed an ironic perversion. For men of Jewish descent—soon to be slated for extermination due to their Semitic "blood"—were the great pioneers in the field of hematology and were singularly responsible for the discovery of the life-saving blessing of blood group classification.

Medical legend has it that the first ever human-to-human blood transfusion took place in that historically fateful year 1492. A Jewish physician used a tube device to exchange the blood of three strapping young lads for that of the ailing Pope Innocent VIII in hopes of rejuvenating him. The results were disastrous for all four subjects. The boys were exsanguinated and his Holiness expired all the sooner, prompting the Jewish doctor to prudently take flight. With the advent of William Harvey's description of the circulation of the blood in the early seventeenth century, with its distinction between the functions of arteries and veins, there came a surge of interest in transfusion. It now appeared that a donor's blood could be pumped by his heart directly into a recipient through a tube connecting the former's arteries to the latter's veins. Experiments in animal-to-human transfusions were briefly in vogue, particularly in France, under the assumption that the characteristics of the donor (say, the calmness of a lamb) would induce similar qualities in the recipient. These were followed by human-to-human transfusions, but after a fatal mishap and a law suit, the medical faculty of the University of Paris virtually outlawed the practice. Human-to-human transfusion was revived early in the nineteenth century, thanks to the introduction of a syringe for this purpose by a London professor. But a survey taken in 1868 revealed that over a third of all transfusions ended fatally. It not infrequently happened that the recipient, far from improving, was immediately seized by chills and fever and went into terminal anaphylactic shock.

In the new age of microscopy and theories of immunity in the late nineteenth century, it became known that a defense mechanism of the blood serum brings about the agglutination (clumping together) of foreign pathogenic bacteria and often their lysis (disintegration). Researchers speculated that the mixing of animal with human blood caused a similar hostile, in fact violent, reaction, which would account for the often tragic outcome of the transfusion of large quantities of lamb's blood to human patients in centuries past. But that such reactions occurred on an apparently hit-or-miss basis in human-to-human transfusions was suspected to involve some underlying pathological disorder on the part of the donor or recipient blood.

Enter now Karl Landsteiner. The son of a prominent Jewish journalist, Dr. Leopold Landsteiner, Karl was born in 1868 in Baden bei Wien, a health-resort town on the slopes of the Vienna Woods. During his medical education at the University of Vienna, he was particularly drawn to the more theoretical subjects of anatomy, physiology, and especially chemistry. The latter brought him to Würzburg for post-M.D. research at the laboratory of the organic chemist and future Nobel laureate Emil Fischer, who coined the term *side-chain* so beloved by Paul Ehrlich. Back in Vienna for his residency, young Dr. Landsteiner watched as the lives of patients ebbed away after an accident or during an operation due to loss of blood, which no doctor dared to replace by transfusion.

Karl Landsteiner had his doubts about the prevailing hypothesis, that the dreaded violent reactions to transfused blood were due to some obscure hematological disease on the part of the donor or recipient. As the twentieth century dawned, Landsteiner undertook to investigate the phenomenon at the University of Vienna Pathological Institute. He choose as his subjects six people—himself and his Institute colleagues Sturli, Erdheim, Pletschnig, Zaritsch, and Störk—who, as far as known, were suffering from no disease.

In test tubes Landsteiner mixed one by one the red blood cells of each subject with each of the other's (cell-free) sera and observed the results under the microscope. He found that the blood cells of Sturli and Erdheim were attacked (agglutinated) by the serum of each of the other four colleagues but not by each other's. Similarly, the blood corpuscles of Pletschnig and Zaritsch were clumped by everyone else's serum but not by one another's. The blood cells of the remaining two, Landsteiner and Störk, were immune from attack by anyone else's serum (including one another's). Thus were established the three major blood groups of humanity, called respectively A, B, and O. (Subsequent research by Sturli on a far larger group further revealed a rarer fourth blood type, AB, whose cells were agglutinated by the sera of all three other types.) Blood transfusion ceased to be a deadly game of Russian roulette, being rendered relatively safe by the typing of donor and recipient for compatibility.

Although a practicing Catholic, Landsteiner, whose blood type was O, was born of Jewish parents into the Jewish faith. The ethnic ancestry and religious background of his five colleagues were not recorded. For the purposes of Landsteiner's research such data would have been quite irrelevant. Yet from an anthropological point of view, interesting questions arose as to possible links between blood group and ethnic or racial origin. The questions were answered by Jewish researchers whose innocent empirical data, when subsequently commandeered by the Nazi pseudoscientists, had potentially deadly consequences for the Jews themselves.

Ludwik Hirszfeld was born in Warsaw in 1884 to a Jewish family well assimilated to the language, culture, and science of Poland, which was then mostly under czarist rule. His chemist uncle headed the capital's Institute of Mineral Water. As a Jew identifying with the Poles, young Ludwik opposed Russification in Poland and became involved in the underground Independence Movement. Like many Jews he was also drawn to socialism in his youth, especially in view of the stormy social developments that accompanied the rapid industrialization of textile manufacturing in Lodz, where he attended the *gymnasium*. Unable to obtain a place at a Polish university, Hirszfeld went to study medicine in Germany, first in Würzburg and then in Berlin. Attracted to bacteriology and immunology in general, the young student's main lifelong focus and the important chapter in the history of medicine he would write were determined by Hermann Oppenheimer's book *Toxin and Antitoxin*. As Hirszfeld later related: "I recall the decisive night when I sat reading this article till early morning. When I got up and closed the book, it was settled that I would become a serologist." Research was, however, not without its costs, and the financially hardpressed student had to hock his watch to help pay his lab fees and buy guinea pigs. After qualifying as a physician, Hirszfeld wrote his M.D. dissertation on blood agglutination under Professors Ulrich Friedemann and Max Rubner.

The first of Hirszfeld's major contributions to medicine came in 1907 with his prescient elucidation of the immunological nature of allergies at the Institute for Cancer Research in Heidelberg. "The organism defends its inviolability no matter whether invaded by a pathogenic germ or by a bit of inorganic matter from space," he wrote. "Climate and food allergies prove that the organism is in consonance with the external world and reacts in a fundamentally identical way to an array of stimuli—irrespective of their character or destructive power." Hirszfeld next set as his goal the elucidation of the immunological processes involved in the body's reaction to cancerous tissue (immunosurveillance, as it is called today). But this research soon brought Hirszfeld and the Institute's director, Emil von Dungern, to the matter of inheritability of the blood types.

Although the laws of heredity had been presented by the Moravian monk Gregor Mendel in 1866, his work remained buried in an obscure publication and the laws had to be independently rediscovered at the turn of the twentieth century. This rediscovery prompted two Jewish scientists, Albert A. Epstein and Reuben Ottenburg, to suggest, in 1908, that the blood types were inherited according to Mendelian principles, just as, say, eye color. It was Hirszfeld and von Dungern, however, who established the patterns of blood heredity and showed, for example, that a child of type B with a mother of type A could never have a type A or type O father; and that a child of type O could never have a type AB father (whatever the mother's type).

An idea now formed in Hirszfeld's mind that the various blood types were not only inheritable, but also that their occurrence and geographic distribution might vary according to race, nationality, or ethnic origin across the world, as do such characteristics as hair and eye color. As Hirszfeld later wrote, the researching of this hypothesis would have entailed "a project which under normal circumstances would have required dozens of years of work; a project of world exploration from the serological point of view. It is possible that the project would not have been realized in our lives."

Unlikely as it may seem, the outbreak of the Great War heralded the partial realization of Hirszfeld's dream. Von Dungern, along with Hirszfeld's other German colleagues, served on the side of the Central Powers. Hirszfeld was a subject of the czar but for this very reason hesitated to join the Allied cause, seeing Russia as the oppressor of his fellow Poles. So strong was his nationalist sentiment that when the Polish uprising had broken out in 1905, Hirszfeld in Germany had bought a gun, intending to return to Poland and take part. But what made Hirszfeld nevertheless choose to aid the Allied side was news of a fearsome typhus epidemic raging among his fellow Slavs, the Serbs (the bullying of whom by German-backed Austria in the wake of the assassination of Archduke Franz Ferdinand in Serajevo had ushered in the war). Hirszfeld and his wife, Hanna, likewise a physician, brought the Serbian doctors the most advanced knowledge of bacteriology and epidemiology. He isolated a new strain of paratyphus, henceforth known as *Salmonella Hirszfeldii,* with which he himself became infected, on top of malaria.

After two years of fighting around Belgrade, the Serbs were evacuated to the Greek port of Salonica, which in ages past had been the great, predominantly Jewish, mercantile emporium of the Mediterranean. There they joined up with an Allied expeditionary force. Unable to advance but politically too embarrassed to evacuate, the Allied force remained bottled up until the end of the war in the "cage" (as they themselves called it) or in "our largest POW-camp" (the Germans' term). As luck would have it, the Allied force was composed not only of various European nationalities (British, French, Greeks, Bulgarians, and the like), but also of colonial troops from the Arab countries, India, and even lands as far away as Senegal, Madagascar, and Vietnam. The mountain had come to Mohammed.

Drawing and analyzing some 8,000 blood samples from as many as 1,000 cooped-up soldiers of disparate nationalities, Hirszfeld discerned a definite geographic distribution pattern of blood type. Whereas close to half the Northern Europeans were of type A, this proportion dropped more and more as one proceeded eastward. On the other hand, about half the Indian soldiers were of type B, and this fell off as one moved westward, so that among the Englishmen hardly one in ten had B blood.

Not being able to publish his results in enemy Germany, Hirszfeld sent an article to the *British Medical Journal,* only to be informed months later that the study would not be of interest to doctors. Fortunately, the *Lancet* thought differently, and its publication of Hirszfeld's work caused a sensation both inside and outside the medical profession. For something about the hitherto mist-shrouded prehistory of mankind seemed to have been revealed at Salonica. As Hirszfeld wrote: "This discovery allowed the conclusion that the group types probably originated in two parts of the world, type A somewhere in Northern Europe, type B in Asia, perhaps in distant Tibet or India. Evidently driven by constant restlessness, these peoples migrated from west to east and from east to west, interbreeding until racial groups came into being which in the forge of a common history were fused into a single people." As for type O, Hirszfeld suggested that it arose comparatively late in human evolution.

The next crucial step in the linking of blood type with hereditary genes was taken by another Jewish scientist, Felix Bernstein, a professor of mathematical statistics and actuarial theory at the University of Göttingen in Germany. Although Göttingen was famed for its constellation of mathematical geniuses—not the least of whom at the time were the Jewish professors Hermann Minkowski and Max Born—Bernstein was drawn to the life sciences as well as to numbers and equations. This was due in part to the influence of his father, Julius, a prominent physiologist. Furthermore, the university's anatomy department boasted an ever-expanding collection, first begun a century earlier, of meticulously measured skulls supposedly defining the various racial subdivisions of mankind. A proponent of exactitude in biology, Bernstein was the world's first teacher of bio-mathematics. As such he built upon the pioneering work of his coreligionist Wilhelm Weinberg, an influential member of the Racial Hygiene Society who in the first decade of the century had accumulated extensive statistics on identical and fraternal twins. to which he applied Mendelian and other genetic principles in order to determine patterns of inherited pathologies and life expectancy. In 1925 Bernstein published an article, "Comprehensive Studies of the Hereditary Blood Structures in Man," which worked out with mathematical precision the genetic mechanisms put forward by Hirszfeld. (One difference with Hirszfeld was Bernstein's suggestion that type O was, evolutionarily, the original blood group, with A and B later mutating from it.)

The discovery and elucidation—albeit almost exclusively by Jews—of the geographic distribution of blood groups that destroy one another *in vitro* and *in vivo* gave a new form to the concerns of racists, particularly in Germany. The threat to Aryan purity by contamination from the east now came in the form of B-type blood rather than the wrong skull shape, as measured by the old-fashioned cephalic index. As one French Aryan supremacist wrote, "One can predict without much fear of error that a child of group B blood will be better suited to the retail trade than to bearing arms." Blood group tests were soon applied to forensic medicine and paternity suits. The supposed Jewish versus Aryan dichotomy was perhaps strengthened in the public mind by a well-publicized case of a mix-up of two babies at a Chicago maternity hospital—Watkins and Bamberger—where a serological test settled the matter of identity after comparison of head shapes, footprints, and the like with those of the parents proved indecisive. Yet in fact, serological tests among the general Jewish population showed them to be 38 percent of type A, not far below the figures for gentile Western Europeans. Furthermore, in virtually every European country where tests have been conducted, the Jewish ABO distribution closely parallels that of the gentiles. (It is in the distribution of the Rh (rhesus) factor that the blood of the various Jewish communities of Europe shows some significant differences compared to their gentile neighbors—apparently due to an old core of Mediterranean ancestry among the Ashkanazim.)

No less disruptive to the dichotomous fantasies of the Aryan racists was the discovery that the most southeasterly group of humanity, the Australian Aborigines, were as much as 40 percent of type A, making them quite Aryan. Similar percentages were found among the native Greenlanders. In the New World, some Indian populations such as the Mayas and the Pueblos had no admixture of B types, while other Indian tribes in Brazil and Peru were exclusively of type O. Hirszfeld suspected that the various blood groups correlated with varying degrees of immunity and susceptibility to certain diseases. The geographic distribution of the different blood groups is today thought to be related to the incidence of smallpox, tuberculosis, cholera, and mosquito-borne diseases such as malaria in the present or past homelands of the respective people. A factor determining whether the serum of blood type x does or does not mount a hostile reaction to the red cells of blood type y may have to do with sensitization of serum x to antigens on certain microorganisms that coincidentally happen to appear on the surface of y's cells as well.

Hirszfeld himself was keen not to allow any improper use of his discovery. "I wish to separate myself from those who attach the blood groups to the mystique of race," he wrote. "We have created the notion of serological race as an analogy to biological race. . . . The actual distribution of groups on the earth reflects the crossing of races and constitutes further proof that humanity presents a mosaic of races." This view accorded with Hirszfeld's overall medical ethics, as indeed had been exemplified by his volunteer work during the war: "Medicine is a synthesis of scientific truth and ethical truth. . . . Therefore the physician most of all must oppose war propaganda, hate, and all propositions which do not recognize the equality of people."

When at war's end a fellow Pole, a colonel serving in the Serbian army, had brought to Ludwik and Hanna Hirszfeld the news of the establishment of an independent Poland in line with Woodrow Wilson's ideal of self-determination, the three of them wept openly for joy. "In one's homeland one has both a past and a future; abroad only a present," Hirszfeld declared as he crossed the border of the new Poland. By then Hirszfeld had converted to Roman Catholicism. Poland's more than three million Jews of the unbaptized variety had less cause to be so unambigiously enthusiastic about the new republic. The concept of self-determination in Wilson's fourteen points enjoined the new Polish government to guarantee the civil and political rights of minorities, but these were never fully implemented, and the celebration of Polish independence was marred by anti-Jewish pogroms. Discriminatory measures ensured that the wealthy and upper-middle-class Jews would remain but a thin stratum in Poland, and that only a meager 6 percent or so of all Jews would be engaged in the professions. (Yet so great was the Jewish striving in medicine that, by one estimate, over half of all Poland's doctors in private practice were eventually drawn from this 6 percent.)

Free from discrimination, thanks to his baptismal certificate, Professor Hirszfeld (the title was conferred upon him in 1931) variously headed the Epidemiology Institute, the Department of Bacteriology and Experimental Medicine, and the Serum Section of the State Institute of Hygiene and the Institute of Science. He turned interbellum Warsaw into an international center for anthropological serology and also showed that within Poland itself, blood type B was more prominent in the south, perhaps as a reflection of a stronger pre-Indo-European element and the later Mongol invasions. Hirszfeld also developed a philosophy of illness as a deviation from the harmony of mutual (or at least nonconflicting) interests of the micro- and macroorganisms—a transitional phase before the symbiosis is reestablished, perhaps with some gentle persuasion on the part of the doctor. This was much in contrast with the philosophy of waging total war against the pathogenic microbes in neighboring Germany.

Germany was long a traditional threat to Polish sovereignty, and Poland had everything to fear from the rise of a revanchist Nazi regime, with its ideal of regaining lost territories to the east and acquiring some new *Lebensraum* for breeding a purer A blood type. But as the '30s wore on, the increasingly authoritarian Polish government introduced anti-Jewish measures that restricted the economic activity of the Jews and limited their numbers at the universities. This affected the medical profession as much as any other, perhaps more so. Thus the Polish authorities consciously aped the actions of their Nazi German enemies, albeit with a bit of moderation.

In at least one sense the exclusion of the Jews from the medical profession in Germany was a blessing to them. For no Jewish doctor would be tainted by the German medical community's systematic involvement in the greatest conceivable breach of the 2,000-year old physician's pledge always to avoid doing harm. Already early in Hitler's reign Germany's two largest medical associations—now *Judenrein*—placed themselves under the leadership of the Führer of the National Socialist Physicians League. (The dentists, veterinarians, and pharmacists were later invited to join in as well.) Politically inclined non-Nazi journals of social medicine were censored or banned. Twelve chairs of racial hygiene were established at various German universities, where attendance at such courses were obligatory. A special SS Physicians Führer School was established at Alt-Rehse in Mecklenburg.

Obsessed with the genetic health of the race, the Nazis initiated programs that sterilized some 350,000 people deemed "genetically unfit"— Germans with feeblemindedness, schizophrenia, Huntington's chorea, severe alcoholism, hereditary blindness or deafness, and congenital malformations. This genetically unfit category included some 500 half-black but otherwise healthy Germans in the Rhineland—the product of radical mixing with French colonial occupation troops—who were likewise sterilized. As a new World War approached, far more draconian measures were deemed appropriate. The previous war had seen the deaths of some half the inmates of German mental asylums (by one estimate, over 40,000 in Prussia alone), not from any coordinated policy of destruction but due to wartime rationing of the necessities of life, which allotted lowest priorities to such institutions. Now, a decision was made for the active and systematic—rather than passive and haphazard—destruction of lives deemed not worth living.

In the context of the perverted legal system of the Third Reich, the lawfulness of this annihilation had its basis in Hitler's direct spoken orders. (His deliberate avoidance of any written legislation on this potentially sensitive matter resulted in some initial confusion when the Reich Ministry of Justice dutifully but naively sought to investigate the reports of illegal killing.) But the implementation of the operation, which claimed an estimated 70,000 lives, was a purely medical affair and totally in the hands of physicians. Prominent psychiatrists and directors of mental institutions—officially working under the name of the "Community Foundation for Institutional Care" and administered by the "Reich Association for Hospitals"—systematically murdered the patients once entrusted to their care. By all accounts, no doctors were coerced into participation; they did so voluntarily.

Although falsified certificates of death and other subterfuges were used to cover up the operation, reports of the mass murder leaked out. Before the extermination was complete, the operation was halted (at least, its systematic as opposed to uncoordinated implementation; another 70,000 or so would perish during the war, through starvation, neglect, and deliberate poisoning). This was due to public pressure, particularly sermons of protest from the Catholic clergy, who had previously also objected to sterilization. Yet no such protests were heard from the pulpit or from the Vatican when, soon after, the "genetically unfit" category was expanded to include millions more people under German control. As Johann von Leers, an SS officer appointed professor at the University of Jena, stated in his book *The Criminal Nature of the Jews:* "If the hereditary criminal nature of Jewry can be demonstrated, then not only is each people morally justified in exterminating the hereditary criminals—but any people that still keeps and protects Jews is just as guilty of an offense against public safety as someone who cultivated cholera-germs without observing the proper precautions." The criminality inherent in Jewish genes was apparently determined with a certain mathematical precision, so that every European with more than two Jewish grandparents was slated for extermination.

This operation, too, was to be a medical procedure. Even before the genocide began in earnest, German physicians were willingly engaged in various systematic experiments with concentration camp inmates and some-times with prisoners of war. At Dachau, high altitude decompression ex-periments were carried out for the Luftwaffe, as were hypothermia ex-periments in which victims were immersed in ice water for various lengths of time to determine the limits of survivability. Subsequently, in Auschwitz twins were deliberately infected with fatal typhoid for the purpose of se-rum and organ analysis. In experiments on the conversion of seawater to drinking water, control group subjects perished after being given only saltwater to drink for twelve days. Women at the Ravensbruck concentra-tion camp were inflicted with simulated battlefield wounds, including gunshot, to test the effectiveness of new drugs. Experiments on castration and sterilization were carried out in order to find an efficient way to de-populate the conquered eastern territories destined to be settled by Ger-mans.

Complicity in these actions extended to the highest echelons of the German medical establishment. University of Kiel medical professors su-pervised the hypothermia experiments, which were reported to a group of almost 100 physicians at the annual meeting of the Luftwaffe Medical Service in Nuremberg and then to the conference of Wehrmach physicians in Berlin. The Ravensbruck experiments were reported openly at the Congress of Reich Physicians and resulted in awards to the researchers from the German Orthopedic Society. E. Eppinger, a pioneering gastroenter-ologist, was involved in the deadly seawater drinking experiments. Ferdinand Sauerbruch, Germany's most renowned surgeon, was part of a select group of physicians who met in Berlin to receive reports on the hypothermia experiments.

When it came time to implement the Final Solution, medical doctors conducted the first experiments (on Russian prisoners of war) of Zyklon B. The results were so favorable that it was then used to kill most of the six million Jewish victims of the Holocaust. To ensure that the genocide re-main a medically approved procedure, concentration camp inmates and new arrivals were, under orders from S.S. chief Heinrich Himmler, screened by licensed medical doctors trained in anthropology and racial hygiene to assure no classification errors were made and to determine who would be sent directly to the gas chambers and who would be worked to death. By all accounts, every German physician who participated in the Holocaust did so voluntarily. (Even at the Nuremberg trials, while some doctors claimed to have merely been following legitimate orders, not one claimed coercion.) For the Jewish doctors, by contrast, compliance with the Nazis could be a life and death matter, for their chances of survival depended on their perceived usefulness to the German war effort. Yet, for example, the Dutch gynecologist Dr. Rosalie Wijnberg (founder and president of the Netherlands Association of Women Physicians) courageously refused to sterilize the Jewish wives of gentile men.

What was the fate of the other Jewish doctors, particularly the hematologists, we have met in this chapter?

Karl Landsteiner died in 1943, not in a Nazi death camp but from a heart attack suffered in his laboratory at the Rockefeller Institute in New York, where he had been department head and was now emeritus. Although he complained about living in an apartment on bustling Madison Avenue, as compared to his villa on the outskirts of Vienna, Landsteiner, who became an American citizen, also fully recognized his great fortune in having escaped from the European abyss. Twenty years earlier he had been brought to the Rockefeller largely through the efforts of Dr. Simon Flexner, the Institute's Jewish director. At the Rockefeller, Landsteiner, together with his Russian-born pupil Dr. Philip Levine, isolated in 1927 yet three more inheritable factors in human blood, namely M, N, and P, whose importance lay primarily in the field of forensic medicine. Three years later Landsteiner received the Nobel Prize.

In 1940, Landsteiner and his Brooklyn-born colleague Dr. Alexander S. Wiener went on to isolate the rhesus (Rh) factor in human blood. Its true importance for medical pathology, namely in the field of obstetrics, was, however, discovered by Levine, who was inspired by a general question posed by Hirszfeld years earlier about possible immunological conflict between mother and fetus. Levine showed that the unborn child of an Rh-positive father and an Rh-negative mother may inherit the former factor, which may then, via the placental circulation, sensitize the mother's system to form antibodies against her own baby's blood, with consequences ranging from mild to fatal (depending on the success of other natural mechanisms in softening the effect). Thus Levine explained the hitherto mysterious instances of anemia and jaundice in the newborn and pointed the way to testing and transfusion techniques by which they could be countered.

Felix Bernstein emigrated upon Hitler's coming to power in 1933, eventually to become professor of biostatistics at Columbia University. Friedrich Schiff, whose laboratory was ironically given the task of identifying the blood groups of SA detachments, emigrated to New York in 1935, where he headed the department of bacteriology and serology at Beth Israel Hospital.

For his part, Ludwik Hirszfeld considered emigrating on the eve of the war but felt obliged to remain in the Poland to whose predominant language, culture, and religion he had assimilated. Thus he organized the blood transfusion services during the defense of Warsaw. With the Nazi occupation came first a stream of regulations isolating Jews from public life. Hirszfeld, Catholic though he was, was deemed to be of non-Aryan blood and was dismissed as director of the Institute for Hygiene. The German occupiers plundered the famous scientist's home, declaring, "Now you're just a Yid." Next came concentration, as Hirszfeld, along with hundreds of thousands of other Jews from Warsaw and other towns in Poland, were herded into the new Ghetto.

With typical perversity, the Nazi propaganda, whether intended for the general public or the SS, justified the ghettoization in medical terms. Readers were told how "the Jew totally lacks any concept of hygiene," how his "environment of filth and sanitary pollution, in a bizarre labyrinth of alleys, multileveled basements and built-up courtyards," was "infested with lice [leading to] the spread of spotted typhus," and how "the German army and population must at all cost be protected from the immune bacillus-carrier of the plagues—the Jew." The Germans then set about to create in reality the very conditions they had fantasized in their scare-mongering propaganda. Typhus and other contagious diseases caused by overcrowding, malnutrition, and lack of sanitation now took their dreadful toll. Offering his services to the *Judenrat*, Hirszfeld was appointed head of the health committee and had some success in combating the epidemics. Yet all the bacteriological skills in the world could do little for a population starving for lack of food and freezing for want of fuel. As Hirszfeld described the scene of one of his house-calls: "On the bed-planks and on the floor, people are lying—not really people but figures that call to mind balloons or living corpses. They're lying naked or in miserable rags, often uncovered with no pillows. It's cold and most rooms have no windowpanes. What are these specters waiting for with their distant-looking eyes? For death. And it comes with merciless inevitability." To keep morale up, the Jewish intelligentsia presented series of educational lectures. Among other things, Professor Hirszfeld organized courses at the Ghetto hospital, predominantly for former medical students. These were of such quality that those few students who survived later received credit for them from postwar Polish academic authorities as equivalent to university medical studies.

Although he had received many offers of hiding places from his "Aryan" former colleagues, who held him in such high esteem (his being a convert to Catholicism didn't hurt either), Hirszfeld remained with his wife and daughter in the Ghetto as long as he felt he could be of use to his erstwhile coreligionists. But when the deportations to the death camps began in earnest and the Ghetto hospital was liquidated, he made his way to the Aryan side. As the heroic but inevitably futile revolt raged among the remaining Jews in the Ghetto, Hirszfeld and his family moved from one undercover place to another in Warsaw and finally found refuge in the countryside, where he was hiding in the woods when liberation by the Russian army came. Although he and his wife survived, their only child, Maria, died of pneumonia. As the distraught Hirszfeld remarked, at least she had been buried in her own grave, even if under a false name. Millions of other people of Jewish "blood" had undergone the ultimate delousing. (I. G. Farben's Zyklon-B had for a quarter century served the Germany military and civil authorities as a tried and true lice-fumigant). They came to rest in mass graves or had their ashes discharged through smokestacks into the Polish sky.

Chapter 15
The War of the Microbes at Oxford

I had to stop where I did. [But] I would have produced penicillin in 1929 if I had had the luck to have a tame refugee chemist at my right hand.
                                     —Alexander Fleming on Ernst Boris Chain

W ith us ther was a Doctour of Phisik,
   In al this world ne was ther noon hym lik,
To speke of phisik and of surgerye,
For he was grounded in astronomye.
He knew the cause of everich maladye,
Were it of hoot, or coold, or moyste, or drye,
And where they engendred, and of what humour.
He was a verray, parfit praktisour.

When Chaucer penned these words in his *Canterbury Tales* late in the fourteenth century, there was hardly a Jew in all England. But this had not always
been the case. In the wake of the Norman invasion in 1066, Jews from
William the Conqueror's French domains had followed him—perhaps at
his personal invitation—to his newly acquired territory across the Channel. Settling in London and other towns, they engaged in finance and usury
and were made to contribute heavily to the treasury of a series of monarchs through highly discriminatory taxes.
     Members of the lesser nobility in their power struggles with the crown
tended to view the Jews as instruments of royal oppression and were also
not very scrupulous as to how they might liquidate their debts to the Jewish financiers. Religious bigotry neatly meshed with economic resentment.
In the twelfth century, riots were encouraged, leading to massacres at Stam-

ford, Norwich, and elsewhere, in which the deeds of debt to the Jews perished along with the Jews themselves. It was in England that the notorious blood libel, which would plague the Jews of Europe for the rest of the Middle Ages and beyond, first made its appearance. Jews were forcibly converted at Dunstable, while in York the community escaped the raging mob only by committing mass suicide.

Among the few thousand Jews of Medieval England, there are references to dozens of physicians. By far the most eminent was Magister Elias. A rabbi, author, and distinguished talmudic authority, as well as businessman and physician, Elias was the acknowledged leader of Anglo-Jewry and a familiar figure at the courts of Henry III and Edward I. Such was Elias's medical reputation that from across the North Sea, the counts of Flanders and Hainault beseeched the king's chancellor over and over again to arrange for "Maistre Eleyes li Juis" (as he was known in the Old French language of court) to come to the aid of the critically ill John of Hainault. (Elias went, and John recovered and lived on for many years, thus further glorifying the doctor's reputation, whether justifiably or not.)

From the contemporary chronicles of William of Newburgh, one gets the impression that Jewish physicians had more chance than their lay coreligionists of escaping a pogrom, but only if discretion formed the better part of valor. As William wrote:

> On the following day [after the massacre] a certain Jew coming up, a distinguished physician, who was friendly with and honored by the Christians, for the sake both of his art and of his own modesty, he commenced to deplore the slaughter of his people in violent terms, and as though prophesying vengeance, thus stirring up again the still-smoldering rage. The Christians soon seized him and made him the last victim of Jewish insolence.

Although, as was common in Europe in the Middle Ages, the English crown in the twelfth century viewed the money-generating Hebrews as "our" Jews and afforded them sanctuary in the royal castles when riots occurred, throughout most of the thirteenth century successive English monarchs proceeded to kill the goose that laid the golden egg by strangling the Jews economically and adopting the Jew badge and other church restrictions. By the time Edward I ascended to the throne in 1270, the impoverished Jewish community was of little value to his treasury. After considering various measures, such as permitting Jews to engage in commerce (of little use since they could not join the Merchants Guild) or rescinding the prohibition on their engaging in usury, Edward finally decided, in 1290, on complete expulsion as the final solution to England's presumed Jewish problem.

A century later, when Chaucer wrote his *Canterbury Tales*, virtually no Englishman, or his parents or grandparents, had ever seen a Jew. Yet supposed Jewish iniquities remained part of the folk memory. At least this was so for Chaucer's hypocritical prioress, whose tale recalled: "Ther was in Asye, in a greet citee, / Amonges Cristene folk, a Jewerye, / Sustened by a lord of that contree / For foule usuer and lucre of vileynye, / Hateful to Crist and his compaignye." The notorious accusation of the ritual murder of the Christian boy Hugh in Lincoln some 150 years earlier is related by the prioress as if it were a recent event: "O yonge Hugh of Lyncoln, slaynd also / With cursed Jewes, as is notable, / For it is but a litel while ago . . ."

Yet alongside such lingering historical anti-Jewish sentiment among Chaucer's pilgrims, one also finds the spirit of the Spanish-born *converso* Moses Sephardi, also known as Pedro Alfonse (or Piers or Peter Alfonce), who likewise "but a litel while ago" had served as court physician to Henry I and whose words of wisdom grace the Tale of Melibeus. (For example: "And Peter Alfonce seith, 'Make no felawshipe with thyne olde enemys; for if thou do hem bountee, they wol perverten it into wikkednesse.' . . . And therfore seith Piers Alfonce: 'Oon of the grettest adversitees of this world is whan a free man by kynde or of burthe is constreyned by poverte to eten the almesse of his enemy.' . . . .")

Although it is quite unlikely that Chaucer's Doctour of Phisik, the "verray, parfit praktisour [who] knew the cause of everich maladye," was Jewish (the journey to Canterbury being, of course, a Christian pilgrimage), there were Jewish doctors in England during the ban—in fact, the sole representatives of their faith. English monarchs, even if bigoted, called in Jewish doctors from abroad when it was a matter of life and death. For example, in 1318, a mere twenty years after the ban, Edward II imported a Jewish physician, and a century later Henry IV brought three Jewish doctors from Italy and France.

The expulsion from Spain in 1492 and from Portugal a few decades later brought Marranos to England, including, of course, physicians. Records from the mid-sixteenth century make mention of Masters Antonio and Diogo in London and Dr. Pedro Brandan and surgeon Pero Vaz in Bristol. Dr. Hector Nunez fled from Portugal to London in mid-century and was elected fellow of the Royal College of Physicians and of the Royal College of Surgeons. But not all Marrano doctors had it so good. The physician Fernando Lopes of St. Helans, London, was arrested, tried before the Lord Mayor, and banished.

A particularly colorful figure in English medical history was the sixteenth-century Marrano physician Rodrigo Lopez. Born in Portugal, he was, according to legend, captured on the high seas by Sir Francis Drake and forcibly brought to England. There he soon flourished as resident officer at St. Bartholomew's Hospital and a distinguished fellow of the College of Physicians. Lopez was appointed physician to Queen Elizabeth I, who granted him a monopoly on the import of anise seed and sumac. His success can be gauged by the commentary of an envious colleague, who was apparently no philo-Semite: "Doctor Lopus, the Queenes Physitian, is descended of Jewes: but himself A Christian, & Portugall. He none of the learnedest, or expertest maketh as great account of himself, as the best: & by a kind of Jewish practis, hath growen to much Wealth, & sum reputation: as well with ye Queen herself, as with sum of ye greatest Lordes, & Ladyes." But Dr. Lopez was to meet a most inglorious end when he got involved in court intrigues. As physician to the earl of Leicester he was accused of helping the earl to poison his rivals. Later Lopez was charged with conspiring against the queen herself, was put on the rack, where he confessed, and was then hanged, drawn, and quartered.

The English Civil War of the 1640s saw the triumph of the Puritans with their Old Testament concept of a Chosen People and their quest for the building anew of (as William Blake would later put it) "Jerusalem in England's green and pleasant land." This provided a potential climate for lifting the ban on the Jews. The Amsterdam rabbi-physician Menasseh ben Israel—who, as we have seen, took a particular interest in Marco Polo's Chinese Jews, whom he assumed to be descendants of the Lost Tribes, and was further delighted by more recent reports of other Lost Tribe descendants among the Indians in Ecuador—negotiated with Oliver Cromwell, the Lord Protector of the Commonwealth, for the legal re-admission of the Jews into England. Manasseh pleaded that the coming of the Millennium had first to wait for the fulfillment of the prophecy in Deuteronomy

(28:64) that the Jews be dispersed "from the one end of the earth even unto the other"—which, of course, had to include England, especially now that descendants of the lost tribes had supposedly been sighted in the New World. To drive the point home to Cromwell, Manasseh cleverly evoked the classical name for England in Medieval Hebrew as "the corner of the earth" (a mistranslation of the Norman French "Angleterre," as meaning "angle" of land).

As things turned out, the resettling of Jews in England was tacitly accepted rather than formally approved during the Commonwealth period, and this policy of toleration continued after the restoration of the monarchy under Charles II. Two founders of the new Jewish community in London were Joseph Mendes Bravo, a practising physician, and the physician-rabbi *Hakam* Jacob Abendana, whose Leiden-educated brother Isaac, likewise a physician, taught Hebrew language and literature at Trinity College, Cambridge, and later at Oxford. Montpellier-educated Ferdinando Mendez served as physician to Queen Catherine of Braganza and to King Charles II and was elected fellow of the Royal College of Physicians in 1687. This was the age of the great (gentile) clinician Thomas Sydenham, the advocate of less convoluted theorizing and more observation and bedside teaching in order to reveal the natural history of each disease. Sydenham's activities earned him the sobriquet "the English Hippocrates," implying that the discrediting of Galenic doctrines went hand in hand with a return to the true spirit and methods of the ancient Greek father of Western medicine.

The Marrano physician Isaac de Sequeyra Samuda became a member of the Royal College of Physicians and was elected fellow of the Royal Society in the first half of the eighteenth century, chiefly for his contributions to astronomy. His namesake Isaac Henrique Sequeira, educated in Bordeaux and Leiden, served as physician extraordinary to the Portuguese embassy at the Court of Saint James and honorary physician extraordinary to the prince regent of Portugal. Wealthy and pompous, with his gold-headed cane, Dr. Sequeira was also blessed with a long life, spanning most of the eighteenth century and part of the nineteenth. At the time of his death just after the Napoleonic Wars, he was the oldest licentiate of the College of Physicians. After practicing medicine in Leghorn, Italy, Dr. David Nieto accepted a call at the turn of the eighteenth century to serve as rabbi of the Portuguese community in London, where he wrote on religion, philosophy, mathematics, and astronomy, as well as medicine. Several Jewish physicians hailed from the New World, either from the British colonies, including the Caribbean, or from the Portuguese domains. The New York–born Joseph Hart Meyers went to the Mother Country (this was still a few years before the outbreak of the American Revolution) to study in London under William Hunter, the renowned anatomist and obstetrician. After obtaining his M.D. from Edinburgh with a dissertation on diabetes, Meyers returned to London and became a licentiate of the College of Physicians and a founding member of the Medical Society of London, as well as physician to the Portuguese Hospital. In the early nineteenth century Jonathon Pereira, a medical doctor and member of the Royal College of Surgeons but originally trained as a pharmacist, served as professor of materia medica at the New Aldersgate Medical School and was also well known for his lectures on pharmacology at the London Hospital. Isaac Alvarenga rose to rear-admiral rank at the Medical Department of the Royal Navy.

Throughout this era, up until the mid-nineteenth century, not a single Jew, physician or otherwise, received his degree from either of England's only two universities, Oxford and Cambridge. The privilege was limited to those subscribing to the articles of the Church of England, a restriction affecting Catholics, Quakers, and other dissenters, as well as Jews. So it was that many English Jewish doctors were educated across the North Sea at Leiden. But there were also university opportunities for them elsewhere in their home island, for the Scottish universities had long been open to students of all faiths.

There was virtually no Jewish community in Scotland prior to the nineteenth century. The exception was a small number of traders, who long enjoyed a tolerance of sorts. (In 1691 the Edinburgh Town Council upheld the right of a Jew to do business there, declaring: "Jewes as such are not to be considered or treated as other infidels. They being the ancient people of God, or the seed of Abraham of whom considering the flesh of Christ came. . . . And though now . . . they are enemies of the gospell, yet for our sake as touching the election they are beloved for their father's sake. Upon which and several other accompts it is that they are allowed the libertie of trade in places of greatest trade where the reformed religione is professed.") This spirit extended to the Scottish universities around the turn of the eighteenth century, as religious tests began to fall into disuse. Through most of the nineteenth century, until the great wave of immigrants fleeing czarist persecution in the 1880s, the Jewish community in Scotland would number only in the hundreds. But the Scottish universities would become the alma mater of generations of mostly non-Scottish Jewish students, typically in the field of medicine. Edinburgh University was the destination of preference. Its medical faculty, established early in the eighteenth century by two former pupils of Herman Boerhaave—Alexander Munro and Robert Whytt—and affiliated with a teaching hospital, became a glorious successor to Leiden, graduating many of the English-speaking world's most prominent doctors. Edinburgh in turn would serve as the inspiration for America's first two medical schools at the College of Philadelphia (the future University of Pennsylvania) and Kings College (Columbia University) later in the century.

Not all of Scotland's medical schools rated so highly, however, and this brings us to the case of Samuel Solomon, perhaps the most successful quack in Jewish medical history. Around the turn of the eighteenth century a German-born Jew, Dr. Bossy Brodum, was hauled before the president and censors of the College of Physicians in London and questioned about his practices. Brodum's "Nervous Cordial" and "Botanical Syrup," advertised in his pamphlet entitled "A Guide to Old Age or a Cure for the Indiscretions of Youth" (which he had the *chutzpah* to dedicate to King George), had gained him a lucrative practice in the fashionable West End. When challenged as to his credentials, Brodum produced a diploma from a certain Marischal College in Aberdeen. Although a chair of medicine had been established there in 1700, there was little teaching, and it was possible to obtain the M.D. degree upon presentation of appropriate testimonials and an appropriate sum of money. Having done this, Dr. Brodum was now apparently free to continue his practice unhindered.

Brodum's career inspired Samuel Solomon to emulate him, with a vengeance. Born to a lower-class Jewish family of itinerant traders in Liverpool, Solomon sold spectacles and shoe polish before coming under Brodum's influence and likewise purchasing, in 1795, an M.D. degree from Marischal College. (In Solomon's case, if not necessarily in Brodum's, the college records express doubt as to the authenticity of the certificates and testimonials presented by him but state that the degree was nevertheless granted.) Shortly thereafter, Solomon began a decades-long publicity campaign for his cure-all, the Balm of Gilead, named after a reference in Jeremiah (8:22). Addressing himself mostly, though not exclusively, to the male market, Solomon focused on the sin of masturbation, whose debilitating effects on mind and body he held responsible for a range of ailments, a partial list of which would include memory loss, weakened sight, melancholy, rheumatic pain, gonorrhea, hemorrhoids, pimples, premature aging, and bad dreams. (In this he was even more fanatical than Maimonides in condemning self-pollution.) Fortunately, there was the Balm of Gilead, available for half a guinea a bottle. This was not an inconsiderable sum in those days, but then again, as Solomon explained in his advertising pamphlets and broadsides: "So, noble, safe and efficaceous a remedy was never [before] offered to mankind." The Balm, he went on, was "the real pure essence of gold, . . . which our alchemists and philosophers have so long sought after in vain, . . . together with some of the choicest balsams and strengtheners in the whole materia medica."

Under the pretense that the Balm's enriching of the blood, bracing of the nervous system, casting off of viscid humors, restoring of muscle fiber tone, and so forth and so on, would also cure those maladies not necessarily caused by onanism, Solomon presented his product as a virtual panacea. Testimonials supposedly poured in from all over the world, telling of how the Balm stopped a yellow fever epidemic in its tracks and cured consumption as well. True, as Solomon conceded in a rare bit of modesty, the Balm "will not give immortality." But, he hastened to add, "if it be in the power of medicine to gild the autumn of declining years, and calmly and serenely protract the close of life beyond its narrow span, this restorative is capable of effecting that grand desideratum."

The Balm seems in reality to have been nothing but French brandy flavored with some spices and herbs. Yet Solomon's brilliant marketing strategy, aided by his popular book *A Guide to Health,* which went through some sixty-six editions, yielded such riches that he could construct in his hometown of Liverpool his imposing Gilead House, a local landmark. There Solomon entertained many notables, including Madame Tussaud, who desired his effigy for her wax museum.

Although, unlike Brodum, Solomon was not hauled before the medical board, he did experience the ire of the husbands of some of his cordial-addicted lady patients, who fell upon him on a country lane one night and, giving him a proverbial taste of his own medicine, forced him to drink all of the many bottles of the Balm he was carrying. The same group of men may have collaborated on a popular ballad about the two Jewish quacks:

Brodum or Solomon with physic,
Like death, despatch the wretch that's sick,
Pursue a sure and thriving trade;
Though patients die, the doctors paid!
Licenced to kill, he gains a palace,
For what another mounts a gallows.
While Solomon flies on the wings of the wind,
His magical Balm of Mount Gilead to find,
Little Brodum stands stewing his herbs in a copper,
And to vend his decoction for gold he thinks proper.

Yet, in all fairness, the hype of Solomon's advertising was not exceptional in his day and age. More important, if the Balm indeed consisted of nothing more potent or toxic than brandy—Solomon specifically stressed that it contained no mercury or cantharide (the dried Spanish fly, poisonous if taken internally in large doses)—patients were probably better off with his nostrum than with the violent concoctions that more honest, mainstream doctors were likely to prescribe.

"Dr." Solomon notwithstanding, the Anglo-Jewish community had been generally poor at the beginning of the nineteenth century. But as the century progressed, they increasingly entered the middle class. This was also a time of striving for legal equality. Particularly noteworthy in this regard was Dr. Barnard van Oven. The grandson of a Leiden-educated immigrant Dutch doctor and son of a founder of the Jews' Hospital in London (all three were elected licentiates of the Royal College of Surgeons), van Oven authored the pamphlets "An Appeal to the British Nation on Behalf of the Jews," and "Ought Baron Rothschild to Sit in Parliament?"

The upward mobility and secularization of nineteenth-century Anglo-Jewry went hand in hand with a yearning for higher education, medical and otherwise, which was still barred to Jews (and Catholics and Protestant dissenters) at Oxford and Cambridge. Thanks in no small measure to the generosity of the eminent emancipationist Isaac Lyon Goldsmid, the secular University College of London, open to all faiths, was established in 1826. Meanwhile, at Oxford and Cambridge there evolved a certain flexibility, permitting some Jews to study and take their lower degrees there. Finally, with the passage of the new Universities Test Act of 1871, all religious restrictions were abolished. This was the decade dominated by the Conservative prime minister Benjamin Disraeli (later Lord Beaconsfield), who, although his family had conveniently accepted Anglican baptism when he was a boy, openly and proudly identified with his Jewish roots. (As for public hygiene, the P.M. declared: "The health of a people is really the foundation upon which all their happiness and all their power as a State depend.")

It was from Cambridge that the man who would make the greatest contribution to medicine of all British Jews received his Ph.D. It was at Oxford that he would conduct the research for which in due course he would receive a knighthood, along with the Nobel Prize. Yet for the first twenty-seven years of his life, up to the coming to power of Hitler in Germany, he never dreamed he would one day become a British subject. He possibly also never imagined he would receive the Nobel Prize in medicine, for he was a chemist with no medical training.

Ernst Boris Chain's grandfather, a tailor in White Russia, was typical of many Jews in the eastern reaches of Europe late in the nineteenth century. His grandson would, many decades later, recall an impressive figure with a large black beard who immersed himself in the study of the Torah and the Talmud whenever he could, while leaving to Ernst's grandmother the day-to-day matters of life. But Ernst was born in Berlin, in 1906, his father, Michael, having like many *Ostjuden* emigrated to Germany near the turn of the century. Michael Chain studied chemical engineering and became yet another successful Jew in the German chemical industry, establishing the Chemische Fabrik Johannisthal, which specialized in the manufacture of metal salts.

As for Ernst's mother, Margarete, her family had deeper roots in Germany. She was furthermore a close relative of Kurt Eisner, the Social Democratic prime minister of Bavaria who, after the First World War, advocated a decentralized, nonmilitaristic Reich (somewhat along the Swiss model) and was assassinated for it. At the Chain home the political atmosphere was, as the conservative Ernst would later call it, "regrettably left wing." But the commitment to Judaism was also strong, as was the Jewish tradition of education. Both his parents took it for granted that Ernst would attend the university and pursue an intellectual career. This attitude was inculcated in their son. Anything short of this goal was (as he recalled) simply "unthinkable."

Although his father died just after the war and the family's savings were wiped out by the ensuing hyperinflation, Ernst did indeed pursue higher education. After graduating from the *Gymnasium,* he attended the Fredrich-Wilhelm University in Berlin, majoring in chemistry and physiology. His next move was to the Kaiser Wilhelm Institute for Physical and Electro-Chemistry, home to many outstanding scientists, a wildly disproportionate number of whom were fellow Jews. These included Hermann Walther Nernst, famed for his pioneering work on ions, and Lise Meitner, who would be instrumental in the birth of nuclear fission. But the most eminent of all was the institute's director, Fritz Haber, Nobel laureate and dean of German chemists. A Lutheran of Jewish descent (his father was a Breslau dye-stuffs manufacturer), Haber was also a staunch German patriot, and it was he who in World War One had almost singlehandedly given the German army the means to hold out under conditions of great shortages by his developing of a process for synthesizing the nitrates essential for war munitions. In the chaos following the war, Haber helped establish the Emergency Fund for German Science, proclaiming that "our existence as a nation depends on our scientific great power status, which is inseparable from our scientific organization and activities." The influential American Jew Abraham Flexner, renowned for his reforming of the American medical education system along German lines earlier in the century (more about which in the next chapter), heeded calls such as Haber's and arranged for the infusion of millions of dollars of Rockefeller Foundation money to the former enemy. (So great and lasting was Haber's reputation that, in 1935, in an act of political defiance similar to the German Ophthalmological Society's testimonial to Carl Koller, and just as tragically rare in the Third Reich, Haber's former Kaiser Wilhelm Institute would host a well-attended memorial meeting to mark the first anniversary of his death.)

For his doctoral research Chain joined the chemistry department of the Pathological Institute of the Charité Hospital. In going to Paul Ehrlich's former institute, Chain was clearly following in Ehrlich's footsteps. As he would one day recall, his scientific career, from its very inception, involved a desire to explain biological phenomena—for example, why bacteria may grow but may also become inhibited or disintegrate, or how metabolic reactions are regulated by hormones—in terms of the "action of well-defined chemical substances," the elucidating of their molecular structures and their means of interacting with the cells that make up all life forms. Yet the two decades after the death of Paul Ehrlich in 1915 were in fact the doldrum years of chemotherapy in Germany as elsewhere. It was as if, in the absence of any other scientist of Ehrlich's stature, no one had the audacity to pursue his vision of shooting chemicals into the bloodstream of human beings. True, there were in this period some advances in chemotherapy. In 1916, Ehrlich's former chief biologist at the Georg-Speyer-Haus, Dr. Wilhelm Roehl, now working at Bayer, developed a "colorless dye," somewhat chauvinistically christened Germanin, as an effective treatment for sleeping sickness. And in the '20s Roehl was instrumental in the development of Plasmoquine, a highly efficient synthetic substitute for quinine in the treatment of malaria. But both sleeping sickness and malaria are caused by protozoa ("first animals"). This is the family of comparatively large microorganisms, sometimes fluke-like in appearance, a few of whose members in fact are even visible to the naked eye. As such, they were deemed particularly easy targets for chemical magic bullets to hit. True, the tiny treponema of syphilis, despite its superficial resemblance to the larger trypanosomes of sleeping sickness, is a bacterium, not a protozoon. But its susceptibility to Ehrlich's arsenic was considered, well, somewhat of a fluke. Researchers in 1920s and 1930s despaired of ever developing other antibacterial drugs, just as, decades later, they would despair of ever developing effective drugs against the still far smaller viruses.

On January 30, 1933, after the National Socialist Party had for the second time won a plurality of votes in the nationwide elections, Adolf Hitler was appointed chancellor of Germany. Unlike many other Jewish (and for that matter, Christian) scientists, whose hard-headedness usually led them to agnosticism, Chain had a deep religious belief that he was always able to reconcile with his love of science. It was his conviction that

> far from being incompatible with the scientific approach, [the capacity to believe] complements it and helps the human mind to integrate the world into an ethical and meaningful whole. There are many ways in which people are made aware of their power to believe in the supremacy of divine guidance and power: through music or visual art, some event or experience

decisively influencing their life, looking through a microscope or telescope, or just by looking at the miraculous manifestations or purposefulness of nature.

Like most German Jews, religious or secular, Chain was at first not greatly alarmed by Hitler's rise, hoping it to be a passing phenomenon. But unlike most German Jews—another prominent exception was Albert Einstein, who happened to share none of Chain's religious orthodoxy—Chain felt sufficiently, in his own words, "disgusted with the Nazi gang" to leave the Fatherland. And so the young biochemist crossed the North Sea to England. Germany's loss was to be England's gain. But more important, a decade later the Axis' loss would be the Allies' gain. All this was unexpectedly linked to an infinitesimal spore of a mold so common and humble that it is found floating around the backyards of most houses in London or Berlin.

Chain arrived in an England whose Jewish population had grown rapidly over the previous half century, due to a massive wave of immigrants from Eastern Europe, whom the longer established Anglo-Jews had done their best to assimilate to middle-class English respectability. The most important single contribution to medicine by one of these Yiddish Englishmen appeared in the 1912 volume of the *Journal of Physiology* under the title "On the Chemical Nature of the Substance which Cures Polyneuritis in Birds Induced by a Diet of Polished Rice." This dull name, which might seem more at home in a poultry farmers' magazine, belies the article's great importance. For it reported how its author, the Polish Jew Dr. Casimir Funk, working at the Lister Institute in London, isolated the active ingredient in the husks of whole rice that prevents beriberi, the vitamin B1 deficiency ailment, once suspected of being a communicable disease caused by microorganisms. It is to the biochemist Funk that we owe the very term *vitamins*, short for "vital amines." (First spelled "vitamines" by Funk, the word lost its final "e" when it was latter determined that not all vitamins are amines.)

In his first year in exile the young refugee Ernst Chain was helped by a 250-pound stipend from the Liberal Jewish Synagogue. He went to Cambridge University and quickly obtained there a second Ph.D., on a dissertation entitled "Some Chemical and Biochemical Investigations on Phospholipids." Meanwhile, at Oxford University an Australian named Howard Florey, recently appointed to the chair of pathology, was intent on attracting scientists to research the biochemical aspects of bacteriology. Chain's dissertation supervisor suggested him to Florey, and so was set in motion a series of events that were to form one of the most important chapters in the history of medicine.

If the two decades after Paul Ehrlch's death were the doldrum years of chemotherapy in Germany, the situation was even more stagnant in Britain. This was due particularly to the influence of the doyen of British immunology, Sir Almroth Wright, the founder and head of the Inoculation Department at St. Mary's Hospital. Somewhat ironically, Wright had been a pupil of Ehrlich and had maintained the closest of contacts with him. But Wright's admiration of Ehrlich was decidedly biased away from his chemotherapy and toward his work on immunotherapy—the harnessing of natural serum antibodies produced by humans or animals themselves. Wright was also influenced by Haffkine and the phagocyte theory of Metchnikoff. As such, he developed a complex synthesis of the humoral and cellular concepts of immunity, and he proposed that by a series of autovaccinations (substances cultured from the patient's own blood and injected back into him) in the course of the infectious process, the offending microorganisms could be targeted for destruction by the body's devouring defense cells. When in 1906 George Berhard Shaw wrote his play *The Doctor's Dilemma*, which was otherwise scathingly critical of the medical profession, he spared his close friend Wright, who provided the model for the play's hero, Sir Colenso Ridgeon. In his "Preface on Doctors," which introduced his play, Shaw explained: "Sir Almroth Wright, following up one of Metchnikoff's most suggestive biological romances, discovered that the white corpuscles or phagocytes which attack and devour disease germs for us, do their work only when we butter the disease germs appetizingly for them with a natural sauce . . . ."

St. Mary's under Wright's leadership was home to a Scottish bacteriologist named Alexander Fleming. In 1922 a drop of the 41-year-old Fleming's nasal mucus fell on a bacteria culture and he noticed that it caused some destruction. Fleming's boss Wright naturally approved of potentially therapeutic substances produced by the body itself, and some further investigation soon showed the active ingredient to be present also in tears and other secretions. Indeed, in a vague way this was long known. The ancient Babylonians recommended the copious production of tears (aided by the chopping of raw onions) for eye infections. The old rabbinical literature similarly lauded the tears induced by mustard. Wright christened the bactericidal substance lysozyme (that is, an enzyme that causes lysis, or disintegration, of pathogenic microorganisms) and had Fleming present his observations in a paper to the Royal Society. But lysozyme's antibacterial properties are not particularly strong, and Fleming soon forgot about it.

In Oxford a decade later, Chain's boss, Florey, happened to have a particular interest in the duodenal intestines and its secretions. He suggested that his new assistant Chain check out the existing literature on lysozyme. This eventually brought Chain to Fleming's forgotten paper, which, like most of the other publications on lysozyme, did not impress him. But then some cross-referencing drew Chain to another obscure and forgotten publication of Fleming's, about a quite different antibacterial compound, a fungal substance not produced by the body at all.

Alexander Fleming had by no means been the first in history to notice the potential medical benefits of certain molds, particularly Penicillium. Nor was he the first to forget about them. Modern researchers have identified the mold-derived antibiotic tetracycline as having contaminated the stored grain in ancient Nubia in southern Egypt, and it has been suggested that it may have reduced the infection rates among those eating the grain. It is probable that forms of Penicillium mold likewise contaminated the grain stocks, with similar potential benefits for the consumers. In the folk medicine of the Ukraine, Yugoslavia, Greece, Finland, and many other lands, molds and moldy bread were used for the treatment of wounds.

What might have, but didn't, become a great medical breakthrough was an event in England in 1876, more than a half century before Chain's arrival in there. The naturalist John Tyndall had become interested in Louis Pasteur's findings of the presence of microorganisms in "fresh air." Tyndall left test tubes of meat exposed and in at least one instance observed: "The mutton in the study gathered over it a thick blanket of *Penicillium*. . . . It had assumed a light brown colour, 'as if by a faint admixture of clay'; but the infusion became transparent. The 'clay' here was the slime of dead or dormant *Bacteria,* the cause of their quiescence being the blanket of *Penicillium.* I found no active life in this tube, while all the others swarmed with *Bacteria*."

There was nothing particularly exotic about Penicillium or about most of its strains. Some, such as *Penicillium expansum* and *Penicillium digitatum*, were known to be undesirable since they attack apples and oranges in winter storage. Other strains, however, had been serving the French cheese industry for ages. The blue veins of roquefort cheese are due to the mold *Penicillium roqueforti,* and *Penicillium camemberti* imparts to camembert its distinctive taste. Tyndall went on to distinguish more strains of the mold, yet it seems not to have occurred to him that the benefit of Penicillium to mankind could extend much beyond the pallets of French cheese gourmets. This, despite the prescient remark made by Louis Pasteur in 1877: "In the inferior and vegetable species, life hinders life. A liquid invaded by an organized ferment, or by an aerobe, makes it difficult for an inferior organism to multiply. . . . These facts may, perhaps, justify the greatest hope from the therapeutic point of view."

In 1928, when Chain had just received his doctorate in Berlin and the Nazis had hardly more than 2 percent of the deputies in the Reichstag, an infinitesimal spore of *Penicillium notatum* mold drifted onto a petri dish in a laboratory at St. Mary's Hospital where Alexander Fleming had been cultivating a teeming colony of staphylococcus microbes. This is the family of bacteria that causes pus formation, whose endotoxins destroy tissue cells and whose enterotoxins cause food poisoning. Fleming himself was not there, having taken a vacation. The petri dish was one of forty or fifty perpetually cluttering up his workbench, for he took a certain pride in not being particularly tidy. (Legend has it that the spore drifted in through the window. But although this story is not in itself implausible—Penicillium is common enough on the streets of London—the window was in fact probably shut, since not only Fleming's workbench, but also his windowsills, were cluttered and the windows were rather inaccessible. The spore more likely floated up from a lower floor in the hospital where allergy testing was taking place.)

On his return, Fleming started to sort through the clutter of cultures with a view toward discarding them, when he remarked, "That's funny." The now famous petri dish had a green and yellow mold in the middle of the plate of once flourishing staphylococci. The bacteria were now to be found only around the rim. In between was a clear fluid where staphylococci had formerly thrived and had now been disintegrated, apparently by some substance secreted by the mold. *Penicillium notatum* spores had no doubt floated onto the petri dishes of other microbe hunters before Fleming.

But lucky circumstances combined to produce penicillin at St. Mary's in 1928. Fleming went away for several weeks, while his laboratory remained at a temperature of around 18–20 C. This was warm enough to let the Penicillium take and multiply and cool enough to make sure that the staphylococci Fleming was cultivating would not reach full strength before the mold's exude could exhibit its antibacterial effect. Even so, in Pasteur's famous words, "In the field of observation, chance favors only those minds that are prepared." Fleming had the habit of first checking his old petri dishes before discarding them. His keen eye recognized Penicillium's potential and he was stimulated to cultivate it and carried out tests. Thus Fleming determined that the mold was harmless to animal tissue and yet retained its bactericidal and bacteristatic properties even when diluted several hundredfold. As he wrote in his paper in the *Journal of Bacteriology* in 1932, penicillin (the name was his) "has been used on a number of septic wounds and has appeared to be superior to dressings containing potent chemicals." However, Fleming also discouragingly remarked that penicillin is difficult and expensive to cultivate and is quite unstable, losing much of its potency within a couple of weeks.

A more important reason for penicillin's sinking back into obscurity for another decade was the general scientific climate at St. Mary's under Almroth Wright. Years later Fleming would say with regard to Paul Ehrlich: "Salvarsan marked the beginning—and a magnificent beginning—of bacterial chemotherapy. I believe it was my experience with Salvarsan which first really stimulated my interest in his branch of science. . . . We are all humble and loyal disciples of the great man." Indeed, early in his career Wright had passed on to Fleming a supply of Salvarsan from his close friend and former teacher Ehrlich, and the Scotsman had become so adept in its use that he was nicknamed "Private 606." But by the '20s, interest in therapeutic chemicals, whether synthesized or occurring in nature, had waned considerably. So it was that Fleming limited his testing of penicillin to local applications. Although he injected healthy mice and rabbits to determine penicillin's nontoxicity, it seems never to have occurred to him to inject rodents that were systemically infected with streptococci or with any other pathogens.

When in 1935 Fleming's article came to Ernst Chain's attention, this was only one of hundreds of papers on substances with antibacterial properties that he was glancing through as part of his search through the literature. It was the good fortune of millions of people who would owe their lives to penicillin that Chain suspected something of potential importance. He realized that Fleming had apparently discovered some kind of mold lysozyme. The cell walls of all those disease-causing bacteria that penicillin inhibited must have something in common—a molecular structure on which the hypothesized enzyme could act. Would it be possible, Chain wondered, to determine just what this shared cellular structure was and isolate in pure form the substance acting on it? When Chain broached the subject with his boss, Florey, during the tea-time break at the Oxford lab, the Australian discouragingly recalled that some years earlier a chemist had found penicillin to be by nature exceptionally unstable and therefore probably of no real therapeutic value. But Chain chimed in with his opinion that a better chemist would produce a stable version. In this, he was echoing the optimism of Paul Ehrlich, one of whose many honorary doctorates was from Oxford. Florey gave Chain the go-ahead, and this marked the beginning of the end of the doldrum years of chemotherapy in Britain.

Curiously, in the land from which Chain had been forced to flee, the doldrum years of chemotherapy were likewise coming to an end, and this, too, owed much to the spirit of Paul Ehrlich, even though the memory of him would soon be systematically obliterated. A half century earlier, in 1885, Ehrlich had spoken of the "miraculous power" of sulfanilic acid, derived from the same coal tar that yields aniline and azo dyes. He would likely have returned to it had he not died so soon after his triumph with the arsenical compounds. But as mentioned earlier, his former chief biologist at the Georg-Speyer-Haus, Dr. Wilhelm Roehl, developed in the year after Ehrlich's death a drug for sleeping sickness called Germanin, a sulfanilic acid compound. In 1932 a member of Roehl's team at Bayer, the physician-chemist Gerhard Domagk, went on to compound a sulphonamide dye called Prontisil Red. Although it proved useless against bacteria *in vitro* (in the test tube), Domagk decided to test Prontisil *in vivo* (in the body). A series of mice injected with deadly streptococci—the bacteria family that causes lombar pneumonia, meningitis, septicemia, empyema, peritonitis, strep throat, scarlet fever, rheumatic fever, puerperal fever, and other woes—were then injected with Prontisil. The bacteria were soon dead and the mice alive and well. Soon after, the drug proved itself in the human body, too, as it brought back from the brink of death women with puerperal fever and men with sepsis.

For this discovery, Domagk was awarded the Nobel Prize in 1939. At the same time, Domagk, although not Jewish, had the additional honor of being detained for a week by the Gestapo. No reason was ever given, but the arrest clearly was linked to the prize. Back in 1914 Domagk had quit his first year of medical studies at the University of Kiel and enthusiastically enlisted in the army, but soon became disillusioned by the carnage and the effects of gas gangrene on the wounded. By war's end he had, in his own words "swor(n) many times before God that I would help with all my strength and energy to meet this madness of destruction in the small way that I could do it—to ease the hopelessness and need in which the nations of this world had got themselves entangled." Domagk's subsequent work for the benefit of humanity was in fact purely medical and not political. Yet in Nazi eyes, the Nobel Prize was tainted. Not only had so many Jews won the Nobel in medicine and other fields, but the peace prize had been awarded to the German pacifist activist Carl von Ossietzky, then already in a concentration camp. Domagk ended up informing the Nobel committee that he could not accept the prize. (He eventually did, retroactively, after the war.)

The giant conglomerate I. G. Farben, whose many subsidiaries included Domagk's employer Bayer, had once been denounced as "Jewish" by the Nazis, who sarcastically referred to it as "Isadore G. Farben" rather than "Interessegemeindschaft Farben" (dye interest collective). In the '30s, however, it came firmly under the control of the Nazi state. (This did not apply to the U.S. Bayer Company, which during the First World War had become totally independent of its German namesake and erstwhile parent company and was in fact its rival in the marketing of aspirin until the companies were reunited in the 1990s.) Yet none of the worldwide commercial benefits of Domagk's discovery flowed into the economy of Hitler's Germany. As mentioned earlier, Pronitsil worked only in the body and not in the test tube. A group of French doctors soon determined that this was because, strictly speaking, the Prontisil itself had no bactericidal effects but was broken down by the body into sulphanilamide, the active agent. Bayer had in fact for decades before Domagk's discovery been producing sulphanilamide by the ton as a by-product of its dye industry but had never tested it as a drug. The original patent was now long expired. So it was that as the world braced itself for war, all nations could benefit from the sulphanilamides without indirectly financing the building of German tanks.

In England, the refugee Ernst Chain sensed that he was becoming engaged in a chemotherapeutic arms race of vital national interest. His first priority was to obtain a suitable culture of the *Penicillium notatum* mold on which to begin experimenting. Here followed another one of those ironies in the history of science, for as it turned out, Chain needed to look no farther than the hallways of his own laboratory, where a lab assistant was walking around with a tray of penicillin cultures. For Fleming, not realizing the great therapeutic potential of his discovery, had recommended it for more mundane purposes, writing that "penicillin is certainly useful to the bacteriologist for its power of inhibiting unwanted microbes in bacterial cultures." And indeed for years the Oxford laboratory had been culturing *Penicillium notatum* simply as a convenient way to keep petri dishes free of contamination.

With the help of a young Jewish Rhodes Scholar, Leslie Epstein, whose doctoral dissertation he was supervising, Chain set about fermenting, extracting, and purifying the mold's exude. It was soon determined that penicillin was not as unstable as had been thought. Florey and Chain together conducted a series of tests showing penicillin's wondrous affects on mice infected with staphylococci, streptococci, and clostridia, the latter being the genus whose toxin-producing bacteria cause tetanus, gas gangrene, and botulism. Chain and Florey also confirmed that, unlike so many other powerful bactericides, penicillin was basically nontoxic to humans, since its action involved interference with metabolic processes peculiar to cell walls of bacteria. A chemist of great manual dexterity, Chain was also the first to elucidate penicillin's structure and side-chains as best as the (by present-day standards) crude laboratory methods would allow.

In the meantime, France had fallen and German troops were massed across the Straits of Dover. The Oxford team took the precaution of smearing the lining of their clothes with the best penicillin strains in the hope that, in a worst-case invasion scenario, the secret mold could be kept dormant there and smuggled to safety. In 1941 the first clinical test—on an

Oxford policeman gravely infected by a scratch from a rosebush—brought the patient miraculously back from the brink of death, only to have him suffer a fatal relapse when the minute supply of the precious drug ran out.

If there was as yet not enough penicillin to save one life—the desperate experimenters had been reduced to recycling traces of penicillin excreted in the ill-fated patient's urine— how could there ever be enough to save tens of thousands of war casualties, now that Hitler's minions were at the gates of Moscow and advancing toward the Suez Canal? The solving of this problem by the Allied scientists has been likened in its importance to the Manhattan Project that produced the atomic bomb. This may be an exaggeration, but there are strong parallels between the two stories, beginning with the fleeing in 1933 from Hitler's Germany of the Jewish scientists Einstein and Chain, who later became instrumental in realizing the respective projects. True, Einstein was not involved in research on the bomb proper. But it was through his great prestige as a scientist and as the author of the formula of the conversion of mass into energy that he was able to alert President Roosevelt to the military potential of nuclear fission and the danger of ongoing German research in this field. Other refugees from European anti-Semitism, Leo Szilard and Edward Teller—along with the American-born Jew Robert Oppenheimer—actually built the bomb and thereby ensured the Allied victory. Most important in this regard was the developing of industrial techniques for producing a critical mass of fissionable uranium. (Incidentally, Szilard would later turn away from nuclear physics and toward the life sciences, developing at the Salk Institute in La Jolla, California, an eloquent theory of antibody formation based on the latest information on molecular genetics. But developments in this field were then proceeding so fast and furiously that his theory, impressive though it was, was immediately eclipsed.)

In the case of penicillin, it was Chain who, as a member of Florey's team, showed the true therapeutic potential of Tyndall's discovery and Fleming's rediscovery and brought this to the attention of his medical colleagues. This initial work had been carried out at Oxford on a shoestring budget of only a few hundred pounds a year from the British Medical Research Council and the Rockefeller Foundation. Much of the Oxford penicillin was grown on bed pans. Now came the matter of finding industrial techniques to generate a "critic mass" of the drug, that is, enough to have a real effect on the war's casualty rates.

As a German by origin, Ernst Chain was familiar with the system of close cooperation between universities and industry that had been going on for decades in Germany. Professor Ehrlich's strong connections with Hoechst and other chemical concerns was just one example of this. The Krupp conglomerate supported biological research; the manufacturer of Odol mouthwash sponsored hygiene exhibitions; the Zeiss Foundation, of optical fame, helped finance the University of Jena; and the famous professor of hygiene Max Pettenkofer invested in beef extract production. The early decades of the twentieth century saw the rise of the Kaiser Wilhelm Institutes (renamed after World War Two as Max Planck Institutes), which were heavily financed by industry and commerce. This symbiosis was facilitated by the prominent positions of German Jews in both academia and industry. The German-Jewish banker James Loeb (also known for his subsidizing of the Loeb classics library) financed the establishment of the Kaiser Wilhelm Institute of Psychiatry in Munich during the First World War. (In a—in retrospect—woefully misplaced gesture of public spirit, his family foundation continued financing the institute's research into the biological and hereditary aspect of criminality throughout the '30s, despite the dismissal of the Jewish staff and the deprival of all Jews of their citizenship.) Chain soon learned that in Britain such collaboration was deemed rather ungentlemanly, not the least in medical circles. This attitude was an apparent holdover of the social distance the landed gentry had been anxious to maintain from the entrepreneurs during the industrial revolution.

Somewhat related to this was Chain's real or imagined perception of latent anti-Semitism in some British circles. Chain's scientific disagreements and personality conflicts with his colleagues may, in truth, have had some basis in ethnic differences. In particular, the reservedness of his boss Florey, a most taciturn Australian, contrasted with Chain's exuberant central-European Jewishness. Chain, short, dark-haired, with a large, bushy moustache, had no interest in any sport or game. More than once he would remark regarding his intercultural problems: "It is because I don't play cricket. If I only played cricket it would all be different." The conflicts came to the fore again later, when in collaborating on a book on the story of penicillin, Chain felt snubbed by what he perceived as Florey's attempt to take a disproportionate share of the credit for himself. Fleming, in turn, was perceived by both as hogging the limelight as the supposed true discoverer. But as the famed physician Sir William Osler had once so rightly put it, "In science, the credit goes to the man who convinced the world, not the man to whom the idea first occurs." And in any case, as we will see later, the personality and priority conflict between two Jewish-American boys, Selman Waksman and Albert Schatz, regarding the development of streptomycin went further than this and ended in the stereotypically Jewish resort to litigation.

Whatever the conflicts, Chain had been proud to become a naturalized British subject in 1939 just as Hitler's troops were massing on the Polish border. Chain felt a certain economic as well as political and sentimental loyalty to his adopted land and its people, and he soon proposed that the Oxford group take out patents for penicillin so that the future financial gains could benefit the British economy. This was much in keeping with the tradition of collaboration between universities and industry in Chain's native Germany. But in England, it, too, was considered a rather ungentlemanly proposal for a medical researcher to make.

As it turned out, the postwar financial benefits of penicillin production would accrue to the United States. For although Chain and the British scientists remained actively involved, the penicillin production research soon became centered in Peoria, Illinois, in the American heartland, far from the German bombing raids, wartime shortages, and danger of invasion. There, at a regional research laboratory of the U.S. Department of Agriculture, a process for massive penicillin culturing was developed using corn steep liquor in deep—rather than surface—fermentation. This new method called for a strain of Penicillium better suited to it. The microbiologists searched through soil samples flown in by the Army Transport Command from all parts of the world under Allied control. Molds from Capetown, Bombay, and Chungking were the front-runners when the most suitable strain of all was discovered on a rotten cantaloupe at a market right there in Peoria.

Soon American drug companies with German names, most notably Pfizer (established in Brooklyn in 1849 by yet another young refugee from the ill-fated revolution in Germany) and Merck (originally, a subsidiary of the firm in enemy Darmstadt), were drawn into the process, contributing their own innovations. Before 1941 was out, a small number of RAF fighter pilots could be treated with penicillin around Oxford. Two years later, there were supplies of the drug, although still limited, in the Allied hospital tents during the North Africa campaign and later in Salerno during the invasion on Italy.

Churchill, in anticipation of D-Day, spurred on penicillin production, publicly praising the drug for having "broken upon the world just at a moment when human beings are being gashed and torn and poisoned by wounds on the field of war in enormous numbers."

The U.S. Army surgeon general and the American secretary of war gave voice to the Allied policy of adhering to the Geneva Convention and not discriminating between one's own and enemy wounded when it came to the use of penicillin in Allied military hospitals. This policy applied, at least in principle, even when supply was limited. But the making available of the drug or its means of production to the enemy was deemed to be another matter, especially since this could potentially put countless thousands of wounded German soldiers back on the battlefield. The existence of penicillin was itself no secret. Reports on the new drug were published in the prestigious British medical journal *The Lancet* even after the outbreak of war. But it was deemed advisable to keep the actual product out of enemy hands. When in 1941 Florey received reports from neutral Switzerland that the Germans were looking for samples to analyze, he recommended that the drug not be sent there and that security around the mold cultures be tightened in Britain. Yet later in the war, Allied planes would parachute consignments of penicillin into Switzerland, in grateful recognition of its government's efforts on behalf of British prisoners-of-war. Some other neutral countries were similarly favored. For, as in the case of fissionable uranium, which was likewise no secret in and of itself, it was the industrial process more than samples of the product that had to be kept under wraps.

The Axis powers attached sufficient importance to penicillin for the Germans to send to Japan by submarines copies of medical journals dealing with the drug. The Japanese set up their own Penicillin Committee and tested thousands of strains of the mold. But the Allied effort to mass produce penicillin, shrouded by the provisions of the British Official Secrets Act and equivalent laws in America, far outdistanced that of the Axis. By the time of the D-Day invasion of Normandy in June 1944, there were some twenty-two penicillin plants in the United States and Canada, producing enough of the drug to treat all 40,000 wounded soldiers.

Predictably, at war's end the three major figures in the penicillin drama, Fleming, Chain, and Florey, were called to Stockholm to receive the 1945 Nobel Prize for Medicine. This was also the time when Chain's worst fears were confirmed: his mother and sister, who had remained in Germany, had been deported to the Theresienstadt concentration camp, never to return. The revelations of the true extent of the Nazi campaign against Chain's coreligionists, together with a personal feeling of blame for not having saved his own family, inevitably prompted new consideration of his role vis-à-vis Judaism. Unlike most other scientists—be they of Jewish or Christian background—Chain attended religious services with a certain regularity, even though he would work on Saturdays if necessary and did not observe the kosher dietary regulations. "The essence of our belief cannot be scientifically proved," he readily conceded

> but this does not mean that its truth value is inferior to that of scientific theories which . . . have the habit to be disproved in the course of time. I consider the power to believe to be one of the great divine gifts to man through which he is allowed in some inexplicable manner to come near to the mysteries of the Universe without understanding them. The capability to believe is as characteristic and as essential a property of the human mind as is the power of logical reasoning.

Chain's scientific involvement in commerce and industry brought him in contact with some of Britain's most prominent Jewish business leaders, such as the first Baron Nathan, chairman of the Wolfson Foundation, and Lord Sieff, chairman of Marks & Spencer, with whom he also cooperated in Jewish causes. At war's end, Chaim Weizmann, first president of the soon-to-be-established State of Israel, endeavored to harness Chain's scientific reputation and energy in service of the Jewish homeland, just as he had done with Paul Ehrlich more than thirty years earlier. Chain was offered a virtual blank check if he would head a department in the new Weizmann Research Center in Rehovoth. Chain went to lecture in Tel Aviv and at the Hebrew University in Jerusalem, the first of many visits that would leave him "inspired and stimulated as we always are after having touched the soil of Israel." Although eventually deciding that the cause of penicillin and antibiotic development would be more effectively served by his residence in Europe rather than in Israel, Chain became a member of the board of governors and executive committee of the Weizmann Institute. In such a capacity he was able to encourage increased contact between the institute and industry.

Ernst Chain's discoveries—which continued in his capacity as director of the Center of Chemical Microbiology in Rome and then head of the new Biochemistry Department at London's Imperial College—earned him a long list of distinctions. These included the French Legion of Honor; the Ehrlich Centennial Medal, awarded on the occasion of the hundredth anniversary of the great scientist's birth; and many honorary doctorates. Perhaps the most important distinction (apart from the Nobel) to come Chain's way was his following Alexander Fleming and Howard Florey to a knighthood—the exuberant Russian-German-Jewish exile who felt himself somewhat of an outsider in English society, the taciturn Scottish representative of the traditional British medical establishment, and the Australian returnee to the Mother Country. (Quoth Sir Alexander regarding Sir Ernst and the history of the wonder drug they developed: "I had to stop where I did. [But] I would have produced penicillin in 1929 if I had had the luck to have a tame refugee chemist at my right hand.")

Yet even as the recipient of one of the highest distinctions that Britannia could bestow on her subjects, Chain had no intention of submerging his cultural and religious heritage. In 1948 he had married within the faith—to a businessman's daughter with a Ph.D. in chemistry from Oxford—and was determined to give his three children a Jewish education and to see the Jewish religion and community survive as a distinct entity. "Assimilation is a loss of orderliness, and therefore a step toward an increase in entropy, i.e. chaos," stated Sir Ernst. "It is most important to realize this and to understand that we benefit *most* the community among which we are living by *preserving* our identity, and not by losing it through an assimilation process."

Chain's religious sentiments led him to question the validity of some aspects of Darwinian evolutionary theory. At first sight, this would seem rather ironic, for much of Chain's later work was devoted to getting around the defenses that mutating strains of microbes throw up against penicillin by producing penicillinase, an enzyme that inactivates most types of the wonder drug. This kind of biological arms race has been going on in the soil for a few billion years, in true Darwinian fashion. The prize of survival goes only to a life form which has evolved so as to get around the defenses of competing but less adept mutants, while also defending itself against them. Now, with the widespread introduction of therapeutic penicillin, those pathogens—reproducing, like most microorganisms, two to four times an hour and generating an almost infinite variety of random mutations—that could manage to thwart the drug were generating resistant strains. Humans, whose generations are measured in quarter centuries rather than in quarter hours, have to rely on their brains rather than on the random mutations of their genes so as to devise in the test tube new drug variants to get around the emerging defenses of the penicillin-resistant pathogens. Yet although concerned with such Darwinian processes on a day-to-day basis in his laboratory, Chain disputed them when it came to man's genesis ("God cannot be explained away by such thoughts") and he was particularly critical of the Darwinian overextrapolation of animal to human behavior ("It is the differences between animal and man, not the similarities, which concern us").

Especially important for Chain were the ethical aspects of Judaism. Here is another parallel with his fellow German refugee Albert Einstein, although Chain's religious beliefs were far more traditionally Jewish than Einstein's. On the occasion of receiving an honorary doctorate from Bar-Ilan University in Israel, Chain spoke of the "ethical neutrality" and value-free nature of scientific observations and theories—even assuming that these theories stand the test of time, which is often not the case. When it comes to dealing with one's fellow men, including the matter of how the results of scientific work may be applied in practice, science itself can provide no ethical basis. One has to look elsewhere. For Chain, his moral source was clear:

> We, the Jewish people, have had the extraordinary privilege to have been given a lasting code of ethical values in the divinely inspired laws and traditions of Judaism which have become the basic pillars of the Western world. These laws and traditions have lasted over three millennia and will remain a guiding force for the Jewish people and many other nations as long as one can foresee.

Chapter 16
Heralding the American Century

[T]he Jew David's or Hebrew Plaster . . . is the most celebrated article known for the cure of all seated or local pains of long standing: such as Rheumatism, Spinal Diseases, Lame Backs, oppressive Pain in the Breast, acute Pain in the Side, Corns, Swellings, Tumors, &c, &c.

—advertising broadside, late nineteenth century.

The thought is now hovering before me that man himself can act as a creator even in living Nature, to form it eventually to his will. . . . Biologists label that the production of monstrosities; [but then] railroads, telegraphy, and the rest of the achievements of the technology of inanimate nature are accordingly monstrosities.

—Jacques Loeb

Research, untrammeled by near reference to practical ends, will go on in every properly organized medical school.

—Abraham Flexner

*E*ven before the arrival of Columbus, Jews and Jewish healers had been inhabiting the New World for centuries, at least in some people's fantasy. In the seventeenth century the Marrano adventurer Antonio de Montezino returned to Amsterdam from Ecuador to report his discovery of the tribes of Reuben and Levi living as Indians near Quito. Among the evidence adduced by adherents of this theory were supposed similarities in circumcision rites, female purification customs, and dietary regulations between the Hebrews and the Indians. In this regard, at least one report made explicit reference to biblical and New World medical men: "[American Indian] Priests are in some things among them, as with the Hebrews, Physicitians, and not habited as other men. . . ." Rabbi Menassah ben Israel—who, as we have seen, supported the view that the Chinese Jews were descendants from the lost tribes—gleefully propagated this discovery, for it encouraged his millenarian hope derived from the book of Daniel that redemption would begin when the Jews were dispersed to all lands.

Lost tribes apart, it may still perhaps be said that there were Jewish doctors in the New World before Columbus. For, according to some accounts, before the great admiral set foot on American soil, three apparently Jewish (or crypto-Jewish) members of his crew had preceded him, one of whom was Maestro Bernel, the ship's physician, and another, Marco, the ship's surgeon. Such a scenario would have been quite fitting. Columbus's voyages were motivated not only by the search for the gold of the Orient but also for the Eastern medicinal plants and spices that had been written about since the time of Pliny the Elder's *Historia Naturalis,* some fourteen centuries earlier. Indeed, the Admiral of the Ocean Sea was prone to misidentifying the plants of the New World as aloes, myrrh, cinnamon, and mastic. (The latter was supposedly good for loose teeth, a consequence of the scurvy that was the curse of seamen until the discovery of sources of vitamin C.) In his quest, Columbus relied on the medical knowledge of the Jewish doctors and scholars aboard his ship as he did upon the celestial navigation devices and charts of the Jewish physician-astronomers who stayed behind in Iberia. On at least one occasion a chart of lunar eclipses drawn up by Joseph Vecinho, the physician-in-ordinary to King João II of Portugal, appears to have saved Columbus and his crew during an encounter with the Indians.

But there was more reason for Jews to accompany Columbus than the medical and scientific knowledge they provided. As we have seen in earlier chapters, the farther reaches of the Portuguese and Spanish empires afforded crypto-Jews greater hope of escaping the Inquisition that was raging in Iberia during the Age of Discovery. This applied to the New World as well as to the eastern colonies of Goa or Macao. So it was that the Marrano Dr. Juan Lopez da Vega in Peru presumably introduced the native feverbark remedy, quinine, to Europe in 1638. Yet not all Marrano physicians were so fortunate in the New World. Among those known to have perished in autos-da-fé in the late sixteenth and early seventeenth centuries were

Drs. Juan Alverez, Thomas (Isaac) Tremino, and Francisco M. da Silva in Lima, and Dr. Alvaro Nunez in La Plata.

Circumstances were quite different in the English colonies. Records in Charles County, Maryland tell of the arrival there on January 24, 1656, of Jacob (formally João) Lumbrozo, "ye Jew doctor, native of Lisbon of the Kingdom of Portugal." Dr. Lombrozo was not only perhaps the first medical doctor in Maryland, but possibly also its first recognized and openly practicing Jew. Arrested in 1658 by some zealots for "blasphemy"—which they interpreted as including denial of the Trinity—Lombrozo was released ten days later as part of a new governor's general amnesty. That Dr. Lombrozo was never again molested—indeed, he was later naturalized and granted commissions to trade with the Indians, by which he became very wealthy—set a precedence of tolerance in Maryland, whose port city of Baltimore would be home to many prominent Jewish doctors in centuries to come.

Eighteenth-century records in the various colonies show the names of other Portuguese-born Jewish physicians, as well as a few from German-speaking lands, Holland, and the West Indies. (About half the Jewish doctors were native born.) Interesting is the case of Dr. Samuel Nunez who in Lisbon was denounced to the Inquisition and imprisoned. So important was his medical knowledge that he was paroled under the condition that two Inquisition officers share his elegant mansion to ensure he and his family not relapse into Judaism. While entertaining some dinner guests, he conspired with the captain of a British brigantine to have himself and his family spirited away to England, whence he made his way, in 1733, to Georgia. In Virginia, another (presumed) Portuguese-Jewish physician, Dr. Siccary, is said to have introduced the tomato into the diet of the colonists, a vegetable highly cultivated by the Indians, especially by the Aztecs, but unknown in the Old World and regarded with suspicion by the Europeans.

The particular importance of these Marrano doctors in the British domains becomes evident from a comparison between medical provisions in the Spanish and the British colonies. At the time of the European exploration of the New World, Iberian medical scholarship—built in large measure upon the works of Jewish physicians—had not yet gone into eclipse.

Already in 1551 the Spanish established a university, including a medical faculty, in Lima, Peru, soon followed by one in Mexico City, where the New World's first medical books were also printed. The Spanish introduced a medical regulatory system, and within 100 years they had also established an extensive network of hospitals, including 125 in Mexico alone.

In the British colonies, by contrast, neither the Mother Country nor the local powers-that-be were inclined to get involved in medical matters in a systematic way. It was not until the decade before the American Revolution that medical faculties came into existence—as part of the new College of Philadelphia (later the University of Pennsylvania) and Kings College (later Columbia University). This was also the time when the colonies' first regular hospital was established in Philadelphia, largely through the efforts of Benjamin Franklin. Although some Americans also went to study in Leiden, Edinburgh, London, and Paris, academically trained physicians were few and far between, and qualified British doctors had little incentive to abandon lucrative practices in the Mother Country for life in the colonies. For medical treatment, the great majority of colonials relied on traditional folk remedies, occasionally supplemented by elements borrowed from the native Indians. Some more formal medical advice was available from nonacademic barber-surgeons and apothecaries and from popular publications such as *Every Man His Own Doctor* and the health tips in Ben Franklin's almanacs. An acquaintance with Galenic theory, along with an overlay of more recent medical concepts, was often part of the general knowledge of literate gentlemen, particularly the clergy. The latter were especially welcome by the sick, since in those days it was generally felt (often quite correctly) that treatment, even from a university-trained doctor, was seldom more effective, and often worse, than simple prayer.

The unenviable state in the healing arts at the time of the birth of the American Republic gave little hint of the enormous contributions the country would make to medical science in later years. The paucity of academically trained doctors and lack of a formal medical structure in the rebellious colonies placed the Continental Army, at least theoretically, at a significant disadvantage compared to the British forces. The Jews in the colonies, numbering only some 3,000, were predominantly drawn to the American cause and to its leader George Washington, who later, as president, assured "the children of the stock of Abraham" of a government that "gives to bigotry no sanction." Several Jewish doctors served with the patriot forces, and Washington became the first of many American leaders to praise a Jewish physician—in this case, Dr. Philip Moses Russell, "for his assiduous and faithful attentions to the sick and wounded," which included the harsh wintering at Valley Forge.

In contrast to the two years of often tumultuous debate in the revolutionary French Assembly, which finally granted civil equality to all French Jews in 1791, the American Jews as a specific group were a non-issue in the new republic. America had become home to a variety of religious dissenters and refugees from the sectarian strife that had plagued Europe for centuries. The Founding Fathers themselves were influenced by the concept of deism, which was far removed from traditional Christian orthodoxy. The Constitutional Convention of 1787 banned in general any religious test for federal office, and in 1791 the first amendment of the Bill of Rights further established the separation of church and state.

From the very beginning of the colonies, Jews were to be found in commerce not only in the ports but on the frontier, where, it is said, they were the only traders not to resort to arms or whiskey in their bartering for the furs of the Indians. As the new nation now expanded, Jewish physicians as well as traders roamed the western frontier. We know, for example, of Dr. Isaac Levy of the wild and woolly Illinois Country, since he was the first there to be involved in what was to become a venerable American (some would say, Jewish-American) tradition, the medical lawsuit. (Levi's case involved a patient who, in the hope of a speedier cure, swallowed all sixty of the doctor's rather toxic pills in two days instead of in the course of a week as prescribed.)

Although the Jews in America numbered only some 10,000 in the early decades of the nineteenth century, they made their mark on the medical profession. Army and Navy archives tell of the services of Jewish physicians and surgeons in the Tripoli Campaign, the War of 1812, and the Mexican War, some of whom received congressional citations. Dr. Moses Albert Levy served with Sam Houston's Army and received from his commander "warmest praise for [his] unremitting attention and assiduity" at the capture of San Antonio. The "Fighting Doctor" David de Leon was decorated by Congress for rallying the troops at the battle of Chapultepec.

On the scientific front, however, the activities of the Jewish-American physicians in the first half of the nineteenth century—indeed, for most of the 1800s—were rather unremarkable, certainly when compared to those of their German brethren. This has to be seen in the context of the overall American contributions to medical science in this period, which were likewise modest though not negligible. To Oliver Wendell Holmes, Sr., gynecologist-obstetrician and later Harvard medical dean as well as great man of letters, goes credit for having pointed, in vain, to the apparent transmission of childbed fever through some matter (he called it "virus," a vague term in those days, related to the Latin word for "virulence") brought by doctors from the autopsy room or elsewhere to the maternity ward. (This was in 1843, three years before similar observations, likewise in vain, were made in Vienna by the legendary Semmelweis.) By far the greatest American gift to suffering humanity in the nineteenth century was general anesthesia. This came about in the mid-1840s when the New England dentists Horace Wells and William Morton got the idea of applying the nitrous oxide and ether popular in traveling laughing-gas shows and student frolics to the less frivolous business of tooth extraction and limb amputation. Some fundamentalist Christians objected to anesthesia—particularly in childbirth— as this would be a violation of the curse in Genesis that "in sorrow thou shalt bring forth children." As one clergyman pamphleteer wrote: "Chloroform is a decoy of Satan, apparently offering itself to bless women; but in the end it will harden society and rob God of the deep, earnest cries which rise in time of trouble for help." Opponents of anesthesia even suggested that William Morton had married a Jewess and that he himself had been circumcised. Yet supporters of anesthesia, who generally carried the day, could resort to a different passage in Genesis (albeit before Eve's transgression), where a merciful God Himself carried out under anesthesia the first operation (which was also, in a sense, an obstetrics procedure) when in order to create Eve He "caused a deep sleep to fall upon Adam, . . . and He took one of his ribs, and closed up the flesh instead thereof" (2:21).

When the Civil War broke out in 1861, northern Jews generally flocked to the banner of the Union cause, and it is said that some of the less sophisticated among them thought Abe Lincoln to be a coreligionist. Among the hundreds of Jewish field officers (including nine generals) who wore the Union blue, there were dozens of Jewish doctors, some losing their lives in the conflict and others rising to high rank. Most notably, Jonathan Phineas Horwitz, who during the Mexican War had been in charge of the Naval Hospital, served through the Civil War as assistant of the Navy's Bureau of Medicine and Surgery and was soon after appointed by unanimous approval of congress and the president to serve as the Bureau's chief—the post that would later become the surgeon general. Yet the Jewish physicians of the Confederacy, though far fewer in number, were not to be outdone by their northern coreligionists. As Benjamin Judah served as secretary of war and then as secretary of state, so the first post of surgeon general of the Armies of the Confederacy went to Dr. David de Leon, the "Fighting Doctor" of Mexican War fame. The post of assistant surgeon general was occupied by his coreligionist Dr. I. Baruch.

As with most wars, the carnage of the Civil War at least came to benefit the art and science of medicine. This is illustrated by the experiences of the young Confederate surgeon Dr. Simon Baruch (who, although he went on to have a quite distinguished medical career spanning more than a half century, never became a medical great but would sooner be more remembered as the father of the famed financier and adviser to presidents Bernard Baruch.) Born in 1840 in the mainly Polish province of Posen in the Kingdom of Prussia, Simon grew up speaking German at home and in school, a language that would later come in most handy when treating captured German immigrant Union soldiers or reading journals such as *Virchow's Archiv.* At age 15 he dropped out of the *gymnasium* in order to seek fame and fortune in America, journeying to South Carolina where some friends of the family lived. Simon subsequently enrolled in the prestigious Medical College of South Carolina, whose comparatively stringent M.D. requirements mandated the student's attendance at nine months of lectures (actually a four-and-a-half month series, repeated verbatim in the second year), his dissecting of a cadaver (which, although it took place in the winter, necessitated fast work in the semi-tropical climes before the age of refrigeration), his writing of a thesis, and his serving a three-year apprenticeship with an established physician. The college, however, temporarily shut its doors at the outbreak of the Civil War (South Carolina was in fact the first state to secede, and it was at Charleston that the first shots were fired), so Simon completed his education at the Medical College of Virginia in the Confederate capital of Richmond.

Even though chance more than anything else had brought him to Dixie, Dr. Baruch felt a solidarity with his friends and neighbors and offered his services to the Confederate army. Many young doctors who, like himself, soon found themselves at the front line with little or no prior practical experience would eventually take back home with them many skills, albeit sometimes acquired at a high cost to the first wounded soldiers they attended. As Baruch later recalled: "Before ever treating a sick person or even having lanced a boil and still under the age of 22, I was appointed assistant Surgeon, it is true, after a rigid examination, and put in charge of a battalion of 500 infantry, with only a hospital steward to assist me." Soon, at the second battle of Manassas, Baruch had his surgical baptism when he amputated a leg as a senior colleague looked on. This was only the first of many injured limbs he would remove as standard procedure, rather than risk the dreaded gangrene (necrosis of the limb due to cut-off of blood circulation, often accompanied by infection), osteomyelitis (pus formation in the injured bones), and pyemia (blood poisoning, with secondary pus formation at sites away from the wound), all of which were still mysterious in the absence of knowledge of pathogenic microorganisms. Baruch's baptismal operation, although based on lectures and books rather than practical experience, went well. Chloroform was administered even though anesthetics were often in short supply and their use in surgery was not yet universally accepted. The opposition was not necessarily on religious grounds; some surgeons were convinced that the patient's "excitement" during non-anesthetized amputations actually increased his chances of surviving the operation. As for asepsis, the idea of a surgeon sterilizing his instruments rather than just wiping off the old blood on a heavily caked apron before his next amputation would have seemed about as sensible as a railroad mechanic boiling his wrenches before going on to his next locomotive repair job.

At the battles of Antietam, Fredericksburg, Chancellorville, and Gettysburg, Simon Baruch found himself operating for as long as thirty-six straight hours as the casualties kept pouring into his primary station nearest the front lines and shells continued to fall. Yet as horrendous as the war's final body count was—some 600,000 soldiers on both sides perished during the four years of conflict—the statistics would have been worse had it not been for some formal innovations, most notably on the Union side but also in the Confederacy. The yellow medical flag—the forerunner of the red cross symbol—was mutually respected and horse-drawn ambulances from both sides were allowed safe passage to convey the wounded from the battlefield to the field hospitals. The surviving injured rode on red-painted hospital trains and even steamships to large, well-ventilated, and relatively sanitary hospital complexes in Washington and New York. Inspired by the great work of Florence Nightingale in the recent Crimean War, a corps of women nurses was organized, both under formal auspices under Dorothea Dix and through the informal efforts of Clara Barton. A high degree of civility was also evident in the gentlemen's agreement between North and South. Surgeons attended the wounded of the opposing side as well as their own. Captured army doctors in gray were aided in their work by their colleagues in blue, and vice versa, and were treated as noncombatants rather than as prisoners of war. Twice, Baruch's makeshift field hospitals were overrun, and twice he was allowed to cross back over the lines.

At the front Simon Baruch wrote his first medical article, on comparisons of damage caused by bayonets and by bullets, and showed that, contrary to the fears common among the soldiers, the former wounds offered a considerably better prognosis for recovery that did the latter. From such observations by military doctors would come America's first world-class contribution to academic medicine, the multivolume *Surgical History of the War of the Rebellion,* containing a wealth of statistics, case histories, and exquisitely executed paintings. (Short of hard cash in the postwar period, Baruch would obtain the first volume by bartering away two older books of his to the Surgeon General's Library.) Baruch's personal and collective war experience in surgical cases was to help him become a prominent eye, ear, and throat surgeon later in civilian life.

But Simon Baruch knew all too well that for each of the hundreds of thousands of soldiers of North and South who fell to bullets or bayonets, two more died of disease. Robust farmboys from the sparsely populated West would be felled by measles and mumps, to which their frailer Eastern comrades were immune, having survived them in childhood. Typhoid and typhus ("camp fever") were less discriminating. Dysentery caused, among other things, the appropriately named "Evacuation of Corinth" (Mississippi), a hollow Union victory, since both armies were reduced to an embarrassing crawl. Disease probably partially or fully incapacitated every general at various times in the war. So it may at least be said that Lee's diarrhea at Gettysburg was somewhat compensated for by Sherman's malaria in his Georgia campaign.

Medical treatment of sick soldiers typically involved the heroic approach. For a recruit with pneumonia, young Dr. Baruch was ordered to apply blisters and administer massive doses of potassium nitrate, mercury, and antimony every three hours to induce evacuation and salivation. As Baruch later remarked: "The disease was practically cured, but the patient died from sheer depletion." This instilled in Baruch a lifelong therapeutic skepticism—a preference for relying on the healing power of nature rather than on dubious drugs. In his later years, in the decades spanning the turn of the twentieth century when Baruch was established as one of New York's most prominent physicians, he would tirelessly campaign for the revival of the ancient art of hydrotherapy and endeavored to turn Saratoga Springs into a spa on the European model. Water, in its various forms and applications, represented for him a benevolent alternative to, on the one hand, dangerous drugs of questionable effectiveness and, on the other hand, the therapeutic nihilism that grew up in reaction to them. (Baruch even claimed that in the case of typhoid fever, hydrotherapy increased the number of Metchnikoff's leucocytes in the blood, whereas an antifever drug such as coal tar decreased them.)

In view of the dismal state of the art in medical treatment in the Civil War period, an ounce of prevention was worth far more than a pound of cure. Baruch's med school notebooks show that he had occasionally been presented with such concepts as "animalcules in the air" and "parasytic [sic] vegetable growth." But it would be more than a decade before the germ theory of transmissible disease gained acceptance in Europe, let alone in America, and not until the twentieth century that the Rickettsia microbe and the body louse, which carried it from human to human, would be identified as the culprits in typhus epidemics. Nevertheless, the general value of good camp sanitation was more appreciated by the army doctors in the Civil War than in any previous war. Inspectors from the U.S. Sanitary Commission gave instructions on camp drainage, placement of latrines, water supply, and cooking. Similar measures were adopted by the South, and not least of all by Baruch, who by his mid-twenties had risen to the post of chief surgeon of Confederate hospitals in North Carolina. As appalling by modern standards as was the two-to-one ratio of disease to battle fatalities among Civil War soldiers, the success of hygienic measures (as distinct from less-than-useless therapeutics) can be gauged by comparison with the nine-to-one ration in the Napoleonic Wars, the seven-to-one ratio in the Mexican War, and the four-to-one ratio in the Crimean War. Simon Baruch would later in life become a public health reformer and indefatigable campaigner for public baths for the tenement neighborhoods of New York, extolling the hygienic blessings of regular bathing or showering, aside from any supposed hydrotherapeutic benefits.

With the concern for better sanitation in the Civil War period came an increasing acceptance of the contagious nature of epidemic diseases. Such enlightenment was slower in coming in America than in Europe. When, for example, in 1832 cholera spread from its traditional endemic center of the Ganges to Europe and then jumped the Atlantic to the United States, the great majority of American physicians maintained that the disease was not at all contagious in the sense of being communicable from person to person. The more learned the doctor, the more likely he was to adhere to some concept of chemical change in the atmosphere, causing the release of some pathogenic toxin. The better-educated laity was inclined to accept this reasoning, but among the general populace the fear of contagion remained strong. Whole neighborhoods rose up in arms at the prospect of even the shabbiest of buildings on one of their streets being converted into a cholera hospital. And despite the lure of high pay, lower-class women were reluctant to serve as nurses in such institutions, perceiving the mortal risks involved. By the time of the next cholera visitation, in 1849, the medical profession had softened its anticontagionism but only somewhat. Yet when just after the Civil War the third epidemic struck, the majority of doctors were of the opinion that the common people had been right all along about the communicability of cholera. (Right they indeed were, but still in a mistaken way, since cholera is typically transmitted not by direct person-to-person contact or through an airborne route, but by contaminated water or food bearing a then still unknown microscopic organism.)

Whereas the earliest Jewish Americans and their physicians were mostly of Sephardic origin, throughout most of the nineteenth century it was in the German-speaking lands of Europe that America's Jewish population, which came to number some quarter million around 1880, had its roots. Often regarded by others as ethnic Germans, the Jews were in any case only one of many immigrant groups, and they could claim a Jewish presence in America extending back to the earliest colonization. As such, they generally escaped being the specific target of nationalist prejudice, which was often the fate of their coreligionists in the nation-states or feuding supranational empires of Europe. Even the South, which had few foreign immigrants and would later carry a stigma of anti-Semitism (whether wholly deserved or not), was hospitable to the Jews. Simon Baruch, despite the economic and social difficulties of postbellum Dixie, eventually built up a thriving practice among both blacks and whites in South Carolina. He became chairman of the Executive Committee of the State Board of Health (the most prestigious and powerful post for a physician), helped found the local Hebrew Benevolent Society, and rode with the Ku Klux Klan. (The thought of a doctor to so many liberated slaves—from whom he accepted corn, poultry, or a little sewing in lieu of cash—donning a white hood and sheet over his mezuzah becomes slightly less anomalous and more forgivable when one recalls that the Klan's prime targets in the Reconstruction era were the carpetbaggers and scalawags rather than blacks and non-Protestants.)

In the North and the expanding West, Jews were looked on with some favor by the Old Testament–oriented Congregationalist descendants of the Puritans and other Protestant sects, who often saved their animosity for the growing number of Catholic immigrants. There was a philosophical harmony in the political sphere as well, certainly in the view of Supreme Court Justice Louis Brandeis, who would declare that the "fundamentals of American law, namely life, liberty, and the pursuit of happiness, are all essentially Judaistic and have been taught by [Jews] for thousands of years." In the economic sphere the Jewish entrepreneurial spirit was in harmony with the general American approval of material gain and, if possible, accumulation of wealth. The deep Puritan spirit in American culture endorsed, indeed enjoined, the pursuit of an earthly "calling" and, where possible, the accumulation of capital as a sign of Election—an attitude that lived on even after the waning of the religious beliefs in which they had been rooted. (Such at least was the controversial thesis of the German-Jewish pioneer of sociology, Max Weber, around the turn of the century.) There may have been more than a grain of truth when, in the age of rapid German industrialization, one of the prominent antimodernist and anti-Semitic prophets of cultural despair, Julius Langbehn, bewailed the activities of the capitalists in Berlin by declaring: "The crude cult of money is a North American, and at the same time Jewish, trait. . . ." If so, this species of latent or manifest anti-Jewish prejudice in Germany, with its Lutheran and Catholic traditions, was less likely to flourish on American's Puritan-Protestant soil, as Jewish merchants rose from peddler to shopkeeper to (in some cases) department store magnate.

In much of Europe—and most particularly in the Germanic lands—the increasingly centralized state with its often massive bureaucracy was commonly seen by its subjects as naturally deserving of its (hopefully beneficent) authority, not least of all in matters of health and in its regulation of the medical profession. The climate was fundamentally different in westward-expanding America, with its origin in revolt against political authoritarianism, its decentralized constitution guaranteeing rights to each state and to each individual, and its tradition of free enterprise. In the field of health care, therefore, government regulation of drugs, licensing of physicians, and provision of hospitals were minimal or nonexistent for most of the nineteenth century. Mainstream doctors—with their "orthodox" arsenal of calomel (mercury), opium, medicinal alcohol, and stimulants—competed with various sects and fringe therapies, foreign and domestic. Homeopathy and hydropathy (the latter being Simon Baruch's passion) were the important imports from Europe. Osteopathy and chiropractic were among the home-grown healing fads. (Although it mattered little in nineteenth-century America where or what type of medicine a healer studied, in the course of the twentieth century colleges of osteopathy would at least provide a haven for would-be doctors who couldn't get into med school and chiropractic colleges for those who couldn't get into osteopathic school.)

From drugstores, mail order catalogues, and traveling medicine shows, suffering humanity could acquire for a quarter dollar or less Swaim's Panacea, Dr. Girard's Ginger Brandy ("a certain cure for cholera, colic, cramps, dysentery, chills & fever") and Mrs. Pinkham's Vegetable Compound ("The Greatest Remedie in the World"). Not to be left out of the present story is the Jew David's or Hebrew Plaster, touted as "The Most Successful Pain Extractor in the World." The text of the advertising broadside for this product, graced with an engraving of a bearded, dark-eyed, hooked-nosed Semite with a brim hat, attested not only to the appeal of exotic remedies in general but also to the age-old mystique surrounding Jews and healing:

This Recipe, obtained of an old Jew, a traveler in the eastern countries, proves to be of immense value to the western world. Since this Plaster has been introduced into America, every other plaster, salve, ointment, or liniment has been discontinued by all who have had an opportunity of testing the superior medical virtues of the Jew David's or Hebrew Plaster. This

Plaster is the most celebrated article known for the cure of all seated or local pains of long standing: such as Rheumatism, Spinal Diseases, Lame Backs, oppressive Pain in the Breast, acute Pain in the Side, Corns, Swellings, Tumors, &c, &c.

If cure-all Ginger Brandies, Vegetable Compounds, and Hebrew Plasters have since gone the way of the leach-jar, some other faddish nineteenth-century health aids have endured to become venerable icons of the American way of life: the corn flakes of Dr. John H. Kellogg's Battle Creek sanitarium; the grape-nuts of his patient and then breakfast food rival C. W. Post; and the easy-to-digest crackers of the vegetarian preacher Sylvester Graham. Coca-Cola, developed in 1886 by the Atlanta physician John S. Pemberton, was originally promoted as an aid to digestion and energizer of the respiratory system, and until relatively recently was strongly associated with the drugstore soda counter, even long after the cocaine in its original formula had been removed.

As was often the case in the American medical profession, some aspiring Jewish physicians received their training as apprentices to older physicians. Others were educated at proprietary schools. The more notable Jewish doctors, however, received their education at medical schools that already were, or would later be, affiliated with universities. Particularly popular among Jewish med students were Philadelphia's Jefferson Medical College and University of Pennsylvania. But even at the university medical schools, the quality of education lagged far behind that of the universities of Europe, particularly in the Germanic lands. So, like their Christian colleagues, a few Jewish doctors who could afford it went to the great European medical centers for postgraduate training. Berlin, Vienna, Prague, and other German-speaking university towns were the main destinations for Jewish-American doctors, although some also trained in Paris and London. Perhaps most notable of this group was Dr. Jacob Mendes da Costa, who was born in 1833 in St. Thomas and studied medicine in Philadelphia before doing postgraduate work in Europe. Back in the States, da Costa became perhaps the most renowned clinical teacher in the East as professor at Jefferson Medical College, whose distinguished faculty members also included the New York–born laryngologist Jacob da Silva Solis-Cohen, author of a definitive textbook on diseases of the throat, and his Philadelphia-born brother Solomon, a leading internist and journal editor as well as poet.

However, approximately half of the Jewish physicians in America in the nineteenth century were European-born, the great majority from Germany and German-speaking lands. Many of them arrived in the New World already with medical degrees from Vienna, Berlin, and Prague, as well as from other German-speaking universities. As mentioned in an earlier chapter, American medicine was much the beneficiary of the failed revolutions of 1848 in Europe, not least in the person of Abraham Jacobi. As America's first professor of pediatrics (at Columbia University's College of Physicians and Surgeons), Jacobi was much influenced by Darwinian theory, as when he wrote: "Nature does not kill and does not heal. If there were consciousness in Nature, she would feel indifferent about what she is, *viz.,* mere evolution." Yet whether as practitioner, teacher, or president of the AMA, Jacobi was concerned with ethics and combined some of the traditional Judeo-Christian thought with the spirit of 1848. ("The magnetic needle of professional rectitude should, in spite of occasional deviations, always point in the direction of pity and humanity." "Aims, methods, and persistency are common to the medical profession of all countries. On its flag is inscribed what should be the life rule of all nations: Fraternity and solidarity.") All told, some two dozen medical schools in the nineteenth century had Jewish professors, both native and foreign-born, among whom were department heads and deans.

The American laissez-faire spirit and political decentralization meant an absence of heavy bureaucratic involvement in medical research. Defense, being largely a function of the federal government under the constitution, was somewhat of an exception. So, as in the Civil War, some world-class American contributions to medicine took place under federal auspices in connection with military matters. During and after the Spanish-American War at the close of the nineteenth century, Walter Reed, an instructor at the recently founded Army Medical School, conducted experiments and epidemiological studies demonstrating the transmission of typhoid fever via well water and the transmission of yellow fever via the mosquito *Aedes aegypti* (the latter achievement immortalized on stage and screen by the play *Yellowjack*). Reed's colleague Dr. William C. Gorgas, along with other army physicians, subsequently instituted anti-mosquito sanitary measures that largely eliminated both yellow fever and malaria from Cuba, the Panama

Canal Zone, Puerto Rico, the Philippines, and other tropical areas that had, temporarily or indefinitely, come under the American flag (some more about which, later).

On the domestic front, a National Board of Health was established in 1879 to enforce quarantine and sanitary regulations in harbor areas. This did not proceed without protest from the various local authorities, not least from Simon Baruch, who along with many Carolinians, viewed with suspicion this further encroachment on states' rights. (Such feelings on Baruch's part were considerably tempered after he moved to New York two years later.) Under the auspices of the Bureau of Animal Industry of the Department of Agriculture, Daniel Salmon elucidated the chain of transmission of the microbe *Salmonella cholera,* which affects pigs and humans, while Theobald Smith showed ticks to be the culprits in the spread of the microorganism causing Texas cattle fever. From the federal Marine Hospital Service evolved the U.S. Public Health Service. Concerned not just with quarantine regulations, this agency was involved in the control of communicable diseases in general, particularly hookworm, typhoid fever, and tularemia.

In this heyday of the microbe hunters, it was believed that pellagra, for two centuries a major cause of death in southern Europe and the American South, was transmitted by insects in the manner of yellow fever and typhus. But in his 1912 paper, the Polish-born British Jew Casimir Funk, who isolated the vitamin that prevents beriberi (see Chapter 15), suggested that pellagra was likewise due to a vitamin deficiency. The hunch was proved correct when two years later Dr. Joseph Goldberger, a Hungarian-born Jew in the U.S. Public Health Service, investigated an outbreak of pellagra in Mississippi. Goldberger had very personal knowledge of the effects of insect-borne infectious diseases malaria and typhus, having contracted both while researching them in the South, with near-fatal results. But Goldberger was struck by certain peculiarities in pellagra's epidemiological pattern. Why, for instance, did it ravage the inmates of prisons, orphanages, and insane asylums but typically spare the staff and administrators? Why, furthermore, were villagers in areas of diverse farming, where most crops and fresh meats were not shipped to distant markets, less prone to the disease than were villagers in cotton-growing and truck-farming regions? In a series of some fifty papers, Goldberger marshaled a combination of clinical, laboratory, and epidemiological arguments that convinced the scientific world that pellagra is a nutritional deficiency and in fact easily prevented or cured by protein-rich food or small quantities of brewer's yeast. (Upon Goldberger's death in 1929, this factor was named vitamin G in his honor but was later classed under the B-complex vitamins.) Yet impressive as were these turn-of-the-century American accomplishments, they were dwarfed by the giant advances in medical science brought about by the likes of Pasteur and Metchnikoff in France and, even more impressively, by Koch and Ehrlich in Germany. And even their work was mostly in the realm of prevention and vaccination, with effective treatment being limited to a handful of diseases such as diphtheria and syphilis. As the therapeutic skeptic Simon Baruch wrote in the last decade of the nineteenth century: "To-day we stand in breathless expectancy, awaiting the dawn of precision in therapeutic. This hope is vain! Recent experience has demonstrated the fallacy of specific therapeutics. . . ."

But the first half of the twentieth century—the American Century—would see the passing of the mantle of world leadership in science in general and medicine in particular from Germany to the United States and such rapid advancements that around mid-century Bernard Baruch would proudly recall his father, Simon, declaring sometime before his death in 1921: "There are no such things as incurable, there are only things for which man has not yet found a cure." Two of the great men who set the trend in motion in the first decade of the new century were brothers, first generation Americans who, like Simon Baruch, were of German-Jewish origin. On the face of it they were a very unlikely pair to fulfill this role. Both were raised in postbellum Louisville, Kentucky, a town that had begun the nineteenth century as a frontier outpost. One was an elementary school drop-out, who received his M.D. from a diploma mill after only a few months of study and, by his own admission, couldn't distinguish malaria from typhoid. The other brother wasn't a physician at all but a classicist with no graduate degree in medicine or anything else.

Simon and Abraham Flexner were part of a family of seven brothers and two sisters. Their father Moritz Flexner, the descendant of rabbis, teachers, and beer brewers, hailed from German-speaking Bohemia, in the Austro-Hungarian Empire. He had taught school in Strasbourg (then as now, but not always, a French city) before hastening to the New World in 1853, perhaps due to involvement in some political intrigue. After some unsuccessful experiences in New York and New Orleans, Morris (as he now called himself) followed some friends to Louisville, home to a German-Jewish community that included the eminent Brandeis family and other intellectuals who had fled Germany after the suppression of the 1848 revolution. There Morris prospered moderately, first as peddler, then as small store owner and wholesaler, and he started bringing his European relatives, one by one, to America's shores. Morris soon married Esther Abraham, who, like him, was a German-speaking Jew with a French overlay. (Born in the German Rhineland, she had lived for five years with relatives in Paris, where she learned dressmaking.) They moved to Lawrenceburg in the bluegrass region and started building their large and illustrious family along with a thriving business.

But with the Civil War came political turmoil. Kentucky, birthplace of Confederate president Jefferson Davis as well as Abraham Lincoln, remained in the Union but continued to allow slavery. Almost as many Kentuckians chose to wear Confederate gray as Union blue, many of the former drawn from the bluegrass region. Although Esther's great-aunt owned a slave, Morris was apparently an abolitionist. Indeed, the German-American community in general, counting among its ranks many refugees from the ill-fated revolution of 1848, was basically sympathetic to Lincoln's ideals, and it was thanks to the action of four "Dutch" regiments in St. Louis in the early days of the conflict that neighboring Missouri, slave state though it was, stayed within the Union. Fearing his business would be burned down by Confederate raiders or their sympathizers, Morris dissolved the firm he had established in Lawrenceburg and moved back to the safety of Louisville. There Simon was born in 1863.

The postbellum period brought a rapid expansion of Morris Flexner's wholesale hat business and he traveled widely, particularly through the South. His family likewise expanded, and Abraham was born in 1866. Father and mother Flexner were reasonably true to Judaism, observing the religious holidays, sanctifying the Friday evening supper, and keeping separate meat and milk tableware. But like many German Jews and German-Jewish immigrants, the Flexners tended toward Reformed Judaism. Two of the Louisville Reformed rabbis were keen to divest the Jewish people of their tribalism and closeness, advocating instead the universal appeal of Judaism. Sermons were given not in Hebrew, and yet not in English either, but in German, a language the nine Flexner children could hardly follow. (Although some German was spoken at home, this was not sufficient for understanding the synagogue services, let alone for scientific purposes later in Simon and Abraham Flexner's lives.) As part of the spirit of the age, the older Flexner children came under the influence of Darwin, Huxley, and, particularly in Abraham's case, the philosopher Herbert Spencer. Their parents, although attached to Judaism, were sufficiently free-thinking as not to offer religious counterarguments to the new rationalism. Simon and Abraham became so universally minded as to marry Christian girls, both of distinguished old American families. Yet all but one of the seven brothers were Bar Mitzvahs at age 13.

The exception was Simon, who dropped out of Sunday Hebrew school and also stopped praying around the time he reached Bar Mitzvah age. One may interpret the irreligious nature of this future great doctor as a refusal to take on faith that which cannot be logically demonstrated and the beginning of a belief in the religion of Science. But the fact was that, as bad as he was in the religious school, he was an even worse student in the secular public school. Totally uninspired by the classroom atmosphere in Louisville, Simon dropped out of the sixth grade and never completed elementary school or attended high school. Going from one odd job to the other, he worked for a year (an unusually long time for him) at a local drugstore. There he learned nothing more scientific than how to roll pills and was eventually fired after being caught throwing advertising leaflets into the sewer instead of handing them out to potential customers. Such were Simon's ne'er-do-well ways that his father conducted him through the local jail, showing him where he would probably end up.

But a watershed in Simon Flexner's life seems to have occurred at age 16, when he unexpectedly survived a serious bout with typhoid fever, which, he would later somewhat flippantly speculate, caused an alteration in his brain chemistry. More likely, it made him psychologically more aware of the precariousness of life and the wisdom of not wasting it. Obtaining another job in a larger drugstore, Simon attended night courses at the Louisville College of Pharmacy and, remarkably for a once so unpromising pupil, was awarded the school's gold medal as the best in the class of 1881–1882. When Simon's elder brother Jacob acquired his own drugstore, Simon, now armed with his diploma, joined him as a registered pharmacist, dispensing sodas alongside the drugs. There was no lack of demand for either product. Hygiene was poor, and people drank the brownish water from the Ohio River or from the corner pump, whose source flowed under the poorly paved open drainage system in the streets above. Typhoid, measles, whooping cough, and diphtheria were common. Whole families often suffered from consumption. Yellow flags in front of houses warned of smallpox, and victims of the yellow fever endemic in New Orleans sometimes made their way up the river to Louisville. And, of course, there was always venereal disease, for which the Flexner pharmacy discreetly kept a supply of unlabeled nostrums, which were about as dubious in their effectiveness as the labeled drugs for all the other scourges.

Jacob's drugstore housed a microscope. In an age when medical scientists in Germany had already been focusing on the subvisible world for decades, the newfangled device was still somewhat of a toy in the eyes of American physicians and was often derided in the medical curriculum, even at the more prestigious universities. But it held a special attraction to Simon. Jacob's drugstore was also the meeting place of leading local doctors taking a break from their housecalls, and they favored his younger brother with specimens of human tissue from autopsies and operations. With the help of Delafield and Prudden's *Handbook of Pathological Anatomy and Histology,* Simon Flexner became perhaps the most skilled microscopist in Louisville, for whatever that distinction was worth.

Although the Flexner family had flourished economically in the postbellum period, their fortunes waned with the Panic of 1873 and declined further with the death of father Morris nine years later. Morris had hoped that his seven sons would become professional men—doctors, lawyers, scholars—and would not have to engage in trade. Through the hardships that followed her husband's death, mother Esther was fond of quoting his words, so typical of new Americans: "Our children will justify us." Simon for a while entertained a vision of improving the family's fortunes by establishing what would perhaps have been the first private pathology lab in America—and certainly the first in his region—where blood, urine, gastric solutions, and surgical specimens could be analyzed and bacteria searched for. Perceiving that an M.D. degree might be handy for such an endeavor, Simon enrolled at the Medical Institute of the so-called University of Louisville. Although this was the best of several local diploma mills, almost his entire instruction consisted of a few lectures on surgery, obstetrics, and gynecology, and the *materia medica*. For this, Simon needed to absent himself from the drugstore merely for an hour every morning for a few months and attend a few dissections in the evening and some demonstrations in chemistry. This would normally have been supplemented by a practical apprenticeship under an established physician, but since Simon made clear his intention not to go into practice, the requirement was waived. So the newly minted Simon Flexner, M.D., could honestly say, "I never made a physical examination. I never heard a heart or lung sound." Indeed, his one and only attempt at treatment—involving a sick cousin—led to his misdiagnosis of malaria for typhoid fever and his avowal never again to try his hand at practicing.

Whereas in Europe, particularly in Germany, university education and scientific research, especially medical, were wholly or largely financed by the state, backed by its formidable powers of taxation, in America such financing was left to wealthy individuals or groups. This fact was central to the critical role the Flexner brothers would play for a half century in the ascendancy of American medicine. In Baltimore, the Quaker merchant-philanthropist Johns Hopkins had, in 1873, bequeathed half of his $7 million fortune for the establishment of a new university and the other half for a new hospital to be associated with the university's medical faculty. The university's first president, Daniel Coit Gilman, was a visionary who, focusing on advanced education and research, began by building America's first top-flight graduate school. Only then did he go on to establish the university's undergraduate college. It was from there that Simon's kid brother Abraham (more on whom shortly) received his B.A. in 1886, and it was he who encouraged Simon to pursue his postgraduate studies in pathology at the Hopkins. For the Hopkins was introducing the most dramatic of its innovations in the field of medical education and research, soon to reverberate throughout American medicine.

Gilman recruited four visionary young doctors to serve as the medical faculty's founding professors, the most famous of whom were the today almost legendary William H. Welch and William Osler. Although none were Jewish, there was a Jewish connection. It was at the urging of Abraham Jacobi, who, although in exile, remained a chauvinist of German science, that Welch went to Germany to study its system of medical education. Welch did research at the laboratories of the Jewish medical men Julius Cohnheim and Karl Weigert in Breslau and left a favorable impression on them for the pioneering study on lung edema he carried out at their Pathology Institute—interrupted only briefly when the young Robert Koch came to demonstrate to Ferdinand Cohn his solution to the anthrax riddle. In search of a dean for his new medical school, Gilman consulted Cohnheim, who recommended his former pupil Welch. Dean Welch, in turn, soon tapped Osler, who had likewise journeyed to Germany and had described the Jews as the "most brilliant ornaments" in the crown of German medicine.

It was on the basis of the German model that Welch and Osler set up—in a somewhat grotesque-looking converted morgue—the Hopkins pathology laboratory. Understandably, in view of their personal experiences with German-Jewish researchers, the founding professors were particularly free of anti-Semitism. So it was that Simon Flexner, with his dubious M.D. degree but obvious talent, was able to get in on the ground floor. This was in 1890. For almost the whole of the last decade of the nineteenth century Simon Flexner worked at the Hopkins, first as a paying postgraduate student, then as a fellow, and soon as a faculty member and resident hospital pathologist. Among his microscopic research, largely based on autopsies, cultures, and tissue and organ sectioning, were the description of an unusual eye tumor due to embryonic misdevelopment, which he termed neuroepithelioma retinae; the discovery of amoebic pathogens in an abscess of the jaw; case studies of lymphosarcoma (a malignant tumor of the lymph nodes); experimental studies on the action of toxins on tissues and organs; and investigations into the gas gangrene bacillus.

During his Hopkins period, Flexner made the almost obligatory pilgrimage to Germany, visiting the medical faculties of Berlin, Freiburg, Tübingen, Heidelberg, and German-annexed Strassburg, before also stopping by Vienna and Prague. Yet in this era of expansive American optimism, it was hoped that the U.S. institutes, and particularly the Hopkins, would come to represent more than just a transplantation of European ideas and methods to the New World. This sentiment was well expressed by the Hopkins's chairman, who, seeing a colleague off on a European trip, predicted that "a nearer view of the fading glories of the older civilizations will send you back to us . . . with your confidence increased in the grand possibilities of your own country." Indeed, all of Simon Flexner's superiors at the Hopkins medical faculty and hospital were American, or, in the case of Osler, Canadian, and although most had received their education in Germany, the new university sought to make such study abroad superfluous in the coming century. While inevitably impressed by the German labs, Simon remarked that "the great attention to specialties seems to me to dwarf all originality." The American emphasis on originality, freedom, and equality of opportunity would, hopefully, show the way to the future. Indeed, a friend of Flexner's at the Hopkins, Walter Reed, was soon to become one of the first internationally renowned American medical men, for his role in the elucidation and conquest of yellow fever.

By the end of the '90s, Flexner had risen to the titular rank of full professor in pathological anatomy. But salaries at the Hopkins were modest; the regular (rather than merely titular) post of professor of pathology would probably not be free for a long time to come, and even then the powers-that-be, despite the Hopkins' liberalism, would probably not appoint a Jew. So Flexner considered other offers. Somewhat ironically, he choose the University of Pennsylvania, America's oldest medical school, where anti-Jewish sentiment was no secret. (In the whole university, only the professor of Semitic languages was Jewish, and he also had to double as university librarian. At least one member of the Medical Faculty Club threatened to resign if the Jew Flexner were admitted.)

Simon Flexner's achievements as professor at Penn began even before he settled in Philadelphia. In 1899, immediately following his appointment, Flexner traveled to the Far East, visiting Japanese bacteriological laboratories and performing autopsies on plague victims in Hong Kong, on his way to the Philippines. There, as a consequence of their victory in the Spanish-American War, the American forces were facing an uprising of native Filipinos but in fact were far more in danger of succumbing to tropical microorganisms than to bullets. Temporarily commissioned in the army, Flexner investigated malaria, typhoid fever, tuberculosis, and dengue fever among the America soldiers, as well as smallpox, leprosy, ringworm, and beriberi among the natives. Various forms of dysentery presented a particular problem, and Flexner isolated a typhoid-like causative agent that came to be known as Flexner's bacillus.

About a year later, Flexner again answered a call from Washington, this time concerning a domestic health crisis. Reports of the Black Death in San Francisco's Chinatown were causing near hysteria on the coast. Doing a delicate constitutional balancing act between the desires of the surgeon general to get at the facts and the Californian authorities' threats of restrictions and censorship out of fear of general panic and economic ruin, Flexner and his group did indeed uncover several cases of the bubonic plague but were also able to show that the crisis was well under control and that the rats, the usual carriers, were not infected.

But field work was secondary to laboratory research. Flexner's testing of a promising snake antitoxin on humans began earlier than planned when one of the rattlers in his Philadelphia lab escaped and bit an unsuspecting college employee, who then had to be treated (successfully, it turned out) with the previously untried serum. Subsequently, Flexner distinguished "neurotoxin" venom, which works on the nervous system rather than on the blood and whose chemical structure was soon elucidated by Paul Ehrlich in Germany. Directing his attention next to pneumonia, Flexner determined that an absence or inactivation of certain enzymes in some pus cells was responsible for their conversion into fibrous tissue, which could leave the otherwise recovered patient with permanently damaged lungs.

Yet during his tenure at Penn, the organizational talents of Simon Flexner—despite a lifelong retiring personality that matched his slightness of physique—were to overshadow his research and set the tone for his greatest achievements. The curriculum at America's oldest med school was rooted in traditional clinical medicine, as was the whole Philadelphia medical establishment. In short order, Flexner set up a pathology laboratory on the Hopkins model for M.D. graduates wishing to study pathology before entering clinical practice. Immunology, though not one of the Hopkins strong points, was likewise given an important place at Penn. Furthermore, Flexner arranged with the municipal authorities for the bodies of the deceased patients at the nearby Bockley Hospital and Almshouse to be made available for autopsy and teaching purposes, thus allowing abundant first-hand study of the effects of chronic and degenerative as well as acute diseases. But all Simon Flexner's administrative innovations at Penn were just a minor prelude to the organizational task that would shortly fall to him, thanks to a so-called robber baron.

As great as had been the wealth of the merchant-philanthropist Mr. Johns Hopkins, this was dwarfed by the assets of John D. Rockefeller, a Protestant of French-Huguenot descent, whose dealings in oil in the era of rapid industrialization had made him the richest man in America by the turn of the twentieth century. Now, in what was still the age of small government and almost no government funding, Rockefeller, too, was seeking a public-spirited outlet for some of his enormous private capital. One of his most trusted assistants, Frederick T. Gates, was an ordained Baptist minister who at one time had also aspired to be a physician. His continuing interest in medicine drew him to William Osler's recent book *The Principles and Practice of Medicine,* which honestly conceded that even some 2,000 years after the birth of rational medicine, doctors were capable of curing only four or five of the multitude of afflictions to which human flesh is heir. Seeing how medical research in America was so poorly endowed compared to chemistry and physics, Gates envisaged, in terms appropriate to a man of the cloth, a medical research institution on Manhattan Island that would be "a sort of theological seminary." "In these several rooms," Gates waxed religiously, God "is whispering His secrets. To these men He is opening the mysterious depths of His being. . . . If God looks down on the world and has His favorites, it must be the men who are studying Him, who are working every day, with limited intelligence, and in the darkness—for clouds and darkness are around Him—and feeling their way to His heart." Although John D. Rockefeller's previous contact with medicine had been mainly limited to his aged and quaint homeopathic physician, he was soon won over to Gates's vision.

A committee of America's top medical men was formed, chaired by William Welch, and the search for the new institute's director was on. First to be approached was microbe-hunter Theobald Smith. But Smith, who in any case felt himself too removed from human diseases (his greatest fame was for his discovery of the tick as the vector in the transmission of Texas cattle fever), was reluctant to leave the security of Harvard. And (although he did not explicitly say so) Smith probably doubted his administrative as opposed to purely scientific talents. So it was that early in 1902 the post at this "temple of pure science" was offered to Dr. Simon Flexner, M.D. (or as Gates waggishly called him, in line with his ecclesiastic metaphor, "Rev. Simon Flexner, D.D.").

His good intentions notwithstanding, there still adhered to John D. Rockefeller much moral condemnation of the way the "robber baron" had systematically smothered smaller competition in building up his gigantic oil trust. Simon's own family had suffered bankruptcy and temporary hardship during the economic crisis in his youth, one of the liabilities of a largely unregulated market. But Simon was also well aware of how, in an era of

great economic expansion and opportunity that was America in the decades spanning the turn of the century, he and his family had brilliantly
risen from their humble beginnings. So it was that Simon Flexner subscribed
to a sort of social, economic, and intellectural Darwinism. His concept of
survival of the fittest in human society being applicable to brains, not brawn,
Flexner saw no problem in using the Rockefeller millions to cure the
physically ill and weak, for, as he pointed out, the cleverest advancers of
the human race were not necessarily the constitutionally strongest.

Although Rockefeller had originally envisaged a small institute that would
gradually expand as needed, Flexner had a vision more worthy of America's
wealthiest philanthropist: The Rockefeller Institute would "cover the entire field of medical research in respect to both men and animals." Each of
the various departments would be autonomous and individual research
would be encouraged, although "when united [they] would still form a whole
allowing for conjoint investigation of comprehensive problems." Each department would be staffed by the best and the brightest (and correspondingly well-paid) directors, assistant directors, and fellows, plus scientists
not on the institute's payroll, conducting research at their own expense. A
small hospital would be attached for the direct study of clinical cases, for
"while the work of the Institute will, of necessity, be highly experimental,
intimate relations with the problems of human diseases should not for a
moment be lost sight of." The personnel would be free of the burdens of
classroom teaching so as to devote themselves to pure investigation.

The Rockefeller Institute's first great success came in 1906 when New
York was struck by a deadly epidemic of cerebrospinal meningitis. Infecting horses with the responsible meningococcus and drawing off their an-
tiserum yielded the "Flexner serum," which effectively ended the recur-
rent epidemics of the disease. Subsequently, Flexner and his co-workers
developed a reasonably effective serum against the dysentery bacilli, the
cause of the "summer diarrheas" that had regularly claimed the lives of so
many infants. When in 1910 a new epidemic, infantile paralysis, struck the
country, Flexner's institute was able to identify the viral causative agent
and by thus giving a face to the enemy help stem the panic, although it
would be another thirty years before Jonas Salk, Albert Sabin, and their
colleagues developed vaccinations and effective antisera. During World
War One, Colonel Flexner (as he was commissioned) established a base
hospital on the Rockefeller's grounds for training army doctors in the treat-

ment of war wounds and then went to France to inspect the army's medical labs.

The structure of the Rockefeller Institute was such that departments were built around—often specially created for—a particularly brilliant scientist in a certain medical field. So it was that, as mentioned in Chapter 14, the Austrian Karl Landsteiner, a man of pure Jewish "blood" in the Nazi mythology, continued his blood group classifications and isolated the rhesus factor. No less a medical superstar, lured by Simon Flexner to Manhattan's Upper East Side, was Jacques Loeb. Born to a middle-class Sephardic family in the German town of Mayen in 1859, Jacques was raised in an intellectual and liberal, rather than religious, environment. His uncle Harry Bresslau, professor extraordinarius of history at the University of Berlin, was a firm believer in Jewish cultural assimilation and exercised a certain influence on young Jacques's intellectual development, especially after his father's untimely death. Through his *gymnasium* curriculum in Berlin and his university studies in Munich, where he received the M.D. degree in 1884, Loeb absorbed the nineteenth-century German concept of *Bildung* and *Wissenschaft*—in the sense of pure science for its own sake. But Loeb also came under the sway of the Austrian-Jewish social philosopher, scientist, and engineer Josef Popper-Lynkeus, whose ideas had some influence on the zeitgeist of the fin-de-siècle. Popper saw not just science but also technology as having great aesthetic and cultural value, in and of itself, regardless of its application. He devoted much energy to aeronautics, viewing it as a testimony to man's mastery of his world and the triumph of the human spirit, comparable to spaceflight and the moon landing a few generations later. (Popper turned out to be wrong in predicting that human flight would be of little or no practical use, but for him this was beside the point, anyhow.)

So it was in that in the biological realm Jacques Loeb, while still in Germany, took it upon himself to do what nature could not, or was loathe to. He began by producing two-headed tubularia by suspending in a fluid some cut pieces of their stems, free from contact with solid surfaces and thus from the irritability that normally stimulates the generation of a tail on one end as reciprocal to the head on the other. This Loeb did more or less for its own sake. "The thought is now hovering before me," he wrote to the famed Austrian philosopher-scientist Ernst Mach, "that man himself can act as a creator even in living Nature, to form it eventually to his will.

. . . Biologists label that the production of monstrosities; [but then] railroads, telegraphy, and the rest of the achievements of the technology of inanimate nature are accordingly monstrosities. In any case, they are not produced by nature; man has never met with them."

Loeb carried out his highly innovative research at Berlin's Landwirtschaftliche Hochschule (Agricultural College), not the most prestigious of German academic institutions but one more concerned with down-to-earth matters. He knew that his Jewishness was a handicap to academic advancement in Germany, although by no means an insurmountable one, as attested to by the number of Jews occupying highly prestigious professorial chairs. Loeb also knew that the introduction of technology—pure or applied, physical or biological—to the *Gymnasium* or university curriculum was often derided as *Amerikansierung* (Americanization), the supposed antithesis of *Kultur*. So in 1891, Loeb set sail for America itself, a land where (in his words) "nationalistic insults play no role, and where there is no hereditary nobility and no royalty." And where, furthermore, "because tradition is lacking, the natural taste for truth can penetrate further [so that] people everywhere pick up not 'classical' Greek and Roman authors, but rather will open a physics book."

Jacques Loeb's sense of time and place was excellent when it came to heralding the American Century and, specifically, the ceding of leadership in medical research from Germany to the United States. Accepting an appointment from the newly established University of Chicago in 1892, Loeb found himself at the site of the great Columbian Exposition (whose grounds were soon to be the university's new home), marking the 400th anniversary of Columbus's arrival in America. There, Loeb shared lab space with the renowned Jewish-American physicist A. A. Michelson, who was to receive the Nobel Prize for his measuring of the speed of light. But also outside the fair grounds and the university campus, fin-de-siècle Chicago, which had started the century as a frontier outpost and had its heart burned out by the great fire of 1871, was now the site of a daringly new, uniquely American architectural phenomenon. The brilliant structural designs of the Jewish architect-engineer Dankmar Adler, utilizing the new concept of steel frames and elevators, gave free reign to the revolutionary, vertically oriented vision of his partner, Louis Sullivan. ("The skyscraper," Sullivan wrote, "must be every inch a proud and soaring thing, rising in sheer exaltation that from bottom to top it is a unit without a single dissenting line").

The year 1904 found Loeb at another great American exposition, the St. Louis World's Fair. In the shadow of Sullivan and Adler's stunning Wainwright building, Loeb addressed the St. Louis Congress of Arts and Sciences on the possibility of creating living matter from nonliving substance. Loeb fully accepted the arguments against spontaneous generation, advanced by scientists, Jewish and non-Jewish, for most of the nineteenth century. Now, for the century that was just beginning, Loeb proposed the task of creating life in the test tube—again, not necessarily for possible practical application, but simply because Nature herself couldn't do it.

A major step in Loeb's ambitious program of human control of biology soon came with his production in the laboratory of a virgin birth, of sorts. Sex is the common form of reproduction of all evolutionarily advanced organisms, even the humble sea urchin. Yet Loeb showed that by varying the inorganic salt content of the sea water, the unfertilized sea urchin eggs could be made to divide and develop without the benefit of a sperm, thus producing a maternal clone rather than offspring containing maternal and paternal genetic characteristics.

What was shown to be feasible with sea urchins could conceivably be applied to mammals, including even humans. "I consider it possible," Loeb wrote, "that only the ions of the blood prevent the parthenogenetic [asexual] origins of embryos in mammalians." He further declared, to the delight of some Christians seeking scientific validity for their religious scriptures, that "an immaculate conception may be a natural result of unusual but natural causes." Meanwhile, childless couples wrote to Loeb beseeching him to produce parthenogeneis in the wife, while some early feminists for their part gleefully envisaged a future in which motherhood need not involve bondage to a husband.

Despite the attention some of his research received among the general public, Loeb's scientific breakthroughs were also much admired in academic circles. So it was that he received a call from Flexner in New York. Loeb gladly accepted this further chance to train, in his terms, "thinking physicians" as opposed to "medical artisans." In the first three decades of the twentieth century New York's skyline included close to 200 buildings of more than 20 storys. Already in 1909 one of them had topped the 50-story mark. The soaring skyscrapers served as monuments not so much to utility as to American technology and to personal and corporate prestige. The Equitable Life Building vied with the Metropolitan Life Building, the Singer Building with the Banker's Trust Building. Architects Ernest Flagg, Cass

Gilbert, and Daniel H. Burnham sought to outdo one another in adapting tradition to the new medium. And Frank W. Woolworth rightly predicted that, regardless of the new Woolworth Building's inherent commercial viability, the publicity value for his chain of five-and-ten-cent stores of this 58-story "Cathedral of Commerce," completed in 1913, would be more than worth the millions invested in it. The Rockefellers were, of course, not to be left out for long. The '20s would see the construction in lower Manhattan of their massive Standard Oil Building in a classically monumental style, followed by the boldly innovative plans for a coordinated group of neat midtown skyscrapers around a 70-story cascading sculptured slab, to be called Rockefeller Center. The group of buildings of the Rockefeller Institute on the East River was, however, of a far more modest scale, reflecting, perhaps, the solemnity of the "Temple of Pure Science" they represented.

For a while in New York Loeb, dedicated though he was to science for science's sake, got involved in political issues. He had definite socialist sympathies and entertained the idea that elucidation of good biological instincts—of parenthood, workmanship, and the desire for happiness for all—might serve for the establishment of ethical social principles and the control of ethically deficient "individual mutants." A firm believer in assimilation—Jewishness was religious and as such a Medieval relic—Loeb saw anti-Semitism as part of a more general problem of racism. As a biologist, he could state with a certain scientific authority that although human talent may be demonstrably greater in certain families or strains, this was not a matter of race. Furthermore, research on plants and animals indicated that hybridization—the equivalent of miscegenation, so dreaded by racial purists—often produced strains superior in many ways to both parent races. As for the notion that cultural traits—as opposed to raw talent and ability—could be genetically transmitted, this was a relic of emotional, pre-scientific romanticism. Not surprisingly, in view of his convictions, Loeb was active in obtaining Rockefeller Foundation funding for the medical school of Howard University, America's preeminent black institute of higher education.

In the course of time, however, Loeb came to view his ethical and political concerns as too divorced from his scientific work. Retreating to his ivory tower, he declared that happiness was only to be found in "quiet work in the laboratory, in the atelier of the artist, or in some other cloistral existence." This was the aspect of Loeb that the brilliant young (gentile) microbiologist Paul De Kruif, the future author of the popular-scientific bestseller *Microbe Hunters,* came to know and love upon joining the Rockefeller Institute in 1920. "Satirical old Jacques Loeb," De Kruif would write. "There is a note of discouragement, of pessimism, of complaint in his voice. He bewails his isolation. He complains that he grows old with the encouraging support of so few of his contemporaries."

It was Paul De Kruif's description of Loeb that provided Sinclair Lewis's model for Max Gottlieb, the figure who intellectually dominates the most famous of all medical novels, *Arrowsmith* (1925), and helped win for Lewis the Pulitzer and Nobel Prizes. "Not once," we are told concerning the aloof German-born Gottlieb, a professor at the fictitious University of Winnemac in the American heartland,

> did he talk of results of the sort called "practical"; not once did he cease warring on the *post hoc propter hoc* conclusions which still make up most of medical lore; not once did he fail to be hated by his colleagues, who were respectful to his face, uncomfortable in feeling his ironic power . . . . They said, with reason, that he was so devoted to Pure Science, to art for art's sake, that he would rather have people die by the right therapy than be cured by the wrong. Having built a shrine for humanity, he wanted to kick out of it all mere human beings.

Although Lewis's Gottlieb was often pessimistic when he thought about the long-term effects for humanity if disease was ever in fact eliminated, this in no way deterred him from continuing his scientific work. He gladly accepted the call to head a department at the McGurk Institute in New York (the fictional equivalent of the Rockefeller), viewing it as possibly America's "soundest and freest organization for pure scientific research . . . a Heavenly laboratory in which scientists might spend eternity in impractical research." Gottlieb, "alternatively proud and amiably sardonic" about his Jewish heritage, had in any case abandoned all traditional belief for faith in science. As he expressed it to his young assistant, Dr. Martin Arrowsmith: "'The scientist is intensely religious—he is so religious that he will not accept quarter-truths, because they are an insult to his faith.'"

Jacques Loeb died in 1924, at age 65, the year before his alter ego, Max Gottlieb, entered the popular imagination. Simon Flexner continued to guide the Rockefeller Institute until his retirement in 1935. He left behind quite a legacy, not only in the institute's research record and the accomplishments of its alumni (many former assistants and fellows under the eminent department heads had in turn gone on to head their own departments at universities throughout the country), but also in the model it provided for other institutions at home and abroad. As a distinguished virologist Peyton Rous put it in retrospect: "Flexner showed that society would be more wise to support men solely for what they might find out, however distant this appeared from stated medical needs; and that men of the right sort could be trusted to have better ideas than others could think up for them." Yet as great as was the transformation brought about in American medical research in this period, it paled before the metamorphosis that took place in American medical education. This, too, was the doing of Flexner. Not of Simon, but of his kid brother Abe.

In their attitudes toward learning, the contrast between the two adolescent Flexner brothers could hardly have been starker. At an age when the drop-out Simon was being led through the local jail—his presumed future home—his brother Abe was devouring every book he could get his hands on. Abe would later speak critically of the standards of public education in Louisville and in the South in general. Nevertheless, his high school did inculcate in him a love of Greek, an interest in literature, and an appreciation of physiology and chemistry. Books were a precious commodity at the Flexner home, which had fallen on hard times in the 1870s. But as luck would have it, high school student Abe was able to contribute to the family chest while surrounding himself with books by working part time in Louisville's private library, which was also the meeting place of the town's intelligentsia.

In 1884, the eldest of the brothers, Jacob, offered to subsidize the further education of his promising kid brother as best he could from his drugstore revenues. This was in keeping with all-for-one and one-for-all spirit of the Flexner family, and it meant that Jacob, who would later become a prominent Louisville physician, had to delay his plans to study medicine. Jacob chose for his younger brother the recently opened undergraduate school at Johns Hopkins. This seemingly arbitrary choice was to have doubly profound consequences for American medicine for a century to come.

Not only did the experience lead Abe, as we have seen, to urge his older brother Simon to go to Welch at the Hopkins medical faculty in order to advance his career in pathology and thus provide him with a model for medical research; it also had a strong formative influence on Abe's pedagogical views, which would be crucial when in due course he was called upon to shape the future of medical education in America.

At the Hopkins undergraduate school, the administrative set-up was informal and the buildings makeshift. Yet the faculty, chosen without regard to age, religion, or ethnic origin, was first-rate and so in turn was the level of scholarship of the students who sought and gained admittance. A guiding principle was the advancement of knowledge for its own sake, without its necessarily having an obvious practical application. Idiosyncrasy was prized. Despite the less-than-sufficient preparation in Greek and Latin Abraham Flexner had received in Louisville, he decided, in view of the temporary nature of the support his brother Jacob could provide, to double up on his courses. In keeping with the informal spirit of the university, there was no required attendance at lectures, although the exams had to be passed. So it was that the keen and ambitious Abe graduated in classical philology after two years instead of the usual three or four.

Returning to Louisville, Abraham Flexner taught Greek, Latin, physiology, and algebra at his former high school. In line with the Hopkins' emphasis on scholarship above professional training, he had never had a practical course on pedagogy and in fact would always deride the idea that teaching could be taught. Flexner drew instead upon his natural love of the transference of knowledge, which was further inspired by philosophical books such Rousseau's *Émile* and the biographies of great educators such as Prussian minister Friedrich von Althoff, the driving force behind the German universities.

After four years before large classrooms in the public high school, Flexner started his own school where pupils could receive individual attention. Such a school typically enrolled children of the well-to-do—but sometimes also the non-paying disadvantaged—who, though promising, were having trouble at the public school and would not otherwise be able to go on to college. Flexner made a point of never letting mediocrity set the standard. Through individual attention in an informal setting with flexible programs, a pupil was encouraged in the areas in which he showed most strength, in the hope that this would stimulate a desire to excel in other subjects as well.

The reputation of Flexner's school as a place of excellence in learning led to a shifting of the bulk of its new enrollment from promising but problematic pupils to the promising and ambitious. "Educational inequality must be prized and sought if democracy is to be lifted over the dead-level of mediocrity," Flexner stated. Decrying the standardized public school system by which the best students were usually allowed to advance through the grades only at the same pace as the average pupil, Flexner tailored his school's program of individual education so as to prepare its best pupils to go on to Harvard and other top colleges at 16 and receive their bachelor's degrees at 19, the age when graduates from other prep schools were first entering college.

Notwithstanding such success, and despite (or perhaps because of) the national attention he began to receive, Abraham Flexner was most dissatisfied with life in the backwaters of Louisville, particularly now that brother Simon was heading the Rockefeller Institute in New York. As Abe wrote to Simon: "I am pathetically anxious to do something. . . . But I am fastened here like Prometheus on his rock with a grinding routine that is almost as hard on the liver as a vulture's beak." It was with Simon's encouragement that Abe, aged 39, closed his school in 1905 to make his way in the world of education beyond Louisville.

The achievements of Flexner's school and its pupils had already attracted the favorable attention of Harvard president Charles W. Eliot. To Harvard, Abraham Flexner now went in order to study subjects that he considered to be related to education. He did some experiments in physiological psychology, supplemented by a trip to New York where Simon let him study the human brain. He followed seminars in philosophy at Harvard and got to know William James, America's preeminent philosopher-psychologist. But more important, Flexner was busy observing the way in which the whole system of college education operated.

The following year, 1906, brought Abe to Berlin. He was not favorably impressed by the amount of granite expended for garish victory arches and unsightly statues of Junker generals rather than monuments to the likes of Goethe, Schiller, Heine, and Mendelsohn—a sign of far worse to come. But Flexner's main objective was observing the German educational system in action, particularly the élite *gymnasia*. These evoked mixed feelings in him. On the one hand, the concept of such a system of special secondary schools was in keeping with Flexner's philosophy that an aristocracy of excellence (irrespective of socioeconomic class origin) is the truest form of democracy. On the other hand, Flexner, who prized individuality and originality in education, could hardly be favorably impressed by German standardization. The *gymnasia* seemed to bear down too heavily on most of the pupils. The atmosphere was unsympathetic and harsh, and not in keeping with Flexner's philosophy that excellence could best be stimulated by a climate of good humor and friendship between teacher and pupil. Whether in Berlin or Louisville, Flexner opposed exams that called for answers based on learning sterile fragments of knowledge rather than on original thought.

Next came Abe Flexner's analysis of the German university system. He was predictably impressed by the great value it put on pure scholarship. He also approved of the way in which full professors *(ordinarii)* were nominated—three names proposed by the university's faculty, of which one would be chosen by the education minister in Berlin—since this prevented the inbreeding common in other countries. But Flexner found fault with the concentration of power in the few full professors and also with the system by which the students' per-lecture fees went directly into the professors' pockets, since this naturally gave the professors financial incentives to mandate heavily attended required lecture courses rather than offer exclusive seminars or tutorials.

On the basis of his experiences in Louisville, Harvard, Berlin, and elsewhere, Flexner wrote his first book, *The American College,* which was severely critical of America's—specifically Harvard's—system of electives, lecturing, and assistantships, all of which, he felt, tended to dampen rather than inspire any love of scholarship among the students. Although his book brought about no immediate reforms, it did receive favorable attention from Henry S. Pritchett, president of the recently established Carnegie Foundation for the Advancement of Teaching. Steel magnate Andrew Carnegie had established his fund initially for providing retirement pensions for professors and teachers, thus making education a securer career more able to attract promising talent. But under Dr. Pritchett, the foundation also focused critically on prevailing academic standards and practices, and he quickly turned to what was arguably the greatest scandal in American education, the medical schools.

There were in the first decade of the twentieth century no fewer than 155 medical schools in the United States and Canada. The great majority were for-profit enterprises in which the fees of the students went directly into the pockets of the professors who granted them diplomas. Some moves toward reform in the system had recently been made by the eminent Jewish ophthalmologist Dr. Aaron Friedenwald. Baltimore-born and educated, Friedenwald was also familiar with the European system, thanks to his post-M.D. studies in Vienna, Prague, and Paris. As president of the Medical and Chirurgical Faculty of the Baltimore's College of Physicians and Surgeons, beginning in 1889, Friedenwald was involved in the developments in medical education taking place at Hopkins and other schools in the area. It was he who, as president of a special meeting of the American Medical Association in 1890 on the subject of medical education, provided the driving force for the establishment of the Association of American Medical Colleges under AMA auspices. However, although the AMA carried out surveys, the tone of its reports was constrained by diplomatic niceties toward fellow physicians.

So it was that when Abraham Flexner was on a visit to the Carnegie Foundation, Pritchett suggested that he conduct an independent and impartial survey of all the med schools in the United States and Canada. Flexner suspected a case of mistaken identity and pointed out that it was Simon who was the director of the Rockefeller Institute for Medical Research, and that he, Abraham, had no medical training. But Dr. Pritchett replied: "That is precisely what I want. I think these professional schools should be studied not from the point of view of the practitioner but from the standpoint of the educator. I know your brother, so I am not laboring under any confusion. This is a layman's job, not a job for a medical man."

In conducting his survey, Abe Flexner may have been aided by a rumor that, since he represented the Carnegie Foundation, there might be funding in the offing, which the med school being surveyed would be more likely to receive by not inflating its qualities. (Flexner did nothing to encourage this rumor, but perhaps he was not particularly strenuous in countering it.) Among the first things to strike Flexner was that entrance requirements, even when they existed on paper, were often nonexistent in practice. Students were commonly admitted without even a high school diploma as long as they could pay the fees. As for the training they received, the fundamental medical sciences were commonly absent. Because the "professors" (they granted themselves the title) were also practitioners who profited from referrals from former students, there was strong motivation to have a "chair" in a specialization such as obstetrics or surgery but not in the more basic or theoretical, and hence less lucrative, medical sciences. When asked by Flexner if there was any physiology lab, the dean of a medical school in Salem, Washington, replied, "Surely, I have it upstairs, I'll bring it to you," and promptly returned with a small sphygmograph (pulse measurer).

But even the practical training was usually woefully inadequate. An important point for Flexner was the extent to which a medical school had rights, or at least privileges, at some local hospital. Ideally, the school should be free to appoint the hospital's physicians and surgeons, who would also be the school's clinical teachers. In practice, however, even when a school supposedly had affiliation with a hospital, there might be no ward visits by the students and no postmortems.

Conditions at medical faculties affiliated with universities were not necessarily better than at the proprietary (for-profit) schools. In some cases, such as the medical department of the "University of Buffalo," the university in question existed only on paper. But even, for example, at the very real State University of North Carolina, the medical building at Raleigh where the med students received their clinical education was devoid of any equipment, though not lacking in grime. (Flexner made sure to photograph every room.) And although Washington University in St. Louis was itself a proud and ambitious institution, its medical department was sooner a source of shame. Even institutions such as Columbia University's College of Physicians and Surgeons and the Tufts College Medical School were not spared severe criticism.

Only one medical school was worthy of being held up as a model: the Johns Hopkins. There, as we have seen, the curriculum included basic medical sciences and labwork, and pure research was prized. On the clinical side, a teaching hospital had been attached to the medical faculty since the university's very inception. For admission to its med school, the Hopkins required that every student already have a college degree, including premed and language courses. As William Osler had wryly commented to his distinguished cofounder: "Welch, we are lucky to get in as professors, for I am sure neither you nor I could get in as students." Indeed, this applied as well to Abe's brother Simon, who, with no high school diploma and an M.D. degree obtained from a proprietary school in a matter of months, was nevertheless able through his talents to become a researcher at the Hopkins and rise to full professor status.

The scathing "Flexner Report" (as it came to be known), resounded as front page news across the nation, with headlines punctuated by words such as "sordid" and "hideous." Understandably, there was shock among the public and state officials and predictable indignation among the medical schools, particularly the owners. Threats of libel suits followed, and even anonymous death threats. But, in fact, the report sounded the death knell not for Flexner but for the majority of North America's medical schools, which soon disappeared as quickly and easily as they had once sprung up. Although it had been cynically predicted that Flexner would go a bit soft when it came to evaluating his home town's medical schools, Louisville was in fact hit particularly hard by the report. Six of its seven medical schools vanished almost overnight.

There then rose the problem of just how the surviving schools should be restructured. Flexner, who soon after his report appeared revisited Germany and received an honorary M.D. from the University of Berlin, generally held up the German model, with its combination of lab research and clinical experience. This was also the Hopkins model, which particularly encouraged pure science. "Research, untrammeled by near reference to practical ends, will go on in every properly organized medical school," Flexner recommended. "[I]ts critical method will dominate all teaching whatsoever; but undergraduate instruction will be throughout explicitly conscious of its professional end and aim." The Hopkins also shared with the German universities certain mechanisms to prevent excessive inbreeding so that the best and the brightest from other universities and cities could be called to the faculty. But even the Hopkins suffered from the fact that its clinical professors—the great Osler was no exception—received only a nominal salary from the university and therefore were usually obliged to divide their time between the academic world and private practice. At other medical schools the situation was far less favorable still, for they mostly lacked the Hopkins' impressive talent of nonpracticing physiologists and anatomists teaching and researching the basic medical sciences. The proposed remedy, the great step in the reform of American medicine, again involved harnessing Rockefeller dollars to Flexner ideals.

Back in 1902, at the time he was founding the Institute for Medical

Science that bears his family's name, John D. Rockefeller also established the General Education Board. Already before that time he had been in the habit of contributing to Negro education and to Baptist colleges. With the founding of the Board, Rockefeller hoped to advance education in a systematic and efficient manner. Now, a decade later, Rockefeller's right-hand man in his charitable endeavors, Frederick T. Gates, who was so instrumental in channeling some of the philanthropist's millions to the Rockefeller Institute under Simon Flexner, was drawn to Abraham Flexner's vision of the future of American medical education. Abe was brought onto the Board.

Flexner's first act was to funnel some $1.5 million of Rockefeller money to the Hopkin's medical faculty to make it possible for professors in the clinical branches—medical, surgical, obstetric, and pediatric—to assume full-time teaching and research schedules. Soon, similar endowments were made to the medical faculties of Washington University and Yale. Important here was that the professors in question were not to cut themselves off from the real world of practice but merely to refrain from accepting personal fees. Thus they could build their practices purely around the academic needs of the university and its students.

This marked only the beginning of the revolution in university medical education for which Rockefeller money was a catalyst. Vast sums were also needed for the construction of new facilities, especially laboratories. Flexner adopted a policy of donating Rockefeller funds in a seemingly arbitrary, but in fact strategic, manner. So, for example, several million dollars were given to build and equip a modern medical school in Iowa, while requests from neighboring midwestern states for similar donations were ignored. The prediction (which turned out to be quite correct) was that, once inspired by envy and rivalry, funding for the medical schools in Missouri, Michigan, Minnesota, and Wisconsin would appear from local sources. Often Flexner made contributions conditional on the raising of matching— or even larger—funds from other donors. Among the achievements in the generous boom years of the Roaring Twenties were the revitalization and expansion of the Cornell Medical School, the reconstruction of the Vanderbilt medical faculty, and the creation of the medical school of the University of Rochester. Jewish philanthropists were prominent in such endeavors as when, at Flexner's prodding, Julius Rosenwald, head of Sears, Robuck and Company; Albert D. Lasker, who had headed the Shipping Board during the war; and the prominent Chicagoan Max Epstein contributed millions toward making the newly founded University of Chicago a center of medical excellence. All in all, Flexner's expenditure of some $50 million of Rockefeller money via the General Education Board from the end of World War One to the stock market crash ten years later was a catalyst in generating over half a billion (many times this amount in present-day dollars) for the development of American medical education.

During this period, Board funds also helped continue the long-standing tradition of young American medical men furthering their education across the Atlantic. But now, with the American Century in medicine gaining steam, the purpose was no longer quite the same. As Abe Flexner put it: "It does not necessarily follow that because a person goes to Oxford or Cambridge or London or Berlin or Paris he will find conditions better, whether it be in medicine or in any other subject, than the conditions which he left at Harvard, Yale, or Johns Hopkins; but he will find them different and it is this difference that stimulates an able, active, mind." It was perhaps symbolic of the shift of the center of gravity in medicine from the Old World to the New that already in 1910, the Germans were taking lessons from the Americans in establishing the privately funded Kaiser Wilhelm Institute in Berlin, which, like Simon Flexner's Rockefeller Institute on which it was directly modeled, offered the most talented scientists the chance to carry out full-time independent research using the most modern facilities, unencumbered by teaching duties.

What could in a sense be called the crowning achievement of the ideals of both Flexner brothers came at the beginning of the '30s with the establishment of the Institute for Advanced Studies in Princeton, New Jersey. There, the best and the brightest scholars, young and old, of many disciplines, were allowed to pursue pure knowledge in any way they wished in an unstructured sphere with no formal teaching responsibilities. Thus were carried to the extreme some of the principles of autonomy and pure research at Simon Flexner's Rockefeller Institute and the respect for independence—indeed, even for idiosyncrasy— that Abraham Flexner so admired at the Hopkins and advocated throughout his career. The Institute for Advanced Studies, inspired in particular by Abraham's paper "The Usefulness of Useless Knowledge" and his philosophy that "academic democracy means letting men of brains alone," was financed in no small measure by contributions Flexner raised from Jewish philanthropists.

The story of the Institute for Advanced Study in the first decade of its existence, the '30s, was highly significant. The shifting of the center of gravity in science—medical and otherwise—from Germany to America, which had been gradually taking place in the preceding decades, was now infinitely accelerated with the advent of Hitler. Among the great Jewish scientists from central Europe to find a new home in Princeton were the mathematician Hermann Weyl, the nuclear physicist John von Neumann, and, most notable of all, Albert Einstein, driven from Berlin by the Nazis.

Being predominantly oriented toward such ethereal disciplines as mathematics and theoretical physics, the Institute for Advanced Studies had on the face of it no relevance to medical science. Yet almost as if to prove that knowledge obtained more or less for its own sake can have dramatic ramifications in medicine, a great breakthrough in man's war against infectious disease was about to occur in the same state of New Jersey, at a rather obscure agricultural college, in a discipline that was derided as "a science without scientists, without foundation, and without application." In contrast to the likes of the Flexner brothers, Abraham Jacobi and Jacques Loeb, the main figures in this new chapter, were not of Jewish-German origin. Rather, they were part of the migration of some 2.5 million Jews from Eastern Europe in the decades spanning the turn of the twentieth century. This great population movement forever changed the face of American Jewry and, with it, the face of American medicine.

Chapter 17
From the Soil of the New World

Little did I dream in 1918 that the "magic bullet" of Ehrlich that fascinated me so much would later be replaced and much further extended by the "wonder drugs" produced by microbes largely derived from the soil.

—Selman Waksman

They told me that the tubercle bacilli were covered with a heavy waxy capsule and nothing could get in. . . . My feeling was that if nothing got in we wouldn't have tuberculosis, because nutrients would have to get in and waste products would have to get out. If food and waste products could get through, so could an antibiotic.

—Albert Schatz

"*B*lessed art Thou, Lord our God, King of the universe, Who hast not created me as a woman." So goes the benediction in the traditional prayer book recited every morning by orthodox Jewish men, a sentiment that long informed the thinking of the Jewish people, particularly in the Eastern reaches of Europe. So it was that when Fradia Waksman was pregnant with her first child, she, her husband, Jacob, and their large circle of relatives and friends of both sexes prayed incessantly that the child be a boy. The place was the Novaia-Priluka in the Ukraine. The time was 1888, the year when another of the czar's subjects, Eli Metchnikoff, left Mother Russia for good to settle in Paris. The rabbis of the Talmud would have considered the Waksmans' prayers admirable in their intention, but nevertheless in vain, for the determination of the male fetus was deemed by the sages to have occurred by the fortieth day, if not at the moment of conception. But Fradia was the youngest of a family of eight daughters and no sons; hence, perhaps, this pleading for the Almighty to, if need be, reverse the course of nature.

Their prayers were apparently answered, and the boy, named Zolmin or Selman, found himself the center of attention in a largely female universe. No other child would come along for seven years, and then it was a girl, Miriam, whose life would be short. At age 2 Miriam came down with diphtheria. This was in 1897, after Emil von Behring and Paul Ehrlich had already developed the diphtheria antitoxin. Novaia-Priluka had no resident doctor. The barber looked after some minor ills, and Selman's mother preferred fish oil as a cure-all (there being, perhaps, a shortage of chicken soup). A shipment of antitoxin was arranged from Kiev, some 200 miles away, but this arrived too late to stop Miriam from suffocating to death. Selman's "youthful mind began to wonder," as he later recalled, at the concept of miracle drugs, although the fascination would lay more or less dormant for another forty years.

Nine-year-old Selman's sorrow at the passing of his only sibling was at least somewhat consoled by even greater doting by the womenfolk. This was all the more so in that Selman's father, Jacob, was often away. For five years after his marriage, Jacob, conscripted into the czar's army, never once saw his wife. And even after Selman's birth, Jacob was often in the neighboring city, attending to the various pieces of real estate bequeathed to him by his father. Possessing limited experience in such matters, Jacob did the best he could to manage and repair the often run-down properties whose tenants rarely paid their rent.

The traditional gender roles in the Jewish community had not prevented the womenfolk in Selman's family tree from becoming somewhat of a success in business in their own right. His maternal grandmother, Eva London, was a prominent merchant, who was able to care financially for her eight children after her husband's death at age 30. For several days every week Eva was out of town, buying goods on a commission basis for the local merchants. In her old age, the menfolk would consult this matriarch for her wisdom in business as well as in personal matters. Some of this self-reliance rubbed off on her youngest daughter, Fradia, for during her husband's five-year absence in the army, she built a house and ran a dry-goods business.

Selman would later recall how visitations of pestilence would form historical reference points in the stories told by grandmother Eva. Her living memory extended back to the aftermath of Napoleon's invasion of Russia, and she was also the repository of a lot of earlier history of the Jews in the Ukraine, particularly the rebellion against the Polish landlords by the Ukrainian peasants led by Bagdan Chmielnicki's Cossacks in the mid-seventeenth century, in which perhaps 100,000 Jews, caught as "between the hammer and the anvil," were systematically massacred. Yet in her narratives, such tumultuous events were dated as coming before, after, or during the great cholera or plague epidemics, which carried away large portions of the helpless population, Jewish and Christian. Ironically, the antidote to such age-old scourges of mankind were all along present in the black soil of the Ukraine—and in the brown soil of distant New Jersey.

The Ukraine was the proverbial breadbasket not only of the Russian Empire, but of much of the rest of Europe as well. Selman would forever be under the spell of the fragrance of the *tchernozem*, the dark Ukrainian earth, especially when it was being plowed in the spring or harvested in the fall. Attracted as he was to the Russian classic writers, he would later be fond of quoting the words of the poet Gogol:

> Can you conceive of the beauty of a Ukrainian night? ... A moon is at the center of heaven; the boundless horizons seem to have parted into ever more limitlessness. A light of silver bathes the earth, the marvelous air is cool and laden with desire and fragrance. ... Peaceful and tranquil are the ponds; the orchid's walls, steeped in green, encircle the cool refreshing waters. ... All the landscape is at rest. A breath that is wondrous, that is solemn, hovers above.

As Novaia-Priluka had no public or government schools, Selman's mother arranged for the precocious and inquisitive boy's education in private schools or at teachers' homes. The Jewish communities of Eastern Europe, and not least the Czarist Empire, were more traditionalist than their brethren to the west. Yet by this time, even in a small town such as Novaia-Priluka, it was deemed advisable for the Yiddish-speaking Jews who could afford it to receive alongside their religious and Hebrew instruction an education in secular subjects and the Russian language.

The science subjects exerted an increasing fascination on young Waksman, and this made him rather apolitical with regard to both Russian and Jewish national affairs. Furthermore, his home lay far from the centers of political, as well as cultural, importance. Yet no one, least of all a Jew, could be oblivious to the tumultuous events taking place early in the twentieth century in the Czarist Empire. Things had gone from bad to worse after the assassination of the relatively liberal Czar Alexander II and the ascension to the throne of his ultrareactionary and blatantly anti-Semitic son Alexander III. It was in this climate of pogroms that the Zionist movement was first set in motion by a Jewish physician in Odessa, Leon Pinsker. His book *Autoemancipation* analyzed the psychological and social roots of anti-Semitism and the prospects for assimilation and concluded that Jews must take it upon themselves to reclaim their ancestral land rather than hope for help from rulers or legislators. Under Dr. Pinsker's inspiration, some 25,000 Eastern European Jews made their way to Palestine in the first Aliyah from 1882 to 1904.

A spurt of emigration to the Holy Land occurred in 1903 when one of the most notorious pogroms took place in the town of Kishinev in the province of Bessarabia. Forty-five Jews were killed, over 500 injured, and some 1,500 homes and shops looted or vandalized. These riots, organized with the compliance, if not active complicity, of local officials, relied on hundreds of drunken thugs brought in from the villages and joined by some religious seminary students. But the atmosphere of anti-Semitism in Kishinev itself was also strong among the middle-class. Gentile merchants were generally less successful than the Jews, and Christian physicians feared the supposed Jewish takeover of the medical profession. The pogrom, the most serious in a series over the next few years, greatly tarnished Russia's image abroad and brought forceful international condemnation, not least from American president Theodore Roosevelt.

The year after the Kishinev riots, 1904, saw Russia's humiliating defeat at the hands of the Japanese, who forced the capitulation of Ft. Arthur and destroyed Russia's obsolete Baltic fleet. In its wake came agitation for the reform of the autocratic, incompetent, and corrupt system of imperial government. The demands were supported by demonstrations, barricades, and a general strike that brought the railways, ships, and factories to a standstill. Czar Nicholas II, who had succeeded Alexander III eleven years earlier, first consented to the granting of constitutional rights and the establishment of a Duma (parliament). Twelve Jews were elected as deputies, even though Jews had no majority in any electoral district. But these reforms were soon followed by a wave of repression by reactionaries.

Nicholas II reverted to the tried and true political tactic of encouraging the peasantry (the older members of whom had been born in the semi-slavery of serfdom) to vent its political frustrations in the form of anti-Semitic pogroms. The notorious forgery *The Protocols of the Elders of Zion,* a supposed secret Jewish blueprint for world domination, was widely distributed. When Jewish towns and villages were raided by Cossacks and police, those arrested on suspicion of subversive activity were liable to be shot or exiled to Siberia.

The government-subsidized extremist organization, the Black Hundreds, revived the ancient blood libel of the Jewish ritual murder of Christian children. The future Soviet premier Nikita Krushchev would one day recall how during cholera epidemics in the Ukraine in 1902 and again in 1910: "[T]he [Jewish] doctors in the area were beaten unmercifully. . . . A rumor started to circulate among the miners that the doctors were poisoning the patients. Witnesses were found who claimed they had seen someone throw powder into the well."

In the Novaia-Priluka region, however, Jews were fortunate in having relatively friendly relations with the local peasantry. Selman Waksman's mother and grandmother, in particular, were well regarded. Although self-defense measures were organized among the Jews of Novaia-Priluka, these fortunately turned out not to have to be put into practice. And although the police raided Selman's home and detained him, he was soon released when it was found that none of his many books was of a revolutionary nature.

Selman Waksman would, however, be directly affected by discriminatory regulations in the Russian secondary school and university system. The number of Jewish students admitted to the *gymnasia* (the secondary schools that prepared for entrance to the university) was strictly limited by quota and even upon admission there was sometimes the extra burden of discriminatory tuition fees. An alternative for obtaining the *gymnasium* diploma was registering as an external student, which meant that the learning had to be acquired other than by classroom instruction but that the student could then present himself for the *gymnasium* exams for a given year. Selman was at least fortunate in that his memory was extraordinarily biased toward the printed rather than the spoken word. Even in later years, he would find it very advantageous to jot down any important lecture he heard; for once he had seen it on paper, the information was easily stored in his photographic memory. For private instruction Selman went to the *Gymnasium* towns of Vinnista and Odessa and was much helped by a teacher who would have been a university lecturer had he not been Jewish. Selman was in turn able to earn some cash by tutoring pupils of lower grades.

The external examination system worked on an all-or-nothing basis, where (unlike for the regular *gymnasium* students) failure in any one subject automatically meant failure in all. Although Selman missed a year due to a single lapse of memory (he forgot that the river flowing through Berlin was the Spree), the following year he obtained the *gymnasium* diploma with grades near the top of the class. Yet his problems with the discriminatory Russian educational system were far from over. Under the spell of the black soil of the Ukraine, Selman wanted to study its life processes at the university. But the anti-Semitic regulations were such that only those Jews who held gold and silver *gymnasium* medals were considered for admission, and external *gymnasium* students, no matter how high their examination marks, were ineligible for such awards.

So, for his university education, Waksman would have to leave the Russian Empire. He was admitted to the prestigious Polytechnic Institute of Zürich, which would soon boast as one of its professors a former graduate named Albert Einstein. Selman would not have lacked stimulating company in Zürich, for it was then home to many expatriate Russian intellectuals. Among them was one V. I. Lenin, whose maternal grandfather, Alexander Dmitrievich Blank (né Srul Moishevich Blank), had converted from Judaism to Christianity in 1818, in order to attend the Medical-Chirugical Academy of St. Petersburg. (Dr. Blank, who married a bourgeois Christian Volga German, rose to the civil service rank of state councilor and retired young to live the life of a landed country gentleman, was wisely skeptical of orthodox medical therapies. He wrote a book, *As Thou Livest, So Heal Thyself*, in which he extolled the virtues of hydrotherapy and even ordered his children, including Lenin's mother, Maria, to go to bed wrapped in damp sheets "in order to strengthen their nerves.") Before Selman Waksman could actually go to Zürich, however, a personal tragedy overtook him when his mother died of an abdominal obstruction. Although he managed to get her to the hospital at Kiev, the doctors couldn't operate, and the drugs they prescribed were without effect. To add to Selman's grief, his father, who had only visited his mother once during her two-week hospitalization, soon remarried. At home in mourning, Selman reread the

Bible, especially the Book of Job and Ecclesiastes. This was perhaps the last time he would ever consult the Scriptures.

Having been deprived of his own mother, there was no bond to keep Selman Waksman in Mother Russia, especially in view of the precarious political situation, particularly for the Jews. If he was going to leave, why not go all the way? Not to Zurich, but to far-off America. He would not be the first. Already in the late nineteenth century the economic and political situation in Russia had produced a tidal wave of Jewish emigration to the United States, often topping 100,000 a year. Selman's neighbors and cousins were already there, and their letters urged him to join them. So in October 1910 young Waksman was among a group from Novaia-Priluka leaving for America. As their train passed over the Russian border, Selman, though far more scientifically than politically oriented, joined in a revolutionary song: "We have shaken the shackles off our feet. We are entering upon a new world, a free world, where Man is free." But the black soil of his native Ukraine would forever remain in his blood.

Among the previously immigrated relatives who welcomed Selman Waksman to the new continent were two specimens of those stereotypically anomalous creatures (at least outside of the Land of Zion): the Jewish farmboy and farmgirl. His cousins Mendel and Molki Kornblatt had learned the art and science of land cultivation as estate managers in America, and they now tilled their own land and raised chickens in Metuchen, New Jersey. It was there that Waksman would live for the next few years, earning his keep by aerating the manure heap into compost.

In choosing his university curriculum, Waksman considered following so many of his coreligionists through the ages and becoming a physician. (One of his American relatives was already a dentist.) Opportunities for Jews in medicine were vastly greater in America than in Russia, as attested to by the brilliant careers of the likes of Simon Flexner and Jacques Loeb. But there was a general current of anti-Jewish sentiment to contend with in America in the first decades of the twentieth century. The Jews arrived in the millions, along with millions of other immigrants. As such, they were part of the target of general nativist sentiment. Furthermore, unlike their German coreligionists who had arrived before them, the new immigrants were obviously and blatantly Jewish in their manners, customs, and speech. Not a few, the more deracinated variety, held socialist views and were considered doubly un-American. And, of course, these masses of new citizens were pushy in their upward striving. For Jews wishing to become doctors, such prejudices translated into *numerus fixus* quotas at medical schools. A lame argument for this restriction was that gentile patients would prefer not to consult Jewish doctors and that proportional representation in the profession was therefore desirable. This pretext, of course, flew in the face of 1,000 years of medical history. Even countries that banned Jews typically made exceptions for Jewish physicians, who were held in such awe. As an anti-Semitic cancer patient in the American South in Selman Waksman's day who eschewed Christian doctors so eloquently put it: only a Jewish physician could "Jew down death."

The problems facing Jews wishing to enter the medical profession were poignantly illustrated in Morton Thomas's famous novel of medicine *Not as a Stranger*. The fictional Dr. Grover Aarons, a brilliant Brooklyn-born professor of pathology at an undistinguished midwestern state university in the 1920s, who had brought to medicine the religious fervor he couldn't muster for traditional Judaism, reflects on his career:

> His mind went back to the days of bitterness, the days when he roamed the wilderness waiting for the Promised Land. He thought of being a Jew and the quota against Jews at medical schools, no more than ten per cent admitted and the fight for marks to put you among the lucky ten per cent and professors marking Jews low. Work, and he groaned under it. Fatigue, and he fell asleep again in class the moment the lights went off and the slides were flashed on the screen. Hunger, and its acids cramped his belly. And one day, when he could struggle no longer, the high plateau reached at last. And he was a doctor. And the first thing to be seen was a sign, the letters, the burning letters of God. NJA. No Jews Allowed. And there was the wilderness again. That was all. Just a little wilderness. And a little work. And finally, reluctantly, there was this professorship. And now, in this backwater, his dreams clawing at him still, he watched while others soared.

Prior to World War I, however, the prestigious College of Physicians and Surgeons of Columbia University was basing its admissions on merit, and almost half the med students were Jewish. (A quota system introduced later would knock this down to less than 7 percent.) So Selman Waksman was offered a place.

But entranced by his composting manure heaps, Selman was convinced that a medical curriculum would not focus enough on his great interest in life, the chemical reactions of living bodies. The nearby Rutgers College of Agriculture, whose bacteriology department was headed by fellow Russian-Jewish immigrant Dr. Jacob G. Lipman (soon to become dean of the college), was only a few miles away from the farm and offered Waksman a free scholarship. His decision, in 1911, to forgo medical school for Rutgers would, ironically enough, eventually lead to one of the greatest breakthroughs in the history of medicine.

Some 15 percent of the class at Rutgers was Jewish, and in his junior year Waksman organized a chapter of the Menorah Society, devoted to the discussion of Jewish culture and issues. Judaism, he wrote later in life, "has given the world its highest code of ethics and morals." But like so many Jews of his day, young Waksman was exchanging the religious messianic vision for a more secular one. As a Jewish "progressive," he also helped organize a chapter of the Intercollegiate Socialist Society, later known as the League for Industrial Democracy.

If Waksman's left-wing ideology persisted much beyond his youth, it was certainly undermined by the generally unfavorable—sometimes downright appalling—impressions made on him by Soviet agriculture, academia, and social and economic life in general during his return visits to Mother Russia later in life. But, in any case, in his student years and for decades to come, his fascination with the soil and the microscopic life processes within it dwarfed all other concerns. It was as a student at Rutgers that Waksman, during a visit to the Department of Agriculture in Washington, D.C., followed the advice of his mentor, went to the local fruit market, and, to the disgust of the dealers, poked his fingers into the molds of various rotting oranges and lemons. Thus he learnt firsthand to distinguish the squishy rot of *Penicillium italicum* from the hard rot of *Penicillium oxalicum* and also their subtly different shades of green. History might have taken a different turn if these fungi, which Waksman also analyzed under the microscope, had captured more than just his passing interest. But they didn't. And so it was left to Fleming a decade later to stumble upon penicillium's bactericidal properties and to Chain and Florey the following decade to rediscover them and put them to practical use.

What did capture the particular interest of the student Selman Waksman was a type of microorganism that in the course of time would turn out to be hardly less important than Penicillium. Digging around at various depths at the college farms, Waksman obtained soil samples and incubated a broad array of microorganisms. The colonies of bacteria and fungi he cultured were familiar enough to him, but he was surprised to see something else growing on the agar plates—small conically-shaped colonies of lifeforms that were similar to the bacteria but upon microscopic examination resembled more the fungi. Some probing with a needle showed them to be leathery and compact, and when Selman isolated them and grew them on various media, they often took on a pigmentation. These lifeforms were finally identified as belonging to an obscure family of microorganisms called the *actinomyces*. For Selman Waksman they were the start of something big. In the course of his career, he would come to adopt the *actinomyces* as his pet microbes, and one day harness them in ways neither he nor anyone else could have imagined when he first set eyes on them.

Rutgers would be home to Waksman for the next half century, as he worked to transform its agricultural college into a multidisciplinary faculty of microbiology. He was fond of the deep snows and heavy frosts of the New Jersey winter and also the proximity to New York City. The only major interlude was two years, beginning in 1916, at the University of California at Berkeley to obtain his Ph.D. Waksman conveniently got married just before he left—to a girl from his hometown in the Ukraine—and so he only had to make a detour through Niagara Falls on the way to the West Coast. The following year, while Waksman was writing his dissertation, America became drawn into the war in Europe, which had already been raging for three years. Waksman, who had become a citizen before leaving New Jersey, considered enlisting, but his draft board saw the completion of his Ph.D. as being more in the national interest. Waksman had already investigated the possible negative effects of fungi in the munitions manufacturing process. Now, with the United States at war, the country had to rapidly become self-sufficient in those bacteriological and chemical fields in which it had previously been so dependent on Germany. Even before receiving his doctorate, Waksman began working part time at a commercial lab where he researched a new kind of peptone, which had until recently been imported from Germany and was necessary for the production of Behring and Ehrlich's diphtheria antitoxin.

Back at Rutgers in 1918, Selman Waksman was temporarily compelled by economic circumstances to spend most of his week away from the college, at the Takamine Laboratory in nearby Clifton, where the pay was considerably better. The Takamine Lab was a lineal descendant of Paul Ehrlich's lab in Frankfurt, with a detour via Japan. Ehrlich's faithful Japanese assistant Sahachiro Hata had established his own lab for the production of Salvarsan upon return to his native land. As the world slid into the global conflagration, with the disruption of the flow of medicines between nations, Hata encouraged his colleague Dr. Takamine to go manufacture Salvarsan in America. Selman Waksman now had the responsibility to test the toxicity of 606 on laboratory animals and see to it that the "magic bullet" conformed to government regulations. "Since I first learned, late in 1910, of Ehrlich's great discovery, I was fascinated by the idea of finding chemical substances which would be effective in the treatment of infectious diseases of man and animals," he later recollected. In Ehrlich's drug a particular molecular structure made it react in a desired way with the specific living cells of a mircoorganism that was the enemy of humankind. But Waksman and his contemporaries knew all too well of the many other devastating pathogens for which there were as yet no magic bullets.

Yet Selman Waksman would not return to chemotherapy for another twenty years or so. During most of this time, as he himself readily admitted, his work was pretty abstract and theoretical. He analyzed all sorts of soil samples at various levels, as well as specimens from various dung heaps, and determined the population of the microscopic inhabitants and tried to figure out how they grew, how they multiplied, what nutrients they took in, and what waste products they exuded. Waksman bore no ill will toward the professor at the University of Illinois who denied him a fellowship on the grounds that the school "could not waste public funds by supporting a student who . . . could hardly be expected to make an important contribution to practical or even scientific farming." The very title of Waksman's great 1927 tome, *The Bible of Soil Microbiology,* seemed to hint at its otherworldly nature.

Nevertheless, almost despite himself, Waksman applied some of his findings to practical matters. The whole question of soil fertility—why some soils such as in his native Ukraine produce abundant crops, whereas other soils grow almost nothing—was, of course, linked to organic chemical content, and this might be dependent on the proportionate populations of various protozoa, bacteria, fungi, and Waksman's favorite actinomyces in the respective soils. This in turn raised the possibility of manipulating the soil so as to shift the equilibrium of the microorganisms toward greater fertility. The population of unfavorable microbes could theoretically be decreased by the introduction of hostile compounds, while the proportion of favorable microorganisms—not least of which, the actinomycetes—might be increased by providing compounds conducive to their flourishing. Waksman also analyzed the microbial and chemical content of horse manure, a traditional fertilizer, in the hope that a substitute could be found, now that the horse was being increasingly replaced by the automobile, which left behind no excretions of use to farmers.

As for practical medical matters, Waksman's only contact in the '20s and for most of the '30s was peripheral—and far removed from therapeutics or pharmacology. Waksman continued to pioneer the concept of germ warfare among the various microorganisms in the soil, some of which may live in a symbiotic relation, others of which compete or feed upon one another in a Darwinian struggle for survival. Of interest to medicine is the fate of pathogenic microbes in the soil: How long do they remain viable and dangerous to man or beast? What causes their ultimate demise (lack of nutrients, attacks by other microbes, etc.)? These were matters that Waksman investigated. Also peripherally related to medicine was Waksman's search for an alternative source of protelytic enzymes. This need arose as a consequence of another triumph of medicine in the New World.

In 1889 in Strassburg (at the time, part of the German Empire), the Jewish doctor Oskar Minkowski conducted a series of animal experiments that demonstrated for the first time that the pancreas secretes a substance (in days past such secretions were called humors but would now soon be known as hormones) the lack of which results in diabetes mellitus. Thus arose a hope among the millions of diabetes sufferers of being reprieved from their death sentences by injections of pancreatic secretions obtained from animals. Such attempts failed, however, because the antidiabetes agent was inactivated by the other juices secreted by the pancreas as a whole. In the early 1920s, Frederick Bantong and Charles Best at the University of Toronto managed to obtain unneutralized extracts of insulin (as it came to be called) directly and exclusively from the part of the pancreas, the islets of Langerhans, that produces it. Better still, the pancreases of fetuses are almost entirely composed of islet cells, and cattle farmers customarily had their cows impregnated before slaughtering for the resulting weight gain.

Thus the fetuses from the world's slaughterhouses could be counted on to yield enough Langerhans islets and insulin to treat the world's diabetics. But there was a downside to this otherwise blessed development. The same fetal pancreases from slaughterhouses had previously gone to the manufacture of products such as protelytic enzymes and were now suddenly in short supply. Here some of Waksman's fungi came to the rescue as an alternative source for generating the desired enzymes.

It was, however, the rise of Nazism in Germany and the gathering anew of war clouds over Europe that led to Selman Waksman's concentrating on some very practical matters of national interest, eventually culminating in one of medicine's greatest triumphs ever. Already in the first two years of the Nazi regime Waksman had resigned from the editorial boards of two prestigious German microbiology journals, when personal friends of his such as Otto Meyerhof were forcibly removed from their posts because of their Jewish origins. Waksman's decision was not made without some initial hesitation and soul-searching, since his "good German" colleagues maintained that his presence on the board was a positive influence. But as the situation got worse instead of better, Waksman felt compelled to write to the editor: "I find no words to give expression to my feelings of shame and disgust at having my name appear on the front page of a journal now published in a country which does not recognize the simplest of human rights."

The late '30s brought Waksman to Palestine to carry out analyses of peat bogs on behalf of Jewish refugees who had previously been familiar only with the peat moss varieties of their native Germany. Waksman maintained cordial contact with his coreligionist Otto Warburg. Not the cell physiologist and future Nobel laureate in Medicine we met in Chapter 14 (although Waksman knew him as well), but rather the botanist Otto Warburg, likewise a scion of the famed German banking family. This Otto Warburg, a renowned professor at the University of Berlin, had seen the writing on the wall early on, became head of the World Zionist Organization, and immigrated to Palestine, where he set up an agricultural research station at Rehovoth and directed the botanical department of the Hebrew University.

As America was once again drawn into a global conflagration, Waksman took on the post of chairman of the War Committee on Bacteriology. One subject he investigated for the Navy was the role played by bacteria in the attachment of fouling microorganisms to the bottoms of ships, which reduced their speed. As for the land forces fighting in tropical climes, a major concern was the molds or fungi that, by decomposing cellulosic and protein material, damaged everything from electrical and optical equipment to clothing, shoes, and tents. This called for the development and testing of antifungal agents.

But overshadowing the problems of hull-fouling and cellulose-devouring microorganisms was a concern with those germs that are pathogenic to human beings. In the previous World War, as we have seen, a young Selman Waksman had tested Paul Ehrlich's Salvarsan, which implanted in him a dream of discovering "other agents which would have broader antimicrobial activity"—a dream that would remain dormant for the two decades when the world was at peace. Now, with the Germans again set to lay waste to Europe, this time with a particular vengeance, there loomed once more the specter of pestilence among the destitute and displaced civilian population and in overcrowded military encampments.

There was no doubt another factor guiding Waksman—if perhaps only subliminally—to seek to combat the scourges of mankind: The concept of the "magic bullet" had become part of the American national consciousness, thanks to that American-Jewish invention called Hollywood. Almost alone, the East European immigrant Jews and their sons (with an occasional German Jew mixed in) had created Tinsel Town. The Jewish moguls built and ran the great studios of Universal, Paramount, Twentieth Century Fox, Metro-Goldwyn-Mayer, and Warner Bros., as well as theaters across the nation, including some garishly opulent cathedral-like structures with a seating capacity of thousands.

In 1936 Jack and Harry Warner, whose parents had fled from the wave of czarist reaction in the 1880s, released *The Story of Louis Pasteur.* The film was a great success, earning an Academy Award for the title role player, a former star of the New York Yiddish theater named Muni Weisenfreund, better known in Hollywood as Paul Muni. Since then, Warner Bros. had been considering making another film in the same genre. Now, with the memory of Paul Ehrlich obliterated from the books and street signs of his German homeland, the thought of a movie about his magic bullet was particularly appealing—and all the more so in view of Hitler's obsession with Jews and venereal disease in page after page of *Mein Kampf.* (Jack Warner is said also to have been motivated by a murder under mysterious circumstance of a Jewish Warner Bros. executive in Germany, but this may be more Hollywood legend than fact.) "There isn't a man or woman alive who isn't afraid of syphilis," declared the movie's story writer, Norman Burnside, "and let them know that a little kike named Ehrlich tamed the scourge. And maybe they can persuade their hoodlum friends to keep their fists off Ehrlich's coreligionists."

Paul Muni was considered for the title role, in view of his success as Louis Pasteur. But Muni had a policy of never portraying a Jew on the screen. The part was, however, gladly taken by another one-time actor in the Yiddish theater, Edward G. Robinson. The Romanian-born Robinson (né Emanuel Goldenberg) was active in Hollywood's anti-Nazi League and had delighted in exposing the subversive activities of the German-American Bund in his role as an undercover G-man in the semi-documentary *Confessions of a Nazi Spy,* released in 1939. (The filming had been accompanied by formal protests from the German embassy, a failed lawsuit from the Bund, and death threats from anonymous callers and letter-writers, the latter of which had moved Jack Warner to hire armed bodyguards and institute tight security at the studio sets and at the film's premiere.) Robinson now welcomed the chance to break out of the police and gangster movie genre in which he was in danger of being forever stereotyped.

As production progressed in 1939–40, the former "Little Caesar" identified with Paul Ehrlich as with none of the more than eighty characters he played in a career spanning half a century. "During the filming I kept to myself, studied the script, practiced gestures before the mirror, read about his life and times, studied pictures of the man, tried to put myself in his mental state, tried to *be* him." As he later told columnist Hedda Hopper: "Playing Ehrlich was the easiest acting job I ever did, because he was so simple, a great figure struggling with terrific problems. These gangsters are twice as hard to do. They're shallow, nothing to them."

Then one day a telephone message was relayed to Robinson from a lady with an indecipherable German name, which turned out to be that of Stefanie Schwerin, née Ehrlich. The great doctor's elder daughter had been forced out of Germany and had managed, not without difficulty, to come to America. Robinson's identification with his role was complete as he welcomed "Steffa" to the studio and "embraced the young lady as if she were my own daughter." (At the time, Stefanie Ehrlich Schwerin was in fact 56, and a decade older than Robinson.) When he heard that Hedwig Ehrlich, Paul's widow, had managed to flee to Switzerland with only the most meager resources just months before the outbreak of the war, Robinson offered aid. The Ehrlichs politely declined, but in her correspondence with Robinson, Hedwig did make a different request: that a print of the film be given the Ehrlich family as a momento. She in turn received a request from Robinson for a letter from the hand of the great doctor. Hedwig was honored to comply, despite the fact that Paul Ehrlich was in the habit of dictating almost all his correspondence and that so much material had been abandoned in the exodus from Nazi Germany.

Yet despite the worsening situation of the German Jews, Warner Bros. decided to exercise caution in the content of *Dr. Ehrlich's Magic Bullet,* lest it appear self-serving. Most of the Hollywood moguls in fact preferred to cultivate an all-American image and shied away from themes of Jewish interest or concern. Until Pearl Harbor suddenly made flag-waving patriotism and Jewish life-and-death issues coincide, the matter of anti-Nazi films was problematic. True, Warner Bros. had made *Confessions of a Nazi Spy*. But reluctant to be perceived as pursuing any Jewish agenda in the Ehrlich film, the studio bosses circulated an internal memorandum stating: "It would be a mistake to make a political propaganda picture out of a biography which could stand on its own feet." So, the words *Jew* and *Jewish* went entirely unmentioned in the film. Anti-Semitism was referred to only indirectly, as when an authoritarian and thoroughly bigoted physician remarks to the hospital director: "I have nothing against Dr. Ehrlich personally, although I must confess to a certain feeling against people of his faith in our profession." At another point in the film, Ehrlich rails "What has race to do with science? . . . In science truth is master, not the state!" This is in response to a Reich commission's objections to the employment at Ehrlich's institute of people other than "of pure German blood." Yet this reference is not to Jews, but, somewhat ironically, to Ehrlich's Japanese colleague Dr. Sahachiro Hata, whose compatriots were allied with Hitler when the film was made and as such enjoyed a sort of honorary Aryan status.

The original version of the film included a deathbed scene, in which Ehrlich refers to the Pentateuch: "And Moses went up from the plains in the mountain that is over Jericho. And the Lord showed him all the land. And the Lord said unto him, this is the land which I have promised unto thy people. I have caused thee to see it with thine eyes, but thou shalt not go hither. So Moses the servant of the Lord died there in Moab according to the words of the Lord."Yet this finale—so reminiscent of the late Sigmund Freud's pronouncement that future generations of psychoanalysts would explore the Promised Land, of which he, like Moses, had only been able to glimpse—ended up on the cutting-room floor. In the deathbed scene in its edited version, Ehrlich as his final testament whispers to his assembled friends and colleagues with his last breath the rather universalist message: "There can be no final victory over the diseases of the body unless the diseases of the soul are also overcome. They feed on each other . . . diseases of the body, diseases of the soul. In days to come, there will be epidemics of greed, hate, ignorance. We must fight them in life as we fought syphilis in the laboratory. We must fight, fight. We must never stop fighting." And in lieu of any spoken quote from the Book of Moses, the film fades out with the pseudobiblical words flashed on the screen: " . . . And the temples to his memory are the bodies of human beings purified and made whole."

The caution of the Hollywood moguls extended beyond their fear of being perceived as pursuing some Jewish agenda. Especially in the '30s, with the rise of anti-Semitic demagogues, the studio heads were ever sensitive to potential public objections to such a powerful medium being almost exclusively in Jewish hands. "Combining good picture-making with good citizenship," was the Warner motto. Harry Warner so cultivated this image that *Fortune* magazine described him as having "two major interests, business and morals." Since 1934, the studios had been adhering to the Production Code of the Motion Pictures Producers and Distributors of America. The Code stipulated, among other things, that "Impure love must not be presented as attractive and beautiful" and that "the sanctity of the institution of marriage and the home shall be upheld." In fact, even a husband and wife had to have separate, albeit adjoining, beds (whence the name "Hollywood bed"). Or if they dared to be seen on the same mattress, at least one of them had to have a foot on the floor. Just as the word *Jew* was never mentioned in the movie, there was also, incredible as it may seem, serious discussion among Warner executives of never mentioning the word *syphilis*. There had been ample precedent for such self-censorship in movie adaptations of plays and books about syphilis, in which the name had been expurgated for the screen. But these had been fictional stories, whereas Paul Ehrlich was real.

By comparison to the wholesome all-American image presented in the films of the other studios, Warner Bros. was generally a bit more daring, portraying rather disreputable and deracinated characters in its crime and action movies. Also, Warner had made VD training films during the First World War. Probably the deciding factor for explicitly including Ehrlich's Salvarsan breakthrough was the opinion of Hal B. Wallis, president of the Motion Pictures Producers association, who, while advising caution, wrote to Warner Bros. that "to make a dramatic picture of the life of Dr. Ehrlich and not include this discovery among his great achievements would be unfair to the record."

Certain precautions were, however, deemed advisable, including some downplaying of syphilis's venereal nature. The very first lines of dialogue the audience heard is Ehrlich telling his syphilitic patient, a distraught young student: "What you have is a contagious disease, an infection just like any other. I've seen cases where it was transmitted by an inanimate object." This dubious assertion is, for good measure, repeated later in the film. Warner Bros. had also promised the Motion Pictures Producers association that "we will not send out any advertising, exploitation or publicity matter on this subject that deals with syphilis, sex hygiene, venereal disease, or anything pertaining thereto." Yet what may have been one of the cleverest subterfuges in the history of censorship (or else an innocent chance occurrence) was to be seen on the lobby card of the film. Zooming upward past Edward G. Robinson's face was a semi-transparent object that the artist would have claimed to be a test tube, but whose fleshy tint far more readily evoked the contribution to the fight against venereal disease not of Dr. Ehrlich but of his eighteenth-century English predecessor Dr. Condom (who may be apocryphal; opinions vary).

Dr. Ehrlich's Magic Bullet was an unprecedented success. No previous movie in the history of cinema—let alone a bio-pic—had in the first two weeks after its premiere grossed as much at the box office. Of course, there was no real chance that the film, no matter how successful, could persuade the Nazis to "keep their fists off [Ehrlich's] coreligionists." But it could help inspire another Jewish scientist, Selman Waksman, to seek yet another magic bullet to eliminate other scourges of mankind. Through the late '30s Waksman had been unaware of the penicillin research Chain and Florey were conducting in Oxford. It would have mattered little to him, in any case, for two decades earlier Waksman had adopted not the fungi but the actinomycetes as his pet microorganisms. Now, in the early 1940s as the first reports on penicillin circulated, it became clear that the new wonder drug was as inactive against some bacteria as it was devastatingly effective against others. A major division in bacterial classification since the heyday of staining in late nineteenth-century Germany was a given bacterium's reaction to Gram's stain. The chemical properties of the cell walls of so-called Gram-negative bacteria are such that they lose their Gram stain when subsequently washed (counterstained) with alcohol. Among the scourges falling into the Gram-negative category are the bacteria that cause typhoid, bacillary dysentery, and the bubonic plague. Against them, penicillin is useless.

And there is another class of bacterium, the mycobacteria, whose cell walls are neither Gram-positive nor Gram-negative. Against these, too, penicillin has no effect. This class includes the slender rod *Mycobacterium tuberculosis,* the cause of the white plague, which in the previous century and a half had claimed an estimated billion lives worldwide. Years before the war Waksman had observed the demise of *Mycobacterium tuberculosis* when introduced into the soil and he had speculated that the actinomycetes were responsible for its undoing. Waksman had once even directly observed under the microscope how this parasitizer of men could itself be parasitzed by other microorganisms. But at the time this was of little more interest to Waksman than the interplay of so many other microorganisms in the earth. Now, when a raving dictator who had declared that "its [Judaism's] effect is that of a racial tuberculosis among the peoples of the world" began re-alizing his dream of reducing the Jews of Europe to ashes, a Jewish soil chemist across the Atlantic began to realize a dream of lifting the scourge of tuberculosis from all humanity.

"The Lord shall smite thee with a consumption, and with a fever, and with an inflammation, and with an extreme burning, and with the sword, and with blasting, and with mildew; and they shall pursue thee until thou per-ish." Thus ran Moses' threat to any of his followers who might disobey Jehovah's commandments and statutes (Deuteronomy 28:22). The Hebrew word *schachepheth,* translated as "consumption" in this text, has also been taken over as the Modern Hebrew word for tuberculosis. Although scholars are not entirely sure that it is the same disease, we know from certain deformities in Egyptian mummy skeletons that TB was present in the ancient Middle East. The Code of Hammurabi in Babylon made apparent reference to tuberculosis, and other archaeological evidence indicates that the disease had made its way in prehistoric times to Europe, East Asia, and the Americas. In the Hippocratic writings, tuberculosis was called phthisis (which meant "wasting away") and was considered the gravest of all diseases—so difficult to cure, in fact, that the physician was advised not to take on patients in advanced stages, lest their virtually inevitable death injure the doctor's reputation.

For centuries in more recent times, consumption occupied a place of honor in literary and artistic fact and fiction unrivaled by any other disease. A short list of cultural greats afflicted by consumption would include Molière, Voltaire, Spinoza, Schiller, Goethe, Kafka, Gorki, Chekhov, Paganini, Chopin, Dr. Johnson, Scott, Keats, the Brontë sisters, D. H. Lawrence, Thoreau, Emerson, Poe, and O'Neill. So impressive is the register of names that TB was thought to physically stimulate intellectual genius. One theory had it that a slight toxemia (bacterial toxins in the bloodstream) exerted an invigorating effect on the nervous system, combined, perhaps, with some relaxation of inhibition. Complementing this on the psychological plane was the concept of *spes phthisica* (literally, "consumption hope")—an optimism perhaps best typified by the beautiful philosophy of the consumptive Spinoza. Much other intellectual output of consumptives was, however, sooner characterized by a certain melancholy or mournfulness—the music of Chopin and the poetry of Keats—in anticipation of a life to be cut short.

The theme of the consumptive hero—or, better yet, heroine—enjoyed wide currency in the arts. Its archetypal form is exemplified in Puccini's *La Bohème,* set in the 1830s. The heroine Mimi develops respiratory problems, pallor, icy hands, and other symptoms of decline—punctuated by some poetic *spes phthisica*—before drifting off to her final sleep. Dickens, who in *David Copperfield* romantically narrated the fading away of Little Blossom, gave a fuller description of consumption in *Nicholas Nickleby:*

> There is a dread disease which so prepares its victim, as it were, for death;
> which so refines it of its grosser aspect, and throws around familiar looks,

unearthly indications of the coming change—a dread disease, in which the struggle between soul and body is so gradual, quiet, and solemn, and the result so sure, that day by day, and grain by grain, the mortal part wastes and withers away, so that the spirit grows light and sanguine with its lightening load, and, feeling immortality at hand, deems it but a new term of mortal life; a disease in which death takes the glow and hue of life, and life the gaunt and grisly form of death; a disease which medicine never cured, wealth warded off, or poverty could boast exemption from; which sometimes moves in giant strides, and sometimes at a tardy pace, but, slow or quick, is ever sure and certain.

Even physicians were inclined toward romanticism in their description of the consumptive patient, particularly the windows of the soul: "Their eyes have a quite unnatural brilliance, seemingly large and beautiful," wrote one doctor. According to the Hippocratic corpus, phthisis causes the growth of extra long eyelashes.

The romanticizing of consumption in the Victorian age is perhaps understandable when one contrasts its course and symptoms with that of a disease such as cholera. During any of the cholera epidemics that struck Europe and America in the nineteenth century, a proper middle-class lady could at one minute be sitting placidly in a crowded tram or even in a fashionable restaurant, and a minute later be seized with a massive, uncontrollable attack of vomiting and diarrhea. For the bourgeoisie, for whom such physical acts had become obsessively private in the course of the Victorian era, this was almost as bad as death itself, which often ensued in a matter of hours but not before the victims were transformed through dehydration into skull-like apparitions. So it was that in Thomas Mann's *Death in Venice,* the protagonist, Gustav von Aschenbach, after having been brought down from his intellectual heights by his illicit sexual longings, is further degraded by succumbing to the cholera epidemic. By contrast, when the reader is informed that the hero of the same author's *The Magic Mountain,* Hans Castorp, is consumptive, it offers the prospect not of rapid degradation but of a long journey filled with refined intelligence and a dose of *spes phthisica.*

The purported links between consumption and genius seem impressive until one considers the staggering statistics on the prevalence of tuberculosis among the population at large, irrespective of talent. Consumption has always been a disease of population concentration. It was highly common in the cities of ancient Greece and Rome, declined during the deurbanization of the Dark Ages, and then reasserted itself with the emergence of overcrowded walled towns in the late Middle Ages and, later, with the coming of large-scale urbanization. In London in the mid-seventeenth century, consumption accounted for one out of five deaths. Yet this already grim mortality figure surged when the Industrial Revolution drew millions of people previously unexposed to TB to the teeming cities. At the beginning of the nineteenth century consumption was responsible for a staggering 30 percent of all deaths in London. Even in New York it accounted for one in four fatalities. Although the TB mortality figures would decline in ensuing decades—not least of all as a result of the great improvement in the standard of living that industrialization itself eventually brought about—it has been estimated that in the nineteenth century the average annual death rate from consumption was some seven million worldwide, and that the total number of fatalities claimed by the TB bacillus from 1800 into the twentieth century topped the billion mark.

Noteworthy in this history are reports of a lower mortality among the late nineteenth-century Jewish population. The Italian-Jewish psychiatrist Cesare Lombroso reported a significantly lower death rate among Jews than among their Catholic compatriots. In the Whitechapel district of London the Jewish mortality rate was half that of gentiles. All this may have been the result of higher Jewish living standards and the age-old hygienic regulations, along with, it has been suggested, some greater inherited immunity built up in the course of centuries of urban living. Yet this did not stop some American xenophobes during the great immigration wave around the turn of the century from labeling TB a "Jewish disease," a sign of physical inferiority.

Consumption's ravages through the ages brought with it many inaccurate or blatantly false conceptions as to its causation and correspondingly futile attempts to treat it. The ancient Greeks, in the framework of their four humors, seem to have speculated that phthisis arose from a distillation in the head that passed through the trachea and brought about an ulceration in the lungs. This obstructed the flow of cooling air and caused the body tissue to burn up. In the Hippocratic writings, honey and dark resinous wine are recommended, along with herbs grown in the Temple of Aesculapius. The tendency of consumption to run in families and its obscure mode of human-to-human transmission led physicians to doubt its contagiousness and see it as an inherited constitutional disease. Galen, however, recognized phthisis as communicable. He recommended a sunny retreat for some of his patients, particularly the area around Vesuvius. To counter fever, Galen prescribed isolation in a cool, well-ventilated underground room, with fresh milk from a donkey or, better yet, drunk directly from a lactating woman. (This latter source remained particularly popular until fairly recent times, to the detriment of the women in question.)

In the sixteenth century, Girolamo Fracastoro, the forerunner of the germ theorists, devoted a chapter of his *De Morbis Contagiosis* to consumption. "We must, therefore, conclude," he wrote, "that in such *fomites* are left behind the seeds of contagion and it is a fact that there is an incredible analogy or selective affinity between these germs and the pulmonary tissue. . . . Were it possible to destroy them by the use of caustics, there would be no better remedy; but since these substances cannot be employed without danger to this organ, one should seek to treat by way of the adjoining ones." The contagiousness of consumption was supported by Sylvius in Leiden in the seventeenth century, who wrote that "the air expired by consumptives having been brought close to the mouth and nose [of other persons] is drawn in, and in this way offensive and irritating emanations are continuously carried from the affected party to others, especially relatives, and when these are finally infected with the same poison, they also fall into phthisis."

The contagious nature of consumption—whether the supposed agent be a "seed," poison, or something else—remained in dispute, notwithstanding the existence of the microscope. In the eighteenth century various municipalities such as Naples drew up strict regulations for the disinfecting with lye or fire of the surroundings of a deceased consumptive. Public health doctors were also fond of Rousseau's remark that "men mutually poison each other by crowding together." Yet even in the early nineteenth century anticontagionists in the medical profession probably outnumbered the contagionists.

In the mid-nineteenth century an English doctor, George Bodington, noticing that rural people were much less prone to consumption than town and city dwellers, made suggestions that (especially when they caught the enthusiasm of the Germans) grew into the worldwide sanitarium movement. This was a boon to towns as far removed as Davos, Switzerland, and

Albuquerque, New Mexico. ("Albuquerque has two businesses," stated a contemporary guidebook, "the Sante Fe Railroad and tuberculosis.") Aside from hopefully strengthening the patient's resistance—there were indeed ample cases of the disease process being reversed, especially when caught early—the sanitoria at the very least served to prevent the patient from infecting others.

All in all, the only real medical advances in the fight against tuberculosis before the twentieth century were in its detection. Hippocrates had stated somewhat dubiously: "If the sputum of a patient when poured on the coals has a heavy smell, the person is suffering from phthisis." In 1761 the Austrian physician Leopold Auenbrugger, who had inherited from his innkeeper father the art of judging the level of wine by tapping the casks and listening to the resonance, wrote a short booklet entitled *A New Discovery of Percussion of the Human Chest for Detecting the Signs of Obscure Disease of the Chest Cavity*. This told how to determine the level of fluid in the lungs and served as a valuable diagnostic technique for consumption. It was augmented a few decades later by the invention of the stethoscope—in its first version, no more than a rolled up sheath of paper—by the French physician René Théophile Laënnec. (Laënnec, who doubted the contagious nature of tuberculosis, apparently infected himself performing one of his many autopsies. He was treated by bloodletting, which ensured that he himself would be dissected all the sooner.) The last decade of the nineteenth century saw the invention of the X ray by the German physicist Wilhelm Conrad Röntgen and the possibility of actually visualizing the tubercles (the nodule lesions in the lung to which TB owes its name) of pulmonary consumptive patients, rather than just feeling or hearing the effects of their presence.

By then, an even more important visualization had taken place. Through a series of inoculations of infected blood and sputum from animal to animal and man to animal in the mid-nineteenth century, the French army doctor Jean-Antoine Villemin definitely established that tuberculosis is transmitted from one consumptive organism to another. This was further confirmed by inoculations into the anterior ocular chamber by the Jewish researchers Julius Cohnheim and Carl Julius Salomonsen (the latter, destined for fame as professor of pathology and rector magnificus of the University of Copenhagen). Villemin went on to demonstrate by several deductive arguments that consumption does not arise spontaneously in an organism no matter how miserable the living conditions and nutrition. Villemin called the causative agent in the blood and sputum a "virus" (the old, vague term) but didn't claim to have seen it. Various other researchers thought they had, but it was Koch who stained, identified, and then cultivated the culprit. (As we have noted, the med student Paul Ehrlich seems to have stained and visualized TB bacilli before Koch but mistook them for crystals. In any case, he did soon improve on Koch's staining technique.) The visualization and identification of the TB bacillus was a psychological boost to suffering mankind in that, as with the identification of the AIDS virus a century later, it gave a face to a previously unseen enemy. Furthermore, the staining of specimens of a patient's sputum to detect the pathogen was a valuable diagnostic tool. This was supplemented, in 1890, by Koch's tuberculin, an extract of tuberculosis bacilli, which when injected causes a reaction (today known to be a delayed-type hypersensitivity, one of the intricacies of the immune system's workings), the strength of which indicates the severity of the patient's infection.

But this huge triumph of Koch was accompanied by the greatest blunder of his career. Having observed the apparent melting away of tubercular tissue after injections of tuberculin, Koch assumed that the bacilli themselves were being annihilated and he rashly announced to the world a cure for the dread disease. Unfortunately, any therapeutic effect brought on by tuberculin was in fact minimal. The debilitated consumptives who rushed to Berlin to be injected were more likely to die of the nausea, vomiting, and fever that accompanied a severe reaction to a supposedly therapeutic dosage of the drug. Some other patients with a milder form of the disease found that tuberculin actually caused it to flare up again after years of dormancy.

With medical science basically unable to do anything more than diagnose tuberculosis, religious and superstitious cures continued to enjoy wide currency well after the waning of the Middle Ages. Prayers were offered not only to the Virgin Mary, but to the patron saints of consumptives, Malo and Bernulphus. In England, from the reign of Edward the Confessor in the eleventh century to that of Queen Anne in the eighteenth, countless thousands of sufferers of scofula (swollen and discharging tuberculous lymph glands) sought relief by means of the King's Touch, a practice also engaged in by the French monarchs. In Belgium, children received regular doses of holy water with a pinch of the ashes of St. John's fire. The butter from cows fed on churchyard grass was another tried and (supposedly) true remedy. Even in the century that produced Paul Ehrlich, Louis Pasteur, and Robert Koch, Europeans were attaching live trout and catfish to their chests, apparently a relic of the Medieval belief that the evil spirit of consumption could be transferred from the patient to other creatures.

Early in the twentieth century, following the amazing success of Paul Ehrlich's arsenical compound against syphilis, various forms of chemotherapy were tried for TB. These included iodine, mercury, cinnamic acid, copper, and even potassium cyanide. All proved as useless as the cordial for which Mimi's fellow garret-dwellers pawned their last possessions in *La Bohème* a century or so earlier. The most costly failure of chemotherapy involved the revival of the alchemist's interest in gold compounds, in which a Swedish pharmaceutical company heavily invested in the 1920s until the drug proved not only ineffective against tuberculosis but damaging to various organs of the patients as well. Recourse was made to invasive techniques. Pus could be removed from the pleural cavity by surgical drainage. Air could be injected between the lung and chest wall, or ribs could be removed, so as to collapse the infected lung and, by thus immobilizing it, hopefully help it to heal. With it all, in the United States alone, tuberculosis continued to carry away some 90,000 victims annually.

Such was the situation when, in the wake of Pearl Harbor, the 53-year-old Ukranian immigant, Selman Waksman, dreamed of harnessing the same actinomycetes that destroy the TB bacilli in the soil to destroy them in the body. Waksman applied to the Committee of Medical Research in Washington, D.C., newly established to appropriate funds for projects deemed useful to the war effort. The federal government recognized the value of penicillin and eventually funded its development to the tune of over half a billion dollars. But in reply to Waksman's request for a grant to develop *antibiotics* (the term itself was coined by him) from microorganisms in the soil, he was informed, in effect, that, in a country at war, all that counted were hard results in the near future that would lead to victory. Resources could not be diverted for pursuits in the rarefied heights of theory or the muck of barnyard soil. The committee's unfavorable reply was supported by a prominent scientist in Washington who declared: "No branch of science [has] yielded so little information of practical value as [has] soil biology."

Although the books of the Apocrypha are not accepted as canonical by Judaism, Selman Waksman was aware of the verses from Ecclesiastes (38:1–4). After enjoining the reader to "Value the services of a doctor, for he has his place assigned to him by the Lord; his skills come from the Most High, and he is rewarded by kings," the Hebrew author, Jesus ben Sirach, goes on to state: "The Lord hath created medicines out of the earth; and he that is wise will not abhor them." These were words that Waksman took to heart. Perhaps he was also vaguely influenced by the Jewish practice of rendering an unclean knife kosher by burying it in the ground for a prescribed period. Fortunately, some of his faith was shared by the nearby Merck & Co., whose German parent concern, now Nazi-controlled, had been forced to permanently relinquish its American subsidiary in the previous world war. Rutgers University and Merck had an agreement by which the company supplied chemical assistance, animal testing facilities, and large-scale production apparatus in exchange for exclusive licensing agreements for any antibiotics it deemed worth manufacturing.

Waksman's research program involved obtaining some 10,000 different microbe strains from various soils and from other natural materials such as dung, cultivating them on various media, and then testing their ability to inhibit the growth of pathogenic bacteria. Attempts were made to induce or augment antituberculosis properties of some microorganisms through selective competition by first adding living and dead TB bacilli to the soil. The first four antibiotics to show promise in the agar dishes proved upon testing *in vivo* to be either too toxic to animal tissue or not sufficiently effective against pathogens. Undiscouraged, Waksman evoked the spirit of the first magic bullet and its creator: "The antibiotics will do it. Just give us time. Sooner or later, we are bound to find one or more chemical agents that will be able to bring this about. They will kill the bacterium not by digesting it, but by interfering with its metabolism and its growth, without injuring the host. After all, this would be based upon the principle of chemotherapy, as enunciated by Paul Ehrlich." The sentiments of the team of twenty or so researchers in those days were perhaps typified by the comments of one of the women scientists: "Dr. Waksman is our great white father. He is wise, demanding yet understanding. He doesn't seem pretentious. His clothing is worn, and his vest always seems to carry traces of his last few meals, maybe a moth hole or two. He wants us to work hard, not waste lots of time studying extraneous things in books. I worship him."

When the great breakthrough came—the magic bullet against tuberculosis called streptomycin—it was thanks in part to the skills of another Jewish farmboy, Albert Schatz. Like Selman Waksman and millions of other American Jews of that generation, Schatz had his roots in the Empire of the czars. It was from the Minsk region that his grandfather had fled with Albert's then 9-year-old father, Julius, around the turn of the century. In the New World the Schatzes became farmers, but their 140 acres of Connecticut soil were hard-yielding. The family led an economically marginal existence, made worse by the Great Depression on the '30s. Yet as with Selman Waksman, the earth made a deep and enduring impression on young Albert. He decided to attend Rutgers Agricultural College, where he majored in soil chemistry and graduated at the top of his class. After being drafted by the Armed Forces early in World War Two and then discharged due to a back ailment, the 23-year-old Schatz decided to go on for a Ph.D. in soil microbiology at Rutgers, and he approached Professor Waksman to be his dissertation supervisor.

Waksman, who had already been favorably impressed by Schatz's undergraduate work, saw the advantages of steering him toward antibiotics and offered a forty-dollar-a-month stipend. Even in those days, this was a paltry sum, and Schatz, coming as he did from a family of such limited means, might have been tempted to postpone his plans and take a better-paying job. But for Schatz's immigrant Jewish parents, his attaining a doctorate would in itself, as he put it, "validate their lives." Furthermore, Rutgers had its perks. There were cheap fruits and vegetables to be gotten from the agricultural testing facilities and free ice cream from the dairy department. As for a place to sleep, Schatz found lodging at a side room of the plant physiology greenhouse, where he watered the plants and swept up in lieu of rent.

Soon enough, however, Schatz would find himself grabbing many a night's sleep in his laboratory instead. This was an eighteen-foot-square room that although it had two windows, was buried half underground. The doctoral research description proposed to the graduate faculty by Schatz and Waksman specified a double goal: the search for a broad-range antibiotic against Gram-negative bacteria and for a specific antimycobacterial, that is, an agent against tuberculosis. Decades of failure had led to great skepticism among scientists. "They told me," Schatz later related, "that the tubercle bacilli were covered with a heavy waxy capsule and nothing could get in. And that's why the drugs were not effective." But Schatz's view of the world of microbes followed the spirit, if not the specific details, of Paul Ehrlich's side-chain theory a half century earlier, with its nutro-ceptors and chemo-ceptors. "My feeling was that if nothing got in we wouldn't have tuberculosis, because nutrients would have to get in and waste products would have to get out. If food and waste products could get through, so could an antibiotic. So that argument did not hold water with me. I therefore kept on working."

Albert Schatz's quest in the summer and early fall of 1943 led him to scrounge not only through soil samples but also manure heaps, drains, and the culture plates of colleagues engaged in unrelated research. As much by some indefinable intuition as by scientific deduction, Schatz discarded some cultures but retained others as promising. These he mixed in agar dishes with dangerous streptococci and mycobacteria. When the first snows came, the night watchman found Schatz lying unconscious as a result of an attack of pneumonia. But after a short stay in the hospital, Schatz, who though short in stature took pride in his physical fitness and gymnastic skills as well as his dark good looks, was back at work. Less than four months after starting—one might just as well have bet beforehand that it would take four years or forever—Schatz found himself witnessing a phenomenon never seen before in a laboratory, although something similar had been occurring in nature for countless millions of years. Tiny quantities of actinomyces cultures isolated from a manure heap were dissolving all mycobacteria even as far away as an inch on the agar plate. "I was too thoroughly exhausted to feel elated," Schatz later told. "I had worked day and night. But nevertheless, I had a good feeling about it."

Waksman recognized the grayish-green pastel shade of Schatz's culture. Three decades earlier, long before the concept of antibiotics dawned on him, the student Waksman had cultivated a quite similar strain, appropriately christened *Actinomyces griseus* (gray). When the amazing effect of the culture *in vitro* was confirmed in a repeat experiment, the strain was rechristened *Streptomyces,* and the bactericidal substance it secreted, streptomycin. The substance was further purified and concentrated.

Tests with guinea pigs infected with tuberculosis soon followed at the Mayo Clinic. The wondrous cures, without adverse side-effects, led to the first human clinical trials, in 1945, with similar results. But this wasn't all. For streptomycin was also shown to be devastatingly effective against a wide range of Gram-negative bacteria, including *Yersinia pestis,* the pathogen of the bubonic plague. Thus the rumor making the rounds in the mid-fourteenth century that a Jewish medical man—even as his coreligionists were poisoning the wells with plague venom—had discovered a cure for the pestilence and was keeping it secret, proved to be true, if 600 years premature.

For in fact Selman Waksman was indeed making all efforts to maintain secrecy and keep the discovery from the public. This was for fear of raising possibly false hopes in terminal TB patients and their families. Yet in January 1945, an article on strepromycin appeared in *Time.* Letters were sent to Waksman from whole wards of servicemen who had contracted tuberculosis overseas and who knew that the doctors were largely powerless and that nature would have to take its course, resulting perhaps in their recovery, perhaps in their death. They would prefer a battlefield or a beachhead to their passive waiting. By writing to Waksman they at least felt they were contributing something to his fight. Yet for years after it was unambiguously confirmed to be a wonder drug, streptomycin would remain in extremely short supply. Merck & Co., public-spirited and also wishing to avoid any hint of profiteering during wartime, quite graciously agreed to Waksman's suggestion that they cancel their exclusive licensing rights to streptomycin and thus allow all pharmaceutical companies to produce the drug. Yet even with eight American companies manufacturing streptomycin, there was in the late '40s only enough to treat about 1 out of every 400 cases in the United States. The situation worldwide was, of course, far worse, with some 5 million people dying of TB every year.

Even while the scientists continued to eschew publicity, more and more sensational reports appeared in the mass media. Heartbreaking requests poured in from terminally ill patients and their doctors and families all over the world, pleading for a vial of the wonder drug. The most unwelcome task of deciding which requests to honor (all letters were individually answered) fell to the streptomycin researchers. Even when the decision was made to provide the drug in some exceptional case abroad, the medicine might not arrive in time. So it was that in the spring of 1946, Waksman received this heartrending letter:

> I would like to express my deepest thanks for your readiness to send, upon the request of the London Daily Express, some of your new drug, strepto-mycin, in an attempt to save the life of my little child as she lay dangerously ill, with tubercular meningitis. I have every faith that if streptomycin could have arrived in time it would have saved her, but unfortunately she died on the Sunday evening that we received news from you that you would supply the drug. . . . I feel the loss very greatly as she was an extraordinary intel-ligent child, showing great promise.

The previously-mentioned TB meningitis is a form of tuberculosis so deadly that hitherto in all medical history only a handful of patients (per-haps misdiagnosed anyhow) had supposedly survived it. Now, as the trickle of the miracle drug slowly turned into a flood, the tide turned. Not atypical was the letter Waksman received from the mother of another TB meningitis patient, a sailor who had contracted the disease overseas. In biblical metaphors, she told how the Valley of the Shadow of Death had been pierced by a ray of hope. Friends and relatives had been praying for their son's recovery. God, she was convinced, was working in His own way when—long before her son was smitten by TB—Selman Waksman and his colleagues had heard similar prayers and felt the calling to devote themselves to finding a cure. When news of his discovery broke, she repeated the word *streptomycin* in a kind of chant— the modern-day version of an ancient shaman's rite.

Yet this period of great rejoicing and adulation included for Waksman "the days that were the most unpleasant of my life," as his former protegé Albert Schatz hired a group of lawyers to engage in that quintissentially American custom of litigation. Waksman had the policy (some would call it overgenerosity) of allowing the names of his students or assistants to pre-cede his own on publications of discoveries they made as part of his re-search programs. So it was that Schatz's name came first on the three important journal articles announcing streptomycin to the medical world. Furthermore, Schatz's as well as Waksman's name was listed on the patent applications for streptomycin filed by the Rutgers Foundation, despite the fact that Schatz had been engaged in antibiotic work for hardly three months and, it was said, had not even wanted to do it in the first place but was persuaded to by Waksman.

Nevertheless, Schatz felt slighted for not being given enough of the lime-light for the streptomycin miracle and he left Rutgers in 1946. Three years later, he was engaged in litigation with Waksman and the university over Waksman's alleged threats to blackball him in the world of microbiology if Schatz did not agree to forgo royalties to himself. (The Rutgers Founda-tion was then receiving two cents for each gram of the drug sold.) A Rutgers lawyer dismissed Schatz as "one of about twenty technical assistants and graduate students who participated in this extensive research from time to time under Dr. Waksman's direction . . . a carefully supervised laboratory assistant . . . a small cog in a large wheel . . . ." But on the other hand, Schatz's undeniable talent, intuition, and drive had played an important role in the discovery. Waksman, though gravely disappointed in Schatz's actions, nevertheless had referred to him as someone "whom I believed capable of becoming one of the brilliant stars in the firmament of my group of students."

Embittered by the affair but also anxious to put an end to the mess so as to begin the construction of a new Institute of Microbiology, Waksman, after "nearly a year of this nightmare existence," advised Rutgers to make an out-of-court settlement. Schatz was granted a lump sum of $125,000, a public statement by Rutgers officially confirming him as codiscoverer of streptomycin, and 3 percent of the royalties. Waksman retained 17 percent but then voluntarily reduced his own portion to 5 percent by sharing 7 percent among all the people who had worked at the lab at the time of the discovery, including the dishwasher, and donating half of the rest to a new Foundation for Microbiology.

But the matter had still not entirely been laid to rest. In 1952 the Nobel committee, wishing to honor the breakthroughs in the fight against tuber-culosis, announced that Selman Waksman would be the sole recipient of that year's prize for Medicine, even though the Nobel regulations allow up to three people to share it. This caused some surprise, since the synthetic chemical drugs PAC (para-aminosalicylic acid) and Conteben (thiosemicarbazone), developed around the same time as streptomycin by, respectively, Jorgen Lehmann in Sweden and Gerhard Domagk in Germany, were also proving useful against TB and were enabling doctors to prescribe combination treatment and forestall the emergence of drug-resistant strains. Schatz, for his part, felt that if indeed only streptomycin was to be honored, he should share the prize as its codiscoverer. A letter writing campaign was begun, and Schatz went so far as to petition King Gustav VI of Sweden. His Majesty's office replied that the Nobel committee was completely independent of the crown, and that in any case all such decisions were final.

Thus Selman Waksman alone journeyed to Stockholm to join the ranks of Jewish medical men to receive the Nobel Prize. We have seen how Waksman several times spoke of the first Jewish Nobel laureate in medicine, Paul Ehrlich, and of the intellectual and spiritual inspiration he imparted, which began with Waksman's testing of the first magic bullet, Salvarsan, during the First World War and culminated—after a long detour through other fields of microbiology—with Waksman's developing his own miraculous chemotherapeutic agent, streptomycin, during the Second. As Waksman wrote near the end of his career (he died in 1973):

> Little did I dream in 1918 that the "magic bullet" of Ehrlich that fascinated me so much would later be replaced and much further extended by the "wonder drugs" produced by microbes largely derived from the soil. Still less did I dream at that time that one such drug, one of the most important of them all, would come from my own laboratory, from a culture of one of the actinomycetes that I had already isolated from the soil three years previously, at the very beginning of my own work on the soil microbes.

Streptomycin, although by far the most miraculous, was one of several antibiotics to come from Waksman's lab. A strain of actinomycin, the first of the antibiotics he produced, was later found useful against malignant tumors of the lymph nodes (Hodgkin's disease). As such, the drug represented a fundamental step in the development of chemotherapeutic agents against cancer, which gained great momentum later in the century. Waksman also discovered in a fungus a substance with an extraordinarily specific inhibiting effect on a single strain of viral influenza in mice. He christened it Ehrlichin.

Aside from the Nobel, Selman Waksman received an array of honors from the governments, scientific bodies, and universities of many countries. Yet perhaps the symbolically most significant event in his life as it relates to the story of Jews in medicine took place in 1950 when he toured Spain at the invitation of the Spanish Scientific Council. For sheer pageantry of almost religious intensity there was nothing to rival this visit. As he moved from town to town, Selman Waksman was showered with flowers, citations, and an occasional honorary doctorate. Mayors greeted him with cannon salutes and entertained him with grand banquets and flamenco dancers. A prominent mountain was renamed in his honor. As Waksman and his wife walked through the streets of various Spanish towns, parents brought their children to be blessed by him as by a Medieval saint. Cured consumptives and their families rushed to kiss his hand. Flashing bulbs, motion picture cameras, and radio microphones accompanied him everywhere. The most dramatic high-point was a nighttime procession through the old Jewish Quarter of Seville. Waksman, who a few days later would be decorated and blessed by Pope Pius XII at St. Peters, was led through the Medieval streets followed by hundreds of worshiping admirers now freed from the curse of some of mankind's most dreaded pestilences.

The procession took place on the very streets where six centuries earlier a rampaging Christian mob brandishing swords and torches had screamed "death or the cross." It took place in the country from which in the mid-fourteenth century a Jewish physician supposedly provided the bubonic plague venom to his coreligionist colleagues elsewhere in Europe for the systematic poisoning of the wells. It took place in a land where hardly any Jew and perhaps not a single Jewish doctor had legally lived since Columbus and his Marrano physician and surgeon set sail westward in search of exotic drugs almost half a millennium earlier. Now the bubonic plague and the white plague of tuberculosis had been stopped in their tracks—by a magic bullet wrung by a wandering Jew from the soil of the New World.

Epilogue

When writing of developments that have shaped the destiny of mankind, a sense of perspective is vital, and this is best gained when events are viewed at some distance. This is one of the reasons why the mid-twentieth century is a good place to break off our present narrative of the Wandering Jewish Doctor.

Today, with the close of the second millennium behind us, we may look back and tentatively declare that mid-century marked the waning of the Heroic Age of medicine. It also marked the consolidation of the triumph of man over microbe, certainly in the industrialized and post-industrial world. The recent eruption of AIDS, scares about ebola viruses, and concerns about emerging resistant tuberculosis strains—apparent exceptions to this statement—have in fact demonstrated how pathogenic microorganisms can be held in check by a biomedical research and industrial complex whose technological sophistication seems to increase exponentially with each passing decade. Long gone now is the 100-year heyday of the great microbe hunter or magic bullet innovator, working largely on intuition and luck, with limited resources under rather Spartan conditions to battle the age-old scourges that once swept away his fellow men by the millions. The new era is sooner defined by billion-dollar investments in high-tech facilities, predominantly involved with the more chronic and complex health problems such as cardiovascular disease, mental and psychosomatic afflictions, cancers, genetic defects, and geriatric care—the concerns of an advanced and prosperous society, where each baby can usually look forward to eight or so decades of life.

The transition in medicine around mid-century was well represented by two developments involving Jewish scientists. The year 1950 found Manhattan-born Dr. Jonas Salk at the virus research laboratory of the University of Pittsburgh and Polish-born Dr. Albert Sabin at the Cincinnati College of Medicine, working on their respective killed-virus and attenuated live-virus vaccines against polio. Their research—an extension of principles developed in the nineteenth century by the likes of Pasteur and Ehrlich—would bring about the elimination of this crippler of children, the last of the major old scourges of the western world. (Incidentally, a breakthrough that made the polio vaccines possible involved the culturing of viruses using as a medium baby foreskins delivered newly severed to the research labs—which a wag was quick to describe as "another great Jewish contribution to medicine.")

The year 1950 also found Rosalind Franklin, the fiercely independent scion of a Jewish banking family, at her laboratory at the University of London where she was developing X-ray diffraction photographs of DNA, the heredity molecule whose great variety of permutations contains the codes for every life form from microbe to man. To her trained eye before anyone else's would soon be revealed some of the most important features—the helical and backbone-outward structure—subsequently to be incorporated by Francis Crick and James Watson into their DNA model and thus open up the age of genetically manipulated therapies.

Our saga of the Jews and medicine throughout the ages has been not only scientific but also cultural, religious, intellectual, and political. We have seen how the great contributions of Jewish doctors to the welfare of humanity have never guaranteed protection against persecution by totalitarian and intolerant regimes. The mid-twentieth century—our break-off point in this story—was unfortunately no exception. In the Soviet Union, the years 1950–51 saw the arrest on Stalin's orders of two top Kremlin physicians on charges of deliberately falsifying diagnoses of Soviet leaders and prescribing destructive rather than helpful treatments. These were the first of several physicians, mostly Jewish, to be implicated in the infamous Doctors' Plot. Like Hitler, Stalin's medical phobias, and his paranoia about Jewish physicians in particular, may have stemmed from childhood. (A Jew, one of the two doctors in his town in Georgia, may have treated him for smallpox. Although Stalin survived the disease—whether thanks to the treatment or not—it left his face, and perhaps also part of his psyche, permanently scarred.) Like virtually all top Party officials in the Soviet Union, Stalin was looked after by Jewish doctors, one of whom removed his appendix in 1919 and in so doing probably saved his life. Yet an ever growing paranoia after his consolidation of absolute power led Stalin to refuse all injections and eventually to revive the ancient myth of the Jewish doctors as poisoners, who had supposedly already murdered several high-ranking Communists and, for good measure, the famed writer Maxim Gorki as well. Just when the cream of Soviet medicine faced annihilation and their fellow Jews possible mass deportation to the far Eastern reaches, Stalin departed this life. His demise was immediately followed by the exoneration of the Jewish doctors and their release from prison.

The close call of the Jews of the Soviet Union, so soon after the Nazi Holocaust, only highlighted the need for a permanent and secure haven where the Jewish people could determine their own destiny. In this respect, mid-century was, of course, one of the great watersheds in Jewish history as the Israelites regained in 1948 the statehood that historical forces had taken away and continued to withhold from them as the Wandering Jew roamed the earth for two millenia.

Jewish medical doctors had been a driving force in the development of the Zionist dream. As noted in Chapter 17, the book *Autoemancipation* by the Odessa physician Dr. Leon Pinsker, published in 1882, inspired the first Aliyah of some 25,000 Eastern European Jews to Palestine in the ensuing two decades. In the early years of the new century, the neurologist and social-philosopher Dr. Max Nordau headed the World Zionist Organization, as the ideals of national rebirth came to be expressed more and more in medical metaphors. "In a sick Jewry, Zionism is the will to live," rang one cry. The radiologist Dr. Ignaz Zollschan, dismayed by the rise of racial anti-Semitism in his native Austria, was a leading light in the Zionist organization Binyan ha-Aretz (Building of the Land), who pushed for the immediate establishment of Jewish towns, farms, and businesses in Palestine. Felix Theilhaber, as we saw in Chapter 14, was initially less concerned with anti-Semitism than with the self-inflicted decline of the Jews in Germany as they lost the "categorical imperative of Judaism" to procreate or else removed themselves from the community through mixed marriages or conversion. Although himself of non-orthodox background, Theilhaber's visit to the Holy Land in 1906 was an almost mystical experience and made him a powerful propagandizer for Zionism as a potential salvation for the Jewish people. ("I had seen the land of my Fathers," he later wrote. "It was full of stones and not one cedar, but for me Eretz Yisrael was no longer an empty concept, but a reality, a piece of earth whose magic power I was never able to shake off.") Among the great stars of medicine, Ehrlich, Freud, Chain, and Waksman contributed their share to the development of the Zionist ideal.

But the actual realization of the Zionist dream involved a century of very down-to-earth practical work in Palestine on the part of less lionized medical men and women. In 1840 when the Holy Land was under Ottoman Turkish control, there was not a single resident doctor to serve a population, mostly Arab, living under highly unsanitary conditions and plagued by cholera, malaria, and other diseases. In 1843, Sir Moses Montifiore brought to Palestine a physician from Upper Silesia, Dr. Simon Frankel, to treat the small Jewish population and, the following year, serve as head of the first hospital in the Holy Land since the Crusades. For the next eight decades, subject to vicissitudes of the rivalries and conflicts between the great powers, steady progress was made in the establishing of hospitals and health services. The Rothschild and Hirsch families provided much financing, and figures such as Otto von Bismarck, Kaiser Wilhelm II, and the duke and duchess of Mecklenburg-Schwerin played some political role. The rebirth of Hebrew as a modern language capable of handling the dramatic new developments in medicine was marked by the compiling in the late nineteenth century of the *Hebrew Dictionary of Medicine and Science* by Dr. A. M. Mazie, physician at the Bikkur Holim Hospital and cofounder of the Association of Jewish Physicians in Eretz Yisrael.

By the eve of the First World War, there were nineteen hospitals in Jerusalem alone—most of them under Jewish auspices—and several more in other cities. The war saw the issuing of the Balfour Declaration, and in its aftermath the transfer of Palestine from Ottoman Turkish rule to British mandate status. Bodies such as the Hadassah Medical Organization saw to the improvement of sanitation and the eradication of malaria, while a network of rural dispensaries and town clinics, together with the building of new hospitals, provided the structure for the health services of the state-in-making. The '30s brought over 200,000 more Jews to Palestine, including some 50,000 from Nazi Germany, among whom physicians were particularly well represented. Among the casualties in Israel's War of Independence in 1948 were some eighty civilian doctors and nurses who were ambushed on their way to the Hadassah Hospital on Mt. Scopus in Jerusalem. Mid-century saw the establishment of the Life Science program at the Weizmann Institute of Science in Rehovoth (the former Daniel Sieff Institute), which would especially distinguish itself in the fields of cancer, immunology, and genetics. While new physicians are graduated from Israel's four university medical schools, their ranks are continually swelled by immigrant doctors from all continents, giving the Jewish State one of the world's highest doctor-to-population ratios as the Wandering Jewish Doctor comes to rest in Israel.

This epilogue would be incomplete if, having devoted hundreds of pages mostly to the scientific contributions of the Jews to medicine, we didn't say at least a bit more about Jewish medical ethics and how this may relate to the future. Today, Jews as a group are on average the most secular of all religious denominations. This applies no less, perhaps even more, to Jewish doctors and scientists. Yet even the most irreligious of Jews and Jewish doctors have inherited something of the moral tradition of their orthodox forebears. Indeed, we have seen in previous chapters how strongly many free-thinking Jewish scientists have concerned themselves with ethical matters. One recalls Freud's words that "in his inner being, the Jew, the true Jew, feels only one eternal guide, one lawgiver, one law. That is morality." None of this is to imply that there is always consensus among Jews on various ethical matters. As a wag once noted, when God made his covenant with Abraham, He must have known He'd be in for thousands of years of argument. Indeed, as we shall see, even among the most pious rabbis there was always room for dissenting opinions, in which they seemed to have reveled.

A fundamental of Jewish ethics is the infinite value of a person's life. This concept, as we have noted in Chapter 2, already emerged in the talmudic age. The traditional Jewish toast L'chaim (to life) so well reflects the Jewish focus on living in this world rather than on the fate of the soul in the afterlife, which has dominated Christian and Moslem theology. Accordingly, Jewish medical ethics—originally applicable to Jews, but subsequently extended to encompass all humanity—distinguished patients who were in mortal danger (pikuach nefresh) or even in potential mortal danger (sofek pikuach nefresh) and placed the Jewish physician's obligation to come to their aid above virtually all other considerations. Only the prohibitions against committing murder, idolatry, or incest were deemed by the rabbinical sages to take precedence over this mandate. Similar rulings have enjoined the patient—or even healthy persons in danger of becoming ill—to place the preservation of life and health above ritual observance.

The highly orthodox physician called to an emergency on the Sabbath or a holy day might write the essential notes with his left hand (if he is right-handed), using special ink that disappears in a day or two (during which time the notes can be copied) so that this manual violation will at least leave no permanent mark on God's creation and will have been carried out in a less natural way. Similarly, the doctor might switch on the emergency apparatus with the elbow of his left arm. Oddly enough, advances in electronics combined with ingenious—some might say disingenuous—exploitation of potential loopholes in Jewish law may better enable the orthodox doctor to fulfill his ethical duties toward his fellow man without violating his ritual obligations to God. For example, an electronic circuit can be left on during the entire Sabbath but prevented by a blocking force from activating the medical device in question until, in an emergency, the blocking force is removed by the flick of a switch. Be this as it may, the bottom line in any consideration, even for the most pious Jewish doctor on the holiest of days, is that nothing can be allowed to jeopardize the patient's life, which must always take precedence.

But if high technology may hold some promise of relieving the conflicts facing the doctor who is a strict follower of Jewish law, it has also brought him or her, and all the less religious colleagues, an array of very real and complex ethical problems that in ages past existed, if at all, only in hypothetical or simple form.

The patient's last stage of life, in particular, often brings the Jewish infinite regard for all human life into conflict with the physician's mandate to relieve suffering. Traditional Jewish law contains the concept of *goses*, a state in which a person is deemed to be in the process of dying. The sixteenth-century rabbi Moses Isserles (the "Maimonides of Polish Jewry") defined the onset of *goses* to occur when a patient "brings up secretion in his throat on account of the narrowing of his chest." Death supposedly then follows three days later. Great advances in medical knowledge, particularly in the late twentieth century, have, of course, yielded a multitude of quite different signs of impending death and sophisticated scoring systems for predicting its occurrence within a given time as a matter of statistical probability rather than certainty. Furthermore, not only the definition of dying, but even the definition of death itself has become problematic in recent years. And rapid developments in medical technology have made possible various "heroic" interventions that are vastly more capable of prolonging life than anything imaginable to Rabbi Isseles in sixteenth-century Cracow.

Much in the traditional rabbinical literature distinguishes the prolongation of life from the prolongation of dying and suggests what active or passive approaches should or should not be taken in the respective cases. The Talmud (as reiterated by Maimonides) regards a patient in *goses* to be still a living person in all respects, and it is out of apparent concern about inadvertently hastening death that the rabbinical literature strongly discourages manipulations of the patient's body in this state. Yet another interpretation holds that this same prohibition extends to unnecessary or basically futile medical interventions. Rabbinical rulings, going back at least to Judah ben Samuel in the thirteenth century and codified in the sixteenth century by Isserles, have explicitly condoned the active removal of obstacles to the departure of the soul of the dying, and at least one rabbinical authority specifically ruled that it is "forbidden to hinder the departure of the soul by the use of medicines." Some recent orthodox rabbinical pronouncements have allowed the administering of drugs that, in relieving pain, may actually increase the possibility of an earlier death (by, for example, depressing the respiratory center), provided that the former and not the latter is the purpose of the treatment.

The modern explosion of sophisticated medical procedures—for use not only near the end of life but at other stages—has increasingly raised questions of the allocation of scarce resources. The Jewish tradition, based on the talmudic passage that no one's blood is redder than anyone else's, prohibits the sacrificing (whether voluntarily or forced) of one person for another. As Maimonides put it: "Logic dictates that in regard to taking the life of an Israelite to cure another individual . . . one may not destroy one human life to save another human life." As we noted in Chapter 2, such a prohibition referred particularly to the ancient practice, which persisted into the Middle Ages, of an ailing king seeking a cure by bathing in the blood of his lesser subjects slain for this (as we now know) therapeutically useless purpose. But far from therapeutically useless as we enter the twenty-first century would be, for example, the transplantation of a healthy heart into a state president or great scholar dying of cardiac failure. Yet Jewish law prohibits even the voluntary sacrificing of a potential donor's own life.

Similarly, a physician adhering to Jewish law may not give the life support system on which one patient is already hooked up and critically dependent to another person, even if the latter is considered morally more deserving of it. But a more difficult ethical situation arises if (to expand this example) no one is on the life-support system when two critically ill patients present themselves, one of whom is wealthy (and therefore able to repay his costs to the hospital or to society at large) and the other poor; or when one is considered highly virtuous and the other a criminal or social outcast. Of course, the matter could be rendered purely hypothetical if medical treatment were always available to everyone in abundance. Such a social policy might be in the spirit of Deuteronomy (15:11), which proscribes that "thou shalt open thine hand unto thy brother, to thy needy, and to thy poor, in thine land," and it would accord with Judaism's general view of the infinite value of every human life. But on the other hand, one may point to the Talmud's discouraging of the payment of excess ransom by the Jewish community to redeem a captive coreligionist (although any individual Jew is free to do so from his own resources). A major reason for this is that society as a whole should not be impoverished for the sake of one person.

Arguably, the greatest ethical problem facing medicine and humankind as we move into the third millennium of the common era involves not the allocation of scarce resources or the prolongation of a patient's final years or days, but rather the intervention of biomedical techniques in the very creation of life, both human and nonhuman. Biblical authority, as supported by rabbinical rulings, holds that all nature was brought into being for use by man for his benefit. The concept of genetic engineering of nonhuman life for medical benefits to humans is thus generally not viewed as posing a great dilemma in the context of traditional Jewish thinking. There are, however, equally ancient prohibitions against needless destruction of or cruelty to animals, these being God's creatures. Also, some rabbinical opinions refer to apparent prohibitions in Leviticus against the mating of diverse animals or the sowing together of diverse seeds as suggesting that any changing of living creation by man shows a lack of faith in the Creator.

The matter of genetic manipulation in the making of human rather than nonhuman life is far more problematic. "The prophets have constantly warned the people of Israel against the belief that man could ever compete with God's creative powers. But there was always a concealed hope in man

that somehow he could solve the riddle of Creation and break the code to
its secrets." So wrote Isaac Bashevis Singer recently in an introduction to a
book about the *Golem*. This artificial man makes only a very brief appearance in the Talmud. But his significance and status (for example, could he
be included in a *minyan*?) were later discussed by many rabbis as a very real
issue. In the sixteenth century the Italian physician and kabbalist Abraham
Yagel, whom we met in Chapter 4, spoke approvingly of the creation of
the *Golem* as a form of natural rather than demonic magic, which could
prove the scientific-occult superiority of the Jews even at a time when the
mainly Christian Renaissance was flourishing outside the Ghetto walls. But,
of course, as the legend of the *Golem* has come down to us in various literary and, later, cinematographic renderings, the outcome was far from
what Yagel would have wished for. The *Golem* created according to legend
in the late sixteenth century by Rabbi Eliahu Ba'al Shem of Chelm or Rabbi
Judah Loew of Prague became uncontrollable and unpredictable.

For the outpouring of Jewish medical accomplishments—and the particularly Jewish approach to medical ethics—to continue in ages to come, there
has to be still a Jewish people. For well over 100 years, since the time of
Jewish emancipation and integration into an increasingly secular Western
society, the metaphor of the Wandering Jew has given way to one of the
Disappearing Jew. We have seen how, particularly in the Germanic lands
before the advent of Hitler, by assimilation, mixed marriage, conversion,
and low birth-rates the Jews were voluntarily following a path to virtual
disappearance as a distinct people. To some extent, the problem of the
Disappearing Jew has been solved with the creation of the State of Israel,
which promises continued cultural and scientific achievements in a uniquely
Jewish environment, while also offering a secure haven to all Jews, secular
or religious, facing persecution elsewhere. But most Jews, by choice, continue to live outside the Holy Land, particularly in America. In a secular-
ized Western world, Jews on average are not only the least religious of all
denominations, but also the one with by far the highest mixed-marriage
rate and the fewest children when they do marry among themselves. This
trend has understandably occasioned much concern by Jewish authors,
ranging from orthodox rabbis to theological skeptics. Their arguments
correspondingly range from the traditional religious to some nebulous
concept of a more or less secular Jewishness worthy of preservation. Yet

even adherents of the latter view place too little emphasis on just how much poorer mankind would have been in the past and will surely be in the future without the great outpouring of Jewish scientific, intellectual, and cultural accomplishments. With regard to medicine in particular, there is surprisingly little appreciation of how much humankind owes its well-being and very existence to the achievements of Jewish doctors and medical scientists. The re-establishment and survival in the Holy Land of a Jewish State and a reborn Hebrew language is an almost biblical miracle of hope and will triumphing against great odds. Yet the Diaspora continues to generate its own wonders, not least in medicine, for there is something miraculous in what the innate Jewish talents and intelligence, together with a Jewish cultural heritage, bring forth when placed in a tolerant and dynamic environment.

And so the saga of the Wandering Jewish Doctor has lived on in the last half of the twentieth century and will continue in the new millennium, so long as there are still Jews in the Diaspora. Just as the Jews were the great luminaries in medicine for 1,000 years from the Islamic period to the Heroic Age, so they have become the superstars of medicine in the high-tech era. Impressive as were the twelve Nobel Prizes in medicine awarded to Jews in the first half of the twentieth century (several of whom have been mentioned in the previous chapters), this number has been dwarfed by the three dozen Jews who were so honored in the five decades after 1950. In any given year, it has been a good bet that some Jewish scientist—man or (increasingly) woman—would win or share the Nobel in medicine. (This from a people who, even at their height, probably never constituted more than a fraction of one percent of the world's population.) Whereas before the Second World War the Jewish medical scientists most often carried the Nobel home to Germany and Austria, in the second half of the century they have brought the prize back to Britain, France, and—by far most often—to America, whose founding principles of liberty have proven to be no mere transient phenomenon.

As in times past, so today and in ages to come, the country that welcomes the Wandering Jewish Doctor and allows him to cease his roaming does more than bring honor to itself. It brings blessings to all humanity.

Bibliography

Shown between brackets [ ] at the end of each reference is the chapter number or numbers in the present book for which that work served as a source or is mostly related (In= Introduction; E=Epilogue; G=General). An asterisk * at the end of the reference indicates a work of particularly valuable biographical or background material, which is especially recommended for further reading.

Ackerknecht, Erwin H. (1953). *Rudolf Virchow: Doctor, Statesman, Anthropologist.* Madison: University of Wisconsin Press. [10]

————. (1979). German Jews, English dissenters, French Protestants: Nineteenth-century pioneers of modern medicine and science. In Charles E. Rosenberg, ed., *Healing and History: Essays for George Rosen.* New York: Dawson. [In]

————. (1959/1982). *A Short History Of Medicine.* Baltimore/London: The Johns Hopkins University Press. (Trans. from German.). [G]

Adler, Elkan Nathan, ed. (1930/1987). *Jewish Travelers in the Middle Ages: 19 Firsthand Accounts.* New York: Dover. [5]

Alexander, Franz G., and Sheldon T. Selesnick. (1966). *The History of Psychiatry.* New York: New American Library. [13]

Allen, William Sheridan. (1965/1973). *The Nazi Seizure of Power: The Experiences of a Single German Town, 1930-1935.* New York: Franklin Watts. [14]

Altschule, Mark D. (1989). *Essays on the Rise and Decline of Beside Medicine.* Philadelphia/London: Totts Gap Medical Research Laboratories/Lea & Febiger. [7-9, 13,15,16]

Anderson, George K. (1965). *The Legend of the Wandering Jew.* Hanover NH/London: Brown University Press. [In]*

Angoff, Charles. (1956). *H.L. Mencken: A Portrait From Memory.* New York: A.S. Barnes (Quoted in Alan Gould, ed. [1991]. *What Did They Think of the Jews?.* Northvale NJ/London: Jason Aronson.). [In]

Anonymous. (January 1855). Advertisement for "Jew David's Poor Man's Plaster." In *Yankee Nation,* 4(1):5. Collection of William H. Helfand, New York. [16]

Anonymous. (1944). Karl Landsteiner: 1866-1943. *Journal Of Immunology*, 48:1-16. [14]

Bakan, David. (1958/1975). Sigmund Freud and the Jewish Mystical Tradition. Boston: Beacon. [13]

———. (1989). Contributions to the history of psychology: LIII. Maimonides' "Freudian" theory of prophecy. *Psychological Reports*, 64:667-675. [13]

Baruch, Simon. (1915). Reminiscences of a Confederate surgeon. *Long Branch Record*, September 24. [16]

Bäumler, Ernst. (1984). *Paul Ehrlich: Scientist for Life*. New York: Holms & Meier. (Grant Edwards, trans., from German). [10,12]*

Behler, Rudy. (1985). *Inside Warner Brothers*. London: Weidenfeld & Nicholson. [17]

Ben Sasson, H.H., ed. (1976). *A History of the Jews*. Cambridge MA: Harvard University Press. [G]

Bernstein, Herman. (1913). *With Master Minds*. New York: Universal Series Publishing Co. [11]

Bettmann, Otto L. (1956). *A Pictorial History of Medicine*. Springfield, IL: Charles C. Thomas. [G]

Beyerchen, Alan D. (1977). *Scientists under Hitler: Politics and the Physics Community in the Third Reich*. New Haven, CT/London: Yale University Press. [14]

Bickerman, Elias J. (1988). *The Jews in the Greek Age*. Cambridge, MA/London: Harvard University Press. [2]

Bildarchiv Preussischer Kulturbesitz. (1984). *Jews in Germany under Prussian Rule*. Berlin. [9,10]

Boxer, C.R. (1951). *The Christian Century in Japan: 1549-1650*. Berkeley, CA/London: University of California Press. [5]

———. (1969). *The Portuguese Seaborne Empire 1415-1825*. London: Hutchinson. [5]

Brim, Charles J. (1936). *Medicine in the Bible*. New York: Froben Press. [1]

Brock, Robert. (1988). *Robert Koch: A Life in Medicine and Bacteriology*. Berlin/New York: Science Tech/Springer Verlag. [9,10]

Brock, Thomas D., ed. (1990). *Microorganisms: From Smallpox to Lyme Disease*. New York: W.H. Freeman. [8,12]

Brock, William H. (1992). *The Fontana History of Chemistry*. London: Fontana Press. [10,12]

Brown, James A. C. (1964). *Freud and the Post-Freudians*. Harmondsworth: Penguin. [13]

Brunel, Jules. (Summer, 1951). Antibiosis from Pasteur to Fleming. *Journal of the History of Medicine*, 287-301. [15]

Bullough, Vern L. (1956). The development of the medical university at Montpellier to the end of the fourteenth century. *Bulletin of the History of Medicine*, 30(6):508-523. [6]

———. (1958). Medieval Bologna and the development of medical education. *Bulletin of the History of Medicine*, 32(3):201-215. [4]

Burkert, Walter. (1992). *The Orientalizing Revolution: Near Eastern Influence on Greek Culture in the Early Archaic Age*. Cambridge, MA/London: Harvard University Press. (Margaret E. Pinder and Walter Burkert, trans., from German.). [2]

Bury, J.P.T., ed. (1964). *The Zenith of European Power: The New Cambridge Modern History* (Vol. X). London: Cambridge University Press. [9,10]

Byck, Robert, ed. (1974). *Cocaine Papers: Sigmund Freud*. New York: Meridian. [13]

Calder, Ritchie. (1974). The chemistry of statesmanship. *Rehovot* (Weizmann Institute of Science), 19-22. [12]

Cambrosio, Albert, Daniel Jacobi, and Peter Keating. (1993). Ehrlich's "beautiful pictures" and the controversial beginnings of immunological imagery. *Isis,* 84:662-699. [10]

Caplan, Arthur C., ed. (1992). *When Medicine Went Mad: Bioethics and the Holocaust*. Totowa NJ: Humana Press. [14]

Capparoni, Pietro. (1923). *Magistri Salernitani Nondum Cogniti: A Contribution to the History of the Medical School of Salerno*. London: John Bale, Sons & Danielsson. [4]

Carmichael, Ann G., and Richard M. Ratzan, eds. (1991). *Medicine: A Treasury of Art and Literature*. New York: Hugh Hauter Levin Associates/Beaux Arts Editions. [11]

Cassedy, James H. (1991). *Medicine in America: A Short History*. Baltimore/London: Johns Hopkins University Press. [16]

Castiglioni, Arturo. (1938). The school of Salerno. *Bulletin of the Institute of the History of Medicine,* 5(8):883-898. [4]

Chauncer, Geoffrey. (c.1390/1992). *Canterbury Tales*. New York: Everyman's Library. [15]

Chernow, Ron. (1993). *The Warburgs: The Twentieth Century Odyssey of a Remarkable Jewish Family*. New York: Vintage Books. [14]

Churchill, Winston S. (1956). *History of the English-Speaking Peoples*. Vol. 1: The Birth of Britain. London: Cassell. [In]

Cipolla, Carlo M. (1989/1992). *Miasmas and Disease: Public Health and the Environment in the Pre-Industrial Age*. New Haven, CT/London: Yale University Press. (Elizabeth Potter, trans., from Italian.). [4]

Clark, Ronald W. (1985). *The Life of Ernst Chain: Penicillin and Beyond*. New York: St. Martin's Press. [15]*

Cohen, Mark Nathan. (1989). *Health and the Rise of Civilization*. New Haven, CT/London: Yale University Press. [1]

Cohen, Mozes Herman. (1920). *Spinoza en de Geneeskunde*. M.D. Dissertation; Universiteit van Amsterdam. [7]

Cohn, Ferdinand. (1901). *Blätter der Erinnerung*. Breslau: J.H. Kern's Verlag. [9]

Cohn, Norman. (1970). *Warrant for Genocide: The Myth of the Jewish World Conspiracy and the Protocols of the Elders of Zion*. Harmondworth: Pelican. [8,14]

Collins, Kenneth. (1988). *Go And Learn: The International Story of Jews and Medicine in Scotland*. Aberdeen: Aberdeen University Press. [15]

Cowan, Paul. (1982). *An Orphan in History: Retrieving a Jewish Legacy.* New York: Doubleday. [In]

Cowen, David L., and William H. Helfand. (1990). *Pharmacy: An Illustrated History.* New York: Harry N. Abrams. [G]

Cumston, C.G. (1926/1987). *An Introduction to the History of Medicine.* New York: Dorset Press. [G]

Dalton, Katherina. (1969). *The Menstrual Cycle.* Harmondsworth: Penguin. [1]

Daniel, Kellner. (1940). *Redders der Menschheid: Doktoren als Nobelprijswinnaars.* Amsterdam: J.M. Meulenhoff (W.B. Huddleston Slater, ed. and trans., from German). [11-13]

Dawidowicz, Lucy. (1975). *The War against the Jews 1933-45.* Harmondsworth: Pelican. [14]

———. (1981). *The Holocaust and the Historians.* Cambridge, MA/London: Harvard University Press. [14]

De Kruif, Paul. (1926/1954). *Microbe Hunters.* San Diego/New York: Harvest/Harcourt Brace Javanovitch. [7-12]

Delaporte, François. (1986). *Disease and Civilization: The Cholera in Paris 1832.* Cambridge, MA/London: MIT Press. (Arthur Goldhammer, trans., from French.). [11]

Dement, William C. (1972). *Some Must Watch While Some Must Sleep.* San Francisco: W.H. Freeman & Co. [13]

Dimont, Max I. (1962). *Jews, God and History.* New York: Signet. [G]

Dinnerstein, Leonard. (1994). *Antisemitism in America.* New York/Oxford: Oxford University Press. [16,17]

Dols, Michael. (1984). *Medieval Islamic Medicine: Ibn Ridwan's Treatise "On The Prevention of Bodily Ills in Egypt."* Berkley: University of California Press. [3]

Dor-Ner, Zvi. (1991). *Columbus and the Age of Discovery.* New York: William Morrow & Co. [5]

Dörr, Wilhelm. (1987). Gleitwort zum Nachdruk. In Moritz Kaposi (1872/1987), *Bösartige Neubildungn.* Stuttgart: Ferdinand Enke Verlag. [13]

Dubos, René. (1960/1988). *Pasteur and Modern Science.* Madison, WI/Berlin: Science Tech Publishers/Springer-Verlag. [9,11]

Duin, Nancy, and Jenny Sutcliffe. (1992). *A History of Medicine: From Prehistory to the Year 2020.* London/New York: Simon & Schuster. [G]

Durant, Will. (1926/1953). *The Story of Philosophy.* New York: Pocket Books/Washington Square Press. [2,7]

Earle, A. Scott, ed. (1983). *Surgery in America: From the Colonial Era to the Twentieth Century.* New York: Praeger Publishers. (Second edition.). [16]

Efron, John M. (1994). *Defenders of the Race: Jewish Doctors and Race Science in Fin-de-Siècle Europe.* New Haven CT/London: Yale University Press. [10,14]

Einstein, Albert. (1954). *Ideas and Opinions.* New York: Bonanza Books. [13]

Encyclopedia Judaica. (1971). Jerusalem: Macmillan. [G]

Evans, Richard J. (1987). *Death In Hamburg: Society and Politics in the Cholera Years 1830-1910.* Oxford: Clarendon Press. [10]

Fast, Howard. (1968). *The Jews: The Story of a People.* New York: Dell. [G]

Feldman, David M. (1986). *Health and Medicine in the Jewish Tradition.* New York: Crossroad. [E]

Feldman, Seymour. (1982). Introduction. In Baruch Spinoza, *The Ethics and Selected Letters.* Indianapolis: Hackett Publishing Company. [7]

Fischer, Richard B. (1977). *Joseph Lister.* New York: Stein and Day. [8]

Flexner, Abraham. (1960). *Abraham Flexner: An Autobiography.* New York: Simon & Schuster. [16]*

Flexner, James Thomas. (1984). *An American Saga: The Story of Helen Thomas and Simon Flexner.* Boston: Little, Brown & Co. [16]*

Flint, Valerie I.J. (1992). *The Imaginative Landscape of Christopher Columbus.* Princeton: Princeton University Press. [16]

Friedenwald, Harry. (1939). Francisco Lopez de Villalobos: Spanish court physician and poet. *Bulletin of the History of Medicine,* 7(10):1129-1139. [4]

——. (1944). *The Jews in Medicine: Essays.* Baltimore: Johns Hopkins Press. [G]*

——. (1946). *Jewish Luminaries in Medical History.* Baltimore: Johns Hopkins Press. [G]

Freud, Sigmund. (1900/1976). *The Interpretation of Dreams.* Harmondsworth: Pelican. [13]

——. (1913/1989). *Totem and Taboo.* New York: Norton. [1]

——. (1927/1989). *The Future of an Illusion.* New York: Norton. [1]

——. (1939/1972). *Moses and Monotheism.* New York: Viking. [1]

Freud, Sigmund and Carl Gustav Jung. (1974). *The Freud/Jung Letters.* Princeton NJ: Princeton University Press/Bollinger. [13]

Gabler, Neal. (1988). *An Empire of Their Own: How the Jews Invented Hollywood.* New York: Anchor/Doubleday. [17]

Gans, Mozes Heiman. (1971). *Memorbook: History of Dutch Jewry from the Renaissance to 1940.* Baarn: Bosch & Keuning. (Trans. from Dutch.). [7]

Gansberg, Alan L. (1983). *Little Caesar: A Biography of Edward G. Robinson.* London: New English Library. [17]

Garcia-Ballester, Luis. (1991). Dietetic and pharmacological therapy: a dilemma among fourteenth-century Jewish practitioners in the Montpellier area. *Cleo Med,* 22:23-37. [6]

Gay, Peter. (1978). *Freud, Jews and Other Germans: Masters and Victims in Modernist Culture.* Oxford/New York: Oxford University Press. [13]

Geehr, Richard S. (1990). *Karl Lueger: Mayor of Fin de Siècle Vienna.* Detroit: Wayne University Press. [13]

Gerber, Jane S. (1992). *The Jews of Spain: A History of the Sephardic Experience.* New York: Free Press/Macmillan. [3,4]

Gersuny, Robert. (1922). *Theodor Billroth.* Vienna/Berlin: Rikola Verlag. [13]

Gickhorn, René. (January, 1969). The Freiberg Period of the Freud Family. *Journal of the History of Medicine*, 37-43. [13]

Gidal, Nachum T. (1988). *Jews in Germany: From Roman Times to the Weimar Republic*. Cologne: Könemann Verlag. (Trans. from German.). [8-10,12,14]

Gilman, Sander L. (1993). *The Case of Sigmund Freud: Medicine and Identity at the Fin de Siècle*. Baltimore/London: Johns Hopkins University Press. [13]

Goodman, L.E. (1992). *Avicenna*. London/New York: Routledge. [3]

Gordon, Richard. (1993). *The Alarming History of Medicine*. London: Mandarin. [G]

Gottfried, Robert S. (1986). *The Black Death: Natural and Human Disease in Medieval Europe*. London: Macmillan. [8]

Greiling, Walter. (1955). *Im Banne der Medizin: Paul Ehrlich—Leben und Werk*. Düsseldorf: Econ Verlag. [10,12]*

Haeger, Knut. (1988). *The Illustrated History of Surgery*. London: Harold Starke. [G]

Haehl, Richard. (1922/1985). *Samuel Hahnemann: His Life and Work*. New Delhi: B. Jain Publishers. (Marie L. Wheeler and W.H.R. Grundy, trans., from German.). [8]

Haggard, Howard W. (1929). *Devils, Drugs, and Doctors: The Story of the Science of Healing, from Medicine-Man to Doctor*. London: Heinemann (Medical). [G]

Hampshire, Stuart. (1951). *Spinoza*. Harmondsworth: Pelican. [7]

Hankinson, R.J., ed. and trans. (1991). *Galen on the Therapeutic Method: Books I and II*. Oxford: Clarendon Press. [2]

Harris, Marvin. (1989). *Our Kind: Who We Are, Where We Came from, and Where We Are Going*. New York: Harper Perennial. [1,11]

Helfand, William H. (1989). Samuel Solomon and the Cordial Balm of Gilead. *Pharmacy in History*, 31(4):151-159. [15]

Henle, Jacob. (1840/1938). *On Miasmata and Contagion*. Baltimore: Johns Hopkins University Press (*Bulletin of the Johns Hopkins University Institute of the History of Medicine*, 6:907-983; George Rosen, ed. and trans., from German.). [8]*

Herzl, Theodor. (1896/1988). *The Jewish State*. New York: Dover. (Sylvie d'Avigdor, trans., from German.). [In]

Hertz, Alexander. (1961/1988). *The Jews in Polish Culture*. Evanston, IL: Northwestern University Press. (Richard Lourie, trans., from Polish.). [11]

Hess, Hindle S. (1980). *Jewish Physicians in the Netherlands*. Assen: Van Gorcum. [7]

Heynick, Frank. (1981). Linguistic aspects of Freud's dream model. *International Review of Psycho-Analysis*, 8(3):299-314. [13]

———. (1983). From Einstein to Whorf: space, time, matter, and reference frames in physical and linguistic relativity. *Semiotica*, 45(1/2):35-64. [13]

———. (1985). Dream dialogue and retrogression: neurobiological origins of Freud's "replay hypothesis." *Journal of the History of the Behavioral Sciences*. 21(4):321-341. [13]

———. (1986). The dream-scripter and the Freudian ego: pragmatic competence and superordinate and subordinate cognitive systems in sleep. *Journal of Mind and Behavior*. 7(2/3):169-201. [13]

————. (1986). A geophysical note on man's free-running circadian rhythm. *Journal of Interdisciplinary Cycle Research.* 17(2):113-119. [2]

————. (1993). *Language and Its Disturbances in Dreams: The Pioneering Work of Freud and Kraepelin Updated.* New York: John Wiley & Sons. [13]

Heynick, Frank, and Herman N. de Lange (1979). Einstein's Dutch connection. *Higher Education and Research in the Netherlands.* 23(3/4):18-21. [13]

Hitti, Philip K. (1943/1996). *The Arabs: A Short History.* Washington: Gateway/Regency. [3]

Hobson, J. Allan. (1988). *The Dreaming Brain.* New York: Basic Books. [13]

Hortzitz, Nicoline. (1994). *Der "Judenartzt": Historische und sprachliche Untersuchungen zur Diskriminierung eines Berufsstands in der frühen Neuzeit.* Heidelberg: Universätsverlag C. Winter. [14]

Hsia, R. Po-chia. (1988). *The Myth of Ritual Murder: Jews and Magic in Reformation Germany.* New Haven, CT/London: Yale University Press. [8]

Huizinga, J.H. (1969). *Dutch Civilization in the Seventeenth Century and Other Essays.* New York: Harper Torchbooks. (Arnold J. Pomerans, trans., from Dutch.). [7]

Jacobi, Jolanda, ed. (1942/1979). *Paracelsus: Selected Writings.* Princeton NJ: Bollingen/Princeton University Press. (Norbert Guterman, trans., from German.). [8]

Jacobs, Aletta. (1924). *Herinneringen.* Amsterdam: Holkema & Warendorf. [7]

Jahoda, Gustav. (1970). *The Psychology of Superstition.* Harmondsworth: Penguin Books. [1]

Janik, Allan, and Stephan Toulmin. (1973). *Wittgenstein's Vienna.* New York: Touchstone. [13]

Jansen, B.C.P. (1959). *Het Levenswerk van Christiaan Eijkman.* Haarlem: De Erven F. Bohn. [15,16]

Janton, Pierre. (1973/1993). *Esperanto: Language, Literature, and Community.* Albany, NY: SUNY Press. (Humphrey Tonkin, ed.; Humphrey Tonkin, Jane Edwards, and Karen Johnson-Weiner, trans., from French.). [11]

Jaworski, Marek. (1980). *Ludwik Hirszfeld: sein Beitrage zu Seriologie und Immunologie.* Leipzig: BSB B.G. Teubner. [14]

Jones, Ernest. (1953-7). *Sigmund Freud: Life and Work.* London: Hogarth Press. [13]

Jüdisches Lexikon. (1927/1982). Berlin: Jüdische Verlag. [G]

Jung, C.G. (1980). *C.G. Jung Speaking: Interviews and Encounters.* (William McGuire and R.F.C. Hull, eds.). London: Picador. [14]

Kagan, Solomon R. (1926). Medicine according to the Talmud. *Medical Journal and Record* (April 7): 21. [2]

————. (1934). *Contributions of Early Jews to American Medicine.* Boston: Boston Medical Publishing. [16]*

————. (1952). *Jewish Medicine.* Boston: Boston Medical Publishing. [G]

Khrushchev, Nikita S. (1970). *Khrushchev Remembers.* Boston/Toronto: Little, Brown. [11]

Kisch, Bruno. (1951). *Forgotten Leaders in Modern Medicine: Valentin, Gruby, Remak, Auerbach.* Philadelphia: American Philosophical Society. (Officially published as *Transactions of the American Philosophical Society*, New Series, 44 (2):139-317.). [8]*

Knoche, G.D. (1938). De voorouders van Paul Ehrlich. *Mensch en Maatschappij.* 14:262-270. [10]

Kottek, Samuel S. (1981). The hospital in Jewish history. *Review of Infectious Diseases*, 3(4):636-639. [8]

Krebs, Hans. (1979/1981). *Otto Warburg: Cell Physiologist, Biochemist, and Eccentric.* Oxford: Clarendon Press. (Hans Krebs and Anne Martin, trans., from German.). [14]*

Laffan, Michael, ed. (1989). *The Burden of German History, 1919-1945: Essays for the Goethe Institute.* London: Methuen. [14]

Langer, Walter C. (1972). *The Mind of Adolf Hitler: The Secret Wartime Report.* New York: Basic Books. [14]

Leibowitz, Joshua O. (1957). Maimonides on medical practice. *Bulletin of the History of Medicine.* 31:309-317. [3]

Leicester, Henry M. (1956/1971). *The Historical Background of Chemistry.* New York: John Wiley & Sons. (Reprint, Dover Publications.). [10,12]

Leoni, Edgar. (1961). *Nostradamus: Life and Literature.* New York: Exposition Press. [6]

Lewis, Bernard. (1984). *The Jews of Islam.* Princeton: Princeton University Press. [3]

Lewis, Sinclair. (1925/1961). *Arrowsmith.* New York: Signet Classics. [16]

Lifton, Robert Jay. (1986). *The Nazi Doctors: Medical Killings and the Psychology of Genocide.* New York: Basic Books. [14]

Lindeboom, G.A. (1954). The story of a blood transfusion to a pope. *Journal of the History of Medicine*, 9:455-462. [14]

Lindemann, Albert S. (1991). *The Jew Accused: Three Anti-Semitic Affairs (Dreyfus, Beilis, Frank) 1894-1915.* Cambridge, MA/New York: Cambridge University Press. [17]

Lloyd, G.E.R., ed. (1979). *Hippocratic Writings.* Harmondsworth: Penguin. [2]

Lynch, John. (1965). *Spain under the Habsburgs.* Oxford: Blackwell. [4,5]

Lyons, Albert, and R. Joseph Petrucelli II. (1978). *Medicine: An Illustrated History.* New York: Harry N. Abrams. [G]

Maidenbaum, Aryeh, and Stephen A. Martin, eds. (1991). *Lingering Shadows: Jungians, Freudians, and Anti-Semitism.* Boston/London: Shambhala. [14]

Majno, Guido. (1975). *The Healing Hand: Man and Wound in the Ancient World.* Cambridge, MA/London: Harvard University Press. [1,2]*

Mallory, J.P. (1989). *In Search of the Indo-Europeans: Language, Archeology and Myth.* New York: Thames & Hudson. [14]

Mann, John. (1992). *Murder, Magic, and Medicine.* Oxford/New York: Oxford University Press. [1,12,15]

Mansfield, Peter. (1978). *The Arabs.* Harmondsworth: Penguin. [3]

Margalith, David. (January, 1957). The ideal doctor as depicted in ancient Hebrew writings. *Journal of the History of Medicine*. 37-41. [1,2]

Marquardt, Martha. (1949). *Paul Ehrlich*. London: Heinemann Medical. [10,12]*

Marshall, Robert. (1993). *Storm from the East: From Genghis Khan to Khubilai Khan*. Berkley/Los Angeles: University of California Press. [5]

Massie, Robert K. (1991). *Dreadnaught: Britain, Germany and the Coming of the Great War*. New York: Ballantine Books. [12]

McIntosh, Christopher. (1969). *The Astrologers and Their Creed*. London/New York: Random House. [2,6]

McNeill, William H. (1976). *Plagues and Peoples*. New York: Anchor/Doubleday. [5,12]

McPherson, James M. (1988). *Battle Cry of Freedom: The American Civil War*. New York/Oxford: Oxford University Press. [16]

Metchnikoff, Olga. (1921/1972). *Life of Eli Metchnikoff: 1845-1916*. Freeport, NY: Books For Libraries Press. (Trans. from French.). [11]*

Miki, Sakae. (1976). *What Is Medicine? Medicine Is Common to East and West. What Is the History of Medicine?* Osaka: Minami Osaka Insatsu Center Press. (Hiromicho Kamimura, trans., from Japanese.). [5]

Miller, Jonathan. (1978). *The Body in Question*. New York: Random House. [G]

Mintz, Jerome R. (1968). *Legends of the Hasidim: An Introduction to Hasidic Culture and Oral Tradition in the New World*. Chicago/London: University of Chicago Press. [8]

Mitchell, Harvey, and Samuel S. Kottek. (1993). An eighteenth-century medical view of the diseases of the Jews of Northeastern France: medical anthropology and the politics of Jewish emancipation. *Bulletin of the History of Medicine*. 67(2): 248-281. [11]

Morgan, David. (1986). *The Mongols*. Cambridge, MA/Oxford: Blackwell. [5]

Morgan, Elaine. (1982). *The Aquatic Ape: A Theory of Human Evolution*. London: Souvenir Press. [1]

Mosse, George I., ed. (1966). *Nazi Culture: Intellectual, Cultural and Social Life in the Third Reich*. New York: Random House. [14]

Nater, J.P. (1994). *De Dood Is in de Pot, Man Gods!: Ziekte en Genezing in de Bijbel*. Rotterdam: Erasmus Publishing. [1]

Nesse, Rudolph M., and George C. Williams. (1994). *Why We Get Sick: The New Science of Darwinian Medicine*. New York: Times Books/Random House. [1]

Netanyahu, Benzion. (1972). *Don Isaac Abravanel: Statesman and Philosopher*. Philadelphia: Jewish Publication Society Of America. [4]

Neufeld, Edward. (October, 1970). Hygiene conditions in ancient Israel (Iron Age). *Journal of the History of Medicine*, 414-437. [1]

Nigel, Allan. (1984). Illustrations from the Wellcome Institute Library: a Jewish physician in the seventeenth century. *Medical History*. 28:324-328. [8]

Nissan, Shmuel. (1995). Medical services in the Holy Land in the nineteenth century: 1842-1914. In Natalia Berger, ed., *Jews and Medicine: Religion, Culture, Science.* Tel Aviv: Beth Hatefutsoth, Nahum Goldman Museum of the Jewish Diaspora. [E]

NOVA. (1986). The rise of a wonder drug. (Transcript of BBC-WGBH television series.). [15]

Nuland, Sherwin B. (1988). *Doctors: The Biography of Medicine.* New York: Alfred A. Knopf. [G]*

————. (1992). *Medicine: The Art of Healing.* New York: High Lauter Levine Assoc./Macmillan. [G]

Pagel, Walter. (1960). Paracelsus and Techellus the Jew. *Bulletin of The History of Medicine,* 34(3):274-277. [8]

Pais, Abraham. (1991). *Niels Bohr's Times: In Physics, Philosophy and Polity.* New York/Oxford: Oxford University Press. [13]

Patai, Raphael. (1984). An unknown Hebrew medical alchemist: a medieval treatise on the quinta essentia. *Medical History,* 28:308-323. [6]

————. (1994). *The Jewish Alchemists: A History and Source Book.* Princeton: Princeton University Press. [6,15]

Patai, Raphael, and Jennifer Patai. (1989). *The Myth of the Jewish Race.* Detroit: Wayne State University Press. [14]

Pauly, Philip J. (1980). *Jacques Loeb and the Control of Life: An Experimental Biologist in Germany and America, 1859-1924.* Unpublished Ph.D. dissertation, Johns Hopkins University. [16]*

Payne, Robert. (1964). *The Life and Death of Lenin.* New York: Simon & Schuster. [17]

Pernick, Martin S. (1985). *A Calculus of Suffering: Pain, Professionalism, and Anesthesia in Nineteenth-century America.* New York: Columbia University Press. [16]

Peters. Edward. (1978). *The Magician, the Witch, and the Law.* Hassocks: Harvester Press. [8]

Poliakov, Léon. (1971/1977). *The Aryan Myth: A History of Racist and Nationalist Ideas in Europe.* New York: Meridian/New American Library. (Edmund Howard, trans., from French.). [14]

Polo, Marco. (1958). *The Travels.* Harmondsworth: Penguin Books. (Ronald Latham, ed. and trans., from Italian and Latin.). [5]

Preuss, Julius. (1911/1993). *Biblical and Talmudic Medicine.* Northvale, NJ/London: Jason Aronson Inc. (Fred Rosner, ed. and trans., from German.). [1,2]*

Proctor, Robert N. (1988). *Racial Hygiene: Medicine under the Nazis.* Cambridge, MA/London: Harvard University Press. [14]

Pulzer, Peter. (1988). *The Rise of Political Antisemitism in Germany and Austria.* London: Peter Halban. [10,13,14]

Quétel, Claude. (1986/1990). *History of Syphilis.* Baltimore: Johns Hopkins University Press. (Judith Braddock and Brian Pike, trans., from French.). [12]

Randi, James. (1990). *The Mask of Nostradamus*. New York: Charles Scribner's Sons. [6]

Rapoport, Louis. (1990). *Stalin's War against the Jews: The Doctor's Plot and the Soviet Solution*. New York: Free Press. [E]

Ring, Melvin E. (1985). *Dentistry: An Illustrated History*. New York/St. Louis: Abradale Press/Mosby-Year Book. [G]

Robert, Marthe. (1974/1977). *From Oedipus to Moses: Freud's Jewish Identity*. London: Routledge & Kegan Paul. (Ralph Manheim, trans., from French.). [13]*

Robinson, Edward G., and Leonard Spiegelgass. (1973). *All My Yesterdays: An Autobiography*. New York: Hawthorn Books. [17]

Robinson, Victor. (1921). *The Life of Jacob Henle*. New York: Medical Life Company. [8]*

Roit, Ivan, Jonathan Brostoff, and David Male. (1986). *Immunology*. London/New York: Churchill Livingston/Glower Medical. (Chapter 9, The generation of antibody diversity; Chapter 17, Immunity to protozoa and worms.). [1,10]

Rosenberg, Charles E. (1962). *The Cholera Years: The United States in 1832, 1849, and 1866*. Chicago/London: University of Chicago Press. [16]

―――. (April, 1965). Review of Milton Terris (ed.), *Goldberger on Pellagra*. *Journal of the History of Medicine*. 20:179-180. [16]

―――. (1992). *Explaining Epidemics, and Other Studies in the History of Medicine*. New York: Cambridge University Press. [9,16]

Rosner, Fred, ed. (1970). *Moses Maimonides' Glossary of Drug Names*. Philadelphia: American Philosophical Society. [3]

―――. (1977). *Medicine in the Bible and the Talmud: Selections from Classical Jewish Sources*. New York: Yeshiva University Press. [1,2]*

―――, ed. (1990). *Medicine and Jewish Law:* Vol 1. Northvale, NJ: Jason Aronson. [E]

―――. (1991). *Modern Medicine and Jewish Ethics*. New York: Yeshiva University Press. [E]

―――, ed. (1993). *Medicine and Jewish Law:* Vol 2. Northvale, NJ: Jason Aronson. [E]

Rosner, Fred, and Samuel S. Kottek, eds. (1993). *Moses Maimonides: Physician, Scientist, and Philosopher*. Northvale, NJ: Jason Aronson. [3]*

Roth, Cecil. (1956). *The Jewish Contribution to Civilization*. London: East and West Library. [G]*

―――. (1970). *A History of the Jews*. New York: Schocken Books. [G]

―――. (1974). *A History of the Marranos* (Fourth Edition). New York: Hermon Press. [4,5]

Roth, Philip. (1967). *Portnoy's Complaint*. New York: Random House. [In]

Ruderman, David B. (1987). *Science, Medicine and Jewish Culture in Early Modern Europe* (*Spiegel Lectures in European Jewish History, Vol. 7*, Lloyd P. Gartner, ed.). Tel Aviv: Tel Aviv University Press. [8]

————. (1988). *Kabbalah, Magic and Science: The Cultural Universe of a Sixteenth-Century Jewish Physician.* Cambridge, MA/London: Harvard University Press. [8]

————. (1995). *Jewish Thought and Scientific Discovery in Early Modern Europe.* New Haven/London: Yale University Press. [4,8]

Russell, Bertrand. (1959). *The Wisdom of the West.* London: Rathbone. [2]

Rutkow, Ira M. (1993). *Surgery: An Illustrated History.* St. Louis: Mosby-Year Book. [G]

Ryan, Frank. (1993). *The Forgotten Plague: How the Battle Against Tuberculosis Was Won—and Lost.* Boston: Little, Brown & Co. [17]*

Schatzmiller, Joseph. (1994). *Jews, Medicine, and Medieval Society.* Berkley: University of California Press. [4]*

Schlich, Thomas. (1990). *Marburger Jüdische Medizin- und Chirurgiestudenten 1800-1832: Herkunft, Berufsweg, Stellung in der Gesellschaft.* Marburg: N.G. Elwert Verlag (Dissertation). [8]

Schneider, William H. (1983). Chance and social setting in the application and discovery of blood groups. *Bulletin of the History of Medicine,* 57:545-562. [14]

Schorer, Mark. (1961). Afterword. In Sinclair Lewis, *Arrowsmith* (1925/1961). New York: New American Library. [16]

Schouten, J. (1967). *The Rod and Serpent of Asklepios: Symbol of Medicine.* Amsterdam: Elsevier Publishing. [1]

Schrire, T. (1966). *Hebrew Amulets: Their Decipherment and Interpretation.* London: Routledge & Kegan Paul. [8]

Seide, Jacob. (1954). Medicine and natural history in the itinerary of Rabbi Benjamin of Tudela (1100-1177). *Bulletin of the History of Medicine,* 28:401-407. [5]

Shapiro, Sidney, ed. (1984). *Jews in Old China: Studies by Chinese Scholars.* New York: Hippocrene Books. [5]*

Shatzsky, Jacob. (1950). On Jewish medical students of Padua. *Journal of the History of Medicine,* 5:444-447. [4]

Shulman, Yaakov Dovid. (1994). *The Rambam: The Story of Rabbi Moshe ben Maimon.* New York: C.I.S. Publishers. [3]

Sigerist, Henry E. (1951). *A History of Medicine: Primitive and Archaic Medicine.* New York/Oxford: Oxford University Press. [1]*

————. (1961). *A History of Medicine: Early Greek, Hindu, and Persian Medicine.* New York/Oxford: Oxford University Press. [2]

Silverstein, Arthur M. (1989). *A History of Immunology.* San Diego: Academic Press. [10-12]*

Singer, Isaac Bashevis. (1988). Forward. In Emily D. Bilski, ed., *Golem: Danger Deliverance and Art.* New York: Jewish Museum. [E]

Siraisi, Nancy G. (1990). *Medieval and Early Renaissance Medicine.* Chicago/London: University of Chicago Press. [4]

Sklar, Dusty. (1977). *The Nazis and the Occult.* New York: Dorset Press. [14]

Smith, Jane S. (1990). *Patenting the Sun: Polio and the Salk Vaccine*. New York: William Morrow. [E]

Smith, Wesley D. (1979). *The Hippocratic Tradition*. Ithaca/London: Cornell University Press. [1]

Soubiran, André. (1935). *Avicenne, Prince des Médecins: Sa Vie et sa Doctrine*. Paris: Librairie Lipschultz. [3]

Speiser, Paul, and Ferdinand G. Smekal. (1975). *Karl Landsteiner*. Vienna: Verlag Brüder Hollinek. [14]*

Stahl, Ernst. (1904). Matthias Jakob Schleiden: Rede gehalten zur Saecularfeier seines Geburtstages. *Universitätsbericht über das Jahr 1903-04*. Jena: Universitätsbuchdruckerei G. Neuenbahn. [8]

Stern, Fritz. (1961). *The Politics of Cultural Despair: A Study in the Rise of the Germanic Ideology*. Berkley: University Of California Press. [10]

———. (1979). *Gold and Iron: Bismarck, Bleichröder and the Building of the German Empire*. New York: Vintage/Random House. [10]

Stratton, Owen Tully. (1989). *Medicine Man*. Norman, OK/London: University of Oklahoma Press. [16]

Strauss, Maurice B., ed. (1968). *Familiar Medical Quotations*. Boston: Little, Brown & Co. [G]

Tauber, Alfred I. (1991). A case of defence: Metchnikoff at the Pasteur Institute. In P.-A. Cazenave and G.P. Talwar, eds., *Immunology: Pasteur's Heritage*. New Delhi: Wiley Eastern. [11]

Tauber, Alfred I., and Leon Chernyak. (1991). *Metchnikoff and the Origins of Immunology: From Metaphor to Theory*. New York/Oxford: Oxford University Press. [11]*

Taylor, A.J.P. (1945/1988). *The Course of German History*. London: Routledge. [10,12,14]

Temkin, Owsei. (1955). Medicine and Graeco-Arabic alchemy. *Bulletin of the History of Medicine*, 29(2):134-149. [2,3]

———. (1991). *Hippocrates in a World of Pagans and Christians*. Baltimore/London: Johns Hopkins University Press. [2]

Thomas, Lewis. (1985). *The Youngest Science: Notes of a Medicine Watcher*. Oxford: Oxford University Press. [16]

Thompson, C.J.S. (1928). *The Quacks of Old London*. London/New York: Brentano. [15]

Thompson, Morton. (1954). *Not As a Stranger*. New York: Charles Scribner's Sons. [17]

Thorowgood, Thomas. (1650). *Iewes in America, or Probablities that the Americans are of that Race. With the removall of some contrary reasonings, and earnest desires for effectual endeavours to make them Christian*. London: Tho. Slater. [16]

Trachtenberg, Josua. (1939/1970). *Jewish Magic and Superstition: A Study in Folk Religion*. New York: Atheneum. [4,8]

————. (1943). *The Devil and the Jews: The Medieval Conception of the Jew and Its Relation to Modern Antisemitism*. New Haven: Yale University Press. [4,8]

Treue, Wilhelm. (1956). *Mit dem Augen Ihrer Leibärzte*. Düsseldorf: Droste Verlag. [6]

Twersky, Isadore, ed. (1985). *Danzig between East and West: Aspects of Modern Jewish History*. Cambridge, Mass/London: Harvard University Press. [8]

Underwood, E. Ashworth. (1977). *Boerhaave's Men: At Leyden and After*. Edinburgh: Edinburgh University Press. [7,15]

Unger, Hellmuth. (1929). *Helfer der Menschheit: der Lebensroman Robert Kochs*. Leipzig: Buchhandlung des Verbandes der Aerzte Deutschlands. (Dutch version in German-occupied Netherlands: *Dienaar der Menschheid: Het Leven van Robert Koch*. Amsterdam: A.J.G. Strenghollt's Uitgevers Mij.). [9,14]

The Universal Jewish Encyclopedia. (1943). New York. [G]

Van den Haag, Ernst. (1969). *The Jewish Mystique*. New York: Stein & Day. [In]*

Van der Post, Laurens. (1977). *Jung and the Story of Our Time*. New York: Vintage. [14]

Veblen, Thorstein. (1913). The mutation theory and the blond race. *Journal of Race Development*, 3(4). (Reprinted in: Thorstein Veblen, *The Place of Science in Modern Civilization and Other Essays*. New York: Russell & Russell, 1961.). [14]

————. (March, 1919). The intellectual pre-eminence of the Jews. *Political Science Quarterly* (Reprinted in *The Portable Veblen*. New York: Viking Press, 1948.). [In]

Waksman, Selman A. (Summer, 1951). Streptomycin: isolation, properties, and utilization. *Journal of the History of Medicine*:318-329. [17]

————. (1954). *My Life with the Microbes*. New York: Simon & Schuster. [17]*

————. (1964). *The Brilliant and Tragic Life of W.M.W. Haffkine, Bacteriologist*. New Brunswick NJ: Rutgers University Press. [11]*

————. (1964). *The Conquest of Tuberculosis*. Berkley/Los Angeles: University Of California Press. [17]*

Walsh, James J. (1911). *Old-Time Makers of Medicine: The Story of the Students and Teachers of the Sciences Related to Medicine during the Middle Ages*. New York: Fordham University Press. [3]

Ward, Patricia Spain. (1994). *Simon Baruch: Rebel in the Ranks of Medicine*. Tuscaloosa/London: University of Alabama Press. [16]*

Watson, James D. (1969). *The Double Helix: A Personal Account of the Discovery of the Structure of DNA*. New York: Mentor. [E]

Weber, Max. (1904-05/1992). *The Protestant Ethic and the Spirit of Capitalism*. London/New York: Routledge. (Talcott Parsons, trans., from German.). [16]

Weindling, Paul. (1989). *Health, Race and German Politics Between National Unification and Nazism, 1870-1945*. Cambridge/New York: Cambridge University Press. [14]*

Yellin, David, and Israel Abrahams. (1903). *Maimonides*. Philadelphia: Jewish Publication Society of America. [3]*

Yerushalmi, Yosef Hayim. (1991). *Freud's Moses: Judaism Terminable and Interminable*. New Haven/London: Yale University Press. [13]*

Yovel, Yirmiyahu. (1989). *Spinoza and Other Heretics: The Marrano of Reason*. Princeton: Princeton University Press. [7]*

————. (1989). *Spinoza and Other Heretics: The Adventures of Immanence*. Princeton: Princeton University Press. [7,13]*

Zeigler, Philip. (1971). *The Black Death*. New York: Harper/Torchbooks. [8]

574 ～ Jews and Medicine: An Epic Saga

Jewish Nobel Laureates in Medicine (to 2000)

Nationality includes country of birth and country to which the scientists immigrated. (Note: Laureates may be of Jewish descent but not of the Jewish religion. Some sources include several more names than given here, especially for Nobel Prize winners in recent years.)

1908 - Paul Ehrlich, *Germany*
1908 - Elie Metchnikoff, *Russia/France*
1914 - Robert Barany, *Austria/Sweden*
1922 - Otto Meyerhof, *Germany/USA*
1930 - Karl Landsteiner, *Austria/USA*
1931 - Otto Warburg, *Germany*
1936 - Otto Loewi, *Germany/Austria/USA*
1944 - Joseph Erlanger, *USA*
1944 - Herbert Gasser, *USA*
1945 - Ernst Chain, *Germany/UK*
1946 - Hermann Muller, *USA*
1950 - Tadeus Reichstein, *Poland/Switzerland*
1952 - Selman Waksman, *Russia/USA*
1953 - Hans Krebs, *Germany/UK*
1953 - Fritz Lipmann, *Germany/USA*
1958 - Joshua Lederberg, *USA*
1959 - Arthur Kornberg, *USA*
1964 - Konrad Bloch, *Germany/USA*
1965 - François Jacob, *France*
1965 - André Lwoff, *France*
1967 - George Wald, *USA*

1968 - Marshall Nirenberg, *USA*
1969 - Salvador Luria, *Italy/USA*
1970 - Julius Axelrod, *USA*
1970 - Bernard Katz, *Germany/UK*
1972 - Gerald Edelman, *USA*
1975 - David Baltimore, *USA*
1975 - Howard Temin, *USA*
1976 - Baruch Blumberg, USA
1977 - Rosalyn Sussman Yalow, *USA*
1977 - Andrew Schally, *Poland/USA*
1978 - Daniel Nathans, *USA*
1980 - Baruj Benacerraf, *Venezuala/USA*
1984 - Cesar Milstein, *Argentina/UK*
1985 - Michael Stuart Brown, *USA*
1985 - Joseph Goldstein, *USA*
1986 - Stanley Cohen, *USA*
1986 - Rita Levi-Montalcini, *Italy/USA*
1988 - Gertrude Elion, *USA*
1989 - Harold Varmus, *USA*
1994 - Alfred Gilman, *USA*
1994 - Martin Rodbell, *USA*
1997 - Stanley Prusiner, *USA*
1998 - Robert Furchgott, *USA*
2000 - Eric Kandel, *Austria/USA*

Person Index

(Note: As is customary, most medieval Hebrew and Arabic names are listed alphabetically under the first name, e.g., *Menasseh ben Israel* and *Hasdai ibn Shaprut*. Exceptions are when the persons are more commonly known under their last names, e.g., *al-Kindi* or under Westernized versions, e.g., *Avicenna*. German and Dutch names are listed alphabetically under the family name without the preposition or article, e.g., *Ende, Frans van den* and *Wassermann, August von*. Romance names are generally listed alphabetically under the family name without the preposition, e.g., *Almeida, Luis d'* and *Leon, David de*.)

99

Subject Index

(Note: Titles of foreign-language books may be listed in the original or in English translation, depending on how they are generally best known.)

About the Author

Dr. Frank Heynick received his doctorate in medicine from the University of Groningen (Netherlands) with a dissertation on cognitive activity in sleep in a Freudian context. His previous degrees include a BA in history (Hunter College) and an MA in applied linguistics (Columbia University). His more than 250 academic, professional, and popular-scientific articles, books, and chapters in the US and Europe have largely focused on medical history and on specifically psychiatric and dental topics. Jewish themes appear regularly in his writings. Dr. Heynick lives in the Midwood section of Brooklyn, but has also taught and lectured extensively abroad.